WITHDRAWN
an introduction to
STRESS
& HEALTH

SAGE has been part of the global academic community since 1965, supporting high quality research and learning that transforms society and our understanding of individuals, groups and cultures. SAGE is the independent, innovative, natural home for authors, editors and societies who share our commitment and passion for the social sciences.

Find out more at: **www.sagepublications.com**

an introduction to
STRESS
& HEALTH

Hymie Anisman

Los Angeles | London | New Delhi
Singapore | Washington DC

Los Angeles | London | New Delhi
Singapore | Washington DC

SAGE Publications Ltd
1 Oliver's Yard
55 City Road
London EC1Y 1SP

SAGE Publications Inc.
2455 Teller Road
Thousand Oaks, California 91320

SAGE Publications India Pvt Ltd
B 1/I 1 Mohan Cooperative Industrial Area
Mathura Road
New Delhi 110 044

SAGE Publications Asia-Pacific Pte Ltd
3 Church Street
#10-04 Samsung Hub
Singapore 049483

Editor: Michael Carmichael
Editorial assistant: Keri Dickens
Production editor: Imogen Roome
Copyeditor: Audrey Scriven
Proofreader: Leigh C. Timmins
Indexer: Cathryn Pritchard
Marketing manager: Alison Borg
Cover design: Wendy Scott
Typeset by: C&M Digitals (P) Ltd, Chennai, India
Printed in India at Replika Press Pvt Ltd

Library of Congress Control Number: 2013938840

British Library Cataloguing in Publication data

A catalogue record for this book is available from
the British Library

ISBN 978-1-4462-7074-5
ISBN 978-1-4462-7075-2 (pbk)

For Simon, Rebecca, Jessica and Max
Contrary to what your sibs say, Max, I love all of you
unconditionally and equally.
BTW, I sent you that coat of many colors by courier.

CONTENTS

ACKNOWLEDGEMENTS

'We are like dwarfs on the shoulders of giants, so that we can see more than they, and things at a greater distance, not by virtue of any sharpness of sight on our part, or any physical distinction, but because we are carried high and raised up by their giant size.' This comment, that has been attributed to Bernard of Chartres (almost a thousand years ago), was subsequently made more famous by Isaac Newton with his statement 'If I have seen further, it is by standing on the shoulders of giants'.

My source for all information, Wikipedia, has told me that a form of this phrase also appeared in the works of Rebbe Isaiah di Trani (c.1180–c.1250), a Jewish tosaphist (a tosaphist is a highly educated and wise scholar who wrote commentaries on the Talmud), in one of his comments regarding our (his) audacity in contradicting an earlier scholar: 'Should Joshua the son of Nun endorse a mistaken position, I would reject it out of hand, I do not hesitate to express my opinion, regarding such matters in accordance with the modicum of intelligence allotted to me. I was never arrogant claiming 'My Wisdom served me well'. Instead I applied to myself the parable of the philosophers. For I heard the following from the philosophers. The wisest of the philosophers asked: 'We admit that our predecessors were wiser than we. At the same time we criticize their comments, often rejecting them and claiming that the truth rests with us. How is this possible?' The wise philosopher responded: 'Who sees further a dwarf or a giant? Surely a giant for his eyes are situated at a higher level than those of the dwarf. But if the dwarf is placed on the shoulders of the giant who sees further? . . . So too we are dwarfs astride the shoulders of giants. We master their wisdom and move beyond it. Due to their wisdom we grow wise and are able to say all that we say, but not because we are greater than they.'

As I was writing these acknowledgements I again realized how lucky I've been. There are so many people who hoisted me onto their shoulders to give me a wonderful view. I'm grateful, not only for their influence in preparing this book, but also for so many other choices I've made. I've been very lucky right from the start in having great mentors, Jane Stewart, Norm Braveman, Gary Waller and Doug Wahlsten, who pointed out the view. I've also been gifted with many, many wonderful collaborators who made research fun and offered a shared perspective. The gang included Zul Merali and Kim Matheson, my oldest collaborators and BFFs, as well as Sandy Livnat, Arun Ravindran, Alex Kusnecov, Robert Zacharko, Dan Stewart, Bruce Pappas, Dan McIntyre, Shawn Hayley, Mike (Fabio) Poulter, Steve Ferguson, David Park, Alfonso Abizaid, John Stead, Matt Holahan, Kim Helleman, and the Montreal affiliate gang members Joe Rochford, Dominique Walker and Alain Gratton, and those who've been teaching me about social psychology, Cath Haslam, Michael Wohl, and

Nyla Branscombe. Alex Haslam, particularly, has given me some wonderful perspectives of social interactions and identity.

I've also been blessed by several wonderful post docs; Shlomit Jacobson, Marie Claude Audet, Pasto Wann, Maia Miguelez, Vincent Roy, Beth Tannenbaum, Tom Borowski, Zheng (James) Wu Lu, and Pardeep Ahluwalia did all sorts of heavy lifting, and made sure that the graduate students were all OK and provided shoulders for them as well.

I've had a bunch of really terrific kids receive their PhD in my lab, who've gone on to establish their careers in universities, medical practices or as clinical psychologists. Larry Kokkinidis, Gary Remington and Lawrence Sklar comprised that first cohort that paved the way to make it easier for those who came later: Jilly Irwin, Angela Corradini, Chris Prince, Nola Shanks, Steve Zalcman, Marliee Zaharia, Sue Lacosta, Nick Turrin, Jenna Griffiths, Shawn Hayley, Owen Kelly, Kathy Michaud, Kerry Sudom, Jullie Gibb, Kate Raspopow, Amy Bombay, Kelly Christie, Sheena Taha, and Miki Talebi. There are also several about to get their PhDs and will soon be off: Robyn McQuaid, Opal McInnis, and Rob Gabrys.

There have also been some pretty terrific students in our group that limited themselves to a Master's degree. Some went to other universities to obtain a PhD (or another degree), some went to medical school or clinical psychology programs, whereas others took positions directly in research venues: Margaret Hamilton, Carolyn Szostak, Venera Bruto, Maxine Morrison, Brenda Hahn, Wayne Bowers, Jason Kotsopoulos, Jamie McIntyre, Karen Lacey, Karen Brebner, Leslie Drummond, Leslie Kerr, Maralyn Kasian, Anna-Marie Danielson, Reno Ghandi, Effie Helis, Priya Parkash, Mark Turcotte, Kelly Brennan, Alexandra Fiocci, Laura Ziebold, Caroline Wayne, Heather Soberman, Ashley Mulligan, Ashlee Charbonneau, Valerie Repta, Andrea Perna, Jeff Scharf, Katlyn Chambers, Adam Neufeld, Faisal Al-Yawer and Jesse Howell. I was also lucky to have Tom Connor in my lab for a spell, although technically he wasn't one of my students.

I've also had a great many research assistants over the decades, but over the past fifteen years Jerzy Kulzcycki and Marzena Szieckos have been my right and left hand, and Diane Trenouth has provided all sorts of help.

I'm exceptionally appreciative of Michael Carmichael, Keri Dickens, and Imogen Roome at SAGE who did the heavy work of shepherding this book through the many steps it went through, and for patiently guiding me through this processes.

Simon and Helen were, without question, most important in every imaginable way. Of course, if not for Maida, the early experiments that Dan Stewart and I conducted would have been a flop (at least that's her story). Simon, Rebecca, Jessica and Max have been the best. We've taken turns standing on each other's shoulders; I hope the view from my shoulders was a good one.

Finally, I'm particularly indebted to the Canadian Institutes of Health Research (CIHR), the Natural Sciences and Engineering Research Council of Canada (NSERC) and the Canadian Foundation for Innovation (CFI) for providing funding for my research, and to the Canada Research Chairs (CRC) program and the Ontario Mental Health Foundation (OMHF) for personal support over many years.

Ottawa, April, 2013

ABOUT THE AUTHOR

Hymie Anisman received his PhD in 1972 (University of Waterloo), and has been a Professor at Carleton University, Ottawa, since that time, while also holding an adjunct appointment with the Institute of Mental Health Research (Royal Ottawa Hospital). Professor Anisman was a Senior Ontario Mental Health Research Fellow (1999–2006), is a Fellow of the Royal Society of Canada, and has held a Canada Research Chair in Neuroscience since 2001. The principle theme of his research has concerned the influence of stressors on neurochemical and neuroendocrine systems, and how these influence psychological (anxiety, depression) and physical (immune-related and neurodegenerative) disorders. His work has spanned animal models to assess stress-related pathology as well as studies in humans to assess stress, coping and appraisal processes. In this regard, he has assessed the impact of chronic strain emanating from discrimination and stigmatization on well-being, depression and posttraumatic stress disorder (PTSD) among refugees from war-torn regions and among Aboriginal groups that suffered childhood traumatization, distress associated with abusive relationships and life transitions, as well as the transmission of trauma effects across generations.

In addition to sitting on the editorial boards of several journals and on numerous grant panels, Professor Anisman has published more than 350 peer-reviewed journal papers and book chapters as well as several review papers within neuroscience and psychology journals, and has edited two books, one dealing with stress processes and the second concerning psychoneuroimmunology. A mainstay of his research program has been the training of students. More than 20 PhD and 50 MA/MSc students have graduated from his laboratory. His research has been funded by the Canadian Institutes of Health Research (CIHR), The Natural Sciences and Engineering Research Council of Canada (NSERC), the Ontario Mental Health Foundation (OMHF), the Canadian Foundation for Innovation (CFI) and the Canada Research Chairs program (CRC).

PREFACE

There's a poem by Edward Arlington Robinson about a character, Richard Cory, who was later made much more famous by the captivating rendition sung by Simon and Garfunkel. It seems that Richard was

> Born into society, a banker's only child,
>
> He had everything a man could want: power, grace, and style.

Clearly, he was the type of person that everyone envied, and might have wished that they could trade places with him, until we learn of his fate at the end of the poem;

> So my mind was filled with wonder when the evening headlines read:
>
> 'Richard Cory went home last night and put a bullet through his head'.

Sure, there are those people with seemingly charmed lives, who appear to float from situation to situation untouched by the chaos and distress affecting others. However, look a little deeper and you'll find that they aren't immune from stressors, despite the outward appearances. To turn to an old cliché, 'nobody gets out of this alive', and odds are that there are few, very few, who don't have some scars earned along the way. We're not entirely sure what was ailing Richard Cory. However, it is clear that he was far from '*happy with everything he's got*'.

Some of the negative events that we encounter might constitute the usual minor unpleasantries, but some may be traumatic, life-threatening events or experiences that suck the soul right out of your head/body, and leave you shattered. We all know of people who have experienced particularly distressing events or multiple horrible events, and we're left wondering how these people survive and even be cheerful at times, and we shake our heads muttering 'there but for the grace of God go I'. Most of us also know people who seem to get stressed-out far too often. Those people who seem to panic over every minor event, and end up stressing everyone around them. The fact is that there are huge differences in how people react to stressors, who deals well and who deals poorly, who succumbs to the effects of stressors and who becomes stronger in the face of adversity. There's no easy solution to getting rid of stressors, and there's similarly no easy way to make yourself invulnerable; however, there are ways to improve your resilience and to limit the damage that might otherwise be engendered by stressors. This book doesn't describe (or prescribe) some form of anti-kryptonite to help you ward off distressing events, and it isn't a self-help book to make you tough. Instead, it aims to provide information, based on empirical research, about the stress process and the factors that generally facilitate stress resilience. However, along the way, some guidance will also be provided that may (or may not) influence your ways of dealing with bad events, and also help you to help others. However, each individual, as you'll see, is very different, and so this book is about stress in general, and not about you in particular. Michelangelo observed that every block of marble has an angel inside it that it is the sculptor's job to set free. I'm certainly no Michelangelo. Nevertheless, with the methods and insights of neuroscience and psychology as my chisel I hope to help you understand how the general processes of stress impact on each of us in different ways, and indeed how our very individuality is a consequence of those processes.

As the reader goes through the chapters of this book it will become clear that there is a simple logic concerning its construction. However, in the hope of the reader getting the most from it, there are some simple considerations on *how to use this book*. The successive chapters build on one another to offer the reader an integrated perspective regarding stress and its relation to well-being and pathology, and the methods that can be used to diminish distress and its pathological consequences. The initial two chapters are meant to inform the reader about the various factors that determine the extent to which stressors might have adverse effects. Among other things, these chapters cover a series of variables that are related to the stressor itself, individual difference factors that govern vulnerability to stressor effects, and processes related to appraisal and coping. Having described these multiple contributions to the stress process, the next three chapters outline some of the biological consequences of stressors, focusing on hormones (Chapter 3), neurotransmitters, growth factors (Chapter 4) and immune processes (Chapter 5). In doing so, every effort was made to demonstrate that these systems are interrelated to one another and thus jointly protect us from pathology, and conversely, that pathology may involve disregulation involving multiple systems. In addition, these biological changes are considered in the context of the variables described in Chapter 1 and 2 that influence the potency of stressors. With an understanding of the biological consequences of stressors and the variables that moderate these outcomes, the next two chapters are concerned with the influence of stressors on physical illnesses, notably immune-related illnesses (Chapter 6) and heart disease (Chapter 7). This is then followed by the analyses of stressors on psychological disturbances, particularly depressive disorders (Chapter 8), anxiety disorders (Chapter 9) and addictions (Chapter 10). In discussing the physical and psychological disorders, the text repeatedly returns to the information concerning what makes stressors more or less potent, our stressor appraisal and coping processes, and the biological sequelae of stressors. Chapter 11 takes a slight detour from the preceding chapters and could well have been included much earlier. This chapter deals with the intergenerational effects of stressors, and includes a consideration of developmental factors, including prenatal and early postnatal stressors, as well as biological processes that might contribute to the effects of adverse experiences being transmitted across generations. Having detailed some of the consequences of stressors, Chapter 12 deals with methods to diminish distress, which go hand-in-hand with methods to diminish psychological disturbances and some features of physical illnesses that might be secondary to the associated distress. Finally, although few texts concerning Health Psychology include a chapter on discrimination and stigma, it is clear that these are exceptionally powerful insults, and failure to seek help owing to self- and other-stigma is likely one of the main blocks to alleviating mental illness. Thus, not including such a chapter would have been counterproductive. One last point regarding the information in these chapters needs to be made. The initial version of this book contained more than five thousand citations to specific articles. However, including all of these would have resulted in the cost of the book being excessive, and thus sharp scissors had to be taken to this aspect of the book. I apologize to the researchers whose very important work was mentioned in the text, but was not specifically attributed to them. Of course, there are several important topics that were not covered in the book (the issue of sleep is the first to come to mind), and I have no excuse for these ommisions.

As we all know, learning and remembering complex sets of information are less difficult when they are appropriately contextualized. In writing this text I made a considerable effort to simplify some of the material and make it practically relevant, particularly the sections that were related to biological processes. This was done by repeatedly placing this information in the context of pathology, most often depressive and anxiety disorders, but other illnesses as well. A case was also made for individualized treatment of psychological disturbances. That is, treating individual patients on the basis of the specific symptoms presented together with biomarkers that might inform treatment strategies and prevention of illness recurrence. Admittedly, this can only be repeated so often before it begins to sound like a broken CD, and there were times when I felt this intensely. In reading this book, or for instructors teaching from it, I would encourage returning to the information in Chapters 1 and 2 when considering the effects of stressors on biological systems, and likewise when dealing with pathologies to put this in the perspective of the information related to behavioral and biological processes. This might sound a bit preachy or patronising, especially as its likely being said to many good teachers as well as their students, but this is how I envisioned the book being used as I composed the different chapters. This approach has worked well for me as I taught the material, and I hope it does for you as well.

1 THE NATURE OF STRESSORS

MONDAY MORNING

Can hardly get myself out of bed. It's just way too early. Why do they have classes at 8:30? It's inhuman. Well, I better move my butt. I've missed a couple of classes already and I'm pretty far behind, and sometimes I can't even figure out what the Prof is talking about. I borrowed some notes, but I might as well be reading hieroglyphics. I wish I had the time to go through the book, but between working at the restaurant at night and meeting with Jesse on weekends, there don't seem to be enough hours in the day. I can't put Jesse off any longer as I'm sensing annoyance because I'm never around. I really don't want to end up being dumped. Until I met Jesse I felt pretty alone, and didn't have much of a social group to hang with. Aw hell, I can't think about that now. I just remembered that the clock's ticking and those two essays and the class presentation are sitting on my head. I don't even know where to start. It almost seems as if my Profs are colluding against me. The exam schedule is nuts. My two toughest exams are on the same day, and then I've got six days to study for that no-brainer course that is easier than what we took in high school. I've also got to get home before the exams to see Dad. He didn't sound good last time I spoke to him and Mom. I really miss them, and I think they're not telling me everything about Dad's heart problems. I don't even know where to begin. I just want to stay in bed and cover my head.

There are certain topics that encourage opinions from everybody and their cousin, and on which people seem willing to make statements with absolute certainty regardless of their knowledge of the subject. It's unlikely you would overhear conversations regarding heavy topics in physics, such as quark-gluon-plasma or the space and time continuum. However, you might catch snippets of conversations about how to fix the ailing economy (opposite opinions all being dogmatically pushed), about how badly international affairs have been bungled by this or that political party, and about the stresses of modern life. Here, though, people often divide into two camps. There are those who view modern life as a grind with a variety of stressors appearing everywhere, exacerbated by work/school and unhelpful mothers and fathers as well as disloyal friends, and there are those who believe that stressors of modern life are vastly over-rated and that the daily challenges that people are said to experience are something of a fiction, or perhaps it's something that only others need to endure. In short, stress is something everybody talks about with the view that they have special insights into the topic.

I confess that this drives me nuts. I'm supposed to be an expert in a field in which everybody feels they also have remarkable expertise. On more than a single occasion one of my relatives (on the other side) has even offered advice as to what direction my research should be going and offered suggested readings (this relative, incidentally, is adamant that we only use 10% of our brain, something he learned from his Grade 2 teacher). The fact that these events bother me as they do also means that I'm not handling it well. It has clearly frustrated me, at least to the extent that I'm venting about it (and I don't even know you!). It seems that although I'm really good at giving advice about stress, I'm just not very good at dealing with my own distress.

Regardless of whether or not this confession has undermined my credibility, you ought to believe me when I say that stressful events are linked to a wide range of mental health problems, and are among the prime suspects in the provocation of several physical illnesses. For this reason, it's important for us to learn how to recognize and deal with stressful events that entangle us every day (have you noticed that it's a jungle out there?), and major life stressors that most of us will invariably encounter at some time or other.

Does the text in the box at the outset of this chapter sound at all familiar? And if it does, upon finding yourself in a similar situation would you do anything about it or would you just hope everything will get better, eventually? As indicated in the Preface, this book might not help you solve your specific problems. However, it will provide you with information about stress and coping processes, and insights into a constellation of psychosocial, experiential and developmental factors and how these relate to a wide variety of illnesses that have been associated with stressful events. You'll also learn about various aspects of our biological defense systems, and some of the psychological consequences of not keeping stressful events in check. In essence, the book's core goal is to give you a comprehensive and integrated understanding of stress processes and their relation to health. What I want to emphasize is not only that these various elements are all important facets of human psychology (and its interaction with other dimensions of the human condition; e.g., biological, social, economic), but also that stressful events can have consequences that you might never have considered. Beyond having immediate effects on your well-being, stressful experiences can also mark you for decades. In fact, the stressors you encounter, depending on when they occurred and how severe they were, can have intergenerational effects.

This chapter will introduce you to some basic definitions and concepts, with the goal of acquainting you with some of the key variables that influence or determine the impact of stressful events. This will entail:

- a description of what a stressor comprises, and that stressors come in various forms. These include challenges that are of a purely psychological nature, those that have direct physical effects, and those that cause a dysregulation of internal processes, but nonetheless act as stressors, even if we aren't consciously aware of them;
- analyses of the attributes of a stressor that result in it having greater or lesser effects. In this regard, we will discuss the contribution of the stressor's severity, controllability, predictability, uncertainty, ambiguity, and chronicity;
- how stressors are assessed in a laboratory context or in community samples, including analyses of those stressors that appear as nothing more than minor inconveniences, and stressors that represent major life events, as well as traumatic experiences that are endured;
- the individual factors that influence vulnerability to the effects of stressors as well as variables that imbue us with resilience so that we can overcome the potential adverse consequences of stressful experiences. To this end, we'll consider the individual and interactive influences of genetic, environmental, experience-related, personality variables, early experiences, and age-related factors on well-being.

SOME BASIC DEFINITIONS AND CONCEPTS

It's a good idea to begin by defining some key terms so that we're all on the same page. For starters, what do we mean when we use the terms 'stress' and 'stressor'? This sounds fairly mundane, doesn't it? Nevertheless, just humor me, and assume that differentiation of these terms might be useful. A 'stressor' is a stimulus or event that is *appraised* or perceived as being aversive and causes a 'stress response' that comprises a series of behavioral, emotional, and biological changes aimed at maintaining an organism's well-being. Among other things, these stress responses involve biological changes that occur so that energy resources are directed towards the places they are needed, and away from processes that are not essential at the moment (e.g., reproduction, eating, digestion). Simultaneously, multiple brain regions are activated to help us appraise and then deal with the stressful event.

So what exactly are these stressors? In fact, there is no easy definition of 'stressor', since appraisals of events may vary with contextual factors and change yet again over time, and they are also interpreted differently across individuals. In response to a similar definitional problem of pornography, US Supreme Court Justice Potter Stewart famously observed 'I can't define it, but I know it when I see it' (Jacobellis vs. Ohio, 1964). In much the same way, what constitutes a stressor may be highly subjective, and it needs to be acknowledged that individual differences that exist can be fairly pronounced. In effect, one person's poison is another person's meat.

There is enormous variability regarding the degree to which stressors can affect different people. Events or stimuli that are stressful to one individual might not be similarly appraised by a second individual. For example, jumping out of a plane (with a parachute, of course) might be exciting for some individuals, whereas it might be exceptionally distressing for others. Even if two individuals appraise a stressor similarly, they might display different emotional reactions. As well, even if their emotional reactions were the same, they might display different methods of coping with the stressor. Finally, the fact that individuals' appraisals, coping, and emotional responses are comparable does not mean that their biological responses will necessarily be the same, and hence different psychological outcomes (including pathologies) might evolve over

TABLE 1.1 Factors that influence the stress response

Stressor type
    Processive (neurogenic or psychogenic)
    Systemic (immune insults)

Stressor characteristics
    Controllability
    Predictability
    Ambiguity/ uncertainty
    Chronicity
    Intermittence

Organismic variables
    Species
    Strain
    Sex
    Age

Experiential variables
    Previous stressor experiences (sensitization/desensitization)
    Prenatal events
    Early life events (maternal factors, trauma)
    Attachment (bonding)

Personal characteristics
    Self-esteem
    Self-efficacy
    Hardiness
    Optimism
    Neuroticism

Social characteristics
Social support and unsupportive interactions
Appraisal styles
Coping skills

time. These individual differences in stress responses might come about as a result of several factors, some of which are listed in Table 1.1. We'll go through each of these systematically, and revisit them in ensuing chapters, as they have important implications for the development of stressor-induced biological and pathological outcomes. Obviously, assessing the link between stressor encounters and the emergence of psychological or physical disturbances isn't easy, but the progress that has been made is significant and has resulted in the development of several effective strategies for preventing illness and treating pathology once it has emerged.

CHARACTERIZING STRESSORS

Even at this very early point you've learned something important about stressors. First, not all stressors have the same impact, and second, individuals differ remarkably with respect to how they appraise stressful events and how they respond to them. You've also learned that there are multiple factors responsible for these individual differences. Some of these differences might be related to the stressor, whereas others might be related to characteristics of the individual and their varied experiences. We'll now move to a more detailed analysis concerning why we respond to certain stressors as we do, beginning with a discussion of their features.

TYPES OF STRESSORS

Stressors generally come in multiple flavors, and we'll start by distinguishing between these as they don't necessarily result in identical outcomes. A stressor that involves information processing (e.g., asking ourselves 'Is that dog drooling and does that glare and posture mean it's dangerous?', or 'Does this guy with the mask covering his face seem like a mugger?') is referred to as a *processive* stressor. Understanding the threat (stressor) involves several complex cognitive processes that engage numerous brain regions. These include neural circuits responsible for executive functioning that involves appraisal and decision making (e.g., frontal cortex; anterior cingulate cortex), memory processes (e.g., hippocampus and several cortical brain regions), and those involved in anxiety and/or fear responses (e.g., prefrontal cortex, amygdala, and hippocampus). Broadly speaking, processive stressors can be of a purely psychological (psychogenic) nature, or of a physical nature (termed 'neurogenic' stressors), such as those associated with certain illnesses or painful stimuli (e.g., burns). Not surprisingly, psychogenic and neurogenic stressors may elicit similar outcomes in some respects, but as we will see, they can also have several very different consequences.

Another type of challenge, referred to as a 'systemic' stressor, does not involve the same type of information processing, as it entails an insult to our biological systems. Systemic challenges include, but are not limited to, marked changes of glucose concentrations in our blood (as occur in diabetes), the presence of inflammation or the production of certain proteins evoked by inflammation (as occurs with heart problems), and numerous other biological changes. In these instances, we might not be processing the information with the question 'Is this a threat to my well-being?', as we do when confronted by some processive stressors, but our body might be interpreting these challenges as threats, and sending messages to the brain so that certain actions are taken to meet the immediate needs. For instance, the pain associated with a broken bone (a processive stressor) might make us more cautious and protective of the injured area, and thus will increase the likelihood that it will heal without being perturbed. Likewise, the fatigue and achiness associated with influenza (a systemic stressor) pushes us into bed so that we can rest and thus recuperate more readily. The behavioral changes that occur in response to processive or systemic insults involve the integration of several biological and cognitive systems. It seems that multidirectional communication occurs between various facets of our brain, peripheral nervous system, hormonal systems and the immune system so that coordinated responses occur.

PSYCHOGENIC STRESSORS

Different types of stressors (psychogenic vs neurogenic vs systemic) do not necessarily lead to identical outcomes. For example, in rodents, a purely psychogenic stressor, such as being exposed to predator odors, gives rise to neurochemical changes within the brain (e.g., the release of chemicals from brain neurons) that are different in several respects from those elicited by a neurogenic stressor (a painful stimulus). In fact, even among psychogenic stressors, marked differences occur as a function of the specific stressor encountered. Those psychological stressors that reflect innate challenges (e.g., predator odors) instigate neurobiological changes that are distinguishable from those elicited by conditioned or learned stressors, such as cues that had previously been associated with a neurogenic stressor. In light of the specific neural circuits activated by these stressful events, it might be expected that they would also be associated with the emergence of different behavioral outputs or even pathophysiological processes, and might require different strategies to attenuate the negative reactions that might occur.

At one time scientists had thought that we had a 'stress center' in our brain, just as it was mistakenly thought that there was a 'pleasure center'. The neural circuitry associated with stressors is much more complex; we do not have 'a' stress system, but instead there appear to be multiple pathways that respond preferentially to different types of stressors (Merali et al., 2004). When we examine these systems from a perspective relevant to humans, their importance takes on more tangible meaning and significance. For example, some stress responses reflect outcomes associated with something that has already happened (the loss of a loved one, a business failure, a hurricane, or being ostracized by your friends), and not surprisingly, these stressors might be associated with different psychological outcomes.

One can intuitively appreciate that certain conditions, particularly those that involve interpersonal events (e.g., the death of a loved one), might favor certain types of responses and lead to depression, but these processes might be distinct from those involving adverse achievement-related events (work-related stress), although these too can favor depressive affect (Mazure et al., 2000). Moreover, gender differences appear to exist with respect to the types of stressors that lead to pathological outcomes. In this regard, it has been suggested that psychosocial stressors may have more dramatic effects in females than in males, whereas those related to job strain/competition may have more profound effects in males (Kendler et al., 2001; Mazure et al., 2000). Other stress responses, especially those that are of an anticipatory nature (e.g., imminent surgery, anticipation of an upcoming exam or public speaking, taking a plane flight if you have a plane phobia, an imminent tax audit, the chance of seeing the bully in the schoolyard), are likely to be accompanied by anxiety (Harkness, 2008). Still other types of stressors, notably those that are ambiguous in nature (e.g., the 'possibility' of a terrorist attack, or a pilot announcing that 'we have to return to the airport' without further explanation) might be accompanied by disorganized cognitions while the situation plays out.

Some stressors involve an evaluative component (e.g., public speaking or asking questions in class, activities in front of an audience, a job interview), a social component (e.g., a fight with your best friend), one that involves a degree of embarrassment (e.g., certain visits to the doctor if you're a 50+ year-old male), and some that instigate particularly aversive emotional responses (e.g., shame, humiliation). Some psychological stressors may have profound effects, but their actions are fairly transient, whereas others may be remarkably powerful, so much so that they can have life-long effects (Robinaugh & McNally, 2010).

NEUROGENIC STRESSORS

Physical stressors can be brief (stubbing your toe), moderate in duration (e.g., a slight burn, a back strain, or a slightly sprained ankle), they can be persistent (e.g., rheumatoid arthritis, sustained or recurrent migraine headaches), or they can be both persistent and severe (severe burns, injuries sustained from accidents, or the pain associated with certain diseases such as cancer). There's little question that the more intense stressors call upon an incredible portion of a person's psychological and physiological resources. As well, these neurogenic stressors typically don't appear in isolation from psychogenic stressors. Whether these entail financial difficulties brought about owing to physical illness, repeated trips to doctors or hospitals, having to rely on others when one would prefer not to, or the anticipation that the distress will continue, it seems that complex multidimensional processes are often at work. As a result, diverse psychological processes might be necessary to cope with these multipronged insults. Often, our abilities may simply be insufficient to deal with events, and external mechanisms that enable us to withstand these challenges (e.g., our social support resources) may become essential.

SYSTEMIC STRESSORS

Psychogenic and neurogenic stressors are all in some sense tangible (i.e., we can see or feel them), but we can encounter stressors that we might not be conscious of, and hence we might not be aware that we are experiencing any strain. Thus, we typically wouldn't think of them as stressors. Nevertheless, it has been suggested that challenges, such as immune activation, should be considered as stressors given that they elicit a cascade of biological changes that in many ways are akin to those associated with psychogenic and neurogenic insults. Among other things, systemic stressors may affect our neuroendocrine functioning, our brain neurochemical processes, and elicit several depression-like behavioral changes (Anisman & Merali, 1999). However, because we might be unaware that something is happening in our body that might adversely affect us (certainly this is the case soon after infection), there is seemingly no opportunity to take steps that might facilitate coping with the challenge. From this perspective, systemic stressors reflect silent, insidious attackers that can have negative repercussions for well-being beyond their potential direct effects. We'll be dealing with this in considerable detail later (see Chapter 5), but for the moment just keep in mind that stressors aren't always obvious, but may nevertheless have pernicious repercussions.

STRESSOR CHARACTERISTICS

Every stressor that we encounter may have unique elements about it and thus may have very different repercussions. By example, let's consider one broad stressor category, that of being ill, and examine the various elements that make up this type of challenge. An illness can be a brief one (a bad case of the flu, or appendicitis requiring surgery), or one that is less intense, but can still wreak havoc on a person's general well-being owing to the fact that the condition lasts for some time, and there are some illnesses that are chronic and/or progressive (gets worse over time). Some illnesses might allow individuals to function more or less normally despite the symptoms being exceptionally disturbing (e.g., tinnitus), whereas in other instances (e.g., arthritis, lupus erythematosus, Parkinson's disease) the features of the illness might interfere with multiple aspects of daily life. There are also illnesses, such as Type 2 diabetes, that necessitate changes in lifestyle, and can have drastic long-term implications for further diseases, but early on might have few discernible negative effects. Worst of all, for the patient and the family members, are disturbances that rob you of yourself (Alzheimer's Disease), illnesses that might or might not lead to death (cancer, heart disease, HIV), or those that are physically incapacitating (e.g., ALS, paralysis). Some illnesses 'just show up' without any apparent cause, whereas others occur as a result of traumatic events (a head injury, paralysis) stemming from one's own behaviors (engaging in certain sports), those of others (drunk or incompetent drivers), or acts of nature (flood, hurricane, earthquake). In each instance the illness trajectory may vary over months and years, and the needs of the affected individuals might differ accordingly. The psychological aspects related to the illness, the attributions regarding the cause of the illness, as well as the extent to which the illness *allows* the engagement of effective coping, differs with the individual's condition.

SEVERITY

Because each stressor we encounter might have numerous unique characteristics, it is difficult to compare whether one stressor is more severe than another. This is made still more difficult as our perception of stressors may be influenced by the context in which they occur and may vary over time. Furthermore, there are stressors that simply can't be compared to one another in terms of their relative severity (e.g., the death of a child vs dealing with a severe incapacitating illness) as they are on entirely different dimensions, and are often so severe that comparisons become meaningless. Nevertheless, most people would agree that certain stressors are more profound than others (e.g., the loss of a loved one vs getting a parking ticket), and thus most of us could guess that some stressors are apt to have greater pathophysiological consequences than others.

CONTROLLABILITY

The notion that control over one's destiny is important in determining psychological health has been around for a long time. The classic studies in the 1950s by Brady (1958) indicated that a monkey that was responsible for making certain responses in order to avoid an aversive stimulus developed ulcers more readily than a monkey that received an identical amount of unpleasant stimulation over which it had no control. Termed the *Executive Monkey Studies*, this research suggested that having control (and responsibility) was a daunting stressor that could lead to stress related pathology. These studies had obvious implications for business leaders and they became an important talking point for psychologists working with executives in large organizations, essentially telling them that being an executive has its hardships. In essence, being in control also means being responsible, and with this comes considerable psychological strain that could lead to pathological outcomes. This view held considerable intuitive appeal, but later studies contradicted these findings, and it is now commonly accepted that having control over both stressor occurrence and its termination is psychologically and physically advantageous.

NASTY LITTLE CREATURES

For some time it was thought that ulcers arose as a result of stressful experiences. However, it seems that the bacterium Helicobacter pylori is responsible for ulcers (Marshall & Warren, 1984), and in recent scientific discussions the contribution of stressful experiences has taken a back seat. Nevertheless, it does appear that stressors may affect gastrointestinal ulcers, and that stressful events and Helicobacter pylori may act synergistically to promote ulceration.

For their work in identifying Helicobacter pylori as the main culprit responsible for peptic ulcer disease, Marshall and Warren received the Nobel Prize in Physiology or Medicine (2005). To make the point concerning their hypothesis, which most scientists had dismissed, Marshall drank a brew of Helicobacter pylori to demonstrate that this bacterium would, indeed, cause ulcers. It would, after all, have been tough to get experimental participants for this study or even to get the study through an ethics review panel.

Experiments conducted almost a decade after the Brady studies, using a similar paradigm, documented one of the best-known phenomena in stress research. In particular, these studies demonstrated a phenomenon known as the 'learned helplessness' effect, whereby stressors over which the animal had no control provoked marked behavioral impairments in animals. It was shown that animals exposed to an escapable stressor (a shock to their feet), or that had not been stressed at all, subsequently displayed proficient performance in a test where they were required to escape from a stressor. However, animals that had been exposed to an uncontrollable stressor (a footshock that they could not escape) later exhibited profound behavioral impairments in an escape test where an active response would have terminated the footshock stressor. In these studies, the animal in the 'uncontrollable' stressor condition received the stressor at exactly the same time and for the same duration as the animal in the escapable shock condition. However, unlike the animals that were exposed to an escapable stressor, those in the uncontrollable condition were unable to control stressor termination. Instead, stressor offset occurred whenever animals in the escape condition made an appropriate response. Thus, animals received the same duration of the stressor, but differed with respect to the psychological dimension of having control over the stressor termination (this is referred to as a 'yoked' paradigm). As only animals in the uncontrollable condition later showed impaired performance, it was concluded that it was not the stressor itself that was responsible for the behavioral impairments. Rather, it was the animal's inability to exert control over stressor termination that was crucial in determining whether or not the adverse effects of the treatment would become apparent (Seligman & Maier, 1967).

In describing the results of these experiments, it was indicated that those animals who confronted an uncontrollable stressor subsequently did not make overt attempts to avoid or escape the footshock, even though they could now escape if they made a simple response of moving from one side of the test chamber to the other. Instead, they seemed to passively accept the stressor. Indeed, when an animal made an occasional escape response, this was not predictive of further escape attempts. The investigators suggested that these animals had learned to become helpless. Cognitive processes were thought to occur whereby they *learned* that their responses were unrelated to outcomes ('nothing I do matters'), and as they had no control over the situation they stopped trying to escape. Indeed, if animals were initially trained to make an appropriate response and then exposed to the uncontrollable situation, they did not display behavioral disturbances when subsequently exposed to a controllable stressor. These animals, having first learned that they control their destiny, were essentially immunized against the effects of the uncontrollable stressor.

The behavioral disturbances elicited by uncontrollable stressors have been seen across a variety of species, but in rodents it is typically seen only in certain situations. It seems that when the stressor is administered to rodents, the high degree of reactivity that is elicited favors an appropriate escape response being emitted (i.e., running from one chamber in which the stressor is administered to an adjacent 'safe' chamber) and thus potential behavioral deficits are obfuscated. Eventually, it was observed that if the response required of the animal to escape entailed a motor response that was relatively difficult to accomplish or where an active response had to be maintained for several seconds before successful escape was possible, then performance deficits could be elicited. Such findings gave rise to the suggestion that performance disruption was not a reflection of a cognitive disturbance, such as helplessness, but instead stemmed from brain biochemical changes that hindered the rodents' ability to maintain prolonged or complex active responses (Anisman et al., 1978; Glazer & Weiss, 1976).

Failure experiences in humans may have effects vaguely reminiscent of those associated with uncontrollable stressors in animals. For instance, university students exposed to unsolvable problems subsequently displayed impaired performance in a problem-solving task, as did depressed students who had not been exposed to the unsolvable task. Although these outcomes have often been attributed to learned helplessness, there are other explanations that might have little to do with helplessness. For instance, there might be a mismatch between the participant's expectancy regarding their performance, and their failure to meet this expectancy might have induced frustration that was responsible for the subsequent impaired performance. These differing positions notwithstanding, since these early studies, much has been made of the importance of stressor controllability in determining later psychological and physical disturbances.

STRESSOR PREDICTABILITY, UNCERTAINTY, AMBIGUITY, AND BLACK SWANS

The impact of stressors on psychological and physical well-being is influenced by their predictability, uncertainty, and ambiguity. There are occasions on which the occurrence of stressors is very predictable, but there are also those where stressors are entirely unpredictable, and our responses in these situations are likely to be quite different. Who among us would have predicted 9/11, or that an earthquake or tsunami would hit a particular region, causing the deaths of thousands upon thousands? In contrast, tax time is a stressor, particularly for accountants or those who owe the government a lot of money, and its occurrence is predictable (the behavior of governments may not always be predictable, but you can count on them being systematic when it comes to taxes).

Uncertainty is related to unpredictability, but they can be distinguished from one another. We all will die eventually (that is a certainty), but when this will happen is often unpredictable. Essentially, when we talk about predictability, it is usually in the context of events that will happen; it is simply a matter of knowing when they might happen, whether there will be a warning of their occurrence, and on what schedule they might occur (e.g., a single event, repeated events, events that occur intermittently). Uncertainty, in contrast, deals with events that might or might not occur (e.g., it is uncertain whether this new flu virus will end up as a pandemic). When there is uncertainty about the occurrence of a stressor, individuals may take on a cavalier attitude that essentially comprises 'whatever happens, happens'. Others, however, seem to have great difficulty dealing with uncertain situations, and for these individuals their stress reactions could potentially be pathogenic.

Another similar construct is that of ambiguity. We say that a situation is ambiguous when the stimulus context does not provide sufficient information, or provides multiple but inconsistent bits of information, so that it becomes difficult to determine whether and when the event might occur. By example, ambiguity exists when one has a set of symptoms, but they do not form a coherent pattern that allows for a firm diagnosis. Likewise, when government agencies are trying to determine the imminence of a terrorist attack they might encounter a set of stimuli that suggests that something is up (e.g., increased internet chatter, certain individuals or groups have suddenly dropped off the grid), but otherwise things seem much the same as they usually are. The situation here is thus an ambiguous one.

An old proverb has it that '*mann tracht unt got lacht*', literally translated as 'man thinks (plans) and god laughs'. On a daily basis, most individuals typically behave as if the events in their lives are predictable and that they can reasonably anticipate what the future holds for them, and that they even have some control over their lives. Even though most of us know that this sense of control is an illusion, many of us operate as if we have some say regarding what happens to us: we have expectations for the future, and planning is viewed as necessary given our apparent need for order and predictability. Thus, it shouldn't be surprising that adverse events that are unpredictable are generally viewed as being more unpleasant than predictable events (Baker & Stephenson, 2000), and are more likely to be associated with disturbed brain neuronal functioning, the excessive activation of some stress hormones, and altered immune functioning (Pitman et al., 1995).

So, what is it about the unpredictability and uncertainty regarding bad events that makes them so aversive? What differentiates the aversiveness of predictable vs unpredictable events is, to a significant extent, related to the anticipatory period. When we know that an event will happen at a particular time, there may be great anxiety about the impending event, and waiting itself, coupled with the probability of events occurring during specified periods, may be stressful (Osuna, 1985). Yet knowing that the event will or is about to happen gives us the opportunity to prepare or adjust our behaviors and expectancies. Unpredictable events, however, don't allow us to prepare in a similar manner, and we may be on edge for extended periods of time. Most people are familiar with the first part of Franklin D. Roosevelt's statement in relation to the Great Depression, but less familiar with the second part; 'the only thing we have to fear is fear itself – nameless, unreasoning, unjustified terror which paralyzes needed efforts to convert retreat into advance'. This very well describes the response to unpredictable, ambiguous, but potentially very stressful situations: irrational, inappropriate and immobilizing behaviors that reflect our inability to appraise and cope with situations, so that our ability to strategize becomes entirely ineffective.

As with unpredictability, in most situations uncertainty is also seen as being more aversive than is certainty. However, there are instances where this isn't the case. For instance, some people who are at risk for a genetic disorder, such as Huntington's Disease, want to know whether they carry the gene for this illness, and hence will invariably be affected. These individuals don't want to live in suspense, essentially with a sword hanging over their heads, and choose to know whether or not they carry the gene. Others, however, would rather not know and appear to be able to vanquish their thoughts so that their daily routine is not affected. It seems that individuals differ in their *intolerance for uncertainty*. The level of uncertainty that can be tolerated is a trait that individuals bring into situations that involve an ambiguous or uncertain component (Rosen et al., 2007). High intolerance for uncertainty has been found to exacerbate the anxiety associated with daily stressors, and increased intolerance for uncertainty, as well as the desire to reduce uncertainty, was found to predict increased information seeking (Rosen et al., 2007), which could potentially increase the adverse effects of stressors. Unpredictable events obviously have the potential for turning our lives upside down. The death of loved ones, sudden illness, catastrophic natural disasters, are all events that we know are possibilities, but we really don't expect them to happen to us. Yet the probability of dying of heart disease is about 34% and that of cancer is about 16–17% (although survival rates have been increasing for several cancers), Type II diabetes occurs in about 3.5% of individuals and is climbing, autoimmune disorders occur at 3.1%, and then there's kidney, pancreatic or liver disease, and serious automobile accidents that lead to severe disability or death at a rate of about 1.7% each year. There is also a chance of being hit by lightning or a brick falling off a building and onto your head (events that are admittedly rare), or the possibility of being in a plane crash (although for the people on the plane or the person hit by the brick, such probabilities simply don't count). The point of all of this is simple. We might not know how we'll fare in the future, but given the number of bad things that can happen to us, and the additive probabilities of these events, we can pretty much count on not getting away untouched. We don't know whether, how, or when we'll encounter these nightmares, but it's almost a certainty that we'll encounter some bad dreams.

Uncertainty and ambiguity are frequent in our experiences and they are known to promote anxiety. For example, consider what your own reactions to symptoms of an illness might be (e.g., 'Is this lump I feel something I should worry about?' 'This feeling in my chest seems like indigestion, but it might also be a heart attack. What do I do now?'). This, in turn, might lead to further uncertainties pertaining to the illness and its prognosis ('What are the odds that the treatment will work?'), and the availability of a competent and experienced medical practitioner ('Does this doctor have the experience and skill that will be needed?').

From what has been said to this point, it's fairly clear that unpredictability, uncertainty and ambiguity can be exceedingly stressful. But there is also a different spin that has been applied regarding the role uncertainty might play in the context of serious illnesses (Mishel, 1999). From this perspective uncertainty involves two distinct appraisal processes, namely *inference* and *illusion*. If uncertainty exists, then individuals can reconstrue a largely negative situation (inference) to extract a glimmer of hope despite the odds (illusion). Because uncertain situations are vague and changeable, in the context of events that are spiraling downward (e.g., when all treatment efforts to stall the progress of a cancer have failed), individuals can capitalize on uncertainty so that their appraisals take on a positive hue, no matter how limited this might be. Uncertainty, essentially, allows a person to expect the worst, but still hope for the best.

DUMBASS GAMBLERS

It seems that for many of us, there is a need to maintain a semblance of control over our own destinies. Even when a situation is entirely unpredictable and individuals have absolutely no control over the outcome, those who are self-assured are more likely to choose to exercise their own judgment in determining that outcome, despite this semblance of control being illusory. The fact is that when situations are unpredictable and where outcomes are entirely out of our control, our participation in decision making (e.g., how to treat an illness) is not that far removed from that of engaging in a game of chance (gambling).

We see this desire or need for control across various domains. For example, when given the opportunity to play a game of chance (say roulette) where individuals either have absolutely no control over outcomes, or are allowed to 'pay' a premium to press a button to stop the wheel (in this instance they have a semblance of control insofar as the wheel will stop, but they have no control with respect to where the ball lands), they will more often pick the latter. Similarly, when people buy lottery tickets, they will often prefer to choose their own numbers rather than have a series of numbers generated through a computer (as if they have a divine connection with the odds maker in the sky, which the computer, of course, doesn't). It also seems that some people feel that they (or others) are endowed with a trait characteristic of being lucky ('I'm a lucky person', as opposed to 'This was my lucky day'), and so might get involved in events that involve high risk (e.g., gambling), which they believe doesn't apply to them since they are, after all, lucky. If that isn't dopey enough, there are others who develop an 'illusion of control by proxy' wherein they find a 'lucky person' to buy their lottery tickets for them (Wohl & Enzle, 2009). One wonders whether stock market players, at least to some extent, are affected by some of these characteristics.

I was recently introduced to the 'Black Swan theory' advanced by Taleb (2007) to explain irrational behaviors that people often endorse in the context of making decisions. The implications of this perspective for the stress field are enormous, and so I figured it should be brought up fairly early in this volume. Essentially, from Taleb's position there are events that occur very infrequently and are essentially unpredictable, have a major impact on the individual (or society, or the economy), and often have people rationalizing, in hindsight, that the event might have been predictable if only the right data had been available. For instance, could we have predicted 9/11 and the ensuing stock market debacle, or in Japan the earthquake and resulting tsunami and the potential for a nuclear meltdown? Probably not, but it can be argued that even though any single event is an outlier (a black swan), there are so many possible things that could go wrong, one or more of these will eventually occur. Black swans don't simply refer to 'major' events like a 9/11, a crash in the housing market, or the possibility of another war breaking out somewhere (the latter aren't really black swans, but more like albino squirrels, which I've seen several times). There are individual tragedies that can also occur, such as being diagnosed with a rare disease, sitting at lunch and having part of a building suddenly collapse with you as collateral damage, or a piece of space junk reentering the atmosphere and taking direct aim at your house. We can't know what will befall us, as there are simply too many 'unknown unknowns'; so many that the odds of dodging all of them are slight. However, they can and do occur, and their ramifications can be enormous.

THE BRAIN'S RESPONSE TO KNOWING AND THE UNKNOWABLE

Given that we often find ourselves in situations where the information available is ambiguous and making decisions entails a degree of risk (e.g., the behavior of stock markets), there has been increasing interest in determining which brain regions might be engaged for decision making under such conditions. For instance, which brain regions are activated under conditions that involve risk (i.e., where the outcome probabilities are known), ambiguity (a situation where there is a lack *information* about outcome probabilities), or ignorance (a condition wherein the outcomes were completely unknown and even unknowable)? It was observed that relative to the risk situation, ambiguous information provoked a greater activation of certain brain regions (inferior frontal gyrus and posterior parietal cortex), and this same outcome was apparent when participants were presented with non-useful information (the ignorance context) (Bach et al., 2009). Perhaps these regions are activated in an effort to make sense of this situation. It might simply be the case that the brain doesn't like uncertainty and tries to set things in order. It has been suggested that the individual differences observed in these situations might be related to differences in intolerance for uncertainty, and it is important to consider this variable in assessing neural systems that are involved in the decision-making process.

CHRONICITY

There are stressors that, unfortunately, must be endured on a chronic basis: these can be psychosocial or family-related issues, financial impositions, health problems, discrimination or stigma, or a combination of different factors. When stressors are chronic and occur on a predictable basis, we are often able to adapt and perhaps even take charge of our situation. Studies of animals suggested that the neurochemical changes that occur in response to acute stressors will diminish with chronic predictable, invariable stressor experiences (stressors that are chronic but don't change are termed 'homotypic' stressors). Sometimes, however, the stressors we experience might be chronic, intermittent, unpredictable, ambiguous and uncontrollable, and vary across days (the latter are referred to as 'heterotypic' stressors), making it difficult to establish adequate coping methods, or even to take preparatory steps to enable effective coping. Under such conditions, the usual adaptation that occurs in response to homotypic stressors might be less likely to develop (Anisman et al., 2008). Thus persistent stressors, such as acting as a caretaker (e.g., for a parent with Alzheimer's or a child with exceptional needs), or dealing with chronic illness or financial problems, each of which involves multiple challenges that might change from day-to-day, might strain our ability to cope effectively and lead to psychological or physical disturbances.

Chronic unpredictable stressors needn't be severe in order to elicit pathophysiological outcomes. Several studies in animals showed that a regimen that comprised a series of mild uncontrollable stressors was effective in this regard (Willner et al., 1992), although this outcome was not universally observed, tending to appear more readily with somewhat stronger stressors. The chronic mild stress model, perhaps because it has a degree of intuitive appeal (i.e., it 'sounds' right), has received wide recognition and attention, but it seems the effects of stressor treatments depend on a number of other factors, such as the individual's previous stressor experiences, the way stressors are appraised, and the coping methods used.

ALLOSTATIC OVERLOAD

In recent years, the concepts of stasis and allostatic overload have evolved to explain the impact of severe or chronic stressors. Under normal conditions biological changes occur to meet the ebb and flow of environmental demands, thus maintaining stability within the organism. This essentially describes homeostasis. In response to strong or sudden stressful challenges, and to severe chronic events, greater and more rapid biological changes are instigated to restore and maintain stability, and we refer to this as allostasis (Sterling & Eyer, 1988). As adaptable as humans and animals might be, when a strain on the system is excessive, our adaptive biological systems might eventually become overly taxed, resulting in *allostatic overload*. Under these conditions the organism may become ill or more vulnerable to the negative impact of new stressors that might be encountered (McEwen, 2000; Schulkin, 2003).

In addition, allostatic overload may occur through a more insidious process. In particular, 'Type 2' allostatic overload occurs as a result of social conflict or other forms of social disturbances. These threats do not necessarily elicit strong coping responses as do severe or traumatic stressors, but over time their toll might become enormous, unless measures are taken to modify the social structure that imposes itself adversely on the individual (McEwen & Wingfield, 2003). This is especially the case as the social challenges that affect us (e.g., in the workplace) might be insidious, essentially creeping up on us without our conscious awareness.

MEASURING STRESSORS

We all seem to know what we mean by a stressor, but for experimental purposes we need to be able to distinguish between different types of stressors and how intense these stressors are perceived to be. Later, we'll be discussing individual differences in how stressors are appraised and perceived, but for the moment we'll examine how stressor experiences are measured, and a few of the limitations of these procedures.

MAJOR LIFE EVENTS

Stressful events are known to promote psychological disturbances, and severe stressors are more likely to do so than are relatively mild stressors. In an effort to analyze the impact of stressors, several variants of major life events scales have been developed, which have been used to predict the relations between stressors and the occurrence of illness or disturbed quality of life. One approach was based on the notion that a stressor ought to be considered in terms of the social adjustment that is required to deal with it (e.g., the Social Readjustment Scale: Holmes & Rahe, 1967). Others simply focus on major life stressors that had been encountered over a set period of time (e.g., six months or one year), basing their severity on responses from a normative group of participants (Paykel et al., 1971). Other questionnaires are available that focus on particular types of events, such as traumatic experiences that might have occurred at some specific time over the course of the life span (e.g., the Traumatic Life Events Questionnaire; Kubany et al., 2000), or particular stress-related pathological conditions, such as posttraumatic stress disorder (PTSD; Weiss & Marmar, 1997). There are also scales that deal with specific types of events ranging from psychological abuse to breast cancer and other types of challenges.

These scales share certain essential attributes (they do, after all, give us an idea of what an individual has experienced), but they also share several deficiencies. First, an evaluation of the distress experienced by an individual over some set period of time is often based on scaled scores. For instance, in the Social Readjustment Scale, 'death of a child' receives a score of 100, 'trouble with in-laws' gets a score of 29, 'changes in work hours' a score of 20, 'revisions of personal habits' 24, and 'pregnancy' 40. So getting pregnant, changing our personal habits, altering our work hours, and having issues with our in-laws are worse than having our own child die. Doesn't make a lot of sense, does it? Furthermore, certain items on the list seem to have a positive valence (e.g., an outstanding personal achievement), others a negative valence (e.g., the death of a close friend), and still others depend on an individual's perspective (e.g., a major change in responsibilities at work, e.g. a promotion, demotion, lateral transfer). So the scale doesn't necessarily reflect adverse events, but instead deals with 'life changes' that might or might not be interpreted as stressors. Of course, the scales don't consider the context in which a stressor had occurred. For instance, the death of a loved one is typically a severe stressor, but it might vary as a function of whether the person had been going through a severe illness or had died suddenly in an accident. Likewise, as we'll see, even apparently minor stressors can have relatively pronounced consequences when these occur within the background of a series of other, more distressing events.

A further problem with each of these approaches is that they ask individuals to report on events that had previously occurred, and hence are subject to 'retrospective bias'. That is, the way individuals interpret or even remember the past may be colored by how they feel at the moment. If an individual is feeling really great, then past negative events might not seem so bad and they might not even recall that certain adverse events had ever occurred. In contrast, if the individual is currently dejected, then all events in their past may be perceived as the slings and arrows of outrageous (mis)fortune and they might even dredge up events that were insignificant. Further to this point, when individuals are ill they often want to know why this occurred. Is it something they did, or something that somebody else did? Or is it just bad luck? In the case of people who are depressed they might be looking for causes and might attribute their depression, sometimes inappropriately, to particular past events. In short, as most defense and prosecution lawyers know, we can't be trusted to recollect our past experiences accurately.

DAILY HASSLES VERSUS MAJOR LIFE EVENTS

One typically presumes that the more intense the stressor the more profound the consequences. To a certain degree this is certainly the case. But what are the consequences of those day-to-day annoyances that can really bug you, especially when they appear repeatedly or are superimposed on the backdrop of other ongoing stressors (it's not from nowhere that we have expressions such as 'the straw that broke the camel's back')? Most of us know the experience of having to deal with a new stressor when were in the midst of dealing with an earlier challenge; our immediate response when this occurs is something like 'Oh no! Not now'. It's hard enough to deal with one event, but when coping resources have to be redirected to a second stressor, even if it's a fairly trivial one, our abilities to deal with these situations may become stretched. Most of us certainly have to deal with multiple concurrent challenges at some time or other. For some, juggling different tasks is so much part of their repertoire that they can't see how anyone would ever have a problem in this respect. For others, however, juggling multiple demands is exceptionally difficult, taxing their resources, and ultimately leading to illness.

Hassles can certainly be a pain and even small increases in these experiences may result in individuals being more prone to illness and mood disturbances. The relations between such 'daily hassles' and pathology have been evident across a range of illnesses, including depression, irritable bowel syndrome and diabetes (Blanchard et al., 2008; Ravindran et al., 1999), although this doesn't necessarily mean that the hassles caused the pathology, as those who are already ill may be more sensitive to day-to-day annoyances. Nevertheless, these seemingly inconsequential stressors, when they continue for long enough, can have a cumulative effect.

The formal publication of the Hassles and Uplifts Scale (Kanner et al., 1981) provided an instrument to show that hassles are related to poor well-being. Since the initial publication of this scale, other similar instruments have been developed for particular groups (e.g., caregivers) or circumstances (e.g., transition to university). Investigations using daily hassles scales typically report an overall score, but it may well be that specific types of hassles are more germane to some individuals than to others. Thus, analyses might be considered in terms of the different types of challenges experienced (e.g., partner, friends and family hassles, as well as those that are related to home, work, health, and financial strains). This hasn't been widely done, but if it were, then it might be observed that illness varies as a function of both the severity and type of the stressor encountered, and that certain illnesses are more closely related to particular types of hassles.

A TAXONOMY OF HASSLES – CHANGING TIMES

In their original report, Kanner et al. outlined the 10 most frequent hassles and uplifts reported. These hassles comprised: (1) Concerns about weight; (2) Health of family member; (3) Rising prices of common goods; (4) Home maintenance; (5) Too many things to do; (6) Misplacing or losing things; (7) Yard work or outside home maintenance; (8) Property, investment, or taxes; (9) Crime; and (10) Physical appearance. This paper was published thirty years ago, but some of those same hassles are still pertinent. Today, however, we might find that frustration with our computer, loud people talking on cell phones, emails from work when you're at home, junk emails (including word that a long-lost cousin in Nicaragua has left you $12.5M) might break into the top 10. Importantly, these were the top 10 items for the population at large, but might not be the top 10 for those dealing with particular issues experienced by some individuals, such as caregivers who deal with illness or any of numerous other major problems. Again, when hassles are superimposed on major life stressors, then we're dealing with exponentially greater problems.

Given that hassles can be draining, you might be asking what can be done about these stressors. Causal observation suggests that having people to whom you can vent and who can help you with minor problems is useful, as social support usually is. However, there are limits to what your social support network is willing to put up with. Using them excessively for the purpose of venting, and putting upon them for very minor reasons (and not giving anything in return), may end up being counterproductive, as friends might abandon you or offer unsupportive reactions and you might get to be known as a whiner. Of course, mutual whining might diminish this problem, and although it doesn't eliminate stressors, it is a way of coping.

Most of us probably already know the key element that needs to be considered in relation to hassles, namely, don't have a meltdown. It's not productive, and excessive reactions to mild events can act as stress generators, causing further problems that need to be dealt with (like fixing the broken laptop that you whacked when you forgot to save the data). Second, put things in perspective; losing your keys or having a minor skin blemish doesn't rate as all that terrible in comparison to some serious events that can be encountered. Heart disease, cancer, and paralysis are all horrible experiences, and are difficult to deal with. Day-to-day hassles aren't, and usually can be dealt with readily. In Chapter 12 we'll be talking about various stress management procedures and treatments. One that is currently in vogue is mindful meditation (mindfulness). A key precept of this procedure is 'think in the moment'. In part, this means appraise the *present* situation properly, without worrying about secondary issues, and don't go into an automatic negative response mood. Once appropriate appraisals have been made (i.e., 'this is just a minor hassle'), then with proper deliberation, effective coping strategies can be used. Of course for some people (especially the perfectionist types and likely the Type A personalities) those little things left undone sit there sneering at them annoyingly, to the extent that they are incapable of focusing on important issues. Basically, the best advice that can be offered is what my kids (annoyingly) say to me when I'm on the verge of a meltdown over something minor, 'Chill, Dad'.

ENOUGH IS ENOUGH

A newspaper headline had a story about a Dalhousie University professor who, after standing in line for about an hour to get a rare on-campus parking pass (even though he'd been teaching at the university for thirty years), walked up to the administration offices and handed in his resignation. I can visualize his frustration when he was likely already very busy with classes about to start, and at a certain point he just said 'Screw it'. A small part of me wondered whether he was a flake, but a larger part was in admiration, given that as a university professor, I know some of the administrative aggravations that are often experienced (like completing form after form after form). Still, the event described had occurred yesterday, and today he's out of work. It may be that he won't miss the job (he was near retirement) and/or has other options. Alternatively, this might be an instance of stress generation. (Incidentally, as a result of such frustration I've developed a 'request a request form' so that when I'm asked to fill out a form, I ask them to complete my form so that I can determine whether they have the authority and justification to request that I complete their form – I'll be happy to share this form if you email me, and you won't have to complete a form to get it.)

STRESSOR INTERVIEWS AND DIARIES

To overcome some of the limitations associated with retrospective analyses, several researchers have attempted to obtain confirmation of stressful experiences by interviewing friends and family members. Although, at first blush, this might seem reasonable, the fact is that such reports can reflect the observers' own spin or bias, and hence can be just as flawed. Besides this, stress, like beauty, is ultimately in the eye of the beholder, and it's hard to know what a particular person feels by asking someone else. Judicial courts don't allow witnesses to testify about what was happening in the mind of someone else, and researchers are equally skeptical of this approach.

Ultimately, the best way to evaluate the relations between stressful events and later outcomes is by prospectively assessing stressor experiences and then relating them to particular outcomes, such as aspects of health. Not unexpectedly, this can be an onerous task that takes an awfully long time to complete, and participant loss (referred to as subject attrition) can be very high. Thus, one might end up with only those participants who are most dedicated to the project, so that the data collected might not be representative of individuals at large. If the study is relatively short term, say for a matter of weeks or even a couple of months, a diary approach can be used (e.g., Holtzman et al., 2004). This can be conducted using a format in which participants answer a brief set of questions at the end of each day (or week) indicating what they've experienced. This requires that the investigator meet with participants and form some sort of relationship with them so that they will be motivated to engage in the study on a daily basis. As useful as this approach might be, its use in long-term studies is obviously limited by logistical considerations.

INDIVIDUAL DIFFERENCE FACTORS

VULNERABILITY AND RESILIENCE

Up until this point, we've focused on the different characteristics of stressors that could potentially influence behavioral or physiological outcomes. Of course, these features are only a few of the many factors that influence how stressors affect us. To a considerable extent, previous life experiences, characteristics of the organism (animal or human), and personality variables determine the nature of the stress responses that occur. In the next section we'll focus on the influence of these variables. In assessing these factors, we will not only think about what makes us vulnerable to pathological outcomes related to stressful experiences, but also what goes into an individual being more or less resilient in the face of different challenges. Some of the factors that seem to make individuals resilient in fending off or preventing the adverse effects of stressors have been identified (see Figure 1.1), but it's certainly the case that there are enormous differences across individuals in this regard.

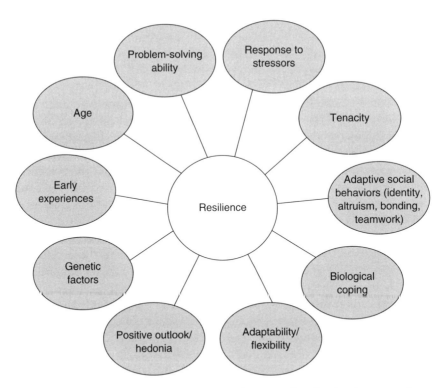

FIGURE 1.1 Numerous factors might be important in preventing the development of stress-related pathology. These range from personality characteristics, genetic factors, and a variety of experiences. Some, but certainly not all, of the important ingredients are provided in Figure 1.1. The effectiveness of these resilience factors is likely dependent on the stressor situation, will vary over time as the stressor is experienced, and will also vary across individuals.

VULNERABILITY VS RESILIENCE

In the context of illness, vulnerability refers to the susceptibility of a person (or a group, or even a whole society) to increased psychological or physical poor health as might occur in response to particular environmental or social challenges. Resilience, by contrast, refers to factors that limit or prevent these events from having adverse effects or, more often, resilience refers to the ability to recover from illness. The two aren't necessarily at opposite ends of a continuum. Moreover, the absence of factors that increase vulnerability doesn't necessarily imbue resilience. A person can, theoretically, have many factors that engender stressor resilience, but a single catastrophic vulnerability factor might be sufficient to undo all that fitness. By example, how often have you heard of a person being perfectly healthy who suddenly dies? It took only one malfunction, an aneurysm or a pulmonary embolism, for instance, to undo all that was 'healthy' about that individual. In this regard, one could take the view that stressors act on weak links within a system. A person may have all sorts of strong links, but when stressors come along, they have the most profound impact on the weakest link, causing damage at that point.

For an individual to be resilient, numerous ingredients might have to come together in exactly the right amounts. Charney (2004) suggested that neural mechanisms related to reward and motivation (hedonia, optimism), responsiveness to fear and fear-related situations, and adaptive social behaviors (altruism, bonding, and teamwork) all acted to influence character traits that affected resilience to severely traumatic events. Another perspective has it that resilience increases with increased tenacity, trust in one's instincts, acceptance of change, control, and spirituality. Still another perspective attributes resilience to the ability to adapt and be flexible to changes, the ability to problem solve, and possessing a positive outlook on life. No doubt, other resiliency factors, including early experiences and genetic factors, contribute to the ability to withstand the potential for stressors to harm us. Moreover, it is possible that certain characteristics exist that might enhance well-being even in the presence of factors that would otherwise increase vulnerability to pathology. For instance, an individual with many factors that make him or her vulnerable to stress-related pathology may overcome challenges by having an excellent social support network or perhaps by espousing a religious belief that allows them to endure the worst challenges. This is not to suggest that religiosity is the way to go, but it seems to work for some people.

Most studies that assessed the relationship between stressful events and pathology have addressed questions related to what makes us ill and what the characteristics are of individuals who are most likely to become ill. Much less information is available regarding what makes us resilient. Where we most often encounter this topic is in considering the resilience of some individuals in coping with illness, and the findings from such studies have been especially constructive. There are some individuals who, in the context of serious illnesses, are particularly resilient and are able to maintain, or regain, their mental health readily. Among individuals who have previously encountered a severe illness, the cognitive restructuring that might have occurred previously (e.g., finding meaning in their illness, which we'll come back to in Chapter 2) may have facilitated their ability to appraise and cope with a further stressor. In other instances, however, the previous stressful experiences might not have served in this capacity, but instead acted against well-being. Having gone through a traumatic experience, individuals might simply be too worn down or they may be sensitized so that later stressors in the form of severe illness might simply be too difficult to handle.

Resilience in relation to illness can be influenced by several personality characteristics, such as self-efficacy, self-esteem, internal locus of control, optimism, mastery, hardiness, hope, self-empowerment, determination, and acceptance of illness. Knowing this, unfortunately, isn't going to be of much help in advising anyone how to deal with illness as we can't easily get people to develop better self-esteem or greater hardiness. However, the way individuals appraise and cope with their illness may have profound repercussions for their well-being. Specifically, positive cognitive appraisal, spirituality, and active coping, which are considered in Chapter 2, were associated with resilience, and these attributes can be promoted with proper training (e.g., using cognitive behavioral therapy or mindfulness training as described in Chapter 12).

GENETIC FACTORS

When I was an undergraduate and first introduced to genetics, it was described in the form of Mendelian inheritance (that stuff about pea plants), and most of us came to believe that we inherited certain genotypes (specific genes we received from our parents) which then affected our phenotype (what we looked like), although it was acknowledged that inheritance could be incomplete and hence we might not be exactly like either of our parents on any given domain. So, unlike pea plants, people aren't simply tall or short, green or yellow, or round or wrinkled: there are all sorts of levels in between. A second premise that was drilled into us was that whatever genes you inherited were those that you were stuck with forever, and that was that. A third premise was that for some unknown reason, genes could interact with the environment, but nobody ever explained how or why this could happen. In the last decade there has been a revolution within molecular biology and all fields of medicine and neuroscience. Scientists have not only unraveled the genome, they have also found ways of modifying genes, and identifying how and where genetic changes occur naturally or in response to environmental factors or in response to stressful events. We now know that the potential actions or effects of genes can be suppressed by environmental triggers or specific experiences and hence might promote (or limit) pathology. We also know that genes can be inserted or deleted, and thus might affect phenotypes, and we have discovered many subtle inherited mutations or variants that occur within genes (referred to as 'polymorphisms') that can have profound effects on pathology.

SO, WHAT'S THIS STUFF ABOUT GENES CAUSING BEHAVIOR?

There is this odd notion that genes cause behavioral phenotypes. That seems pretty vague; it's as if you inherit some gene or set of genes, et voila, a behavior appears as if by magic. Moreover, it's often thought that the effects of genes are immutable. In fact, however, the job of genes is to produce proteins, including hormones, peptides, neurotransmitters, enzymes and receptors that, in turn, influence behaviors. The effects of these genes aren't immutable, but are influenced by environmental factors that moderate how these gene effects are expressed. So, you might have genes that dispose you to particular characteristics, but whether these characteristics are expressed can be influenced by day-to-day events or events that occurred way back when, even when you were just a fetus.

As you know, the chromosomes you inherit from your parents comprise a lengthy DNA strand that's made of many genes, each of which comprises a set of nucleotide bases (guanine, adenine, cytosine, and thymine; the latter is replaced by uracil in an RNA strand) that reflect the gene playbook. Using the DNA as a template, RNA is formed through a process called transcription. The messenger RNA (mRNA) produced through this process is then decoded so that a specific amino acid chain, or polypeptide, is created that will in turn produce a protein (e.g., a hormone or neurotransmitter). When the characteristics of the DNA are altered, as occurs when even a single nucleotide is changed, the message that's delivered can potentially change and have some pretty significant consequences.

The genes on a DNA strand are interspaced by a bunch of additional nucleotides, much of which we know little about. But, in this pile of 'junk DNA' we also find strands that precede the gene. These are known as 'promoters' or 'promoter regions' (there are other names used as well, such as 'response elements') that are thought to act as activators or repressors. Essentially, the promoter serves as an instruction manual for the gene that follows it. These promoter regions can tell a gene when to turn on or off, or even when to interact with other genes. Importantly, environmental events, including stressors, influence these promoters by affecting other chemicals present in cells as well as extracellularly, which can then affect the influence of the gene on hormonal and neurotransmitter processes, and all those other biological factors that come to affect behavior.

Genes, therefore, have the potential to affect behavior in one way or another (e.g., increasing certain proteins that favor a disposition towards behavioral phenotypes, such as depression or anxiety), but in most instances they don't directly cause the behaviors. Ultimately, what we do is dictated by much more than just our genes. Face it, whether it's God or Nature, neither fully transcribes our lives before we are born. That would be pretty boring. Instead, we're faced with multiple paths that can be taken, ways to deal with environmental insults and social relations, and these affect the way genes get to express themselves.

APPROACHES IN HUMANS

There have been many studies showing that genetic factors might be related to various psychopathological states. These studies have included pedigree analysis in which a particular phenotype has been traced through families in an attempt to identify the presence of particular genes, and studies that compared pathology in monozygotic and dizygotic twins (identical vs fraternal twins) to determine the degree to which a particular phenotype was inherited or induced by environmental factors, and often these phenotypes were linked to inheriting certain biological substrates. In more recent years, one of the most common approaches has involved the identification of particular genes or gene polymorphisms in relation to the presence of pathological states. In some instances this has entailed finding a sample (cohort) of affected and non-affected individuals (who have, or do not have, a particular phenotype or a family history for a particular phenotype), and then doing genomic analyses to see whether there is a match between the presence of certain genes or mutations and the appearance of a pathology. The idea is that if we could identify the gene associated with an illness, then determining what proteins this gene is responsible for making (e.g., levels of hormones and neurotransmitters and their receptors, and all sorts of other essential biological factors) would facilitate the development of treatments to attenuate or prevent pathology.

It sounds simple enough to find a proper cohort and then do the genetic analysis. However, if it actually were that simple, then many of the problems in the field might already have been solved. First, the diagnosis of an illness needs to be correct, which isn't always a simple matter as different illnesses have overlapping symptoms. Second, individuals might have similar symptoms, but that doesn't necessarily mean that these stem from the same underlying biological causes (including genetic and biochemical processes). Two individuals can come to have a particular chemical modification, but this might have involved different routes (much in the same way as your bank account can be low either because you're spending too much, not earning enough, a bank error, or unknown to you someone had been removing money from your account). Finally, there are potentially millions of mutations that can occur across the genome (more than a single mutation can also appear on any given gene), and most of these will be entirely unrelated to the pathology being studied. As a result the number of participants needed to do the studies appropriately is huge. In retrospect, it is understandable that the data from studies that have been conducted, probably because so many mutations occur concurrently and due to the small numbers of participants used, have not been particularly reliable. What has been clear, however, is that for certain pathologies, as well as the underlying biological processes, the expression of genetic effects was not always evident. Instead, the contribution of genetic factors was most evident in the presence of particular challenges, such as life stressors.

APPROACHES IN ANIMALS

Studies conducted using rodents have made it clear that genetic factors are fundamental in determining several stress responses and the pathological outcomes associated with stressors. In this regard, several approaches can be adopted to evaluate these relationships. A good first step is the use of inbred strains that naturally differ with respect to a given phenotype (the behavior or physiological characteristics of the animal) and genotype (the animal's genetic makeup) and relating these characteristics to neurochemical or hormonal differences in response to stressors (Crawley et al., 1997). Of course, simply because a strain is high (or low) with respect to both a given behavioral outcome and particular biological change doesn't mean that these factors are connected. But as described in the insert, this observation can be followed by further analyses to determine whether a correspondence between behavioral and biological factors is evident when various crosses between the strains are assessed (e.g., within F_1, F_2 and backcross generations).

GENETIC ANALYSES IN PAST DECADES

There are occasions on which it might be suspected that the effect of a stressor is determined by the genetic backdrop upon which it is superimposed; that is, having a particular gene doesn't cause the development of a particular psychological or physical illness, but it might be permissive in that it allows for stressors to have adverse effects. There are some fairly simple, if somewhat tedious, manipulations that can be conducted to evaluate these possibilities.

When two inbred strains are crossed, the offspring (referred to as the F_1 generation) will all be genetically identical to one another. For example, one parent might be dominant for both components of a gene (AA), whereas the other parent may be homozygous recessive (aa). As the offspring inherit one gene from each parent, the offspring will necessarily be Aa. With respect to another gene, both parents may be BB, and so the offspring will necessarily be BB. The same will apply to every gene and hence all F_1 animals will be identical to all others. When we cross two F_1s, we can then begin to see differences in the genotype: the offspring of an Aa × Aa cross can potentially carry the AA, aa, or Aa combination. Within this F_2 generation (also referred to as the 'first segregating generation') we can determine whether a particular gene and phenotype are linked to one another (either in the absence of a stressor or following exposure to a stressor). For instance, if every mouse that has inherited the 'AA' genotype exhibits a particular phenotype, and every mouse with the 'aa' genotype exhibits a different characteristic, then the two might be related. This doesn't mean they are causally related, as this is once again simply a correlation between variables. However, if those mice that exhibit a given phenotype carry the AA, Aa, or the aa combination, then we would know with a fair degree of certainty that these genotypes and the phenotype are unrelated. There are still more sophisticated variations of this approach (e.g., QTL analysis), but their description will have to be passed over for now.

There are occasions where a single gene can have more than a single phenotypic outcome. This is referred to as 'pleiotropy'. Pleiotropy can occur because genes on a chromosome are inherited as a group (termed 'linkage') or because one phenotype (e.g., a biological change) may directly or indirectly lead to a second phenotypic change. Assessing genes across successive crosses also allows us to see whether certain characteristics always appear together (e.g., Does a certain chemical always end up being present in conjunction with a particular heart problem?; Does having a certain coat color predict the occurrence of epilepsy?). In effect, we could be able to develop 'biomarkers' that predict later disease occurrence.

As well, one could determine whether genetic influences interact with maternal factors in determining outcomes. As we have just learned, all F_1s of inbred strains are identical to one another. If a particular trait is entirely due to genetic factors, then it shouldn't matter who their mom is (i.e., from one strain or the other). However, F_1 mice can be produced where the dam (mom) is a member of a particular strain, whereas in another cross the dam is of the alternative strain (this is referred to as a 'diallel cross'). In this instance the F_1s will all be identical, but if they differ from one another on some phenotype, then we'd likely ascribe this to characteristics of the mom.

With the remarkable advances in our understanding of molecular biological processes and the related technologies, newer and more sophisticated methods have been developed, including those in which specific strains of mice can be engineered. Specifically, mice (and in some instances rats) have been developed in which genes can be directly manipulated (engineered). Thus, one can assess the effects of stressors on a particular outcome in the presence of a specific genotype. For instance, a gene can be deleted from (knock-out) or added to (knock-in or transgenic) the genome of a mouse, and then bred so that numerous identical mice are obtained. This allows for analysis of the role of a particular gene or small set of genes in relation to particular pathophysiological outcomes, and how stressors influence vulnerability to pathology. So, if one believes that stressors cause a rise in chemical X, which then promotes depressive-like symptoms, then strains can be developed that lack the gene responsible for producing chemical X and thus determine whether the depressive-like behaviors are prevented. Conversely, mice can be developed that overexpress the gene that determines the presence of chemical X, with the expectation that depressive-like features would be more prominent. In theory, this approach is potentially revealing and might prompt important hints for human pathology. Yet, as most complex human pathologies likely involve many genes, the effectiveness of this approach is necessarily limited, and certainly doesn't reflect the full spectrum of the disorder. Furthermore, in mice born with a particular gene deleted, there is a fair possibility that other genes may compensate for the deleted genes. With respect to the latter issue, approaches have been developed so that the gene deletion will occur at specific times in life (thereby handling the adaptations that could occur through early development) and these can be targeted at specific brain regions. The possibility of using this 'conditional knockout' in relation to pathology has been very exciting, and opportunities exist to assess the combined role of more than a single gene.

The key point for us here is that when these genetic approaches are coupled with the analysis of stressor effects (and other factors that may favor the provocation of behavioral disturbances) and other experiential factors (e.g., early life experiences), it may be possible to identify the array of factors that contribute to stress-related disturbances. This approach can also be used to identify the relative contribution of different biological processes to specific features (symptoms) of illness, and may ultimately provide markers that can be used to predict an individual's vulnerability to disease states.

As will be seen in ensuing sections, the data supporting genetic involvement in stress-related pathology are overwhelming, and the data derived from such studies have been critical in the development of new targets for the treatment of several illnesses. One can't say, however, to what extent genetic and environmental factors influence pathology, as among other things, their relative contributions likely vary with the specific disease being assessed. Understandably, most of the molecular genetic analyses that have been conducted have involved animals (primarily mice), and studies of the interactive effects of stressors and genes in affecting illness in humans have been limited. Nevertheless, as we'll see, when these factors were examined concurrently, the results obtained were impressive.

ENDOPHENOTYPIC ANALYSES

Before closing off this section one further issue ought to be introduced. Because of the diversity of symptoms associated with most psychiatric disturbances, the variability in the effectiveness of pharmacological treatments of such disorders, and the presumed array of neurochemical and hormonal processes that might underlie these disorders, it was suggested that analyses of these illnesses might not be best served by assessing them as syndromes. Instead, as illustrated in Figure 1.2, it might be more profitable to assess the 'endophenotypes' that comprise the disorder. This would involve tying specific *symptoms* of a disorder to specific genetic components and neurochemical processes that might be related to the efficacy of treatment responses (e.g., Gottesman & Gould, 2003). This is not an easy thing to do, but calls for this approach have become more common, and it has led to the idea that rather than treating all individuals diagnosed with a syndrome in a particular way, it would be propitious to identify the biological and behavioral characteristics of each individual, and then to apply 'individualized' treatments accordingly. This might be expensive in the short run, but more economically sensible over the long term.

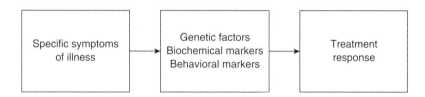

FIGURE 1.2   An endophenotypic approach attempts to link the specific symptoms of an illness to specific biological factors, such as genetic markers, and then to link these factors to particular treatment responses. There are likely many factors that are associated with illness, but not all will be predictive of a treatment response. However, identifying those that do, even if they are not causally related to the illness, may be an important element in developing individualized treatment strategies.

PERSONALITY

We all know those individuals who, given the least encouragement, seem to turn into Henny-Penny shouting that the sky is falling, and others, in contrast, who seem stoic even under the worst of conditions. As we've already seen, there are several factors that make us different from one another in this regard. An important set of characteristics engendering diversity of responses to stressors concerns personality attributes. In particular, there appear to be relatively stable features of individuals that appear to be important in determining whether they will be more or less vulnerable or resilient to the impact of stressors (Suls et al., 1996). Certain personality traits might influence the stress process by affecting the way we appraise or cope with stressors, whereas others might make us more sensitive or reactive to stressors, and there seem to be characteristics that are actually instrumental in getting us into aversive situations (e.g., high risk takers are more likely to get into certain stressful situations relative to those low in this feature). Many of these factors may have evolved through the parenting individuals received, the socialization that occurred in early life, experiences that shaped particular responses, and it is probable that genetic factors also contribute in this regard.

One of the best studied views of personality has comprised the analysis of the Big Five or Five Factor Model. This conceptual framework has a lengthy history that culminated (more or less) with the model provided by Costa and McCrae (1992). The Five Factors comprise Openness, Conscientiousness, Extraversion, Agreeableness, and Neuroticism. One could argue that each of these dimensions could influence stress responses indirectly, but it is Neuroticism (or emotional stability) which largely comprises the disposition to experience unpleasant emotions readily (anger, anxiety, depression, or vulnerability), which seems most closely related to stressor reactivity. In this regard, some of the questions from the Big Five Factor inventory ('I get stressed out easily'; 'I worry about things'; 'I get irritated easily') tell us this factor is indeed targeted at stress-related reactivity (Vollrath, 2001).

Of course, the Big Five represent only one perspective concerning the personality dimensions that might influence the stress response. In fact, because of the broadness of this framework, it isn't clear that it is the best approach to evaluate predictors of stress reactivity, and numerous other factors have been proposed that are viewed as personality-based moderators of the stress response. Of these, *resilience* has received increasing attention, although it is not viewed as a trait. Resilience is seen as a process (or a constellation of factors) leading to changes that make individuals better able to deal with stressors or to bounce back from the adverse effects otherwise elicited by stressful experiences. Based on the many components that influence the stress response, it can be deduced that there are certain characteristics that lead to an individual being more or less resilient (e.g., early life experiences, developmental trajectory related to dealing with novel events, appraisals and coping abilities), taking into account that stress responses are governed by multiple contextual factors.

Not surprisingly, individuals who approach situations with an upbeat and optimistic outlook will have a very different view of that situation than do individuals who enter it with a pessimistic perspective. Scheier and Carver (1985) developed the Life Orientation Test (LOT), which was later revised (LOT-R), to measure the attributes of personality that make up optimism/pessimism. There are other instruments to measure this characteristic, but it seems that the LOT-R is the most widely used. Based on studies using the LOT-R it was shown that optimism/pessimism represents a personality trait that was associated with stress reactions and the ability to meet fairly severe life challenges. In this regard optimism/pessimism influenced how individuals deal with severe stressors, including breast cancer in females and radical prostatectomy in men, moderated hormonal changes and immune responses ordinarily elicited by stressors, and was related to stress reactions, such as burnout (Carver & Connor-Smith, 2010; Carver et al., 1993).

As in the case of optimism, it seems that an individual's *self-efficacy* (the belief that tasks can be accomplished and difficulties resolved through one's own efforts) can act as a moderator of the stress response, and thus influence well-being. Likewise, it seems that our *locus of control* may influence how we appraise or respond to stressful events. Specifically, those with a high internal locus of control tend to have the view that events in life arise primarily because of their own behaviors and actions, whereas individuals with a low internal locus of control generally believe that fate, chance, or powerful others determine what events they encounter. These characteristics are thought to influence how individuals interpret or appraise situations and their own abilities to deal with them, and thus will affect psychological stress responses (we'll be coming back to this in Chapter 8, when we discuss depressive illness).

There are many personality factors that play into how we deal with stressors, but only a small number of these have even been mentioned to this point. Numerous volumes have been written on this issue, and trying to cover this broad field wouldn't do it any justice, certainly not in just a few pages. As we move forward, however, the contribution of several of these many personality traits will emerge, but for the moment, the important message here is that you should not assume that the things that bother you, and the way you think stressful issues should be dealt with, necessarily apply to everyone.

AGE

An individual's age has a lot to do with how they react to stressors emotionally and physically, and whether pathology will arise. Lupien et al. (2009), in their timely and thoughtful review, indicated that regardless of whether stressors occur prenatally, in infancy, childhood, adolescence, adulthood or in those who are aged, profound brain changes and mental health poroblems can emerge. These outcomes, as already mentioned, can reflect the interaction with genetic and other psychosocial factors, but the nature of the pathology that emerges may be dependent on the timing of the stressor experience. My inclination is to start this section with a discussion of older age, as this is of particular importance to me at the moment. But for the sake of a good orderly description, we'll follow a chronological order.

PRENATAL EXPERIENCES

Stressors experienced by a pregnant female may have effects on the fetus that will be manifested at various times following birth. In humans, the offspring of mothers who had experienced chronic or severe stress during pregnancy subsequently exhibited cognitive, behavioral and emotional problems during both childhood and adulthood. However, studies that evaluated these relations in retrospective analyses were troubled by some of the factors typical of self-report studies. Moreover, prospective analyses of children born following natural disasters were confounded by changes in quality of life that extended well beyond the primary stressful period (e.g., earthquakes, hurricanes, and tsunami are followed by multiple financial and health repercussions). This, however, does not belie the fact that the perceived severity of natural disasters was a strong predictor of mental health problems among pregnant and postpartum women, which was related to perinatal health outcomes in the offspring.

The fetus' intrauterine environment might profoundly influence its brain development, and hence stressful events that influence this prenatal environment may have repercussions that carry through postnatal periods. For example, stressful events will give rise to elevated levels of a stress hormone (corticotropin releasing hormone), which may appear in the placenta, ultimately affecting the fetal brain (Charil et al., 2010). In addition, among rodents, the offspring of mothers that had been stressed during pregnancy showed elevated activity of the stress hormone corticosterone when they encountered stressors postnatally, and this outcome was evident even when the pregnant dam had experienced a stressor on only a single occasion. Furthermore, these experiences influenced particular neurochemical receptors present within the hippocampus, a brain region that is fundamental in regulating biological stress responses and cognitive functioning. It might be particularly relevant that the effects of maternal stressors have especially profound effects in female offspring, and might be an important element responsible for differences between males and females in the development of stress-related pathology. In Chapter 11, which largely deals with the intergenerational transmission of trauma, a lengthier discussion of prenatal stressor effects is provided.

STRESSORS AS TERATOGENS

Teratogenic agents (those that cause disturbances and malformations of the fetus) are dependent on the stage of development at which the compound is encountered. Typically, the most harmful effects occur during the first trimester, but can vary with the species, the nature of the teratogenic agent, as well as particular phases of developmental growth. In the case of stressors, it has been suggested that the mid-term period is particularly sensitive to the adverse effects of stressors, possibly because placental adaptation can be achieved early in pregnancy, thus limiting adverse outcomes. However, the data from human studies and those from non-human primates and rodents have not been entirely uniform, and this issue has yet to be fully resolved. This is particularly the case as most strong stressors encountered by humans are often chronic in nature (especially when the aftermath of the initial trauma is considered) and hence span a lengthy period of fetal development (Charil et al., 2010).

EARLY POSTNATAL EXPERIENCES

Stressors have profound effects on children, and events early in life may subsequently affect biological responses to stressors in adulthood (see Chapters 3–5), and encourage psychological disturbances, such as depressive disorders, a variety of anxiety disorders and drug addiction (Chapters 8, 9 and 10), and may even have effects that are manifested across generations (Chapter 11). There are a wide range of stressors that infants and children can experience, ranging from physical, psychological, or sexual abuse, through to neglect or socioeconomic difficulties (poverty). However, children may not appraise specific challenges in the same way that adults do and therefore it is sometimes difficult to discern how they are being affected by adverse events (e.g., Compas et al., 2001). As well, the social, cognitive, emotional, and tangible resources to deal with stressors are not as well developed in children as they are in adults. Thus, it can reasonably be expected that stressful events might have marked immediate effects on children's well-being, and the notion is intuitively appealing that stressors experienced early in life would have profound repercussions on long-term well-being.

Early studies conducted by Harlow indeed revealed that monkeys raised in isolated environments later became asocial and had vastly deficient parenting skills. It has likewise been known for decades that raising children in deprived environments where they were not stimulated by touch or caress, as in the case of hospitals or orphanages, gave rise to frequent psychological and physical disturbances and exceptionally high levels of infant mortality. In fact, profound behavioral and biological disturbances are seen even when humans or rodents are brought up in environments that are not nearly as severe as those experienced by children in orphanages or monkeys in Harlow's studies. Early experiences, and in particular maternal care and factors related to socioeconomic status, most certainly influence developmental trajectories and ultimately adult behaviors (Shonkoff et al., 2009). Among other things, children from a nurturing early life environment were subsequently found to have a hippocampus that was larger (by about 10%) than children from a less nurturing environment (Luby et al., 2012), which could have enormous repercussions for stress responses and mental health, as well as learning and memory processes. Furthermore, stressful early life experiences have been associated with greater adult anxiety, depression, and chronic fatigue syndrome, and have also been implicated in favoring the development of a variety of diseases of aging, such as vascular disease and autoimmune disorders, and premature mortality (Shonkoff et al., 2009).

RE-PROGRAMMING BIOLOGICAL FUNCTIONS AND EPIGENETIC PROCESSES

To account for why early events might have repercussions many years later, it was proposed that psychological stressors result in the programming of various types of biological signals, including those that involve hormonal and immunological processes. Further, adverse early life experiences give rise to several behavioral and cognitive changes (e.g., high threat vigilance, mistrust of others, disrupted social relations, disturbed self-regulation, and unhealthy lifestyle choices) that might engender further stressors or result in these individuals being highly reactive to threats. These behavioral factors, and the stress reactions they elicit, might exacerbate already disturbed hormonal and immunological functioning associated with the early experiences, and eventually might culminate in pathology.

In considering the effects of early life experiences, one should not just focus on severe cases, such as abuse. Indeed, simply having an inattentive or neglectful parent can have profound and lasting repercussions on cognitive functioning and on vulnerability to stress-related disturbances. Studies with rodents indicated that early life neglect may engender disturbed adult behavioral and biological functioning, whereas stimulation may enhance an animal's ability to contend with later stressor experiences. In this regard, it seems that if pups had an attentive mom who cared for them well (in the case of rodents this involves lots of licking and grooming of pups), then these animals grew up to be fairly resilient in the face of stressors (Kaffman & Meaney, 2007). In contrast, extended periods of separation from the mom, or having an inattentive mom, resulted in animals being more stress reactive as adults, relatively resistant to the extinction of fear responses, and even after extinction had taken place, the fear response could readily be reinstated (Callaghan & Richardson, 2011). Essential questions that have emerged have concerned which neurobiological processes are involved in these outcomes, and whether the adverse effects of early adverse experiences can be reversed, or if there are variables that may compensate for poor parenting.

In their influential review and commentary, Shonkoff et al. (2009) indicated that numerous diseases that appear in adulthood, including psychiatric disorders, diabetes, heart disease, and various immune-related disorders, might have their roots in childhood stressor experiences. They suggested that the cumulative effects of life stresses contribute to allostatic overload that might eventually lead to pathology, or alternatively, that stressful experiences in childhood may become biologically 'embedded' (either through epigenetic processes or via sensitized biological responses) so that their consequences might appear years later. These investigators distinguished between 'positive' or 'tolerable' stressors that, with appropriate social support, might allow individuals to learn how to cope with such events, from those described as 'toxic' stressors (extreme poverty, psychological or physical abuse, neglect, maternal depression, parental substance abuse, and family violence) that are more likely to lead to pathology. In effect, there are challenges that are basically part of growing up, that have positive effects as they allow individuals to learn how to appraise and cope with events properly. However, there are also 'toxic' challenges that no one should have to endure. Shonkoff et al. didn't simply indicate that there were problems, rather they called for changes in public policy to attenuate these problems. They suggested that an increased focus be placed on: (a) reducing toxic childhood environments; (b) greater provision of early care and education programs that might not only serve as appropriate learning environments, but could also foster 'safe, stable and responsive environments; (c) evidence-informed interventions and treatments to deal with family mental health problems; and (d) expanding the role of child welfare services so that they undertake comprehensive developmental assessments in order that professionals be able to apply appropriate interventions. To what extent these straightforward suggestions will be endorsed by policy makers will be seen.

EPIGENETIC PROCESSES

A fairly hot topic in recent years has been the possibility that stressful events (as well as other factors) may affect the expression of genes, without altering the sequence of amino acids that make up these genes. This has been termed 'epigenetics', which essentially refers to the study of heritable changes in gene expression that result in a phenotypic change, but without fundamentally altering changes in the underlying DNA sequence (Bird, 2007). Some event, say one that had been experienced early in life, may have caused a series of changes within cells, so that the expression of the gene is suppressed. This gene suppression could affect whether or not certain neurochemical processes, including the neurochemical receptors, are operating appropriately, and hence could have effects with respect to how individuals deal with stressors, or they could have effects directly on processes that lead to illness. Importantly, these changes could persist over the course of an organism's life, and could also be transmitted across successive generations (if the epigenetic change occurred within the germ line, i.e., the sperm or ovum), hence affecting the biological and behavioral processes of the children and grandchildren of the individual that had initially been affected. Epigenetic changes have been shown to contribute to some forms of cancer, as well as autoimmune disorders, such as rheumatoid arthritis. Although epigenetic mechanisms have been linked to stressful experiences encountered at any time in life, there has been considerable interest in determining to what extent early life events (abuse or neglect) might have long-term consequences owing to epigenetic changes. In this regard, analyses of the brain tissue of depressed individuals who died by suicide revealed epigenetic changes in the genes associated with stress-relevant neurochemical responses among those individuals that had experienced early life parental neglect (McGowan & Szyf, 2010; Poulter et al., 2008).

TRANSITIONAL PERIODS

In addition to the impact of prenatal and early postnatal periods, there are other developmental times during which an organism might be especially sensitive to stressors. These include those phases of life that are referred to as transitional periods. We all go through events in life that involve change or transitions that call upon our adaptive resources. Entering kindergarten, for instance, is one of these life transitions. You're suddenly a big boy or big girl, having graduated from day care, but you also suddenly find yourself in a new social context, where it's not just you, mom and dad anymore. Likewise, entering high school, college, university, or the workforce is also an exciting major life transition during which we might experience insecurities and may be particularly vulnerable to the adverse effects of stressors. Leaving home, living with someone else, getting married (or divorced), moving cities and retirement, represent life transitions, and at these times the responses to stressors might be altered.

Most animal studies that assessed the effects of early life events on later stressor vulnerability have focused on events experienced during the early postnatal period (postnatal days 1–10), and as we've seen, stressors experienced at this time alter the developmental trajectory of stress relevant processes. However, it also seems that the juvenile (early adolescent) period, spanning postnatal days 28–35 in rodents, is exquisitely sensitive to stressors and has protracted ramifications on vulnerability to the stressor-provoked neurochemical and behavioral changes that occur in adulthood (Jacobson-Pick et al., 2008; Spear, 2009). The sensitivity of this developmental phase may be related to reorganization of many neurotransmitter systems that occur at this time. As well, it is a developmental phase during which rodents display increased socialization (play) with conspecifics and increased independence from the dam. In fact, stressors in the form of social instability encountered at this age may influence brain development, particularly the hippocampus, and thus may affect some forms of memory in adulthood, including those associated with fear (McCormick et al., 2011). Moreover, as adults, these rats exhibited elevated levels of the stress hormone corticosterone and reduced numbers of receptors in the hippocampus that are sensitive to corticoids. Interestingly, in both rodents and humans, the adolescent period is one during which fear responses are especially difficult to overcome relative to those seen in younger or older individuals. Once an anxiety or fear response is established it may persist even after the danger is no longer present, and among adults with fear-related disorders, about 75% of cases have their roots in anxiety that developed at earlier ages. These fear responses are not immutable, as they could be attenuated with appropriate treatment; however, this was more difficult to achieve in adolescent rodents and humans (Uys et al., 2006).

Adolescence in humans is a period in which individuals are highly focused on 'fitting in', developing an adult-like identity, finding a peer group that will accept them and with whom they feel comfortable, showing interest in a sexual partner, and even concerns about events that they will be facing some time down the road. These issues become particularly acute as young people move from secondary school to university, as this transition requires considerable adaptation in the face of psychosocial and environmental changes. During this stage of life, many individuals leave behind long-standing social networks and form new ones, including changes in their romantic relationships, and efforts to gain social, economic, and emotional independence. In effect, just when young people are expected to establish their independence, they encounter a transition replete with factors that destabilize their support systems, and individuals may struggle with a collision between expectations of autonomy and contending with a series of novel and stressful experiences that would be best met with the support of others.

Given the distress associated with transitions into adulthood, a considerable number of young people experience clinical levels of major depression, dysthymia (i.e., chronic low-grade depression), and anxiety disorders that were estimated to be as high as 25% (Mackenzie et al., 2011). Moreover, many may have undiagnosed or subsyndromal symptoms of depression and anxiety that could reflect the antecedent conditions of major depression (Offer & Spiro, 1987). Thus, although the transition into adulthood can be seamless and exciting for some, for many others it is a challenging process that seems to last forever, and every day is filled with hardships.

OLDER AGE

Before starting a discussion of stress and aging, we need to distinguish what we mean by aged or aging. When I was young, and the mean life span was somewhere around 75 for females and 70 for males, someone at retirement age (65) was considered to be fairly old. With changes in lifestyle (diet, exercise) and medical treatments, life expectancy has increased appreciably, and 65 is hardly seen as 'old', and certainly not by others who are about that age (am I sounding a bit defensive?). Still, being old is no picnic, and getting old also has significant down-sides. With age comes a decaying system; young guys no longer want to play tennis as they 'want a good game', and flirting is interpreted as coming from an 'old lech'. Worse still, disease states generally become more common: neurodegenerative and cardiovascular diseases appear; kidney, liver, and lung diseases are on the horizon; and prostate problems, even those of a minor sort, can cause social distress (if this is too ambiguous, think of 'Depends'). Aging also influences the extent to which stressors affect well-being. Whether an individual ages 'successfully' or not depends (there's that word again) on, among other things, complex interactions that involve genetic factors, environmental influences, concurrent morbidities, and the ability to cope with stressors.

Studies in rats have pointed to yet another age-related factor that interferes with well-being in association with stressors. In older rats, the release of several brain neurotransmitters, such as norepinephrine, as well as the stress hormone corticosterone, is elevated under basal conditions (as it is in humans), and increases appreciably in response to acute stressors. However, normalization (the return to basal levels) may take longer to occur than it does in younger animals. It is thought that hormonal and neurochemical responses elicited by stressors are of adaptive value, but once the stressor terminates, things ought to return to normal relatively quickly. The sluggish normalization of neurotransmitter release and corticosterone levels, as we'll see in Chapters 3–5, in older individuals might have some fairly unfavorable repercussions.

A good conceptual framework to use in regard to stress and aging is that of allostasis and allostatic overload (Goldstein, 2011). Let's face it, the wear and tear on a 70 year-old person (like a 70 year-old car), will be much greater than the load that has been put on a much younger model. The greater the strain an individual had encountered previously, and the greater the challenge they are currently undergoing, the more likely it is that the bumper will fall off. However, as individuals age, vulnerability to pathology might not only stem from decaying biological processes, but might also be a result of the dwindling availability of resources that lend themselves to effective coping, including the reduced availability of social support from family and from friends who might not be able to help (or who might have predeceased them).

WHO WOULD SCAM OLD PEOPLE?

Of the many illnesses faced by older people, one of the most dreaded is dementia. The loss of self and the indignities that can be experienced in relation to many diseases are often beyond what anyone envisions for themselves. Significantly, among the elderly, cognitive decline is linked to stressful experiences. A prospective study among elderly individuals conducted over just 2.5 years revealed that protracted, highly stressful experiences were associated with increased conversion from individuals exhibiting mild cognitive impairments to moderate levels of dementia. Studies in rats also suggested that cognitive deficits and 'tau pathology' (a substance implicated in Alzheimer's disease) are influenced by cumulative stressor experiences (Sotiropoulos et al., 2011).

(Continued)

(Continued)

There are all sorts of scams being perpetrated, particularly through the internet. Over the course of two days I learned that my long-lost cousin in Italy, Giorgio Anisman, and my similarly lost cousin in Russia, Yvegeny Anisman, had died suddenly and I was their only known living relative. I stood to inherit millions! Who falls for these transparent and patently ridiculous efforts? Apparently there are some people who do, but it's a subset of older folks that are the most frequent victims of telephone and internet scams. It could potentially be that an age-related loss of neurons has made them 'less smart', or it might be that they're more trusting or, phrased differently, that they are deficient in their ability to 'doubt' information that would ordinarily appear suspicious. It seems that with age, a region in the brain associated with appraisals and decision making, the prefrontal cortex, may undergo changes for the worse. In this regard, even among otherwise intelligent people, when the dysfunctionality occurred in one aspect of this region, namely the ventral medial prefrontal cortex, individuals experienced difficulty in the effortful process necessary for disbelief, and hence they were more likely to be the victims of fraud. Being scammed is embarrassing and stressful for pretty well anyone, but for the elderly it's yet another slap in the face that highlights their limitations.

For some 'seniors', particularly those who've aged successfully (healthy in body and mind), this time of life can be wonderful. For many others, however, aging is the pits, and they certainly don't refer to it as 'the golden years'. Besides being accompanied by health problems and repeated visits to different doctors, aging is associated with difficulties getting around, the loss of friends (through death or translocation), the dispersal of family members as children find employment or other opportunities elsewhere, and diminished coping resources, including a progressively smaller social support network. In fact, loneliness, which is stressful for individuals of any age, is often notable in the elderly as their social network might have dissipated, and certain types of stressors produce especially marked physiological changes (e.g., cardiovascular responses) relative to those apparent at earlier ages (Ong et al., 2011). Beyond these stressors, aged individuals might suffer multiple indignities, including unsupportive interactions (often being patronised, talked down to, dismissed, made to feel invisible, or made to feel like a burden) and stigmatization. In light of these factors, it seems that the coping strategies endorsed by older individuals might shift away from ones that reflect a sense of control over their own lives, to those that are reliant on others. Is there any wonder that depression rates in older people are as high as they are?

SEX

It's hardly news that women in much of the world have it much harder than do men. Whether it involves issues related to the job front, taking care of the home or children, or illness, women seem to carry a greater load than do men. Certain illnesses, such as mood disorders and autoimmune disorders (those in which the immune system turns on the individual, as in the case of multiple sclerosis, lupus erythematosus, arthritis) also occur more frequently in women than in men. In the case of major depression the ratio is about 2:1, and this increases to 3:1 in the case of atypical depression (i.e., where symptoms comprise increased sleep, increased eating, and mood reactivity). Likewise, posttraumatic stress disorder (PTSD) that develops in response to traumatic events occurs more frequently among females than males. These sex differences might occur for any number of reasons, including differences in the stressors actually experienced, greater stress-relevant neurochemical disturbances in females, the influence of particular sex hormones, socialization processes that promote certain behavioral styles being adopted, the endorsement of less adaptive coping strategies to deal with stressors, or psychosocial or personality factors that favor the development of illness. To the extent that sensitivity or reactivity to stressors differs between sexes, one might expect to find that the treatment of stress-related disorders would likewise differ in this regard.

In animal studies sexual dimorphisms (differences in phenotypes as a function of gender) are also apparent in neurobiological responses to stressors. In rodents, females are generally more behaviorally reactive to stressors than males, typically being associated with greater stressor-related neuroendocrine changes, such as variations of the stress hormone corticosterone (Rivier, 1999). Moreover, neuronal activity is increased in numerous brain regions that govern behavioral and cognitive responses to stressors (e.g., frontal, cingulate, and piriform cortices, and the hippocampus, hypothalamic paraventricular nucleus, medial amygdala, and lateral septum), and the extent of the activation varies over the estrous cycle, implicating a role for sex hormones in determining these outcomes (Figueiredo et al., 2002).

In humans, however, the effects of stressors on cortisol (the equivalent of corticosterone in rodents) were greater in males than in females, or were found not to differ as a function of gender (Kajantie & Phillips, 2006). It seems that these effects might vary with the estrous cycle, with greatest cortisol responses in women occurring during the luteal phase (the later part of the menstrual cycle during which the hormone progesterone is very high). It was also reported that the effects of social stressors on cortisol levels in women are blunted among those using oral contraceptives, indicating interactions between stressors and estrogen in provoking the stress response. No doubt there are numerous factors that could account for the difference between cortisol responses in human males and females, including those related to the nature of the stressor (intrapersonal stressors might have greater effects in females, whereas performance pressures have greater effects in males) and the appraisal/coping that might be instigated by the stressor in particular situations.

As we cover successive topics, it will become clear that the greater stress-vulnerability of females regarding depressive and anxiety disorders is also apparent with respect to autoimmune disorders and some types of heart disease. Despite these health inequities, it seems that on average, women still outlive men just as they did fifty years ago, although the gap has been closing. This is not simply due to a bias regarding who is in the workforce, as the same statistics are apparent in both industrialized and non-industrialized countries.

IF THEY'RE THE WEAKER SEX, HOW COME WOMEN LIVE LONGER THAN MEN?

The greater life span of women doesn't seem to simply be a result of estrogen levels, although it can't readily be ruled out that estrogen can interact with other factors to increase well-being. It could be related to women having two XX chromosomes, whereas men have an X chromosome replaced by a puny Y. Tom Persl had an interesting perspective on this (Lauara Blue, *Time Magazine*, 6 August 2006; www.time.com/time/health/article/0,8599,1827162,00.html). He suggested that several factors converge to produce the gap. First, men *smoke a lot more than women (or at least they used to)*; second, *they eat more food that promotes elevated cholesterol levels*; third, *men generally are not as effective in coping with stressors, tending to internalize rather than letting go and externalizing*. This said, I've heard from women that men complain vociferously about every little thing, and if, God forbid, they get a cold you'd think the world was coming to an end (incidentally, these women even referred to this as a 'man cold'). There is another factor that should be considered: it is possible that *testosterone may somehow come to affect longevity*. It has, in fact, been reported that eunuchs in Korea between the fourteenth and nineteenth centuries lived about fifteen years longer than other people. Doesn't sound like a great method for extending life, does it?

PREVIOUS EXPERIENCES AND SENSITIZATION

There is no question, as we've seen in our discussion of early life experiences, that an individual's previous experiences may influence the response to later stressor encounters. It's not simply a matter of our memories of previous experiences influencing our responses to stressors. The characteristics of the neurons themselves may have changed, so that the response to later stimulation is enhanced (this is known as 'sensitization').

Studies in animals indicated that stressor encounters influence the neurochemical responses elicited by subsequent insults. For instance, the brain's neurochemical changes exerted by acute stressors can be induced more readily if mice had previously encountered stressful experiences (Anisman et al., 2008). It's still a bit early in the book to explain how stressful events might come to change the characteristics of neurons so that they would become more responsive (or conversely, less responsive, which is termed 'desensitized' or 'down-regulated') to later challenges. In fact, there are several ways in which these sensitized responses can develop, but what must be recognized at this point is that many biological systems are subject to this sort of effect. You might come across the concept of plasticity in regard to neuronal processes. This refers to the ability of the synapses to change, or the connection between neurons to change in strength as a result of experiences (use) or lack of use. Plasticity is a fundamental feature of the brain that is required for, among other things, learning and memory, and sensitization is an instance of this neural plasticity. However, when we deal with sensitization it should be considered that processes responsible for the sensitization of a given neurotransmitter system may differ from those associated with the sensitization of a second transmitter system. For instance, it is possible that sensitization of some systems may involve altered expression or sensitivity of relevant receptors, whereas sensitization of other systems may involve the synergistic (multiplicative) effects of two or more biological substrates. Finally, the effects of stressors on sensitized neuronal responses may persist for many months following a stressor event, and it is possible that sensitization processes contribute to the long-term influence of stressors on psychological states.

Based on such findings, it was suggested (Post, 1992) that the biological substrates of depressive illness may evolve over time with repeated stressor experiences and recurrent depressive episodes. With each stressor experience, or with each episode of depression, the stressor severity needed to elicit the depressive mood becomes smaller, until eventually, very little is needed to encourage a depressive state. There have, indeed, been numerous reports showing that although the first episode of depression is preceded by fairly strong stressors, the severity of the stressor necessary to cause illness recurrence is smaller (Kendler et al., 1995). In fact, among individuals who experienced recurrent episodes of depression, very mild stressors were needed to re-induce the depressive state, and even reminders of stressful experiences were sufficient to produce this outcome (Monroe & Harkness, 2005).

In addition to sensitization of biological systems, how we appraise (evaluate) the world around us can be influenced by our previous stressor experiences. By example, it isn't hard to imagine that if individuals encounter a stressor that traumatized them, later reminders of these same experiences will have profound psychological and physical repercussions. This also applies to adverse experiences that occurred in early childhood. Children who experience a trauma will, as adults, be much more likely to develop depressive illness (Kendler et al., 2004), and importantly, this is apparent even when statistically controlling for the family and contextual factors that have been associated with depressive illness. This effect of early life adversity is not limited to young children, having similarly been observed in women that had experienced physical or sexual abuse in adolescence (Harkness et al., 2006). It might be the case that when certain stressors are encountered, they cause changes in numerous aspects of an individual's life, altering the trajectory of life experiences (friendships and other support networks, coping processes, lifestyles, general world view, and even the propensity for further stress encounters), and culminating in a greater vulnerability to psychological and physical illness.

STRESS GENERATION

Stress generation refers to occasions on which individuals, because of their circumstances, may bring stress onto themselves. This doesn't mean that we should blame the victim for finding themselves in adverse situations. Instead, it means that sometimes, through any number of factors, people are disposed to doing the wrong thing at the wrong time, and they might even do this repeatedly. Depressed individuals, by their behaviors, are thought to be a particularly vulnerable group for stress generation (Liu & Alloy, 2010). For instance, one partner in a romantic relationship may tire of always having to deal with the other person's depressive state (poor mood, negativity, lethargy, and aggressive behaviors that might occur), hence leading to the dissolution of the relationship. Essentially, the depressed partner, by not altering their negative behaviors (typically these involve behaviors of a dependent nature), contributed to the break-up and the loss of an important relationship that might have served as a stress buffer. Likewise, the depressed individual, who tends to be inactive and withdrawn, may also alienate their co-workers, and ultimately find themselves out of a job. Stress generation is also more common among those high in neuroticism (emotional instability), which is not surprising as their emotional sensitivity might favor interpersonal conflicts (Poulton & Andrews, 1992). It has also been reported that perfectionism contributed to interpersonal stressors (Flett et al., 1996), as did sociotropy (a personality trait in which individuals exhibit high levels of dependence and an excessive need to please others; Daley et al., 1997). This is in line with the perspective that individuals whose self-esteem is based largely on their relationship with others place themselves in a situation where interpersonal conflicts will be tied to depression and thus will contribute to further stress generation.

In a sense, it seems that stress breeds stress. In fact, in some instances, by their behaviors and attitudes individuals are able to make their worst fears turn into reality. Let's have a look at one example where this appears, namely that of dating abuse, which occurs in about 20% of dating relationships among university-aged individuals (the abuse, incidentally, goes in both directions, as males when asked are as likely to report psychological abuse as are women). Significantly, however, women who had previously been abused were reported to be at increased risk of being in further abusive relationships. In our research conducted with undergraduate women, 70.4% of those who encountered dating abuse reported a previous assaultive experience (childhood assault, assault by a previous partner), whereas only 24.6% of those in non-abusive relationships had such a history (Matheson et al., 2007). It was not a matter of women who experienced abuse generally being more likely to encounter traumatic experiences, as other forms of trauma (e.g., accidents, witnessing violent events, and the death of someone close to them) were not more common among abused women. Instead, it seemed as if an experience of abuse that occurred earlier in life effectively set in motion a cascade of changes that favored increased vulnerability to later stressors, which provoked depression and PTSD. What exactly this process entails isn't known, but it is possible that the initial abusive experience engendered a set of beliefs and learned coping responses that facilitated women's ability to endure or tolerate their abusive situations, or alternatively, the experience may have limited their capability to leave a bad relationship. Additionally, early abuse experiences may limit the development of social and emotional intelligence skills, and such skill deficits undermined the ability to appraise and respond appropriately to emotionally charged stressor situations (Terrance & Matheson, 2003). In view of the relations between dating abuse and earlier abusive experiences, increased incidence of stress generation, diminished self-esteem and self-worth, depression and PTSD, it would be inappropriate to consider an adult experience in isolation from other factors that might be tied to stress generation.

CONCLUSION

Stressful events are common life experiences whose effects can be negligible and brushed off readily, or they can be extremely severe, affecting individuals for years. Numerous factors can contribute to our vulnerability to stressor-elicited illnesses, and likewise being resilient in the face of severe stressors and pathology involves complex interactions between a constellation of variables. To a significant extent, however, the impact of stressors will be determined by how these stressors are viewed or appraised and how individuals cope with them. In Chapter 2 we'll be covering these topics in the hope that this will give us a better perspective of what to do when we encounter adverse events. However, if there's a single take-home message from Chapter 1, it's that stressful events and their effects are not only complex, but also that there are marked interindividual differences in their effects. What might be stressful to you might be a walk in the park for someone else, and conversely someone else's greatest distress may be a mild annoyance for others. Without considerable experience (and perhaps not even then), don't presume to understand another person's stress responses.

SUMMARY

- Stressors come in multiple flavors and vary across numerous dimensions. The extent to which stressors affect our well-being is related to the nature of the stressor and the psychological attributes of that stressor, such as the controllability, predictability uncertainty, and ambiguity of stressors or threats of impending stressors.
- The impact of stressors may be governed by the chronicity of stressor experiences as well as stressors that had previously been encountered (e.g., early in life).
- Individual difference factors are fundamental in determining to what extent a stressor might have severe adverse consequences. In this regard, genetic make-up, age, gender, and personality factors all are effective in moderating stress responses.
- Factors that contribute to these individual differences, including the phenotypic expression of genes, can be influenced by previous stressor experiences that can potentially shape the way in which individuals respond to psychological, physical, or even systemic challenges.

2 APPRAISALS, COPING, AND WELL-BEING

THE IDIOT DEFENSE

One strategy that has been used in legal proceedings, often termed the 'idiot defense' (but also termed the 'ostrich defense'), is that of maintaining that the defendant was unaware of certain events that had occurred, even though they ought to have been aware of them. In many scandals that involved corporate fraud (e.g., Enron, WorldCom), chief executives maintained that their job was to run the company as a whole, and leave certain aspects of the corporation to experts in specific sectors. Typically, this defense didn't do much for them.

When little kids see a clown, some of these kids laugh whereas others might find them scary. Obviously, how the clown is perceived is in the eye of the beholder. Of those kids who find the clown scary, some might cover their eyes or put their head under a blanket, and for that moment the stressor doesn't exist. In kids this ostrich defense might be viewed as cute, but comparable behaviors in adults (e.g., don't look or touch that swelling or lump and you can pretend that it's not there) are referred to as avoidance or denial, and are also seen to be illogical, not at all cute, and even less useful than the 'idiot defense' adopted in legal cases.

In Chapter 1 we learned that stressor features as well as our individual characteristics, regardless of whether they're due to genetic contributions, previous experiences, personality or age, will influence the extent to which negative experiences affect our well-being. To a significant extent, these variables influence how potential stressors are appraised or viewed, and the methods that are used to minimize or eliminate their impact (Lazarus & Folkman, 1984). In this chapter we'll consider appraisal and coping processes and how they might come to promote negative outcomes. The reader ought to come away with an understanding of:

- what's meant by stressor appraisal, and how to identify the factors that influence the appraisal process and decision making, as well as how misappraisals of events might occur and how illogical thinking might play into these;
- how appraisals influence emotions, and how emotions might affect appraisals;
- the various ways in which individuals cope with stressors, and some of the moderators of a coping response. They should also be able to identify how coping styles and strategies (styles refer to a dispositional or trait characteristic; strategies are viewed as a state characteristic that may be dependent on situational factors) might influence the emergence or exacerbation of pathological states;
- the extent to which some coping methods can be used to deal with stressors more effectively than others, and the circumstances under which this might be the case;
- how social support resources can be used to deal with stressors, and what happens when instead of obtaining support one ends up with unsupportive interactions.

APPRAISALS AND COPING SKILLS

How we perceive potentially threatening events, and which methods we use to cope with them, have been linked to both psychological and physical pathologies. Indeed there has been a deluge of studies showing that the impacts of stressors were modified by both personal and coping resources, thus influencing whether or not particular disturbances would emerge. Likewise, the occurrence of depression in the context of particular illnesses

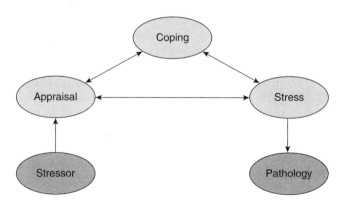

The appraisal-coping-stress triad

FIGURE 2.1 The triad above indicates that our appraisals influence the coping strategies that we use to deal with stressful experiences. Once a stressful event occurs we make an appraisal of this event, which, in turn, leads to coping strategies being engaged in an effort to attenuate or diminish the impact of the stressor. If the event is seen as aversive, and especially one that is out of our control, then the event will be perceived as stressful and a stress reaction will be engendered, which might provoke or exacerbate a pathological condition.

(e.g., HIV, cancer, renal transplants, and cardiac problems) has been related to the individual's coping ability (Tennen et al., 2000), and it seems that aspects of coping may be fundamental in dealing with specific stressors, such as caregiving, the loss of a child, stigma and discrimination, as well as in response to severe trauma (Branscombe & Ellemers, 1998). As depicted in Figure 2.1, how we perceive or cognitively appraise (interpret) stressors has a lot to do with the coping strategies we invoke to deal with them (Lazarus & Folkman, 1984), which in turn might contribute to whether or not pathological outcomes will emerge. Conversely, the coping styles or strategies we use to deal with stressors might also come to influence how we appraise stressors.

APPRAISALS OF STRESSORS

Appraisals refer to the evaluations that individuals make in response to a potential stressor. These appraisals comprise the threat or risk associated with the event (i.e., the potential for harm or loss, and the degree of challenge the event represents), as well as an assessment of the severity, controllability, predictability, ambiguity, and the meaning associated with this potential threat. When faced with a potentially stressful event, appraisals ought to be adaptive, as they should enable individuals to distinguish those situations that require action from those that do not, along with the type of action that will most effectively address the stressor. To a considerable extent, appraisals are based on the individual's specific abilities, beliefs, previous experiences in dealing with similar and dissimilar events, and the resources available to contend with the challenge. Thus, appraisals define the extent of the threat that an event imposes, and influence the coping methods that are selected to deal with the stressor. For example, although threat and challenge are similar in so far as they both might promote action, they also have important distinguishing features. Specifically, an appraisal of threat is often associated with negative emotions (e.g., fear, anxiety, or anger) as it signifies the potential for harm or loss. Challenge, in contrast, might signify the potential for growth or gain and hence might be associated with positive emotions (e.g., exhilaration, eagerness, excitement). However, this might not be the case for all individuals encountering a given event: for one individual the event might reflect a challenge, but for another, the same event might be viewed as a threat.

PRIMARY AND SECONDARY APPRAISALS

Potentially stressful events are thought to give rise to two interpretive processes, termed 'primary' and 'secondary' appraisal. Primary appraisal comprises perceptions associated with the impact of a potentially stressful event or stimulus: for example, the impact of an event may be perceived as benign (or even positive), and hence no immediate action might be deemed necessary. Alternatively, the event or stimulus might be construed as a threat, and as such, additional interpretations concerning the event might be evoked: these include the potential for the event to induce harm, whether it threatens the individual, and to what extent it is a challenge (Lazarus & Folkman, 1984).

Threat might not always be identified easily in some situations, but individuals will infer that a threat is present based on experience and previously acquired knowledge (Lazarus, 1966). Moreover, the positive or negative outcomes associated with earlier experiences might provide individuals with information relevant to threat appraisals (Gallagher, 1990). Having identified a threat, individuals ought to engage in behaviors to limit the threat or its impact. Needless to say, remaining in a heightened or repeated state of arousal owing to perceptions of impending threats is hardly adaptive, and might confer increased vulnerability to illness. Indeed, individuals who tend to appraise events as threatening may be at increased risk for greater long-term health problems relative to those who make more positive appraisals (Hemenover & Dienstbier, 1996).

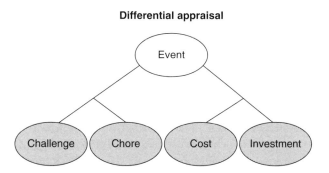

FIGURE 2.2 This differentiates between possible appraisals that can be made with respect to a given situation. For instance, an individual being sent on a training course to upgrade their skills can see this as being either a challenge ('This will be super. I've always wanted to be able to get the maximum out of the internet and here's my chance to learn.') or a chore ('Oh brother. Now I have to leave the comforts of home for two weeks to take a dippy course that I could do on my own.'). They can also see it as a cost ('I've got a ton to do and when I get back the pile will have become that much higher') or an investment ('Once I get this under my belt, I'll be able to do searches twice as fast and that'll increase my productivity and give me yet more leisure time').

As indicated in Chapter 1, the response to stressors is governed by numerous factors (e.g., previous experiences, age), and true to this, appraisals of stressful events may be influenced by several antecedent experiences as well as numerous dispositional factors (e.g., Power & Hill, 2010; Roesch & Rowley, 2005). In this regard, general appraisal styles have been associated with several global personality constructs, including hardiness, optimism, hope, hostility, trait negative/positive affectivity, and extraversion and neuroticism. Given the large number of factors that can influence how individuals might appraise a potential threat, it's perfectly predictable that unanimity is often lacking as to how certain stressors are appraised. Certainly there are stressors that virtually all people will perceive in a similar fashion (e.g. war, natural disasters). However, there are many less intense stressors that are somewhat ambiguous, which will be associated with diverse appraisals.

Whereas primary appraisals are mainly concerned with the perceived impact of a stressful event, secondary appraisals encompass those perceptions related to the resources available for successfully eliminating or attenuating a stressor. Essentially, the secondary appraisal poses the question 'Can I cope with this threat?'. For example, when confronted with potential unemployment (an occurrence likely to be perceived as threatening or distressing), a secondary appraisal would comprise an assessment of the financial resources available to deal with the stressor (e.g., employment insurance) relative to the demands that will be placed on the individual (e.g., mortgage payments, tuition for kids, gasoline, food; along with other stressors that accompany being 'let go', including diminished self-esteem, anger, or shame). Thus, the apparent stressfulness of the event will depend, in part, on the degree to which that individual's resources are perceived to enable them to meet these demands. Of course, the appraisals that individuals make regarding a threat are influenced by a variety of contextual or experiential factors. For instance, in the case of potential job loss the appraisals might be affected by whether the individual is supporting others, whether they're near retirement and would have left the job soon, as well as the extent to which their identity was tied to the job.

SECONDARY APPRAISALS AND CONTROL DIMENSIONS

One of the most fundamental aspects of secondary appraisals concerns our perceived control over the situation. Control can involve several different components or subtypes. *Behavioral control* comprises the ability to influence a stressful situation through the initiation of some sort of action, whereas *cognitive control* can be conceptualized as the ability to influence the situation by using some sort of mental strategy (Cohen et al., 1986). Another aspect of control comprises *decisional control*, which entails having a choice over the coping strategies available to deal with a stressor, provided that the situation allows for such choices to be made. Another element of control is concerned with *informational control*, which reflects the degree to which the individual is able to predict and prepare for stressful events. Although each type of control appears to be important in determining strategies to reduce distress, cognitive control likely promotes the most beneficial effects on well-being.

APPRAISALS, DECISION MAKING, AND FAST AND SLOW THINKING

As described in Figure 2.2, the way we appraise stressors goes a long way in determining the way in which we choose to cope with challenges. The model described by Lazarus is, in several respects, very reminiscent of a framework that has been adopted in decision-making theory, and it has much to offer theorizing related to stress processes and the development of stress-related psychopathological conditions. To a significant extent we make decisions or attributions based on what Tversky and Kahneman (1974) termed the 'representative heuristic' (Kahneman, by the way, won a Nobel Prize in economics for his work, but sadly Tversky died before he could be a recipient of this award). Generally, heuristics refer to strategies (or shortcuts) that are made on the basis of information that is easily accessed. These shortcuts might be based on an individual's experiences or rules that had previously been established. Thus, rather than going through lengthy processes to make decisions, individuals might simply resort to past practices, educated guesses, or rules of thumb. The representative heuristic is employed when individuals consider whether their current hypothesis regarding the occurrence of an event is consistent with everyday experiences instead of strict probabilistic considerations. When individuals are in stressful situations new learning is often difficult, but well-entrenched performance, memory, and decision making are not usually impaired. Evidently, in a problem-solving situation that occurs soon after being exposed to a stressor, problem-solving abilities may be compromised, and individuals are more likely to fall back on using a representative heuristic. Another heuristic comprises *attribute substitution*, which essentially means that when a situation is fairly complex, individuals will make decisions based on a simpler question, but without necessarily being aware that they are doing so. In this instance, they might choose certain attributes of a complex situation or a person, and apply these attributes more broadly. It also seems, as we'll see shortly, that certain emotions and personality variables might influence the way we appraise events and the decisions we make. Fearful individuals tend to exhibit pessimistic risk assessments and are risk averse, whereas angry people are more optimistic in their assessments and less risk adverse. Unfortunately, anger may also be associated with a heuristic in which individuals might not select from all the options available to them in a decision-making situation (Lerner & Tiedens, 2006).

In discussing the cognitive processes related to decision making, it was suggested that dual systems are in operation: an automatic operations system (dubbed System 1 or Fast Thinking) and a more cognitively-based system, termed System 2 or Slow Thinking. Kahneman (2011) explained that System 1, the automatic, fast thinking system, is highly influenced by our experiences, so that it is *primed* to react in a particular way in response to environmental events, whereas the cognitively-oriented slow thinking System 2 might kick in when more complex decisions need to be made.

DECIDING ON THE FLY

Some decisions that we make are based on lots of thought and reasoning, but sometimes we need to make decisions rapidly and there might not be much time to do so. It seems that although the prefrontal cortex is generally involved in decision making, some aspects of this cortical region might be responsible for decision making that occurs on the spur of the moment, whereas others are based on experience and habits that had been formed earlier (Jones et al., 2012). It has been thought that 'value-based' decisions, such as those that occur when an individual appraises options and potential consequences, involve the functioning of the orbital frontal cortex. Based on studies among individuals that had sustained damage to this region, it was concluded that the orbital cortex is necessary when decisions must be computed quickly or that must be inferred. However, other cortical regions likely are involved when the decisions are based on 'cached' values that were determined by previous experiences. It will be recognized that this is not far

(Continued)

(Continued)

removed from the Fast and Slow Thinking described by Kahneman, but anchors the notion to particular brain regions. Essentially, when the orbital frontal cortex is disturbed, decision making 'on the fly' suffers from an impaired ability to base decisions on prior experiences that allow options to be weighed appropriately. This has obvious implications for an individual's ability to learn from their mistakes, and may be relevant for the propensity to make bad decisions related to repeated drug abuse, especially as drugs such as cocaine markedly influence the orbital frontal cortex.

To a considerable extent our experiences and memories of experiences might prime our responses to particular events (Morewedge & Kahneman, 2010). In this regard, three factors will largely govern our response biases; associative coherence, attribute substitution, and processing fluency. Associative coherence refers to a particular stimulus eliciting a coherent and self-reinforcing pattern of associative processes; what this means is that the stimulus or event is consistent with our preconceived or primed 'intuitions'. The second component, attribute substitution, means that when we have made a judgment about a particular stimulus, we might form further unconscious attributes about this stimulus, based on what we had learned previously in similar situations. So if we are primed to believe that Sarah is a charitable person, we might make further attributions about that person, such as Sarah is also kind, warm, and even a kindred spirit. Even though we know virtually nothing about Sarah, except for one characteristic (she is charitable), it primes us to readily believe or accept other features of her personality. Finally, processing fluency, or our subjective experience concerning the relative ease/difficulty involved in a given cognitive task, is influential in determining whether particular judgments will be made. There are a variety of factors that influence processing fluency in addition to previous experiences and priming, including the clarity and ease with which the information is obtained.

Turning back to primary appraisals in the context of stress responses, it seems that when we make an initial decision or appraisal about an event, this involves a semi-automatic process that might be enacted on the basis of the very same principles described by Kahneman in regard to decision making. Essentially, associative coherence, stimulus substitution, and processing fluency may be fundamental in defining our initial appraisals of a potentially threatening situation. Consider for a moment a sudden stressful occurrence that you experienced. If it was one that you had previously experienced or one that was similar to other events, then you might engage in responses that are 'second nature' to you and the resulting actions seem well rehearsed (hence, when going into some situations, a realistic practice run, even cognitively, is well advised). However, if the stressful situation is entirely out of the range of your expectations or experiences, then it may give rise to a confused response (or even an 'out of body experience') and it takes a few seconds or even milliseconds for you to 'understand' what is actually happening. It is then that System 2, or secondary appraisals, come into the picture so that appropriate decisions can be made.

There are situations that we get into where decision making is not clear cut. Indeed, we might find ourselves in circumstances where the conditions seem ambiguous because we don't have the knowledge or background to see it for what it is. By example, most of us won't have a clue concerning the value of a car or a house when we start out looking to make a purchase. Instead, we look at 'anchors' that help us make a decision (Kahneman, 2011). In this case, the anchor is the asking price (or what other houses in the area have sold for, or advice from an agent who is actually not on our side, but simply wants to make a sale), and after some negotiation we might come up with a number that is reasonable both to ourselves and from the perspective of the vendor. However, the seller could have asked for an amount that was 10 or 20% higher (or lower) and we would have gone through the very same process, simply because we have no idea what the actual value of the house or car might be. Of course, in some instances the starting point might be so far off the mark that we wouldn't even consider the purchase, but if it is 'in the ball park' then we might proceed with our negotiations none the wiser.

The very same thing holds true when it comes to making appraisals regarding threats to our well-being. We need an anchor to tell us what the threat means. When a government agency pronounces that the risk of a pandemic is high, we might ask 'what's meant by high?'. Does 'high' mean that 99% of people will be affected, or is 'high' 30%, and what does this mean when it comes to the risk for me or those close to me? Furthermore, given the past track record of the agencies that inform us about all sorts of events (e.g., the media, government, or even some celebrity who holds forth on a subject in which s/he hasn't any expertise), to what extent should these anchors be discounted? After all, we've had numerous warnings from government agencies of things that simply haven't materialized. Even though we are able to process a fair amount of information, and we're able to appraise its value, it is often the case that our appraisals aren't at all sophisticated and might actually be tied to anchors that comprise nothing more than 'what some guy said' or list prices on a sign.

APPRAISALS AND MISAPPRAISALS

Before we go any further, an important caveat needs to be introduced. We often assume that our appraisals of situations are, in fact, accurate. In part, this is likely correct. This also means that, in part, this conclusion is wrong. How accurate are our appraisals of situations? You probably know that when you're in a slump everything looks bad (this is your appraisal), and when you're riding high, then just about everything looks good, and even the obviously bad things look manageable. Essentially, when a person comes into a situation in a poor state of mind, then in dealing with stressors they might not see the world the way it really is, but instead see it from a narrow, dark, and gloomy place. It's under these conditions that we might want to look to our friends to get their reaction to events, as it's often easier for an outside observer to see things 'in perspective'.

Just as we might make appraisals based on our own previous experiences, we also do so based on what others tell us or on the basis of what we believe that others think. Individuals frequently make social comparisons, and then form their appraisals accordingly. Experiments from decades ago illustrated that we tend to conform to what others do when making certain types of appraisals, and it seems that social comparisons are also made when it comes to some fairly stressful situations. Obviously, when you need to rely on the judgment of others over a certain issue, make sure that they're in the right state of mind for properly assessing a situation. At times, a person might find themselves asking for advice from a group of friends. However, as you have heard at some time or another, the appraisals and actions made by groups might be very different from those that any single individual might make. Specifically, when appraisals and decisions are made by a group, it is more likely that they will engage in greater risk taking than might be the case if they do so as individuals. This phenomenon, known as the 'risky shift', can come about owing to a diffusion of responsibility ('we're all in this together, and we'll share the blame if things don't work out well'). Alternatively, it might be that individuals follow the example of others who are seen as more inclined to take on a risky position. Regardless of the source of the risky shift, this tells us that when we, as individuals, make appraisals of situations, the perspectives we come up with might differ from those made by a group.

There are also numerous situations in which individuals don't make evaluations of events on the basis of their own intuitions, but on the basis of what norms they believe exist. In a recent study we recruited college-aged women who were in psychologically abusive dating relationships and in whom symptoms of depression were elevated. When these women were shown a nine-minute video clip of a young woman describing her steadily increasing abusive relationship (escalating from mild criticism through to verbal and psychological abuse, and finally to clear physical harm), our abused participants, who we had expected would be upset by what they heard, were for the most part not at all upset. Indeed, some were upbeat, and even giddy. Our experimental probing suggested that these women seemed to be making social comparisons to justify the fact that they were staying in their current relationship, and the film clip served to validate their view that their relationship was actually normal. Essentially, some of these women indicated that 'My relationship isn't all that great. But if my boyfriend treated me that way [referring to the video clip] I'd leave him'. Remarkably, however, when we measured the stress hormone (cortisol) that is detectable in saliva, their hormone levels were elevated in comparison to those of women who were in non-abusive relationships. So although their *stated* appraisal of the situation was that it did not distress them, their biological stress system seemed to tell us otherwise, and just witnessing the video and answering questions related to their own lives were sufficient to produce this outcome. Their verbal statements might have reflected a social comparison process, but we don't discount the possibility that their statements concerning their relationship might well have been a cover to avoid admitting that their situation was actually as abusive as it was (Matheson & Anisman, 2012).

SEEMED LIKE A GOOD IDEA AT THE TIME

Most of us have misappraised situations. Sometimes we make commitments to do things which at the time 'didn't seem like bad idea'; however, our sense of dread increases as the time for action approaches. Ask any plane phobic about a holiday planned six months earlier, or the person with a fear of public speaking who agreed, many months earlier, to talk to a large group, and they'll say that it didn't seem like a bad idea at the time. When things are far off, there is an 'illusion of courage' that makes us less fearful of an event even though we've had lots of experience knowing that we won't deal with this well when the time comes (Van Boven et al., 2012). We're just not very good at appraising the distress of distal events. Clearly, what we need to do at the time of the invitation is perceive how we will actually react when the moment of truth comes along, and importantly, act on these feeling, rather than fool ourselves into thinking that things will be different next time.

Related to the fact that experiences influence how we appraise events is the notion that even subtle cues can prime us to perceive events around us in a particular way. We know, for example, that eye witness testimonies are frequently unreliable, and that our memories of events can be altered through subtle suggestions (Loftus, 2003). Priming, as Kahneman (2011) has indicated, can likewise be based on subtle factors as well as comments made by individuals in regard to a person or situation. If my best friend thinks someone is two-faced, and he tells me this, then when I meet this person I might well be very cautious or even negative. Related to this, stereotypes about certain groups or cultures can influence our appraisals, even if we are not consciously aware that this is occurring. Likewise, if an individual is primed to believe that a certain drug will reduce the pain that they're experiencing, they will report diminished pain after consuming the drug, even if it was only a placebo (see more on this in Chapter 12). A person in a 'uniform' or a relatively tall person is viewed as more authoritative than others, even if there's not a hint that this person is in the least competent. Our appraisals, and our misappraisals, intrude on a huge number of things that we do on a day-to-day basis, and often we might not have a clue concerning the subtle effects of such priming.

As mentioned earlier, our appraisals concerning the controllability of a stressor may have considerable importance in defining the coping strategies that we use and the behavioral and psychological outcomes that ensue. If we believe that we can influence a situation, then appraisals of that situation obviously ought to differ from those evident when we believe a situation is beyond our control. However, individuals frequently overestimate the degree to which they are able to exert control over otherwise chance events, and might be motivated to perceive control over their environment. It goes without saying that these misappraisals might produce difficulties that hadn't been anticipated, but this illusion of control might also have some positive attributes. When we perceive events as controllable, we are generally better able to deal with stressors through the adoption of problem-focused coping strategies (trying to diminish or eliminate stressors or somehow dealing with them in thoughtful systematic ways), which is usually considered a good way of coping. In a sense, the illusory sense of control may actually reflect an adaptive process for dealing with challenges. For instances, cancer patients who had the perception that they had some control over their illness exhibited lower levels of distress than did individuals who did not have these control perceptions (Ranchor et al., 2010). Illusory control in this instance might not affect disease progression, but at the very least, it allows for lower daily distress.

Finally, there are many instances in which situations, especially those of a social nature, are relatively unclear, as the messages we receive are subtle or may have multiple meanings. What does a slight frown by my colleague mean, and was it actually directed at me or was it a frown that wasn't directed at anybody in particular? If a situation is uncertain or ambiguous, it's fairly difficult to make proper appraisals. Often, this is compounded by the fact that appraisals regarding stressors are made at the very time when we might be least well prepared to make accurate appraisals – that is, while we are in a threatening situation our judgment may be influenced by our emotions or our inability to see things objectively.

APPRAISALS AND IRRATIONAL THINKING

There is yet another aspect of uncertainty/ambiguity that is central to our analysis of appraisal processes. This issue also falls into the category of decision making rather than appraisals, but appraisals of choices and making decisions are (obviously) intricately linked. Kahneman and Tversky have made the point that individuals often behave in apparently odd ways, often making seemingly irrational decisions. In one interesting study, students were placed in a situation where they were told to imagine that they had sat a very important exam that would determine their future. They were then asked to imagine that the grades would be posted in two days' time. Some students were told they had passed the exam, whereas others were told they had failed. At this point they were also told that they had the opportunity to take a nice holiday trip, and were asked whether they would take this trip. Those students who had passed and those who failed frequently indicated that they would take the trip – presumably those who passed saw it as a reward for their hard efforts, and those who failed saw it as a chance to diminish their despair. Essentially, all the students indicated that they would indeed take the trip, although they would do so for different reasons. Now comes the really interesting part. In a second study, students were told that the exams would be posted in two days' time, but this time they were given the option of either (a) going on the trip immediately (before the results of exam were released), (b) foregoing the trip, or (c) paying a $5 fee to hold their ticket (delay the trip) until they had received their grades. The students did what you would probably do – they paid the $5 to have the ticket held. Does this decision make any sense at all? In the first experiment students indicated that they would be taking the trip regardless of whether they passed or failed! Yet when offered the option of waiting (and paying $5) they tended to choose this, despite the fact that they would likely opt to take the trip irrespective of their grade. So what might have motivated this behavior? It seems that uncertainty gives rise to some interesting ways of coping that are understandable, even if they are irrational.

TOO MANY CHOICES

Retailers know that giving the consumer too many choices isn't always the best idea; when faced with too many choices, with varying attributes and prices and confusing information, the potential consumer goes away to 'think' about it. My friend, a retailer, tells me that when she hears this she wants to scream 'Think about it? What's there to freakin think about? We're talking about a toaster. A toaster! Not whether you should go for chemo vs. mastectomy!'.

We can go on with numerous examples of the irrational decisions that people make, but the main topic of this book is about stress, and in this context we often witness people make bad decisions that then have negative repercussions. You might recall from our earlier discussion of stress generation that stressed individuals seem to get themselves into increasingly distressing situations. They make poor appraisals and then choose the wrong methods of coping, and they do this repeatedly. Let's use a very simple example of this. At the end of this chapter there is a questionnaire to measure how individuals cope with stressors. In our research we use this coping inventory a fair bit. In some experiments we ask participants to indicate, on a 5-point rating scale, to what extent they use each of the coping responses to deal with particular stressors. In some of our experiments we also asked participants to indicate how effective they thought these coping strategies would be in dealing with a given stressor. For many people, particularly those who seemed fairly well adjusted, there was a match between the coping method they chose and how effective they thought it might be. However, others, particularly individuals with high levels of depressive symptoms, favored particular coping styles, despite their belief that this coping method wouldn't be effective. I can almost hear them saying 'I know my coping responses weren't good, but I just didn't know what else to do'. You might want to complete the questionnaire in relation to a recent stressor you experienced, and then go through it a second time to determine whether you think the coping behaviors you selected were effective.

There are, of course, many factors that go into the irrational behaviors that individuals display. For some, their personality characteristics don't allow them to do what's necessary. There are individuals who are so afraid of making wrong decisions, or who can't abide with feelings of regret, that they end up not making any decisions. For others, too many choices are daunting and they too end up making no selection at all. In still other situations procrastination might be a way of dealing with the anxiety associated with making decisions (putting off seeing a doctor regarding certain suspicious symptoms), and they continue with these clearly maladaptive behaviors in the full knowledge that their procrastination might have negative consequences (Steel, 2007). (I'm told this is a 'guy thing', but I'm not so certain of that.) Not surprisingly, perhaps, the greater the stakes the more difficult it might be for decisions to be made. For instance, decision making by parents regarding pediatric medical procedures can be an enormous strain (Lipstein et al., 2012), especially when once the decision is made, it can't be unmade. Sometimes the decisions individuals have to make are at an entirely different level, such as moral decision making. In an experimental setting, individuals might be presented with a scenario that entails choices that are difficult to resolve (e.g., in experimental paradigms in which the participant is given the choice of actively sacrificing one person in order to save the lives of several others). You'd think that such decisions would be based on logic or empathy, but there are actually a large number of factors that influence outcomes. Not unexpectedly, perhaps, the decisions made in these situations are very much influenced by the recent stressors that individuals had encountered (Youssef et al., 2011).

Human behaviors in response to stressors are, in several respects, not all that far removed from the responses that rodents show under adverse conditions. When animals are in stressful situations, their defensive repertoire may narrow to those responses that are highest in their repertoire, and other response strategies will emerge only as the predominant strategies are rejected; however, there are occasions where animals might persist in emitting these incorrect responses despite the fact that they are never reinforced. In a sense, this is not unlike human behavior under the conditions of strong challenges, wherein individuals fall back on those strategies that are highest in their repertoires (resorting to the tried and true), even if this approach isn't the most logical or effective. However, humans have a System 2 that kicks in when the reactions of System 1 are clearly not productive, and this serves us well in decision making even when we find ourselves in some very stressful situations.

TRUSTING YOUR BRAIN AND TRUSTING YOUR GUT

As we learn new things and retain this information, millions of neurons within the prefrontal cortex are firing, and the repeated activation of these neurons is necessary to keep short-term memories in place. Should these neurons stop their systematic vollies, the memory will quickly be lost (think of how quickly you forget a phone number when you're interrupted). Understandably, when stressful events occur, our short-term memory will be disrupted, possibly because some of the neurons that were working to maintain that memory were now engaged with some other task. As memory processes are integral to problem solving and decision making, in the face of stressors it's efficient and practical to rely on heuristics that are well entrenched. People working in high-pressure situations (surgeons, air-traffic controllers, soldiers), need to be well trained so that when stressors erupt, as they invariably do, they have the short-cuts available to them that allow for rapid and appropriate decision making.

There are situations that are somewhat ambiguous and making decisions is understandably difficult. In these situations we might make decisions based on our intuitions (or trusting our gut). Perhaps not surprisingly, even though the situation was ambiguous, those with expertise fared better with respect to their decisions even though they relied on gut responses compared to those without the same level of expertise. Interestingly, however, when told to ignore their gut instincts and rely on a strict analytical basis, the experts and non-experts performed equally. It may be that there are heuristics here that kick in when making gut decisions that can take us some way if the gut instincts are based on brain processes (Dane et al., 2012).

Most students, at one time or another, have been faced with the dilemma of whether they should accept their first response in a multiple choice exam, or rethink it and perhaps change their initial answer. From the research described here, it seems that if you know your stuff, then go with your first instinct. If you don't know your stuff, then an analytical process won't help you much, so you might as well go with your gut. However, if you fail the exam don't blame me for giving bad advice. Maybe you should have been attending classes more often …

APPRAISALS AND PERSONALITY FACTORS

The meaning that a person constructs about any given situation, as well as their own capabilities in dealing with these events, might not only be related to events that involved similar experiences, but can vary with the individual's global self-constructs that emanate from a lifetime of experiences, including those that occurred during childhood (Carver & Connor-Smith, 2010). In this respect, uncontrollable adverse events during childhood (e.g., abuse, neglect, or parental loss) may lead to the emergence of dysfunctional beliefs that can distort the individual's evaluation of their own coping capabilities or competency. These evaluations might influence the individual's self-efficacy and the way the individual appraises the specific characteristics of stressful encounters. Unfortunately, once these negative self-referential attitudes are well entrenched they're not easily dislodged, and misappraisals of situations might be more common than we'd imagine. It also seems that highly extraverted individuals tend to appraise situations as challenges, whereas individuals high in neuroticism are apt to appraise situations as more threatening (Gallagher, 1990; Hemenover & Dienstbier, 1996). We won't go through the numerous personality factors that affect stressor appraisals, but we can readily understand that several other global personality constructs, including hardiness, optimism, hope, hostility, trait negative/positive and affectivity, would influence our appraisals of potentially stressful events.

Of the methods used to diminish distress and the illnesses that stem from stressful experiences, several include attempts to change the way individuals appraise events. Rather than engaging in negative thinking, individuals are taught to appraise events in a more positive or more realistic manner, and then to deal with stressors based on these appraisals, even though this might be a personality feature that is difficult to modify. Fundamental to these approaches is the avoidance of entering situations with a negative perspective. Thus, while some aspects of stress management entail proper ways of getting rid of or coping with distress, an important aspect involves changing an individual's appraisals of events around them. A whole school of thought, now termed 'positive psychology', has formed around the concept that positive perspectives and expressions of particular personal characteristics can be essential to foster well-being (Seligman & Csikszentmihalyi, 2000). What this means is that rather than follow the medical model in which attempts are made to diminish the symptoms of illness, the aim of positive psychology is to promote well-being by acting prophylactically to prevent the development of stress-related pathology (Schueller & Seligman, 2008). In this regard, a treatment referred to as positive psychotherapy (or

PPT), which essentially comprises a series of exercises to instill positivity, reduces signs of depression in a subclinical population as well as in clinically depressed individuals, and this procedure was superior to antidepressant medication (Schueller & Seligman, 2008).

THE FORECAST

… how many will pass from the earth and how many will be created; who will live and who will die; who will die at his predestined time and who before his time; who by water and who by fire, who by sword, who by beast, who by famine, who by thirst, who by upheaval, who by plague, who by strangling, and who by stoning.

Who will rest and who will wander, who will live in harmony and who will be harried, who will enjoy tranquility and who will suffer, who will be impoverished and who will be enriched, who will be degraded and who will be exalted.

Fans of Leonard Cohen might recognize that this Rosh Hashana prayer of atonement might be at the root of his poem/song, 'Who by Fire'. Our take-home message might be that while life isn't all that predictable, most of us don't spend our time worrying about all the 'ifs' and 'maybes'. Although we know we're eventually going to get hammered in some form or other, we manage not to think about it. Illnesses are a long way off, and might even happen to someone else and not me. Perhaps this is an excellent strategy to deal with uncertainty, since focusing on potential catastrophes likely isn't profitable. What we can do, however, is recognize that there are certain behaviors (or lifestyle factors) that can affect the risk of bad outcomes and we're probably better off dealing with those.

APPRAISALS IN RELATION TO LEARNING, MEMORY, AUTOMATICITY, AND HABIT

Years ago, Hebb (1955) formulated the view that as we learn new information the connections between neurons are strengthened, and the assembly of cells involved in recognizing objects and responding to them appropriately is both strengthened and widened. Complex learning and memory involve still broader cell assemblies or networks, and once the connections are sufficiently strengthened, stimulating one aspect of the network will result in the entire cell assembly being triggered. So, for example, if I tell you that a word in this sentence (the one you are reading at this moment) is actually spelled incorrectly, you might have to go back again to find the error. Likewise, you won't have any trouble understanding the statement 'a frnd in ned is a frnd indd'. This is because your cell assemblies are in place, and once a component of the cell assembly is activated, you can interpret the sentence appropriately.

According to this formulation, learning occurs via a top–down approach; we learn through a trial-and-error process, through associations being made, by being rewarded for certain responses, and generalization (a grizzly bear is a grizzly bear regardless of whether we see it from the front or from the side) and discrimination (grizzly bears are dangerous, but not when they're in an enclosed area within a zoo). As topics become more difficult, the networks involved become more complex, but we take advantage of already developed networks so we can build on these. Some perceptions and responses are so deeply ingrained that we will respond reflexively to particularly stimuli, essentially working on auto-pilot or using automatic thoughts (Kahneman's Fast Thinking or Negative Thinking biases displayed by some individuals). Related to this, some of our behaviors are so exceptionally well entrenched that we can engage in them repeatedly (habits), which essentially reflects a bottom–up approach. When we try to solve problems we often use methods that were successful in the past, with the attitude that if the wheel has already been invented, why should we try to build something new? This axiom has been around for a long time, but it isn't always a correct perspective (for that matter, I can see somebody, somewhere, having said that if we already have a perfectly useful abacus, why try something new?). Sometimes, we simply need novel approaches to old problems.

These same processes are pertinent to how we appraise and cope with stressors. To a certain extent we are hard-wired to respond to environmental stimuli in a standard manner (fixed action patterns). Young birds, for instance, respond in a stereotypic fashion to a visual image of a hawk moving across their visual field, and animals often respond to warning signals from other animals without having had previous relevant experiences. These automatic responses are essential; an antelope might not get a second chance to discover that a lion running at it is, in fact, a threat. In other cases, factors related to learning (attention, memory) are fundamental in stress processes being established. Essentially, we are equipped with both top–down (experience–dependent) circuits, and those that develop through a bottom–up approach (prewired).

There is considerable evidence that our cognitive functioning, particularly in relation to appraisals of stressors, may be warped by previous experiences. In the preceding sections we saw this repeatedly, but what is particularly noteworthy is that certain appraisals may come to occur in an automatic fashion. For some individuals, depending on their personality attributes and previous experiences, these automatic thoughts involve a negative bias. Thus, for example, when we ask depressed individuals to recall previous experiences, they tend to recall more negative than positive events (Ingram et al., 1995), and also tend to recall a greater number of negative emotional words than those that have a positive valence (Taylor & John, 2004). Essentially, by experiencing and learning about events in a particular way, automatic response sequences (or habits) may be established so that we will appraise these events in a stereotyped negative way when we later encounter them. Unfortunately, habits are hard to break, and getting ourselves out of negative mind sets takes some doing.

EMOTIONAL RESPONSES

Just about everyone realizes that positive and negative events will give rise to different emotional responses. The nature of these emotional responses will depend on how an individual appraises an event (conversely, emotional responses can also influence appraisals), and the context in which the event occurs, as well as previous experiences, personality factors, and motivation. In this brief section we'll discuss emotions associated with stressful experiences, but I have to admit here that one can hardly do justice to such a complex and fascinating topic in only a few pages, particularly given the vast literature that exists (see for example the work of Damasio, 1999).

A given event might elicit different emotional responses across individuals owing to particular experiences, various developmental factors and other related socialization processes. As well, damage to certain parts of the brain owing to a stroke or lesions may profoundly influence emotionality, ranging from a loss of emotion and affect through to excessive responses to certain types of stimuli. Moreover, just as individuals may differ in their intellectual capacity and social intelligence, there are individual differences concerning emotional intelligence (Salovey & Mayer, 1990). Essentially, emotional intelligence is thought of as an ability that involves multiple skills related to emotional perception and expression, the emotional facilitation of thinking, emotional understanding and emotional regulation, as well as personality characteristics and other traits (e.g., optimism, motivation). Some people are adept in this regard, whereas others seem to express their emotions in odd ways and also seem unable to read the emotions of others. An extreme form of this inability to understand emotions is alexithymia, a trait in which individuals seem to have difficulty in identifying their own feelings, describing their feelings, or understanding the feelings of others, and in fact, they might look to others in emotional situations to see how they ought to react.

DISTINGUISHING BETWEEN EMOTIONS

There are subtle differences that exist in emotional responses to stressors and, as seen in Table 2.1, our vocabulary is replete with descriptors that reflect these differences. In addition to these individual emotions, several emotions can also occur concurrently in response to a single event (seeing a certain person can elicit jealousy, hatred, and anger concurrently), and sometimes it's difficult for us to even understand the emotion that we are feeling. Likewise, a particular event can instigate one emotion in a given context, but a very different one in a second situation. By example, a racial or religious epithet can cause an individual to feel anger when it occurs, but if this occurs in front of others, and the individual thinks that these other people believe the slur, then it might cause feelings of shame. Some emotions differ from one another in ways that might be related to the context in which certain events occur. For instance, fear and angst are very similar, but fear is thought to be directed to a specific stimulus, whereas angst is sometimes thought of as a non-directed emotion. Likewise, shame and embarrassment/humiliation are very similar in that they each occur in response to one's own socially or professionally unacceptable behavior that comes to the attention or is witnessed by others. Each also involves the loss of honor (dignity). However, whereas embarrassment and humiliation are emotions that occur in front of others, shame can also occur as a result of an unacceptable behavior that only the individual knows about.

The emotions mentioned up until this point have been largely those of a negative nature, but there are also many positive emotions that can alter the way we appraise stressful events: desire, ecstasy, excitement, enthusiasm, euphoria, hope, joy, love, lust, passion, pleasure, pride, trust, and zest are just a few of these. They're as complicated as the negative emotions, and obviously appear under different conditions. Sometimes these emotions can combine with those of a negative nature to elicit 'mixed emotions' or those that are 'bittersweet'. Watching adult kids leave home can leave an individual feeling both pride and loss/loneliness, and having a loved one pass after a lengthy illness can similarly result in both relief and sadness. Of particular relevance to the present discussion is that if positive emotions can alter the way we appraise and hence respond to stressful events, then the positive psychology mentioned earlier can potentially be an effective way of precluding the despair and depression that might otherwise be endured in negative situations.

TABLE 2.1 Negative emotional responses across situations

Situation	Emotion
Irritating situation	Annoyance
Traumatic event	Shock, horror, surprise, awe
Loss	Grief, depression, sorrow, despair, sadness, misery, hopelessness
Anticipation of adverse events	Fear, anxiety, worry, angst
Absence of tangible or social stimulation	Boredom, loneliness
Failure, that occurs in the context of a public forum	Disappointment, embarrassment, humiliation, shame
Threat directed toward ourselves or at our group	Fear, anger, hostility, rage
People who have engaged in abhorrent behaviors or wronged us	Contempt, hatred, loathing, disgust
Our own engagement in untoward behavior	Guilt, regret, remorse, self-shame
Perceptions of what others have	Jealousy
Inability to reach a goal	Frustration
Emotions triggered by the discomfort of others	Empathy, apathy
Emotions shared by members	Collective guilt, collective sham, collective angst

STRESS-RELATED EMOTIONS

Clearly, emotions can involve multiple mechanisms, and because more than a single emotion can occur at the same time, they are often difficult to study, certainly in the context of identifying biological correlates of emotions. Further, we often resort to animal studies to analyze the biological responses associated with certain emotions (e.g., fear, anxiety), but there are limitations to what can actually be evaluated in animals (Do mice feel emotions such as shame or guilt, and if they do, how can we tell?). What does seem to be the case is that while there are wide arrays of emotions that emerge under diverse conditions, these all serve several common or interrelated functions. Among other things, they provide us with information about events around us. They also let others know how we're feeling (unless we can successfully hide our emotions), allowing them to take measures that are corrective (apologize), supportive (sympathy), or defensive (aggressive, indignant). However, there are nuances to these emotions that give us more detailed information than simply 'things are bad' or 'everything seems to be okay'.

You're probably aware that there are different types of pain, and they have different meanings and implications (e.g., to a physician). There are sharp pains and dull pains, those that continue or are intermittent, pain that throbs and that which is steady, pain that is localized or that which is widespread or radiates. Likewise, different emotions can tell us about the situation we're in and whether defensive actions should be taken, and what these actions should comprise. By example, anger is an activating emotion, so that in response to some transgression (e.g., a slur against one's group), an individual might want to take an angry or aggressive stance toward the perpetrator. Concurrently, that person may feel shame/embarrassment, which is an emotion associated with withdrawal or suppression, and as a result they might be less likely to act on their anger. This decision might potentially save them from the ill-feelings of a group of bystanders who might view aggression as socially unacceptable, although the individual might later experience a period of pervasive rumination about the event and what they should have or could have done differently. Yet it is exactly this experience that provides individuals with critical information, namely that they can't deal with this issue on their own and that collective action by group members will be needed instead (Matheson & Anisman, 2012).

Just as emotions can influence cognitive processes, cognitions can influence emotions or the way emotions are expressed. For instance, an aggrieved party ordinarily might become aggressive towards the person who angered them. However, the expression of that aggression might be more likely if the potential victim of this aggression was appraised to be smaller and weaker, and less likely when that person looks strong and able. The 'aggrieved' person may be angry, but in some instances they seem to have executive control regarding behavioral outputs. We often hear the statement 'I just lost control'. This might be true in some instances, but it may also be the case that individuals 'allow' themselves the luxury of losing control when the opponent is viewed as weaker.

As we've already seen, positive or negative moods have a lot to do with how we appraise or interpret events around us. Likewise, being angry or envious will alter appraisals of events related to the person who we are angry with or of whom we are envious. More than that, however, our emotions can alter our general disposition to react in particular ways to unrelated events. There's nothing very surprising in this, but even though we all seem to know it, it is remarkable how often we ignore this basic bit of knowledge. We've all heard of the boss who, when in a bad mood, might pick on an employee, or the parent who, having had a rough day, then takes it out on a partner/child. These individuals can't seem to compartmentalize their responses, and their mood increases their own stress reactions, giving rise to stress in others, and concurrently they lose potential sources of support that might otherwise have helped them deal with their own distress. Most of us also know that our emotional responses will affect our decision-making ability, particularly if this entails complex and/or stressful aspects. By example, in his (1993) book on negotiating, *Getting Past No*, Ury offers the sound advice that when stress levels are high and emotions are peaking, it's best to 'go to the balcony' (meaning, remove yourself from the situation and see what's going on as an observer, rather than being enmeshed in the turmoil). In this way we can see the scene for what it is, unhampered by our emotional responses.

We've known for a long time that the limbic portion of the brain plays an integral role in emotional outputs. For instance, fear and anxiety are associated with the central portion of the amygdala and the extended amygdala (a region referred to as the bed nucleus of the stria terminalis), whereas the ventral tegmentum and nucleus accumbens (midbrain regions that we'll talk much more about later) seem to be involved in reward/motivational processes. However, these brain regions do not operate in isolation from other regions, but cooperate with one another to produce organized outputs. Connections exist between the prefrontal cortex and the amygdala, so the brain regions involved in decision making (the cingulate cortex, prefrontal cortex) can influence those involved in anxiety (the amygdala). It also seems that some brain regions, such as the nucleus accumbens, may contribute to more than a single type of stimulus, being activated in stressful as well as rewarding situations. Presumably, complex emotions that entail an amalgam of primary emotions involve multiple brain regions interacting with one another.

It might be expected that different emotions may also be tied to diverse peripheral physiological changes. Just as specific events can give rise to different emotional responses, distinct patterns of cardiac and respiratory activity have been associated with fear, anger, sadness and happiness (Rainville et al., 2006). Likewise, the release of the classic stress hormone cortisol occurs preferentially if the stressful event elicits shame (Dickerson & Kemeny, 2004) or anger (Moons et al., 2010), and the immune responses elicited by stressors similarly depend on the specific emotions elicited (Danielson et al., 2011).

COPING WITH STRESSORS

Appraising stressors appropriately is only half the story regarding how stressors can influence well-being. The other half is concerned with how individuals cope with stressors. Some theorists have viewed coping as a *style* (i.e., a dispositional feature that is relatively stable), whereas others have seen this as a *strategy* that varies in response to situational factors and varies over time as the stressor and its ramifications unfold (Tennen et al., 2000). There is also a middle ground in which it is supposed that the coping methods used vary as a function of the particular situation encountered, but these methods are guided by the particular coping styles that individuals bring with them to the situation. This hardly seems surprising, but it had at one time been a topic of some debate. In the section that follows we'll go into a fair bit of detail regarding coping processes, but as we do, keep in mind that coping may stem from the way individuals appraise events, but it also may affect appraisals. We're dealing with dynamic processes that are subject to feedback and frequent adjustments.

THE STRESS–APPRAISAL–COPING TRIAD

There are numerous coping methods that can be used to deal with stressful experiences. These can be in the order of a couple of hundred actions or behaviors, but they are usually classified into about a dozen different subtypes that fall into two or three general types that comprise problem-focused, emotion-focused, and avoidant strategies (disengagement). There have been other names for these strategies, and other classification systems described, but these categories are probably the most widely used. Emotional coping subsumes multiple strategies (e.g., emotional expression, emotional containment, rumination, self- or other-blame, withdrawal, denial, and passive resignation) as does avoidant coping (avoidance, denial). Problem-focused coping, as the name implies, primarily involves coping through problem solving, or through other cognitive processes that can be used to deal with stressors, such as cognitive restructuring (re-evaluating the threat, or finding meaning in a bad event). In addition, there are methods of coping that don't fall comfortably into any single class as they can be used in multiple capacities. For instance, one can use social support in an emotion-focused capacity (a shoulder to cry on), in problem-focused coping ('Help me find a way out of this jam'), or in an avoidant capacity (e.g., through distraction). Likewise, active distraction (e.g., going to the gym to 'work off' anxiety) and humor can fit into each of the categories, but more often they align most closely with problem-focused coping. Both wishful thinking and rumination are usually viewed as emotion-focused coping methods, but this may depend on what other coping methods are used concurrently. Thus, if individuals ruminate and feel sorry for themselves, then this is clearly emotion-focused coping, but some individuals use rumination together with problem solving, in which case it is not part of an emotion-focused strategy. Finally, religion doesn't fit well within any of these categories; it may represent an avoidant strategy, but it can also be used as a problem-oriented strategy or one that involves obtaining social support from like-minded people (Ysseldyk et al., 2010).

COPING THROUGH RELIGION

Religion is potentially a very effective coping strategy, even if it doesn't (necessarily) have healing powers that some have attributed to it. For religious individuals, it may provide comfort when all else fails. Religion can provide a system of beliefs that allows individuals to find meaning in an experience, and to appraise events as predictable and at the very least 'under God's control'. In addition, it often provides a social support network that enables problem-oriented coping, or even emotion-focused strategies that bring about solace and peace of mind.

Marx disparagingly stated that 'Religion is the sigh of the oppressed creature, the heart of a heartless world, just as it is the spirit of a spiritless situation. It is the opium of the people'. The response to this might be 'Whatever gets you through the night' (Lennon, 1974; this should of course be distinguished from the other Lenin), provided, of course, that this is not used as an alternative to potentially more effective coping strategies. Indeed, rather than seeing religion as the opium of the people (masses), it can be argued that among some groups it serves as the SSRI (or the CBT) of the masses.

HOW TO COPE

It is often thought that when appraisals and coping strategies are ineffective, then the development of pathology might ensue, whereas effective coping will limit such outcomes. If only it were this simple. Trying to analyze the relations between stressful events, coping strategies, and the emergence of pathological states isn't as straightforward as simply correlating individual coping strategies with particular outcomes. Appraisals and coping strategies not only vary across situations, they also do so with the passage of time (DeLongis & Holtzman, 2005; Tennen et al., 2000) and the subjective construal of the stressor. Added to this, individuals won't use a single strategy at a time, but may use several strategies concurrently, or flip from one to another as the situation demands, as well as on the basis of the opportunities and resources available.

The specific coping strategies that individuals endorse might serve different functions as a stressor evolves over time. By example, when an individual first learns that they have a potentially fatal illness, one of their first reactions (once the shock has worn off) might be one of seeking support from their relatives (spouse, children) or close friends. The function of this might simply be to use the support as an emotional-coping method. This might be followed soon after by the use of this support group to obtain information (e.g., to find out whether alternative treatment strategies are available). Later still, the support may become one of an instrumental nature (taking the person to treatment sessions, supplying food), and finally, in a worst case scenario, social support may be used to provide social comfort, distraction, and finding peace.

It is often taken as axiomatic that in situations in which the individual has control, problem-focused strategies (e.g., problem solving, cognitive restructuring or positive growth) that are seen to be adaptive will predominate, whereas those strategies that encourage an undue focus on emotions (e.g., rumination, emotional venting, self-blame) are viewed as counterproductive and maladaptive. This simple view is intuitively appealing. Yet it is also a bit simplistic, especially as emotion-focused coping ought to be viewed as comprising either emotion-approach or emotion-avoidant features. In certain situations the latter coping method (e.g., using avoidance/denial) might be an optimum strategy (e.g., when learning that one has a terminal illness). Likewise, although avoidance often works against individuals' well-being in the long run, it may provide temporary relief from an ongoing stressor, giving someone the opportunity to adopt (or develop) more effective strategies. As well, emotional approach strategies that allow the individual to modify or regulate negative emotional responses can have positive effects in several stressful situations. This coping method can generally be subdivided into emotional processing (e.g., attempts aimed at acknowledging, exploring, and understanding emotional responses to challenges) and emotional expression (reflecting verbal and non-verbal messages concerning the emotions felt). In emotionally-charged situations, emotion-focused coping might be particularly beneficial as it facilitates the individual's ability to come to terms with their feelings, and in so doing distress may be reduced (Stanton et al., 1994). To be sure, emotional expression without coming to an understanding of these emotions can be disruptive, especially when this coping method involves inappropriate rumination or gives rise to negative affect and appraisals.

Table 2.2 provides a description of several coping strategies that individuals might use in dealing with distressing events. As we've seen, any given coping strategy may serve different functions, or operate to facilitate or inhibit other strategies. Despite the frequent discussion of which coping strategies are good and which are bad, keep in mind that individuals do not endorse coping strategies in isolation of one another, and different coping strategies are used concurrently and/or sequentially. Individuals can ruminate and problem solve concurrently, and they can ruminate and blame at the same time. And in addition to this, they can shift from one strategy to another and then to yet another all within a short time-span.

TABLE 2.2 Coping strategies

Problem-focused strategies

Problem solving: Finding a solution to limit or eliminate the impact or presence of the stressor.

Cognitive restructuring (positive reframing): Re-assessing the situation or putting a new spin on the situation. This can entail finding a silver lining to a black cloud, e.g., "My kid flunked out of university, but hey, I save on paying his tuition", through to finding meaning (benefit finding) in adverse experiences.

Avoidant or disengagement strategies

Active distraction: Using active behaviors to distract ourselves from ongoing problems. This can include working out, going to the movies.

Cognitive distraction: Distracting ourselves through thinking about issues unrelated to the stressor, such as immersing ourselves in our work, or engaging in hobbies.

Denial/emotional containment: Not thinking about the issue or simply convincing oneself that it's not particularly serious.

Humor: Engaging in humor to diminish the stress of a given situation, or simply to put on a brave face.

Drug use: Aside from the positive feelings that individuals might obtain from using certain drugs, drugs can also serve as a means of dealing with stressors.

Emotion-focused strategies

Emotional expression: Coping with an event through emotions such as crying, anger and even aggressive behaviors.

Other-blame: Comprises blaming others for adverse events. It can be used in an effort to avoid being the one blamed, or as a way to make sense of some situations.

Self-blame: This comprises blaming ourselves for the events that occurred. Sometimes, of course, we are guilty and should be blaming ourselves, but there will also be instances where we inappropriately lay the blame at our own feet.

Rumination: This comprises continued, sometimes unremitting thoughts about an issue or event; these thoughts often entail self-pity, revenge, or replaying the events and the strategies that could have been used to deal with events. Rumination often accompanies depression, and individuals with certain ruminative styles are at increased risk of depressive illness.

Wishful thinking: This entails thoughts regarding what it would be like if the stressor were gone, or what it was like in happier times when the stressor had not surfaced.

Passive resignation: This comprises acceptance of a situation as it is. It might be a reflection of helplessness when an individual believes that they have no control over the stressor or their own destiny, or it may simply be one of accepting the future without regret or malice ("it is what it is").

Religion

Religiosity (internal): Using a belief in God to deal with adverse events. It can represent the simple belief in a better hereafter, a belief that a merciful god will help attenuate the event, and when things don't work out, falling back onto 'God works in mysterious ways".

Religiosity (external): Religion may involve a social component where similar-minded people come together (congregate) and serve as supports or buffers for one another to facilitate the individual's ability to cope with a stressor.

Social support

Social support seeking: Finding people who can help us cope with stressful experiences is one of the most common methods of dealing with stressors. This is especially the case given that social support may serve multiple functions in relation to stressors.

One would think that if a particular strategy proves ineffective in attenuating the impact of a stressor, then it would be advantageous for an alternative strategy to be adopted. Yet, under certain conditions, cognitive functioning may be impaired, limiting the adoption of new responses. In times of distress our repertoire of responses may be narrowed so that only our prepotent (or well-entrenched) responses will be used, whereas other coping methods, as effective as they might potentially be, will fall by the wayside. In still other situations, particularly those that involve a high degree of ambiguity (e.g., 'Will the biopsy show the tumor to be malignant or benign?', 'Can we expect biological terrorism?'), individuals may find themselves uncertain about what to do, and end up taking few coping initiatives on their own. In these instances, a good role model or leader can be especially worthwhile.

So, what differentiates individuals who are good at dealing with stressors from those who are not? As already indicated, how we appraise situations is fundamental in this regard. However, assuming that an appropriate appraisal is made, it seems that those individuals who are adept at using a relatively broad range of coping strategies, and prepared to be flexible in their use (i.e., able to shift from one strategy to another as necessary), may be best suited to deal with stressors. In contrast, stressors will most negatively affect those individuals with a restricted range of coping methods, or rigidity in turning away from ineffective coping strategies. Further to this same point, the functional effectiveness of coping is not simply determined by which strategy is used, but also by how various strategies are used in conjunction with one another (Matheson & Anisman, 2003). As a case in point, although rumination is frequently associated with depressive illness (Nolen-Hoeksema, 1998), it typically occurs together with other coping strategies. In fact, in non-depressed individuals rumination co-occurred with a broad constellation of problem- and emotion-focused strategies, as well as cognitive disengagement (e.g., 'I'm going through some pretty bad times, but if I talk to the guys at work they might have some ideas about what I can do'). In contrast, among dysthymic patients (those with chronic, low grade depression), rumination was primarily associated with emotion-focused coping, and inversely related to efforts to disengage (e.g., 'I'm going through some pretty bad times, and it's because I'm just a failure at everything I do or ever will do; I just want to lie here and never see the world again') (Kelly et al., 2007). We don't know what came first; the depression might have preceded the narrowed coping methods, but it is often thought that poor coping favors the emergence of depression. In either event, poor coping seems to involve the use of rumination in conjunction with emotion-focused coping strategies rather than with an array of other strategies.

There is yet another oddity in the way individuals cope or problem solve that varies as function depending on whether they had previously been stressed. When placed in a problem-solving situation, individuals who had not been stressed tended to consciously take the simplest approach to figure out how things worked, and concurrently their hippocampal activity was high (the hippocampus is involved in memory and its activation serves participants well in this problem solving situation). Stressed participants, in contrast, tended to use excessively complex strategies, even if they could not verbally express why they chose the strategy that they did (i.e., it seemed to be a subconscious undertaking). In this instance, brain imaging revealed that the problem-solving effort was accompanied by activation of the striatum that might be more aligned with unconscious learning. In effect, stressful events may influence the way we deal with situations, moving us away from purposeful, conscious approaches.

THE GOOD FIGHT

For as long as I can remember, there has been this notion that fighting against an illness might increase survival, whereas feelings of helplessness and hopelessness would have the opposite effect. This is epitomized in movies where the doctor says about the star that has just undergone some brutal surgery to remove a bullet or a tumor 'Well, it's up to him/her now. But, I think Matt/Marlene is strong and has a will to live'. It's as if the patient has some control over events (does this also mean that if they were to die, then they'd be to blame?). In fact, feelings of helplessness and hopelessness have been negatively related to five- and ten-year survival following breast cancer treatment (although the strength of the relationship was only moderate). However, there have also been reports that having a 'fighting spirit' was unrelated to survival. So, although negative appraisals and mood might lead to poorer outcomes, having a positive spirit and the will to fight simply doesn't impress or worry cancer cells.

The advice that is commonly given to those who are critically ill is 'don't give up', 'be strong', or 'fight against your illness', and obituaries make reference to 'the valiant battle' or 'fought bravely to the end'. Most (or maybe only some) of us also know the words from Dylan Thomas's famous poem: 'Do not go gentle into that good night, Old age should burn and rage at close of day; Rage, rage against the dying of the light.' There is certainly much to say for putting up the good fight, and there's no doubt that social support can help in this regard. Yet in reading Thomas's poem you might want to note the use of the term 'good' in referring to night in the very first line, even though there is the encouragement to 'rage against the dying of the light'. Perhaps the night can be good, especially when raging against the dying of the light has proven to be useless and the person has suffered a long and painful illness. It is under these conditions that the social support a person receives can serve as a comfort that might help the person let go and die peacefully. In fact, I believe (although there's obviously no evidence to support this belief) that sometimes a dying person is waiting for their family to allow them to go gentle into that good night.

ASSESSING APPRAISALS AND COPING

Several instruments have been developed to assess the coping styles or strategies that individuals endorse in stressful situations. In general, methods of evaluating appraisals of events are less common than those assessing coping methods. Often, participants are asked to think of an event or are provided with a depiction of an event, and then simply asked how threatening and stressful they perceived that event to be, and how much control they think they had over it. There have also been scales developed to assess stressor appraisals, with one of the most commonly used being the Stress Appraisal Measure (SAM) (Peacock & Wong, 1990). The SAM is thought to measure three aspects of primary appraisals, namely challenge, threat, and centrality, as well as secondary appraisals comprising resources available to contend with a particular event. This widely-used instrument typically has much to offer, especially when used in conjunction with an analysis of the coping methods used.

Coping methods have been assessed through various scales. One of the earliest measures in this regard was the Ways of Coping Questionnaire (WOC), which assesses the degree to which individuals endorse specific coping strategies in response to a specific stressor that the participant indicates they had recently encountered (Folkman & Lazarus, 1988). This scale comprises eight subscales, six of which assess problem-focused coping, and two which reflect emotion-focused coping. A degree of dissatisfaction with this approach has been expressed (e.g., Endler & Parker, 1994), which has prompted the development of still other scales.

The Coping Response Inventory (CRI) developed by Moos et al. (1990) assesses the individual's appraisal of a specific stressor and then divides coping into approach and avoidance responses, as well as cognitive and behavioral coping. The Coping Orientation to Problem Experience (COPE) inventory developed by Carver et al. (1989) assesses how individuals generally deal with stressful events. This measure comprises 15 strategies that are typically organized into problem-focused coping (e.g., planning), adaptive emotion-focused coping (e.g., humor), and finally, maladaptive emotion-focused coping (e.g., denial). Similarly, the Coping Inventory for Stressful Situations (CISS) developed by Endler and Parker (1994) assesses the frequency with which individuals endorse particular coping strategies for dealing with stressful events. Finally, Matheson and Anisman (2003) developed the Survey of Coping Profile Endorsement (SCOPE) to assess coping styles and strategies, and subsequently used this scale to measure appraisals of coping effectiveness (see Table 2.3). This questionnaire asks participants how they would cope with stressors in general (coping styles) or in response to specific events (strategies). The SCOPE comprises 14 subscales aligned with those described in Table 2.1.

These coping scales have a fair bit in common with one another: there is overlap in some of the items, dimensions of coping, and when factor analyzed (a statistical method to determine which of several variables link or cluster together to create distinct factors), they all provide either the two- or three-dimensional structure already described (e.g., problem-focused, emotion-focused or avoidant coping). Thus, the choice of instrument an investigator might use depends on the stressor of interest as well as the fit with the researcher's own theoretical approach to understanding the issues at hand, or with how they wish to use the data. There are also other coping scales available that focus on specific situations or variables (e.g., Quality of Social Support Scale), particular illnesses (e.g., Mental Adjustment to HIV Scale; Mental Adjustment to Cancer Scale), or coping within specific subgroups of individuals.

What follows is a sample version of the most recent rendition of the SCOPE as well as the scoring used for this instrument. If you are curious and decide to assess your own coping methods using this questionnaire, bear in mind that you can't use this to make diagnoses about yourself (e.g., 'My profile looks like someone who is very unhappy'). The scores provided in the ensuing section are 'group' scores, and comparing yourself to these 'averaged' profiles might not mean much. Further, the scale can be used to measure coping 'styles' or 'strategies' depending on the wording of the question. If the question asks you to respond on the basis of 'stressful events experienced over the past two weeks', then

TABLE 2.3 A coping scale

Survey of Coping Profile Encorsement (SCOPE)
The purpose of this questionnaire is to find out how people deal with more general problems or stresses in their lives. The following are activities that you may have done. After each activity, please indicate the extent to which you would use this as a way of dealing with problems or stresses in recent weeks.

Ordinarily, in recent weeks have you:	Never	Seldom	Sometimes	Often	Almost always
1. accepted that there was nothing you could do to change your situation?	0	1	2	3	4
2. tried to just take whatever came your way?	0	1	2	3	4
3. talked with friends or relatives about your problems?	0	1	2	3	4
4. tried to do things which you typically enjoy?	0	1	2	3	4
5. sought out information that would help you resolve your problems?	0	1	2	3	4
6. blamed others for creating your problems or making them worse?	0	1	2	3	4
7. sought the advice of others to resolve your problems?	0	1	2	3	4
8. blamed yourself for your problems?	0	1	2	3	4
9. exercised?	0	1	2	3	4
10. fantasized or thought about unreal things (e.g., the perfect revenge, or winning a million dollars) to feel better?	0	1	2	3	4
11. been very emotional compared to your usual self?	0	1	2	3	4
12. gone over your problem in your mind over and over again?	0	1	2	3	4
13. asked others for help?	0	1	2	3	4
14. thought about your problem a lot?	0	1	2	3	4
15. become involved in recreation or pleasure activities?	0	1	2	3	4
16. worried about your problem a lot?	0	1	2	3	4
17. tried to keep your mind off things that are upsetting you?	0	1	2	3	4
18. tried to distract yourself from your troubles?	0	1	2	3	4
19. avoided thinking about your problems?	0	1	2	3	4
20. made plans to overcome your problems?	0	1	2	3	4
21. told jokes about your situation?	0	1	2	3	4
22. thought a lot about who is responsible for you problem (besides yourself)?	0	1	2	3	4
23. shared humorous stories etc. to cheer yourself and others up?	0	1	2	3	4
24. told yourself that other people have dealt with problems such as yours?	0	1	2	3	4
25. thought a lot about how you have brought your problem on yourself?	0	1	2	3	4
26. decided to wait and see how things turn out?	0	1	2	3	4
27. wished the situation would go away or be over with?	0	1	2	3	4
28. decided that your current problems are a result of your own past actions?	0	1	2	3	4
29. gone shopping?	0	1	2	3	4
30. asserted yourself and taken positive action on problems that are getting you down?	0	1	2	3	4

Ordinarily, in recent weeks have you:

	Never	Seldom	Sometimes	Often	Almost always
31. sought reassurance and moral support from others?	0	1	2	3	4
32. resigned yourself to your problem?	0	1	2	3	4
33. thought about how your problems have been caused by other people?	0	1	2	3	4
34. daydreamed about how things may turn out?	0	1	2	3	4
35. been very emotional in how you react, even to little things?	0	1	2	3	4
36. decided that you can grow and learn through your problem?	0	1	2	3	4
37. told yourself that other people have problems like your own?	0	1	2	3	4
38. wished you were a stronger person or better at dealing with problems?	0	1	2	3	4
39. looked for how you can learn something out of your bad situation?	0	1	2	3	4
40. asked for God's guidance?	0	1	2	3	4
41. kept your feelings bottled up inside?	0	1	2	3	4
42. found yourself crying more than usual?	0	1	2	3	4
43. tried to act as if you were not upset?	0	1	2	3	4
44. prayed for help?	0	1	2	3	4
45. gone out?	0	1	2	3	4
46. held in your feelings?	0	1	2	3	4
47. tried to act as if you weren't feeling bad?	0	1	2	3	4
48. taken steps to overcome your problems?	0	1	2	3	4
49. made humorous comments or wise cracks?	0	1	2	3	4
50. told others that you were depressed or emotionally upset?	0	1	2	3	4
51. distracted yourself with food?	0	1	2	3	4
52. found comfort in your favorite foods?	0	1	2	3	4
53. spent time cooking a big meal?	0	1	2	3	4
54. gone out for food with friends?	0	1	2	3	4

To determine your score, add up the items for each type of coping method and divide by the number of items (questions) in that category. Below you will find the questions that are relevant for each of the coping methods.

Problem solving: 5, 20, 30, 48
Cognitive restructuring: 24, 36, 37, 39
Avoidance: 17, 18, 19
Active distraction: 4, 8, 15, 29, 45
Rumination: 12, 14, 16
Humor: 21, 23, 49
Social support seeking : 3, 7, 13, 31
Emotional expression: 11, 35, 42, 50
Other-blame: 6, 22, 33
Self-blame: 8, 25, 28
Emotional containment: 41, 43, 46, 47
Passive resignation: 1, 2, 26, 32
Religion: 40, 44
Wishful thinking: 10, 27, 34, 38
Eating: 51, 52, 53, 54

you'll be examining coping style. If, however, the question is framed as asking about coping with a particular event (e.g., a fight with your spouse, an argument with your boss, distress over not getting things completed, etc), then you'll be looking at coping strategies. If you do each of these assessments, starting with coping styles, and then at later times assess your coping strategies in regard to particular stressors, you might find that your coping methods differ across stressor situations, but there will be some similarity to your coping disposition (style).

COPING AS A PROFILE OF RESPONSES

In most studies that involve numerous subtypes of coping, a 'factor analysis' is conducted to reduce the number of variables that need to be dealt with as responses to certain questions will often cluster together. Thus, although a given coping inventory might comprise many subscales, the factor analysis might group these into two or three more manageable units. As indicated earlier, emotion-focused coping comprises several coping strategies, such as emotion-based strategies, self- and other-blame, rumination, and so forth, and hence these are essentially pooled to represent a single factor. Likewise, problem-focused coping might comprise problem solving and cognitive restructuring, and these are combined as a single unit for purposes of analysis.

Factor analyzing the data and combining categories may be fine in many situations, but there are occasions where this might not be desirable, and to a certain extent might even be counterproductive. The factor structure evident under one set of conditions (e.g., in a group of individuals who are healthy or non-stressed) might not match up with that evident under certain stressor conditions or among individuals dealing with a particular experience. For instance, in a non-stressed group of individuals, social support may fall into a factor that is aligned with emotion-focused coping. However, in response to a certain illness, it might more comfortably fall into the category of problem solving, as social support would be used in this capacity (e.g., 'help me find out if there is an alternative treatment strategy available'). Still later, if the illness progresses, social support might fall into an emotion-focused framework. Obviously, across these circumstances social support would appear as part of a different factor (as a source of problem solving or instrumental support vs one that involves emotional support), and hence they would not be statistically comparable to one another.

A second issue concerns the fact that although having a factor structure simplifies analysis, coping processes entail complex interactions that cannot be deduced using simple methods. In fact, creating broad categories that involve multiple coping strategies might not allow for the identification of subtle factors that could distinguish groups from one another. It is ironic, parenthetically, that while social psychologists have focused on reducing the number of variables into broad factors (although some, such as Carver, have made the point that the researcher might feel more comfortable not factor analyzing the data and assessing strategies individually), those involved in the creation of tests and measurements of other characteristics have not done so, and have recognized the value of treating categories distinctly. For instance, an IQ score provides an overall index of intelligence/ability or separate

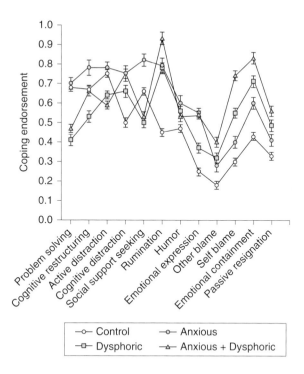

FIGURE 2.3 Coping profiles among university students who exhibited dysphoria (moderate depression), anxiety, both dysphoria and anxiety, or low levels of both.

indices for verbal and performance measures. However, most tests are not limited to these broad categories. Instead, these tests involve multiple categories that allow the identification of more subtle problems that might be present. For instance, Johnny can score comparably across all components of the IQ test, or he might score low in those dealing with language, but high in those that involve creativity. In both instances he might have an average overall IQ score, but these different profiles might have very different implications. Likewise, the profile of coping responses endorsed may provide important clues as to the subtle differences that exist between groups or between individuals, which might otherwise be obfuscated by pooling data across the several strategies that make up a factor.

Figure 2.3 shows the coping strategies adopted in a normative sample of university students. In general, those coping methods that are often considered to be adaptive, including problem solving (PSV), cognitive restructuring (CR), active distraction (ADIS), cognitive distraction (CDIS), and social support seeking (SS), were found to be more highly endorsed than the emotion-focused strategies comprising emotional expression (EE), other-blame (OB), self-blame (SB), emotional containment (EC), passive resignation (PR). An exception to this was that rumination, which is not usually thought of as an effective strategy (but consider the comments made earlier about its conjoint use with other strategies), was also found to be used frequently. For the most part, the coping strategies were comparable between men and women, although women tended to exhibit higher levels of cognitive distraction and rumination, as well as social support seeking and emotional expression.

When coping styles were assessed among individuals who differed with respect to depressed mood, the differences in coping profiles were pronounced (Figure 2.3). The Beck Depression Inventory (BDI), a self-report questionnaire that asks individuals about various aspects of their mood, was used to divide participants into groups. Among individuals with some degree of depressive symptoms (a moderate BDI score >9, termed 'dysphoric' in the figure), the coping profile could readily be distinguished from those of individuals who were not at all depressed (a low BDI score <4). The dysphoric individuals used less problem-focused coping and social support seeking than individuals with low or mild symptoms of depression. They also used more rumination, emotional expression, other-blame, self-blame, and emotional containment than non-depressed individuals. Evidently, even in the face of mild depressive symptoms (nowhere near clinical levels), some coping methods were very much like those of individuals with higher levels of depression that we had seen in earlier analyses.

As anxiety often appears in conjunction with depression (anxiety is often comorbid with depression), we wondered whether the coping profiles of those with anxiety or dysphoria alone could be distinguished from that evident among individuals with both sets of features. Figure 2.3 shows that the coping profile of individuals in these categories differed from one another in several respects. Specifically, anxious participants displayed problem-focused coping just like that of the controls, whereas those with dysphoria or dysphoria plus anxiety showed much lower problem-solving efforts. A similar pattern was evident with respect to active distraction. However, all three of the symptomatic groups reported greater rumination than that of the controls. Moreover, the degree of emotional expression, other-blame, self-blame, and emotional containment varied as a function of the symptoms presented. Individuals with a combination of anxiety and dysphoria reported higher levels of these coping methods than did those with only one class of symptoms. It seems that the profiles of coping responses effectively distinguished between individuals with different psychological symptoms, which might not have been detected as readily if the coping methods had been grouped into broad categories.

The point of these various examples is that psychological illness, and even mental health characteristics below the clinical threshold, might be accompanied by distinct coping profiles. Using this profile approach may also provide clinicians with information regarding where their focus should lie in helping patients deal with their stressors or illnesses. Specifically, if a clinician believes a patient is not coping well, it might be useful to identify which specific aspects of their coping methods deviate most from the norm, and then focus therapy on these particular aspects of coping as well as on particular appraisals.

A TWENTY-FIRST-CENTURY COPING RESPONSE

In response to severe stressors, as in the case of severe depression, food consumption typically declines. However, in response to moderate stressors there are a fair number of people who display increased eating, particularly in the form of junk food rich in carbohydrates (Dallman, 2010). Negative emotions among 'emotional eaters' might elicit this outcome owing to particular hormonal changes (Raspopow et al., 2010). Alternatively, emotional eaters might not accurately recognize bodily sensations when under duress, essentially mistaking arousal for hunger. Yet another view is that distress results in disinhibition which 'allows' for increased eating to occur, and that eating acts as a coping mechanism to alleviate the negative emotions otherwise evoked by stressful events. With respect to the latter view, eating might actually be a way of coping with adverse events (as either a disengagement strategy or in an effort to 'self medicate' through increased glucose availability).

Long ago, when human-like critters spent a large portion of their time hunting (a dangerous pastime as the prey could easily become the predator), the increased release of the stress hormone cortisol might have been essential for proper defensive actions, and this cortisol also prompted the consumption of food. This increased consumption was necessary, especially for the strength and endurance to partake in the next hunt, when it would readily be burned off. As my friend and associate Sonia Lupien has indicated, today, when the hunt comprises a visit to the supermarket and stressors consist of sitting on our butts while being stuck in traffic, the cortisol release that leads to eating might turn out to be counterproductive. Therefore eating may be a vestigial response associated with cortisol release, but its value in relation to stressors in Western society (which often comprises eating comfort foods high in calories) is less apparent.

FINDING MEANING AND PERSONAL GROWTH

In some situations, cognitive restructuring may be a particularly effective problem-oriented method of dealing with severe stressors. A common form of this coping method has comprised changes in the meaning and importance of the aversive event. It has been suggested that living through traumatic circumstances may result in two independent processes occurring, namely trying to make sense of the event and finding some benefit from the experience (Davis et al., 1998). For instance, although cancer occurrence can take an enormous physical, psychological, and social toll on individuals, cancer survivors might use their experience as an opportunity to improve their physical and mental health. Indeed, individuals report gaining benefits from living through a cancer experience; they might recognize the positive implications or experience post-traumatic growth following their experience of cancer (Cohen & Numa, 2011; Sherman et al., 2010). Beyond the positive effects of this coping method, it also limits negative post-traumatic stress outcomes and the adverse effects of intrusive thoughts on positive affect, life satisfaction, and spiritual well-being (Park et al., 2010).

Not unexpectedly, the positive effects associated with finding meaning or benefit finding ('meaning making' is a related concept that will be treated together with finding meaning and benefit finding) occur in a variety of other venues, such as caregiving for spouses with dementia, family members with cancer, and among parents with severely ill children. The fact is that benefit finding stemming from a severe adverse experience is not at all uncommon. Women treated for breast cancer frequently become engaged in 'walks' to support breast cancer research, and other groups have similarly made heroic efforts to raise funds for certain charities (e.g., the Terry Fox Foundation; Rick Hansen's Man in Motion campaign; the Michael J. Fox Foundation; the Milken Family Foundation).

It is vital to distinguish between two subtle characteristics regarding meaning making, namely those of searching for meaning ('meaning-making efforts') and arriving at a meaning ('meaning made') (Park, 2010). Perhaps not unexpectedly, simply searching for meaning doesn't necessarily result in appreciable benefits, whereas finding or arriving at some meaning might. In fact, seeking meaning can in some instances have adverse effects or might be indicative of a persistent preoccupation with an adverse event (Park, 2010). Later, when we deal with methods of stress management, a theme that will be repeated is that there aren't any treatments that work for everyone. So, too, it seems that finding meaning might be an effective coping method for some individuals but not for others, and it might also vary with the situation that culminated in the severe trauma. It is one thing to find meaning in the death of a loved one that can be ascribed to the negligence of others (e.g., legally taking on an automobile company when death was caused by cars bursting into flames upon a moderate back-end collision), it's quite another to find meaning from a person tripping over their coffee table, hitting their head, and subsequently dying (although these cases are often chalked up to being 'God's will').

There are several factors that predict which individuals adjust (sometimes referred to as acceptance of the diagnosis and the treatment) to their condition. These comprise the sustained use of proper coping methods, the ability to manage non-illness related stressors, and a belief system that resulted in an altered meaning of the cancer experience. Thus, the well-being of women in this situation would be well served by providing resources to reduce distress, providing effective support systems, which include the opportunity to talk about their experiences, and helping women in reframing their beliefs about the illness. As powerful as finding meaning or post-traumatic growth might be as a coping method, its effectiveness in dealing with some disorders might be better than with others. For instance, post-traumatic growth is a cogent factor in dealing with cancer, cardiac disease, multiple sclerosis, and rheumatoid arthritis, and has been reported to be a prominent coping method among parents dealing with a child with a severe illness. However, the jury is still out regarding the efficacy of this coping method in dealing with HIV/AIDS. As effective as finding meaning might be, it doesn't cover every situation, nor is it for everyone. Some people simply won't find any meaning in their illness, which might simply be seen as something that they must endure.

SOCIAL SUPPORT

There has been a vast amount of research concerned with the benefits of social support in dealing with day-to-day stressors and those of a traumatic nature. As indicated earlier, social support has many functions, serving as a shoulder to cry on and a source of information, guidance, instrumental help, reliable alliances, social integration, attachment, reassurance of worth, and an opportunity to provide nurturance. The value of these components of social support varies across situations as the needs of individuals differ under various circumstances, and may also vary over time in relation to a given stressor (e.g., in response to a serious illness).

SOCIAL SUPPORT AS A BUFFER

Social support might not be effective in getting rid of every stressor (e.g., getting the tax department off your back, unless you're really well connected), but it could serve as a buffer against some of the adverse effects of stressors, thereby preventing the psychological disturbances that might otherwise occur (depression, anxiety; Lakey & Cronin, 2008), improving physical health, and promoting recovery from illness (Carod-Artal & Egido, 2009). For instance, elevated depressive symptoms were highly related to having poor social support, and obtaining social support may limit the development of depression. These studies, which included retrospective and prospective analyses, have involved a wide range of stressful situations and taken in several age groups. Of course, the positive actions of social support may vary with a great number of factors, and so blanket statements concerning the value of social support need to be somewhat tempered.

POSITIVITY AND SOCIAL SUPPORT

There are many physicians and scientists who believe that social support, along with other aspects of 'positive psychology', may have great benefits in the healing process, even for some diseases that don't seem to respond well to drugs (e.g., some types of cancer). There are, however, others who believe that positive psychology and social support are all well and good, but they don't cure illnesses. The data provide a degree of support for the view that positive outcomes may come about in relation to social support, but are the magnitude of the effects meaningful with respect to illness attenuation? For instance, a 10 or 20% rise in immune functioning may be statistically significant, but does this translate into a greater ability to fight infection or cancer? Regardless of whether it does or doesn't, social support will lessen the psychological burden of those in distress.

The beneficial effects of social support aren't new. In the Talmud, which preceded modern psychology by a fair bit, there is the statement that 'whoever visits the sick takes away 1/60th of their illness'. I don't know where they got this number, and I suspect that it's not evidence-based. That aside, this statement doesn't necessarily mean that you acquire 1/60th of the other person's illness (although I've seen this argument actually made), nor does it mean that a tumor will have shrunk by 1.66% with each visitor. I guess it also doesn't mean that if 60 people visit you simultaneously, then you'll be entirely cured. What the statement is intended to mean is that social support lightens the burden (even temporarily) carried by the sick person.

The mechanism through which social support has its positive actions is not fully understood. Support can act as a distraction, or a way of limiting the psychic damage that might otherwise be provoked by stressors, and it also limits many of the stressor-elicited biological changes (hormonal, neurochemical, and immunological) that might have adverse consequences. For instance, social support availability was inversely related to levels of stress hormones (e.g., cortisol), both in laboratory stress tests and in natural settings (Heinrichs et al., 2003). For instance, women with metastatic breast cancer with a high quality of social support showed lower cortisol levels than those with a lower quality of support. In fact, based on a meta-analyses (see the box below as to what is meant by 'meta-analysis') it was concluded that social support diminished the cortisol response elicited by laboratory stressors (Heinrichs et al., 2003). Further, it was reported that in a stress test where psychosocial support resources were available, brain activity changes occurred (comprising right prefrontal cortex activation and diminished amygdala activity) that were associated with appraisal and fear/anxiety processes (Taylor et al., 2008). Further, individuals who had received social support over several days displayed a blunted cortisol response and elevated neuronal activity within the anterior cingulate cortex in response to a social stressor (Eisenberger et al., 2007).

META-ANALYSIS

The use of meta-analyses has become increasingly popular to identify the key variables that determine the processes associated with various pathologies and stressor effects. A meta-analysis is a statistical procedure in which the results of many studies already published in peer-reviewed outlets are combined in order to evaluate a particular research question. The aim of this type of analysis is not simply to say that a significant effect was associated with a particular condition or treatment, instead it assesses the effect size in each study (effect size is an index of the strength of associations that exist between two variables) taking into account the number of participants included in that study. Hence it is thought that this sort of analysis provides a more realistic estimate of how variables are related to one another. In some reports, the meta-analysis is also accompanied by a thorough review of the literature, pointing out some of the variables that might not have been included in the primary analysis, and which variables might either mediate or moderate relations that were uncovered by the meta-analysis.

It is likely that *actually* having support may not count nearly as much as the *perception* that social support is available. Indeed, when individuals perceived support as being available, their well-being improved irrespective of whether and to what extent the support was actually proffered (Wills & Shinar, 2000). Moreover, it is likely that the quality of the support available, rather than simply having support, may be essential in determining changes in psychological symptoms. In some instances social support groups are particularly effective in buffering stressor effects, especially if members of the group are all encountering similar problems (say a suicide support group, or one that involves the parents of children with particular illnesses). It seems that support coming from someone 'who understands my pain' is better than that coming from someone, no matter how well intentioned they might be, who seems less able to 'put themselves in my shoes'.

SOCIAL SUPPORT IN RELATION TO IDENTITY

The benefits that might be derived from social support depend on the motives and goals of the individuals (or groups) that provide the support, how the recipient of the support perceives and interprets the motives of the supportive individual or group, and the broad context associated with the conditions where the support was offered (Haslam et al., 2012). If the support provider and recipient are both part of the same ingroup (i.e., they share an identity, meaning that they see themselves as being part of the same religion or culture, and in this case it can also mean individuals who share similar problems), then the positive effects of the support in a stressful situation may be more beneficial than those obtained from someone who does not share the same identity (Haslam et al., 2005). Thus, social support that comes from a parent who has a child with a heart problem similar to one experienced by the child of the support recipient might be more valued and effective than support obtained from someone who does not have a sick child. However, there are also cases where support from an outgroup member can be exceptionally well received (e.g., support in relation to a political stance), as this reinforces the idea that 'my cause is just, and is widely recognized'.

Typically, when the influence of support is assessed, this is considered within the context of the benefits obtained by the support recipient, and not in the context of benefits to the support provider. As we'll see, for some individuals acting as a support provider (a caregiver) can be meaningful and rewarding, and it seems that charitable giving and working for charitable causes can have a similar impact. Prosocial behaviors, such as the provision of support, have indeed been associated with specific brain activity changes, including increased neuronal activity in the ventral striatum, a brain region involved in reward processes. Evidently, giving support elicits positive outcomes in the support giver, and in some instances diminishes their own distress.

FORGIVENESS AND TRUST

Among the most common stressors experienced are those that entail interpersonal relations. These can take the form of disputes, let-downs, or transgressions between family members, close friends, traditional enemies, authority figures, or between groups of individuals. There are many instances in which a victimized individual or group is asked to forgive (or voluntarily might choose to forgive) the behaviors of the transgressor. Apologies can be offered by one party in the hope that forgiveness can be obtained from the other. In a best-case scenario one individual sees that they were in the wrong and values the relationship, and hence apologizes. The recipient of the apology then views this as sincere, and forgives the other person. It is not uncommon for transgressions within our intimate relationships to be the greatest challenge regarding our ability to forgive. Depending on the severity and chronicity of the conflict (e.g., abuse or partner dissolution or betrayal), such transgressions may engender shame and/or anger, anxiety, depression, and considerable rumination that can be exceedingly damaging, and often these transgressions are hard to forgive. In other instances, the transgression might be perceived as being just too great, the hurt too strong, and forgiveness is virtually impossible. Of course, there are numerous other factors that might also come into play that could undermine a reconciliation (e.g., ego, trust, self-righteousness, financial concerns).

So who benefits from forgiveness? Both parties, I suppose, but it may be particularly beneficial for the forgiver. The view has often been expressed that forgiveness of interpersonal transgressions might limit the adverse impact of these events on well-being, particularly by limiting the ruminations that go with them (e.g., McCullough, 2000). Essentially, rather than focusing and ruminating on the transgression, by forgiving the transgressor the victim allows themself the freedom to walk away. Of course, this doesn't mean that offering forgiveness results in forgetting, but for the moment it allows them to 'let go' or 'move on'. As a result, forgiving someone else for their behaviors might actually be, as is often said, 'a gift to the forgiver' (Brown & Phillips, 2005; McCullough et al., 1998).

As difficult as apologies and forgiveness might be to achieve between two individuals, it is often more difficult to achieve a reconciliation between groups. However, there are notable cases in which this has happened. By example, the Australian government, and later the Canadian Government, via their respective prime ministers, apologized to Aboriginal groups for wrongdoings related to the treatment of children who had been forcibly removed from their homes and sent to 'residential schools' in order to socialize them. The intent of the apology was to have the Aboriginal people forgive them (and the people of the country) for past wrongs. It seems as if this should have been an easy thing to do, but it took years for this to be enacted (see Chapter 11 for a discussion regarding intergenerational trauma effects).

You might ask what sort of effect this apology could possibly have as it didn't come from those who committed the atrocities, but from others who were actually far removed from those who were responsible, and sometimes the apology came with considerable reluctance as it might have had implications for reparation for the wrongdoing. Well, if nothing else, it's a message that says 'We don't condone the past egregious behaviors, and we would like better relations with you'. Typically, the response from groups that receive an apology is a positive one, but with caveats attached: 'We are happy to receive your apology and it means a lot to us. Although, we can't forget the past, we would like to move forward. Thus, your apology will mean much more *if it comes with actions that improve quality of life for our group.*' In effect, the apology serves as vindication for the oppressed group's experiences, and it might represent a first step for future improvement. There is a down-side to this, of course, as improvements for the aggrieved group may not occur, and they will thus see this as yet another betrayal (and in the meantime, members of the oppressor group may well say 'Heck, we gave them an apology, now what do they want?').

Conceptualizations of forgiveness, regardless of the framework from which a researcher comes, share the view that forgiveness influences perceptions of an interpersonal interaction so that negative thoughts, feelings, and behaviors are reduced (McCullough, 2000). It is believed that to a certain extent forgiveness (or the ability to forgive) may be a dispositional characteristic (Ysseldyk et al., 2009), but not unexpectedly, this also varies with specific transgressions. Ultimately, however, forgiveness might act to reduce vengeful and avoidant motivations and increase benevolent feelings or behaviors. In effect, forgiveness should not be viewed as an end in itself, but might be an act that influences cognitive, behavioral, and affective responses in relation to the transgression.

Although forgiveness is typically associated with positive psychological outcomes, a forgiving response can also have the opposite effect. In the case of an abusive relationship, forgiveness might serve to perpetuate women's (or men's) illusion of long-term safety and well-being, and thus reinforce the individual to stay in a clearly unhealthy relationship. For example, forgiveness of a currently abusive partner might act to diminish the perceived severity of the transgression (e.g., 'Oh, maybe I'm being a bit too sensitive'), which might undermine an individual's well-being in the long run (e.g., through self-blame, avoidance and social isolation, and continued experiences of abuse). As a result, rather than serving as a buffer against distress, in some situations forgiveness may alter appraisals and coping efforts, culminating in a greater probability of stress-related symptoms evolving.

In order for genuine forgiveness to occur it is essential that the behavior of the protagonist can be trusted. Trust is an essential component not only in interpersonal relationships, but also in intergroup relations, and it is a fundamental component in politics and in commerce. Of course, it is also essential in conflict resolution as forgiveness requires trust that the other person or group will not subsequently repeat their objectionable behavior. When we trust another person we are essentially leaving ourselves uncloaked and unprotected, believing that no harm will come to us.

Not surprisingly, just as trust might make for good relationships, a breach of trust may have exceptionally stressful and damaging effects. We see this frequently in cases of separation/divorce where an individual may feel that 'I trusted you, and you have gone and severed this trust in the worst possible way'. Obviously, this would be most evident if there was a third party involved. This type of situation, predictably, might be accompanied by rumination, and in particular, thoughts concerning retribution (which is the saintly way of saying revenge). As indicated earlier, however, this might be the worst possible way of coping. Rumination can have some positive attributes when it's used in combination with problem solving or cognitive restructuring. However, in the case of rumination associated with divorce/separation, the cognitive restructuring that will be evident (if indeed it is) will likely be focused on less productive issues. Revenge can be satisfying, but only transiently, particularly as it may cause the other side to escalate the battle. At the very least, it becomes a vicious circle wherein the individual ruminates more, thinks about all the wrong things, and even becomes obsessed with the idea. Sometimes it's best to just walk away, have this person out of your life, and to do so quickly and efficiently. Of course, there are occasions when the other side is unreasonable (e.g., on financial issues) and you don't want to be pushed around and have someone take advantage of you, especially when you believe that the circumstances that led to the split are not your doing. In this instance, you might have good cause to stand your ground, but at the same time you ought to appraise the down-side of the battle that will evolve, and consider how far you want to take it, before making your next move. In a game of chess lots of pawns die, and there may be sacrifices.

Trust comes into our lives in various ways, and trust in the workplace (in this case, trust in the organization and trusting other employees) influences our well-being and our satisfaction with the organization. Investigators often view 'trustworthiness' as reflecting the benevolence, integrity, and ability of a trustee (person or organization), and 'trust' as already described as comprising an intention or willingness to accept (or allow oneself) to become vulnerable with the expectation that the trustee will behave appropriately. It seems that trust has much to do with job satisfaction: Helliwell et al. (2009) indicated that one unit of trust (on a 10-point scale) has an effect on well-being that is comparable to a 30% salary increase. In effect, if you offer people the equivalent of an extra 20% of their salary (i.e., some amount less than 30%) or the opportunity to work in a trusting environment, they would likely pick the latter. To be sure, within many settings trust also needs to be accompanied by several related factors, including integrity, loyalty, consistency, and openness. And added to this, whether it's close interpersonal relationships, workplace situations, or intergroup conflicts, an essential factor concerns the view that individuals often think that talk is cheap: their trust will be dependent not on what is said, but on what is done.

UNSUPPORTIVE INTERACTIONS

Social support can go a long way in helping individuals deal with stressors, and this appears to be especially true in regard to illness. One not only sees the influence of social support in relation to psychological illness, such as depression, but also in relation to adjusting to neurological illnesses, such as Huntington's disease, motor neuron disease, multiple sclerosis and Parkinson's disease. Support can come from different sources, and social support from family members may have particularly pronounced positive effects on chronic illness outcomes, especially when family cohesion is high and there is an emphasis on self-reliance and personal achievement. In contrast, negative patient outcomes were tied to critical, overprotective, controlling, and distracting family responses to illness management.

Social support is unquestionably positive for our well-being, yet there may also be a downside to receiving support. Among other things, receiving support could negatively influence self-esteem, as it might result in the individual feeling less competent in contending with the situation without assistance. In addition, individuals might feel indebted to the support provider, which may serve as an additional stressor for an already stressed individual. Finally, attempts to obtain social support may sometimes promote ineffective responses from others, or may cause inaccurate advice to be obtained as the other person might simply not have the 'right' answer.

This brings us to yet another potential risk related to social support; specifically, we often approach others for support, usually with a reasonable expectation that that support will be forthcoming. Typically, our friends listen and offer their support. There will be times, however, when that support isn't offered, or comments are made that are not quite in line with our expectations. Such experiences, referred to as 'unsupportive relations' or 'unsupportive interactions', might take us by surprise, and in some instances may have marked negative repercussions (Ingram et al., 2001) that far exceed those of simply not having support. Clearly, being unsupported is not the same as having a lack of support, and the ramifications can be pertinent to the evolution of pathological outcomes. Unsupportive responses may come in several forms, including minimizing (e.g., 'felt that I was overreacting'), blame (e.g., 'I told you so'), bumbling (e.g., 'did not seem to know what to say, or seemed afraid of saying or doing the *wrong* thing', as well as forced optimism) or distancing or disconnecting (e.g., 'did not seem to want to hear about it').

SITTING ON THE FENCE

There are times when individuals might expect support, even if they don't explicitly seek it. When victims of discrimination, threats of genocide, or of harsh treatment by their government do not receive support from others (as we've seen often), then the behavior of other countries and people might be viewed as an instance of an unsupportive relationship, and the effects on later relationships can be very disturbing: '*In the end we will remember not the words of our enemies, but the silence of our friends*' (Martin Luther King; Nobel Laureate, 1964) and '. . . *to remain silent and indifferent is the greatest sin of all*' (Elie Wiesel; Nobel Laureate, 1986).

This said, there are times when others might intervene, without sufficient understanding or knowledge, basing their behaviors on instinctive gut responses, media manipulation, well-orchestrated political campaigns, or simply in taking the side of the perceived underdog. With respect to international and national politics, ideologies become confused with realities, and discerning what is true and what reflects bias becomes exceedingly difficult. Decisions that are made in this regard likely follow the heuristics described by Kahneman and Tversky as opposed to well thought-out, reasoned decisions.

There are times when our friends fail to support us properly, but there are also times when we misinterpret what can be done or we have warped expectations concerning what our friends ought to do. For instance, some progressive, chronic illnesses can be devastating emotionally and financially, but social support might not be as forthcoming as it might be when a person has been diagnosed with cancer. Friends might not rally around as readily when a person is diagnosed with MS or lupus, and certainly not if it's a mental condition. Moreover, even if they do, there's a time-stamp on this behavior as people are able or willing to provide support for only so long before they tire or need to get on with their own lives. Unfortunately, the ill person might see this withdrawal of support as a betrayal or unsupport ('you know who your friends are when the chips are down'), which can exacerbate the depression that might be associated with illness.

Connected to unsupport is the premise that support was expected, but wasn't obtained (or did not reach the level that was expected). Of course, there are some people who are entirely unreasonable and have expectations of others that simply can't be met. There are also those who demand loyalty to an extent that supporting them fully would be contrary to anything reasonable. In most cases, however, the support expected is not unreasonable, and often the support is sought from those to whom we are closest. Thus, when your best friend forever (BFF), partner, parent, or sib doesn't come through as expected, it's particularly distressing, and adds to the distress you were dealing with in the first place. Think of a time when you counted on your two best friends to help you out, but both had more important commitments, or said things that were just plain thoughtless ('well, you know, there are two sides to every story'), or worse still, blamed you for the situation you found yourself in ('well, maybe you brought it on yourself'). How long was it before you spoke to them again?

Unsupportive interactions have been linked to reduced psychological well-being, over and above the perceived unavailability of social support, or the effects of the stressor experience itself (Ingram et al., 2001; Song & Ingram, 2002). We've all heard of cases where family members distance themselves from one of their own who has been diagnosed with HIV/ AIDS. The stigma of this illness is enormous and having family members turn on an individual is obviously counterproductive for the patient. But the unsupport might even come from those who are close to the affected person simply because they may feel uncertain about how to act and what to say due to a lack of experience. As a result, and despite good intentions, responses can be interpreted as unsupportive, causing further distress in those individuals living with the disease, thus exacerbating depressive symptoms and poor emotional well-being. Remarkably, the stigma associated with HIV/AIDS is so profound that even children who contracted the disease prenatally or through transfusions are victimized by unsupport. Specifically, although the families of children with HIV/AIDS and those with cancer exhibited comparable family functioning and both groups tended to seek support from family members, the parents of children with HIV/AIDS were more reluctant to seek support from outside the family. Once more, HIV/AIDS has a stigma attached to it that affects whole families regardless of how or in whom the disease appeared, and thus the benefits of support might not be sought or ever obtained.

Yet another example of how unsupport affects outcomes derives from work with young women who end up in abusive dating relationships. Dating abuse is not an uncommon circumstance, as more than 20% of college women are subjected to physical abuse and the number is still greater for psychological abuse (however, I would remind you, before you start becoming unsupportive of all males, that the incidents of abuse perpetrated by women against men are just as high). The problems for abused women may be compounded by other unsupportive relations that develop. Specifically, when abused women disclose information regarding their situation, family and friends may become frustrated and react negatively when their advice is not accepted, especially if the victim of abuse refuses to terminate the relationship. Predictably, these women may feel that that they can no longer rely on their social network for support or advice, and will stop confiding in them, thus further isolating themselves. With no one to turn to, their partner may become their sole source of support, despite the abuse (reminiscent of the child who turns to the abusive parent for support and protection).

In addition to direct effects on well-being, unsupportive relationships may undermine the use of other coping methods. In this regard, among HIV patients, perceived distancing and the disinterested responses of others predicted greater use of ineffective coping strategies, such as disengagement and denial, which in turn was associated with greater mood disturbance. Likewise, among bereaved respondents, unsupportive interactions with members of their social network were associated with diminished coping efforts and reduced perceived effectiveness of the coping strategies that were used. The net result of these unsupportive experiences is that individuals might become reluctant to seek support, and may limit or re-orient their help-seeking behaviors in an ineffective fashion. Rather than seeking help from friends or family, individuals might turn to anonymous sources of support (e.g., internet chat groups) where judgments are not tied to the individual's sense of self-worth (i.e., rejection from an anonymous stranger may be less distressing than rejection by a close other).

One final comment is in order before closing off this section. Unsupport is particularly notable in the elderly, and especially among those with severe neurological problems, such as Alzeheimer's Disease, Parkinson's, and stroke. In fact, there have been many reports of the elderly being subjected to abuse as a result of frustrations experienced by caregivers. A new position statement by the American Academy of Neurology has, in fact, called on clinical neurologists to screen patients for abusive experiences. We may as well be upfront about this. Not all caregivers are meant to do this sort of sensitive work and their frustrations might emerge inappropriately. Of course, abuse is manifested in many contexts beyond elder abuse, and when patients show up for neurological testing, it is wise to assess whether these problems are secondary to some sort of abuse, as not doing so might leave the patient open to still greater problems.

TAKING ADVANTAGE OF A FRIEND

There is a cute and interesting laboratory manipulation that has been conducted to see how individuals might (or not) deal with decisions that involve unfairness, and represent an unsupportive interaction. The 'ultimatum game' (or a slight variant called the 'dictator game') is one in which a sum of money is offered to two individuals provided that they can come to an agreement on how to split the booty. If the proposer makes an offer that is accepted then they both win, but if the proposal is not accepted then they both lose. Typically, if the offer is an unfair one (say an 80:20 split), then the second person will reject the offer. It can be imagined that if the total prize were $100 the individual offered $20 would simply say, 'Screw this. I'd rather lose the $20 than be suckered'. But what if the total prize were $100,000, would they be as likely to walk away from $20,000?

In this paradigm the unfair offer is coupled with a neurophysiological profile in which electrical activity in the medial frontal region becomes very negative (Boksem & De Cremer, 2010). However, if the unfair offer comes from a friend, then it's less likely that it will be rejected, and the negative activity within the frontal cortex is not apparent, possibly owing to activation evident in other regions, such as in the anterior prefrontal cortex (Campanha et al., 2011). Apparently, we respond more positively to unfair offers from friends than from strangers. Frankly, I'm a bit surprised by the results. I would have thought that when one is taken advantage of by a friend the emotional and negative cognitive responses would be that much greater than when this knife in the back came from a stranger. However, events in a laboratory might not mean the same thing to an individual relative to the betrayals that occur in real life.

SOCIAL REJECTION

A particularly potent stressor that social beings, like us, might encounter is one that entails social rejection. Groups of individuals can be rejected, as seen in cases of discrimination related to gender, sexual orientation, race, or religion. Rejection can occur at a group or personal level. Social rejection is, in fact, fairly common as in the case of stigmatization and discrimination against those with mental disorders, or those with illnesses such as AIDS. Social rejection can also occur in the absence of these factors, occurring either because the individual is somewhat different from the rest of their ingroup or is viewed as being an embarrassment to the group. This is often referred to as the 'black sheep effect', where members of the ingroup don't want their group's identity tarnished by a particular individual. When group members feel that they are a unified social entity (entitativity), outliers from the group who negatively represent them are denigrated in order to preserve the good standing of the group as a whole (Lewis & Sherman, 2010). Predictably, the stronger the ingroup cohesion (ingroup identification), the more likely a deviant member would be viewed as being atypical and hence rejected. In fact, individuals will derogate an unfavorable group member to a greater extent than they would an unsavory outgroup member. This could be a means of protecting the group, but it is equally possible that this differential derogation is an individual protection strategy as it serves to limit the threat of being associatively miscast ('He's not one of us, and I'm not like him at all') (Eidelman & Biernat, 2003).

Some adolescents will know the feeling of having their two best friends turn on them or simply ignore them, leaving them out of social events and generally feeling diminished by them. In general, unsupportive relationships, especially those that involve targeted rejection, can be especially damaging, and have been linked to an exacerbation of depressive feelings. No matter the age, the impact of social rejection can be intense and undermine individuals' abilities to contend with ongoing stressors, just as unsupportive responses act in this capacity. You'd think that on-line social exclusion might not be as bad as it is when it occurs in a real social setting, but it is actually hurtful, even if you don't know the people who are excluding you. However, when excluded from an on-line forum, it might be a bit easier to say to yourself 'It's not me, they have a problem', and hence your self-esteem might not be as drastically affected as it may otherwise be. Then again, think about being excluded as a 'friend' on your erstwhile friend's Facebook page, especially when everybody under the sun is included. It's already happening that a slap to the face now occurs in the form of being 'defriended'.

Our fear of social rejection is in itself a very powerful negative emotion that may be linked to elevations of the stress hormone cortisol, and if this fear is sufficiently persistent, the overall biological profile that is observed is not unlike that characteristic of other chronic stressors and those that accompany PTSD. Essentially, fear of social rejection reflects a trait that is accompanied by chronic distress, leading to an adaptation to limit the excessive physiological activation that might culminate in allostatic overload.

Given the powerful actions of social rejection on psychological well-being, there have been several paradigms developed to assess this in a laboratory context. One increasingly popular approach to studying this is a computer game, referred to as cyberball, in which a virtual ball is tossed between three characters (Blackhart et al., 2007). One of the icons is controlled by the participant, and the others are presumed to be controlled by other individuals. Initially, the ball is tossed evenly between the players, but shortly afterward, it is passed between the other two virtual participants and the actual participant is excluded.

This has the effect of eliciting negative ruminative thoughts, an altered mood, hostility, and elevated cortisol levels. In addition to these behavioral and hormonal effects, social rejection in the cyberball paradigm markedly influences the brain processes associated with appraisals and decision making as well as with depressed mood. In particular, following rejection the self-reported distress was accompanied by increased activity (as measured by functional magnetic resonance imaging (fMRI)) in the dorsal anterior cingulate cortex, although this outcome was diminished among individuals who had experienced rich social support in the days prior to testing. Not unexpectedly, the effects of rejection on brain processes were marked in adolescents, especially in those with a higher rejection sensitivity who might be most vigilant regarding peer acceptance.

What makes these findings particularly interesting is that the very same brain activation profile has also been seen in studies assessing the effects of physical pain (Eisenberger et al., 2003). Given this similarity it was suggested that the anterior cingulate cortex is fundamental in the neural circuitry that supports physical and social pain, and may be part of a broader 'neural alarm system' (Eisenberger & Lieberman, 2004). Similar effects were observed in adolescents, and in this instance rejection was also accompanied by decreased neuronal activity in the ventral striatum (a region associated with reward processes), suggesting that the rewarding experience that could accompany a game with others had lost its luster. Moreover, these brain changes were most prominent in those individuals who were especially sensitive to rejection (Masten et al., 2009). Furthermore, the way in which an adolescent's anterior cingulate cortex responded to social rejection was predictive of their disposition toward later depression (Masten et al., 2011). In particular, those who showed the greatest changes of the anterior cingulate cortex activity in response to social rejection in an online social interaction subsequently showed the greatest depressive behaviors (as judged by parents) over the ensuing year. Thus, this index of social exclusion might be a marker for future depression. It is of particular significance in this regard that social support during adolescence, reflected by the time spent with friends, can serve to diminish the brain changes associated with peer rejection even when measured in the ball-tossing game two years later. In effect, reactions in a social rejection test might be a marker for later mood disturbances that accompany social interactions.

In an effort to provide a comprehensive perspective of how social rejection comes to promote depression, Slavich, O'Donovan et al. (2010) incorporated emotional, cognitive and psychobiological factors in an interesting manner. Essentially, it was suggested that social rejection may result in the activation of neurons within brain regions (e.g., the dorsal anterior cingulate cortex) involved in the processing of information related to negative events and reflection-based distress. These experiences give rise to negative self-referential cognitions ('people just don't like me') and emotions that are related to these feelings, especially shame and humiliation. This, in turn, would activate brain regions that are involved in regulating mood, and may affect certain aspects of the immune system (inducing inflammatory effects) that might also contribute to depressive-like states.

Aside from the informative nature of these studies with social rejection, what struck me was that the observed emotional responses and the changes of brain activity occurred even in a relatively contrived laboratory situation, where a virtual ball was being tossed around. How much stronger would the brain react to social rejection in a genuine life context that involves friends or family? As King Lear said, 'Turn all her mother's pains and benefits to laughter and contempt; that she may feel how sharper than a serpent's tooth it is to have a thankless child!'

CONCLUSION

Adverse events, especially those that occurred during critical periods early in life or possibly during adolescence, result in increased vulnerability to later stressor induced pathology. However, some individuals are able to emerge less scathed than others even in the face of the most traumatic events. It is possible that this occurs owing to an inherent biological resilience, the availability of effective coping resources, a sense of mastery, or other psychosocial factors. In fact, stressful events in some cases may imbue individuals with greater resilience (e.g., by putting them in a situation that favors finding meaning or personal growth). Individuals may have learned from adverse experiences that with appropriate behaviors and coping methods it is possible to transcend current strife (Seery, 2011), indeed there might be something to the tiresome cliche 'that which doesn't kill you makes you stronger'. From a practical research perspective, knowing which behavioral or biological factors distinguish those who succumb to illness in the face of severe trauma and those who do not might prove exceptionally valuable in defining strategies to immunize or treat individuals so that traumatic events do not have the severe repercussions that might otherwise occur.

It seems that appraisals of events and how we cope with them can be influenced by prior stressful experiences as well as our current affective state. There are some individuals who tend to put a negative spin on events, so that others often perceive them as being a negative or pessimistic person (they, in contrast, would say that they are not pessimists, they're realists). Likewise, the coping strategies they typically endorse are stereotypical (fixed), even when the situation might call for a different approach. Breaking well-entrenched behavioral styles (habits) is exceedingly difficult (e.g., emotional rumination in response to stressors), but there are times when these coping methods are entirely inappropriate and hence ineffective. In contrast, an effective way of dealing with stressors is to be flexible in using particular coping strategies, and to recognize that this flexibility needs to be maintained over time and across situations. That sounds like good advice, but it doesn't tell you how to do it, and might be about as helpful as advising me to become taller if I want to play in the NBA. However, when we come to Chapter 12 (dealing with treatment and intervention strategies) we'll discuss ways that might help individuals adopt a more flexible pattern of responses to the challenges they encounter.

SUMMARY

- How we appraise stressors may influence the way in which we cope with them.
- Appraisals of events can influence our decision-making process that also feeds into our choice of coping methods, although individuals often behave in irrational ways, appraise events inappropriately, and make poor decisions.

- It isn't that the coping methods adopted aren't inherently good or bad, it is instead that the effectiveness of particularly coping strategies is likely situation-dependent.
- Several coping methods can be used concurrently, and the array of coping strategies used can determine their usefulness. In addition, in dealing with stressors it is important to maintain flexibility so that various strategies are available as needed.
- Social support is often one of our most potent coping strategies, but expected support that does not materialize, or is viewed as less than ideal, may be interpreted as unsupportive, and can thus have very negative repercussions.

3 HORMONAL CHANGES ASSOCIATED WITH STRESSORS

SEARCHING FOR THE SOURCE OF ILLNESS

Perhaps this comment should have appeared earlier, but this really seemed like the right place to bring it up. When people think of scientists, they often think of nerdy people standing at a lab bench and throwing around big words. In contrast, someone who works as a CSI or an NCIS agent, or as a behavioral profiler, seems pretty cool (can you tell I'm a television junkie?). Likewise, archeologists and anthropologists all seem, at least in the last two decades, to be stereotyped as Indiana Jones. I see neuroscientists more like detectives who are hunting down culprits that cause the brain or other organs to act in particular ways. They find certain clues (or associates) related to a disease state, rule out those that are either simply bystanders or just associated with the pathology, but not directly involved in its provocation (i.e., dismiss those with alibis), and then once they have a very good suspect, they tie the behavior of that variable (person) of interest to the pathology (crime). Among other things, they try to simulate the crime by administering drugs (or other treatments, including creating mice with or without a certain biological make up) to determine whether a pathological state emerges (recreating the crime scene), assess whether this happens all of the time or only under certain circumstances (serial killer or a unique event), and finally evaluate whether the pathological state can be reversed by eliminating or blocking certain chemical systems. As we go through the next sections, keep in mind that the basic approaches to evaluating the role of different hormonal and neurochemical systems in the stress process or identifying the cause of pathology are not really complicated, involve some keen detective work, and at the end, any judgment comes from a jury of peers (journal or grant reviewers, who when they make negative decisions are thought of as 'sleazy lawyers that graduated into being corrupt politicos').

The stress response, as we've seen, is determined by a constellation of factors related to stressor characteristics and various individual difference factors, as well as how we appraise and cope with challenges. But what exactly are the stress responses we've been talking about? Well, some comprise anxiety, worry, rumination, and poor mood, whereas others might entail psychological illnesses (depression, PTSD) and physical pathologies, such as heart disease and diabetes. In a very general sense, stressful events promote numerous biological changes, some of which might be acting in an adaptive capacity. Others, however, reflect the consequences of the strain on biological systems becoming too intense or long lasting. Ultimately, something will give. It could be that adaptive biological systems stop operating properly, allowing for pathological states to emerge, or it might be that pathology reflects the side effects or secondary consequences of the adaptive system's efforts to deal with the challenge. In theory, each of us has a weak link(s) or struts, and when the load becomes too heavy this link might break and lead to pathology. The specific link(s) that break will presumably contribute to the specific pathology that will be elicited.

Numerous papers have been written documenting the impact of stressors on adaptive hormonal systems, and the factors that influence their effectiveness. Likewise, there have been many reports indicating that stressful events either provoke or aggravate pathophysiological outcomes, including those of a psychological, immunological, cardiovascular, muscular, or gastrointestinal nature – you name it, and stressors affect it. The trick is defining which specific stressor-related biological processes, or sets of biological processes, are responsible for particular pathologies. In this chapter, we'll consider one set of systems activated in response to stressors, namely hormonal processes that not only have adaptive consequences and maintain our well-being, but also contribute to pathological outcomes. By the end of this chapter, you should appreciate that:

- multiple hormonal systems exist that interact with one another, and that each of the hormones have multiple actions;
- some systems, such as one that leads to an elevation of the prototypical stress hormone cortisol, have received particular attention. However, stressful events influence numerous hormones and their receptors, each of which play a fundamental adaptive role to meet the organism's needs in response to a variety of challenges;
- some hormones are usually considered in the context of stressors, and have profound effects on mood states, such as anxiety and depression. There are also hormones, such as leptin, insulin, bombesin, neuropeptide Y, and ghrelin, that are associated with eating and energy balances. Others, such as estrogens and testosterone, are usually considered to have primary effects on sexual characteristics and sex-related behaviors, while oxytocin is often viewed as a hormone related to prosocial behaviors. In each of these instances, however, these hormones are influenced by stressful events, and coordination exists so that appropriate defensive actions can be initiated, whereas responses and processes that are not essential at the moment are suppressed;
- pathological outcomes can arise as a result of the dysfunction of one or another hormonal process.

HORMONES AND BEHAVIOR

To fully understand how stressful events come to affect our health, it's necessary to understand that stressors might do so by virtue of their actions on multiple biological systems. If you come from a biological background this might be easy-peasy, but if you have less

FIGURE 3.1 Several sites within the body from which particular hormones are released.

(Illustration created by Lucas J. Wareing)

experience in the biological sciences and are more interested in the psychosocial or developmental aspects of stressor effects, you might find these biochemical interactions somewhat complicated or view them as peripherally interesting but not *really* relevant to you. Be assured here, I'm not trying to prime you so that you'll back away thinking 'I don't understand this stuff, and I don't care to learn about it'. On the contrary, if you read this stuff in the context of how hormonal factors might provoke or aggravate certain illnesses, you'll find that it's not all that difficult. So, with an open mind (and none of that 'I don't like math' routine) let's assess to what extent stressors affect physiological processes, and then we'll be able to consider their role in the emergence of pathology. This chapter will primarily consider the hormonal processes related to stressors, and in Figure 3.1 you can see where these hormones originate. In the ensuing two chapters we'll be considering neurotransmitters and growth factors as well as immune system changes. These systems are highly inter-related with one another, and we'll consistently be referring back and forth between them.

WHAT'S A HORMONE?

A hormone is a chemical released by a cell or gland in response to external or internal signals (e.g., stressors, altered sugar levels), which then travels to a distal site where it affects other cells of the body. Typically, hormones are transported in the blood, and cells respond when a hormone triggers specific receptors that are present, which then provoke a series of changes that culminate in a cellular response. There may be several different types of receptors for any given hormone, and triggering them may engender different outcomes.

Hormone molecules that are released directly into the bloodstream are referred to as 'endocrine' hormones, whereas those secreted directly into a duct and then flow either into the bloodstream, or from cell to cell by diffusion, are referred to as 'exocrine' hormones (this process is known as 'paracrine signaling'). When the hormone stimulates the very cell that actually released it (yes, this happens, and there are reasons for this as we'll see later), this is referred to as 'autocrine signaling'.

Hormones come in several flavors. There are hormones that are derived from lipids and phospholipids (these are naturally produced substances, such as fats, sterols, mono-, di- and triglycerides, and an assortment of vitamins). The hormones that are of particular interest to us are the steroid hormones, such as corticoids and sex hormones (e.g., estrogen). Glucocorticoids (GC) refer to a class of steroid hormones that bind to the glucocorticoid receptor (GR), which is present in virtually every cell, with cortisol (corticosterone in rodents) being the prototypical stress hormone.

A second class of hormones made up of lengthy amino acid chains are peptide hormones (usually just referred to simply as peptides). These comprise those that are on the relatively small side (e.g., vasopressin), and those that are large as they comprise numerous amino acid chains (e.g., growth hormone and insulin). There are some hormones, such as adrenaline (also called epinephrine), that are manufactured (synthesized) and released in the periphery and by neurons in the brain, and in the latter capacity they are referred to as neurotransmitters (see Chapter 4).

Tables 3.1 and 3.2 provide a broad overview concerning the functions of a number of hormones that are found in the hypothalamus and the pituitary gland, respectively. The hormones

TABLE 3.1 Hypothalamic hormones and their effects

Secreted hormone	Biological effect
Corticotropin-releasing hormone (CRH)	Released from paraventricular nucleus of hypothalamus: stimulates adrenocorticotropic hormone (ACTH) release from anterior pituitary
Dopamine (DA)	Released from the arcuate nucleus: inhibits prolactin secretion from anterior pituitary
Growth hormone-releasing hormone (GHRH)	Released from the arcuate nucleus: stimulates growth hormone (GH) release from anterior pituitary
Somatostatin (SS)	Released from the periventricular nucleus: inhibits growth hormone (GH) and thyroid-stimulating hormone (TSH) release from anterior pituitary
Gonadotropin-releasing hormone (GnRH)	Released from the preoptic area: stimulates the release of follicle-stimulating hormone (FSH) and luteinizing hormone (LH) from anterior pituitary
Oxytocin (OXT)	Released from both the supraoptic and paraventricular nucleus: promotes uterine contraction, milk ejection
Melanocyte stimulating hormone (MSH)	Produced in the lateral hypothalamus: associated with feeding, motivation
Vasopressin (VP)	Released by both the paraventricular and supraoptic nucleus: promotes water reabsorption and increased blood volume
Orexin (hypocretin)	Produced within the hypothalamus, but orexin receptors are found throughout the brain: involved in arousal, wakefulness, and appetite

TABLE 3.2 Pituitary hormones and their effects

Secreted hormone	Biological effect
Anterior portion	
Growth hormone (GH)	Stimulates growth and cell reproduction, and Insulin-like growth factor (IGF-1) secretion from liver
Thyroid-stimulating hormone (TSH)	Stimulates thyroxine (T4) and triiodothyronine (T3) synthesis and release from thyroid gland, and stimulates iodine absorption by thyroid gland
Adrenocorticotropic hormone (ACTH)	Stimulates corticosteroid (glucocorticoid and mineralcorticoid) release from adrenocortical cells and promotes androgen synthesis
Beta-endorphin	Inhibits perception of pain
Follicle-stimulating hormone (FSH)	In females: stimulates maturation of ovarian follicles in ovary. In males: stimulates spermatogenesis, production of androgen-binding protein
Luteinizing hormone (LH)	In females: stimulates ovulation and formation of corpus luteum; In males: stimulates testosterone synthesis
Prolactin (PRL)	Stimulates milk synthesis and release from mammary glands; involved in sexual gratification
Melanocyte-stimulating hormone (MSH)	Stimulates melanin synthesis and release

Secreted hormone	Biological effect
Posterior portion	
Oxytocin (OXT)	Elicits uterine contraction; lactation
Vasopressin (AVP)	Water reabsorption and increased blood volume

released from the adrenal gland are provided in Table 3.3. Many of these hormones are fundamental to the stress process. Among other things, they affect our ability to contend with stressful events by influencing our readiness to make appropriate behavioral or emotional responses, modify cognitive processes, and promote the physiological changes (e.g., variations in immune and heart functioning, as well as energy regulation) that are essential for survival. In general, hormones have functions beyond that of stress regulation, being fundamental to our basic functioning, metabolic processes, the initiation and cessation of eating, regulating immune activity, reproductive processes, preparing the body for transitional phases of life (puberty, parenting, bonding, the menopause), and the production and release of yet more hormones. Moreover, they contribute to cell death (apoptosis) and the stimulation or inhibition of cell growth, and they influence our mood states and cognitive functioning.

TABLE 3.3 Adrenal hormones and their effects

Secreted hormone	Biological effect
Adrenal cortex	
Cortisol (corticosterone in rodents)	Stimulates gluconeogenesis and fat breakdown in adipose tissue; inhibits protein synthesis; inhibits glucose uptake in muscle and adipose tissue, promotes immune suppression and acts as an anti-inflammatory
Mineralocorticoids (e.g., aldosterone)	Stimulate active sodium reabsorption and passive water reabsorption, thus increasing blood volume and blood pressure
Androgens (e.g., DHEA and testosterone)	Masculinization (limited compared to effects of androgens from testes); in females this has masculinizing effects
Adrenal medulla	
Epinephrine (adrenaline) and norepinephrine (noradrenaline) (Epi and NE)	Elicits flight or fight response; increases oxygen and glucose to the brain and muscles; promotes vasodilation, increases catalysis of glycogen in liver and the breakdown of lipids in fat cells; suppresses bodily processes (e.g., digestion) during emergency responses; influences immune system activity
Dopamine (DA)	Increased heart rate and blood pressure
Enkephalin (Enk)	Involved in pain regulation

ASSESSING THE RELATIONSHIP BETWEEN HORMONES AND BEHAVIORS

There are several approaches that can be used to assess the relationship between hormones and behaviors. As usual, this is fairly simple in animals, but a bit more complicated in humans. In animals the effects of the hormone can be assessed simply by administering it (by injection or in their food or water), and conversely, treatments can be given to block the receptor or block the source of the hormone through surgical interventions (e.g., by adrenal-ectomy to reduce adrenal hormones, or ovariectomy to reduce female sex hormones). Alternatively, mice can be genetically engineered so that the hormone or receptors are diminished or the hormone levels can be increased. Once the hormone is reduced and the consequences assessed, one can then determine whether these effects are reversed by the exogenous administration of that hormone (i.e., a replacement therapy). Things can become a bit complicated as hormones may interact with one another, as well as other biological processes and life experiences, so it often requires sophisticated experimentation to determine how and when this occurs.

In humans the analyses of hormones in relation to behavior require different approaches. In some cases one can assess individuals with diseases that involve hormonal disturbances. For instance, it is possible to study those with Addisons's disease in which an adrenal insufficiency exists. Alternatively, pituitary adenoma and adrenal adenoma (an adenoma refers to a benign tumor of glandular origin; they can eventually become malignant, and the term 'adenocarcinoma' is then applied) are accompanied by high cortisol levels, and thus one could determine the influence of hypercortisolemia. The same types of procedures could be used to assess the behavioral influence of sex hormones, varied pituitary hormones, thyroid hormones, and so on. In some cases hormones are administered clinically (corticoids, estrogen, progesterone) or experimentally, and in these conditions the potential behavioral effects can be deduced. Yet another approach is to rely on individual differences in hormonal levels and simply determine whether individuals with high (or low) levels of a given hormone exhibit differences with respect to certain behaviors, reactivity to stressors, or the development of particular pathologies.

Another frequent approach to assess the connection between hormones and behaviors has been to determine whether a variant of a gene is associated with reduced levels of a hormone or disturbances of a hormone receptor, and then relate this to particular behavioral phenotypes. You will recall from Chapter 1 that variants of a gene can arise because the code that makes up the gene is altered (referred to as a polymorphism). Genes are composed of a long string of nucleotides, namely adenine, guanine, cytosine, and thymine. Each set of three nucleotides makes up an amino acid, and lengthy strings of amino acids make up proteins (much like a group of letters make up a word, and a string of words make a sentence, and so forth). These nucleotides, and the amino acids they form, comprise genes that code for particular proteins. If a nucleotide is altered at an important place on the gene, then this polymorphism can have dramatic effects (just as a letter in a word, or a word in a sentence, can alter the meaning of an entire sentence). Often, the polymorphism can involve just a single nucleotide, in which case it is referred to as a single nucleotide polymorphism (SNP), or it can also involve multiple nucleotides. The greater the number of mutations (it might be better to call them 'variants', since mutation is often used as a pejorative, and not all mutations have negative consequences), the more likely one or more will appear at critical sites on a gene, and hence the greater the risk of a bad outcome. There are all sorts of factors that could influence the appearance of mutations. For instance, mutations in a newborn arc tied to the age of the mother, and it also appears that polymorphisms might be tied to the age of the father.

HOW BACTERIA DEAL WITH HOSTILE ENVIRONMENTS: A CASE FOR MUTAGENESIS

Studies in bacteria have given us an interesting perspective concerning the conditions under which stressors might promote genetic mutations. Specifically, Dr Susan Rosenberg and her team reported that when Escherichia coli (E. coli) were under stress, which in bacteria comprises starvation or the presence of an antibiotic challenge, the rate of gene mutations increased very appreciably. Ordinarily, DNA breaks can occur frequently and there is a process that is involved in DNA repair. One might have thought that perhaps stressor conditions disrupted this DNA repair process, but this didn't turn out to be the case. Instead, it seemed that in the face of a challenging environment the rate of mutation (referred to as mutagenesis) increased provided that the cells were not well adapted to that environment. In effect, the nature of the cell may be changing in an effort to adapt to the relatively hostile conditions that were present (Amar et al., 2012).

This work, importantly, was not only indicative of why the mutagenesis increased, but also identified the essential network hubs that controlled this process. Cells are best off when diversity exists, and many proteins are invested in maintaining this diversity, often functioning to detect threats within the environment, which then trigger specific changes that increase mutagenesis.

BIOLOGICAL STRESS RESPONSES

The brain and peripheral nervous system, as well as many other organs, contain several hormones and receptors that influence every aspect of our functioning. As we'll see, too little or too much of any hormone creates its own characteristic set of problems. As one would expect from well-regulated processes, there are many checks and balances within and between the systems in our body and brain, but when these are sufficiently disturbed, pathophysiological outcomes might appear. Unfortunately, because there are so many biological changes that occur concurrently and interact with one another, it's sometimes difficult to determine where the problem is, which biological systems contributed to the imbalance, and how to repair the problem or at least patch it up for the moment.

When we encounter a stressor, a series of biological changes occur that might reflect adaptive responses to deal with the stressor or its repercussions. These might be important for appraisal processes, serve to diminish the physical or emotional pain associated with the stressor, prepare the individual to deal with ongoing or impending insults (e.g., enhancing arousal, vigilance, and the cognitive processes necessary for effective coping), increase energy substrates that may be needed for survival, and limit potential adverse effects that might otherwise be provoked. However, there are also instances in which hormones can have negative consequences for our well-being. We'll deal with why this occurs later, but for the moment we can use the analogy of pain perception, and the obvious questions of 'What's it good for? Wouldn't we be better off if there were no such thing?'. As indicated earlier, pain gives us a clear message that things are amiss, and that some actions need to be taken to avoid further problems. Individuals with a congenital lack of pain receptors wouldn't know if they had their hand on a hot stove, and thus would suffer severe tissue damage. In the same fashion, the biological changes associated with stressors send out the message that we ought to be doing something about the situation we're in.

THE HYPOTHALAMIC–PITUITARY–ADRENAL (HPA) AXIS AND GLUCOCORTICOIDS

Several hormones play essential regulatory roles to make sure that the body's needs are being met. Some of these are fundamental to the stress process (including behavioral responses, such as fighting or fleeing) and are activated very soon after an adverse event is experienced, whereas others seem to kick in a little later, but they too have important actions in dealing with the challenges that might be encountered.

CORTISOL/CORTICOSTERONE RESPONSE TO AN ACUTE STRESSOR

Within seconds of a stressor being encountered, several neuronal changes occur in cortical brain regions that are involved in stressor appraisal processes and in those associated with decision making (e.g., the prefrontal, including the anterior cingulate cortices). At roughly the same time the sympathetic portion of the autonomic nervous system is activated, which entails the release of epinephrine and norepinephrine that stimulate several organs in the body (e.g., causing increased cardiovascular tone). As illustrated in Figure 3.2, owing to the activation of neurons within the prefrontal cortex, a series of biological changes occur that culminate in the release of cortisol (corticosterone) from the adrenal gland. Cortisol released into the bloodstream then reaches the brain where it stimulates neurons in the hypothalamus and hippocampus, which will have the effect of stemming a further release of the hormone. This self-regulating HPA loop (referred to as a negative feedback loop) is of fundamental importance as a persistent gluco-corticoid (GC) increase may have damaging effects. Specifically, if the glucocorticoid receptors (GR) on hippocampal cells (where the receptors appear in high densities) are excessively stimulated, they may be damaged, and thus a component of the shut-down mechanisms will not be operating. As a result, corticosterone will continue to be released, leading to still greater hippocampal cell loss. If this continues unabated, then disturbances of cognitive functioning

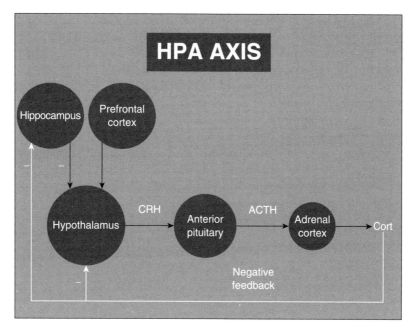

FIGURE 3.2 Depiction of the effects of a stressor on hypothalamic–pituitary–adrenal (HPA) functioning, and the feedback loop involved in its regulation. Stressors induce the activation of neurons within the prefrontal cortex as well as in certain aspects of the amygdala, which then influence neuronal activity in the paraventricular nucleus (PVN) of the hypothalamus, promoting the release of corticotropin releasing hormone (CRH) from the terminals of the PVN neurons. Within a few seconds the CRH released from these PVN neurons stimulates the anterior (front) portion of the pituitary gland, causing the release of adrenocorticotropic hormone (ACTH). This ACTH enters the bloodstream and eventually reaches the adrenal glands (located just above the kidneys), where it stimulates the release of cortisol (corticosterone is the rodent equivalent) into the bloodstream. Once in circulation, corticosterone will reach the brain, where it influences the hypothalamus and the hippocampus, causing CRH release to be diminished, and hence the HPA activation will subside. In effect, this is a self-regulating loop, wherein corticosterone, the final product of the HPA activation, comes to inhibit the CRH that was involved in the initiation of the HPA cascade.

(Illustration created by Lucas J. Wareing)

will ultimately ensue. During the normal aging process neurons are typically lost, but this could be exacerbated by treatments that cause sustained cortisol elevations (McEwen & Gianaros, 2011).

Of particular significance, as described in Figure 3.2, is that the regulation of HPA functioning is determined by neuronal processes in regions other than the hypothalamus. For instance, following a stressor experience, the activation of neurons within the prefrontal cortex and amygdala, which are critically involved in stressor appraisals and emotional responses, serves to activate HPA activity. It's obviously important to have a nicely regulated corticoid response to stressors, so that mild stressors elicit a moderate corticosterone release from the adrenal gland, whereas stronger stressors should elicit a greater release. In addition, as in the case of most stress systems, the release of the hormone should diminish relatively quickly after the stressor has terminated. Indeed, the magnitude of the corticosterone rise, as well as the time needed for normalization to occur (i.e., the time before corticoids return to their resting levels), varies as a function of factors related to the stressor itself, such as its nature and severity, although it seems that there are some stressors (e.g., social defeat) that result in the duration of the corticosterone rise being relatively persistent (Audet et al., 2011). As well, these neuroendocrine changes vary as a function of the strain of animal examined, its gender (female rodents ordinarily exhibit a greater response), and age (older animals take longer to normalize following stressor termination), as well as the constellation of variables listed in Figure 3.3 that were discussed in Chapters 1 and 2.

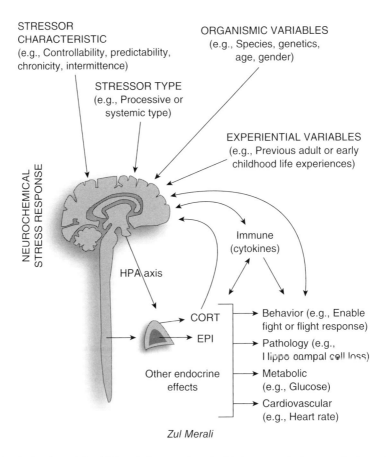

Zul Merali

FIGURE 3.3 Activation of the HPA axis is associated with hormonal changes that can influence the multiple biological systems, body organs, and brain regions that will ultimately affect well-being. The extent to which hormonal changes occur is determined by the type and characteristics of the stressor, a series of organismic variables, as well as the organism's previous experiences, including those that occurred prenatally and early in life.

WHAT CORTISOL (CORTICOSTERONE) DOES FOR US

Corticosterone has numerous positive actions, many of which will not be evident on the target tissues for some time following the stressor (e.g., an hour or so). Among its many regulatory actions, corticosterone increases blood sugar through gluconeogenesis in the liver and in muscle (this simply means the production of glucose from substrates such as lactate and glycogen). In addition, corticosterone aids in the metabolism of fats, carbohydrates, and proteins, and limits immune over-activation that might otherwise occur in response to stressors. Owing to some of these actions, glucocorticoid acting agents are widely used clinically (e.g., hydrocortisone, prednisone, prednisolone, and dexamethasone). In low doses they are used to treat Addison's disease (a condition, as we saw earlier, where the adrenal glands do not make sufficient cortisol), and because of its immunosuppressive effects at high doses, it is also used to suppress allergic and inflammatory responses. It is also utilized to manage disorders in which the immune system attacks certain parts of the self (rheumatoid arthritis is an example of one of these autoimmune disorders) as well as to prevent tissue rejection following an organ transplant and in graft-versus-host disease (where the transplanted tissue, the graft, attacks the recipient or host).

Although corticosterone is often thought of uniquely in terms of the HPA axis, it also affects neuronal functioning in several other brain regions. For example, chronic glucocorticoid elevation increased the release of peptides (bombesin and corticotrophin releasing hormone) in stress-sensitive brain regions, such as the prefrontal cortex and amygdala (Merali et al., 2008). Corticosterone activation of neuronal activity at the amygdala has diverse effects, including changes in visceral and somatic pain sensitivity among female rodents, and these effects varied with the estrus cycle, possibly owing to interactions with ovarian hormones (Gustafsson et al., 2011). Glucocorticoids may also impair working memory (i.e., the processes that are engaged for the memory involved in ongoing tasks), but it also seems that glucocorticoid stimulation of the prefrontal cortex can enhance memory consolidation (Barsegyan et al., 2010), a process in which short-term memories are firmed up so that they become part of our long-term memory.

Sapolsky et al. (2000) described corticoids as having four primary actions in relation to stressful experiences. Corticoids can be permissive, stimulating, preparative, or suppressive, although more than a single action of corticoids can be evident at the same time. When glucocorticoids allow for the effects of other stressor-provoked hormonal changes to occur or be amplified, then we refer to it as having permissive actions. Thus glucocorticoids may permit the effects of other hormones (e.g., epinephrine and norepinephrine) to be expressed, thereby affecting cardiovascular tone. Likewise, this combination may also be involved in the release of free fatty acids and hence energy availability, or in allowing certain types of immunological factors to affect cells in our body. In addition to the permissive actions, glucocorticoid release in response to stressors may stimulate (or suppress) the actions of other hormones. Importantly, it seems that the function of corticosterone under normative conditions (in the absence of a challenge) and that associated with a stressor might differ somewhat.

There are actions of glucocorticoids that are not only essential during a stress reaction, but also influence the response to impending stressors. That is, they may set the stage so that the organism is prepared to deal with a potential stressor being encountered (preparative changes). In a sense, this represents the plasticity or malleability of this system, as it implies that the basal state may be altered in anticipation of forthcoming events. We know that these types of changes can occur in animals that had previously encountered stressors (e.g., the sensitization we discussed earlier), including those experienced during early life, and it seems that when encountered repeatedly, certain stressor conditions may result in the corticoid response being diminished or having reduced actions (suppressive).

In animals, the corticosterone changes are exquisitely sensitive to stressors, and various characteristics regarding the glucocorticoid changes have been described in remarkable detail, including the moment-to-moment surges of corticosterone release that are elicited by stressors (Lightman et al., 2000). Although factors related to the appraisal of stressors are fundamental in determining the corticosterone response, the contribution of variables, such as stressor controllability, in governing this response, is a bit more complex. When an animal is first confronted by a novel stressor, there is uncertainty as to whether this stressor will be brief or prolonged, and controllable or uncontrollable. Adaptive biological systems can't sit around idly waiting for the brain to figure out all the contingencies of the situation, and often must react rapidly to deal with threats. Essentially, it would be advantageous to mount a strong defensive response to maintain well-being, and then, as information is acquired regarding the characteristics of the stressor (e.g., its controllability, chronicity), it might be appropriate for this neuroendocrine response to be adjusted accordingly. For example, if the stressor turns out to be controllable, then the extent of the cortisol release could be turned down.

MINERALOCORTICOIDS

In addition to glucocorticoids, another class of corticoid exists, referred to as mineralocorticoids, which have their own receptors (MR). The mineralocorticoids were historically linked to the retention of sodium in the body, and were not typically associated with stress responses, although we now know that they are influenced by stressful events and have implications for stress-related pathology. For instance, MRs are present within the hippocampus, where they temper (or balance) the effects of GR activation, and may also affect hippocampal neuronal activity. Likewise, early in a stress response, when the corticosterone levels are at their peak, MR activation occurs, resulting in a hippocampal neuronal excitation that could potentially be important for other stress responses (de Kloet et al., 2008; Groeneweg et al., 2011). Furthermore, illnesses that have been associated with stressors, such as metabolic syndrome (characterized by obesity and insulin resistance) and diabetes, are tied to the elevated production and release of aldosterone (a hormone that is part of the mineralocorticoid family) from the adrenal gland, and this contributes to sodium levels, water retention, and blood pressure. Added to this, MR stimulation may be associated with cardiac problems (heart failure and hypertension), and MR antagonists may have a clinically beneficial effect for metabolic syndrome.

CHRONIC STRESSORS

As we saw with respect to the behavioral effects of stressors, adaptation-like effects may occur in response to chronic stressors so that the corticosterone response is less pronounced.

Ordinarily, the adaptation occurs fairly readily if the stressor is the same on each occasion, whereas the adaptation occurs slowly, if at all, when the stressor occurs on an intermittent, unpredictable basis, and when the nature of the stressor varies over days (Anisman et al., 2008). Predictably, this sort of stressor regimen is also associated with greater pathology of various sorts. Interestingly, although the corticosterone response diminished with repeated exposure to a given stressor, if animals were then exposed to a novel stressor the increased corticosterone response was again evident, and in some instances was even exaggerated. It seems that the adaptation that occurs is specific to particular events or stimuli, and might not reflect the down-regulation of the biological processes associated with corticosterone release, but instead represents an adaptation that is somewhat unique to specific events or cues. What these findings tell us is that even if it appears as if the organism has 'adapted' to stressor experiences, this is not actually the case, and its vulnerability to exaggerated neuroendocrine changes, as well as behavioral disturbances, may be elevated.

TRACING THE PAST THROUGH YOUR HAIR

The release of cortisol following stressor exposure, typically determined in blood or saliva, persists for a matter of minutes, and in some cases hours. But can it be used to measure more distal stressor experiences, or to track stressful periods over weeks or months? It seems that cortisol accumulates in hair, and as hair grows at about 1 cm a month, by assessing cortisol in snippets of hair a diary of cortisol (and hence stressor experiences) can be determined (Russell et al., 2011). This is a relatively novel approach to the analysis of stressor effects, and its ultimate usefulness remains to be determined. However, it strikes me that it holds some promise for studies assessing the link between cortisol and a variety of stress-related pathologies. In fact, even after controlling for several other pertinent factors, elevated levels of hair cortisol were a good predictor of the risk of acute myocardial infarction (Pereg et al., 2011).

PRENATAL AND EARLY POSTNATAL EVENTS INFLUENCE THE CORTICOSTERONE RESPONSE

Stressful events experienced by a pregnant female rodent or human can have multiple effects on the offspring. In Chapter 11 we'll be discussing the intergenerational effects of stressors, including those that occur with respect to corticosterone, so we won't cover this topic here. However, consider that stressing a rat while she is pregnant results in elevated levels of corticosterone in both the mother and the fetus. This, in turn, results in further downstream effects, including structural changes within stress-sensitive brain regions. Given the fundamental involvement of these regions in cognitive and behavioral processes, a variety of behavioral disorders may be observed in the offspring, such as attention and learning deficits, as well as a disposition toward anxiety and depression, and some investigators have suggested that the risk for schizophrenia is elevated as well. Essentially, by promoting excessive prenatal levels of glucocorticoids, the programming of fetal neurons may be altered, thereby affecting later behavior throughout the life span. As will be seen, however, these effects, like others described up until this point, are subject to moderation by genetic factors and the postnatal environment, including the care that pups receive from their mom.

Stressors encountered early in life may also have profound long-term ramifications on well-being in responses to later stressor challenges. These early experiences can alter the developmental trajectory of stress relevant processes so that biological reactivity is altered in adulthood. It has also been reported that through epigenetic processes (recall that these involve the suppression of genes without actually modifying the genes' code) glucocorticoid receptor functioning may be modified so that the adult responses to stressors are altered (e.g., Szyf, 2011).

As with the early-life period, as described in Chapter 1, the juvenile (adolescent) period in rodents is also a highly stress-sensitive one. Stressors experienced during this period have protracted ramifications on vulnerability to stressor-provoked neurochemical and behavioral changes in adulthood (Tsoory et al., 2007). The adolescent phase in rodents is also exquisitely sensitive to stressors that involve social instability (e.g., changing cage mates on successive days) and may have effects that are more enduring than similar stressors experienced in adulthood (Morrissey et al., 2011).

STRESSOR-INDUCED GLUCOCORTICOID EFFECTS IN HUMANS

Based on studies in animals, one would think that stressor-provoked corticoid elevations would also be readily apparent in humans. In fact, this is not the case at all. In rodents, 200–300% increases of corticosterone are introduced simply by placing the animal in a novel environment, and 400–800% increases of corticosterone are ordinarily seen in response to relatively strong stressors. In humans, by contrast, the effects of stressors are far less marked. The anticipation of heart surgery, for instance, only caused a cortisol increase of about 30–50%, academic exams typically are not associated with cortisol elevations or the elevations are limited, and only half the graduate students assessed immediately prior to their thesis oral exams showed elevated cortisol levels, even though virtually all reported high levels of anxiety. The effects of other naturally occurring stressors have likewise been associated with limited cortisol changes (Michaud et al., 2008). Yet cortisol levels can be elevated in association with stressors that we often don't think about, including a threat to our social identity, such as sexism or racial discrimination (Matheson & Anisman, 2012), and under conditions where shame (or anger) is elicited (Dickerson & Kemeny, 2004).

CORTISOL RELEASE IS AS AN ADAPTIVE RESPONSE, NOT AN INDEX OF DISTRESS

Because stressors often cause an increase of cortisol, there are those who think of cortisol as an index for the stress experienced. This is simply incorrect. In fact, in some instances, such as among individuals experiencing chronic distress or in those with PTSD, cortisol levels are lower than in those who were not stressed (Yehuda, 2002). Furthermore, upon being presented with an attractive member of the opposite sex, males and females both exhibited elevated cortisol levels. If cortisol were an 'index of stress' then one might infer that there is some equivalence regarding social interaction with a potential date and that of impending heart surgery. It might be better to consider cortisol as an adaptive response to particular types of challenges, and not as an index of distress.

Some years ago, one of my female graduate students undertook a project to assess the influence of problem-solving situations on cortisol levels among undergraduate students. We had expected that certain situations would lead to elevated cortisol more readily than others (e.g., manipulating uncertainty and uncontrollability). Among females the results were in line with our expectations, with some stressor situations having greater effects than others. Among males, however, the cortisol levels were quite high even at baseline (before the manipulation was applied), and continued to rise over the session. It eventually dawned on us that the presence of an attractive nurse (who patted the arm of male students before inserting the catheter needle and occasionally commenting on their muscular arms) might have had something to do with the results obtained.

CORTISOL CHANGES ASSOCIATED WITH LABORATORY-BASED STRESSORS

Several basic approaches have been used to assess cortisol changes in relation to stressors within a laboratory context. The first entails an assessment of cortisol levels in response to a challenge that may or may not include reminders of previous stressor experiences (auditory or visual representations, or written scripts). These paradigms may be associated with cortisol variations, but contrary to what might be expected, the magnitude of these effects is typically modest (Matheson & Anisman, 2012). The most common stressor challenge paradigm used is one that involves public speaking in front of a small panel of judges followed by a verbal arithmetic test. This paradigm, known as the Trier Social Stress Test, or the TSST (Kirschbaum et al., 1993), promotes an increase of cortisol that is evident in blood or saliva within 10–15 minutes and returns to basal levels in less than one hour. The extent of the reported cortisol rise varies across laboratories, ranging from 40–100%, although increases of as much as 200–300% were also reported. Predictably, the extent of the cortisol rise varied with several factors known to influence stress responses, such as previous stressful experiences, whether women were using oral contraceptives, and as a function of the menstrual cycle (Foley & Kirschbaum, 2010).

It might seem curious that this relatively contrived laboratory stressor would promote greater cortisol elevations than the anticipation of real-life stressors, such as open heart surgery or the distress among students preceding their thesis oral exam (Michaud et al., 2008). So what does this mean? Is open heart surgery appraised as being less stressful than the TSST? This is hardly likely (even given how terrifying public speaking can be), but these findings suggest that there's more to the cortisol response than just the potential threat associated with the stressor. There are multiple differences between the TSST and a stressor such as impending surgery. First, participants in the TSST are typically unaware of what the test will be like before they get to the experimental setting and hence have no opportunity to prepare themselves. In contrast, surgery patients will usually have been forewarned about their procedures and some degree of 'adaptation' may have occurred. Importantly, as well, cortisol levels in the TSST are determined in blood (or saliva) taken *after* the stressor test, whereas in the case of heart surgery or the academic oral examination, blood samples were taken before (i.e., in anticipation of) the primary stressor. In addition, it seems that the cortisol response may be tied to particular emotional responses associated with a stressor. It was suggested that uncontrollable social-evaluative threats (e.g., when there is an audience appraising the person being stressed) may give rise to emotions such as shame, that are particularly effective in provoking cortisol elevations (Dickerson & Kemeny, 2004).

We likewise found that cortisol levels were elevated in other situations that elicited shame and/or anger (e.g., when women who had been abused were provided with reminders of the abuse). In our case, however, only anger accounted for the unique variance; shame was related to the anger, but once the influence of anger was accounted for, the contribution of the shame was negligible (Matheson & Anisman, 2012). This doesn't mean that shame was not involved, as it might have promoted the self-directed anger ('I'm so embarrassed I can't stand myself – I'd like to just kick myself around the block') that was ultimately responsible for the cortisol response.

PREVIOUS EXPERIENCES INFLUENCE THE CORTISOL CHANGES ELICITED BY LABORATORY CHALLENGES

As many serious stressors involve a chronic component as well as worry or rumination secondary to the stressor, it is necessary to consider whether acute and chronic stressors have different effects. Although the cortisol rise associated with acute stressors has multiple adaptive attributes, sustained cortisol release, as we discussed earlier, may have adverse consequences. Therefore, it might be a good thing that some of the neuroendocrine responses elicited by acute stressors are limited following chronic challenges.

The down-regulated HPA response associated with certain trauma experiences was also evident in response to certain pharmacological challenges. It turns out that these studies are exceptionally informative from a broad perspective concerning how stressors operate. Ordinarily, when a person is injected with CRH (the peptide that causes ACTH release from the pituitary), a rise of ACTH is evident in blood. However, the ACTH release in response to a CRH challenge was diminished among depressed women who had been abused when they were young, indicating that their HPA functioning was down-regulated. Of particular significance, when these women were placed in a situation that elicited a social evaluative threat (the Trier test), their HPA response was exaggerated (Heim et al., 2008). We likewise observed that among women who had experienced psychological and/or physical abuse in a dating relationship, cortisol levels were low if they exhibited PTSD symptoms. However, when these women were presented with reminders of their abuse, their cortisol levels increased markedly, particularly among those who exhibited the highest PTSD scores (Matheson & Anisman,

2012). In effect, it seems that despite the down-regulated ACTH and cortisol response, in the presence of a *meaningful* stressor, an exaggerated cortisol response occurs.

Intuitively, these data make sense. Following trauma, individuals might become hyper-reactive to environmental cues that were potentially stressful, but if HPA activation were engendered by every aversive stimulus encountered, then the system would become overly taxed (allostatic overload), and pathology would be more likely to occur. Thus, it would be advantageous for HPA down-regulation to occur to prevent excessive cortisol release. Yet it would be counterproductive for the HPA system to be down-regulated all of the time, as activation of this system might occasionally be necessary. Therefore, the cues that are particularly relevant or those that elicit strong emotional responses might effectively promote the activation of the brain regions (e.g., the prefrontal cortex or amygdala) involved in stressor-appraisal processes, which would then influence HPA functioning, essentially over-riding the down-regulation that would otherwise occur.

PROBING IN THE DARK

When I was a young researcher, and the data concerning neurochemical changes induced by stressors were sparse, a strategy I took to guide my work was to imagine how adaptive biological systems ought to act and how these would change across situations. Or to put this another way, if I were Nature or God, how would I develop a system so that it would be most effective in dealing with challenges? At the time, this seemed like a nifty idea ('nifty', appropriately, is a word from that era), although it was doomed from the beginning owing to a large number of reasons, least of all that we had limited knowledge about how the brain worked, as well as about how chemical messengers were produced, what receptors entailed, and so on. At every turn I discovered that nature was, in fact, much more creative, intuitive, and thoughtful in creating ways of protecting animals and humans relative to my best plans. The down-regulated HPA system at baseline and the hyper-reactivity in response to relevant stimuli are examples of just one dimension that I hadn't even considered. Einstein, in suggesting that things in nature don't just happen by accident, is famously quoted as saying that 'God doesn't play dice with the universe'. A corollary would be that 'only an idiot would try to play God'.

THE MORNING CORTISOL RESPONSE IN RELATION TO STRESSFUL EXPERIENCES

Another approach used to assess cortisol responses in relation to recently experienced or ongoing stressful events has focused on the changes in diurnal cortisol variations. Circulating cortisol levels typically rise over the first 30 minutes following our waking up (a 40% increase is typical in saliva) and will then begin to decline (Schmidt-Reinwald et al., 1999). By late afternoon the rate of this decline is more limited, and our cortisol levels will eventually reach their nadir around midnight, before climbing to the high levels seen on awakening. A primary research focus has been on the initial cortisol rise following awakening, as it seems that the cortisol rise is particularly great among individuals dealing with ongoing or recent stressors, such as job strain, or among those individuals who perceive their life circumstances as being hopeless (Schlotz et al., 2004). Likewise, after the cortisol has reached its peak, the subsequent decline occurs less readily in those with low social positions, and this outcome was related to poorer health and sleep, older age, smoking, and stressors experienced on the day of sampling.

Although stressful experiences were accompanied by exaggerated morning cortisol elevations, among individuals who had experienced a traumatic stressor that led to PTSD, as well as under conditions of excessive or prolonged strain (e.g., job-related burnout or fatigue, exhaustion related to distress), the diurnal cortisol profile might be flattened (i.e., the morning cortisol levels are reduced, and the evening cortisol levels elevated). As described earlier, excessive cortisol release over extended periods could have adverse effects, including hippocampal cell loss, and the down-regulated morning HPA response might be adaptive, limiting the negative outcomes that might otherwise occur.

CORTISOL AS A BIOMARKER

The cortisol response (or that of other hormones) observed in response to stressors brings up another issue. Specifically, if one wanted to assess the potential for illness based on hormone levels (i.e., develop markers to predict illness), it might be sufficient simply to measure the basal levels of a hormone and on this basis predict who might (or might not) develop a pathology. However, what hormone levels are like under basal conditions might be very different from those evident in response to a challenge. As a result, it would be propitious to measure the basal levels of a hormone, and then apply a challenge and determine (a) the extent to which the hormone level changed, and (b) how long it took for the hormone level to normalize (i.e., return to basal levels). Presumably, the hormonal release should drop off quickly once a threat is no longer present, and thus sustained activation might be indicative of a system that is not working optimally, and might thus be predictive of the potential for pathological outcomes to arise.

Let's examine this from another perspective and you'll see why I'm suggesting that the hormone should be measured after a challenge. If you want to have your heart checked, a doctor can simply examine your heart rate and blood pressure, which will provide some good information. Better information can be obtained when an electrocardiogram (EKG) is used in conjunction with an index of blood pressure, and even better information can be accessed when a load or challenge is placed on the system (termed a 'stress test') in which you're placed on a treadmill and measures are taken when your system is being strained. In this case, one might want to know how high your heart rate climbs, as well as how long it takes for it to settle down after you've stopped running, with faster normalization being preferable. Essentially, when we place a load (strain) on the system and examine how it's handled, then we get a better idea of how the organ (or specific biochemical) is doing and perhaps how it will function in the near future. This approach is used in testing cars and bridges, and it would be useful for neuroendocrine systems as well.

CORTICOTROPIN RELEASING HORMONE (CRH)

In addition to being a fundamental regulator of the HPA system, CRH has actions beyond those involving the hypothalamus. Indeed, CRH and its receptors are key players in the stress response at several other brain sites, including the prefrontal cortex and amygdala, regions that are associated with emotional responses (Herman & Cullinan, 1997).

STRESSOR EFFECTS ON CRH FUNCTIONING

Beyond the hypothalamic CRH release that accompanies an acute stressor, CRH mRNA expression (see the box concerning the meaning of mRNA expression) and *in vivo* CRH release (i.e., the release of the peptide measured in a freely moving animal) are also increased at the central amygdala (CeA) (Lee & Davis, 1997; Merali et al., 1998). It is interesting that unlike the suppression of the hypothalamic CRH release elicited by cortisol (i.e., the negative feedback loop that occurs after cortisol is released), in the central amygdala and bed nucleus of the stria terminalis, cortisol increases CRH expression, as well as $GABA_A$ neuronal functioning, that may act to provoke anxiety (Schulkin, 2006). It seems that the regulation of CRH at sites outside of the hypothalamus (extrahypothalamic) involves processes distinct from those that operate at the hypothalamus.

The extrahypothalamic activity of CRH may directly influence behavioral outputs, or it may do so by influencing still other neurochemical processes. Among other things, CRH may regulate a subpopulation of neurons within the raphe nucleus (this is a region in the hindbrain that is the site of cell bodies for neurons that send their trajectories to the hippocampus and frontal cortex), promoting the release of the neurotransmitter serotonin at terminal' regions (Hammack et al., 2003). Likewise, the infusion of CRH into the locus coeruleus (a site of norepinephrine cell bodies) increases forebrain norepinephrine neuronal activity, whereas CRH antagonists (drugs that block CRH receptors) attenuated these effects. These data obviously raise the possibility that CRH has notable effects beyond its involvement in HPA functioning, and that the effect of CRH on behavior might involve a series of biochemical changes. As we'll see, the prefrontal cortical regions and the hippocampus play an essential role in appraisals, decision making, and memory, and one might suspect that stressors might have some effects by altering CRH and other neurotransmitters at these sites.

WHAT DOES MRNA EXPRESSION MEAN?

You'll recall, I hope, that genes comprise lengthy stretches of DNA that contain a code for the eventual production of an individual's many phenotypes (e.g., hormones and neurotransmitters, as well as more visible characteristics such as eye and hair color). One of the two strands that

(Continued)

(Continued)

make up DNA serves as a template or blueprint for the production of RNA, which occurs through a process called transcription. In a series of steps a type of RNA (messenger RNA or mRNA) is formed that carries the code for the synthesis of one or more proteins. Thus when the mRNA that codes for a specific protein is expressed, it is likely that more of this protein is being made. In theory, the presence of more mRNA that code for a particular protein, the more of that protein is being synthesized, although this isn't always the case. It is often (usually) not sufficient to simply measure mRNA expression, and this needs to be backed up by a demonstration that the protein levels have actually changed. Phrases such as 'expression of CRH mRNA is increased' mean that an experimental treatment has the potential of increasing the synthesis of the protein (CRH in this instance).

There are some genes that are continually transcribed (constitutive genes), whereas others are transcribed as needed (facultative genes), and there are those that are transcribed in response to environmental change. The stressor-induced changes of CRH mRNA expression are an example of an environmental event triggering the transcription of a specific gene.

FEAR AND ANXIETY

Fear and anxiety are often thought of as being negative emotions, especially if these emotions are strong. However, in many instances in which fear and anxiety are moderate, they may have important positive functions, keeping us alert and apprehensive in the face of potential threats. Fear and anxiety are essential parts of the defensive or survival repertoire, and events or brain changes that impede these processes may have severe negative repercussions on an organism's ability to survive.

As you probably will know, the amygdala is a brain region that has been associated with emotions such as fear and anxiety. Given that stressors increase CRH mRNA expression (essentially reflecting increased production of this hormone) and CRH release at the central amygdala (CeA) of freely moving animals, this peptide is thought to play a major role in stress-provoked emotions. Although the terms 'fear' and 'anxiety' are frequently used interchangeably, they are actually distinct from one another. Fear is a directed emotion that is elicited in response to stimuli that have been paired with an aversive stimulus (i.e., when an individual fears some things or places). Essentially, fear is a classically conditioned response, and as such is not something that we can readily control. Anxiety, in contrast, is usually elicited by diffuse stimuli (e.g., a general environmental context, but anxiety can also be independent of prior experiences) or it can reflect a free-floating emotion, or one that is felt in anticipation of a threatening event.

It also seems that fear and anxiety involve the activation of CRH neurons within different aspects of the amygdala (Lee & Davis, 1997). Whereas fear-eliciting stimuli increase CRH expression within the various portions of the amygdala, diffuse stimuli that promote general anxiety are more closely aligned with CRH variations that occur within extended aspects of the amygdala, such as the bed nucleus of the stria terminalis (BNST), which is a major output pathway that runs from the amygdala to the hypothalamus (Davis, 1992). It also seems that the function of the central, medial, and basolateral aspects of the amygdala may not necessarily be the same (e.g., in regard to the acquisition, expression, or extinction of a fear response) (LeDoux, 2000). Moreover, although psychogenic and systemic stressors (the presence of inflammation) induce many similar effects, their actions on amygdala functioning are not identical as they seem to engage different aspects of this region. Whereas systemic stressors markedly influence central amygdala activity, psychogenic stressors have more potent effects on the medial amygdala.

Finally, the mechanisms involved in fear/anxiety reactions might depend on the presence of particular environmental triggers. Specifically, numerous psychogenic (e.g., learned fear cues) and neurogenic (physical) stressors provoke CRH release from amygdala neurons and, conversely, the anxiety associated with these treatments can be attenuated by agents that antagonize CRH. However, unlike these stressors, anxiety elicited by a naturalistic stressor (e.g., exposure to an unfamiliar environment), which might involve pre-wired neural circuits, was not altered by CRH antagonists. It was thus suggested that anxiety associated with a naturalistic stressor might involve processes other than, or in addition to, CRH (Merali, Khan et al., 2004). Evidently, although it might be correct to believe that the amygdala contributes to stressor-elicited emotions, not all aspects of the amygdala act in the same way in response to varied challenges, and may have different implications for the behavioral and emotional responses that emerge. These findings, and others like them, also raise the possibility that treatment strategies ought to consider the nature of the stressor encountered (i.e., is it a learned stress response or one that engages prewired systems?).

CRH RECEPTORS

Although a correspondence might be expected between the amount of hormone or neuro-transmitter present and particular emotional or behavioral outcomes, the functional effectiveness of hormones and neurotransmitters is dependent upon whether they successfully trigger particular receptors that instigate further downstream biological effects. In this regard, several receptors have been identified for many of the neurochemicals that are pertinent to behavioral changes, and their activation may have consequences that might be very different from one another. Moreover, treatments that promote neurochemical changes may dose-dependently activate certain receptor subtypes preferentially. Clearly, analyzing the effects of various treatments on behavioral outcomes is not simply a matter of measuring the levels, synthesis, or release of a neurochemical, but also necessitates an examination of receptor changes and their downstream effects. If this weren't difficult enough, the behavior of the receptors themselves may be influenced by the presence of still other receptor types (i.e., receptor–receptor interactions may occur) or other neurotransmitters (Magalhaes et al., 2010).

The primary CRH receptors that have been investigated are the CRH_1 and CRH_2 receptors. Consistent with the view that CRH activation was directly linked to elevated anxiety, administration of a CRH receptor antagonist attenuated the depression-like behavior provoked by an uncontrollable stressor (Mansbach et al., 1997). Moreover, in mice that had been genetically engineered so that the expression of CRH receptors was altered (elevated or reduced), predictable changes of anxiety and depressive-like behaviors were apparent (Keck & Muller, 2005). Mice that overproduced CRH had higher levels of anxiety, whereas reduced anxiety was seen in mice with the CRH_1 receptors deleted. Likewise, diminished anxiety was elicited when the CRH_1 receptor was antagonized pharmacologically (Muller et al., 2003). Such findings suggested that CRH_1 receptor expression in limbic forebrain regions may be especially pertinent to the development of anxiety states.

The information regarding the involvement of CRH_2 receptors in anxiety is less extensive than that associated with CRH_1 receptors. It initially appeared that the contribution of CRH_2 to the promotion of anxiety was limited, but it has since been shown that when CRH_2 receptors were knocked out, elevated anxiety was apparent, particularly among males. Interestingly, studies in double mutants (where both the CRH_1 and CRH_2 were knocked out) indicated that both CRH_1 and CRH_2 receptors may influence anxiety, and it also seemed that early experiences, especially those related to maternal care, moderated the actions of these receptors on anxiety. However, as seen with numerous other hormone responses, the effects observed in males and females were different from one another, suggesting that anxiety was mediated by more than just specific CRH receptor subtypes (Bale & Vale, 2003).

The involvement or interactions between CRH_1 and CRH_2 in relation to anxiety has yet to be fully deduced. One view has it that the two CRH receptor subtypes selectively mediate different aspects of the behavioral stress response. In particular, CRH_1 receptors might contribute primarily to emotional responses, whereas CRH_2 receptors principally subserve the regulation of coping responses (Liebsch et al., 1999). It was similarly suggested that CRH_1 may be fundamental in regulating explicit processes, including attention, executive functions, the conscious experience of emotions, and even learning about these emotions, whereas CRH_2 might contribute mainly to the implicit processes necessary for survival, largely involving motivated behaviors such as feeding, reproduction, and defense. Based on this supposition it might be considered that patients presenting with anxiety and depression might benefit most from drug treatments that antagonize CRH_1 receptors, whereas patients with eating disorders would be best served by drugs targeted at CRH_2. This said, there has been fairly compelling evidence implicating CRH_2 in anxiety-related processes. For instance, anxiety brought about by a stressor could be attenuated by CRH_2 antagonist administration directly to the dorsal raphe nucleus, the site of serotonin cell bodies, potentially suggesting that anxiety is mediated by tandem CRH_2 and serotonin processes (Hammack et al., 2003). There is little question that CRH contributes to the negative emotional responses associated with stressors, and once the involvement of receptor subtypes in mediating these emotions is clarified, improved treatment strategies for anxiety-related disorders might be in the offing.

STRESS, ENERGY BALANCES, AND EATING TO COPE

There are a great number of hormonal and environmental factors that influence eating-related behaviors. Our circadian cycle plays a prominent role in this regard; we tend to eat at prescribed times, and various hormonal changes might be important signaling factors. Added to this, specific environmental stimuli, such as the smell of fresh baked bread or a smoked meat sandwich, will rouse our appetite, and some good-looking, carbohydrate rich foods are tempting even when we've just finished a large meal. The presence of danger will have the opposite effect on our inclination to eat. Whether its elk, deer, rodents, or even grasshoppers, when a predator is in the vicinity, the search for food diminishes and animals tend to eat less. For that matter, for nocturnal eaters, such as rodents, the amount of food consumed is lower on clear moon-lit nights than on dark nights, possibly reflecting the danger of exposing themselves to predators. Apparently, hard-wired biological processes might exist across species in order that the danger cues that elicit vigilance and anxiety/fear will diminish the search for food, with the result that it's less likely that these animals will become some other critter's supper.

There's good reason to suppose that appetitive and aversive systems act in opposition to one another so that when an individual is stressed, the resulting CRH release that encourages defensive behaviors might also inhibit eating or other processes related to reward processes, but this depends on the nature or severity of the stressor. In the next chapter we'll be covering a series of neurotransmitters, such as dopamine (DA), which are integral to feelings of reward and pleasure. It seems that in response to an acute, moderate stressor the release of CRH and the excitation of CRH_1 and CRH_2 receptors promote the release of DA at the nucleus accumbens, possibly making

TABLE 3.4 Hormones related to energy regulation and eating

Secreted hormone	Biological effect
Corticotropin releasing hormone (CRH)	Formed in the paraventricular nucleus of the hypothalamus. In addition to being fundamental to stress responses, it diminishes food intake and increases metabolic rate.
Cortisol (Cort)	Released from the adrenal gland it is the prototypical stress hormone; also stimulates caloric intake, and may promote a preference for high calorie foods under stressful circumstances (stimulates the consumption of comfort foods).
Leptin	Produced by fat cells: reduces food intake, and is involved in changes in brain cytokines.
Ghrelin	Produced in gut: serves to stimulate increased eating; may affect reward processes; modulates stress responses.
Insulin	Produced in the pancreas: regulates fat and carbohydrate metabolism; involved in getting glucose from the blood into various body cells and storing it as glycogen.
Bombesin (in humans neuromedin B [NMB] and gastrin relasing peptide [GRP])	Produced in gut and in several brain regions: acts as a satiety peptide (signals when an individual is full) and promotes anxiety
Neuropeptide Y (NPY)	Hypothalamic hormone: increases food intake and reduces physical activity; increases energy stored in the form of fat; blocks nociceptive (noxious) signals to the brain; increases vasoconstrictor actions of norepinephrine.

rewards more salient, and could thus lead to increased consumption of tasty foods. However, if the stressor was relatively intense the effect on DA was abolished, and this effect could persist for months. This switch in the CRH–DA relationship was accompanied by a shift in reaction to CRH from one that was associated with appetitive responses to one that was in line with more common emotional responses to aversive stimuli (Lemos et al., 2012).

Given the intersection between eating and stress processes, the section that follows describes some of the hormones implicated in energy regulation and stress responses (see Table 3.4). Moreover, in Chapter 10, we will be discussing the possibility that eating can act as a coping mechanism among some individuals, and it also appears that in many ways eating shares some of the characteristics of the addiction associated with drugs of abuse, such as alcohol, heroin, and cocaine.

I EAT WHEN I'M STRESSED

We've likely all heard someone say 'I eat when I'm stressed', sometimes mumbled through a mouthful of cake, a slobber of ice cream, or both. There's selectivity, however, as to what's eaten when a person is stressed. You'll just never hear anyone say 'I'm really stressed out. I think I'll have a nice celery stick'. What we're looking for in response to moderate distress are comfort foods. It could be that these make us feel better, and in this sense such foods act as a way of coping. Alternatively, there may be chemical changes in the brain and body that are activated by stressors that drive us to crave comfort foods. It is equally possible that the fast caloric fix provided by sugars and carbohydrates, and the ensuing biological changes instigated by these comfort foods, are responsible for providing sufficient energy to keep animals one step ahead of predators and may facilitate coping with psychological stressors. It seems that eating comfort foods essentially reflects the brain's attempt to reduce the activity of a chronic stress-response network that would otherwise promote anxiety.

Dallman (2010) has suggested that with continued distress, the persistently high concentrations of glucocorticoids contribute to the eating changes that are observed. Specifically, the glucocorticoid elevations cause an increase of CRH activity within the central amygdala, promoting strong emotional responses and setting other stress systems in play. Glucocorticoids are also important in stimulating caloric intake, and in the presence of insulin may contribute to the preference for high calorie foods, especially under stressful circumstances. Essentially, the increase of glucocorticoids causes the salience of pleasurable or compulsive activities (ingesting sucrose, fat, drugs) to be increased, so that comfort foods promote greater pleasure than they would otherwise. That sounds pretty good so far, but as you know, there's not a whole lot that tastes good that's good for you. Glucocorticoids are also involved in the redistribution of stored energy (fat) so that it appears as abdominal fat depots. In fact, given the link between stress, cortisol, eating, and metabolic processes, Dallman also suggested that these factors might contribute to the current obesity epidemic. Moreover, given the link between stress and heart disease, abdominal fat may be predictive of chronic heart disease.

LEPTIN, INSULIN, BOMBESIN, NEUROPEPTIDE Y, AND GHRELIN INVOLVEMENT IN EATING

The discovery of the hormone leptin has been considered among the most significant research findings in the field of energy balance. Produced primarily by adipocytes (fat cells), this hormone enters circulation, and then, by affecting the brain and peripheral organs, has the effect of reducing food intake, increasing energy expenditure, and reducing adiposity (fat) (Zhang et al., 1994). In addition, leptin influences HPA axis activity, and might also influence the effects of stressors on processes related to mood states; it also influences the release of neurotransmitters such as serotonin (5-HT) and DA (Fulton et al., 2006). As will be discussed in Chapter 4, 5-HT and DA are likely associated with reward processes, and therefore it is conceivable that by virtue of its effects on these transmitters, leptin might influence reward-seeking behaviors and affective tone related to feeding. In addition to leptin, mammalian analogues of the amphibian hormone bombesin (BB), namely neuromedin B (NMB) and gastrin-releasing peptide (GRP), contribute to the regulation of eating, essentially serving as a satiety signal just as leptin acts in this capacity.

There are also hormones that are involved in getting us to begin eating. In this regard, when elevated, both ghrelin and neuropeptide Y (NPY) are associated with increased food consumption (Abizaid & Horvath, 2008). Generally, the levels of ghrelin increase just before mealtime, presumably signaling us to eat (or acting as a preparatory response for the food we're about to eat), and then decline after we've eaten. The dysfunction of the ghrelin-related process can have adverse effects related to energy and feeding processes. For instance, ghrelin levels are altered among women with clinical levels of eating disorders, being elevated in anorexia and bulimia nervosa, whereas binge eating is associated with decreased ghrelin (Geliebter et al., 2005). This doesn't necessarily mean that these hormones cause eating disorders, although they might contribute in this regard.

As with other eating-related peptides, ghrelin activates dopamine neurons that are involved in reward processes, and could thus be an intermediary step for the rewarding feelings derived from food (Abizaid, 2009). In fact, eating was increased when ghrelin was injected directly into the ventral tegmental region of the brain, which is known to be involved in reward processes, whereas ghrelin antagonists had the opposite effect. Ghrelin also directly stimulates orexin cells in the lateral hypothalamus (orexin is a hormone that has been associated with food craving), as well as cells in several other hypothalamic nuclei. Furthermore, in humans, ghrelin administration increases food-related imagery and stimulates reward pathways, thereby implicating ghrelin in appetitive responses to incentive cues (i.e., the secondary stimuli that have been associated with reward) as well as the visual and olfactory cues that promote food cravings (Schmid et al., 2005).

There are few readers who don't know at least a little bit about insulin (e.g., it has something to do with diabetes). This hormone, like others we've discussed, is involved in the regulation of energy balances. Ordinarily, insulin's main job is one of regulating fat and carbohydrate metabolism, and it is instrumental in getting various cells in the body to take up glucose from the blood, and to then store it as glycogen inside these tissues. In addition to these vital peripheral actions, insulin also inhibits NPY release from the arcuate nucleus of the hypothalamus, which has the effect of reducing food intake. Insulin also interacts with glucocorticoids, as well as leptin and other regulatory hormones that have been implicated in the development of obesity and metabolic disturbances associated with chronic stressors (Landsberg, 2001).

THERE'S NO GOOD NEWS FOR THOSE WITH METABOLIC SYNDROME

There have been quite a few definitions of metabolic syndrome that differ modestly from one another. It has been defined by the World Health Organization (WHO) as the presence of diabetes, disturbed glucose tolerance, fasting glucose, or insulin resistance. One of these features must also be accompanied by two of the following: elevated blood pressure, high triglycerides, diminished level high-density lipoprotein cholesterol (HDL), obesity, and an elevated urinary albumin excretion ratio.

Metabolic syndrome, which is promoted by poor lifestyle habits (excessive eating and limited exercise) and stressful events, is accompanied by elevated visceral fat. The fat cells (adipocytes) release chemicals, such as those related to inflammatory processes (see Chapters 5 and 6) that can have numerous adverse consequences. It is known, for instance, that they can encourage heart disease and depression. Metabolic syndrome is also associated with the promotion of Type 2 diabetes and rheumatic diseases. If all this weren't bad enough, it has now been found that Type 2 diabetes is accompanied by a doubling in the occurrence of Alzheimer's disease. Although this could just be a correlation and the two aren't causally related, it seems that insulin signaling might be relevant to the tau tangles and amyloid β plaques that are characteristic of Alzheimer's disease.

LEPTIN, INSULIN, BOMBESIN, NEUROPEPTIDE Y, AND GHRELIN INVOLVEMENT IN STRESS PROCESSES

Stressful events, as already indicated, influence each of the peptides involved in feeding and energy regulation. In this regard, leptin and ghrelin might also be related to stress responses and might contribute to stress-related pathology, such as depression, or certain eating-related symptoms associated with depressive illness. The data from animal studies have been fairly impressive in this regard. Among other things, it was shown that the depressive-like behavioral disturbances provoked by a chronic stressor regimen could be antagonized by leptin administration. In contrast to these animal-based studies, however, leptin variations in relation to depression in humans have not been entirely consistent, and the factors that determine leptin levels in relation to mood disorders have yet to be determined. Nonetheless, as leptin and ghrelin are tied to eating processes, it is possible that the neurovegetative features of depression, particularly the altered eating common in depression, might be linked to these hormones as well as inflammatory processes (Abizaid et al., 2013).

Paralleling the effects of leptin, it seems that bombesin-like peptides (neuromedin B and GRP) that act to trigger satiety are able to promote anxiety, whereas receptor antagonists had the opposite effect (Kent et al., 2001; Moody & Merali, 2004). In general, GRP and NMB have not been examined as extensively as other stress and feeding hormones, but the changes associated with these peptides and the conditions in which they are altered suggest that they are part of complex circuits that link appetitive and stress processes to one another (Moody & Merali, 2004). It also seems that bombesin influences the neurotransmitter serotonin in brain regions associated with emotional responses, and these peptides have been implicated as potential processes related to anxiety.

Stressors were shown to elicit the release of bombesin-like peptides from the central amygdala (Merali et al., 1998), and caused HPA activation (Kent et al., 2001; Merali et al., 2004), whereas the elevated release of ACTH elicited by bombesin was attenuated by pretreatment with a CRH antagonist (Kent et al., 2001). As well, stressor exposure may increase 5-HT activity, but this outcome was absent in mice genetically engineered so that the BB_1 receptor was absent (Yamano et al., 2002), supporting the view that this receptor may be critical for this particular stress response.

As in the case of leptin, there is good reason to believe that insulin plays an essential role in response to acute stressors, acting to promote the mobilization of energy stores and uptake of glucose into cells that are vital in dealing with environmental challenges. However, with chronic exposure to stressors, insulin insensitivity may develop, possibly through glucocorticoid actions (Black, 2006). This essentially means that following sufficiently protracted stressor experiences, pancreatic cells will no longer release insulin as readily, leading to Type II diabetes. Interestingly, glucocorticoids ordinarily contribute to stress-induced obesity, and stressors have been associated with the increased consumption of foods with a high caloric content, i.e., comfort foods (Dallman, 2010). However, with insulin depletion (and presumably with insulin insensitivity), some of the obesity-inducing actions of glucocorticoids were prevented. It seems likely that in the absence of insulin, the positive, soothing aspects of comfort foods might be precluded, thereby altering their use as a coping response.

When insulin changes are considered in the context of stress responses, the focus is typically placed on its secretion from the pancreas, which can account for the eating and obesity changes that occur. However, there's more to insulin's actions than just that. Dopamine neurons in the ventral tegmental area (this is one of the regions associated with reward processes) express insulin receptors, making it possible that insulin influences these dopamine cells and could thus affect the hedonic or pleasurable component of eating (Könner et al., 2011). Moreover, problematic over-eating might represent an altered balance (or a disconnect) between hypothalamic regulatory functioning and midbrain reward circuits that involve dopamine activity. Indeed, for problematic eating to persist, those hormones that provide satiety signals, such as leptin and insulin, might have lost their ability to regulate the circuits that engender pleasure (Egecioglu et al., 2011).

MULTIPLE PROCESSES REGULATE EATING AND ENERGY BALANCES

So why do we have so many systems that are involved in feeding initiation and feeding cessation? Wouldn't one of each have been enough? The fact is that each of the peptides has multiple functions, and their actions go beyond that of feeding processes or those associated with stressors.

(Continued)

(Continued)

Furthermore, simply because two peptides might be involved in initiating eating doesn't mean that their actions are identical. Feeding is more complex than simply knowing that you're hungry, putting stuff in your mouth, chewing for a while, and then swallowing. There are anticipatory responses that get the juices going so that eating will be facilitated, certain eating responses are tied to environmental cues that tell us it's time to eat (there are circadian clocks that work in this capacity), and there are processes that coordinate eating responses with those involved in decision making, stress responses, and so forth. Of course, the actions of these various processes aren't perfect as many eating-related disturbances can occur, including anorexia, bulimia, emotional eating, binge eating, Prader Willy syndrome (a rare genetic disorder in which children exhibit an insatiable appetite), and the recent epidemic of other obesity-related conditions, such as metabolic disorder and diabetes.

PROLACTIN

Prolactin is a particularly interesting hormone that is released from the anterior pituitary following stimulation by thyrotropin-releasing hormone, and its release is inhibited by the secretion of dopamine from the arcuate nucleus of the hypothalamus. It was initially thought that the prime function of prolactin was that of promoting lactation (secretion of milk from the mammary glands), but it is now known that it also contributes to several other essential biological processes, including sexual behavior and sexual pleasure, eating-related processes, pain perception, and responses to emotional stressors. Indeed, prolactin receptors and mRNA expression for these receptors have been detected in several stress-sensitive brain regions, such as the central amygdala, the bed nucleus of the stria terminalis, and the nucleus accumbens, so that this peptide can activate neurons in these brain regions. Moreover, the stressors that ordinarily affect neuronal activity within these regions appear to affect prolactin functioning and might contribute to HPA activation (Lin, 2008).

The finding that lactation and stressors are associated with prolactin processes, and that prolactin influences other stress-endocrine functioning, has resulted in an interesting perspective regarding the stress responses that occur during pregnancy and subsequently during lactation. Although HPA activity is very responsive to stressors in rodents, it is blunted during the last trimester of pregnancy and during the lactation period. Presumably, this suppression is essential so that excessive corticosterone does not reach the fetus or pups (postnatally through the mother's milk). Any of several factors could be responsible for this outcome, including alterations in the function of hormones such as oxytocin, prolactin, and opioids, and the diminished ability of norepinephrine to elicit the hypothalamic responses that promote CRH and arginine vasopressin release (Tu et al., 2005). Whatever the process, it seems that during this period moms are protected from biological changes ordinarily associated with anxiety (although postpartum depression is an obvious deviation from these findings). Interestingly, however, a critical feature for this was that the mom and her pups had to have been in contact with one another within the preceding few hours. In the absence of this contact, the effects of stressors on HPA functioning in the moms were not attenuated (Walker, 2010).

There is likely an important evolutionary need for stress hormone responses to be inhibited during the lactation period. However, there seems to be a degree of selectivity regarding the effects of different stressors or where these challenges are directed. Specifically, unlike the effects of stressors directed at the mom, the corticosterone release is marked when the threat is aimed at the pups. In effect, while caring for their young, animals distinguish between or 'filter' relevant from irrelevant stimuli, as well as different types of relevant stressors. However, when the threat is directed at offspring, the HPA response in the mother is particularly activated, presumably to offer the resources needed to maintain the well-being of the young (Walker et al., 2004).

ESTROGEN AND TESTOSTERONE

The greater prevalence of depression and anxiety disorders in women than in men might simply mean that women are 'more sensitive' to life experiences, and generally more emotional, possibly owing to factors related to socialization processes. Alternatively, it

TABLE 3.5 Sex hormones and their effects

Secreted hormone	Biological effect
Testosterone	Male steroid hormone produced in the testis in males and ovaries in females. Involved in the development and sexual differentiation of brain and reproductive organs, and is fundamental in secondary sexual features developing, including body hair, muscle, and bone mass.
Dehydroepiandrosterone (DHEA)	In males, produced in adrenals, gonads, and brain, and is involved in the production of androgens and estrogens. Has been implicated in maintaining youth.
Estrogens (estrone, estradiol, estriol)	Estradiol is predominant of the three estrogens produced in the ovaries; involved in female reproductive processes, sexual development; affects bone density, liver, arterial blood flow, and has multiple functions in brain; involved in protein synthesis, fluid balances, gastrointestinal functioning and coagulation, cholesterol levels and fat depositions.
Progesterone	Formed in the ovary; precursor for several hormones; involved in triggering menstruation, and for maintaining pregnancy (e.g., inhibits immune response directed at embryo; reduces uterine smooth muscle contraction; inhibits lactation and the onset of labor); influences the resilience of various tissues (bones, joints, tendons, ligaments, skin).

(Continued)

TABLE 3.5 (Continued)

Secreted hormone	Biological effect
Luteinizing hormone (LH)	Produced in the anterior pituitary gland. In females, an 'LH surge' triggers ovulation and development of the corpus luteum, an endocrine structure that develops from an ovarian follicle during the luteal phase of the estrous cycle. In males, LH stimulates leydig cells to produce testosterone.
Follicle stimulating hormone (FSH)	Secreted by gonadotrophs of the anterior pituitary gland; regulates development, growth, pubertal maturation, and reproductive processes. With LH it acts synergistically in reproduction and ovulation.

might be that relative to men, women actually encounter more and greater stressors or life restrictions that favor the development of illness. They also tend to use emotion-focused coping to a greater degree (although not necessarily at the expense of problem-focused efforts), and some hormonal and neurochemical responses to stressors may be greater in women than in men. In the latter regard, particular attention has been devoted to the analysis of the impact of ovarian hormones in depression and anxiety (see Table 3.5). Studies in animals have shown that estradiol (the primary sex hormone present in women) can have a range of different effects, including the modulation of several neurotransmitters within limbic brain regions, and may influence HPA activity. Further, over the course of the estrus cycle, several hormonal changes occur that can influence neuronal growth factors in the brain (e.g., brain derived neurotrophic factor) that have been implicated in depressive illness.

STRESS RESPONSES IN MALES AND FEMALES

In rodents, females generally exhibit more pronounced stressor-elicited corticosterone elevations than do males, but it seems that in humans these effects are comparable in the two sexes, and in some studies males displayed greater hormonal changes. However, the effects observed in females may depend on the menstrual cycle, and may be diminished in women using oral contraceptives. When estrogen levels are high (or following the administration of estradiol, the primary type of estrogen), stress responsiveness is reduced. It was also reported, based on fMRI analyses, that in women, stress-arousing stimuli provoked especially marked neuronal activity in stress-relevant brain regions (amygdala, orbitofrontal cortex). These effects, however, were more pronounced during the early follicular phase (prior to ovulation during which the follicles in the ovary mature and during which estrogen levels climb) compared with mid-cycle. Based on such studies, it seems that estradiol acts as a brake on HPA axis functioning, whereas progesterone (a steroid hormone involved in the menstrual cycle, pregnancy, and embryogenesis, which peaks during the latter half of the cycle) may result in disturbed negative glucocorticoid feedback. In effect, sex hormones in women might influence the biological processes that govern stress responses and may therefore affect mood states.

TESTOSTERONE'S BAD RAP

Testosterone is important for male development and several behaviors, but it's been receiving a bad rap. I've heard of a macho guy being referred to derisively as 'Mr Testosterone', and the link to aggression is usually used as a put-down. But of all of the nasty things said about testosterone (even more than the notion that it encourages aggression and violence), what cuts to the quick most are reports that testosterone disrupts collaborative behaviors and causes males to be egocentric (Wright et al., 2012). Specifically, it was reported that treatments that increased testosterone also promoted behaviors that reduced the benefits that would be accrued by operating collaboratively with others. This seemed to be a result of individuals giving greater weight to their own judgments relative to those of others (egocentric choices) during joint decision making.

As you read this, you likely saw the term 'egocentric' as a pejorative. In fact, I'm afraid of commenting on this as it might cause some folk to turn on me, but this is how our biology works, possibly because there might be some benefit to it. It has been suggested that there are times when collaborative behaviors need to be balanced against those that are self-oriented, depending on the social environment. In a sense, this egocentrism may have high survival value, not only for the individual, but also for the group as a whole. As a result, testosterone-driven guys might be getting a bad rap, despite the fact that what they do might actually have positive attributes. And one more thing: testosterone administration is also associated with reduced lying in men (Wibral et al., 2012). I don't know what the implications of this are, but when I described this to a female colleague recently, she suggested that excessive testosterone levels get to the brain and make males too dumb to lie effectively.

The primary sex hormone in males is testosterone, which is formed in the testes, and to a limited extent is also produced in the adrenal glands. As with HPA hormones, testosterone is influenced by hypothalamic and pituitary processes through a negative feedback mechanism. Testosterone is known to play a pivotal role in the production of male reproductive tissues, and is also involved in the development of secondary features, such as the growth of body hair, as well as muscle growth and bone density, and it is for the latter reasons that it has been abused by athletes. In addition, this hormone has been deemed important in dominance challenges and aggressive behaviors, as well as cognitive processes. The effects of stressors on testosterone have been inconsistent, but it does seem that testosterone levels are also particularly elevated in those animals that had won in competitions or were higher in a dominance hierarchy.

ANABOLIC ANDROGENIC STEROIDS (AAS) AREN'T A GREAT BET, BUT WHAT ABOUT THAT STUFF TO PREVENT HAIR LOSS?

Anabolic (tissue building) androgenic steroids (more commonly referred to as anabolic steroids) have become relatively popular in some circles, especially among some professional athletes and

(Continued)

(Continued)

wannabees. These agents have medical uses in low doses, but at higher doses have masculanizing effects, building greater muscles and hence improved strength and athletic performance. Of course, they don't only affect muscles in the arms and legs, they also affect the heart muscles and may adversely affect other organs, such as the liver. They may also promote immune system problems, coronary artery disease, and disturbed cholesterol levels, and they don't do any favors for users' complexions.

It's not often talked about, but they also affect the brain, as do virtually all hormones. Among other things, these hormones interact with neurotransmitters and can have emotional effects (particularly anxiety) and could potentially affect cognitive functioning. Increasingly, the use of anabolic steroids has filtered down to adolescents, where these agents can have permanent, or at least very long-lasting, effects on brain neurons and on behaviors including elevated levels of aggressiveness.

There's been lots of talk about the adverse consequences of anabolic steroids. However, given the balance between health risks on the one side and potential stardom on the other, it's not altogether surprising which way individuals will move, especially among young people who by nature are risk takers.

It's not just anabolic steroids that have adverse effects on mood and behavior, but these do seem to have received the most attention. What's less known is that certain drugs that affect hormones, like those that are used to minimize hair loss, can also have a curse associated with them. Propecia and Proscar (that contain finasteride) are the commonly used treatments for this condition. Finasteride can have several negative side effects, such as impotence, abnormal ejaculation, abnormal sexual function, gynecomastia (developing breasts), erectile dysfunction, and testicular pain, and may also be associated with high-grade prostate cancer.

Ordinarily, finasteride inhibits the enzyme 5-alpha-reductase, that is involved in the conversion of testosterone into the potent androgen DHT, and thus finasteride may result in testosterone levels being elevated. It also contributes to the conversion of progesterone to dihydroprogesterone (DHP) and then to allopregnenolone. The allopregnanolone modulates the receptors for the neurotransmitter $GABA_A$, and might therefore cause the anxiety and depression that have been increasingly reported among finasteride users. Moreover, when the treatment is discontinued, libido increases remarkably in some patients, and they might be especially vulnerable to depression, including suicidal thoughts. So it might be an ego-boost not to lose much hair, but in some individuals this comes with a greater cost than the one bargained for.

STRESS AND REPRODUCTION

As many of us will know, when a person is distressed their sexual desires may be altered. When stressed, females are less inclined to engage in the behaviors that lead to sex (proceptive behaviors), and less inclined to respond to male overtures (receptivity), and male sexual behavior is often altered as well (although it might take a bit more distress for males to lose interest) (Carter, 1992). Essentially, the person may suffer a bit of anhedonia ('I just don't feel like it'), and they may be anxious and distracted.

Wingfield and Sapolsky (2003) in reviewing this topic indicated that, in general, ongoing stressors have a suppressive effect on reproductive behaviors and on reproduction itself. In females this comes about because these stressors disrupt ovulation (and gonadal hormone production in males), disturb the uterine changes that are necessary for implantation (in males, erectile functioning is impaired), and proceptive and receptive behaviors are inhibited. As described earlier, multiple hormonal cascades occur in response to stressors. Included in these is the secretion of β-endorphin (an opioid peptide that is produced in the pituitary and hypothalamus, and is involved in analgesia), which has the effect of inhibiting the release of gonadotropin-releasing hormone (GnRH) coupled with a diminished sensitivity of pituitary gonadotropes (the cells in the anterior pituitary that produce luteinizing hormone, a hormone that is involved in provoking ovulation) (Carter, 1992). Added to this, the corticoids that are released in response to stressors will influence the ovaries so that responsiveness to luteinizing hormone is reduced. The net result of this complex set of hormonal changes is that the reproductive cycle lengthens and becomes irregular. Not surprisingly, the decline in receptivity among female rodents can be reversed by treatment with the female hormone progesterone.

It is not just stressors in mature adults that influence sexual behavior. It seems that stressors at various earlier times of life may influence later adult sexual behavior. For instance, among juvenile mice, even a stressor such as being shipped from the breeder to the laboratory, or being exposed to mild infection, reduces receptivity among females, and reduces behavioral responsiveness to estradiol and progesterone in adulthood, possibly owing to an enduring reduction of estrogen receptors in several brain regions (Ismail et al., 2011). As well, in rodents, stressful events encountered during the prenatal period came to affect the behavior of male pups when they were subsequently assessed as adults, and these outcomes could be attenuated by neonatal administration of testosterone (Pereira et al., 2006). In addition, prenatal stressors, including infection in the pregnant dam, resulted in later maternal behaviors being disturbed, and as adults the male pups exhibited disrupted sexual behavior. Clearly, stressful events can have enduring behavioral repercussions, some of which might be related to estrogen and testosterone variations.

OXYTOCIN

A PROSOCIAL HORMONE

Oxytocin is a particularly interesting hormone that is associated with a variety of prosocial behaviors, such as attachment, maternal behaviors and bonding, social perception, love, generosity, altruism, empathy, sacrifice, the motivation to be with others (social motivation), and even the ability to infer the emotions of others based on their facial cues. Moreover, oxytocin is one of several factors (together with vasopressin, dopamine, and serotonin) that contributes to various facets of love, such as trust, pleasure, and reward, and when the oxytocin receptors are altered (through a gene variant), individuals will see the world as more threatening and have a tendency to be less generous (Campbell, 2010).

The importance of oxytocin cannot be overstated, particularly as so much of our lives is dictated by social interactions and our social identity. By example, consider the development of trust, one of the features affected by oxytocin (Kosfeld et al., 2005). Trust, as we've already seen, is an essential element in intergroup, intragroup, and interindividual relationships, and a necessary ingredient in politics and in commerce – even in some of our most basic social interactions. Trust is also a fundamental element needed for coping with certain types of stressors, including those associated with conflict resolution, especially as oxytocin may help us reach out to others in an effort to gain their support. As we saw in Chapter 2, in order to end a social conflict we might accept an apology from another person by offering genuine forgiveness. This might come about if we *trust* that the other person will not repeat their duplicitous behavior, but for this to occur oxytocin functioning must be adequate.

To a certain extent, each of these emotions and behaviors might be thought to be uniquely human, but in certain rodent species (e.g., prairie voles) strong pair bonds developed, and social interaction was accompanied by changes of oxytocin (Insel & Young, 2001). Moreover, when prairie voles were isolated they exhibited depressive-like behavioral disturbances that could be attenuated by the administration of oxytocin. Therefore, oxytocin might not only be involved in that hopey-changey stuff (as Sarah Palin might put it), but also may prove exceptionally influential in determining mood states and mood disorders.

TRUST COMES FROM A HORMONE?

Oxytocin, a hormone that acts peripherally and in the brain, has been implicated as being causally involved in prosocial behaviors, including trust. Intranasal (through a spray) administration of oxytocin in humans increased *trust*, and also increased the benefits gained from social interactions. This change in trust did not appear to represent an increase in the willingness to take risks (trusting someone may entail some risk, after all) as the effects of oxytocin on trust uniquely occurred in the context of social interactions. It was also reported that upon learning that their trust had been breached, participants in a placebo condition understandably reduced their subsequent trust. In contrast, under these same conditions, participants who received oxytocin through a nasal spray did not reduce their trust (Baumgartner et al., 2008). The effect of oxytocin was accompanied by brain activity changes that might reflect fear processing (the amygdala and midbrain regions) and adaptations that occur in response to a breach of trust (the dorsal striatum).

When I described this study to a (non-scientist) friend, his response was 'So what are you saying? Having this oxytocin makes you into a sucker; it turns people into social dopes?'. I suppose that is an alternative explanation for these data, but there is actually a fair degree of research that supports the trust hypothesis regarding oxytocin, my buddy's interpretation notwithstanding.

MODERATION OF THE STRESS RESPONSE

Variations of oxytocin levels are not only instigated by social stressors, they can also be provoked by other psychogenic and neurogenic stressors. Moreover intracerebroventricular administration (i.e., directly into one of the ventricles in the brain) of oxytocin diminished the expression of CRH mRNA elevations ordinarily elicited by acute stressors (Zheng et al., 2010). Thus, oxytocin may be involved in the regulation of CRH that is ordinarily released as a response to stressors, and might therefore influence anxiety. Oxytocin administered to humans (via a spray) also attenuated the negative cognitive appraisals otherwise evident in trait anxious individuals, and together with vasopressin appeared to be a key regulator for stress coping, anxiety, and depression. In fact, intranasal oxytocin administration effectively reduced the cortisol elevations associated with stressors. Interestingly, in response to a Trier Social Stress test, dynamic changes readily occurred in the methylation of the oxytocin receptor, suggesting that the stressor instigated an epigenetic change of this gene sequence. Whether this plays out in a relevant fashion with respect to psychopathology is uncertain, nor is it known whether earlier stressful events dispose individuals to these epigenetic changes. Yet given that the oxytocin receptor is sensitive to this moderate level stressor attests to the potential role of this hormone in regulating stress responses that could be elicited by strong life challenges.

As in the case of other stressor-related hormonal changes, a social stressor encountered early in life seems to have enduring effects on the behavior of prairie voles. After six weeks of isolation beginning just after weaning, they exhibited high levels of anxiety coupled with enhanced mRNA expression of oxytocin as well as CRH and AVP. Likewise, the maternal care that rats received during the early postnatal period may influence the appearance of oxytocin receptors in females during subsequent adulthood (Francis et al., 2002). Beyond the effects of early life events, the prenatal stressors experienced by pregnant rats resulted in diminished social interaction and the quality of the interactions with conspecifics, and this treatment also reduced oxytocin expression in the amygdala. This apparent social incompetence was, however, reversed by administering oxytocin directly to the amygdala, but was not affected by postnatal experiences, such as having the pups of the stressed dams fostered by mothers that had not been stressed (Lee et al., 2007). Thus, although the effects of prenatal stressors can be altered, simply having a mother that had not been stressed was not sufficient to attenuate the effects of prenatal insults.

WHAT HAPPENS WHEN THE OXYTOCIN RECEPTORS ARE ALTERED?

It seems that individuals may differ with respect to the presence of the gene for the oxytocin receptor (OXTR), and this may have implications regarding the factors that make some individuals engage in more prosocial behaviors than others. For instance, this gene was related to

(Continued)

(Continued)

whether or not individuals sought social support under conditions of distress, and may also have repercussions regarding the influence of social support in moderating the neuroendocrine responses to stressors. As described earlier, the cortisol rise elicited in the Trier Social Stress Test was limited if participants had a friend accompany them to the test situation (social support). It seems that a single nucleotide polymorphism exists regarding the oxytocin receptor, so that in the presence of this mutation the effect of having a friend accompany the person to the stress test was less effective. These findings not only indicate that social support may buttress individuals against a social stressor, they also show that oxytocin functioning is likely critical in this respect.

Oxytocin also seems to play a role in relation to parochial altruism (altruism refers to helping fellow group members despite the cost to oneself; parochialism refers to hostility towards members of other groups; parochial altruism refers to a blend between the two in which group members are true to their own, and warn and defend one another in relation to other groups) (Israel et al., 2012). For instance, despite the financial consequences, in the presence of high levels of oxytocin, individuals exhibited a 'tend and befriend' attitude, comprising cooperation and trust, towards members of their own group, while simultaneously displaying a 'tend and defend' (defensive aggression) attitude towards competing outgroup members

So, while some people have referred to oxytocin as the 'love chemical' or the 'nice chemical', it more likely represents the 'adapt well to your social surroundings chemical', although this doesn't sound nearly so sexy.

Paralleling the adverse effects of early life stressors in rodents, childhood maltreatment in humans (particularly emotional abuse) has enduring effects in the form of reduced oxytocin levels measured in cerebrospinal fluid. Moreover, this outcome was inversely related to the number of different types of stressors the individual had experienced, the severity and duration of the abuse, and current anxiety ratings (Opacka-Juffry & Mohiyeddini, 2012). Of particular significance was the finding that it wasn't just any childhood stressor that elicited the oxytocin variations in response to subsequent adult challenges. Specifically, using the TSST it was found that oxytocin levels were altered to a greater extent among women who had experienced childhood abuse than in those that had experienced childhood cancer (Pierrehumbert et al., 2010). Evidently, early experiences involving social challenges have protracted actions on adult stressor responses that might not be evident among individuals who had experienced childhood medically-related stressors. Thus, these negative social or parental early experiences may have long long-term consequences on behaviors (e.g., bonding, trust) that are mediated by oxytocin.

Several studies assessed whether oxytocin administration would influence social interaction and bonding-related behaviors, particularly in the context of stressful conditions. In fact, among individuals with impaired emotional regulation, oxytocin administration reduced the cortisol response ordinarily associated with the TSST or in response to social rejection, and reduced anxiety in response to an interpersonal stressor (Quirin et al., 2011). As well, in response to an interpersonal stressor, anxiety was reduced among individuals who had been treated with oxytocin and tended to have an emotion-focused coping style, and might thus have been particularly sensitive to the effects of stressors (Cardoso et al., 2011). Together, these data suggest that oxytocin may influence the way in which social stressors are appraised, but it is still premature to conclude that oxytocin would be effective in reducing distress once it is present.

Given that oxytocin together with other peptides such as vasopressin are related to social factors as well as anxiety, it was suggested that this hormone might also be related to generalized social anxiety disorder, possibly involving amygdala neural functioning. Moreover, in view of the importance of social factors in facilitating coping abilities, oxytocin may be a fundamental factor associated with our well-being, especially in the context of social stressors or in situations in which social support might be useful in attenuating the impact of stressors.

CONCLUSION

Stressful events have marked effects on numerous hormonal processes. Some reflect adaptive responses to help the organisms deal with potential or actual challenges, whereas others may contribute to the adverse effects of the stressor. In this chapter we've only touched on some of the hormones affected by stressors, and really dealt with those that are best known. In fact, stressors also affect various other substrates, including hypothalamic hormones (e.g., thyrotropin-releasing hormone) and pituitary hormones (growth hormone, β-endorphin, melanocyte-stimulating hormone, as well as somatostatin and histamine), all of which have been implicated in various stress-related pathologies. Yet, given the complex interactions that occur between hormones, neurotransmitters, and other processes, understanding the immediate and long-term impact of stressors will ultimately require analyses that focus on the synergistic and antagonistic effects of stressors, and how these change over the course of a stressor experience.

SUMMARY

- Numerous hormones are available that are necessary for day-to-day functioning, being essential for energy regulatory processes and eating, characteristics related to sex-based phenotypes, growth and maturation, as well as adaptation to the effects of stressors.
- Many of the hormonal changes are determined by stressor characteristics, as well as individual difference factors related to age, gender, genetic factors, and previous stressor experiences, as described in Chapters 1 and 2.
- Hormonal processes are exquisitely sensitive to stressors, and many of these stress-based hormonal responses are fundamental in determining whether the challenges will promote pathological outcomes.

4 NEUROTRANSMITTER PROCESSES AND GROWTH FACTOR CHANGES

GRANDMA GETS A NEUROSCIENCE LESSON

'The brain is amazing, Grandma. There are billions of cells in it; these neurons have long tentacles coming off of them and each of these tentacles has a bunch of branch-like projections – thousands upon thousands of them. And on each of these branches there are little connectors through which messages can be received. These messages come in different forms, so that they can receive messages of various types – sort of like someone working at the UN and being able to understand different languages. OK, that's a bad example; those people at the UN don't understand each other and never will. Anyway, Grandma, if all that isn't enough, these neurons also have a long projection through which they can send messages to other neurons. It's like an electric cord, but once you get to the end, chemicals come out of it and send messages to other neurons. They call these chemicals neurotransmitters because they're transmitting information from one neuron to another. And that isn't half of it, Grandma; inside each of these neurons are little factories churning out a whole bunch of these chemicals so that messages keep going down the track. The amazing thing is that all these neurons, and their little connectors, have to work in coordination with one another, otherwise we wouldn't know what we're doing.'

Sagely and thoughtfully, and with the hint of a frown, she says 'Very interesting . . . But it seems to me these little neurons aren't always working so good. Have you seen your Aunt Gertie's son lately? He never knows what he's doing. Can they fix a broken brain?'

Behavioral and cognitive responses to stressors are largely governed by the efficiency of brain neurons in communicating with one another as well as the presence of growth factors that influence the synaptic plasticity that is essential for this process. In this chapter we'll explore the effects of stressors on brain neurotransmitter functioning as well as on several growth factors. In this regard, we'll consider:

- how individual neurons work and the contribution of particular neural circuits to cognitive, emotional, and motivational functioning. To this end, we'll examine the impact of stressors on neurotransmitter functioning and the conditions that lead to such changes, with particular reference to how these neurotransmitter variations might be related to psychopathology. It will be clear that most of the factors outlined in Chapters 1 and 2 that affect stressor aversiveness, and how stressors are appraised and coped with, also play a prominent role in determining how stressful events will affect neurotransmitter functioning;
- the effects of stressors on the classic neurotransmitters, norepinephrine, dopamine, and serotonin, that have long been linked to anxiety disorders, depression, drug addiction, and schizophrenia. We'll also consider the effects of stressors on other neurotransmitter systems, including GABA, acetylcholine, and cannabinoids, and their interactions with other neurotransmitters and the hormones described in Chapter 3;
- the impact of stressors on growth or the neurotrophic factors that play an essential role in synaptogenesis and neurogenesis (new synaptic or neuronal growth), keeping neurons viable, and synaptic plasticity. These factors are essential for memory processes and may be critical for psychological disturbances.

NEURONAL AND GLIAL PROCESSES IN RELATION TO CHALLENGES

The billions of cells within the brain, and the still greater number of dendrites with their multiple connections, must operate in a coordinated fashion. This essentially involves different cells speaking to one another in a way that is clear, fast, and precise (and unlike events in my house at supper, the participating neurons likely don't interrupt one another). Essentially, this means that there ought to be the capacity for neurons not only to be activated, but also to be inhibited when appropriate. Communication between neurons involves a series of events that need to be understood before delving into how stressors influence our psychological and physical well-being. As you'll see, the dance that goes on between neurons is remarkably elegant, and the integration that exists between neuronal systems is awesome. Every once in a while, when I consider the complexity of the brain, and even the complexity of a single cell and its immense and coordinated machinery, I have to wonder whether it's possible that all of this came about through a process as 'simple' as natural selection.

GLIAL CELLS

The brain has two basic types of cells: neurons and glial cells. It was thought that neurons act to communicate information, and glial cells served as support cells for neurons. However, glial cells do much more than just that. Several types of glial cells exist, but those of particular interest to us at the moment are astrocytes and microglia (oligodendrocytes are also a type of glial cell in the brain that is involved in the myelination of neurons;

in the periphery, Schwann cells serve in this capacity). Astrocytes provide nutrients to neurons, maintain the ion balances within fluid outside of the brain cells, and are important in the repair and scarring of cells within the brain and spinal cord. Astrocytes are able to communicate with neurons in that they respond to and release particular neurotransmitters (e.g., GABA). Microglia, like particular types of cells in the periphery (macrophages, a type of cell present within our immune system), are essential for the functioning of the central nervous system (CNS), acting as the primary form of active immune defense. Microglia constantly search for potential CNS damage, as well as plaque and infectious agents, and ordinarily respond quickly to destroy agents that pose a risk to neurons (Rivest, 2009). Moreover, microglia are believed to play a fundamental role in the stress response. As we'll see when we discuss immune and inflammatory processes (Chapters 5 and 6), activated microglia can also have some fairly adverse effects. Among other things, by promoting strong inflammatory responses that cause neurodestruction, they might contribute to neurodegenerative disorders (e.g., Alzheimer's and Parkinson's disease). Specifically, as part of their antimicrobial response, microglia also produce free oxygen radicals that promote cell death. Thus, despite having some positive effects, microglia end up as the bad guys, and it was even suggested that their presence might serve as a biomarker for neurodegenerative processes (Litteljohn & Hayley, 2012).

NEURONS

How we respond to environmental stimuli, including stressors, is governed, to a considerable extent, by the activity of neurons in higher brain centers. Even if you are not sophisticated in physiological processes you will know at least a bit about neurotransmission, but we'll briefly go over a couple of key points, just to remind you. Brain neurons communicate with one another by releasing a chemical (termed a 'neurotransmitter') which stimulates (or inhibits) the adjacent cells that are contacted. Once this neurotransmitter is released from vesicles (located at the terminals of axons) into the space between two cells (synaptic cleft) it influences the adjacent neuron by triggering the receptors that are present. Some of the released transmitter is degraded by enzymes present in the synaptic cleft, and in the case of many transmitters, some may be transported back into the cell (through a process called 'reuptake') to be recycled. The longer the neurotransmitter stays in the synaptic cleft, the greater the opportunity for that neurotransmitter to activate the receptors. Thus, the efficiency of the neurotransmitter can be increased by extending its time in the synaptic cleft either by inhibiting enzymes that ordinarily destroy the transmitter or by inhibiting the reuptake into the neuron. In addition to this, there are agents that can simulate a neurotransmitter and go directly to the receptor and stimulate it (agonists), whereas other agents can block the receptor (antagonists) thus diminishing neuronal functioning. As indicated when we discussed hormones, there are different types of receptors that may, once stimulated, promote varied effects, and as well as these, there are receptors present on the cell that release the neurotransmitter (presynaptic receptors or autoreceptors) that, once triggered, have the effect of reducing the rate of transmitter production.

ECO-FRIENDLY NEURONS

Neurotransmitter systems are the poster boys (or girls) for going green. When more transmitter is needed, rather than just making a bunch more, some of it stays in the synaptic cleft to make maximal use of what's already there. Furthermore, after it has done its job it's taken back up into the neuron to be used again (recycling) through a process called 'reuptake'. Our neurons, it seems, are conscious of the importance of recycling, even if some of us aren't.

Regulation of the neurotransmitter also occurs through other processes. When the receptors that are present on a presynaptic neuron (autoreceptors) are triggered (as would occur more readily when large amounts of neurotransmitter are in the synaptic cleft), this tells the neuron to stop producing further transmitter. The process regarding neurotransmitter production, release and reuptake is reminiscent of industrial processes: the factory sends cars to the dealers; however, if the lot fills with unsold cars, the dealer might contact the plant to ask for production and delivery to slow down to avoid flooding the market and using up the resources to make further products. (Incidentally, this car lot example has nothing to do with the word 'auto'receptor.)

There is a common heuristic that certain neurotransmitters are responsible for particular behavioral processes. For instance, it might be thought that serotonin (5-HT) is involved in depressive illness, norepinephrine (NE) and 5-HT are involved in anxiety, dopamine (DA) is responsible for reward processes, and so on. To an extent this type of formulation is accurate, and treatments that affect one or another neurotransmitter might influence particular behaviors. However, this is an overly simplistic perspective, as the neurons triggered by different neurotransmitters might have conjoint actions with several other transmitters, and can elicit additive or synergistic actions. Furthermore, multiple brain regions and many neurochemical processes might be involved in any given behavior. In the ensuing sections we will be dealing with several neurotransmitters, each in turn, but keep in mind that we're actually dealing with a community of neurons, involving several brain regions, that do things in sync with one another.

It wasn't all that long ago that we thought of a transmitter and a receptor as a lock and key arrangement in which little key-like chemicals floated across the synaptic cleft and fitted into little locks that resided on the dendrites or cell bodies of neurons. There have been many changes to this conceptualization. For starters, we no longer see the receptors as locks that (semi)permanently reside on the cell surface, but as chemical attachment sites that are continuously synthesized (and thus the number of receptors changes as a function of numerous variables) and can be internalized (essentially being sucked into the cell), so that at a given time the complement of receptors present on the cell surface can vary. Moreover, for a given transmitter there may be several types of receptors present that upon being triggered might have different downstream effects. Hence, only certain types of DA receptors have been implicated in schizophrenia, whereas other DA receptors subtypes might be associated with other normal or abnormal behaviors. Likewise, only certain 5-HT receptors may contribute to depressive illness. Clearly, when assessing the effects of stressors on neuronal functioning, it is not enough to consider only the amount of transmitter available, the amount released, or even that a receptor has been triggered, but also, as we'll see in Chapters 8 and 9, to take into account the impact of the transmitter on specific types of receptors.

NEUROTRANSMITTER CHANGES ELICITED BY STRESSORS

As in the case of the earlier chapter concerning stressor-induced hormonal changes, the sections that follow rely heavily on data from animal studies that pertain to stressor-provoked neurochemical alterations. There's no doubt that studies of this sort have enhanced our understanding of the stressor effects on mood, cognitive processes, mental disorders, and illnesses involving neurodegenerative processes, as well as illnesses that involve immune functioning. At the same time, it is sometimes difficult to generalize animal-based findings to human pathologies in view of the fundamental role of cognitive processes (e.g., stressor appraisal) in accounting for the reaction to stressors. Furthermore, in humans, certain types of stressors (e.g., those dealing with social threats or ostracism) may engage neuronal processes that differ from those involving other forms of distress, such as shame, loss, and rumination. Moreover, unlike hormones that can be detected in blood, analyzing brain neurotransmitters in humans is difficult. Although analyses using positron emission tomography (PET) can offer some clues regarding neurotransmitter and receptor changes in the brain, they don't inform us about the moment-to-moment changes attributable to specific emotional or cognitive changes that occur during stressful events.

READING FACIAL EXPRESSIONS

As useful as studies in rodents might be, there are limitations regarding the possibility of gauging emotional responses in these critters and how these might be related to particular neurotransmitter or endocrine changes. Attempts were made to determine whether facial gestures in mice can tell us something about what they are feeling. Mogil and his associates developed the mouse grimace scale that entails a standardized behavioral coding system to assess the facial responses elicited by noxious (painful) stimuli of moderate duration (Langford et al., 2010). It seemed that mouse facial expressions were reliable and could potentially be used to assess the efficacy of treatments meant to act as analgesics. I'm not sure whether this would be possible with respect to complex emotions such as shame. I don't know what would humiliate or shame a mouse, or what they would look like when they do feel shame.

Those with pets, typically cats and dogs, will tell you that they communicate with them readily and can read their expressions with little difficulty. I knew a cat that when let into the house would rub against my leg, and he did the same thing when a can of food was being opened. I used to think this was such a smart cat, and would always politely say 'you're welcome' in response to his apparent leg-rubbing 'thank you'. I've since been told that the cat was actually 'marking me' as if I were part of his territory. I was a bit disappointed to hear this, but was simultaneously grateful that he hadn't chosen another method to mark me.

Stressful events in rodents markedly influenced central neurochemical processes that may be fundamental to psychological well-being. In fact, of the more than 60 different molecules that can act as neurotransmitters, including a variety of amines, peptides, and gases, a fair number are affected by stressful events. These neurochemical changes, as indicated earlier, likely serve in an adaptive capacity, being fundamental in maintaining allostasis. Among other things, the neurochemical alterations that are elicited might prepare the organism to deal (cope) with the stressor, blunt its psychological impact, and engage appropriate cognitive appraisals systems and those necessary for effective coping (Anisman et al., 2008).

Although stressors have ubiquitous consequences, studies on animals indicated that not all stressors have the same effects, as different neural circuits may be engaged, depending on the nature of the stressor encountered. By example, processive stressors (those that involve higher-order processing) that entail physically aversive properties (neurogenic stressors), and those of a psychological origin (psychogenic stressors, including learned as well as innate threats) might engage different neural circuits, just as we saw earlier in the case of CRH. To be sure, it is difficult to compare the influence of different types of stressors, given that they might not be appraised similarly or they may not be equally aversive. Nevertheless, given that psychogenic and neurogenic insults differentially influence several neurotransmitters within the amygdala or prefrontal cortex, the regions associated with stressor appraisals and fear/anxiety, these challenges might also have different behavioral consequences (Merali et al., 2006).

BIOGENIC AMINES: NOREPINEPHRINE, DOPAMINE, AND SEROTONIN

ACUTE STRESSOR EFFECTS ON UTILIZATION AND LEVELS

A fairly large number of neurotransmitters and their receptors have been identified, and treatments for psychiatric disorders often target these systems. Among the earliest neurotransmitters identified were NE, 5-HT, and DA, collectively referred to as biogenic amines. These neurotransmitters and their receptors are rich in the limbic brain regions (e.g., hippocampus, amygdala, and prefrontal cortex) that are associated with executive functioning (appraisals, decision making), emotions, and memory processes, and contribute to several forms of psychopathology. These amines are also present in hypothalamic nuclei (e.g., paraventricular nucleus, arcuate nucleus) and are essential for hormonal functioning, including HPA and hypothalamic–pituitary–gonadal (HPG) activation, as well as basic biological responses such as energy regulation, feeding, and sexual behaviors.

As depicted in Figure 4.1, the rate at which a neurotransmitter is used (released from the neuron) is ordinarily met by an equivalent rate at which it is manufactured (synthesized), and so the level of the neurotransmitter doesn't change. This is the 'steady state' of the transmitter. In response to stressful stimuli, the rate at which neurotransmitters are used increases, presumably in order to facilitate coping efforts or to set in motion the processes that maintain well-being. Predictably, the increased neurotransmitter utilization is accompanied by increased synthesis so that levels remain stable. However, in response to sufficiently severe challenges, particularly those that are uncontrollable, the amine release increases still further and the rate of utilization may exceed the rate of synthesis, and consequently the amine levels will decline. The reduced monoamine reserves, in theory, would render the organism less able to contend with further insults, and consequently it would be more vulnerable to pathology. In more prosaic terms, this is akin to taking more money out of your bank account than you're depositing, and eventually your balance will reach zero, and your ability to make any further commitments will be limited.

As you saw earlier, when an animal first encounters a stressor, it is uncertain whether the stressor is controllable or uncontrollable, and it ought to respond strongly irrespective of stressor controllability. After all, when a potential threat emerges, a rapid response is needed given that there might not be any second chances. Only if the stressor is controllable can the organism afford to temper the biological responses that would otherwise be provoked. It would seem reasonable to expect that those brain regions involved in appraisal/coping processes ought to be more sensitive to this differentiation relative to those brain regions that are more fundamental to vegetative or basic life processes. Consistent with this view, inescapable stressors are likely to cause excessive utilization of NE and 5-HT and promote a reduction in the levels of these neurotransmitters. Furthermore, if rats were first trained in an escapable test (a treatment that protects [immunizes] animals against the behavioral disturbances elicited by an uncontrollable stressor), the increased 5-HT release ordinarily elicited by an inescapable stressor was prevented in frontal brain regions associated with cognitive appraisals (Bland et al., 2003).

Stressors also markedly influence the release of DA, but these stressor-provoked changes seem to be less widespread than those of NE and 5-HT. Of particular significance, however, was that the DA changes were evident within the arcuate nucleus of the hypothalamus (a region that is involved in the regulation of several hormones), the nucleus accumbens, and the cortical and limbic sites that are important in mediating reward and appraisal processes. Studies conducted in freely moving animals indicated that amine alterations could be induced in these brain regions even by relatively mild stimuli (tailpinch, novelty) and by psychosocial stressors. It has been speculated that the DA changes elicited by stressors might be responsible for the anhedonia (the diminished reward gained from otherwise rewarding stimuli) that occurs in response to stressors and might thus contribute to syndromes, such as depressive disorder, in which anhedonia is a key feature. In Chapters 8 and 10 we'll be discussing the impact of stressors on DA systems in relation to depression and addiction processes, respectively. At that point it will become clear that the stressor-elicited changes of some DA systems might play a fundamental role in the instigation and maintenance of behavioral pathologies.

SNAPSHOTS OF DYNAMIC EVENTS

In assessing brain neurochemicals, the most common procedure comprises analysis of the levels of specific neurochemicals and their metabolites (the latter are products of the neurotransmitter that is degraded). The accumulation of metabolites tells us approximately how active the neurons have been in response to the stressor experience. In most studies, brain tissue is typically collected at a single time point following a stressor experience, and hence this provides only a static measure (a snapshot) of what has occurred in a dynamic system. An alternative approach, referred to as 'in vivo microdialysis', involves placing a cannulae (a very thin tube) into the brain, and then collecting fluid outside of the neurons (interstitial fluid) that contain transmitters that have been released from the local neurons. By analyzing brain fluids (dialysates) at successive time points, an index can be obtained regarding the transmitter that is actually released at various times before and after the stressor, rather than inferring this from the metabolite that has accumulated. In this way, a perspective can be gained concerning what happens over time as the animal contends with a stressful situation.

Regardless of whether studies are conducted in animals or in humans, or whether they involve emotional, cognitive, or behavioral processes, or those related to hormonal, neurotransmitter, or immune mechanisms, we're almost always dealing with systems in flux, and so, whenever possible, it's best to measure changes on an ongoing basis.

IMPACT OF CHRONIC STRESSORS: ADAPTATION AND ALLOSTATIC OVERLOAD

Do we adapt to adverse experiences, or are the effects of stressors more and more damaging the longer we endure them? From a behavioral and a neurochemical perspective, both could be correct, but this would largely depend on many of the factors described earlier (previous experiences, genetic disposition, stressor characteristics). Moreover, there is no reason to believe that all biological systems will operate in the same way. It is entirely possible for an adaptation-like effect to evolve with respect to a particular neurotransmitter in a given brain region, whereas changes in the levels or utilization of other transmitters (or even the same transmitter in other brain regions) may become more pronounced with repeated stressor experiences.

Reductions of a neurotransmitter's levels for extended periods may render the organism vulnerable to pathology and there are multiple adaptive biological mechanisms that act to limit the sustained reductions of a neurotransmitter. Typically, the reduced levels of NE, DA, and 5-HT associated with strong acute stressors are not evident after protracted or repeated insults. As described earlier, this appears to result from a compensatory enhancement of synthesis in the case of NE and 5-HT (see Figure 4.1), and in the case of DA the utilization of the stressor may be somewhat curtailed as well.

Again this is reminiscent of how we deal with our financial expenditures. In times of emergency (e.g., paying off old school loans, repairing the roof), the amount that leaves our bank account might exceed our earnings, and so our account balance drops. To compensate for this we might take on part-time work in order that our balance returns to what it was before. Yet simply because our balance has been reinstated doesn't mean everything is back to normal. Things have changed and the pressures on us have increased, and we have less room to maneuver now that we have this part-time work. Not only does the possibility exist that we might be unable to maintain this heavy workload, but should yet another emergency arise, we might be less able to contend with the challenge. In a sense, our biological stress systems operate in just this way. With repeated stressful experiences, or with a prolonged stressor, we might manage in some fashion or other to gain the biological (and psychological) resources that are needed to meet our immediate demands. But make no mistake, ultimately the burden may become too great and our adaptive systems may fail. In effect, there seem to be several checks and counterchecks to maintain allostasis in response to chronic stressors. However, we should not be misled into thinking that things are 'back to normal'. Our amine levels might have been reestablished, but this occurred through increased neurochemical production, elevated utilization, and receptor activation which could potentially take a toll on our system. Indeed, if a stressor experience is sufficiently severe and/or long lasting, the load placed on our critical systems may be excessive, and the resulting allostatic overload might ultimately result in our increased vulnerability to pathology (McEwen, 2000).

There's more to this adaptation than just a moderate change of synthesis or use of a transmitter. In chronically stressed animals, amine levels sometimes don't simply return to prestress levels, but might actually come to exceed basal levels. Ordinarily, when animals are exposed to a stressor, the synthesis and utilization of NE and 5-HT increase, and then normalize quickly when the stressor terminates. That is, once the threat or stressor is gone, neuronal activity quickly reverts to the prestress state. However, when an animal is stressed day after day, and the risk of utilization exceeding synthesis is persistent, yet another adaptive change occurs. In this case, it seems that when the stressor terminates, the utilization of the transmitter normalizes readily as it should, whereas the elevated synthesis of the transmitter does not, but instead continues for some time. The elevated production, in the absence of heightened utilization, results in transmitter levels being elevated above the initial baseline, potentially rendering animals better prepared to deal with subsequent stressors. This represents a fairly elegant adaptive mechanism. If the stressor occurs day after day in a predictable fashion, then the right thing for the system might be to build up a reserve of neurotransmitters that would be available for use when the stressor reoccurs the next day. However, at a certain point too much neuronal activation may actually be counterproductive (e.g., leading to sustained anxiety, or causing peripheral effects, such as excessive immune activation), and so further adaptive changes occur to induce the down regulation of β-NE and 5-HT receptor activity and the processes activated by these receptors (Anisman et al., 2008).

There are certain chronic conditions that don't lend themselves to adaptation at all. Specifically, if the chronic stressor varies over time, occurs unpredictably, is uncontrollable, and actually involves a series of different types of challenges, the pressure on biological systems might be especially marked and a risk exists that this overloaded system might collapse. In this regard, the 'adaptation' of biogenic mine functioning ordinarily associated with a predictable stressor regimen may be absent or less pronounced following an intermittent chronic stressor regimen (Tannenbaum et al., 2002). Moreover, chronic variable stressors may set the stage so that exaggerated neurochemical responses are elicited when the organism encounters yet another adverse experience long after the original stressor experiences. Of course, genetic or other experiential factors (e.g., early life events) might influence the

Neurochemical change in response to different stressor conditions

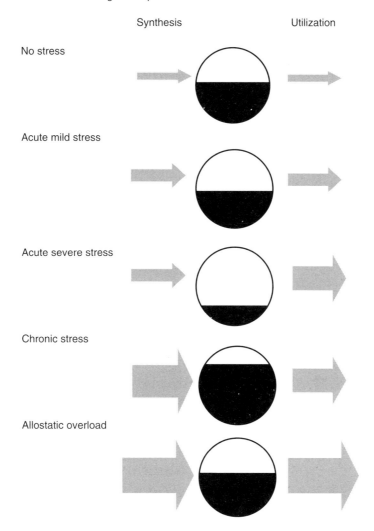

FIGURE 4.1   The changes of monoamine synthesis, utilization, and consequently the levels, vary with the nature of the stressor. Under nonstress conditions the synthesis and utilization of a transmitter are comparable and the levels thus remain stable. When a stressor is administered that is mild/moderate the utilization of the transmitter occurs in order for the organism to deal with the stressor. This is met by increased synthesis, and thus once more the level of the transmitter remains stable. As the stressor severity increases, or if the stressor is uncontrollable, the burden of coping rests on biological systems, and in this case utilization of the transmitter may increase sufficiently, outstripping synthesis, and hence the transmitter levels will decline. If the stressor continues, a compensatory increase in utilization occurs, possibly because of a down regulation in autoreceptors, and consequently the levels may again revert to a steady state. However, the increased synthesis and utilization under these conditions can go on for only so long, and eventually the adaptive processes may be overwhelmed (allostatic overload), thus favoring the development of pathology. There are multiple processes affected by stressors simultaneously, and this represents only one way in which pathology might arise in relation to stressors.

organism's adaptive capacity (or resilience) in dealing with such insults, and it is likely that these factors, among others, also moderate the stress response that accompanies a chronic variable stressor regimen.

MONOAMINE RECEPTOR CHANGES ASSOCIATED WITH STRESSORS

Various receptor subtypes can be differentially affected by stressors, depending on the brain region examined. In this regard, receptors can be up-regulated or down-regulated with respect to their number (density) or their sensitivity to agonists (agents that directly stimulate receptors). By example, 24 hours following a forced swim stressor, 5-HT_{1A} receptor density was down-regulated in the dorsal raphe nucleus (where the serotonin cell bodies reside, and where this type of receptor acts as an autoreceptor) and in the hippocampus, but was elevated in the thalamus, hypothalamus, and amygdala. It also appeared that behavioral impairments following stressor exposure were related to yet other receptor changes. For example, a stressor regimen that engendered behavioral impairments in a learned helplessness paradigm was associated with an increase of mRNA expression of 5-HT_{1B} receptors within the dorsal raphe nucleus, without affecting postsynaptic 5-HT_{1B} expression within the hippocampus or prefrontal cortex (reviewed in Anisman et al., 2008).

At first blush this diversity of effects might seem a bit puzzling. Then again, why should the neurotransmitter or receptor changes be the same in all brain regions, particularly as neurons at various brain sites might serve in different capacities? Some may be involved in appraisals, others in mediating either psychological or physical coping responses, or they might contribute to energy regulation, and still others might be involved in the regulation of neurotransmitter synthesis (as occurs when autoreceptors are altered). Thus, from an adaptive perspective, selectivity would be advantageous with respect to which transmitters and receptors are altered, either directly or in a compensatory fashion. But what gets these neurons and receptors to do what they do, and how do they know when they're supposed to do these things, to say nothing of how they know when to stop?

STRESSOR CHARACTERISTICS INFLUENCE AMINE CHANGES

The severity and predictability of a stressor can influence the nature and magnitude of the neurochemical changes elicited, and psychogenic insults that are ethologically significant (e.g., predator odor, social defeat) are particularly effective in promoting NE and 5-HT release from neurons within limbic brain regions. Moreover, it seems that those stressors that involve social challenges (e.g., social defeat or changes in the social environment) may have longer-lasting neurochemical effects than do other challenges. Thus, to some extent, the circuitry associated with certain stressful experiences may be hard-wired, and how threats are appraised likely influences to what extent the neuronal processes will be activated. Yet the behavioral or emotional changes that accompanied the stressor-provoked 5-HT variations (e.g., anxiety), even if they were elicited by very different challenges, were attenuated by chronic antidepressant treatment as well as other manipulations that enhance neuronal functioning (Beitia et al., 2005). Evidently, despite some differences in the effects of diverse stressors, there are common paths (or endpoints) for the effects of stressors, and these could potentially involve processes that might be amenable to the same therapeutic treatments.

ASYMMETRICAL NEURONAL CHANGES ELICITED BY STRESSORS

It had been believed that, with only a few exceptions (e.g., in relation to language), the left and right brain were mirror images of one another, and there wasn't much attention devoted to whether they might have different functions. It was subsequently suggested that the left and right hemispheres each had unique functions. For instance, the left prefrontal cortex was thought to play a role as an 'interpreter' of information, and with the development of imaging techniques several psychological conditions were found to be associated with brain changes in one or the other hemisphere (e.g., depression, ADHD). It seems that this is also the case in response to stressors, as even mild insults differentially influence left and right prefrontal cortex DA activity (Sullivan & Gratton, 2002). Essentially, right prefrontal cortex DA activity was most closely linked with stress regulatory systems, including HPA functioning. Likewise, in non-depressed individuals, the activation of neuronal functioning in the left prefrontal cortex occurred when participants were attempting to minimize their negative affect, whereas bilateral prefrontal cortex activation occurred among depressed individuals who were focused on their negative affect. Hence, under normal conditions, the left prefrontal predominates in dealing with challenges. However, among depressed individuals inappropriate engagement of the right prefrontal cortex, and the ensuing stimulation of the amygdala, might contribute to the regulation of affective and perhaps cognitive responses to negative stimuli (Johnstone et al., 2007). At some point it may be possible to take advantage of this asymmetry in predicting the development of depression and whether certain types of treatment ought to be administered (e.g., cognitive behavioral therapy vs certain types of medications). And in addition, normalization of the hemispheric responses to threat cues might be useful in predicting whether the influence of a given treatment strategy has been fully effective, thereby diminishing the odds of illness recurrence.

ACETYLCHOLINE (ACH)

Acetylcholine (ACh) was among the first neurotransmitters discovered, and it plays a fundamental role in peripheral and central nervous system functioning. In the peripheral nervous system it usually acts as a countervailing force to the excitatory effects of epinephrine and norepinephrine. For instance, whereas epinephrine stimulates sympathetic functioning (e.g., increasing heart rate), ACh has the opposite effect. As a result, there is a system to get things going, and one to calm things down, and these systems ought to work cooperatively.

Despite the fact that ACh has been studied for decades, analyses of the effects of stressors on this neurotransmitter within the brain have been sparse. Nevertheless, psychogenic stressors, such as predator odor and immobilization, are known to increase the release of ACh within the prefrontal cortex and hippocampus, and cholinergic functioning was regulated by input from other neurotransmitters, such as GABA, glutamate, corticotropin-releasing hormone (CRH), and DA (e.g., Pepeu & Blandina, 1998). Consistent with the view linking anxiety and ACh functioning, stressor-provoked ACh variations could be attenuated by the anti-anxiety agent chlordiazepoxide (Smith et al., 2006). In addition to influencing ACh itself, aversive stimuli promoted changes in the density of certain ACh receptors, notably the muscarinic receptors (this is one of the two types of ACh receptors, the other being nicotinic receptors) (Mauck et al., 2010).

As in the case of other neurotransmitters, the effects of stressors on ACh release varied with different organismic and experiential variables. Specifically, vulnerability to stressor-induced ACh changes is increased appreciably if rats had also experienced an early-life stressor, whereas the effects of stressors on ACh activity were attenuated by raising rats in an enriched environment (Segovia et al., 2009). And added to this, the ACh variations were more pronounced in females than in males, particularly during diestrus and proestrus phases of the estrus cycle (during the first half of the estrus cycle), suggesting the involvement of estrogen (or related factors) in determining the stressor-elicited ACh changes.

WHAT ELSE IS THERE TO KNOW ABOUT ACETYLCHOLINE?

During the first few months of 2013, reports from Syria pointed to the possibility that chemical weapons were being made available to the Assad regime and could potentially be used against those trying to overthrow the government. There have also been reports that Assad transferred chemical weapons to Hezbollah in Lebanon, and there are fears that such weapons might also fall into the hands of al-Qaeda operatives who have mingled with anti-Assad forces. All of this showed that the situation had reached new levels of *sturm und drang*, much of it indirectly related to ACh.

ACh has a somewhat tainted history as several of the gases used in WWI involved effects on this transmitter. These gases were the type that blocked the enzyme acetylcholinesterase, which normally degrades ACh, resulting in excessive levels of this transmitter, culminating in death. Today, there are more than 70 agents that can be used as war gases to either kill or incapacitate. Some of the more infamous agents are sarin, soman, and tabun that were made in secrecy in Germany both before and during World War II for use as chemical weapons through their effects on ACh. Other war gases include mustard gas, chlorine, hydrogen cyanide, and several that have scary names, such as VX, VR, and agent 15. To this list one can also add ricin and botulinum toxin, although they are not technically 'gases'. Zyklon B, developed by the Nazi regime, was not used on battlefields, but was used instead to execute noncombatants in concentration camps.

Most countries have not prescribed the use of poison gas in warfare. The 1925 Geneva Protocol for the Prohibition of Poisonous Gases and Bacteriological Methods of Warfare stated that 'the use in war of asphyxiating, poisonous or other gases, and of all analogous liquids, materials or devices, has been justly condemned by the general opinion of the civilized world'. Of course, this hasn't stopped the development of new poison agents, and it didn't stop its use in the Sino Japanese war, the Iran Iraq war, WWII, the North Yemen Civil war, and Iraq's war on the Kurds, as well as its alleged use in Chechnya, and at the time of this writing it seems that the Syrian army has used sarin against civilian populations.

> The Conference on Disarmament (1992) submitted the Chemical Weapons Convention to the UN General Assembly (although it was not signed for about five years) which banned chemical weapons (but, oddly, it didn't include biological weapons). Given the 'politics' of the UN, did anyone possibly believe that the results of that agreement would be any more credible than the Geneva Protocol almost seventy years earlier?

γ-AMINOBUTYRIC ACID (GABA)

GABA, the most abundant neurotransmitter in the brain, acts as the principle inhibitory neurotransmitter within the mammalian CNS, essentially acting as a brake so that neuronal functioning is properly regulated. It's all well and good to have a powerful engine that gets a car moving from 0 to 60 in seven seconds, but at the end of the road, brakes can come in pretty handy, and GABA serves in this capacity.

THE GABA$_A$ RECEPTOR

You'll remember the description previously given of receptors for neurotransmitters. Well, GABA involves a different form of receptor. The GABA receptor essentially comprises a channel that under certain conditions will allow electrically charged particles (ions) into the cell where they cause that cell to be activated. Two types of the GABA receptor have been identified (GABA$_A$ and GABA$_B$), but for the moment, we'll focus on the former. The GABA$_A$ receptor is made up of five subunits (or components) that basically 'hold hands' with one another, forming a ring, where the central region comprises the channel through which ions can pass. The subunits that make up the five-unit receptor comprise α subunits (of which there are six forms, $\alpha_1, \alpha_2, \alpha_3, \alpha_4, \alpha_5, \alpha_5$), three types of β subunits, and three types of γ subunits, as well as an ε, π, and δ subunit. Most receptors have two αs, two βs, and a γ.

Given the number of different subunits and their multiple combinations that make up the five-unit cassette (receptor), there are a huge number of variants of the receptor. Importantly, the combinations of subunits determine the characteristics of the receptor, including the specific drugs that can act upon it. Most GABA$_A$ receptors that have $\alpha_1, \alpha_2, \alpha_3$, or α_5 subunits are sensitive to the anti-anxiety agents that fall into the benzodiazepine class, whereas those containing α_4 or α_6 subunits are insensitive to benzodiazepines, and instead are sensitive to other GABA acting agents, such as neurosteroids (e.g., estrogen) and alcohol.

GABA-RELATED CHANGES ELICITED BY STRESSORS

The view that GABA is important in the stress response comes from multiple sources of evidence, aside from the fact that anti-anxiety medications act through GABA receptors. In particular, GABA levels in plasma and cerebrospinal fluid are elevated in anxiety-provoking situations, and when assessed *in vivo*, GABA$_A$ release was increased in response to certain stressors (de Groote & Linthorst, 2007). In addition, the GABA$_A$ subunits that make up receptors within stress-sensitive brain regions were elevated in response to stressors, an outcome that was particularly strong when the stressor involved a series of different challenges administered over several weeks. These effects, additionally, varied with the basal anxiety that mice displayed, being more pronounced in a very anxious mouse strain (BALB/cByJ) than in hardy, stress-resilient mice (C57BL/6ByJ) (Poulter et al., 2010). It also appeared that chronic stressor treatments reduced GABA$_A$ in several brain regions, and consistent with a role for GABA in depressive illness, these stressor effects were attenuated by antidepressant treatment (Shalaby & Kamal, 2012).

As in the case of several hormones, stressors experienced in early life provoked long-lasting changes of GABA$_A$ receptor activity, especially among animals that were again exposed to the stressor in adulthood (Skilbeck et al., 2010). Moreover, rats that had been stressed as juveniles (recall that this is the equivalent of adolescence in humans) more readily exhibited GABA subunit variations in response to later stressors, and were more sensitive to the anti-anxiety diazepam, indicating that the early stressor experience had functional outcomes stemming from the altered GABA$_A$ subunit expression (Jacobson-Pick et al., 2008). Findings such as these have led to the view that early life stressful experiences, by influencing the trajectory of biological processes related to GABA functioning, determine the basal and stressor elicited levels of anxiety in adulthood.

Limited data are available concerning the impact of stressors on GABA neuronal functioning in humans. Nonetheless, it was shown using an imaging procedure (magnetic resonance spectroscopy: MRS) that in the face of a threat, GABA activity decreased relative to that which was evident during a safe period (Hasler et al., 2010). Likewise, in depressed humans who died by suicide, GABA$_A$ subunit expression was disturbed relative to that of individuals who died of factors unrelated to suicide (Merali, Du et al., 2004). The latter findings don't necessarily tie GABA functioning causally to depression (or to suicide), but these data are certainly in line with the suppositions offered concerning stress, depression, and GABA functioning.

INTERACTIONS OF GABA AND OTHER NEUROBIOLOGICAL FACTORS

Given that GABA's function is to act as a brake, serving to limit the influence of excitatory transmitters, it is understandable that it acts in concert with other neurotransmitters and hormones in the modulation of stress responses and in provoking stress-related behavioral disturbances, such as anxiety and depression. For instance, GABA$_A$ and 5-HT processes influence one another (reciprocal innervation) within the prefrontal cortex and hippocampus (both of which have been associated with depression), and it seems that 5HT$_{1A}$ receptors regulate GABA$_A$ receptor expression (Sibille et al., 2000). In view of the fundamental role of GABAergic inhibitory transmission in prefrontal cortex functioning, coupled with its interactions with 5-HT, it is possible that antidepressant treatments (as well as those related to anxiety) might ultimately have their therapeutic effects through actions on GABA processes.

The interactions involving GABA are not limited to 5-HT, as intimate relations exist between GABA and CRH functioning. In this regard, GABA might serve as an essential mediator by which CRH (and possibly stressors) come to influence 5-HT functioning, and such relationships again may be reciprocal (Waselus et al., 2005). If this weren't sufficiently complex, further GABA-related interactions exist that could influence depressive illnesses. By example, GABA$_A$ subunit expression may be altered by ovarian hormones, such as progesterone and its metabolite allopregnanolone, which might then contribute to the sex differences that exist with respect to depression and anxiety (Maguire & Mody, 2007). This certainly appears confusing, but there's a simple way of thinking about this that may be useful for the moment. Specifically, there are several neurotransmitters, including 5-HT and CRH, that influence one another and thereby influence behavioral outputs. To make sure that this mutual regulation functions smoothly, GABA acts as a coordinator (much like an orchestra conductor) to make sure that these transmitters are working together, hushing (inhibiting) one or the other as the situation requires. But when we say 'as the situation requires', this doesn't just mean the presence or absence of a stressor, but also the broad context concerning what else may be happening in the body or brain. Therefore, changes in the hormonal milieu that accompanies the estrus cycle, for example, may influence how the conductor behaves.

GLUTAMATE

Glutamate is the precursor for the synthesis of GABA through the actions of the enzyme glutamate decarboxylase (GAD) within GABA neurons. Aside from this, glutamate is a neurotransmitter in its own right, being the most abundant excitatory neurotransmitter within the CNS, stimulating N-methyl-D-aspartate (NMDA) and α-amino-3-hydroxy-5-methyl-4-isoxazole-propionic acid (AMPA) receptors on adjacent cells. Ordinarily, glutamate transporters present in neuronal and glial membranes remove glutamate after it has been released. However, under certain conditions, such as brain injury (e.g., a stroke), glutamate can accumulate in extracellular space, which can promote cell damage and cell death, referred to as 'excitotoxicity'.

It appears that the increased corticoids elicited in response to acute stressors augment the release of glutamate at the prefrontal cortex, amygdala, and hippocampus. It also appears that the prenatal or early life stressors that induce anxiety in adulthood might be due to persistent variations of glutamate functioning. Consistent with the suggestion that this transmitter might play a role in the emergence of behavioral disturbances, repeated treatments with antidepressants attenuated the glutamate changes otherwise induced by an uncontrollable stressor, just as antidepressants had the effect of attenuating the behavioral disturbances engendered. Although corticosterone likely was responsible for the glutamate variations, it is unlikely that corticosterone contributed to the effects of antidepressants as the corticoid and glutamate changes could be divorced from one another. Unlike the effects of acute stressors, the impact of chronic stressors on glutamate release have not been extensively assessed, although it appears that a degree of adaptation occurs in the prefrontal cortex, but this diminution of glutamate release is less notable in other brain regions. The implications of these brain region-specific changes in regard to behavioral outcomes are uncertain given the paucity of data that have been collected in this regard.

Beyond the changes of glutamate release, acute stressors can increase the expression of NMDA and AMPA receptors at postsynaptic sites, thereby increasing synaptic transmission. These effects occur rapidly in the hippocampus, but are generally not immediately apparent in the prefrontal cortex. Instead, they appear more than one hour after stressor termination, but persist up to and beyond 24 hours. Given the temporal changes that were observed, the possibility exists that glutamate in some brain regions (e.g., the rapid changes in hippocampus) might be fundamental for defensive responses, including those that involve experience-based (learned) behaviors.

Among other things, glutamate is fundamental to synaptic plasticity (i.e., the moldability or changeability of synapses), and is therefore important for learning memory processes. It seems that acute stressors inhibit plasticity within limbic and cortical brain regions, and this outcome can be attenuated by antidepressant treatment or by glucocorticoid receptor antagonism. Interestingly, unlike the sensitization effects seen with respect to other transmitter systems, a stressor experience can impair the neuroplasticity otherwise induced by a later stressor, and it is thought that this could influence fear memories. Once again, the data that are available have also suggested that in response to chronic stressors plasticity might be disrupted within the prefrontal cortex and hippocampus, and could thus disrupt behavioral flexibility and working memory. Indeed, it seems that such effects might be mediated by glucocorticoid functioning (Popoli et al., 2011).

As a variety of stressors affect glutamate transmission in limbic and cortical brain regions, and promote dendritic remodeling as well as diminished synapses and reductions of brain volume, it is conceivable that the glutamatergic system is involved in the evolution of stress-related psychopathology. In this regard, it has even been suggested that glutamate may be a component of a final common pathway underlying the therapeutic action of antidepressant agents (Sanacora et al., 2012). In this regard, the suggestion is that this entails a paradigm shift in which the emergence of pathology likely entails a change of neuroplasticity, rather than considering too little or too much of a given neurotransmitter.

CANNABINOIDS

We can't leave this section without some commentary on the relation between stress and cannabinoids, especially as cannabis has long been known to reduce anxiety in addition to promoting mood-elevating effects. An excellent review of the relationship between stress and the cannabinoid system was published (Hill et al., 2010) that went far beyond the simple stress-reducing effects of cannabis. The psychoactive component of cannabis, Δ9-tetrahydrocannabinol (THC), can bind to specific cannabinoid receptors (CB_1) within the brain (e.g., in the paraventricular nucleus of the hypothalamu, as well as in the hippocampus, prefrontal cortex, and amygdala), and there are specific naturally occurring ligands (molecules that bind to particular receptors) in the brain that are referred to as 'endocannabinoids' (eCBs).

Activation of the eCB system and the CB_1 receptors can regulate the release of other neurotransmitters, including GABA and glutamate, thereby inducing a variety of behavioral outcomes. Indeed, eCB signaling of CB_1 receptors plays a key role in regulating stress reactions, and a pharmacological blockade of CB_1 receptors or altering these receptors through other means increases HPA activity both under basal conditions and in response to acute psychogenic stressors. Moreover, the administration of a CB_1 receptor agonist directly into the basolateral amygdala reduced stressor-induced activation of the HPA axis, indicating that cannabinoids influenced the link between the amygdala and the hypothalamus that regulated stress responses. It was also suggested that CB_1 receptors influenced the release of glutamate within the amygdala, thereby inhibiting the processes leading to altered HPA

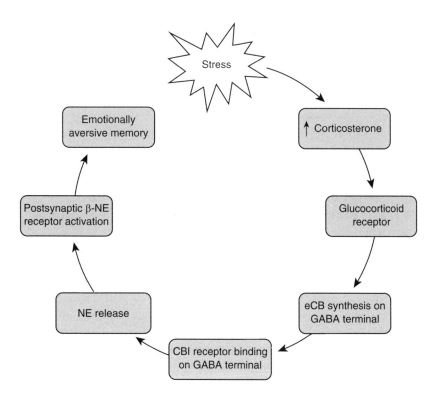

FIGURE 4.2 According to Hill and McEwen (2010), endocannibinoids within the basolateral portion of the amygdala cooperate with glucocorticoids in the establishment of aversive memories. Specifically, they suggest that in response to a stressor corticosterone binds to a particular type of glucocorticoid receptor that activates a pathway that stimulates endocannabinoid (eCB) synthesis. Once released, the endocannabinoids will bind to CB_1 receptors present on GADAergic terminals, thereby inhibiting GABA release. As GABA ordinarily inhibits norepinephrine (NE) release, shutting down (inhibiting) GABA release also allows (disinhibits) NE release and the ensuing activation of postsynaptic β-NE receptors, which augments the consolidation of emotionally-aversive memories.

activity. Conversely, the administration of corticosterone affects eCB signaling, indicating that these systems have reciprocal functions.

As glucocorticoids within the basolateral amygdala contribute to the consolidation of emotionally-arousing memories, and also affect eCB signaling, it is possible that the interaction between these factors might be fundamental for the emotional responses associated with a stressor, or the emotional memory related to stressors. In line with this view, infusions of a CB_1 receptor agonist soon after animals were trained to avoid a stressor enhanced the retention of this response, just as glucocorticoids administered soon after initial training had this effect (Hill et al., 2010). As depicted in Figure 4.2, a sequence of changes that involve corticosterone and endocannabinoid processes might contribute to the consolidation of emotionally-aversive memories.

As most of us know, cannabis can have effects on our appraisal of events, and thus quite apart from the other processes that have been delineated, some of the stress-altering effects of cannabis might simply come from the way individuals appraise (or misappraise) the events they encounter. In a recent theoretical report Hill and Tasker (2012) offered a somewhat related perspective regarding the role of cannabinoids, particularly within the amygdala and prefrontal cortex, in modulating stress responses. Basically, they suggested that endocannabinoids act as 'gatekeepers' of the stress response. The CB_1 receptor, which is presynaptic, is thought to suppress the release of other neurotransmitters that would ordinarily have an excitatory action, thereby assuring that the organism will remain calm (unstressed). When postsynaptic receptors are stimulated two endocannabinoids are produced, and these are released into the synaptic cleft (this is essentially a backward process as usually chemicals are released into the synaptic cleft from the presynaptic neuron). These substances, anandanine (AEA) and 2-arachodonoylglycerol (2-AG), inhibit the release of other transmitters and thus reduce HPA activity. Just as activation of the CB_1 receptor keeps us anxiety-free, disruption of the CB_1 receptor has the opposite effect so that our basal and stressor-induced HPA axis activity is elevated. What is particularly important to the proposed models is that AEA tonically (continuously) affects the CB1 receptor, whereas 2-AG appears phasically (in response to certain stimuli, and hence they might interact at some times, but not others).

It was also suggested that in response to stressors CRH is released at the amygdala, which ultimately reduces the signaling by AEA. This, in turn, increases amygdala neuronal activity and hence promotes anxiety and further HPA activity. Conversely, administration of corticosterone affects eCB signaling, indicating that these systems have reciprocal functions. In essence, like the feedback mechanism we talked about earlier regarding the HPA axis, there is another route by which this occurs, namely through an amygdala-hypothalamic process that involves the CRH-endocannabinoid (AEA)-glutamate-corticosterone-AEA process.

It is particularly significant to this model that just as variations of activity within the amygdala affect HPA functioning, elevations of corticosterone elicited by stressors will promote CRH release at the amygdala (ordinarily, within the HPA system CRH stimulates the subsequent release of corticosterone, but within the amygdala it's the other way around in that corticosterone stimulates CRH functioning). Thus, under chronic stress conditions corticosterone increases CRH signaling, resulting in sustained variations of AEA so that high levels of anxiety persist well after the stressor has terminated. In fact, it is possible that chronic stressors promote persistent reduction of AEA signaling that might lead to the sensitization of amygdala neuronal functioning, thereby engendering pathological anxiety.

Let's now turn to the other important component related to endocannabinoid functioning, 2-AG. As with AEA, stressors increase 2-AG, particularly within the prefrontal cortex and hippocampus, but this effect is slower to occur than that of AEA, and seems to be dependent on the corticosterone activation of glucocorticoid receptors. When 2-AG is activated it has the effect of turning off the HPA stress response, unlike the effect of AEA. This 2-AG response is only apparent during the stressor, and its role is believed to be one of keeping the stress response in check; it also likely contributes to the adaptation associated with chronic stressor exposure.

So, from the perspective of Hill and Tasker (2012), the endocannabinoid amygdala system, through AEA, is responsible for maintaining individuals in a relaxed state during non-stress periods, and is essential for the HPA stress response and anxiety that develops with an acute and chronic stress response. In essence, they suggested that AEA is the gatekeeper that allows us to remain mellow, but can also contribute to the development of anxiety. In response to stressors, the 2-AG system kicks in, but it does so a bit later, and serves to turn off the stress response. Essentially, from this perspective the stress response is not something that simply fades with time, but instead its decline entails an active 2-AG response. Hence, persistent anxiety might involve AEA functioning or the absence (or failure) of a 2-AG response.

GROWTH FACTORS

For the longest time, researchers focused on electrical activity and neurotransmission in relation to behavioral functioning. However, in the 1990s it became clear that growth factors existed that were fundamental to the well-being of neurons. In general, growth factors (neurotrophins), as the name implies, refer to endogenous substances that support the survival of cells, and promote cellular growth and proliferation, as well as cellular differentiation (the latter refers to the processes where cells become more specialized). For instance, growth hormone-releasing hormone (GHRH) and insulin-like growth factor 1 (IGF-1) decline with advancing age and might contribute to age-related neurodegenerative disorders, such as Alzheimer's disease. In fact, a study with a human form of GHRH (tesamorelin) revealed that among older patients cognitive functioning was improved over 10 to 20 weeks of this treatment (Baker et al., 2012).

There exists a lengthy list of growth factors, but in this section we'll focus on only a few of these neurotrophins that primarily influence brain functioning. Many of us who came into research in the 1970s and 80s were taught that whatever neurons you were endowed with at birth were what you were stuck with, and that invariably cell loss would occur as you aged. We now know that this isn't entirely correct. Although most of our neurons might have been formed prenatally, in some parts of the adult brain new neurons can be formed from neural stem cells (a process termed 'neurogenesis') and new synapses are formed on a regular basis. These processes are dependent on the presence of certain growth factors, which can be affected by stressors (another class of molecules, termed 'cytokines', are also classic growth factors, but as they are heavily involved in immune functioning, we'll cover these in Chapter 5, which deals with immunity).

The growth factors that have been of most interest in relation to stressors have been brain-derived neurotrophic factor (BDNF) and others that are structurally related to BDNF, such as nerve growth factor (NGF), neurotrophin-3 (NT-3) and neurotrophin-4 (NT-4), glial cell line-derived neurotrophic factor (GDNF), and basic fibroblast growth factor (bFGF or FGF-2). As some of these growth factors influence neurons and their neurotransmitters, including 5-HT, it was suggested that they might contribute to depression and anxiety. Furthermore, because of their fundamental role in neuronal development, plasticity, and in maintaining the well-being of individual cells, there has also been a prominent focus on the relation between growth factors and learning/memory, as well as those related to psychological disturbances such as addiction and dysfunctional eating (Evans et al., 2004; Turner et al., 2006).

BRAIN-DERIVED NEUROTROPHIC FACTOR (BDNF)

In rodents, acute stressors reduce BDNF in limbic brain regions that are associated with mood states (Duman & Monteggia, 2006), and are particularly notable within the hippocampus. These effects were not only provoked by neurogenic or psychogenic stressors, but could also be elicited by reminder stimuli that comprised cues that had previously been paired with a stressor (Rasmusson et al., 2002). Somewhat unexpectedly, however, the BDNF changes associated with controllable and uncontrollable stressors were unlike some of the neurotransmitter effects described earlier. For instance, both a controllable and an uncontrollable stressor reduced BDNF mRNA expression within the dentate gyrus, a region of the hippocampus in which new neuronal growth occurs, suggesting that the stressor itself, rather than its controllability, was responsible for the BDNF changes (Bland et al., 2007). In other respects, however, the BDNF changes elicited by stressors were in line with those of the transmitters described earlier. Specifically, following exposure to a chronic, uniform stressor (restraint) the magnitude of the BDNF reduction in the hippocampus was less pronounced than after acute treatment, but if the chronic stressor involved a series of different challenges administered over several weeks, the BDNF reductions persisted (Grønli et al., 2006). These data are in keeping with the view that an aversive event, if sufficiently powerful, leads to disturbed BDNF levels, and the same variables that favor the development of a depressive-like state (e.g., a chronic variable stressor) also promoted reduced BDNF.

Although both the prefrontal cortex and hippocampus are likely involved in depressive illness, there are data suggesting that stressors do not uniformly induce common effects on BDNF in these brain regions. Rather than reducing the levels of BDNF, stressor treatments were accompanied by increased BDNF mRNA expression in several aspects of the prefrontal cortex (the anterior cingulate, prelimbic and infralimbic). Likewise, intermittent social defeat among rats was accompanied by elevated BDNF in the amygdala two hours after the stressor, and 28 days later these effects were also apparent in the ventral tegmentum, a brain region that has been associated with reward processes (Fanous et al., 2010). To be sure, BDNF mRNA expression needs to be distinguished from changes in the BDNF protein level, as the increased mRNA expression might not be translated into increased levels of the BDNF protein itself. In fact, it is even possible that the increased mRNA expression, which might be indicative of BDNF production, results from a compensatory change stemming from diminished protein levels. However, there have been reports that BDNF protein (as opposed to the BDNF mRNA) was also elevated in the prefrontal cortex. It isn't certain what the significance of this elevation might be. However, the frontal cortex has many sub-regions, often with very distinct functions regarding cognitive processes, and so there has been increasing attention given to differentiating the changes of BDNF at discrete cortical sites.

In the anterior cingulate cortex, which is important for the processing of emotionally salient events as well as in decision making, the rise of BDNF mRNA expression was actually greater after escapable shock than after inescapable shock (Bland et al., 2007). It was also reported that the appearance of learned helplessness, which has been used to model depression, isn't always accompanied by BDNF reductions, nor are reduced levels of BDNF necessarily accompanied by behavioral disturbances. Findings such as these point to the importance of distinguishing between the hippocampus and aspects of the prefrontal cortex in determining stress responses, even though both these regions are considered stress sensitive and both have been implicated in stressor-related psychological disorders. For instance, reduced BDNF and neurogenesis in the hippocampus may be aligned with some attributes of reduced mood, but altered BDNF within aspects of the prefrontal cortex might serve to strengthen the cognitive and behavioral responses that support the negative thinking and poor appraisals that are apparent in depressive illness. Moreover, since the effects of an escapable stressor are *more* pronounced than those of an inescapable stressor (in opposition to the neurochemical changes that are often elicited by controllable vs uncontrollable stressors), it is possible that BDNF is involved in emitting coping responses and remembering which responses are effective in diminishing stressors.

As the stressors that elicit psychopathology are often of a chronic nature and the psychological illnesses are typically chronic as well, considerable attention has focused on the BDNF changes that accompany repeated and sustained stressor experiences. A detailed analysis of the effects of chronic stressors has revealed an interesting pattern of stressor-elicited BDNF changes within forebrain cortical regions. Specifically, in keeping with the view that stressors ought to promote adaptive changes, acute challenges increased BDNF within cortical brain regions, although this effect was relatively transient (Molteni et al., 2001). In contrast to the actions of acute stressors, BDNF reductions were apparent in the prefrontal cortex following a chronic stressor. Although there may be several processes by which this could occur, it was reported that a chronic social stressor (defeat) was accompanied by epigenetic changes of the BDNF promoter gene (suppression of the gene that codes for the production BDNF), which might have influenced the expression of this growth factor (Tsankova et al., 2006).

Clearly, stressor effects on BDNF in various brain regions aren't nearly as uniform as one would like in order to provide a simple explanation concerning the relation between stressors, BDNF, and the emergence of pathology. We can't be sure whether the diverse BDNF changes that have been reported are due to the passage of time following the stressor, the characteristics of the animals being tested (species, strain), or nature of the stressor (the type, severity, predictability). Although there are many reports of reduced BDNF under conditions that might result in depression, other factors likely contribute to the nature of the BDNF changes that are elicited by stressors and how these might be related to behavioral disturbances.

If one were to think of depression and anxiety simply reflecting a one-to-one correspondence with growth factors (i.e., increased depression is associated with reduced BDNF, and diminished depression with increased BDNF), then some of the data reported wouldn't be understandable. Neither depression nor anxiety disorders (e.g., PTSD) involve static processes, but instead the characteristics of the illnesses change over time (increase or decrease and involve the incorporation of new symptoms), and even the symptom severity may ebb and wane. Moreover, although depression is often considered a 'passive' state in some regards (e.g., increased sleep, increased lethargy and fatigue, avoidance of social encounters), it is a very active process in other respects. One would think, for instance, that the rumination that accompanies depression likely involves considerable neuronal activity, often building on itself, and this is especially persistent.

BDNF VARIATIONS ASSOCIATED WITH EARLY LIFE EXPERIENCES

As described earlier regarding the effects of early experiences on HPA hormonal processes, prenatal and early postnatal stressors (e.g., separation from the mom) have long-lasting effects on the cortical expression of BDNF (Fumagalli et al., 2004). These persistent effects may be related to epigenetic factors, as repeated periods of separation resulted in reduced mRNA expression of BDNF, accompanied by elevated methylation of genes on the BDNF promoter region that would have resulted in BDNF production being shut down (Roth et al., 2009). In effect, adverse early experiences might have long-lasting (perhaps permanent) suppressive effects on the regulatory genes that permit BDNF activation, and hence these early experiences may profoundly influence adult responses to stressors, and from there the development of pathology such as a major depressive illness.

Although early adversity can have negative consequences on our later neuronal function, it might also have the effect of augmenting our ability to respond to subsequent stressors, including through compensatory elevations in the release of neurotrophic factors. To the extent that early life stressors might shape our ability to contend with later challenges, exposure to moderate stressors that are not overly long lasting might alter the developmental trajectory so that we may be better equipped to deal with the various insults we might encounter later. Essentially, while strong early life stressors might impair our adaptive biological networks, hence rendering us more vulnerable to stressor-related pathology, mild or moderate stressors might prime our essential biological systems so that when we subsequently encounter stressors, these systems will be ready to respond appropriately.

BASIC FIBROBLAST GROWTH FACTOR (BFGF OR FGF-2)

Like BDNF, the basic fibroblast growth factor (FGF-2) system contributes to cell proliferation, differentiation, and survival involving neurons and glial cells. Of particular significance to behavior is that FGF-2 appears to be associated with hippocampal neurogenesis, and the expression of FGF-2 is influenced by stressful events (Molteni et al., 2001). In particular, in response to an acute stressor, the levels of FGF-2 were transiently reduced in some brain regions (prefrontal cortex), but increased in others (the entorhinal cortex, hippocampus, hypothalamus). As in the case of BDNF, a stressor experience could also increase FGF-2 mRNA expression in several parts of the prefrontal cortex and hippocampus, and these effects occurred more rapidly and were more pronounced following an escapable stressor than after an inescapable stressor (Bland et al., 2007). As a result, having the ability to control (cope with) a stressor, rather than simply experience a stressor, may be more pertinent in altering FGF production. Furthermore, it was observed that chronic stressor exposure led to more pronounced FGF-2 changes than did those elicited by acute stressors, at least within the entorhinal and prefrontal cortex. In effect, the increase of this growth factor might reflect an adaptive change to minimize the potential negative effects of stressors, or it could reflect the activation of behavioral processes that are essential to engage in effective behavioral coping responses.

Just as the stressors that occur during early life or the prenatal period markedly influence other processes, those experienced during late gestation may also influence adult hippocampal FGF-2. Specifically, when rats were stressed late in pregnancy, their offspring exhibited reduced levels of FGF-2 in adulthood, and the adult behavioral responses to a stressor were disturbed. Essentially, stressors in a pregnant dam had the effect of altering the trajectory of the developmental changes of FGF-2 in the offspring, thereby potentially rendering them less prepared to deal with stressors during adulthood (Fumagalli et al., 2005). Conversely, treatments that alleviate depression increased FGF-2 in cortical and hippocampal sites. This outcome was observed with regard to chronic antidepressant or anxiolytic medications, as well as chronic (noninjurious) electroconvulsive shock. As might be expected if FGF-2 plays a role in promoting depressive-like states, FGF-2 administered directly into the brain of rodents enhanced behavioral performance in tests that modelled depression in humans.

GLIAL CELL LINE-DERIVED NEUROTROPHIC FACTOR (GDNF)

Yet another neurotrophic factor, GDNF, was implicated in stressor-elicited depressive features, although there has been far less research conducted concerning the contribution of GDNF to stressor-related behavioral outcomes. Nevertheless, reduced circulating GDNF levels were associated with depressive illness, and among drug treatment-resistant patients who showed a positive response to electroconvulsive therapy, GDNF levels were found to increase. Likewise, using a chronic stress model of depression in rats, hippocampal GDNF was reduced in parallel with several behavioral impairments, and treatment with an antidepressant reversed these effects. It also seemed that the influence of stressors and GDNF on depressive-like states varied with genetic factors. Using the stress reactive BALB/c and the resilient C57BL/6 strains of mice, for instance, it was shown that these strains behaved differently in response to chronic stressors, and this was matched by the differential epigenetic status of the GDNF gene in the ventral striatum. In essence, epigenetic modifications of

GDNF might influence the behavioral responses that follow chronic stressor treatments (Uchida et al., 2011).

SENSITIZED NEURONAL RESPONSES

In movies and novels, the psychological effects of stressors are portrayed as being profound and the repercussions of stressors may last for many years. Childhood trauma can have especially persistent effects even if we don't remember having been traumatized. So how can traumatic events have such effects, especially as some of these could have even occurred before an individual has the ability to remember events as a cohesive and understandable narrative (i.e., before the individual had acquired language) as opposed to one that existed simply in symbolic form? The Freudians would have told us that these memories were buried as unconscious thoughts that fought to emerge in some manner. Maybe so, but there are other explanations that are more parsimonious or at least testable.

THE PAST INFLUENCES THE FUTURE

There is a very interesting aspect about stressors that needs to be considered from both a psychological as well as a neuronal perspective. As we've already seen, stressful events can have pronounced effects on multiple hormonal and neurotransmitter systems as well as growth factors. Many of these biological changes are relatively transient, typically being measured in minutes or hours, although there are instances in which the effects can be lasting. Thus from a biological perspective we need to ask how is it that events that happened years earlier, including during infancy, might actually come to affect our later vulnerability to psychopathology?

Some years ago, we demonstrated that once neuronal activity had returned to normal, this didn't mean that the reactivity of neuronal systems had also returned to their original state. These neurons might have become 'sensitized', so that if a stressor was encountered at some later time they might be more readily activated, and the brain neurotransmitter changes might be greater and more readily provoked (Anisman et al., 2003). Conversely, in some instances a stressful experience may have the opposite effect, diminishing the response to a subsequent stressor (desensitization). It seems that: (a) a given set of stressor conditions may differentially influence various systems, provoking sensitized responses within one system, but desensitized responses in other systems; (b) the nature of the changes observed may be brain region-specific; and (c) the expression of the sensitization may vary over time following the initial stressor experience. Hence, even though the emotional and biological effects of a relatively severe stressor may have subsided with the passage of time, the recurrence of the stressor (or even reminders of the event) may have pronounced repercussions on some neurotransmitters and thus on the later emergence of pathology. So, with apologies to Yogi Berra (and to Lenny Kravitz, if you're too young to remember Yogi), it ain't over *even* when it's over.

CROSS-SENSITIZATION: DRUGS AND STRESS ARE A BAD MIX

Exaggerated changes in NE, DA, and 5-HT neuronal functioning have been demonstrated upon stressor (or cue) reexposure among animals that had initially been exposed to either acute or chronic stressors. Such effects are also apparent when the second exposure involves a different type of insult (cross-sensitization), and is even evident in response to some pharmacological treatments (e.g., amphetamine, cocaine) that act on these same neurotransmitter systems (Anisman et al., 2003). The implications of this cross-sensitization are fairly broad. Among other things, these mean that a stressor experience might not only influence responses when this or similar insults are later encountered, but also that it may have ramifications regarding the impact of virtually any life stressor that might be experienced subsequently. Furthermore, we can also see that the way certain drug treatments affect us might be altered by our previous stressor experiences, leading to the possibility of some particularly adverse effects occurring. Incidentally, given that stressors influence the response to later amphetamine and cocaine treatment, is it also the case that these drugs influence responses to stressors that might subsequently be encountered? You bet. There have been several reports showing this with respect to both behavioral changes and neurochemical functioning. Using these substances, even once, may alter neuronal processes so that later stressor responses are exaggerated and might thus favor pathology emerging (Barr et al., 2002).

The sensitization associated with stressor experiences is not restricted to biogenic amines. As we discussed earlier, there is ample reason to believe that early life experiences influence adult BDNF responses upon further stressor experiences as well as in response to drugs such as cocaine. In this regard, BDNF may be instrumental in modifying (or controlling) the responsivity of neurons to particular transmitters, such as DA, and might thus influence pathologies that have been associated with this transmitter, including drug addiction, schizophrenia, depression, and Parkinson's disease (Guillin et al., 2001). There is similarly impressive evidence indicating that FGF-2 may be fundamental for the neuronal plasticity associated with the protracted effects elicited by stressors and by catecholamine stimulants, and it is thought that this growth factor might be particularly crucial for the reinstatement of a drug addiction (by drug-related cues) among those who had ceased their drug intake (e.g., Flores & Stewart, 2000).

The development of sensitized responses also seems to be relevant to the responses that occur following exposure to repeated stressors. You will recall that when animals are exposed to a series of stressors that involve the same insult, an adaptation may develop so that monoamine utilization becomes less pronounced. However, if chronically stressed animals are later exposed to a novel stressor (termed a 'heterotypic' stressor), then the diminished stress response is not seen and instead exaggerated monoamine changes may be elicited. As depicted in Figure 4.3, it is almost as if a chronic treatment provokes two distinct responses that are antagonistic to one another. Specifically, in response to a chronic stressor the processes that give rise to the release of the transmitter become increasingly more pronounced (essentially a sensitization response), but at the same time other antagonistic (or countervailing) processes may be set in motion, which might be tied to the contextual cues associated

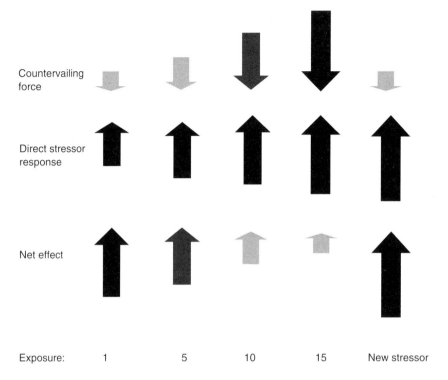

FIGURE 4.3 Hypothetical responses to repeated exposure to the same stressor over successive days, after which a novel stressor is introduced. On successive days the direct stressor actions become progressively stronger owing to a sensitization of the processes that promote these effects, as do the countervailing responses, leading to a diminished net response. However, when a new stressor is encountered the direct, sensitized responses are instigated, but the countervailing actions, which are determined through their association with the stress cues (likely through classical conditioning processes), are limited, resulting in an exaggerated response.

with the initial stressor, making it appear 'as if' an adaptation had developed (i.e., counter-conditioning occurs to diminish the stress response). As a result, when a new stressor is encountered, the sensitized processes burst into action (a cross-sensitization) so that the neurochemical changes are elevated. However, as the stressor is a new one, the compensatory countervailing response typically triggered by cues associated with the earlier stressor no longer occurs, thereby allowing the full measure of the sensitization to become evident. This view isn't all that novel, as similar explanations, based on 'opponent process theory', have been used to describe several stress-related emotional responses, and a similar conditioning model was proposed to explain processes related to drug addiction and overdose (Siegel, 1999; see Chapter 10).

It is of clinical and therapeutic interest that although anxiolytics (drugs that act to reduce anxiety), such as diazepam, limit the NE and DA release elicited by acute stressors, this was not apparent in rats that had been chronically stressed previously. It seems that once the neurochemical changes are pronounced, such as those associated with stressor reexposure, these are less well managed by anxiolytics. In effect, chronic, unpredictable stressors might not only promote greater vulnerability to psychological problems, they might also instigate treatment resistance. It likewise seems that once the neuronal systems have become sensitized so that further stressors provoke greater responses, drug treatments are less effective in antagonizing these outcomes.

In summary, although stressful events may have short-lasting neurochemical effects, these experiences may have long-lasting repercussions. If neuronal systems can be programmed by stressful events, then these experiences could potentially (and likely do) influence our responses to later adverse experiences. We needn't even remember having had these experiences, such as those that occurred when we were infants, but they may nevertheless shape how we subsequently behave. In a sense, our biological systems are preprogrammed to be flexible and able to be molded by experiences. In an ideal world these sensitized responses might help us deal very quickly and efficiently with later stressor encounters. However, depending on the severity of the initial challenge or vulnerability factors that influence our response to this challenge, aversive events might instigate excessive neuronal sensitivity or reactivity to further challenges, thereby favoring the development of certain pathologies.

CONCLUSION

Stressful events clearly induce multiple neurochemical changes, many of which occur across several brain regions. Although activation of these neurochemical processes might have adaptive value, the capacity for these variations to be sustained may be limited, and when biological systems are overworked (which can happen after severe acute stressors as well as after chronic stressors), behavioral and physical disturbances might ensue. Furthermore, if sufficiently intense, stressful events can alter the characteristics of neurons so that later stressor experiences are more likely to engender neurochemical changes, increasing the likelihood of an overload and hence the development of pathological outcomes.

In earlier chapters the point was made that a vulnerability to pathology could come about as a result of dysfunction in any of numerous systems aggravated by stressors. In this chapter we saw that many neurotransmitter systems and growth factors could similarly be affected by stressors, especially when these were unremitting, uncontrollable, and unpredictable. As a result, several questions come to mind when considering the association between stressor-related biological changes and threats to mental or physical health. Specifically, which of the many changes elicited by stressors are helpful to us, acting to attenuate the psychological or physiological disturbances that might otherwise occur? Which changes are involved in the provocation of stressors' damaging effects? And finally, which biological changes are simply bystanders that don't have a relevant function either way? We covered several neurotransmitters that can serve in an adaptive capacity, and some conditions were pointed out where stressful events could lead to pathological outcomes.

As complicated as you might think things might be based on the small amount we've covered, consider that there are very many neurotransmitters that could be affected by stressors that we haven't touched upon. Currently, more than 50 peptides have been identified, many of which can act as neurotransmitters (e.g., neuropeptides such as β-endorphin, dynorphin, enkephalin), and that are certainly influenced by stressful events. In the same way, there are other monoamine neurotransmitters that can be affected by stressors which we haven't dealt with (histamine, melatonin, as well as octapamine and tyramine). Gaseous substances, such as nitric oxide, can also act like neurotransmitters, and these substances can likewise be affected by stressors. Clearly, all of these transmitters can't be covered in a broad overview like the one being presented in this book, and hence only those that seemed particularly germane have been discussed. However, as we learn more about the effects of stressors on varied processes, it won't be surprising to find that these also contribute to pathological outcomes in response to stressful experiences.

A second aspect of the stress response that needs to be considered is that since many of the central actions of stressors can have effects on peripheral processes, it needs to be asked whether any of these, as well as hormonal variations, can serve as the 'biomarkers' of illness. That is, can they tell us about pathological outcomes that are imminent or can they be useful in predicting which treatments might be best suited for an existent pathology? A stressor may give rise to the peripheral release of factors such as cortisol, epinephrine, norepinephrine, and cytokines (immune messengers), and to this we can add several brain neurotransmitter responses. Other biological changes may also occur, possibly reflecting compensatory effects comprising the under- or over-production of primary neurotransmitter and endocrine changes. Among others, these include variations in insulin, glucose, total cholesterol, high density lipoprotein cholesterol, and triglycerides, as well as immune (cytokine) markers and acute phase protein (C-reactive protein) that might contribute to a variety of pathological conditions. Given that these factors are presumed to change with stressor experiences, we could reason that it might be possible to use the changes of neuroendocrine, immune, metabolic, and cardiovascular system functioning as an index of allostatic load. Essentially, these might be biomarkers for the stress systems becoming overly taxed and also indicative of which systems would be apt to fail and hence which types of pathology might ensue. It's still a bit too early to determine how these multiple biological substrates will be used. For instance, do they have additive predictive power, or are some factors redundant with one another so that we don't need all of them to make a prognosis? Likewise, are some more pertinent to particular pathologies and not others? Whatever the case, it seems that the search for stress-related biomarkers is a reasonable approach to determine the predictors of impending illness and the treatments that might be most efficacious.

SUMMARY

- Stressful events give rise to multiple neurochemical and growth factor changes. These outcomes are thought to reflect the adaptive responses necessary to meet the demands being placed on the organism.
- The effectiveness of neurotransmitter and growth factor changes in dealing with stressors is limited, and their positive effects can be diminished with severe, unpredictable challenges, and possibly

influenced by previous stressful experiences, genetic variables, and numerous other features of the stressor as well as individual difference characteristics.

- With repeated stressor exposure compensatory changes may occur to assure adequate neurotransmitter functioning. However, these come with a cost as excessive neuronal activation may result in systems becoming overloaded and thus increase our vulnerability to pathology.
- Multiple neurochemical interactions occur, and it similarly appears that growth factors can affect neurotransmitter functioning, and vice versa. These changes may govern the effects of stressors on the emergence and recurrence of behavioral disturbances.

5 THE IMMUNOLOGICAL EFFECTS OF STRESSORS

SCIENCE, NON-SCIENCE, AND NONSENSE

There's something to be said about folk-wisdom or what some prefer to call, dismissively, old wives' tales or grandmother tales. These can seem quaint, and typically aren't considered seriously. There are also all sorts of superstitious behaviors that seem to be inherited across generations (don't hit the ball on the label of the bat; don't kick the football on the laces; squashing a spider will cause it to rain; you only use 10% of your brain).

It's also widely thought that if you're sufficiently stressed, you'll end up with any one of several immunologically-based illnesses. Over the years there have been repeated suggestions that stress is associated with a vulnerability to the common cold, or fatigue-related syndromes. In fact, when your doctor can't figure out what's causing your ailment, s/he might resort to suggesting that stress might be the causative agent for what's been bothering you. Stress is also thought to make you old before your years (and since cancer is often a disease of aging, the link between stress and cancer, according to my mom, is undeniable!). There is certainly a lot of folk wisdom that fits into the baloney category, but that doesn't mean all of it is delicatessen grade.

Beyond the hormonal and neurotransmitter processes discussed in Chapters 3 and 4, the immune system is essential for our survival. Our immune system serves to fend off the challenges that we encounter every day in the form of bacteria, virsuses, and other microscopic creatures that seem to be determined to cause us harm. In this chapter you'll hopefully get to understand:

- the function of the immune system and the various different cell types and processes that make up this system;
- how the hormonal systems described in Chapter 3 interact with the immune system;

- the effects of stressors on immune functioning and some of the moderating variables, particularly those discussed in Chapters 1 and 2 that affect immunocompetence;
- that immune cells communicate with one another through chemicals referred to as cytokines;
- that cytokines can gain entry to the brain and are also manufactured within cells located within the brain, and could potentially play a causal role in promoting a variety of psychopathologies, including mood disturbances and schizophrenia as well as neurodegenerative illnesses.

WHAT THE IMMUNE SYSTEM IS SUPPOSED TO DO

Most people know something about the functions of the immune system, including that it's supposed to protect us from all manner of foreign microscopic invaders. Knowing this, you might wonder why we ever get ill. Is the system not very effective? Does it fail us only on some unique occasions? Are some of us more vulnerable to illness than others? Are there factors that cause our immune systems to malfunction, thereby leaving us vulnerable to the ravages of all sorts of microbes that are hanging around?

At some level most individuals also seem to know that stressful events increase vulnerability to illnesses involving the immune system. This notion is intuitively appealing, and we're likely to accept it even in the absence of hard data. Indeed, you might have noticed that stressful events sometimes precede becoming ill. Of course, if you've made this observation it doesn't qualify as a valid scientific inquiry, nor does it suggest causality, and yet in controlled studies it was found that among participants exposed to a respiratory virus, the greater the life stressors individuals had experienced in the recent past, the more likely it was that they would develop respiratory symptoms and clinical colds. Conversely, positive emotions were associated with greater resistance to colds, and coping related to social support limited the adverse effects of stressors on immune functioning (Cohen et al., 2001).

In line with the findings that stressful events are associated with illness, it seems that stressors, or the behaviors elicited by stressors, influence immune functioning. This begs the question as to whether the data that have been gathered can be used to aid clinical practice. Unfortunately, there are many variables that influence the nature of the immune system changes elicited by stressors, and coming up with appropriate answers isn't simple. Nevertheless, it has become ever-more certain that psychological events influence immune functioning, and conversely, this circuitry has huge implications for the development of psychopathological conditions and their treatment (Haroon et al., 2012).

Most psychology and neuroscience students will have covered material related to hormones and neurotransmitters, and so in Chapters 3 and 4 some short-cuts were taken in describing these systems. It's less likely that these students will have dealt with the immune system in much detail. Thus, before delving into immune-stress relations, a brief primer concerning the immune system is provided, which will then be followed by an overview of how stressors influence the immune system. If you are interested, many more detailed treatments of the immune system can be consulted (Janeway & Travers, 2001).

THE IMMUNE SYSTEM (A VERY BRIEF PRIMER)

Most analogies of the immune system rely on the simple perspective that the components of this system comprise an army whose function is to beat the enemy forces. This army, like any other army, has lots of needs and functions. First, an essential component of any army is to recognize the enemy forces, since your immune system doesn't want the death of its own cells by 'friendly fire' (what an oxymoron!), nor is it desirable to incur 'collateral damage'. Second, an effective communication system needs to be present so that different functions can be carried out by your forces in synchrony and at the right time. Third, there need to be generals who direct troops, and there need to be troops who engage the enemy at the front line, those that make up the heavy artillery units, those units that search and destroy (the latter is referred to as 'cell trafficking' in the immune system), and those that are in hiding, waiting to ambush the enemy. Fourth, there needs to be a way of getting new recruits into the battle ('the surge', to use a recently developed term). Fifth, there needs to be a mechanism by which soldiers are called off, especially if they become too voracious in their appetite for killing, eventually turning on their own. Finally, the soldiers need to have a memory of the enemy and be able to mount a fast and strong response should that enemy decide at some future date to re-engage.

COMPONENTS OF THE IMMUNE SYSTEM

The primary function of the immune system is to monitor the organism's internal environment for indications of tissue damage and the presence of bacteria and viruses (termed 'microbial infection'). To a very great extent this involves knowing what the 'self' comprises, and then anything that isn't 'self' can be treated as foreign. Much of this information is established in the developing fetus. During that time the immune cells are 'learning' what's you and what's not. We term this aspect of the immune system 'innate immunity'. Once you're a real, living, sentient being, your immune cells will acquire still further information (through experiences) about what's what, which is referred to as 'adaptive' or 'acquired' immunity.

Ordinarily, once your immune cells are exposed to an antigen (i.e., foreign particles or molecules from damaged tissues), an exquisitely orchestrated immune response occurs. To a considerable extent, this is achieved by lymphocytes, a type of white blood cell, that circulate throughout the body and provide immunological protection against microbial antigens (essentially engaging in surveillance and search-and-destroy missions).

MACROPHAGES AND MICROGLIA

Macrophages are among the key players involved during the early stages of an immune response being mounted. These cells have several functions, including the breakdown of foreign cells (e.g., bacteria) and necrotic (dead) tissue through a process referred to as *phagocytosis*. In addition, macrophages are essential in the presentation of foreign particles (antigens) to other immune cells (lymphocytes), which then destroy these foreign particles. In particular, macrophages capture foreign particles, and after processing them (i.e., digesting and breaking them down), they present aspects of this particle to certain types of T cells that then make decisions about whether these cells belong to the individual (self) or are actually foreign.

Besides macrophages, there are other cells that act as antigen presenting cells (APCs). These include monocytes, although it might be noted that macrophages are actually monocytes in a mature, more differentiated state. Another type of APC that has been receiving increased attention is the dendritic cell, and as we'll see, there are cells present in the brain, namely microglial cells, that operate in a similar capacity. These cells had, for a long time, been given limited attention, but in recent years their multiple functions have become much more evident.

ANTIGEN PRESENTING CELLS

In 1973 Ralph Steinman and Zanvil Cohn published a paper describing dendritic cells which turned out to be a type of antigen presenting cell (APC). It was a while before immunologists started paying attention to the importance of this cell type (in fact, this didn't occur until the 1990s), and in 2011 Ralph Steinman won the Nobel Prize for Physiology or Medicine for his discovery. Although the Nobel Prize isn't given posthumously (Cohn died in 1993), an exception was made in the case of Steinman, who died three days before the announcement of the prize. The committee members were unaware of his death, and once announced, retracting the prize would have been a pretty miserable thing to do.

Microglia and other cells of this class (astrocytes, oligodendrocytes) appear in the brain in enormous numbers, but virtually all of our attention was focused on neurons, and these glial cells were described simply as cells that surrounded neurons to keep them in place and to insulate neurons from one another, to provide neurons with food supplies, and to remove garbage. Given their numbers and even these basic functions, why didn't it occur to us that we should be asking fundamental questions about whether they do anything else, and what causes them to become active or quiescent? I think that part of our shortsightedness was based on our social biases – neurons are the intelligentsia of the brain, and glial cells are 'the help'. As we'll see shortly, microglia might have a lot to do with the development of psychological pathology.

LYMPHOCYTES: T AND B CELLS

The primary lymphoid organs, namely, the thymus and bone marrow, are the sites for the generation of lymphocytes that comprise T and B cells, respectively, that have the capability of differentiating between self and non-self tissue. In addition to the primary lymphoid organs, there are *secondary* lymphoid organs, such as the lymph nodes as well as the spleen and lungs, where immune responses can be amplified (as lymphocytes divide and multiply during infection, this is often reflected by a swelling of the lymph nodes).

Once the macrophage has captured a foreign particle it presents it to lymphocytes, thereby promoting their activation, ultimately leading to cytotoxicity (the destruction of infected cells). As we've already seen, there are two main types of lymphocytes: B lymphocytes whose primary function is antibody production (a substance used to recognize and indirectly destroy foreign matter), and T lymphocytes that have regulatory and cytotoxic functions. The responses of T cells are often referred to as *cellular* immune responses, whereas those of B cells are termed *humoral* immune responses. The latter term has been used because the main function of B lymphocytes is the production of antibodies or immunoglobulin molecules (abbreviated as Ig) within bodily fluids (humors refers to body fluid), such as blood, that serve to mark invaders for destruction.

It might sound as if the function of B and T cells is redundant, but this isn't at all the case. Specifically, B cells are responsible for neutralizing foreign products and do so by attacking them when they're travelling within our body. T cells work in a different way. Ordinarily, a virus gets into a cell and then into the nucleus where it uses the cell's own DNA machinery to replicate itself (as these crafty little devils don't have their own capacity to multiply, they hijack host cells to do their dirty work). T cells have evolved to attack your own cells that have been infected by a virus, and to do so directly. Thus, in killing an infected cell, the T cell is destroying whole factories that would otherwise be making the virus.

The T cells fall into several classes, and we can tell them apart by their name tags. In this case the name tags are made up of molecules present on the cell surface that can be identified (e.g., you'll see terms such as CD4 and CD8, as well as CD16 and CD56, among others, that essentially let you know the T-cell type). One type of T cell, referred to as a cytotoxic T cell, can directly lyse virally infected cells (lysis occurs when the T cell attaches is itself to the target and ruptures the cellular membrane, thereby causing the viral contents to be destroyed), bacteria, and tumor cells. A second type of T cell is the T helper (Th) cell that takes its name from the fact that they help B cells produce antibodies against antigenic stimuli. Th cells don't kill infected cells as cytotoxic T cells do, nor do they remove debris like macrophages do. Instead, they act like information couriers that direct and stimulate the actions of other cells. In this regard, they recognize something as being foreign and then promote the multiplication of cytotoxic T cells to attack the enemy. Conversely, they can also cause a down-regulation of immune activity, which is an essential self-regulatory feature to limit the risk of autoimmunity (i.e., this refers to a variety of diseases in which the immune system turns against the self, thus provoking an autoimmune disorder). Those Th cells that are associated with cellular immune responses that activate cytotoxic lymphocytes and natural killer (NK) cells are referred to as Th_1 cells, whereas Th_2 cells are associated with the suppression of certain immune responses and also in the regulation of antibody functioning. Of particular relevance is that the Th_1 cells release chemical substances that promote inflammatory responses, whereas the Th_2 cells release chemicals that have anti-inflammatory actions (i.e., they act against (inhibit) the proinflammatory responses) (Reiche et al., 2004).

For the fairly complex set of events involved in an immune response being mounted, as described in Figure 5.1, there necessarily must be a fair bit of cross talk between different types of cells. Messages are sent from one immune cell to another through a chemical process that, in some respects, is reminiscent of how neurons in the brain communicate with

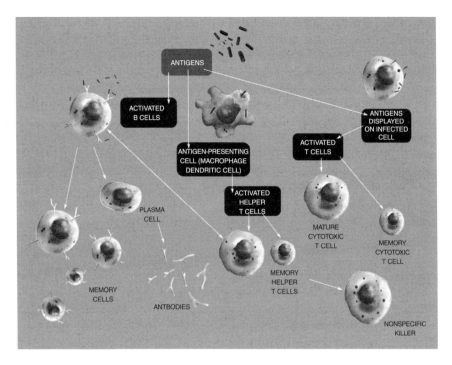

FIGURE 5.1 Upon exposure to an antigen, macrophages engulf the foreign particle and then display aspects of it to T and B cells that may either be naïve or have a memory of the foreign substance. They then go about mounting a strong immune response to eliminate the foreign matter. The speed of the response and its strength is superior if immune cells had previously encountered this antigen (modified from J.W. Bastien (http://www.uta.edu/chagas/html/biolImS1. html).

(Illustration modified by Lucas J. Wareing)

one another. This occurs through the secretion of signaling molecules referred to as cytokines. These cytokines are synthesized and released by various immune cells (macrophages and lymphocytes in the periphery, and by astrocytes and microglia present in the brain). Within the periphery these cytokines act as signals for growth and the differentiation of lympho-cytes, and act in a paracrine or autocrine fashion (stimulation of cells that are close or self-regulation, respectively). There are certain cytokines, named interleukin (IL)-1β, IL-6, tumor necrosis factor-α (TNF-α), and interferons (IFN), that are classified as pro-inflammatory (largely produced by Th$_1$ cells) as they encourage inflammation. Others, such as IL-4 and IL-10 that are produced by Th$_2$ cells, act against the pro-inflammatory cytokines and hence are referred to as anti-inflammatory cytokines. Ideally, the pro- and anti-inflammatory cytokines are 'in balance' with one another. In response to challenges the pro-inflammatory cytokines go into action, and when the job is done the anti-inflammatory cytokines kick in to get things stopped. There are many other cytokines, some of which we'll be dealing with in passing, but these players will be introduced as we get to them.

NATURAL KILLER CELLS

Another immune cell that is important for our protection is the Natural Killer (NK) cell. This cytotoxic lymphocyte is a component of the innate immune system, playing a prominent role early in an immune reaction. The NK cells have the innate ability to recognize cancer cells or those that are infected with a virus, and so travel about examining cells for appropriate markers. From their name, NK cells sound as if they're the tough guys of the immune world. In fact, they're not all that tough, and serve primarily to contain an invading enemy, giving the adaptive immune system the opportunity to mount a strong cytotoxic T cell response to deal with the virus. In effect, NK cells execute a holding action, allowing the big guns to multiply, and then they bring those forces to the battle.

SCARY CELLS

Once an NK cell finds a cell that is suspected of being a tumor cell or one that contains a virus, it deploys a tentacle to attach itself to the cell thought to be infected. It then searches, using another tentacle, for a marker or switch that will inform it whether that the cell is, in fact, not dangerous, whereupon the NK cell will back off and go on its way. However, if this marker is not found, the NK cell attacks the target cell, penetrating its outer shell and injecting chemicals (e.g., *perforin* and *granzyme*) into the target cell, causing its death and disintegration, along with the virus that might reside inside the cell. Scenes such as this play out again and again, day after day, and represent part of the surveillance system that protects us from tumors and some viruses, but under certain conditions it may fail, and the result can be disastrous.

Given the behavior of NK cells and what they look like, it seems as if they were scripted by some Hollywood B-movie director of science fiction horror films. Maybe some of these folks are reading journal articles to help them come up with nifty ideas for films.

ANTIBODIES AND ANTIGENS

At the ouset of this chapter, a primary function of certain immune cells was said to be that of learning about the enemy as there is a possibility that this force will return at a later date, and we would be well served if our immune cells recognized the enemy as soon as they returned. In fact, 'immunological memory' (also referred to as acquired characteristics) is the hallmark of some immune cells, so that a rapid and robust response is mounted to an antigen that the immune system had previously encountered.

Ordinarily, B cells are capable of producing antibodies that are fundamental in this recognition process. There are five classes (isotypes) of antibody (or immunoglobulin; Ig) molecules: IgA, IgD, IgE, IgM, and IgG. Following their activation, B cells differentiate into either (1) antibody-producing cells (also referred to as plasma cells) that secrete soluble antibody, or (2) memory cells that can survive in the body for years and whose function is that of remembering an antigen and responding quickly should that antigen be encountered again. As depicted in Figure 5.2, the general make-up of all antibodies is very similar, comprising a

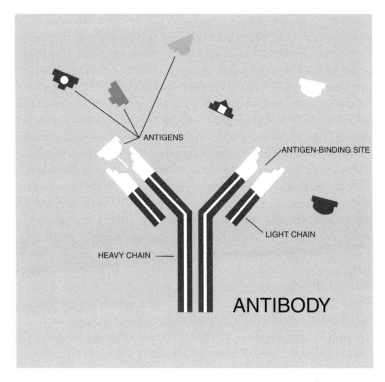

FIGURE 5.2   Antigens have external characteristics which can bind with the end parts of an antibody, provided that the antigen binding site is compatible with the antigenic features. The five types of immunoglobulins appear during different periods of infection and are not equally distributed in different parts of an individual.

IgA is present in mucosal areas, such as the respiratory tract, urogenital tract and the gut, as well as in saliva and tears, and thus might be the first to encounter foreign substances that enter the body.

IgE binds to antigens that provoke parasatic infections, but in some individuals it binds to environmental substances that can elicit allergies (allergens). When this occurs, histamine is released from mast cells and basophils, resulting in the common symptoms of allergies.

IgD appears on the surface of naïve B cells (i.e., those that have not previously been stimulated), serving as receptors for antigens. Ig activates aspects of the immune system, including mast cells and basophils that are involved in actions that enhance immune functioning.

IgG contributes to antibody-based immunity against previously encountered invading pathogens. As IgG is capable of passing into the placenta it can also provide passive immunity to the developing fetus.

IgM is involved in eliminating pathogens upon initial encounters with them. This antibody is activated during the early phase of a B cell mediated response, acting as the first line of defense.

(Illustration created by Lucas J. Wareing)

Y-shaped structure composed of two light and two heavy polypeptide chains. The ends of the two arms of the Y of this protein are variable, meaning that their composition can differ from other antibodies. This part of an antibody is essential for recognizing a foreign particle. As there are millions of these antibodies, each with slightly different tip or end structures (referred to as antigen binding sites), they are capable of recognizing a very wide range of foreign particles (antigens). These recognition sites don't need to identify the entire antigen, they only need to see a part of the whole in order to promote an immune response (you don't need to see every element of your friends to recognize them, just seeing their face is enough). Once an antigen is recognized as being foreign it is 'tagged' so as to signal its removal by other immune cells. As well, antibodies can neutralize targets directly by binding to a part of a pathogen and activating the 'complement pathway' (several small proteins present in the blood), which contributes to the formation of a complex that helps antibodies kill the pathogen. As described in Figure 5.2, there are five classes of antibodies that serve somewhat different functions and are concentrated at differents points in our bodies.

During the primary immune response, which occurs the first time a particular antigen is met, most classes of antibody molecules are produced, with the production of IgM predominating. Having been exposed to the antigen, a memory for the antigen is established so that when these memory B cells subsequently encounter the antigen again (or something that looks sufficiently similar to it), a rapid and strong immune response occurs during which the IgG isotype predominates. Because of the magnitude and speed of the sensitized (secondary) immune response being mounted, the illness is not likely to reappear. Thus, for instance, when exposed to the chicken pox virus for the first time, we might end up with a bunch of sores and feel poorly for days. However, when years later we again encounter this virus, the immune system mounts a strong secondary response and the virus is destroyed before it has the opportunity to make us ill. In the case of some illnesses, such as chicken pox, a related illness, shingles (also known as Herpes Zoster, which is very different from Herpes Simplex that some readers might be more familiar with), can occur because the virus was not fully eliminated from the body, hiding in nerve cells or other places, and may re-emerge years later to create very considerable discomfort. Most viruses don't act in this way, and once we've seen an end to their initial assault, we won't likely be *plagued* by them again.

INTERPLANETARY VIRUSES?

Well before the discipline of immunology came about, or even before much was understood about viruses and bacteria, at a time when blood-letting and leeches were used as cures, there was clearly a rudimentary understanding of some immunological concepts. For instance, the history of diseases is replete with examples where affected individuals were isolated (and even shipped off to islands) for fear of the illness being spread (think of the poor lepers). During times when the Black Death rampaged through Europe, ships that had reached port on the Italian shore were kept out at sea for a period of time to make sure that the silent killer wasn't brought on to shore, thus infecting the populace. Typically, ships were kept away for a period of 40 days, referred to as 'quarantena', and it is from this that we've got our word 'quarantine'. The duration of this quarantine ought to vary with the disease being considered as infectious periods can vary depending on the virus.

When astronauts from some of the Apollo missions returned to earth, they were quarantined for a period to prevent the transmission of any infection they might have picked up. I wonder how administrators knew how long the quarantine should last. Would a moon virus, if there were such a thing, follow the same rules as an earth virus?

CHANGES IN IMMUNE COMPETENCE

Obviously, if we're going to assess the effects of stressors (or any other treatment) on the capability of the immune system, we need appropriate markers of competence and ways to measure these. Analyses of various treatments on immune functioning can be conducted through several *in vitro* procedures (in parts of an organism, or in a test tube or petri dish) and *in vivo* (in the living organism) that are essential to determine the specific nature of the effects of treatments. Specifically, is a problem present owing to the altered killing ability of immune cells? Are immune cells not proliferating quickly enough to deal with an intruder? Is there a failure to recognize the intruder? Analyses of immune functioning can include counting the number of specific types of immune cells (per a fixed volume of blood), but this doesn't provide a *functional* index of immune competence (i.e., the extent that immune cells doing what they were programmed to do, namely multiply, search out and indentify invaders, and then kill them).

It is necessary to determine, among other things, whether a treatment such as a stressor influences 'cell trafficking pattern'. For example, where are lymphocytes actually residing? Are they in circulation or are they hanging out at secondary immune organs, such as the spleen? In addition, it is essential to determine the rate of T or B cell proliferation (i.e., their multiplication in blood or in secondary immune organs, such as the spleen) in response to specific stimulants (called 'mitogens'), as well as the antibody responses evident upon exposure to foreign substances (antigenic stimuli), or the killing ability of specific immune cells upon being challenged. Of course, knowing whether and which components of immune functioning are altered by a treatment is very important, but what we really want to know is whether or not a treatment has positive or negative effects on the organism's well-being in the face of an infectious challenge (i.e., has their vulnerability to pathology been altered?). This question is typically examined by assessing the vulnerability to viral or bacterial insults, recovery from illnesses or rate of wound healing, and the development or exacerbation of pathological symptoms (including those related to autoimmune disorders).

IMMUNE–HORMONE INTERACTIONS

The regulation of hormones, neurotransmitters and growth factors, as we've already seen, is essential for well-being, and this holds for immune functioning as well. The Goldilocks analogy (not too much, not too little) seems to be particularly applicable, especially as different pathological outcomes may occur when our immune activity goes off the rails in one direction or another. There are fine reciprocal balances between and within different aspects of the immune system, and there also appear to be regulatory factors that are external to the immune system. In this regard, it has been suggested that endocrine and immune processes act to signal one another, and that this bidirectional signaling is essential for the effective functioning of our defensive systems (Blalock, 1994).

GLUCOCORTICOIDS AND OTHER HORMONES

Glucocorticoids (such as corticosterone/cortisol) are not only activated by stressors, but also by inflammatory stimuli (Sternberg, 2006). And added to this, at physiological levels (i.e., those that naturally occur in the body in response to a challenge) this hormone modulates immune functioning, preventing excessive immune activity. At pharmacological doses (high levels engendered by administration of the compound at doses exceeding those that ordinarily appear in the body) glucocorticoids act as potent immunosuppressants. Given the pronounced effects of stressors on glucocorticoid release, it is reasonable to assume that stressors will also affect immune functioning by virtue of these corticoid variations (Raison & Miller, 2003). However, in doing so, it is necessary to bear in mind that the corticoid changes might be dependent on whether the stressor is acute or chronic, and whether it is a strong stressor versus one that is traumatizing, as well as in relation to previous stressor experiences. That said, there are circumstances in which glucocorticoids can have the effect of increasing, rather than reducing, immune functioning and inflammatory responses (Sorrels & Sapolsky, 2007). This is especially evident in the case of CNS inflammation, including that which is evident following a stroke, and in response to stressors that might have occurred prior to experiencing an inflammatory immune challenge.

The interactions with the immune system are not limited to glucocorticoids, and indeed several hormonal processes have long been known to act in this capacity. Sex hormones, such as estrogen and progesterone, as well as epinephrine, thyroid hormones, melanocortin, and many others, may influence immune activity and hence the emergence of pathological states. As we've already seen, stressful events are likewise known to affect a variety of neuroendocrine processes, and thus the potential effects on immune functioning aren't limited to glucocorticoids. Accordingly, the identification of unique environmental factors that interact with multiple hormonal and immunological processes has garnered increasing interest.

INTERACTIONS BETWEEN THE IMMUNE SYSTEM AND THE BRAIN

Not very long ago (in the 1970s and before), it had been maintained that the immune system and the brain were independent of one another. Immunological activity was thought to be restricted to peripheral domains, and was not influenced by psychological events. This position was eventually abandoned, and replaced with the view that multi-directional communication occurs between the immune, endocrine, autonomic and central nervous systems. Recognition that hormones could affect immune functioning came early, but figuring out how the immune system communicated with the brain (and vice versa) has proven to be another matter entirely.

The brain was held to be 'an immunologically privileged organ' (i.e., not affected by peripheral immune functioning), but it was also thought that perhaps a message could get to the brain through the same messenger molecules, namely cytokines, by which immune cells communicated with one another. Although cytokines are large molecules and thus have only limited access to the brain, they can get there to influence neuronal functioning. This occurs at regions at the edge of the brain or where the barriers to the brain are not as pronounced, including around the ventricles (termed 'circumventricular organs', such as the the organum vasculosum of the lamina terminalis), the posterior pituitary, the median eminence, and the area postrema (Nadeau & Rivest, 1999). In fact, it is now well established that activation of the inflammatory immune system will result in HPA activation and will affect neurotransmitter functioning in several forebrain regions that are associated with mood processes and decision making. To an appreciable extent the neurochemical changes elicited by inflammatory factors are reminiscent of those elicited by psychogenic and neurogenic stressors, and it was suggested that the brain was interpreting a peripheral immune challenge as if it were a stressor. Essentially, the immune system may be part of a regulatory loop that, through its actions on neuroendocrine, neuro-chemical, and growth factors, might contribute to the symptoms of mood and anxiety-related disorders as well as several neurological disturbances (Anisman & Merali, 1999).

It is particularly significant that cytokine synthesis is not only generated within immune cells that circulate through the body, but also occurs within microglia present in the brain and might even occur within neurons. In this regard, cytokine activity within the brain increases appreciably in response to physical and chemical insults (e.g., brain injury, concus-sive injury, seizure, cerebral ischemia, chemically induced brain lesions), as well as a systemic or central challenge with a bacterial endotoxin (a substance that is structurally like a bacte-ria and is recognized as such by immune cells) or viruses (Rothwell & Luheshi, 2000). Moreover, as with CNS insults, stressors affect the production and levels of cytokines within the brain, and it was speculated that through the actions of these central cytokine changes on hormonal and neurotransmitter activity, stressors might come to affect psychopathology. It is thought that an increase of cytokines in the brain stemming from brain insults might reflect their involvement in a reparatory capacity; however, when the concentration of these cytokines is too high, they might act in a destructive manner (Rothwell & Luheshi, 2000). Of course, they might also simply be bystanders that don't have any particular action other than serving as the markers of ongoing problems.

STRESS, CENTRAL PROCESSES, AND IMMUNOLOGICAL ALTERATIONS: ANIMAL STUDIES

In describing the effects of stressors on immune functioning, we've been painting with a very broad brush, and there may be many subtle routes by which stressors might come to affect immune functioning. There are multiple elements that make up the immune system, any of which could be subject to disruption by stressful events. Even if NK cytotoxicity in any given individual is strong, it may be that the B cell or T cell system is weak, or these lympho-cytes don't proliferate as they should, or maybe they simply don't recognize invaders prop-erly. And in addition to this, there are so many factors that govern each aspect of immunity, and so many processes that can be affected by stressors, it's a wonder that we can get through so many adverse situations as we do. Essentially, the immune system is very power-ful and protects us fairly well, but it isn't perfect and the fact is that diseases occur, and it is possible that stressors can exacerbate these.

As much as one would like to make some very simple and straightforward conclusions concerning the impact of stressors on immunity and our vulnerability to pathology, as in the case of other stress-related biological factors, we haven't yet got the full picture. There are numerous factors that seem to influence the way in which stressors affect immune function-ing, and stressors might not affect all the components of immunity in the same way. Of course, as most of us know, viruses are not simple little critters that just hang around wait-ing to be destroyed by the immune system, but instead they evolve and engage in multiple strategies to evade their detection and destruction. As our immune systems learn about how to deal with one variant of a virus or bacteria, new variants emerge that could be learning how to evade our protective processes. Moreover, it might be that stressful experiences limit the adaptability of the immune system to deal with these ever-changing challenges.

Stressful events influence immune functioning across a range of different species, including laboratory animals (mice, rats) and domesticated farm animals (fowl, pigs, cattle). Not unexpectedly, the immune changes are dependent on the stressor severity and chronicity, and are influenced by experiential, developmental, and organismic factors, such as those described in Chapter 1. Altered immune functioning is frequently seen in response to neurogenic (physical) challenges, but stressor effects on immune activity are not attributable simply to tissue damage, as they are also provoked by psychological stressors, such as stressor-related odors or cues that had been associated with stressors, as well as variations in social stability.

TRAUMA AND SEPSIS

It is important to differentiate between the effects of different stressor severities as they can have markedly different ramifications. Among stressors in the mild to moderate range, diverse immune changes may be observed. In contrast, there is a common, highly reproducible genomic response to injury, irrespective of whether it involves major trauma or serious burns, or if recovery is rapid or complicated. The 'Inflammation and Host Response to Injury consortium' assessed the human response to injury and identified the specific factors that instigated excessive, uncontrolled body-wide infection (i.e., sepsis) or multi-organ dysfunction (Xiao et al., 2011). To this end, whole-genome expression patterns were assessed in white blood cells from traumatized patients obtained within 12 hours of the injury and at various times over the ensuing month. The gene expression pattern changes were compared to those of serious burns patients and those of healthy controls.

In both the trauma and burns patients there was an immediate increase in the gene expression of pathways involved with inflammation and with the innate immune system, but there was a concurrent suppression of adaptive immune pathways. In fact, differences between patients with and without complications were primarily evident with respect to the magnitude of gene expression changes and how long they lasted. These findings may be instrumental in designing therapies to promote improvement in trauma patients who would otherwise have complicated recoveries.

STRONG AND WEAK STRESSORS

Stressors influence several components of the immune system. Among other things, stressors affect the number of immune cells in circulation, the cytotoxicity (killing potential of cells) of T and NK cells, the multiplication (proliferation) of immune cells upon being challenged, immune responses to bacteria and viruses, and susceptibility to experimentally administered cold viruses, as well as the time it takes for a wound to heal (Anisman et al., 2008; Dantzer et al., 2007). However, not all stressors have the same effects. It generally appears that mild stressors may augment immunity, whereas more protracted or severe stressors have the opposite effect. For instance, stressors such as exposing animals to a predator (but without permitting them to be hurt) enhanced the proliferative response of B cells, but as we'll see shortly, this did not occur if mice had been exposed to the stressor on a chronic basis. To be sure, an acute stressor ought to result in a surge of immune functioning to deal with the challenges that might have to be dealt with, and at the same time those functions that aren't essential at the moment, such as digestion or reproduction, ought to be shut down. Moreover, stressors should result in the redeployment of immune cells so that they appear at tissues where they might be needed rather than at secondary lymphoid organs (i.e., cell trafficking is altered).

These suggestions seem reasonable enough, but there are instances in which acute stressors might not have precisely these effects, and might actually result in diminished immune functioning, as observed in response to severe stressors (Sorrells et al., 2009). Moreover, an elevated immune response isn't always advantageous, and might actually have damaging effects (leading to autimmune disorders), and so there are mechanisms present that might limit immune activation (e.g., the corticoid response associated with stressors) so that this response doesn't become excessive.

In addition to the immediate effects on immune functioning, stressors can also affect the very powerful secondary immune response. It was demonstrated using an *in vivo* measure of cell mediated immunity that acute stressors enhanced T cell reactivity (Dhabhar, 2009). In this particular experiment the delayed type hypersensitivity response (DTH) was used as a measure of immune functioning. In this test animals are initially treated with an antigen, and then days to weeks later they are challenged with the same (sensitizing) antigen. Ordinarily, the latter treatment promotes an inflammatory response characterized by increased redness and swelling of the challenged body part (typically the footpad or pinnae of the ear). In this study it was found that if rats received a single stressor session just prior to the challenge with a sensitizing chemical, the DTH response of challenged rats was increased, indicating augmented immune functioning. In contrast, immune activity was suppressed following chronic insults (applied over three to five weeks).

There have also been reports that showed some paradoxical results in regard to stressor effects on secondary immune responses. Strong stressors that initially suppressed lymphocyte proliferation (this is unlike the immunoenhancement elicited by milder stressors) for some reason had the effect of enhancing the proliferative response of cells that had previously been sensitized to cholera toxin (i.e., those cells that had a memory for this antigen and hence would ordinarily respond readily upon re-exposure). Evidently, the impact of stressors may depend on the status of the immune factors being examined (e.g., a primary vs a secondary immune response). What might be responsible for these different effects isn't certain, but it does tell us that the immune response to stressors is likely governed by an array of factors beyond that of stressor severity.

One key element that needs to be considered with respect to stressor effects on immune functioning is that we are dealing with a dynamic system and hence the influence of a given manipulation can vary over time. Indeed, it has been shown that a stressor's effects on immune functioning, circulating cytokine levels, and the production of cytokines within the brain, varies with the timing of the stressor relative to an immune challenge (Dhabhar, 2009). If animals are exposed to a stressor and they then encounter an antigenic challenge not long afterward (say, within 24 hours), their immune response is augmented and certain cytokines may be elevated. In contrast, if animals were first exposed to an immunogenic challenge and then exposed to the stressor, the immune suppression might be apparent. It likewise appears that corticoid treatment administered hours prior to an immune challenge leads to immunoenhancement, whereas this does not occur if the corticoid treatment and the immune challenge occur together. It seems that the stressor (or corticoid) serves as a priming stimulus so that the immune system is ready to respond if necessary. Some of the research that examined the effects of stressors on cancer progression has similarly indicated that an acute stressor makes things worse if it occurs well before tumor inoculation (or tumor cell transplantation) or after the tumor has just begun to grow, but has less of an effect when administered at other times. It is as if the initial stressor might have caused the deployment of essential immune cells, but once the emergency has abated and the immune cells are again 'relaxed', a sneak attack in the form of an immugenic challenge is particularly effective in getting around the protective capacity of immune cells (Sklar & Anisman, 1981).

ACUTE VERSUS CHRONIC CHALLENGES

As already alluded to, acute stressors of moderate intensity may enhance immunity, whereas chronic stressors are more likely to be immunosuppressive (Dhabhar, 2009). This makes sense from an adaptive perspective, as clear threats to the organism's well-being should encourage enhanced immunity in order to maintain that organism's well-being. But as the stressor continues, the availability of biological resources may decline, thus rendering the organism more vulnerable to immunological disturbances. Moreover, as we've already seen, having dealt with an initial challenge (such as a stressor) the capacity of the immune system to deal with a second threat that comes along may be diminished, either because of hormonal activation that elicits immune suppression, or because the immune system has become, in a sense, fatigued by the first experience. With still further stressors these negative immunological reactions might become ever more pronounced.

SURGERY AS A CHALLENGE

As long as we're on the topic of stress and immunity, we might consider that surgery is a stressor. Thus, a surgical treatment that is meant to attenuate or eliminate problems can, in some instances, make things worse. Surgery, for example, has effects like other stressors, inducing the suppression of immune activity, and may be associated with post-operative complications related to sepsis and even tumor metastases (Hogan et al., 2011).

The nature of surgery has been changing over the years. Some procedures that required opening the body cavity have been replaced with keyhole surgery in which a small cut allows access to organs. As a result, surgery is less traumatic and recovery is much faster. There will come a day when tiny robots the size of just a few cells will be doing this work and extensive surgery won't be necessary at all. You know how we perceive blood letting that was used years ago? Well, in the future people will be saying 'Oh yuckers! Can you believe it! In the twentieth century and the first part of the twenty first century they used to cut people open!'.

One of the most potent stressors for social animals, as in the case of humans, concerns social disruption (or social defeat), and this insult may also have particularly marked effects on immune functioning and susceptibility to infectious disease. This is especially the case as social stressors likely don't occur on an occasional basis, but represent the norm among communal animals. Ordinarily, corticoids inhibit immune functioning and could potentially regulate (limit) the actions of stressors on immunity. However, after a week of social disruption, resistance was evident with respect to the immunosuppressive effects of glucocorticoids (Stark et al., 2001). Although this should enhance the ability of the immune system to fight off invaders, it is also possible that the absence of the suppressive effects of glucocorticoids might allow for excessive cytokine production that might result in increased autoimmune responses as well as mortality in response to inflammatory immune challenges. It seems, once again, that there are limits to the adaptive changes that might be associated with stressors, and persistent or repeated social stressor experiences may instead give rise to changes that could promote or exacerbate serious health complications. It won't be the least surprising to learn that there are many variables that could potentially influence the impact of social stressors (as well as other psychogenic and neurogenic stressors) on immune functioning, as well as vulnerability to disease. Among other things, the animal's age, sex, and numerous other variables influence immune-related functioning and determine stressor impact. As well, some strains of mice are exceptionally affected by stressors, and there are hardy strains that can deal with some very tough situations; similar individual differences likely exist in humans (Gibb et al., 2011).

STERILE INFLAMMATION

The immune system is not only activated by pathogenic stimuli, but is also affected by challenges of a non-pathogenic nature, which has been referred to as sterile inflammation (Fleshner, 2013). Traumatic events can produce effects akin to those associated with systemic pathogenic stimuli and can lead to multi-organ failure. A protein complex, referred to as the 'inflammasome', might be responsible for the effects of traumatic stressors, acting via a series of steps that promote activation of IL-1β and IL-18. It seems that the immune system is able to detect danger through what is referred to as 'danger (or damage) molecular pattern molecules' (DAMPs), that can both initiate and prolong the non-infectious immune response. These endogenous molecules are released by damaged or dying cells, and although their function is meant to be positive, they can wreak havoc, as in the case of the overwhelming inflammatory response that is too frequently seen in patients with an acute lung injury or acute respiratory distress syndrome after they have been placed on a ventilator. The interaction between DAMPs and dendritic cells is also thought to play a key role in tumor immunity, autoimmunity, chronic inflammatory conditions, and tissue transplantation, as well as ischemia reperfusion injury (i.e., upon the blood supply returning to tissues following a period of oxygen deprivation). But as we've seen so many times up until this point, there are times when processes such as these seem to backfire, leaving us in a bad state.

STRESSOR EFFECTS ON IMMUNE FUNCTIONING IN HUMANS

Studies in humans have largely relied on blood measures in which *in vitro* immune functioning was assessed (e.g., NK cytotoxicity or lymphocyte proliferation induced by a mitogen), but there have been studies that addressed the *in vivo* outcomes of stressors on functional changes related to immune activity (Kemeny & Schedlowski, 2007). Within a laboratory context, psychological stressors provoke an increase of immune functioning (e.g., Pace et al., 2006). In contrast to the effects of acute laboratory challenges, chronic life stressors generally had the effect of impairing immune functioning. By example, chronic life stressors, such as caregiving (e.g., for a partner with a neurodegenerative disorder such as Alzheimer's), was associated with reduced immune activity and impaired wound healing (Glaser et al., 1999). Paralleling these findings, antibody production in response to immunization showed that humoral immune responses can be modulated by stressors (Cohen et al., 2001). It has also been reported that the distress associated with academic examinations among medical students was accompanied by reduced T cells (of all varieties), as well as diminished killing of Epstein-Barr virus by memory T cells (Maes et al., 1998). Similarly, reduced immune responses were evident among dementia caregivers in response to the Herpes simplex virus-1 antigen (HSV-1; this is the form associated with cold sores, whereas HSV-2 is associated with genital herpes), attesting to the negative impact of a chronic stressor experience. Like T and B cell production, stressful experiences, particularly those of a chronic nature, were associated with reduced NK cell activity. Not unexpectedly, immune responses varied with personality and emotional factors. For instance, NK cell activity was particularly low among individuals who were hostile or those who were especially negative (Kiecolt-Glazer et al., 2002).

It seems that stressful events during early life in humans might also influence immune functioning and may therefore affect well-being throughout the life span (Miller et al., 2011). Such an outcome was found in studies using rodents challenged with a bacterial endotoxin (e.g., lipopolysaccharide (LPS) or to an influenza virus. It was similarly reported that among women raised in a harsh family environment, the cytokine response (measured in response to an *in vitro* challenge) was markedly increased, accompanied by a reduction in the sensitivity of glucocorticoid receptors, possibly suggesting that these glucocorticoids had a diminished ability to regulate immune responses (Miller et al., 2011). These investigators suggested that if such immune and hormone alterations persisted, as they apparently do, it would render individuals at increased risk for disorders that were promoted by pro-inflammatory cytokines.

There have been several studies showing that stressors administered within a laboratory context can alter various facets of immune and cytokine activity. For instance, in response to a Trier Social Stress Test the levels of IL-6 in blood as well as that of NK cells was elevated among depressed individuals that had experienced an early-life stressor, potentially pointing to the influence of these combined experiences (Pace et al., 2006). It was also observed that social rejection within a laboratory context, which was found to increase neuronal activity within the anterior cingulate cortex, was also reported to increase the soluble receptor (one that is not bound to a membrane) for TNF-α and that of IL-6 (Slavich, Way et al., 2010). Remarkably, when taken for three weeks, the anti-inflammatory acetaminophen, which is used to reduce physical pain, was also found to diminish the pain of social rejection and diminished the brain neural responses associated with rejection (Dewall et al., 2010). It seems that the inflammatory actions of social stressors can be exceptionally powerful, and the mood effects elicited by rejection might be causally related to the inflammatory effects provoked. When we discuss the influence of inflammatory processes (and the beneficial effects of anti-inflammatory medications) on depressive illness, the data provided by Slavich, Way et al. (2010) will be seen to fall into a framework that links numerous biological processes to affective illness.

STRESSORS AND CYTOKINE CHANGES

Proinflammatory cytokines have been implicated in psychiatric, cardiovascular, and various neuropathological disorders, and hence there has been increasing emphasis on the assessment of circulating proinflammatory cytokines in response to stressors. Cytokines are particularly sensitive to neuroendocrine factors, and thus the stressor-induced alterations of cytokine production might stem from neuroendocrine changes. This view is certainly the simplest explanation for the effects of stressors on cytokine levels and activity, and the one that makes the fewest new assumptions. However, in the case of stressor effects on biological processes we've seen again and again that the simplest explanations often fall by the wayside. Science has a way of humbling us. Often, I think that I've got a handle on the characteristics of a stress-related biological outcome, only to be disappointed by the data. Instead of the law of parsimony (Occam's razor; the simplest solution is likely the correct one), I'm reminded of Gilbert and Sullivan's *HMS Pinafore*;

> 'Things are seldom what they seem,
>
> Skim milk masquerades as cream'

TH$_1$ AND TH$_2$ DERIVED CYTOKINES

Th$_1$ and Th$_2$ cells, as we've seen, have different functions, as do the cytokines produced by these systems. Whereas Th$_1$ cells are involved in protection against intracellular bacteria, Th$_2$ cells play a role in allergic reactions and the inhibition of Th$_1$ cells, and the more recently identified Th$_{17}$ cells appear to deal with bacteria and have also been implicated in the amplification of autoimmune disorders. As described earlier, these cells and the cytokines released by them (Th$_1$ cytokines comprise IL-2, IFNγ, and TNF-α, and Th$_2$ cytokines comprise IL-4 and IL-10, among others) need to act cooperatively in dealing with varied conditions. Shifts in the balance towards Th$_1$ reflect a bias towards proinflammatory processes, whereas a shift toward Th$_2$ reflects the opposite effect. Excessive and prolonged skewing in either direction may have adverse effects. Early in an immune response to a pathogen, the predominance of Th$_1$ cell function promotes increased phagocytic functions (engulfing and absorbing waste material and potentially harmful microorgainisms) through the activation of macrophages and stimulation of antibodies. These actions are subsequently down-regulated by Th$_2$ cell cytokines (particularly IL-10). The latter effects essentially shift the immune response away from the development of an unnecessarily protracted and potentially damaging impact on tissue function. As a result, there is an appropriate temporal sequence that ought to be followed upon exposure to a pathogen.

Stressors modify the production of Th_1 and Th_2 cytokines and may consequently provoke imbalances in their mutual regulatory functional relationship. As stressors influence several cytokines, it might not be enough to simply determine which cytokines go up or which go down in response to stressors. Instead, as in the case of other biological systems, it might be especially pertinent to evaluate the relationships between multiple cytokine perturbations in relation to the emergence of stressor-elicited challenges to well-being. This sort of analysis may, however, be difficult as stressor effects on cytokines may vary over time, and not every cytokine follows the same temporal trajectory. In fact, if one were to examine the effects of a stressor at one point in time, the impression that might be gained is that the treatment elicited immune enhancement. However, at a different point in time, just a few hours later, the analysis might suggest that the stressor inhibited immune functioning. And to make things still more complicated, what one observes in the periphery may be far different from that which occurs in the brain (Gibb et al., 2013). Stressors and immune challenges both set in motion dynamic processes, and finding a single rule that predicts what would happen at different times is exceedingly difficult.

IMPACT OF STRESSORS ON PRO-INFLAMMATORY CYTOKINES (IL-1β, IL-6, AND TNF-α)

Analyses of the effects of stressors on cytokine production have involved measurement of circulating cytokines, or the *in vitro* determination of their production in the blood, spleen, or other lymphoid organs. When cytokine production is determined *in vitro* there is the problem of biological meaningfulness (i.e., Is what happens in a petri dish actually representative of what happens in the body, especially as the influence of other factors, such as hormones, are no longer present?). This is often dealt with through *in vivo* studies using challenges such as the immune activating agent lipopolysaccharide (LPS; this is the outer coat for E. coli bacteria) that reliably has both *in vitro* and *in vivo* actions. Using this approach, it was observed that the production of proinflammatory cytokines, such as IL-1β, were present in higher concentrations after stressor exposure, and after several days of social disruption mice exhibited greater amounts of IL-1β and TNF-α in lymphoid regions (e.g., spleen and lung) and in the brain. Typically, these changes are matched or followed by variations of IL-10 so that the pro-inflammatory effects of the stressor are appropriately regulated, but this is not always the case, especially when stressors are sustained and unremitting (Gibb et al., 2013).

For some time, analyses of IL-1β and TNF-α seemed to be predominant in research concerning pro-inflammatory cytokine actions. Increasingly, however, attention has also focused on the impact of stressors on IL-6. One of the major functions of this cytokine is the promotion of cell growth and the differentiation of B cells, and it seems that neuronal growth is also influenced by IL-6. Thus, alterations in the production and/or release of IL-6 would likely influence humoral immune processes, the functional status of immune cells, and perhaps CNS activity. In fact, there have been studies on humans which have suggested that life stressors can affect cytokine production, depending on the nature of the stressor. Specifically, parents of young cancer patients, who were no doubt undergoing considerable distress, showed suppressed IL-6 production (Miller et al., 2002). In contrast, the distress of academic exams, public speaking, or exercise was associated with augmented *in vitro* IL-6 production (Maes et al., 1998; Paik et al., 2000). There are any number of factors that could have led to the differences in the effects observed, although it is likely that they were related to the chronicity and intensity of the stressor experience. However, if individuals that had been undergoing a chronic stress are exposed to an acute laboratory stressor, a different picture emerges. For instance, among older women (but not men) who had been experiencing chronic loneliness, the laboratory challenge provoked a greater increase of IL-6 and IL-1Ra (this is an endogenous antagonist of the IL-1 receptor), while cortisol elevations were less marked than those in women who were not experiencing loneliness (Hackett et al., 2012). It is tempting to suggest that even though chronic strain may diminish cytokine activity, this stressor prepares these cytokines to react strongly to novel challenges just as such an outcome occurs with respect to cortisol.

It shouldn't be surprising to learn that dispositional factors may also influence immune functioning. For instance, in response to an acute stressor IL-6 rose in direct relation to optimism. However, this association was absent when individuals experienced a laboratory stressor, leading to the suggestion that the improved health reported among optimists might be due to this trait counteracting stress-induced increases in inflammation that could potentially be harmful (Brydon et al., 2009). Likewise, it was reported that higher self-esteem was accompanied by limited TNF-α and IL-1Ra (interleukin-1 receptor agonist) responses in response to an acute stressor relative to those with lower self-esteem (O'Donnell et al., 2008), prompting the suggestion that this might be one way in which self-esteem protects against the development of disease. Paralleling these results, the rise of IL-6 and IL-10 in blood samples was reported to be directly related to individuals' propensity for exhibiting shame or anger (but not anxiety) following a laboratory challenge comprising the TSST (Danielson et al., 2011). Thus, it seems that the cytokine responses to stressors are subject to moderation by personality factors or the emotional responses that are elicited.

Another class of cytokines that has been studied for some time, and that has received increasing attention, is that of interferons (IFN), so named because they interfere with viral replication. Interferons come in different forms (e.g., IFN-α, IFN-β, IFN-γ, and several others), each of which has a somewhat different function, although they all influence viral replication and can fight tumors. As described in Chapter 6, IFN-α is now commonly used in the treatment of hepatitis C and in certain types of cancer, whereas IFN-β-1a and IFN-β-1b are used to treat the autoimmune disorder, multiple sclerosis.

The effects of stressors on IFN have not been as widely studied as other cytokines, and some of the data that have been obtained might not be as relevant as they could have been. Specifically, in many studies conducted in rats or mice the human form of recombinant IFN-α was used, but this form might not be biologically active in rodents, or might induce effects that would not be elicited by forms of the cytokine that are species appropriate. In studies in mice where the murine (mouse) form of IFN-α was used, the behaviors seen were somewhat similar to those elicited by other cytokines, such as IL-1β, but were far less pronounced. Likewise, the increase of corticosterone elicited by IFN-α was less prominent than that seen after IL-1β administration. There have been a small number of studies that assessed the impact of stressors on the actions of IFN-γ (which is related to IFN-α). For instance, stressor exposure reduced IFN-γ production in spleen lymphocytes, and following repeated daily restraint the production of IFN-γ was diminished in response to tetanus toxin, herpes simplex virus, influenza virus, or tumor antigens, suggesting that individuals experiencing chronic strain might also be more vulnerable to the effects of pathogens.

What was particularly interesting, and potentially relevant with respect to the clinical use of IFN-α, is that when mice had been moderately stressed (through social disruption), the effects of IFN-α were greatly increased. It seems that as in the case of other cytokines, the adverse behavioral actions of IFN-α are exaggerated when administered on a stressful background (Anisman et al., 2007). As we'll discuss later, this is of clinical significance as humans undergoing immunotherapy with this cytokine (i.e., in the treatment of hepatitis C or certain cancers) are typically affected by considerable distress, and the effects of the treatments might reflect the synergistic (multiplicative) actions of the cytokine and the ongoing stressor conditions (Anisman et al., 2008).

The research that has been conducted concerning stressors and cytokines has largely focused on those discussed to this point. One cytokine that has received recent attention is that of IL-18, which is thought to play a role in several diseases (infectious illness, cancer, autoimmune disorders, diabetes, and atherosclerosis). In addition to being derived from immune cells, it is found in the adrenal and pituitary as well as in the brain, where it is produced by microglia and possibly by neurons. This cytokine, like other proinflammatory cytokines can be affected by stressors, and thus might contribute to stress-related pathology (Sugama & Conti, 2008). It would be reasonable to expect that stressors affect other cytokines as well, but at this point the available data are scant.

IMPACT OF STRESSORS ON INHIBITORY CYTOKINES

As described earlier, IL-4 and IL-10 are inhibitory (anti-inflammatory) cytokines that are responsible for maintaining the balances between various aspects of cytokine-related processes (by countering the actions of pro-inflammatory cytokines). Studies of stressor effects in humans within natural contexts have revealed fairly consistent patterns of inhibitory cytokine changes. Chronic stressors, such as caregiving, were associated with elevated production of the anti-inflammatory IL-10 (Glaser et al., 2001). A similar outcome was observed in association with the distress of academic examinations (Marshall et al., 1998; Paik et al., 2000). In general, it appeared that stressors increased IL-10 and might thus inhibit pro-inflammatory effects, thereby undermining immune responses that might otherwise act against potential pathogens. Of course, it is also possible that the observed increases of IL-10 might reflect compensatory changes elicited by the elevated pro-inflammatory cytokines, and hence may serve to regulate the actions of pro-inflammatory cytokines.

Other factors that act in a similar capacity are naturally occuring antagonists of cytokines, such as IL-1Ra and SOCS-3 (suppressors of cytokine). Whereas the actions of stressors on IL-4 have received some attention, there is less information available regarding the effects of stressors on IL-1Ra and SOCS-3. Nevertheless, it seems likely that these factors will turn out to be important players in the adaptive responses to stressors, and their dysfunction might be related to the pathological effects of stressors.

Although there have been a fair number of studies assessing the influence of stressors on cytokine (and immune) functioning in humans, there is still much that we don't know concerning the impact of stressors on these processes. Among other things, it remains to be determined whether stressors differentially influence cytokine activity within different immune compartments (e.g., spleen vs blood), whether the effects observed are unique to certain types of stressor regimens, and whether the effects of stressors vary with the constellation of individual factors described in Chapter 1. As more studies are conducted that consider individual difference factors and various stressor characteristics, interpretations may arise that will provide a uniform picture of how stressors affect Th_1 and Th_2 cytokine functioning and their balances. For the moment, however, it appears that acute stressful events of moderate severity may increase immune and cytokine functioning, but given a strong enough stressor the immune enhancement might not be evident. Moreover, the immune and cytokine variations associated with stressors likely vary in a dynamic fashion over time, but most studies have evaluated these changes at one time point or over a restricted time window (e.g., one or two hours). Ultimately, to understand the effects of stressors on immune and cytokine functioning as well as their effects on well-being, it will be necessary to conduct large-scale studies that can evaluate changes that occur over time.

SENSITIZATION

When we discussed the impact of stressors on neuroendocrine and neurotransmitter functioning, the point was made that stressful events typically had short-lasting neurochemical effects, usually measured in minutes or hours. This type of transient response would be seen as highly adaptive, since our defense systems ought to be engaged only so long as the stressor is present, and then terminated when the stressor disappears or is dealt with effectively. However, stressors might also result in the 'sensitization' of biological systems so that upon later stressor encounters the biological responses would be greatly increased, even if these stressors differed from the initial experience. Although a sensitized response ought to help us react swiftly to further stressor encounters, this process might also contribute to the emergence or re-emergence of psychological pathologies.

Commensurate with reports that a stressful event sensitizes biological processes related to neuroendocrine and neurotransmitter functioning, comparable outcomes can be induced with respect to aspects of the inflammatory immune response (Anisman et al., 2003). Among animals that had been exposed to a chronic cold stressor, a later challenge with LPS provoked exaggerated changes of IL-1β, IL-6, and other inflammatory factors within the hypothalamus and prefrontal cortex. In addition, in pups treated with a strong immunological challenge, the subsequent adult response to stressors was altered (e.g., Shanks et al., 2000). Among other things, neonatal endotoxin exposure promoted elevated corticosterone levels, and during adulthood these animals displayed altered brain dopamine functioning and greater stressor-induced suppression of lymphocyte proliferation. Likewise, such a treatment markedly impaired NK cell functioning. The findings concerning the impact of neonatal challenges are especially interesting as they not only point to the possibility that these events may have repercussions for later physical well-being, just as they do regarding psychological disturbances; indeed, the persistent changes of dopamine stemming from early experiences, including immunological insults that occur prenatally, could be involved in disorders such as schizophrenia. In Chapter 10 we'll be examining this further, particularly with respect to the impact of immune insults that occur prenatally and how these might promote later pathology, such as schizophrenia and perhaps autism.

CONCLUSION

Although there have been a fair number of studies assessing the influence of stressors on cytokine and immune functioning, as indicated repeatedly, there is still much that we don't know concerning the impact of stressors on these processes. Among other things, it is uncertain whether the effects that have been observed are unique to certain types of stressor regimens or certain types of immune challenges (e.g., being unique to bacterial or viral challenges, or for that matter whether the effects differ in relation to different types of viral challenges), and whether the effects of stressors will vary with the constellation of individual difference factors. It also remains to be determined whether stressors differentially influence the activity of various cytokines within the brain, and to what extent these differ across specific brain regions.

As more studies are conducted that vary stressor parameters and consider individual differences, a uniform picture may evolve as to how stressors affect Th_1 and Th_2 cytokine functioning and their balances. For the moment, however, it appears that acute stressors of moderate severity may increase immune and cytokine functioning, but given a strong enough stressor the immune enhancement might not be evident. Moreover, it seems that the immunoenhancement that follows an acute stressor might be absent following a chronic stressor, and may actually turn to an immunosuppression. However, these conclusions need to be considered as being highly provisional. The cytokine variations associated with stressors likely vary in a dynamic fashion over time, but most studies have evaluated these changes at a single time point or over a restricted time window. Ultimately, to understand the effects of stressors on immune and cytokine functioning, as well as their effects on well-being, large-scale studies will be needed to evaluate the changes that occur over time, how individual difference factors moderate these outcomes, and what the implications might be for disease states.

SUMMARY

- The immune system has both an innate, non-specific component and an acquired or adaptive component that deals with specific challenges.
- Studies in both humans and animals have indicated that stressful events can influence both aspects of immunity and result in an altered vulnerability to pathogens.
- As well as affecting various immune cells, stressors may also influence both peripheral and central cytokine levels and functioning, which could affect vulnerability to physical illnesses and may have neuropathological consequences.
- The effects of stressors on immune functioning in the periphery as well as cytokine changes in the brain are influenced by a constellation of hormonal changes.
- The many specific attributes of stressors, and the moderating influence of experiential, social, developmental, and genetic factors in determining immunocompetence and central cytokine functioning, have not been fully worked out. However, it does seem that there are some instances (e.g., modest, acute challenges) that enhance immune functioning, but others where the opposite outcome occurs (severe or chronic insults).

6 STRESS, IMMUNITY, AND DISEASE

THE DREADED DISEASES

The very words 'You have cancer' or 'The tests came back positive', or even that horribly ambiguous statement that has lots of undertones 'Can you come back in as the tests showed an anomaly?', send a fright through most individuals. Even though heart disease is responsible for more deaths than cancer, it seems that cancer instigates a particular dread. We have special names for cancer, such as 'the big C', as if saying it this way will ward off the evil eye.

The suggestion that cancer may be associated with stressful events or that it occurs more frequently among individuals with mood disorders has been around not just for decades, but for many centuries. We still don't have definitive answers concerning how this comes about, as the link between stressful events and disease likely involves multiple processes, including prenatal and early postnatal events that can shape the competency of our various biological systems that ought to protect us from disease. Of course, cancer creeps us out more than other diseases, but it's a certainty that stressors have effects on numerous illnesses in addition to cancer. Stressors influence our ability to fend off infection, allergies, and viral-based illnesses, and exacerbate the symptoms or flares of autoimmune disorders.

The fact that stressful events under certain conditions might compromise immune functioning is interesting, but you might still be wondering about the bottom line – namely, do stressful events actually cause immune-related disease and permit diseases to develop or grow worse, or is all of this simply an academic exercise without any practical relevance? Furthermore, if stressors have this function, then what can we do about it? Once again, it seems that the questions are simple enough, but the answers are more complicated. There are numerous immune-related diseases, and although some individuals might succumb to one disease or another, many individuals seem to travel through life unmolested by immune-related diseases, despite numerous stressful experiences (it is possible, of course, that some other illness caused their death before an immune-related disorder had the opportunity to show up). In contrast, there are individuals without extraordinarily stressful lives who succumb to immunological disturbances, likely owing to other risk factors related to gender, genetic factors, diet, and environmental toxins. With this in mind we'll look at several broad disease categories to assess the evidence that stressful events play some role in the provocation or exacerbation of disease states. In this chapter you will learn about:

- infectious diseases and how they come about, as well as the contribution of stressful events in affecting these illnesses;
- a class of illnesses, termed 'autoimmune disorders', in which the immune system turns on the self, creating illnesses such as multiple sclerosis, lupus erythematosus, and rheumatoid arthritis;
- the cancer processes, and the possibility that the course of this illness can be exacerbated by stressors. Cancer can come about through factors unrelated to immune disturbances, and thus this chapter will also deal with the stressor effects that involve processes described in Chapter 3 when we dealt with hormones, as well as Chapter 6 that involved immunity;
- the fact that in addition to the stressors affecting immune-related disturbances, illness can exact a heavy toll on an individual's ability to contend with other stressors, thus increasing their vulnerability to a constellation of illnesses.

IMMUNITY AND DISEASE

Immune-related illnesses can come about for any number of reasons. These could occur because of disturbances within the immune system itself, or they may develop because of disturbances of those processes (e.g., neuroendocrine factors) that ordinarily regulate immune activity. The nature of the illness itself might also vary with the specific component of the immune system affected. For instance, reduced T and B cell activity have been associated with human immunodeficiency syndromes, whereas diminished NK cell activity has been related to viral illness and cancer. Disease states may also arise because the recognition abilities of the immune cell may be compromised. In addition, if suppressor cells (or inhibitory cytokines) do not operate efficiently, then the immune system may attack the self, leading to the development of autoimmune disorders, such as lupus erythematosus, multiple sclerosis, and rheumatoid arthritis.

In their review regarding the influence of psychosocial stressors and immune-related disease, Kemeny and Schedlowski (2007) indicated that in the early days of psychoneuroimmunology (defined in that case as pre-1996), most of the work on stress and pathology was prompted by clinical reports showing relationships between stressful life events and autoimmune disorders, as well as skin diseases, infectious illnesses, and cancer. Animal models for some of these illnesses were still fairly limited, and the data from human studies came from retrospective analyses that have many limitations, and many findings that had been reported as often inconsistent. Considerable progress has since been made, although we admittedly still don't thoroughly understand the processes through which stressors influence pathology. Furthermore, it is almost certain in the case of some illnesses that stressful events do not *cause* these as such, but will exacerbate the illness symptoms once the disease state is present. With respect to the converse, namely, whether leading a good healthy lifestyle, keeping fit, eating well, sleeping properly, and dealing with stressors properly will extend our life span – to this, I can provide a very definitive maybe. Maybe you can, provided that you have the right genes, if you don't do anything really dumb, and if you're lucky.

WEAK LINKS AND VULNERABILITY

At the funeral of a close friend, one of my buddies turned to me saying 'David worked out every day, ate properly, got plenty of rest, balanced his home and work life … he died a healthy man'. There are several messages embedded in that statement, including the philosophical and practical. The philosophical side isn't new, and can seem a bit hokey (e.g., live every day as if it were your last … yada, yada, yada), but the practical view is that it takes only one weak link in our physiology to bring down even the toughest individual. In studying the stress–pathology relationship it is good to take a holistic approach, but not at the expense of ignoring molecular analyses that could potentially pinpoint the specific weak links that make individuals vulnerable to pathological outcomes.

INFECTIOUS ILLNESS

Diseases arise when pathogenic biological agents (e.g., viruses) are transmitted from a carrier to a host in which the foreign substance can flourish. Communicable or transmissible diseases have been around for centuries (smallpox, bubonic plague), and virtually everyone knows about the Spanish Flu that killed more than 50 million people (possibly as high as 130 million) between 1918 and 1920, various STDs, HIV/AIDS, and more recently, SARS, West Nile Virus, and H1N1. Many individuals have become aware of the potential threats of viral illnesses, particularly as they hear about them more frequently, and in regard to a pandemic you might have heard the statement that 'It's not a matter of if, but when'. Yet when we were recently threatened by H1N1, only about 40% of people (varying slightly across countries) were inoculated, despite the World Health Organization (WHO) and various governments and the media encouraging us to take preventive measures. There are several reasons that might have contributed to this low level of inoculation: a lack of trust in media and government agencies, ineffective communication, and apathy on the part of the population owing to 'flu fatigue' (stemming from the frequent false alarms issued by health agencies), as well as a strange sense of invulnerability ('Relative to others, it's less likely that

I'll get sick, and if I do get sick the symptoms will also be less pronounced than my neighbors' symptoms'). Fortunately, H1N1 turned out to be less of a danger than originally feared. Eventually, we might not be as lucky, and there's an even chance that when a new strain of virus comes along, a vaccine will not be ready in time (as we saw in relation to H1N1), and we'll be relying on our innate and adaptive immune responses without external help. A pandemic and attacks by terrorists share a crucial and common aspect: we can be successful a whole lot of the time in our preventive measures, but all of these successes will be forgotten if we're unsuccessful even once.

DON'T GIVE A DOSE TO THE ONE YOU LOVE MOST

I asked students in one of my graduate classes (17 kids in all) how many of them had been inoculated against H1N1. The response wasn't surprising. None of them had. I then asked them how many planned on getting a flu shot this year. Again, none planned to do so. I asked them if it was a matter of it being either a pain to walk over to the clinic on campus, whether they were concerned with vaccine safety, or whether it was more macho to not be inoculated. The majority selected the first choice, a few selected the last, and one woosey chose 'other' (he was afraid of needles). I then asked them how they'd feel about the prospect of getting sick, and most of the students more or less shrugged it off. Then, finally, I asked how they'd feel if they passed the flu on to their parents, brothers or sisters (and in one case, to their child). Lots of silence followed as this sank in, although I'm not sure they actually planned on being inoculated.

It's a real shame that so few people have heard of Shel Silverstein, an absolute genius who had multiple talents, including being a remarkably gifted cartoonist, author of incredibly wonderful children's books, poet, singer and songwriter, musician, and composer. He was well known from the late 50s through to the late 80s. Once you look at anything he's ever done, you're hooked (check him out on the web). At any rate, one of his great songs was 'Don't give a dose to the one you love most (it may get back to you)', which really says it all, and I'm surprised that it's not used in campaigns regarding safe sex or the need to deal with yearly viruses in a thoughtful way (even though those yearly flu inoculations aren't nearly as effective as we're led to believe).

Infectious agents are not limited to viruses, but also include bacteria, fungi, multicellular parasites, protozoa, and prions (the latter are associated with Mad Cow Disease). Factors responsible for diseases can be transmitted through foods, bodily fluids, contact with an infected person, or via an airborne route. Some infections arise when an individual's defensive systems are compromised (as observed in people with AIDS), in which case we refer to these as opportunistic pathogens. In addition, infectious disease can be transmitted through a vector, which refers to an intermediate that is responsible for the transfer of a disease, as in the case of mosquitoes or ticks transmitting malaria or Lyme's disease to humans. If you're interested in this topic, including how diseases jump from animals to humans and how they spread, read Nathan Wolfe's exceptionally readable (2011) book, *The Viral Storm*. And as well as this, in their wonderful (2012) book, *Zoobiquity*, Natterson-Horowitz and Bowers describe a large number of examples where diseases are transmitted from animals to humans. The most widely known of these is HIV, which is thought to have been passed to humans ages ago through the Simian immunodeficiency virus (SIV) that is frequent in some species of non-human primates. It was probably transmitted to human hunters through eating the meat of their primate neighbours or having had the blood of these critters get onto their hands and into wounds that might have been present. Once in the human, SIV could have mutated into HIV and then transmitted to others.

In earlier times, bubonic plague, or the Black Death, was the bacterial-based disease that was the scourge that affected huge numbers of people. This zoonotic disease occurs in rodents through bacterial infection with Yersinia pestis. Fleas that had contracted the bacteria from rats could transmit it to humans, usually through the skin, where it continued to spread, killing about 65% of individuals within about four days of infection. Other zoonotic diseases, such as bubonic plague and its cousins pneumonic plague and septicemic plague, were responsible for the plague that killed approximately 25 million people, somewhere near half the population of Europe, in the fourteenth century.

OH, YUCK

It's been estimated that when we enter a room, there's a huge spike of detectable bacteria. These largely comprise medium-sized bacterial particles and larger-sized fungal particles that emanate from us or we stir up from the floor (Qian et al., 2012). The senior author of this work (J. Peccia) was quoted as saying that 'we live in a microbial soup, and a big ingredient is our own microorganisms'.

As grubby as this might sound, you might consider that there are lots of microorganisms that are good for us. In fact, our gut is filled with these organisms and they're essential for the digestive processes to operate properly. Too clean can actually be a problem. There is the view, referred to as 'the hygiene hypothesis', that exposure to all sorts of stuff when we're kids strengthens our immune system. In fact, over the past decades allergies have increased remarkably in Western countries, as have autoimmune disorders, but a comparable increase has not been seen in those countries where obsessive cleanliness hasn't been notable. This correlation might be just that, i.e., a correlation that has no bearing on causality. But you can still use this as a good rationale for living like a slob.

STRESSOR EFFECTS ON INFECTIOUS ILLNESS

Whether or not an individual will contract a virus or encounter other infectious agents depends on a number of factors. Some are related to lifestyle (e.g., hand washing, work environment in relation to people being met, travel, foods eaten), whereas others are related to the nature of the contagious agent. Obviously, having an appropriate antibody or T cell response is fundamental in preventing or attenuating illness. As we know, however, our immune system may not be prepared to deal with new viruses, and factors that further compromise our immune system may render us still more vulnerable to pathology. In fact, some toxins, including bacteria such as anthrax lethal factor and C. difficile, may disturb the glucocorticoid receptors and hence disrupt our immune capacity (Webster et al., 2003). As well, the gender differences associated with the occurrence of bacterial or parasitic infection (Falagas et al., 2007) might be tied to corticoid and progesterone variations.

Given the marked effects of stressors on immune functioning and the hormones that act on immune processes, it is reasonable to expect that stressors would influence vulnerability to infection or the ability of a host organism to fight off an ongoing infection. Indeed, stressors influence our susceptibility to the common cold, the reactivation of the herpes simplex virus (HSV), cytomegalovirus (CMV), and the antibody response to the Epstein Barr virus (Cohen et al., 1991). In addition, stressful events may promote the loss of helper T cells, and hence promote the onset of AIDS symptoms in HIV positive individuals. Of particular interest, in this regard, was the finding that certain aspects of psychosocial events appeared to be particularly tied to HIV progression. Both personality type and ineffective coping styles were more closely aligned with HIV progression than were the specific stress stimuli encountered. Results similar to those associated with HIV were also observed in relation to herpes simplex virus recurrence (Chida & Mao, 2009). Essentially, perceptions of stressors or the coping methods used to deal with these challenges were particularly important in determining the response to existent infection.

WHAT'S A VACCINE?

Vaccines against illnesses are based on the same principles that are involved in memory in immune cells. Essentially, vaccination comprises the administration of dead or weakened virus, but because the agent is not alive (or is weakened) the individual likely won't get the disease as a result of the treatment. Yet the dead virus is recognized as being foreign, leading to an immune response being mounted, and memory cells will retain the information about this virus. Thus, when we later encounter the viral threat again, our immune system will recognize and destroy the virus quickly and therefore sickness will not occur. Of course, in some cases (most commonly seasonal flu bugs) the virus might mutate (change its recognition characteristics), and thereby evade detection, and so we're stuck being unprotected. It's no easy trick to predict these mutations, and sometimes the makers of vaccines can be taken by surprise resulting in vaccine shortages. Remember the hassles encountered in getting the H1N1 vaccines out to the public? Good thing it wasn't as virulent or as deadly as it could have been.

Incidentally, as the response to a vaccine is an immune response much like that elicited by live vaccine (except that the virus isn't multiplying), the effects of vaccination in promoting swelling at the site of administration can be used to assess the strength of the immune response following stressor experiences.

Research in humans that focused on the impact of stressors on infection has, understandably, been limited, as studies typically can't be conducted in which the illness was induced, although it was shown that stressed individuals were more vulnerable to colds following the administration of the cold virus. In general, studies that attempted to relate naturally occurring viral illness to stressful experiences have indicated that such events were associated with elevated susceptibility and the frequency of illnesses, delay in recovery from illness, and more frequent complications related to infection (Bailey et al., 2007).

There have also been studies in animals assessing how stressful events affect virally-related illnesses. The limited number of studies in this regard likely stems from the necessity of conducting these studies in containment facilities to prevent the spread of the virus. In an effort to circumvent issues related to viral transmission, some investigators have assessed the effects of stressors on the response to challenge with polyinosinic: polycytidylic acid (poly I:C), which structurally resembles a viral challenge, but lacks the ability to replicate within the nucleus of the host. The latter studies do not have a bearing on the important aspects of genuine viruses, namely their ability to multiply, but it was nevertheless shown that the effects of stressors on responses elicited by poly I:C were in line with those seen with other challenges.

IMMUNOLOGICAL FORESIGHT

Stressors might compromise our immune ability, and the presence of infection influences neuronal functioning and hormonal outputs, culminating in mood changes. The brain changes induced by immune challenges may be sending us an important message, and this may actually occur even before the full symptoms of an illness have emerged. Indeed, have you ever noticed that you're a bit more lethargic just before showing the symptoms of a cold? In fact, your friends might seem to notice this with comments such as 'You seem to be a bit off today. Maybe you're coming down with something?'. It might simply be that your immune system is aware of a viral insult, and is giving your brain a message to slow down to conserve energy in order to deal with the cold that you're about to experience.

It has been observed that in mice that had been infected with the influenza A/PR8 virus, a stressor reduced IL-1β and NK cell activity (Tseng et al., 2005), thereby increasing vulnerability to illness. Indeed, in rodents, three consecutive days of exercise (on a treadmill) leading to fatigue exacerbated intestinal lymphocyte loss through cell death and increased symptoms of illness brought on by influenza virus that was administered intranasally (Hoffman-Goetz & Quadrilatero, 2003). Likewise, using a herpes simplex virus type 1 infection model, stressors applied early in infection reduced viral clearance and worsened the course of the illness, and this outcome was tied to the immunosuppressive effects of increased corticoids elicited by the stressor (Elftman et al., 2010). Paralleling the findings using viral models, stressors delayed wound healing and diminished the clearance of opportunistic bacteria, such as Staphylococcus aureus, likely owing to the elevation of glucocorticoids stemming from the stressor (Bailey et al., 2003). Incidentally, S. Aureus is a bacteria you might have heard of because it is so common (affecting 20% of the Western population at some time) and has so many nasty effects. Among other things, it can promote skin infections, impetigo (a very infectious skin condition that is seen in children), pimples, boils, carbuncles (a contagious skin condition associated with an abscess that oozes pus), and scalded skin syndrome (widespread formation of blisters filled with fluid). Beyond these skin conditions, S. Aureus can cause several life-threatening conditions, including endocarditis, toxic shock syndrome (TSS), meningitis, pneumonia, bacteria in the blood (bacteremia), and a state of whole-body inflammatory (sepsis), and is the most frequent cause of postsurgical wound infection. Thus, the fact that stressful events can affect S. Aureus has enormous implications for physical well-being, particularly in the elderly, in whom it can aggravate behavioral and cognitive disturbances.

In addition to affecting the response to a newly encountered virus, there are effects of stressors that may be relatively far reaching. For instance, HSV-1 can be a recurrent disorder that stems from the reactivation of a latent virus that might have migrated to the trigeminal ganglia, but is usually inactive (the trigeminal nerve is involved in facial sensations and movement). Stressful events may promote virus reactivation by affecting certain cells of the immune system, namely CD8+ T cells, leading to the reappearance of the cold sores associated with HSV-1. Interestingly, the effects of stressors on HSV-1 infection were less pronounced in female rodents than in males, but after ovariectomy, the susceptibility of females was like that of males. So something about the ovaries might be imbuing them with resistance; however, as the resistance to the stressor effects could not be reinstated by administration of estradiol, the reduced susceptibility in females was likely due to ovarian factors other than that of estrogen (Brown et al., 2007).

In addition to having immediate effects on immunity, stressful events may influence the development of immunological memory. In this regard, however, it was reported that the immune response associated with a chronic stressor was enhanced rather than impaired. In particular, repeated social defeat prior to influenza infection increased the presence of memory T cells as well as their functionality (Mays et al., 2010). It seems that a chronic stressor experience may also alter the microenvironment so that dendritic cells (antigen presenting cells) are more effective in producing cytokine responses (Powell et al., 2011). Although it was repeatedly emphasized in earlier portions of this chapter that acute stressors ought to enhance immunity, whereas chronic stressors have the opposite effect, this profile is clearly not always apparent. At this time there are simply too many procedural differences across studies to allow for a unified story to emerge concerning the link between stressors, immune functioning, and disease.

WET HEAD, GO TO BED

Have you ever wondered why going out with your hair wet in the winter might lead to you getting a cold? One possibility is that viruses communicate with one another and are attracted to people with wet heads ('Hey, there's Murray, he's got wet hair. Get him!'). Since this isn't likely, another possibility is that your body temperature declines, making for a comfortable environment for viruses. Perhaps the heat loss associated with going out with wet hair when it's −10°C reduces your immune capacity, resulting in a cold if the virus happens to be around. However, your core body temperature would have to drop quite a bit before this would happen, making this unlikely.

It's also possible that the premise is wrong and that we aren't actually more likely to get sick because of going out with a wet head in the winter. It might simply be the case that we're more likely to get a cold in the winter than in the summer, wet head or not, because we spend more time indoors and thus are more likely to come into close contact with people who are sick or encounter the germs that they've left behind. The wet head notion, however, has been passed down from mothers and grandmothers (and fathers and grandfathers) for years, and it would be pointless to try to dissuade them of this well-entrenched myth. Besides, it wouldn't hurt to listen to your mother and wear a hat when it's cold.

AUTOIMMUNE DISORDERS

Stressful events have been associated with a variety of immunologically-related disorders. Some of these illnesses, as we just discussed, are those in which stressors might weaken immune functioning, thereby allowing viruses to do their nasty work. In other instances stressors influence disorders in which aspects of the immune system attack the self. As we'll see, there is little evidence that stressors cause these illnesses, but they do appear to aggravate the symptoms of an illness that is already present.

MULTIPLE SCLEROSIS (MS)

CHARACTERISTICS OF THE ILLNESS

Multiple sclerosis (MS) is an autoimmune disease wherein immune responses are directed toward the fatty sheaths (myelin) surrounding the brain and spinal cord axons, thus leading to scarring (also referred to as plaques or lesions). Myelin is necessary for the rapid propagation of an action potential down an axon, and when demyelination occurs, conduction speed is slowed, leading to compromised signals between neurons and between the brain and periphery. Demyelination is common in several neurodegenerative diseases, and may also be a hallmark of Guillain-Barré Syndrome, acute disseminated encephalomyelitis, and chronic inflammatory demyelinating polyneuropathy, among others.

The disease most commonly first appears in young adults, most often in women. Symptoms of MS can be broad, and can include changes in physical sensation, such as loss of sensitivity or tingling, pricking or numbness, muscle weakness, muscle spasms, or difficulty in moving. Moreover, symptoms may include problems with coordination and balance, or with speech and with swallowing, as well as visual problems and fatigue. Cognitive impairments are common as the disease progresses, and depression is a frequent comorbid condition.

Generally, MS can appear in a form in which new symptoms present as discrete attacks (relapsing forms) followed by months or years without further incidents (relapsing-remitting form). Deceptively, although symptoms may disappear entirely between episodes, the underlying neurological disturbances may persist and even progress. Another form, secondary progressive MS (with the telling alternative name of 'galloping MS'), refers to a subtype in which patients who initially were diagnosed with relapsing-remitting MS experience progressive neurologic decline between episodes and where definite periods of remission are not apparent, although false signs of abatement may appear. Still another form of the disease, primary progressive MS that affects about 15% of patients, is not accompanied by remission following the initial symptoms. In both of the latter forms, the progressive phase commonly occurs when individuals are about 40 years old, but the prognosis for the disease is difficult to predict (Compston & Cole, 2008).

There is no known cure for MS, and at present there are only 'disease-modifying treatments' that limit the course of the relapsing-remitting form of the illness, and in the progressive-remitting form even these treatments are largely ineffective. Treatments are those that affect immune functioning, comprising either IFN-α1a, IFN-α1b, immunosuppressive agents, or a monoclonal antibody immunomodulator (monoclonal refers to cells that are products of a single ancestral cell that were derived by repeated cellular replication). Because of their very broad effects, these powerful agents can have adverse effects or be poorly tolerated, sometimes making treatment difficult.

IMPACT OF STRESSORS

Based on a detailed meta-analysis, it was concluded that stressful experiences contribute to the exacerbation of MS symptoms as well as the presence of new brain lesions (Mohr et al., 2004). In a summary of research, MS flares were attributed to a constellation of factors, including disability level, medication usage, cardiovascular reactivity, baseline heart rate, and life events, which accounted for 30% of the variance in illness (Ackerman et al., 2002). It seems that psychological factors may also play a significant role in this respect as new brain lesions were most prominent among individuals that focused on their illness through emotion-based coping and was least evident in patients who used avoidance/distraction to cope (Mohr et al., 2002). Likewise, there have been reports that distressing events were more likely to occur during the period prior to relapse of MS symptoms relative to well periods (Ackerman et al., 2002). Further, viral infection was associated with a rise of MS relapse, possibly owing to the immune activation that accompanies infection. As viral illness itself may be influenced by antecedent stressors, and may activate stress pathways, MS exacerbation might be due to a combination of psychological and viral insults.

Most studies that assessed the relationship between MS and stress involved a small number of participants, were of a retrospective nature, involved self-reports of stress (which could be biased), and the effect sizes were modest (i.e., the variance accounted for was small). Under the scrutiny of a well-controlled study, largely unburdened by recall biases, it was concluded that the data available had not been impressive (Brown et al., 2005). Nevertheless, a modest relation between stressful experiences and MS was detected, indicating that the frequency of stressful experiences and not the severity of acute stressors were most germane in predicting the worsening of MS symptoms. Curiously, the frequency of relapse was diminished relative to that evident during the preceding period if individuals experienced a strong stressor (e.g., major surgery or fractures; Mohr et al., 2000) and following periods of high threat. The processes responsible for these paradoxical outcomes are uncertain, but it will be recalled that moderate vs severe or chronic stressors differentially influence immune and corticoid functioning, and the paradoxical effects observed in relation to MS may involve such mechanisms.

Animal-based studies relevant to MS had suggested that stressful events, particularly those of a chronic nature, contributed to illness exacerbation (Griffin et al., 1993). In contrast, acute stressors may have the opposite effect, possibly owing to the immunosuppressive effects elicited by corticosterone (Levine & Saltzman, 1987). It will be recognized that these findings are not quite in keeping with the data from human studies, indicating that strong stressful events transiently inhibited MS aggravation. Although animal studies are often effective models of human conditions, this is obviously not always the case. This said, however, attempting to equate stressor severity in rodents and humans is difficult, and consequently it is uncertain what to make of these contradictory findings.

One of the better known animal models of MS is that of Theiler's murine encephalomyelitis virus (TMEV) infection (named after the 1937 Nobel laureate, virologist Max Theiler). There were reports indicating that stressors exacerbated several aspects of MS in mice using this model. Interestingly, the timing of the stressor relative to infection was critical in promoting this outcome, just as it was in determining other immune/cytokine changes. In fact, when social defeat coincided with infection (as opposed to preceding infection), the course of the disease was actually less severe and the extent of inflammation was limited. It seemed that IL-6 changes associated with the stressor were fundamental in provoking enhanced symptoms, although it is unclear why IL-6 would be relevant to the effects of timing of the stressor in relation to viral challenge (Meagher et al., 2007).

Summarizing, it seems that stressful events may instigate symptom recurrence among MS patients, depending on the nature of the stressor encountered, and might even contribute to the neurodegeneration associated with this disorder. It may be of particular significance that MS is frequently comorbid with depressive illness, which has been associated with previous stressful experiences. It would be understandable if depressive features followed an MS diagnosis, but it is frequently the case that depressive disorders precede MS, and depression in MS patients is more common than would be expected in illnesses of a chronic nature. Thus, it is likely that MS and depression share some common underlying features. These can be related to antecedent stressful events and/or the involvement of common mechanisms, including neuroendocrine factors or cytokine variations, both of which may be connected to stressful experiences. Not unexpectedly, having a potent coping strategy, particularly social support, predicted a better psychological adjustment among those diagnosed with MS; however, it did not appear that social support was related to the effects of stressful experiences on symptom remission. Thus, social support may help individuals deal with their situation, but once present, the illness is not abated by having this support.

LUPUS ERYTHEMATOSUS

CHARACTERISTICS OF THE ILLNESS

Systemic lupus erythematosus (SLE) is a systemic autoimmune disease wherein the immune system attacks any of several parts of the body, such as the heart, joints, nervous system, liver, kidneys, skin, lungs, and blood vessels, promoting inflammation and damage to these tissues. The disease is most common in women (about 90% of cases), and usually manifests between 15–35 years of age. The symptoms of the disease vary appreciably, but typically include joint pains, fatigue, myalgia (muscle pain), and fever, which may appear and disappear on an unpredictable basis. Because this pattern of symptoms is also common to other illnesses, it may be difficult for a firm diagnosis to be established initially. As the disease progresses, bouts or flares of illness occur, often preceded by signs such as increased fatigue, pain, rash, fever, abdominal discomfort, headache, and dizziness, and with disease progression increased risk occurs for cardiovascular disease, infections, osteoporosis, and cancer. It is possible that inflammatory factors, notably cytokines such as IFNs, contribute to pathological outcomes such as cardiovascular disease (Kahlenberg & Kaplan, 2011).

The neurological and psychiatric manifestations of SLE are of great concern as SLE may be accompanied by periventricular white matter hyperintensities (high intensity of white or grey matter on certain types of MRI scans, possibly indicating demyelination), hemorrhages and infarcts (lesions that stem from cell death brought on by a lack of oxygen), cell loss in several brain regions, impaired hippocampal neurogenesis, and cerebral atrophy. As well, microstructural abnormalities may be present that affect processing speed and executive functioning. There is also reason to believe that memory impairments that sometimes occur in association with SLE might be tied to diminished hippocampal volume and glutamate dysfunction.

The marked brain disturbances associated with SLE have been attributed to antibodies that are directed against proteins in the brain (these are referred to as brain reactive autoantibodies). Although antibodies don't typically get into the brain, these antibodies could potentially gain access because SLE is frequently accompanied by compromised blood–brain barrier efficiency, thereby allowing antibodies access to different aspects of the brain where they might cause damage (Williams et al., 2010). A related accounting of the central actions associated with SLE is that lupus antibodies can cross-react with particular subunits of NMDA receptors, which might cause cell death (Faust et al., 2010). It has also been suggested that the presence of auto-antibodies (these are antibodies that are directed at the self) in a mouse model of SLE was related to the development of depressive-like symptoms as well as to cognitive disturbances in humans (Kowal et al., 2006).

The fact that SLE occurs primarily in women points to the possibility that sex hormones might be a fundamental feature in this illness. In fact, estrogen enhances autoantibody production, whereas testosterone has the opposite effect. Moreover, estrogens may interact with other processes (e.g., DA functioning) to influence behavioral outputs. Whether such factors are responsible for the observed difference between males and females warrants further assessment, but it should also be considered that other factors, including elevated stress reactivity in females, might also contribute in this regard. To be sure, various hormone and neuropeptide changes may have profound effects on immune functioning, and as stressful events influence these hormones, the course of the illness may be altered (Sternberg, 2001).

At the moment SLE is incurable and the available treatments are essentially used to manage (rather than eliminate) the illness. Typically, when symptoms are mild or remittent, treatment is limited to nonsteroidal anti-inflammatory drugs (e.g., prednisone). With more severe cases, drugs that affect immune functioning are used, such as corticosteroids, and immunosuppressants such as cyclophosphamide. These agents can have marked adverse effects and care is taken to avoid such outcomes. More recently, drug development has focused on targeting particular immune cells rather than treatments that affect the immune system broadly, including treatments using drugs such as belimumab and atacicept.

IMPACT OF STRESSORS

Among SLE patients, stressors provoked immune and cytokine responses that were readily distinguishable from that of healthy controls (Jacobs et al., 2001). Interestingly, as in MS patients, SLE symptoms were not exaggerated in response to major life stresses, whereas day-to-day irritations aggravated symptoms. Likewise, daily hassles, particularly those associated with social relationships, were predictive of flares in SLE patients that were reflected by increased use of steroid medication, and appeared to be tied to disturbed cognitive functioning, impaired total attention speed, and visual memory performance (Peralta-Ramirez et al., 2004).

As in the case of other stressor-related disorders, uniform changes were not evident among all afflicted individuals who encountered stressful experiences, but it appeared that SLE flares varied across individuals based on distinct biological features. Flares associated with stressors were most prominent among individuals that carried a particular form of the 5-HT$_{1A}$ gene (the 1019G allele) that might result in increased stressor sensitivity (Birmingham et al., 2006). Of particular significance is that this genotype has also been associated with depressive illness (Lemonde et al., 2003), which is influenced by stressful events. In light of this commonality, it would not be unreasonable to wonder whether this genotype, coupled with environmental stressors, are responsible for the high comorbidity seen between SLE and depressive illness.

It is understandable that a diagnosis of SLE can be devastating to the individual and may promote other stress-related disorders, such as depressive illness. However, even when stressful experiences were controlled for, depression among SLE patients was elevated, possibly suggesting that the depressive features were a manifestation of the neurological consequences of SLE. Nevertheless, the way in which individuals cope with the distress related to SLE has been associated with health-related quality of life (Hyphantis et al., 2011). Furthermore, depressive illness and diminished quality of life among SLE patients was particularly prominent in those who used disengagement or emotion-focused coping strategies, whereas quality of life was best among individuals who used coping that entailed positive reinterpretation and growth (Rinaldi et al., 2006). As expected, depressive symptoms and quality of life could be improved through cognitive behavioral therapy (CBT). Importantly, however, although stressful experiences can affect disease-related processes, psychosocial and coping factors have more of an impact on indices of quality of life than on organ damage (Bricou et al., 2006).

ARTHRITIS

CHARACTERISTICS OF THE ILLNESS

Arthritis is a disorder that entails inflammation of a single joint or multiple joints, and like other autoimmune disorders it is more common in females than males. The symptoms of arthritis may comprise joint pain, difficulty using the hands, moving joints or even walking, muscle aches and pains, tenderness, general malaise or feelings of fatigue, weight loss, and poor sleep, as well as fever. A frequent form of arthritic illness, osteoarthritis or degenerative joint disease, often appears as a consequence of aging, infection, injury, or trauma to the joint. Another common form is that of rheumatoid arthritis, an autoimmune disorder that is characterized as a chronic inflammatory disease that affects the synovial joints (the movable joints surrounded by a capsule containing a lubricating synovial fluid), including the membrane that lines joints and tendon sheaths as well as cartilage, primarily in the fingers, wrists, knees, and elbows, and cervical spine. Several forms of arthritis may occur in children or young adolescents (under the age of 16), with juvenile idiopathic arthritis (juvenile rheumatoid arthritis) being the most common.

Rheumatoid arthritis has been associated with auto-antibodies directed at portions of the IgG molecule, known as rheumatoid factors (RF), as well as those that are directed at other proteins (these are known as antibodies to citrullinated peptides). Importantly, these factors may be apparent in advance of clinical signs of rheumatoid arthritis, implicating them as either causal agents or biomarkers (McInnes & Schett, 2007). Cytokines, such as IL-1β and TNF-α, have also been implicated as culprits in the rheumatoid arthritis process. Treatments of the illness can include physiotherapy, lifestyle changes, and exercise, but primarily comprise drug treatments like anti-inflammatories, corticosteroids, and monoclonal antibodies, as well as analgesics. There have also been promising outcomes using disease-modifying anti-rheumatic drugs (DMARDs), which slow down disease progression. Within this group are TNF-α inhibitors (e.g., adalimumab, etanercept, infliximab, and golimumab), and drugs that inhibit both IL-1β and TNF-α. Unfortunately, the disease is often refractory to treatments and many patients do not reach sustained remission (Polido-Pereira et al., 2011).

IMPACT OF STRESSORS

A sizeable portion (22%) of patients with rheumatoid arthritis attributed their illness to stressful experiences, 45% believed that these exacerbated their illness or provoked flares, and 21% attributed improvements in their condition to a decline of stress (Affleck et al., 1987). A review of autoimmune disorders, including rheumatoid arthritis, indicated that day-to-day stressful events exacerbated pathology, and that social support was fundamental in attenuating these adverse effects (Herrmann et al., 2000). In line with this, chronic interpersonal stress among rheumatoid arthritis patients was associated with greater *in vitro* production of IL-6, coupled with impaired ability of glucocorticoids to inhibit this cellular inflammatory response. As stressful events may influence peripheral cytokine activity, and chronic stressful events may lead to glucocorticoid resistance, thereby limiting the inhibition of cytokines otherwise provoked by corticoids, it is tempting to surmise that arthritic flares may involve a stress component (Straub et al., 2005).

Paralleling these findings, a diary-based analysis of workers with rheumatoid arthritis revealed that pain levels were elevated on days with more undesirable work events compared to days with fewer events. Moreover, individuals with jobs that entailed high 'strain' reported the highest levels of mid-day pain. Such findings complemented those that showed that chronic stressful events influence both juvenile and rheumatoid arthritis, with the former being affected more readily, and it seems that both α-adrenergic receptor functioning and cortisol activity contributed to the symptoms of arthritis and the stress-related flares (Straub et al., 2005).

INFLAMMATORY FACTORS INFLUENCE NEURODEGENERATIVE DISORDERS

Inflammatory processes have, understandably, typically been linked to immune-related disorders, but it seems they might also contribute to the progression of Alzheimer's disease (AD) as well as Parkinson's disease. Alzheimer's disease is usually characterized by neuropathological hallmarks, such as increased β-amyloid plaques, neurofibrillary tangles, and misfolded tau protein. However, it also seems that inflammatory and anti-inflammatory processes, secondary to the misfolded tau or to other brain anomalies or that are brought about by stressors, might contribute to AD (Zilka et al., 2012). It has also been reported that the plaques associated with Alzheimer's disease are surrounded by microglia, which ought to be involved in getting rid of plaques and dead neurons, but they also release IL-1β that might serve to produce neuronal damage. Likewise, traumatic brain injury can serve as a risk factor for the later development of AD, possibly through the initiation of the disease processes that involve apoptotic or epigenetic mechanisms, or instigation of the inflammatory processes that influence cell death. The inflammatory factors that might be related to AD include over-expression of IL-1β, IL-6, IL-18, and TNF-α, as well as changes of inhibitory processes, such as IL-1 receptor antagonist (IL-1Ra), IL-4, IL-10, and transforming growth factor (TGF)-β that could protect the brain from inflammatory factors. In fact, epidemiological studies revealed that intake of nonsteroidal anti-inflammatory drugs (NSAIDs) reduced the risk of developing AD. While clinical trials using NSAIDs in treating AD patients have not yielded impressive outcomes (Rubio-Perez & Morillas-Ruiz, 2012), it seems that the suppressor of proinflammatory cytokine upregulation, Minozac, had positive effects in a mouse model of AD, although it remains to be seen whether this holds up in humans.

CANCER

As indicated at the outset of this chapter, the notion has been tossed around for years that stressful events or stress-related illnesses, such as depression, might contribute to the emergence or exacerbation of certain types of cancer (Costanzo et al., 2011) Obviously, this isn't the place to try to provide extensive information on the cancer process, but it's important that some basic terms and concepts be explained before we enter into a discussion of how stress might influence the development and growth of cancer cells.

THE CANCER PROCESS

There are several different types of cancers, as indicated in Table 6.1, and these can be further subdivided on the basis of several of their inherent characteristics. Cancer, which may stem from either genetic (e.g., breast cancer genes such as BRCA1 or BRCA2) or environmental factors, refers to disease conditions in which certain cells undergo uncontrolled growth so that adjacent tissues may be destroyed. As well, cancer cells can leave a place of origin (i.e., from the primary tumor site), acquire the ability to get into blood vessels or penetrate the lymphatic walls, make an arduous trip through the blood or lymphatic system, our body's superhighways, and then find a comfortable home to establish a new cancer colony. This process, referred to as metastasis, distinguishes malignant from benign tumors, as the latter typically neither invade adjacent tissues nor metastasize, although some benign tumors do metastasize, and conversely, some malignant cancers rarely metastasize.

So, how does cancer come about? How do first cancer cells occur, and why do they multiply without apparent restraint? One of the earliest views concerning the cancer process, the immunosurveillance hypothesis, was that lymphocytes served as sentinels responsible for recognizing and eliminating cancer cells, and hence cancer development was due to some sort of immune malfunction. However, cancer cells are a wily enemy that can find ways of escaping detection, and thus flourish and form a tumor mass. Besides, as cancer cells are mutated forms of our own cells, they might not readily be seen as foreign and hence would not be attacked. In theory, environmental events (including stressors) that reduce immune functioning might act to limit attacks of the immune system on the cancer cells that might be present. However, immune surveillance is only one component of a complex set of factors

TABLE 6.1 Cancer subtypes

Carcinoma: subtype that involves epithelial cells that comprise tissues that line surfaces and cavities within the body, including the skin. Thus, cancers that affect the breast, prostate, colon, and lung are typically carcinomas.

Sarcoma: a cancer that affects connective tissues that largely comprise blood, cartilage, bone, tendons, adipose tissue, as well as lymphatic tissue.

Lymphoma and leukemia: generally refer to cancer of blood forming (or hematopoietic) cells.

Blastoma: a type of cancer that stems from precursor cells (often referred to as blasts) that are essentially primitive and incompletely differentiated cells. There are several types of blastoma, one of which is a cancer type that is seen in children.

Germ cell tumor: derived from pluripotent cells (i.e., those that come from a stem cell and thus have the capacity to differentiate into several different germ lines). This type of cancer is also the type that is seen in children and babies.

A cancer's development is typically described through staging terms. Stage 0 (carcinoma in situ) refers to an early form of cancer characterized by the absence of invasion of tumor cells into the surrounding tissue. Stage I cancers are localized to a single part of the body, and Stage II cancers are also local, but fairly advanced. Stage III cancers are also locally advanced, but may involve lymph nodes being affected. Stage IV cancers are those that have metastasized, or spread to other organs.

that serve to protect us, and disruption of any of several components within our defense networks may place us at risk (Reiche et al., 2004). In essence, cancer could potentially be a result of immune dysfunction, but there are many other ways through which a tumor can come about that have nothing at all to do with immune disturbances.

Earlier, in discussing DNA and its replication, it was indicated that mutations occur when there is a change in the nucleotide sequences that make up genes (either a deletion or a substitution, for instance). These polymorphisms happen frequently, and could potentially appear in daughter cells of the initially mutated cell, and then appear in their daughter cells, and in subsequent replications. Fortunately, during replication, proofreading and editing occurs so that the errors in the transcribed code are fixed. Moreover, even if the errors get by this editing process, the mutation may show up at a point in the DNA strand where its effects are not all that meaningful. Then again, as we've seen, they can also show up in genes that influence all sorts of pathological outcomes.

Ordinarily, our genes contain a section that, when activated or uncovered, causes cell death or suicide, which is referred to as apoptosis. Obviously, if a cell is damaged or could cause harmful effects, it would be advantageous for cells to die off. However, a mutation can also occur in the segment of a gene containing these apoptotic messages so that these cells would not die. In the absence of this regulatory mechanism, this cell would multiply again and again, as would its progeny, ultimately creating a tumor mass. If cells from this tumor have the ability to metastasize, then the mortal danger of this cancer is exponentially greater.

Mutated genes can be passed down from a parent to their offspring, making them especially vulnerable to certain types of cancer. For instance, in the case of breast cancer, the presence of certain mutations in the BRCA1 gene places women at a potentially high risk for developing breast cancer. This mutation varies across cultural groups, being relatively high among Ashkenazi Jews (~8% of women), but less so in Hispanic (~3.5%) and Asian American patients (0.5%). BRCA1, which appears in the breast, is responsible for DNA repair and for the destruction of the DNA if repair of the gene isn't possible. However, if this gene is mutated, then the risk of breast cancer (and to a lesser extent ovarian cancer) increases appreciably. The risk (>60%) is sufficiently great that some women have opted for double mastectomy to be assured that they would not be victimized by cancer.

The presence of the BRCA1 mutation, however, doesn't guarantee that cancer will develop, and there are evidently other factors that might contribute in this regard. The presence of certain hormones or immune factors or environmental toxins that affect these hormones, for example, could trigger the development of cancer in those with the BRCA1 mutation. This 'second hit' hypothesis has understandably encouraged a search for the factors that could enable cancer-related mutations to become expressed as tumors, or conversely the factors that might hinder the development of cancer. In their intriguing book, Natterson-Horowitz and Bowers (2012) indicated that breast cancer appears across species, and this varies as a function of how frequently these species become pregnant and thus lactate. The same thing happens in humans, leading to the possibility that pregnancy or lactation (or both) or the hormones associated with these processes might serve in a protective capacity.

Certain chemicals or environmental stimuli may be carcinogenic. They can instigate DNA mutations that can be especially harmful if they disturb DNA repair processes or tumor suppressor genes. We've heard a lot about cigarettes and sun rays, but there are a vast number of agents that have carcinogenic properties, including many that are found in the workplace. As well, lifestyle, including exercise and diet, might influence the development of cancers, and might be responsible for the differences in certain types of cancer (e.g., gastrointestinal) across countries, regions, and cultures. The cancer process could involve a cell's ability to correct errors (mutations) or apoptotic processes, or reflect a second hit that allows for the adverse effects of mutations to be manifested.

This brings us to the case of how stressful events might affect the cancer process. It seems that certain environments may trigger these types of errors, and these carcinogens are widely believed to be the major cause of cancers (Merlo et al., 2006). The ones we've heard most about, of course, concern cigarettes and sun rays, but there are a vast number of agents that have carcinogenic properties, including some that are common in the workplace. And as mentioned above, lifestyle, including exercise and diet that are affected by stressful events, is also believed to influence the progression of cancers, and might be responsible for the differences in certain types of cancer (e.g., gastrointestinal) that occur across countries, regions, and cultures (Park et al., 2008). However, for the most part the evidence for stress causing cancer is unimpressive, and it is more likely that it promotes the exacerbation of already existing cancers.

Cancer can also be provoked by viruses (i.e., oncovirus), such as the human papillomavirus (cervical carcinoma) that has received a lot of press lately because of efforts to have young women immunized against this virus. You've probably also heard of Kaposi's sarcoma herpes virus, an opportunistic infection often associated with HIV/AIDS, Epstein-Barr virus that may be related to B-cell lympho-proliferative disease, as well as Human T-cell leukemia virus-1 (Pagano et al., 2004). Although stressors can influence virally-related processes, the evidence suggesting some sort of role concerning potential effects of stressors on these virally-related cancers isn't there.

IMPLICATIONS FOR CANCER TREATMENT

Cancer treatments have evolved considerably over the decades. Whereas it was once seen as a death sentence, there are some cancers that are now treated with appreciable success, although admittedly, there are some cancer types that have not been treatable. The treatment (or management) of cancer includes better and more focused chemotherapy, radiation therapy, surgery, and the newer arsenal of treatments that comprise immunotherapy as well as monoclonal antibody therapy. Despite the promising advances in the treatment of cancers, make no mistake, in each case the treatment process is an arduous one, with numerous obstacles, stumbles, and backward steps frequently being encountered. As well, the long-term ramifications of the treatments can be a heavy load to carry, and thus the stress of treatment itself could potentially influence the course of the illness.

As different cancer types can be differentially sensitive to certain hormone treatments (and thus could be more amenable to being affected by stressors) or to certain chemotherapies or other forms of treatment, it is unlikely that any single treatment will emerge to treat all cancers. Of course, the effectiveness of individual treatments will likely vary with the type of tumor being dealt with, its aggressiveness, stage, and location, as well as the genetic characteristics of that cancer. As for so many other illnesses, the treatment of cancers requires an individualized approach.

STRESS STEMMING FROM CANCER

Following the initial shock comes a series of tests, some of which may be invasive and dehumanizing. The treatments themselves reflect yet another series of stressors as these can include amputation or the removal of certain organs or parts of organs, as well as damage to other functions secondary to the surgical procedures. In the case of chemotherapy or radiation, patients often experience sickness, nausea, vomiting, chemo-brain (cognitive disturbances associated with chemotherapy), extreme fatigue, and as a result of the multiple stressors, depression or PTSD may evolve.

If the treatment ends up not doing the patient much good, then there are additional needs, including those from a palliative care team and other health professionals as well as from family members and friends. Home care may be difficult and hospice care might be required to permit the person to die with as little pain and as much dignity as possible. In the case of the treatment being effective, this does not mean that the stress has been alleviated. After treatment the patient may have to spend time in physical or occupational rehabilitation, and this too can be demanding. And added to this, patients often require regular medical testing to see if the cancer has returned or whether other illnesses associated with the disease or its treatment need attention. There are clearly lots of anticipatory stressors that persist well after the initial treatment. Then there's the issue of survival beyond one year, beyond two years, and beyond five years, as well as the possibility that another form of cancer might show up (the risks of this are increased appreciably in cancer patients). Clearly, classification as a 'cancer survivor' doesn't mean back to life as it was before. To be sure, the cancer survivor may develop a better appreciation for the good aspects of life, but they may also be subject to enormous strain and uncertainty about the future.

SOCIAL SUPPORT FOLLOWING CANCER TREATMENT

Patients undergoing cancer treatment need lots of social support, and this support needs to go on for a considerable time following the treatment ending. Two fairly recent experiences in this regard warrant sharing. The first concerned a friend who had just completed chemotherapy. Although he was feeling relatively well, his comment to me was 'To this point I've been kept alive by the chemo. Now, I'm on my own. And, I'm scared'. Unfortunately, he had good reason for this feeling.

The second came from another friend who had been treated for breast cancer. She says that she received a lot of support from friends when she was first diagnosed and during the course of

(Continued)

(Continued)

treatment. Once her chemo- and radiation therapy were completed, her friends seemed to feel she was 'cured', and they thus became relatively scarce. Even though she was frightened and could have used the support, she met with all sorts of unsupportive responses if she so much as hinted at her discomfort: 'I'd think you'd be a little less neurotic about this' or, remarkably, 'why don't you just thank God for getting this far, instead of always being such a downer'.

A STRESS–CANCER LINK

Let's have a look at the possibility that stressful events might actually have an effect on the cancer process itself. As already mentioned, there's not much evidence that stressful life experiences can cause cancer, but studies in animals and humans indicated that stressors could influence the growth of induced or transplanted tumors, possibly by affecting endocrine functioning or diminished cytotoxic responses against these tumor cells (Sklar & Anisman, 1979). Several studies in humans indicated that stressful life events were associated with increased cancer progression (Antoni et al., 2006; Duijts et al., 2003; Hamer et al., 2009), increased cancer-related mortality (Hamer et al., 2009), and earlier death among individuals who had undergone stem cell transplantation in an effort to beat the disease (Park et al., 2010). Moreover, anxiety and depression were accompanied by a poorer response to neoadjuvant chemotherapy (i.e., the administration of therapeutic agents prior to the primary treatment being initiated, such as hormone treatment administered prior to radical treatments) relative to that evident in individuals who were less depressed or anxious.

In line with a stress–cancer perspective, it was reported that among breast cancer patients with high levels of psychological stress, NK cell functioning was impaired relative to that seen in patients with lower stress levels (recall that one job of NK cells is to destroy tumor cells, at least early in the battle). For instance, among women monitored for 18 months following surgery, those who indicated greater levels of distress exhibited diminished NK cell activity and reduced lymphocyte proliferative responses (Varker et al., 2007). Conversely, providing men with stress management tools enhanced postoperative (radical prostatectomy) mood, and this was accompanied by augmented immune functioning reflected by elevated proinflammatory cytokine levels. Predictably, the most rapid decline of distress following surgery was accompanied by the most rapid recovery of NK cell activity (Thornton et al., 2007). It was also observed in patients diagnosed with breast cancer that several measures reflecting coping ability, such as social support, benefit finding, and optimism, were related to NK cell activity and lymphocyte proliferative responses. Similar outcomes were also reported with other forms of cancer, such as gynecologic, prostate, gastrointestinal, digestive tract, and liver malignancies.

An extensive meta-analysis of stress-related psychosocial factors and cancer exacerbation suggested that survival was poorer as stressful events increased and that these outcomes could be tied to several fundamental features that were relevant across different types of cancer (Chida et al., 2008). Although recent or ongoing stressful life experiences were associated with poorer cancer survival and higher mortality, these stressful experiences were not related to increased cancer incidence (i.e., causing cancer). Of particular importance, individual difference factors were predictive of the effects of stressors in that higher cancer mortality was apparent among individuals who displayed a stress-prone personality, had poor coping styles, negative emotional responses, or poor quality of life. In addition, early adverse experiences were also associated with increased incidence of breast cancer, paralleling studies showing that adverse early life experiences may have protracted consequences with respect to adult psychological disorders.

In line with these findings, loss of a parent and poverty during early development were associated with increased adult cancer incidence (Schuler & Auger, 2011). This increase was particularly notable if the stressor involved physical or emotional abuse, especially if it came from a same-sex parent. The effects of adverse early experiences have also been associated with one form of skin cancer, namely the recurrence of basal cell carcinoma. Specifically, among individuals that experienced a major life stressor in the preceding year and who also reported poor early life maternal or paternal care, immune responses were impaired and the recurrence of this form of cancer was increased. It is tempting to speculate that stressors increased the incidence of depression, which led to the tumor occurrences, but a history of depression did not correspond with the recurrence of cancer. Nevertheless, such findings suggest that early adverse experiences together with those events encountered in adulthood might contribute to the storm that emerges as a form of cancer.

The studies in humans that assessed the stress–cancer relationship have largely been of a correlational nature often relying on retrospective analyses that attempted to tie a current cancer state to past stressful events. These studies suffer from the usual problems associated with retrospective analyses; the way an individual perceives their past might be colored by their current state of health, and memories of the past might not be all that accurate owing to age, the secondary effects of the cancer, and a constellation of other factors.

OH, WHY ME?

When women with breast cancer were questioned regarding factors that might have been responsible for their illness, 58% attributed it to stress, whereas the next two leading attributions concerned previous hormone therapy (17%) and genetic factors (10%). Clearly, patients believed that stress was an important etiological factor for their illness, but this doesn't necessarily make it so. Often, when distressed or ill, individuals want to know why this happened to them. Were they responsible for their own destiny, or did someone or something cause it? Sometimes there simply isn't an answer: it might just be a matter of bad luck, or it might be because of environmental agents or events.

(Continued)

(Continued)

Many people simply need a reason for why something bad happened to them. Sometimes people make the statement 'Why me?', and the answer, while not pleasant, simply amounts to 'Why not you?'. As we saw earlier, people often have beliefs that don't align well with reality; one was that of a 'just world', in which individuals believe that the world is fundamentally just and thus when things go wrong there must be a reason for it. Yet, as individuals believe that they are basically good, then their misfortune needs to be due to external forces, possibly stressful experiences. The relevance here is that when we ask a person in distress about their past experiences, what we get in return may (or may not) be a biased perspective.

There have been attempts to assess the stress–cancer relationship in a prospective manner, but these have been few. As well, even when a relation between stressors and cancer was evident, as in the case of a twenty-year prospective study in Israeli individuals that had lost a son in war or by accident, this was a weak one, and in all likelihood other risk factors need to be included in the equation, including lifestyle changes related to the trauma (Reiche et al., 2004). There have also been findings suggesting that appropriate social support and coping might diminish the course of cancer progression, but once again, the data were not strong, despite the fact that stressors were reliably found to reduce NK cell activity.

Yet another approach to assess the stress–cancer relationship involves assessing patients' stressor history when a tumor is first suspected and a biopsy is performed, but before the biopsy results have been received. If distress is a factor in the cancer process, then it would be expected that greater stress reports would be apparent in those individuals later found with malignant tumors than in those with benign tumors. In contrast, if reported stressor experiences stemmed from biased appraisals, then elevated negative life events would be evident in both the malignant and benign groups relative to that apparent in control individuals. In fact, women diagnosed with malignant cancer had experienced greater life stressor events than did healthy controls or women that were found to have a benign condition. As well, among women with a suspected ovarian cancer, nocturnal cortisol levels were higher among those who turned out to have malignant tumors than among those with benign tumors (Weinrib et al., 2010). Furthermore, patients awaiting assessment for ovarian cancer reported elevated vegetative and affective depressive symptoms and exhibited greater plasma IL-6 and cortisol relative to women with tumors that were of low malignant potential (Lutgendorf et al., 2008). Findings such as these lend credence to the view that stress, aspects of depression, and cancer might be linked, and that neuroendocrine factors and cytokines might mediate these relationships. However, don't be misled into thinking that the case supporting a link between stress and cancer progression is a done deal. There are lots of researchers that have not accepted this perspective, and often there have been good reasons, including frequent failures to find a correspondence between these factors. Cancer is a complex molecular biological disease and it would be overly simplistic to attempt to boil it down to the simple notion that stressful events are the primary contributors to disease progression (especially when numerous other psychosocial factors, such as appraisals, coping, and early life events, to name but a few, were not considered). Frankly, I don't think there are many researchers who would argue that stressor events are the major player accounting for the course of illness, although stressful events might contribute to the general well-being associated with cancer, and might be one of a constellation of factors that influences the course of the disease.

PSYCHO-ONCOLOGY

At one time, the notion that stressful events might influence the cancer process was viewed as wacky stuff. Today, it is not unusual to find health care workers accepting the notion that stressful events, lifestyle, and patient comfort could influence cancer progression and the efficacy of treatments. As well, even if these variables didn't affect cancer progression, considering them as part of the treatment regimen may have positive effects on the patient's psychological well-being. However, there are some oncologists, and some individuals in the cancer research field, who see this as an interesting epiphenomenon to which they give lip service, but I get the feeling that they don't actually believe that it is as important as patient advocates would have us believe. This is not to say that these oncologists are not concerned with patients' psychological well-being, but they might think that they should be doing what they do best, namely treating the cancer, whereas other aspects of the patient's well-being should be someone else's job. Phrased that way, maybe they're right, particularly as they may be ill-equipped to deal with psychological interventions, aimed at certain diseases, cancer being among them. Thus, cancer patients might be best treated by medical teams rather than any single individual. Yet patients typically pin their greatest hope for a positive treatment outcome on the oncologist, and thus this is the person who has the greatest sway on a patient's psychological state.

Animal studies are in many ways more amenable to the experimental analysis of the stress–cancer link, and there have been reports indicating that stressors could influence tumor growth as well as metastasis (Moreno-Smith et al., 2010; Reiche et al., 2004). As discussed earlier, this could develop through several routes, the most obvious being that the stressor treatments caused the release of corticosterone, which could act against immune functioning, thereby allowing for less restrained tumor growth. As well, glucocorticoids can inhibit chemotherapy-induced cancer cell apoptosis and may promote cancer cell survival, and stressors can also disrupt DNA repair, thus allowing mutated cells to multiply. In addition to corticoids, the stressor-induced NE release and the consequent β-NE receptor signaling can affect cancer cells (by stimulating cell migration and invasion). Another factor that might contribute to stressor-induced enhancement of tumor growth concerns possible effects on angiogenesis (the growth of new blood vessels that might be important in order for the growing tumor to receive an adequate blood supply), just as stress-related hormones have such effects (Thaker et al., 2006).

Studies in animals have also shown that 'personality characteristics' in mice may be related to stressor-provoked tumor progression. Specifically, a social stressor and later re-exposure to this stressor shortly after tumor cell inoculation, resulted in pulmonary metastases being increased five-fold. However, this was most pronounced in mice that responded to the stressor with a passive coping style compared to those that engaged in active coping. As well, early life stressors, such as social isolation, were associated with increased growth of carcinogen-induced tumors (Williams et al., 2009), although there may be critical periods in development that would be more likely to result in such outcomes. In fact, epigenetic changes might be more readily induced during the early postnatal period, and would thus have greater effects on the later neuroendocrine processes that influence carcinogen-induced tumor growth.

SO, HOW DO STRESSORS COME TO AFFECT METASTASIS?

One way we could think of answering this question is to examine characteristics of the tumor cells that have metastasized or are attempting to do so. Have they become stronger? Do they have some sort of protective coating or cloak that protects them from destruction by immune cells or by specialized proteins (e.g., metastasis suppressors) that are on the lookout for cancer cells? Are they buddying-up to regular cells in the body and thereby disguising themselves to avoid being destroyed by immune defenses (following the adage that a friend of my friend is also my friend)? Each of these approaches has, to varying degrees, received attention in the search to limit or prevent metastasis.

Another perspective to assess the stress–cancer relationship is based on the possibility that stressors might result in the general environment being more hospitable, so that tumor cells can thrive more readily. It has been known for some time that cancer metastasis is accompanied by the growth of a new network of blood vessels (angiogenesis) that feed the tumor cells, and it is possible that stress hormones could contribute to this process. Related to this, stressful events, through their action on sympathetic nervous system activity, might favor the survival and growth of cancer cells that have migrated to bone tissue. Specifically, sympathetic activation and the release of norepinephrine might result in an environment conducive for cancer cells to flourish. When breast cancer cells were injected into the hearts of mice (simulating cancer cells that have left the main tumor mass, and thus are at an early stage of metastasis), these cells caused more cancer lesions on bone of stressed than nonstressed mice. Importantly, reducing norepinephrine's effects by blocking its β-receptors using propranolol reduced the number of cancer lesions. It's a bit premature to say whether these data will actually be relevant to metastasis in humans, but the possibility that a simple anti-stress treatment would have such positive effects is very exciting.

STRESS AND ITS IMPLICATIONS FOR CANCER TREATMENT

So far we've addressed the question of whether stress causes or augments cancer growth. Even if we knew the answer to this, what would it do for us? At best, it might help us to develop methods of attenuating the aspects of the disease aggravated by distress. Yet this might just be pie-in-the-sky as we can't just advise people to avoid stress in the hope that they would or could do so. Yet it would be possible to have individuals in treatment for cancer take up stress reduction procedures (described in Chapter 12). Even if this treatment didn't have an impact on tumor progression, it might diminish distress associated with the illness and thereby enhance quality of life.

It is not surprising that being informed of a malignant tumor and having to undergo treatment might be associated with psychopathological states such as depression, anxiety, and PTSD (Goncalves et al., 2011). Likewise, these symptoms are frequently evident when family members are affected, and are particularly severe when the patient is the individual's child. Several stress management procedures have been used in an effort to diminish distress associated with cancer. Some have used traditional methods of stress reduction, whereas others have dealt with less traditional methods. Traditional therapies, such as cognitive behavior therapy (CBT) or CBT in combination with a biobehavioral intervention, may diminish the depression and distress associated with cancer, as has mindfulness-based stress reduction (MBSR). Chapter 12 provides more information about mindfulness; however, for the moment, suffice it that this procedure, derived to some extent from CBT, involves individuals learning to deal with events in the moment and not to focus on future events that they have no control over. In their review of this literature, McGregor and Antoni (2009) indicated that psychological interventions may not only affect subjective indices of psychological well-being, but might also affect neuroendocrine functioning, lymphocyte proliferation, and proinflammatory cytokine production (Matchim et al., 2011).

As often happens with severe adverse events, such as cancer, some individuals find especially effective methods of coping, and may even be able to find something positive in bad experiences (finding meaning). For some people, it's a matter of appreciating life more, and for others it may involve devoting themselves to a cause to improve the lives of others. This 'benefit finding' or 'posttraumatic growth' has repeatedly been associated with reduced stress and reduced psychological disturbances. But as indicated earlier, only some patients are able to find meaning from adverse events, and one can't push people in this regard. Nonetheless, teaching individuals about their disease and facilitating meaning making, especially if this is incorporated with other approaches to diminish cancer-related distress (such as CBT), might prove useful.

Beyond the antidepressant effects that have been observed, stress reduction treatments (e.g., supportive group therapy) enhanced survival time among women with metastatic breast cancer, as well as gastrointestinal cancer, and a combination of psychotherapy and drug treatments enhanced NK cell functioning (Fawzy et al., 1993). However, there have also been reports indicating that psychological intervention did not have positive effects on the course of the illness. It would have been nice to see consistent results in such studies, but frankly, it is not surprising that this wasn't the case. The proposition that psychological interventions might enhance the effectiveness of traditional cancer treatments was a longshot. As much as I think that stressful events could exacerbate tumor growth, I'm less certain that the opposite effect would readily be obtained through treatments that reduce distress as there are too many variables that need to be considered. For starters, the outcomes observed might be dependent on the nature of the stress-reduction intervention, how effective it actually is in diminishing distress, anxiety, and depression, and when the treatment was applied (e.g., has the tumor escaped from processes that might limit its growth, and hence is essentially unalterable?). Nevertheless, as indicated repeatedly, even if the de-stressing treatment doesn't impact tumor progression, if it helps the individual cope with day-to-day burdens, and perhaps instigates benefit finding, then this treatment ought to be viewed as highly beneficial.

CONCLUSION

The immune system plays a fundamental role in protecting us from foreign pathogens, and in the main it does a fairly good job. However, there are occasions where we do get sick. Immune functioning does not operate independent of other systems as it reciprocally interacts with peripheral and central nervous system functions. Thus, stressful events that affect hormone and neurotransmitter functioning also affect immune activity, and the activation of inflammatory factors has profound repercussions on CNS processes and hence on psychological and behavioral processes. The questions that need to be answered concern which factors moderate these relationships. What makes individuals more or less vulnerable to stress-related biological disturbances, or conversely which factors create resilience, and given this knowledge, what can we do to mitigate these stressor effects?

SUMMARY

- Effective immune functioning is instrumental in protecting us from several diseases, but there are occasions wherein the immune system turns on the self, producing autoimmune disorders.
- Stressful experiences, by virtue of effects on immune functioning, can influence our susceptibility to bacterial and viral infection, and may exacerbate the symptoms of autoimmune disorder and perhaps cancer as well.
- These illnesses are portent stressors that can further impair immunity and other biological processes and may be a source for comorbid illnesses.

7 CARDIOVASCULAR DISEASE

THE HEART: YOU GOTTA ♡ IT

Most people don't think much about their heart or heart problems, and certainly not when they're fairly young, but as we age its functioning (or more appropriately, its malfunctioning) comes to mind more often. It's an amazing little organ made up of 'involuntary' muscle and connective tissue, and regulated by various hormones and receptors. The heart is not all that large, about the size of a fist, typically weighing 250–300 gm in females and 300–350 gm in males, but it's got a big job.

The human heart beat can be detected at about five weeks after conception. The embryonic heart beats at a very rapid rate, reaching 165–185 beats per minute (BPM) at about seven weeks' gestation, and then begins to slow down, eventually reaching about 72 BPM after birth. This beat ought to be sustained for our entire lives. Think about it. That's about 2.65 billion beats over a 70-year life span. With all the technology available, no car motor or any other type of machine could last that long without breaking down, even with maintenance every 20,000 km.

The human heart has one main function, and that's to pump blood, which occurs with every beat. To do this, those millions of cells that make up the heart have to be coordinated. You can't very well have one cell doing one thing, and another cell doing something else. Think of what would happen if some cells decided to pump, while others decided to rest. It turns out that there's a pacemaker present in the human heart (the sinoatrial node) that sets the rate and timing for all the cardiac muscle cells to contract. What a cooperative organ the heart is.

It's smart too, or at least it seems to know what it's doing. The right atrium of the heart in mammals collects de-oxygenated blood from the body (via the superior and

(Continued)

(Continued)

inferior vena cavae), pumps it through the tricuspid valve into the right ventricle and then to the lungs, where carbon dioxide is removed and oxygen obtained. The left atrium then receives the oxygenated blood from the lungs, pumps it through the bicuspid valve into the left ventricle, which then pumps it to the body through the aorta, so that nice clean, oxygenated blood serves all those other organs that depend on it.

So remember to take care of your heart, and it'll take care of you.

As good as the heart might be, there are limits to its durability and eventually problems can arise. In fact, illnesses that involve the heart, arteries and/or veins, referred to as 'cardiovascular' or 'circulatory' diseases, represent the greatest causes of death worldwide, typically being 20–30% in most Western countries. There are several types of heart disease and a very great number of factors that might contribute to some of them. In this chapter we obviously can't deal with each of these, and so we'll focus on only a few issues that might be especially pertinent to stress processes. The messages that you should come away with from this chapter concern:

- how coronary heart disease comes about;
- how stressful events might come to influence coronary heart disease, the influence of social support resources in modifying this outcome, and how socioeconomic status might be linked to heart disease;
- the common finding that depression is a comorbid feature of heart disease, and this has significant implications with respect to its cause and treatment;
- the possibility that personality factors might contribute to heart disease, but there have been serious questions raised about this;
- reports that several stressor-induced biological changes might contribute to heart disease, but of these inflammatory processes, as described in Chapter 6, might be particularly relevant.

DISEASES OF THE HEART

In general, cardiac illnesses fall into several categories, as described in Table 7.1. In this chapter we'll primarily be concerned with coronary artery disease (CAD) and heart failure (HF) and some of the factors that contribute to their onset and progression, but some of these same variables also affect other forms of heart disease. The primary factors that influence or are associated with CAD include gender, family history, stressor experiences and the presence of depressive illness and PTSD, high blood pressure, dyslipidaemia (high levels of 'bad' cholesterol or fat), excessive alcohol consumption, obesity (especially abdominal fat distribution), low physical activity, smoking, and diabetes, and of course the inevitable process of aging. We won't go through all of these in detail, but instead we'll focus on those that

TABLE 7.1 Types of heart disease

- Coronary artery disease (CAD) encompasses illnesses that involve diminished blood flow to the heart so that ischemia (lack of oxygen) occurs
- Hypertensive heart disease refers to cardiac illness that arises due to elevated blood pressure
- Heart failure or congestive heart failure refers to instances in which the heart is unable to pump enough blood to meet the needs of the body and organs
- Cardiomyopathy comprise diseases of the cardiac muscle
- Cardiac arrhythmia entails abnormal electrical activity of the heart so that it beats irregularly (too slowly or too quickly)
- Inflammatory heart disease includes endocarditis (inflammation of the inner layer of the heart), myocarditis (inflammation of the muscle portion of the heart), and inflammatory cardiomegaly associated with enlargement of the heart

are particularly relevant to the processes by which stressors might come to affect heart disease. Kop and Mommersteeg (2013) have provided an excellent, detailed review of many of the factors that contribute to CAD, and the reader is encouraged to consult their work.

Coronary artery disease, which is also referred to as coronary heart disease (CHD), comes about as a result of a buildup of plaque within the coronary arteries (plaque is made up of cholesterol, fat, calcium, and fibrin that is normally involved in blood clotting). Over the course of a lifetime, damage may occur to the endothelium (the cell layer inside veins that comes into direct contact with blood) as a result of excessive cholesterol (or other factors), leading to an inflammatory response. This entails a buildup of monocytes (that later form into macrophages) and T cells that infiltrate the site of damage or infection within the arterial wall (i.e., into endothelial lesions). These macrophages and T cells release cytokines that promote inflammation and the formation of plaque, as well as further lesions to the more inner layers of the vascular cell wall (Hansson, 2005). At this stage, damage to the vessel wall is still primarily at the level of the the innermost layer or component of arteries and veins (referred to as 'intima'), but the accumulation of potential hazardous factors continues. These comprise macrophages and debris, and calcium, as well lipids (cholesterol and fatty acids) and fibrous connective tissue (collectively referred to as atheromatous plaques). The lesions and plaque that build up on the endothelium are typically covered by a thin fibrous layer made up of collagen and smooth muscle cells that can rupture, resulting in vascular lesions and the formation of clots. The accumulation of plaque over time might eventually restrict the flow of oxygen-rich blood to the heart muscle (i.e., atherosclerosis), which culminates in CAD. In addition, an event such as a stressor which increases blood flow (referred to as 'hemodynamic stress') can result in a piece of plaque breaking off and an embolus or blood clot may occur that could lead to a myocardial infarction (MI; a heart attack), or the clot can lodge elsewhere causing other problems.

Coronary artery disease is most often diagnosed in men in their fifties and in women who are somewhat older, most often in their sixties. Of course, plaque buildup begins years earlier, but only comes to clinical attention when patients feel the pain of angina pectoris (chest pain) that arises as a result of diminished blood perfusion (i.e., lack of blood getting to the heart, usually referred to as 'ischemia'), or experience an MI. Ordinarily, ischemia comes about when the supply of blood to the heart doesn't keep pace with the demands placed on it (e.g., in response to physical exertion that increases the heart rate and blood pressure). The term 'stable CAD' refers to a condition in which myocardial ischemia is fairly transient and resolves upon the discontinuation of behaviors that place a load on the heart (e.g., exercise) or via medications that have the effect of promoting blood supply (e.g., nitro-glycerine). Of course, there are other symptoms that will signal something is amiss (e.g., shortness of breath, fatigue related to exertion, or pain in places other than the chest) that need to be considered seriously, especially in high-risk groups. Yet a large number of people seem to choose an odd coping strategy that comprises avoidance or denial.

In general, the link between the atherosclerosis and the severity of acute syndromes might involve numerous factors, and the disease progression might not be gradual (but, instead, might involve growth spurts). For most people CAD is asymptomatic until things get really bad and they run into a life-threatening coronary event or syndrome (Krantz et al., 1996). It seems that symptoms of CAD don't show up until the blood flow is fairly con-stricted, typically when it is reduced by more than 75%. As heart disease progresses, ischemia may become more persistent and last longer (more than ten minutes) and can cause unstable angina (i.e, where angina is present with minimal energy output or even when individuals are at rest), myocardial infarction, arrhythmias, and sudden cardiac death (Naghavi et al., 2003). These acute coronary syndromes develop as a result of plaque rupture or erosion of the endothelium, coupled with the formation of clots that occlude arteries (Libby & Theroux, 2005). When an MI occurs, the ability of the heart to pump blood may become impaired, which culminates in heart failure that comprises difficulty in the filling or ejection phase of cardiac functioning.

THE WIDOW MAKER

The name itself tells you a lot. This is a nickname for a condition that comprises a marked narrowing (stenosis) of either the left main coronary artery or proximal left anterior descending coronary artery of the heart. If the artery is abruptly and completely blocked (occluded), then a massive heart attack occurs that results in 'sudden death'. For instance, when a cholesterol plaque ruptures, for whatever reason, platelets flow to the site of the rupture, forming a blockage, and hence an MI ensues.

Once a widow maker occurs, a person might last for only a few minutes, but it can extend to a couple of hours. There are symptoms that precede the full attack, although they progress rapidly, and sometimes there may be little warning at all. These signs include shortness of breath, nausea, pain in the head, jaw, arms or chest, numbness in the fingers. It's not uncommon for these early signs to be mistaken for flu, indigestion, or food poisoning, and individuals might prefer to believe that 'it's nothing', but the symptoms unfortunately intensify rapidly.

We might prefer to believe that a person experienced 'sudden death', and we have all sorts of expressions, such as 's/he was dead before s/he hit the ground', so that we believe that the person was unaware of their imminent death. In fact, when a widow maker hits, we don't die instantly;

with cardiac arrest and the ensuing absence of blood circulating, a person can last many minutes (as long as 10 to 20). There is, after all, some oxygen stored in the blood that keeps organs alive. Thus, with very fast action it is possible to have individuals survive, but having the right equipment and a trained individual available to take action isn't typically an option.

THE HEART'S TYPICAL RESPONSE TO A STRESSOR

When a stressor occurs, whether it's a physical one such as running for a certain period of time, lifting heavy loads, or whether a frightening event occurs, the need for oxygen to reach our various organs increases markedly. Pumping speeds up from its usual resting rate of about 60–80 beats per minute to somewhere in the range of 100–140 (depending on fitness), which is referred to as 'tachycardia'. Although tachycardia is a normal response to increased exertion or fear, there are many forms of tachycardia that are indicative of problems being present.

In times of distress one of the first biological responses elicited is that of the autonomic nervous system being activated. This initially involves activation of the sympathetic nerve fibers stimulating the heart, which entails the release of epinephrine (adrenaline) that promotes an increased heart rate. Once the stress has passed, the heart begins to slow down through the help of the parasympathetic nervous system's inhibitory influence that involves the release of the peripheral transmitter, acetylcholine. There are occasions following a stressor in which the parasympathetic response may predominate, leading to a lowered heart rate (bradycardia) that in some instances can be fairly dangerous, as insufficient blood flow may cause damage. Commonly, bradycardia may result in fainting, or feeling dizzy, light headed, or nauseous, sweating, weakness, or heart palpitations. Many of us might have experienced these symptoms after a sudden stressful experience, such as a near miss in a car, receiving some very bad news, or that really yucky feeling that one gets when having to make a presentation in front of an audience.

Heart rate and blood pressure, which are intricately linked, are controlled by a set of hormones, including epinephrine and norepinephrine as well as atrial-natriuretic peptide (ANP) and brain natriuretic peptide (BNP). As the heart rate goes up, more pressure is required to make sure that the blood is pushed through the heart with sufficient strength or pressure. Thus, in association with distress, increased blood pressure accompanies the elevated heart rate. When a block exists somewhere in the arterial circulatory system, such as a narrowing of the arteries, the pressure will also rise (as occurs when you place your thumb at the end of a hose to get more distance when watering the garden). Therefore, an elevated resting blood pressure is a sign of something being amiss, and these signs are more pronounced under the conditions (e.g., distress) that increase heart rate. Blood pressure is usually expressed as systolic blood pressure and diastolic blood pressure. Systolic pressure refers to the peak pressure in the arteries when the ventricles are contracting, whereas diastolic pressure reflects the minimum pressure present once the ventricles are filled with blood, just before the pressure of the heart is applied.

PSYCHOSOCIAL FACTORS ASSOCIATED WITH HEART DISEASE

A fundamental goal for researchers and clinicians dealing with heart disease has been the identification of factors that increase vulnerability to illness, and developing tactics to prevent its occurrence. Many risk factors of heart disease are well known (e.g., high blood pressure, high levels of low-density lipoprotein (LDL) cholesterol and low levels of high-density lipoprotein (HDL) cholesterol, large waist circumference or waist–hip ratio). Some of these reflect lifestyle choices and consequences (e.g., smoking), whereas other premorbid factors, such as certain stressor experiences and coming from a lower socioeconomic class, might not be of our own making. In addition, the social environment, including social isolation and low social support, early life negative experiences, and emotional factors such a depression, anxiety, anger, and hostility, has been implicated in the development and progression of CAD, and the risk increases cumulatively with the presence of multiple risk factors (Steptoe & Kivimäki, 2013).

STRESSFUL EXPERIENCES INFLUENCE HEART DISEASE

Stressful events, even those of an acute nature, could promote heart problems. Indeed, a major life trauma or catastrophic event can take its toll on well-being, and in some individuals may provoke an MI leading to death. For instance, following the 1994 Los Angeles earthquake a five-fold increase in cardiac deaths occurred (Leor et al., 1996), and an increase in such deaths was associated with Iraqi scud missile attacks on Israel during the first Gulf war (1991). As a comparable increase was not evident with respect to mortality involving other heart-related events or due to other illnesses, these findings suggest that particular triggers acted to instigate an MI in those at risk. Of course, the occurrence of MIs is not restricted to sudden, frightening events, but can be elicited by other stressful conditions. In the first month of bereavement, by example, the incidence of mortality associated with cardiac events increased two- and three-fold in men and women, respectively.

The occurrence of mental stress-induced cardiac events or those provoked by physical challenges is not uncommon, being estimated at about 20% of occurrences (Kop, 1999), although these don't necessarily occur in those with known underlying heart problems (Brodov et al., 2008). One of the important factors found to elicit such events is expression of anger, which likely encourages autonomic changes that comprise an imbalance between blood flow to the heart relative to that needed to maintain proper functioning (Krantz et al., 1996). Beyond the effects of such acute stressors, CAD is most often associated with non-traumatic life events, especially those of a fairly persistent nature. In this regard, several prospective studies indicated that the risk for new diagnoses of CAD and CAD-related mortality was increased by more than 25% among individuals who perceived high levels of distress relative to those with low levels of distress. It is also the case that the influence of stressors on CAD is apparent in specific situations. The stress of caregiving was accompanied by an increased risk of heart disease (Capistrant et al., 2012), as well as a marked increase in mortality related to inflammatory processes linked to heart disease.

Given the enormous portion of our lives that directly involve our jobs, this could be an important source of distress or joy, and could potentially affect our well-being. It seems fairly certain that certain types of jobs are aligned with heart disease to a greater extent than are others. The largest study to assess the relationship between socioeconomic status, rank (pecking order) within an organization, and numerous indices of health and well-being was the Whitehall study that involved more than 18,000 British civil servants, with the ensuing Whitehall II study covering more than 10,000 participants. In general, these studies indicated that individuals in more senior ranks had a lower mortality rate than those in lower ranks. Of particular interest was the fact that this mortality was associated with a variety of causes, although it was especially notable with respect to heart disease (Marmot et al., 1978). The later Whitehall II studies confirmed these findings and indicated that the outcomes were apparent among women as well as men, and that social rank was also related to certain forms of cancer, gastrointestinal illnesses, chronic lung disease, and back pain, as well as depression and suicide. Given the enormous implications of the Whitehall findings, similar studies were conducted in other countries that largely confirmed the contribution of work-related stressors to cardiovascular and other disturbances.

Several factors influence the relation regarding health risk and job status (socioeconomic status), including lifestyle factors; however, these variables accounted for only a modest amount of the health risk. One factor that seemed to be particularly pertinent to the increased health risk in the lower job grades was that workers were experiencing greater levels of psychological distress, which then influenced their well-being. In this regard, individuals with low decision latitude (essentially, not being in charge) but high job demands, a combination that is often referred to as 'job strain', were at greatest risk of heart disease. Moreover, if chronic job strain was accompanied by the perception of unfairness or injustice within the workplace, individuals had an increased risk of metabolic syndrome (this refers to a constellation of conditions that as a group increase the risk of developing Type 2 diabetes) and coronary heart disease.

In line with these findings, a meta-analysis of 14 prospective studies indicated that after adjusting for age and gender, a combination of high work efforts and low rewards was associated with a 50% increase in coronary heart disease (Kivimäki et al., 2006). Later studies comprising the individual records of about 197,000 participants from 13 European cohort studies confirmed these findings across genders, several age groups, and socioeconomic strata (Kivimäki et al., 2012). As well as this, experiences at work that were described as reflecting a lack of justice (fairness) were accompanied by increased risk for CAD, and a similar outcome was associated with ongoing distress that promoted anxiety, irritability, and poor sleep in the preceding years. Not surprisingly, marital problems were accompanied by increased heart-related mortality (more so among men than women), and the double whammy of a poor work life and poor home life have particularly adverse outcomes. Conversely, having a good home life could buffer against the adverse consequences of job strain.

It seems that in those individuals already at risk, acute emotional events or emotional upset can serve as a trigger to elicit an MI. This triggering event might provoke an increase in blood pressure that favors a clot being thrown from a plaque, or as in the case of sensitized biological systems described earlier, an emotionally significant event can instigate the neurobiological changes that favor an acute cardiac event. Establishing this relationship may be complicated by the finding that stressor-related transient ischemic episodes may be of a 'silent' nature (i.e., in a subset of individuals ischemia is not accompanied by chest pains or other discomfort) and these occurred even in the absence of an elevated heart rate. Furthermore, the identification of specific triggering factors that might contribute to MI is difficult given the problems inherent in attempting to follow individuals for extended periods of time. As a result, most studies that assessed stress–MI relations comprised retrospective analyses, and when asked about potential triggering events, as discussed earlier, individuals might try to make sense of their situation and thus make unwarranted appraisals of events (or an emotional state) that preceded their MI.

In an effort to deal with these biases, patients may be asked to report on potential triggers that occurred in the period that immediately preceded the MI versus a period of comparable duration 24 hours earlier. Using this approach, it has been shown that anger was associated with increased MI occurrence, as was 'emotional upset' and depressed mood. The chance of MI occurring in association with these triggers was elevated still further if individuals had encountered major life changes in the preceding four-week period. Hence, the effect of acute events can be influenced by the psychological backdrop against which these events occur. As much as the procedures are an improvement over those that simply ask 'What was your emotional state like before the MI?' or 'Did any significant event precede the MI?', the fact remains that biases can still exist, and the data need to be considered cautiously even though the conclusions feel right.

There are ample data that support the conclusion that chronic stressful events give rise to an increased risk of coronary heart disease by directly affecting particular biological processes. Among other things, stressors could influence autonomic and hormonal homeostasis that promotes metabolic abnormalities, inflammation, insulin resistance, and endothelial dysfunction. However, stressors could also affect other factors that influence the risk of heart disease (e.g., smoking, alcohol consumption, reduced sleep), as well as non-compliance with medications and other self-destructive behaviors. Although the influence of chronic strain on heart disease is now well established, the role of stressors on a related disease, namely that of stroke, is not as well established. Nevertheless, it was reported that along with diabetes, high blood pressure, high cholesterol, heart rhythm abnormalities, daytime sleepiness, smoking (and a history of smoking), high levels of anger and hostility, and the experience of chronic strain beyond six months were high risk factors for stroke.

Several psychosocial stressors (e.g., job strain, marital discord, caregiving), as indicated earlier, have been linked to cardiovascular problems, and a large study that comprised over 24,000 patients and age- and sex-matched controls across several continents (the INTERHEART study), indicated that an MI was associated with elevated levels of perceived stress, depression, and lower levels of internal locus of control, as well as work and home distress. When considered together with several other factors, such as daily consumption of fruits and vegetables, regular exercise, avoiding tobacco, and regular exercise, abnormal lipids accounted for most of the variance related to heart disease. In considering the influence of stressors and emotions in relation to heart disease, it was suggested (Kop &

Mommersteeg, 2013) that these be considered as falling into three categories: those that involve chronic conditions, such as low socioeconomic status or personality traits that are of a negative nature (e.g., hostility); aversive events that are fairly chronic, but that resolve after a few months or years, including emotional disturbances and depression; acute events or triggers such as sudden, brief stressors or brief periods of anger.

CAN YOU DIE OF A BROKEN HEART?

Those who've been scorned in love might be familiar with the feeling of having a broken heart, and poems and plays tell us of characters who died of a broken heart. Is this an urban myth or can it actually happen?

We've known for some time that with severe stress in animals, as observed when they are kept immobile thus creating fright, capture myopathy may ensue (myopathy refers to an occasion in which a muscle doesn't work properly), creating signs not unlike a heart attack. More recently, a somewhat similar phenomenon has been identified in humans. Takotsubo cardiomyopathy, also known as 'broken heart syndrome' or 'stress-induced cardiomyopathy', first described by Japanese researchers in the 1990s, has been receiving growing attention, especially as in 1–2% of cases it is initially thought to be a case of MI. This syndrome is typically preceded by intense emotional or physiologic stress. Individuals that present with this syndrome report signs of an MI, including chest tightness and/or dyspnea, ECG changes, and mildly elevated levels of cardiac enzymes. However, unlike an MI, the coronary arteries are normal. Physiologically, this syndrome is characterized by the ballooning of certain aspects of the left ventricle (hence it has also been called 'left ventricular apical ballooning syndrome'), thus limiting the heart's ability to pump blood properly (Steptoe & Kivimäki, 2012).

The pathophysiology of this syndrome is still unclear, although there have been several suspects, such as coronary artery vasospasm, microcirculation dysfunction, and transient obstruction of the left ventricular outflow, as well as excessive epinephrine activation. Because of the uncertain cause of the disorder, its management has not been formalized. Nevertheless, treatment has involved beta blockers, statins, and aspirin. There has been the suggestion that Takotsubo cardiomyopathy can actually be protective as it acts against the effects of excessive epinephrine activation that could potentially be damaging. Typically, the symptoms resolve, but there are cases of broken heart syndrome leading to death, especially when genetic risk factors are present.

ACUTE LABORATORY STRESSOR EFFECTS

There has been considerable research assessing the cardiovascular effects of stressors in a laboratory context. It was observed that in CAD patients in whom myocardial ischemia could be induced by exercise, about one half likewise displayed ischemia in response to the psychological stressors applied in a laboratory setting. The frequency and magnitude of psychological stressor-induced ischemia depended on the nature of the mental stressor encountered. Emotionally laden and/or personally relevant stressors, such as a speaking assignment concerning personal faults, provoked greater frequency and magnitude of inducible left ventricular wall motion abnormalities than did relatively non-specific mental stressors, such as the performance of mental arithmetic or the Stroop Color-Word task. Attesting to the efficacy of laboratory-based studies, those patients who exhibited myocardial ischemia during the course of a laboratory stressor were also more likely to exhibit myocardial ischemia in electrocardiogram (ECG) monitoring during ongoing daily-life activity, and were at increased risk of later cardiac events.

Ordinarily, blood pressure elevations during mental stress are substantial, often approaching those evident in response to exercise, indicating that mental stress is accompanied by increased oxygen demand. It seems that in response to mental stress, as in the case of exercise, hemodynamic responses (increased blood flow) may be altered. Specifically, systemic vascular resistance (this refers to the resistance to flow that needs to be overcome to push blood through the circulatory system) is elevated during psychological or physical challenges, possibly owing to coronary vasoconstriction, especially among CAD patients, and the possibility was considered that systemic vascular resistance might serve as a biomarker of cardiac dysfunction.

SOCIOECONOMIC STATUS (SES)

Low SES has been linked to increased occurrence of CAD (Philbin et al., 2001). Multiple factors might act to promote this relationship, including job strain and lifestyle factors (smoking, alcohol consumption, food choices). Moreover, low SES is associated with greater stressor encounters, including psychosocial stressors (conflict), as well as elevated threat or actual loss/harm, which might promote greater negative emotions and cognitions. In addition, depending on the country of residence, those in lower SES categories might have poorer access to medical care, and might experience diminished preventive care and health knowledge. As we discussed earlier, stressful events can give rise to various neurochemical and hormonal changes that might come to affect heart functioning, and these effects can be influenced by psychosocial factors, such as coping methods and social support. However, when multiple adverse processes conspire to limit an individual's ability to cope, and when multiple stressors are encountered across different domains, biological limits can be reached. This could be the case in low SES individuals who might maintain a smaller arsenal or 'resource capacity' made up of interpersonal and intrapersonal ways of coping with stressors. Essentially, in response to stressors, those of low SES may be relatively prone to allostatic overload, leading to the biological changes that favor atherosclerosis and CAD. In Chapter 11 we'll talk about the influence of early life and prenatal stressors on illness that occurs over the life span and across generations. Suffice it for the moment that being born into poverty (or simply low SES) can affect individuals' general well-being and vulnerability to illness throughout their lives.

DEPRESSIVE ILLNESS IN RELATION TO HEART DISEASE

One of the most consistent findings in this field has been that depressive illness was highly predictive of the occurrence of CAD, and that the risk of heart disease was directly proportional to depression severity, especially given the presence of hopelessness and pessimism (Kop & Mommersteeg, 2013; Nicholson et al., 2006). In fact, CAD occurs about twice as often in those with depression than in the remainder of the population, and the mortality risk was appreciably increased. Of course, depressed mood, sometimes at clinically significant levels, may accompany physical illnesses, which is hardly unexpected as illness can strain our physiological and psychological resources. In fact, it is especially relevant that the presence of depression may hinder recovery following cardiac events. Likewise, depression is common following a stroke, and among patients displaying poststroke depression poor functional recovery is apparent, and is also a potent predictor of further strokes.

The link between depression and heart disease has been apparent across several countries, among both men and women, and the degree of risk imparted by depression was as great as that provoked by smoking and high cholesterol levels. Furthermore, as in the case of depression, anxiety may be linked to aspects of heart disturbances, having been associated with sudden cardiac death, and anxiety-related disorders (e.g., panic disorder) have been associated with increased CAD. The comorbidity that exists between these illnesses might speak to the cardiovascular impact of poor coping that is often associated with depression, or alternatively, these findings may be pertinent to the view that depression, stroke, and heart disease share some biological processes; indeed, it has been suggested that illnesses themselves might be important biomarkers for the occurrence of yet more disorders (Anisman & Hayley, 2012a). For the moment, the key point is that psychological and physical illnesses are linked to one another, and an holistic approach to their treatment might be of considerable value.

VITAL EXHAUSTION

This syndrome has been described as occurring when the resources to deal with stressors have been depleted. Vital exhaustion comprises feelings of excessive fatigue and a lack of energy, increasing irritability, and feelings of demoralization, and in several regards it is reminiscent of the signs associated with an excessive workload or other adverse life events that could not readily be resolved. The syndrome is also reminiscent of the features of depressive disorder, and indices of depression and vital exhaustion were found to be highly correlated.

Like depressive disorder, vital exhaustion was predictive of a later MI, and indeed, fatigue is a fundamental predictor of cardiovascular problems (Kop, 1999). In a large-scale prospective study among middle-aged men (and subsequently in women) who were free of CAD, vital exhaustion predicted a later MI, angina, and sudden cardiac death, even when controlling for blood pressure,

(Continued)

(Continued)

cholesterol levels, smoking, and hypertensive drug usage (Appels & Mulder, 1988). Later studies similarly confirmed the fundamental predictive nature of vital exhaustion in age, gender and race adjusted analyses, and controlling for blood pressure, body-mass index, and diabetes. In addition, vital exhaustion acts synergistically with other factors (e.g., smoking) in predicting the long-term risk for cardiac events. However, not all aspects of the syndrome were equally tied to the cardiac events. Tiredness was highly related to recurrent cardiac problems and demoralization was only slightly related to these occurrences, whereas neither irritability nor insomnia had much predictive value.

Like vital exhaustion, depressive illness is predictive of later CAD, but this might not be the case for all forms of depression. The presence of 'somatic depressive symptoms' that comprise fatigability, sleep problems, appetite changes, and psychomotor alterations, is predictive of post-myocardial infarction mortality, whereas this was not the case for the cognitive-affective depressive symptoms (depressed mood, anhedonia, negative feelings about self, concentration problems, and suicidal ideation) (Smolderen et al., 2009). It may be that the former symptoms are indicative of the presence of the inflammatory factors that also influence CAD.

There are numerous biological factors that might be tied to vital exhaustion, especially as its correlates, depression and distress, are linked to several neurobiological factors. Indeed, variations of HPA functioning, including reduced basal cortisol levels, were linked to this syndrome, as was the balance between proinflammatory cytokines (IL-6 and TNF-α) and anti-inflammatories (IL-10). Moreover, vital exhaustion was related to elevated leukocytes and C-reactive protein, elevated antibody titers for cytomegalovirus, and an overall increase of viral load. Together, these data point to the possibility that vital exhaustion might be influenced by inflammatory processes, just as CAD was linked to inflammation.

Having seen that negative events and mood states are associated with an increased risk of heart disease, the obvious question is whether positive events and mood are accompanied by improved heart functioning. It is known, after all, that people with positive dispositions tend to have relatively low levels of cortisol output, and it is certainly possible that improved heart functioning would be evident in these positive people. In fact, in a large prospective study that spanned about fifteen years, those individuals who reported greater positive well-being were at much lower risk for chronic heart disease than those who did not report positive well-being, even after controlling for several other risk factors for CAD. A meta-analysis that included studies of individuals before they had signs of illness, and those that involved individuals with an already established illness, also supported the view that positive well-being was associated with lower levels of mortality (Chida & Steptoe, 2008). This analysis suggested that the action of positive mood was protective with respect to CAD over and above the contribution of simply not encountering emotional distress. Thus, regardless of stressful conditions, positive events seem to be associated with good heart functioning.

COMORBIDITY BETWEEN DEPRESSION AND HEART DISEASE

The relationship between depression and heart disease has been known for some time, but it turns out that this relation may be even greater than previously thought. Specifically, among individuals between 17 and 39 years of age, the presence of depression was highly predictive of later heart disease, to the extent that antecedent depression was associated with a 3 and 2.4 (women and men) times greater risk of dying from cardiovascular disease, and 14 and 3.5 times (women and men) more likely to die of a heart attack in particular. In fact, among women, depression was a better predictor of later heart disease than were the traditional risk factors, such as smoking, obesity, hypertension, and diabetes (Shah et al., 2011). In addition, among individuals who presented with depressive symptoms following a heart attack, the probability of a future attack was markedly greater than among those who had not been depressed.

The finding that depression and heart disease are comorbid conditions is interesting from several perspectives, but the fundamental question is this: why does this comorbidity occur at all? It might be thought that depression itself is very stressful, and hence may place excessive strain on the heart. Indeed, there is good reason to believe that the combination of excessive exposure to chronic stressors (particularly in women), and interpersonal stress responsiveness, coupled with an internalizing coping style, might instigate the physiological processes (alterations in the HPA axis and autonomic nervous system functioning) that promote heart disease. A related view that has been expressed is the cardiovascular reactivity (CVR) hypothesis, which suggests that vascular alterations might arise in depressed individuals because they are highly reactive to stressful stimuli. Thus, it is not the depression per se that is responsible for the heart disease, but rather the high stress reactivity in these individuals that might be responsible. In effect, the stress reactivity could potentially be the common mediator of both illnesses.

Despite the strong relations between depression and heart disease, psychological interventions to reduce depression did not diminish the risk for CAD. But here again, it needs to be underscored that the processes leading to CAD reflect a chronic condition and some researchers believe that this is true of depression as well. Thus while depression interventions might have relatively short-lived benefits (depression is frequently recurrent, even when a positive outcome is initially obtained with treatment), it shouldn't be overly surprising to find that CAD would still be evident. Furthermore, even if the two were causally linked, by the time depressed patients actually sought medical attention, damage to the heart may already have been under way and might not be reversible, although this doesn't imply that the treatment would not be effective in preventing further damage.

THE DRAG OF LONELINESS

Loneliness can be part of the depressive profile and in some instances loneliness can have negative effects above and beyond those associated with depression. Isolation and loneliness can be exceptionally powerful stressors in their own right, and they can be lethal. Among individuals with an already existent heart condition, loneliness was related to earlier death. Moreover, in a large-scale (nearly 45,000 participants) four-year prospective study of people at risk for heart disease, those who lived alone were more likely to die from heart attack, stroke, or other heart-related problems relative to those who lived with others. It seemed that this outcome was age dependent. Among individuals of 45 to 65 years of age, living alone increased the risk of early death by 24%, whereas this difference was less pronounced (12%) in people aged 66 to 80, and absent in the 80+ age group. Any number of factors could account for the age-related effects. Living alone is unusual in those aged 45–65 years and could be indicative of still other problems. Alternatively, it may be that living alone in older individuals may be an index of independence or resilience, or simply indicative of the good health that allows them to live alone (living alone at this age is a reflection of hardiness). It seems that the impact of living alone is not the critical feature accounting for findings such as these. Rather, feeling lonely, regardless of living conditions, was fundamental in the relationship with heart disease.

GENDER DIFFERENCES IN HEART DISEASE AND STRESSOR RESPONSES

Chronic heart disease is the leading cause of death in women, and is generally more closely linked to psychosocial stressors and depression relative to that evident in men. Ordinarily, premenopausal women are far less prone to heart disease than men of the same age, but thereafter the rate of illness equals that of men. There is reason to believe that estrogen levels play a role in the 'female protection' against heart disease that is evident in premenopausal women. In fact, menstrual irregularities or variability and abnormalities or failure of the production of estrogen accelerates atherosclerosis in premenopausal women, consequently increasing their vulnerability to CAD (Kallen & Pal, 2011).

In addition to sex hormones, low socioeconomic status is a predictor of heart disease in women and an even stronger predictor than in men. Likewise, in both sexes CAD was lower in those who were employed than in the unemployed, and women in higher administrative positions had lower rates of CAD than did women in the lower ranks. However, in women dealing with the double load of working and taking care of a family, the positive effects of working were eliminated and the risk of CAD increased. Evidently, although work can provide a way of coping with other stressors, when the load becomes excessive and attacks appear from different directions, the very factors that serve as buffers can become stressors in their own right.

PERSONALITY FACTORS IN RELATION TO HEART DISEASE

TYPE A PERSONALITY, HOSTILITY, AND AGGRESSION

It was thought at one time that certain personality types might be at particular risk for heart disease. Most people will have heard that the Type A personality, characterized as a person who is ambitious, competitive, impatient, hostile, and rushed, will have an increased risk of heart disease (e.g., Rosenman et al., 1975). The initial reports on this created considerable excitement, but since then detailed reviews and analyses have not supported this contention, although it was suggested that one element of this personality type, namely that of hostility, might be predictive of heart disease (Barefoot et al., 1983). Despite some negative findings in the latter regard, based on a meta-analysis, Chida and Steptoe (2010) concluded that anger and hostility were related to heart disease, particularly in men, and that hostility was associated with both more severe CAD as well as an increased risk of a subsequent MI. This said, anger/hostility can be outwardly directed or can be directed at the self (anger-in), and there is reason to believe that individuals who exhibit this anger-in characteristic (or those who do not overtly express their anger) are more prone to CAD than those who express their anger. I'm reminded of the quote attributed to Buddha: 'Holding onto anger is like drinking poison and expecting the other person to die.'

TYPE D PERSONALITY

In recent years another personality construct has been described that may be relevant to CAD. The Type D or 'distressed' personality was proposed on the basis of characteristics displayed by males with this illness (Denollet, 2000). This personality subtype was characterized by the tendency to experience negative emotions (e.g., depressed mood, anxiety, anger, and hostile feelings), and like the negative personality type, they are particularly attentive to negative stimuli. As well, these individuals tend to be gloomy, anxious, and given to being socially inept worriers who tend to have limited personal ties with other people, and importantly, they display an inhibition of self-expression in social interactions. They are typically uncomfortable with strangers, generally feeling inhibited, tense, and insecure when they encounter other people.

Among patients undergoing cardiac rehabilitation, those characterized as having a Type D personality were markedly more likely to experience further heart problems (MI, angina, ischemic heart disease) and to die of cardiac-related causes, even when controlling for other risk factors (Denollet et al., 2010). It had initially been thought that the odds of such problems were increased from four- to seven-fold in Type D individuals relative to others, although a recent meta-analysis indicated that the odds were actually greatly overestimated (Grande et al., 2012). This is not to say that other psychological factors are not important, but that many such factors (including depression, anxiety, anger and hostility, and the avoidance of social contact and hence social support) often cluster together, with the Type D personality being a root factor in this regard.

The biological process by which a Type D personality comes to be manifested as heart disease is uncertain. As stressful events are accompanied by increased HPA activity, and this is especially notable with respect to individuals who exhibit elevated anger, it has been considered that HPA hormones might be related to CAD in some fashion (Kop & Mommersteeg, 2013). Indeed, this is reinforced by the view that cortisol is involved in both inflammatory processes and depression, both of which have been linked to CAD, and elevated levels of cortisol are especially notable when effective social coping is not used to deal with stressors. Furthermore, it seems that in Type D individuals the elevated cortisol levels that occur following an acute cardiac event may be relatively persistent and might thus contribute to further cardiac morbidity.

Under conditions of chronic strain, or among individuals who tend to be highly stressor-reactive (or appraise events negatively), cortisol elevations may come to affect the brain processes (e.g., the hippocampus) that ordinarily shut off HPA functioning, thereby allowing for further cortisol elevations and still greater effects that could favor the development of CAD. Thus, a Type D personality and chronic depression may have especially notable effects on heart disease, and aging, which is normally accompanied by elevated cortisol levels, may summate with a Type D personality to encourage heart disease.

Given the broad effects attributable to personality dimensions, it was suggested that the Type D personality ought to be considered as a premorbid condition for numerous illnesses, especially CAD. Indeed, it might be profitable for individuals with a Type D personality to receive psychological treatment to diminish the behavioral characteristics that comprise these personality characteristics. Admittedly, however, personality traits are difficult to change, and so the efficacy of such programs might be limited.

PHYSIOLOGICAL STRESS RESPONSES THAT AFFECT HEART DISEASE

SYMPATHETIC NERVOUS SYSTEM HYPER-RESPONSIVITY

One of the most common responses to stressors is activation of the autonomic nervous system, which comprises sympathetic and the parasympathetic components. Excessive sympathetic system activation may contribute to endothelial disturbances, hypertension and atherosclerosis, left ventricular hypertrophy (thickening of the left ventricle that can be indicative of further cardiac problems, including enlargement of the heart), and arrhythmia. As norepinephrine and epinephrine are the fundamental neurotransmitters associated with sympathetic functioning, treatments to diminish excessive pressure brought about by sympathetic activation have involved blocking β-receptors, which may have unfortunate untoward effects. For instance, β-blockers reduce blood pressure, but don't get to the root of the problem responsible for the elevated blood pressure that is otherwise evident, and might thus leave individuals with a false sense that their heart problem has been resolved. Furthermore, the diminished heart rate produced by these agents, in some instances, may be accompanied by heart attack and stroke.

Among some individuals there is a tendency for sympathetic hyperreactivity in response to various challenges, and it seems that these 'hot reactors' are more prone to atherosclerosis than are 'cold reactors' who tend to exhibit less sympathetic activity activation. The factors that make some individuals either hot or cold responders aren't certain, but they likely involve brain processes that are tied to appraisals of stressors, and potentially involve genetic factors and stressor experiences. Studies in monkeys revealed that among hot responders, those that received a high-fat diet displayed far greater atherosclerotic lesions than did cold responders. Thus, sympathetic activation may interact with dietary factors in promoting cardiac disease. Whether hot responders correspond to those with a Type D personality isn't certain, but this possibility certainly follows on from what we know about these individuals.

BRAIN INFLUENCES ON CARDIAC FUNCTIONING AND DISEASE

The sympathetic nervous system is determined by neuronal activity within the hypothalamus. Indeed, when administered directly to the brain β ⁻ ᵀ ckers are more effective than when administered systemically. Further⁻ r antagonists (which block the activity of glutamate) ⁻ᵈ icular nucleus of the hypothalamus m⁻ᵇˡ ᵗ affect heart functioning (Garcia Pe₁ ᵉ fundamental role of the hypothalam ᵛascular functioning.

It was th₁ ⁻ocesses, and particularly baroreceptor. ᵃ type of receptor sensitive to blood ᵢ ₁cluding cardiac disturbances, actua₁ ₁ding several that are involved in em₁ ᵃted to energy regulation. It is of par₁ ₁r-evoked blood pressure reactivity w ᵢcal and limbic brain areas that are in⁻ ₁essors. These brain regions include t ₁s the cortical and subcortical netwo₁ ₁bolic changes that accompany behavi₁

STRESS-RELATl

Emotional stressors a₁ s) that contribute to blood coagulat₁ ₁mote such an outcome. Indeed, seve ⁻tant element involved in blood coagu ₁n, and could thus be a common deno₁ ₁ease. In this regard, an acute mental ₁ extent, but among patients with athe ₁lly high so that a hypercoagulable sta ₁nctioning. It is uncertain whether stressor-₁ ₁portant for the development of heart disease irrespective or whether adverse outcomes occur primarily when individuals are already at risk. It may be significant, however, that in response to a laboratory stressor the fibrinogen response was less pronounced among happy people than in unhappy people, again speaking to the potential influence of a positive mood in limiting inflammatory responses and hence heart disease (Dockray & Steptoe, 2010), or it might be that happy people are less distressed and hence don't exhibit the elevated fibrinogen levels that might otherwise occur.

INFLAMMATORY PROCESSES IN HEART DISEASE

Although the inflammatory immune system is meant to protect us from invading pathogens, we've learned that there are times when this system can have unfortunate adverse actions. This may be case with respect to psychological disturbances, such as depression, as well as physical disturbances such as diabetes, and inflammatory factors may also influence cardiac problems, including MI, heart failure, atherosclerosis, and viral myocarditis (Coggins & Rosenzweig, 2012). It has indeed been offered that atherosclerosis may develop as a result of low-grade inflammation that develops as a result of persistent stressor experiences (Kop & Cohen, 2007). Furthermore, following an MI an inflammatory cascade is set in motion (possibly in an effort to be helpful) that results in a further increase of atherosclerotic plaques as well as enzymes that could cause the cap of a plaque to rupture.

The suggestion that immune factors might be related to heart disease has come from various sources. Among other things, several immune-related disorders, including rheumatoid arthritis and HIV, were associated with negative cardiovascular outcomes, and following a splenectomy (a major warehouse for immune cells), patients were at increased risk of myocardial infarction. Moreover, as described earlier, over the evolution of CAD, immune factors (macrophages and cytokines) infiltrate the endothelium in an effort to facilitate healing, but they may also create further damage that leads to still further cytokine changes, and so on.

TOLL-LIKE RECEPTORS IN RELATION TO CARDIAC ILLNESS

In the presence of some types of challenges, notably pathogens (infectious agents) or in response to tissue injury, receptors sensitive to immune-related agents may be activated. One class of receptors that fall into this category is the toll-like receptors (TLRs), of which there are several subtypes (typically labeled as TLR1 through TLR13) that are present in various parts of the organism (the cell surface or specific compartments) that can be activated, depending on the challenge present. Once stimulated, these TLRs will promote, among other things, the release of cytokines that promote an inflammatory response. The TLRs that are most common in cardiomyocytes (the cells that make up heart muscle) are TLR2, TLR3, and TLR4 and some of these, particularly TLR4, are elevated in association with heart failure. As with other inflammatory responses that were discussed in earlier chapters, TLR signaling can have either beneficial or adverse consequences. At low levels or when acutely elevated, inflammatory factors can have protective effects and augment cardiomyocyte function, but sustained TLR activation can result in a worsening of left ventricular dysfunction and favor larger infarct size. Essentially, just as excessive cytokine elevations can have neurotoxic effects in the brain, when activated for protracted periods, TLRs can have adverse consequences on the heart (Hodgkinson & Ye, 2011).

CYTOKINES AND STRESSORS

As we saw earlier, stressful events can give rise to marked changes of brain and circulating cytokines, and it seems that the release of TNF-α, IL-1β, and IL-6 contribute greatly to cardiac functioning and pathological conditions (ischemic heart disease, heart failure, hypertension), and both IL-6 and TNF-α have been used to predict the development of heart failure (Pasic et al., 2003). As in the case of other cytokine actions, the effects on cardiac pathology depend on the level and duration of the cytokine elevation, as well as on the precise mix of cytokines that are present (including anti-inflammatory factors), as they can act synergistically or antagonistically with one another. In this regard, myocardial strain is known to increase the IL-6 production that affects cardiac functioning, whereas treatments that antagonize the inflammatory cascade may diminish heart failure. Furthermore, an infusion of IL-1β or TNF-α directly into the brain may increase arterial blood pressure and sympathetic activity, and influence the synthesis of several hormones that have been implicated in heart disease (Mollace et al., 2001). Conversely, in rats with induced myocardial injury, the administration of a TNF-α antagonist effectively attenuated some of the effects ordinarily associated with heart failure (Wang et al., 2011).

In addition to the classic proinflammatory cytokines, it seems that yet another inflammatory cytokine, IL-18, may be particularly relevant to CAD. This cytokine can be released from various cell types, such as cardiomyocytes, fibroblasts, endothelial cells, and vascular smooth muscle cells, and may contribute to the production of other cytokines. It also appears to be involved in the initiation and progression of what has been referred to as 'vascular remodeling' (Reddy et al., 2010). This essentially involves the degradation and subsequent reorganization (or remodeling) of the extra-cellular matrix (ECM) scaffold of the vessel wall, which can result in atherosclerotic lesions. Put in very simple terms, the ECM is the web or scaffolding upon which tissue forms, not unlike that involved in a building being constructed. When this scaffolding is broken down and then reestablished, lesions can appear that set in motion a cascade of events that can lead to atherosclerosis. The processes associated with the ECM being degraded involves matrix metalloproteinases (MMPs), which also contribute to cell proliferation and migration, and serve as a signal for the production and secretion of growth factors and cytokines, and are essential in a great many processes related to organ development, wound healing, and vascular remodeling. This sounds as if they're the good guys, but MPPs are also involved in the recurrence of stenosis (the narrowing of blood vessels leading to diminished blood flow), atherosclerosis progression, acute coronary syndromes, myocardial infarction, and cardiomyopathy, and they have also been implicated in other types of illnesses, such as cancer, arthritis, and chronic inflammatory diseases.

Yet another immune-related component, that comprises caspases, may also be relevant to inflammation-elicited cardiovascular disturbances. Caspases play a fundamental role in apoptosis (programmed cell death), necrosis, the maturation of lymphocytes, and inflammation. In the latter regard, one of the caspases, namely caspase-1, is involved in the activation of IL-1β and IL-18, and in the production of IL-6 and TNF-α. Caspase-1 was implicated in heart disease given that its deletion in mice resulted in the elimination of left ventricular remodeling after myocardial infarction. Conversely the over-expression of caspase-1 was accompanied by enhanced apoptosis in myocardium sites, even those remote from an induced infarct (Merkle et al., 2007).

THE COURSE AND SOURCE OF CHRONIC INFLAMMATORY EFFECTS

Exogenous factors, such as pathogens, can trigger immune molecules that eventually culminate in heart disease. However, antibiotic treatments are ineffective in treating CAD, and it is generally difficult to link cardiac problems to specific pathogens. Nonetheless, it is possible that the gut microbes we discussed earlier could create inflammation that might come to affect CAD, and it was similarly suggested that the presence of other pathogens might be related to CAD. Indeed, as described by Kop and Mommersteeg (2013), elevated levels of antibodies (indicative of pathogen presence) have been found in CAD patients, and even chronic infection, such as gingivitis, was accompanied by an increased risk of cardiac illness, as were other pathogens, including Helicobacter pylori (also associated with ulcers), Chlamydia pneumoniae (which is associated with pneumonia), and cytomegalovirus (CMV, which is associated with forms of herpes). It is unlikely that any single bacterial challenge is uniquely responsible for cardiovascular outcomes, but the total number of infections experienced (referred to as the 'pathogen burden') were aligned with CAD. Beyond the strain provoked by these bacterial challenges, other types of insults (e.g., mechanical stresses, such as shear stress) can initiate inflammation, and tissue damage originating from chemical or physical trauma can also create an inflammatory environment that contributes to CAD.

Essentially, when thinking about the contribution of inflammatory factors to CAD, one shouldn't focus exclusively on pathogens, as inflammation can come about through other sources, including stressors. Moreover, when stressors and immune activating agents are present at the same time, they can synergistically influence several hormones and brain processes, and could potentially affect cardiovascular functioning. In fact, in response to the combined stressor and immune treatments a notable rise of plasma atrial natriuretic peptide (ANP) was evident as were left ventricular ANP levels (Wann et al., 2010), both of which are heart hormones that have been considered potential markers of cardiovascular disturbance.

GUT BACTERIA AND YOUR HEART

There are trillions of immune cells in our body, most of which are situated in the intestine, and microbial factors present in the gut might be involved in inflammatory processes. Gut bacteria come in either a good or a bad variety. On the negative side, the bacteria might cause release of inflammatory factors that promote destructive outcomes or could contribute to plaque formation. On the good side, it is possible to differentiate gut bacteria among stroke patients and healthy controls in that the latter had higher levels of a particular carotenoid in their blood. Carotenoids act as an antioxidant and thus might protect individuals, to some extent, against heart disease and stroke. This isn't all that new and for years people have been taking dietary supplements containing carotinoids in an effort to improve their health. However, the data supporting benefits for these supplements aren't at all clear. Thus, it might be better, according to some scientists, to consume the bacteria that make carotinoids (these bacteria could, after all, be doing something more than just making the antioxidant). This might be true, but marketing bacteria to make you healthier might be tough, although the yogurt people seem to be doing just fine.

Incidentally, a couple of glasses of red wine have also been offered as a protective strategy to prevent CAD. This occurs either because red wine increases good cholesterol (HLD) or because it acts as an antioxidant. So, choose your (anti)poison … bacteria or wine.

ADIPOSITY AND CYTOKINES IN RELATION TO HEART DISEASE

Being overweight may be a risk factor for heart disease among both men and women, and an increased risk may even be evident with a moderate elevation of body mass index. But, how does this come about? Is being heavy a strain that wears down the heart? Or is being heavy associated with less exercise that could potentially improve heart functioning? Obesity actually encourages a variety of outcomes that could lead to heart disease. It is related to metabolic syndrome, impaired glucose tolerance, diabetes, insulin resistance and the consequent hyperinsulinemia, hypertension, and dyslipidemia, particularly reductions in HDL cholesterol, all of which are associated with heart disease. Prospective studies revealed that BMI and body fat distribution predicted atherosclerosis; however, the relation between obesity and CAD did not appear in all groups of individuals examined, being diminished in Hispanics and African-American women, and there is, in fact, considerable variability concerning the extent to which obesity was related to CAD.

In view of these findings it seems that although each of the factors mentioned might contribute to the effects of obesity on heart disease, there's more to it than just that. Fat cells (adipose tissue) are a rich source for IL-6 and TNF-α, and it is possible that their sustained, elevated release might contribute to heart disease. As atherosclerosis and obesity are associated with comparable inflammatory changes as well as morphological variations, this form of heart disease is often thought of as an inflammatory disease. Abizaid et al. (2013) traced the influence of obesity on various hormones, and the role of hormones on obesity, and their review makes it clear that the cytokines released from adipocytes might contribute to several disease states, with heart disease being one of many.

C-REACTIVE PROTEIN

There has been a great deal of interest in C-reactive protein (CRP) as a marker of systemic inflammation. C-reactive protein and fibrinogen are released from the liver, and are ordinarily found in blood. Both rise remarkably in response to inflammation, with CRP elevations being evident within two hours (and persisting for several days, peaking at about 48 hours). Because of its sensitivity it is used to determine whether inflammation is present, but it says nothing about the source of the inflammation. Nevertheless, because heart disease often involves an inflammatory component, and as longitudinal epidemiological studies revealed that CRP was associated with increased risk for cardiovascular events (Danesh et al., 2004), CRP is used as a biomarker to predict subsequent cardiovascular problems.

Consistent with a role for stress in the induction of inflammatory processes, CRP is elevated following acute stressors, and has also been associated with major depressive disorder. Conversely, in women (but, curiously, not in men), positive mood was accompanied by lower CRP levels. The data concerning the relationship between C-reactive protein and stress reactions and depression have been used as evidence suggesting a link between mood disorders and immune functioning, and are in line with the view that inflammatory factors might be a common denominator for the comorbidity that exists between depression and heart disease. To be absolutely clear, however, the link between CRP and depression has been based on correlational analyses. CRP is an index of inflammation being present, but is likely not a factor that promotes inflammation.

IMPLICATIONS FOR TREATMENT

One would think that if inflammatory factors contribute to CAD, then manipulating these immune-related processes would influence heart disease. In fact, it has been shown that the anti-inflammatory celecoxib enhanced the antidepressant effects of a standard SSRI, but the data in regard to anti-inflammatory effects on CAD have not been overly encouraging. Despite the data suggesting TNF-α involvement in heart disease, the anti-TNF-α agents etanercept and infliximab were not effective treatments for CAD and even caused further problems. There had been indications that TNF-α antagonists might be useful in the treatment of cardiac problems related to rheumatoid arthritis, but such treatments have now been contraindicated (Cacciapaglia et al., 2011). As with so many other pathologies, multiple processes are likely involved in heart disease and thus altering only one process might not be sufficient to yield a cure. Furthermore, in many patients there may be other comorbid features present that could limit the effectiveness of treatments. In effect, it might be important to target specific immune factors that might differ between patients, and deal with still other processes that co-occur or are secondary to the initial problem. Finally, these treatments are usually started once individuals show signs of heart problems, meaning that the damage is already present, whereas the treatments are probably best suited to prevent the development of damage, rather than reverse already existent damage.

CAN A HEART DISEASE VACCINE BE CREATED?

If heart disease is an immunologically related disorder, is it possible that a vaccine can be developed to prevent cardiovascular illness related to some immunogens (Rosas-Jorquera et al., 2013)? It seems that T helper cells (CD4 cells) that are responsible for orchestrating a good deal of the immune response may also be responsible for attacks on the artery wall that lead to atherosclerosis. These helper cells behave as if they had previously come into contact with an antigen residing in the artery wall and thus prompt a large and rapid attack, not unlike that seen in autoimmune disorders in which these immune cells are attacking the self.

Traditionally, vaccines were used to immunize people against the effects of foreign particles. That term is now also used to describe other methods that can be used to generate protective effects against microbial pathogens, including the use of agents that allow for tolerance to develop to limit or turn off antigen specific immune responses (i.e., those with a memory). This approach is being explored in the development of treatment for autoimmune disorders such as multiple sclerosis and diabetes. If T helper cells are, in fact, responsible for the build-up of plaque through an auto-immune-like process, then it might be possible to develop a vaccine that promotes a tolerance for whatever these T cells are singling out for attack.

DIABETES

In this chapter, as well as in our earlier discussion of comorbidity, it was mentioned that diabetes was often comorbid with heart disease, virally-related illnesses, and depression. Diabetes is among the most common diseases world-wide, affecting more than 200 million people. Within the United States, with a population of 350 million, about 19 million people have been diagnosed with diabetes, 7 million more are estimated to be undiagnosed diabetics, and pre-diabetes (meaning high glucose levels, but not yet reaching the diagnostic level) occurs in about 80 million people. It affects men and women equally, and appears in both younger and older people, although in the 65+ age group, more than 25% have been diagnosed with diabetes. We don't hear as much about this illness as we do about cancer and heart disease, but its impact is especially marked. Given its increasing appearance and its relation to other illnesses, it seemed sensible to devote a bit of attention to diabetes in relation to heart disease, and the role of stressors in promoting its appearance.

Diabetes is a metabolic disorder in which blood sugar levels are elevated owing either to insufficient insulin being produced by the pancreas so that glucose is not taken up into cells (insulin is needed for this process) or because cells have become resistant to the effects of insulin and hence do not respond. The former, typically referred to as Type 1 diabetes, is usually treated by insulin injection (or by pump in some instances), whereas the latter (Type 2 diabetes) is usually treated by drugs that limit the release of sugars by the liver. There is a third form of the disorder, gestational diabetes, which occurs among pregnant women even if they had not previously shown indications of the illness. This form of diabetes usually disappears after delivery, but it may be a precursor to Type 2 diabetes.

The symptoms of untreated diabetes typically comprise weight loss, polyuria (frequent urination), polydipsia (increased thirst), and polyphagia (increased hunger), and when the illness is left untreated for a prolonged time glucose absorption occurs in the lens of the eye leading to blurred vision. Over time, numerous complications may occur in association with diabetes, particularly those that involve damage to blood vessels, which leads to atherosclerosis, ischemic heart disease (angina and myocardial infarction), peripheral vascular disease, and stroke. Moreover, because of vascular disturbances engendered by the illness, wound healing is disturbed, and difficult-to-treat foot problems (e.g., ulcers) may develop that can result in amputation. If this weren't bad enough, diabetes can lead to eye damage and blindness, neuropathy in 60–70% of individuals (tingling, numbness, or weakness in the hands and feet owing to disorder of nerves that connect to the spinal cord), and kidney disease that requires dialysis (in fact, diabetes is the leading cause of kidney failure). As well, diabetes is accompanied by elevated levels of amyloid beta and tau protein, particular in brain cells that surround blood vessels, and might thus contribute to Alzheimer's disease.

The frequency of Type 2 diabetes has increased remarkably over the past few decades across all Western countries as well as China and India. It is thought that this increase stems from lifestyle factors, including the types of food eaten, limited exercise, and obesity, and there is also a heredity component that makes some individuals more prone to the disorder. Of relevance in the present context, stressful lifestyles and events have also been linked to the appearance of diabetes, and the presence of psychosocial stressors has also been tied to poor control over the management of diabetes once it is present. The effects of stressors on the development of diabetes appear to be more pronounced in combination with other risk factors, such as obesity. Predictably, factors that diminish the impact of stressors, including the availability of effective coping resources, may limit the impact of adverse events.

The development of metabolic syndrome, which is known to be influenced by stressful experiences and is a frequent antecedent of diabetes, is accompanied by indications of inflammation, including the presence of elevated C-reactive protein. Furthermore, inflammatory mediators, including TNF-α and IL-6, as well as fibrinogen, are elevated in Type 2 diabetes. The elevated levels of these inflammatory factors are evident within the liver and adipose (fat) tissue, and could act as a mediator between obesity and both diabetes and heart disease. Indeed, elevated levels of adipokines (cytokines and related factors derived from adipose tissue) worsen insulin resistance and promote atherogenesis, and polymorphisms related to the TNF-α and IL-6 have been identified that increase the risk of insulin resistance. As stressful events increase levels of these cytokines, including their release from fat cells, it is likely that the ravages attributable to stressors in obese individuals might occur through inflammatory mediators.

CONCLUSION

Psychosocial stressors seem to exert independent negative effects on cardiovascular health, and may actually account for about 30% of the risk for MI. Based on both retrospective and prospective analyses certain personality features, such as the Type D personality, as well as hostility, depression, and anxiety, are associated with an increased risk of coronary heart disease and mortality, and strong negative emotional responses (e.g., anger) can act as a trigger for MI in those with existent cardiovascular problems (even if they had previously been undetected). Other stressors or personality factors, such as those related to time urgency and impatience, in contrast, have generally not been related to an increased risk of CAD, although these factors might contribute to an increased likelihood of hypertension occurring. The effects of stressors on CAD can be exacerbated in those with low SES as well as in those with low levels of social support, and the presence of depression is highly predictive of later coronary heart disease.

Increasingly, the view has been adopted that stressful events can instigate cytokine changes peripherally and in the brain, and these cytokines can give rise to altered levels and turnover of neurotransmitters such as 5-HT, elevated levels of CRH, and lowered BDNF. Individually, and as a group, these biological changes favor the development of depression. As some of these variables, particularly elevated cytokine levels, could potentially affect heart disease, the possibility exists that cytokines (or cytokine–stressor combinations) serve as a link between these very different pathologies. That said, both depression and CAD are complex illnesses that involve multiple factors, and therefore the perspective that was just offered is likely a bit too simplistic; ultimately there will no doubt be other processes identified that link these pathological conditions.

SUMMARY

- Heart disease, which is at the moment the greatest cause of death world-wide, is usually a progressive illness that involves numerous antecedent psychological conditions, socioeconomic factors, the presence of other illnesses, and biological influences.
- The psychological factors associated with heart disease have comprised chronic stressor conditions coupled with an inability to take control of situations, as well as particular personality factors.
- A constellation of hormonal and inflammatory factors may contribute to heart disease, and these are moderated by psychosocial factors and stressor experiences.

8 DEPRESSIVE ILLNESSES

DEPRESSION'S TOLL

Major depression is the single most common mental disorder, affecting more than 10% of the population (some say it is as high as 20%) within Western countries, and the recurrence rate is very high, exceeding 50%. It appears across socioeconomic, educational, and cultural backgrounds: it doesn't discriminate. Depression frequently begins relatively early in life, presenting in teenage years: 6% of college-aged males and 11% of women of this age may be clinically depressed, and suicide is the second leading cause of death in youth (after automobile accidents). Moreover, antidepressants are the most prevalent prescription drugs used on university and college campuses. The prevalence of depression in the elderly population is also exceptionally high, with over 45% of seniors in residential care homes being affected.

Aside from its cost on individuals and their families, mental illness has staggering economic costs on health-care systems and contributes greatly to a marked loss of potential labour supply (e.g., through sick leave and reduced work productivity). In fact, upwards of 50% of new disability benefit claims in some countries are for reasons of poor mental health, with depression being the fastest growing category of disability costs. A recent report by the Institute for Clinical Evaluative Studies indicated that within Ontario (Canada) the burden of mental illness and addiction is more than one and a half times that of all cancers, and seven times that of all infectious diseases combined. Predictably, depression carried the greatest burden, exceeding that of lung, colorectal, breast and prostate cancer combined. With depression being forecasted to become the No.1 burden of disease world-wide by 2030, the days ahead could be pretty gloomy unless a very concerted effort is made to change our approach to treatment and diminish the stigmatization of individuals with this illness.

Depressive disorders have clearly become the plague of the twentieth and twenty-first centuries, and so far the cures have had limited success, many pharmaceutical firms having given up the search for effective drug treatments to deal with this illness. In this chapter we'll be dealing with several aspects of depression with the hope that you can take home several messages:

- depressive disorders comprise a series of different symptoms that vary across individuals, and it probably is better to refer to depressive symptoms or depressive disorders (plural) than to depression or depressive illness (although in this book the terms are used interchangeably);
- depressive disorders can come about through cognitive disturbances, such as the development of feelings of helplessness or hopelessness;
- brain neurochemical changes elicited by stressors, including variations of serotonin, CRH, and GABA, have all been implicated in depressive disorders. Likewise, there is evidence implicating growth factors in the etiology of depressive disorders, and still more compelling evidence indicating that treatments that affect growth factors might be useful in attenuating depressive disorders;
- inflammatory processes, particularly cytokines, contribute to depressive disorders, including poststroke depression;
- factors that affect stress processes and stressor-provoked biological changes, as described in Chapters 1 and 2, also affect the potential for stressors to instigate the appearance of depressive symptoms;
- treatment for depressive disorders might call for an individualized approach based on the specific symptoms and biomarkers with which individuals present.

WHAT IS DEPRESSION?

Most people experience periods when they feel down, possibly because things aren't going right, or because they're overworked, or maybe because they woke up cranky. 'Depression' would be the wrong term for this type of mood, and 'down' or 'sort of sad' would be more appropriate. However, in some individuals, poor mood may be more than just being 'sort of down' and could reflect a depressive disorder. As most people have down-days or down-periods at one time or another, and the characteristics of depression may appear in other illnesses, it is not always simple to make a proper diagnosis, especially as there are several subtypes of the illness, the symptoms may vary across individuals, and these features can also change over time. Some individuals may also exhibit one or more episodes of mania, in which case a diagnosis of bipolar depression is made (this mania can comprise hypomania, where manic symptoms are not excessive, but nevertheless represent a mood swing away from that of the depressed state).

In general, episodes of depression can occur on rare or isolated occasions or prove recurrent. Their severity can be mild, where relatively few symptoms are evident, or severe, in which someone's social or occupational functioning is impaired. Overall, depression is twice as frequent in women compared to men, but in certain subtypes of depression (e.g., atypical depression; see Table 8.1) the ratio is closer to 3:1, and may begin fairly early in life. The illness is amenable to cognitive therapy or drug treatments (although drug treatment efficacy isn't as great as one would have liked), but owing to the stigma associated with mental illness, or because individuals don't recognize their depression as being abnormal, it is not uncommon for people to decide not to seek treatment, and often to suffer in silence. If you haven't already seen a presentation on YouTube titled 'I had a Black Dog' do take a look at it (www.youtube.com/watch?v=LDcdebcH-yA).

DIAGNOSING DEPRESSION

The *Diagnostic and Statistical Manual – 5th edition (DSM-5)* is where you can find detailed symptoms of depressive disorders and other mental illnesses. The *DSM* is a source that provides standard criteria for the classification of mental disorders so that clinicians will all define syndromes using the same criteria. The World Health Organization's *International Statistical Classification of Diseases and Related Health Problems (ICD-10)* is a similar instrument that is more commonly used in Europe. As we'll see shortly, as much as having clear diagnostic criteria for depression is obviously important, as it is for any other illness, this can also create problems in treating the disorder.

TABLE 8.1 Symptoms of depression

Based on the DSM criteria, major depressive disorder (MDD) is diagnosed when an individual presents with the following symptoms for at least a two-week period:

(a) Depressed mood

OR

(b) anhedonia (i.e., no longer receiving from pleasure from events or stimuli that had previously been rewarding)

And at least four of the following symptoms must be present:

(a) significant weight loss or weight gain
(b) insomnia or hypersomnia almost every day
(c) psychomotor agitation or retardation that is observable by others
(d) fatigue or loss of energy
(e) feelings of worthlessness or excessive, inappropriate guilt
(f) diminished cognitive abilities (impaired concentration, difficulty making decisions)
(g) recurrent thoughts of death, recurrent suicidal ideation.

In addition, individuals who are affected with MDD may display feelings of helplessness, hopelessness, and even self-hatred, as well as impaired concentration and/or memory, social withdrawal, and especially low self-esteem and high levels of rumination.

IS THERE A PROBLEM WITH DIAGNOSING DEPRESSION?

With a bit of insight you'll recognize that there's a problem inherent in the diagnostic features associated with depression. Let's change the framework for a moment. Imagine that you go to a doctor and present with a certain set of symptoms, say, a runny nose, muscle fatigue, and fever. The doctor tells you that you've got a cold and prescribes bed rest. Imagine that a month later you go to the doctor again, this time complaining of nasal dryness, and an abnormally low body temperature, but otherwise you feel fit and strong. Once again the doctor tells you that you've got a cold and prescribes bed rest. Does this sound suspicious? Well, that's exactly what one faces when it comes to depression. Two individuals can have entirely different symptoms (opposites in some instances) and still be said to be suffering from depression. Furthermore, ask yourself what's being treated? Is it the specific symptoms or is it the amorphous concept 'depression'? Should individuals with different symptoms get the same treatment or is there something fishy in the way depressive illness is conceptualized and hence treated?

There are many clinicians and researchers who believe that a classification system that applies labels to illnesses may be counterproductive, especially as it might dictate standard treatments for all the individuals placed in a particular category. As we've already seen, it may be more appropriate to treat individuals on the basis of the specific symptoms they express, together with the presence of biochemical and genetic markers.

DEPRESSIVE SUBTYPES

There are subtypes of depression, as described in Table 8.2, that share several common features, but can also be distinguished from one another. Given that these subtypes differ from each other, one might question whether they are, in fact, part of the same syndrome of illnesses, and whether they might have very different etiologies. Remarkably, some physicians without extensive psychiatric training might prescribe the same treatment for all individuals who seem depressed, and in many research studies these illnesses are similarly thrown into a single category. In this book, we repeatedly call for personalized (individualized) treatment strategies not only because individuals might show different symptoms and might thus have different illnesses, but also because individuals with similar overt behavioral symptoms might not be equally responsive to a given treatment, possibly because different underlying biological processes can lead to comparable symptoms. Identifying the proper biological factors responsible for an illness might lead to more effective treatment strategies.

TABLE 8.2 Subtypes of depression

Typical vs atypical depression: Both involve mood changes and/or anhedonia, and a constellation of other symptoms. Whereas typical depression is associated with reduced eating, weight loss, and sleep disturbances (e.g., early morning awakening), atypical depression is associated with reversed neurovegetative features (increased eating, weight gain, and increased sleep) as well as a tendency towards persistent rejection sensitivity (often causing the impairment of social functioning), a feeling of heaviness in the limbs (often dubbed 'leaden paralysis'), and mood reactivity (mood enhancement in response to positive stimuli), even during well periods. These conditions are differentially affected by certain pharmacological treatments, raising the possibility that they involve different biochemical processes.

Melancholic depression: Characterized by a severely depressed mood that exceeds that of grief or loss. Individuals display pronounced anhedonia, with symptoms being worst in the early mornings, and psychomotor agitation, early morning awakening, excessive weight loss, or excessive guilt are common. The atypical features of depression are not evident in melancholia.

(Continued)

TABLE 8.2 (Continued)

Dysthymia: Chronic low-grade depressive symptoms present for at least two years, although the normal course is that symptoms will wax and wane. Symptoms can take typical or atypical features, and may develop prior to or after age 21 (early or late onset dysthymia). If not effectively treated, major depression may develop, superimposed on a dysthymia background, wherein symptoms are much more difficult to treat. This is often termed 'double depression'.

Seasonal affective disorder (SAD): This form of depression is tied to the seasons (or the duration of light over the course of a day), coming on in the autumn or winter, and then resolving in the spring. This diagnosis is made if, over a period of two years, two (or more) episodes have occurred in colder months, but without episodes occurring at other times.

Recurrent brief depression: This disorder is characterized by intermittent depressive episodes that occur, on average, at least once a month over at least one year, but are not tied to any particular cycles (e.g., the menstrual cycle). The diagnostic criteria for recurrent brief depression are the same as those for major depressive disorder; however, as the name implies, it occurs for brief periods (typically two–four days). These episodes can be particularly severe, and may be accompanied by suicidal ideation and suicide attempts.

Minor depression: This diagnosis is made when a mood disorder does not fully meet the criteria for major depressive disorder, but individuals present with at least two depressive symptoms for two weeks.

Postpartum depression: As the name applies, this form of depression occurs after childbirth and affects about 5-10% of women. Symptoms are much like those of major depression, including sadness, fatigue, insomnia, appetite changes, reduced libido, crying episodes, anxiety, and irritability. The depression may be linked to the hormonal changes that accompany pregnancy, or those that occur in association with pregnancy or childbirth, but hormonal therapy has not been found to be an effective treatment strategy. There is also the belief that childbirth may give rise to PTSD in a good number of women, and the PTSD may be comorbid with depression.

Treatment resistant depression: A large number of patients are not helped by antidepressant treatments, even after repeated efforts (treatment resistance is usually defined as the failure of three different medications). Knowledgeable psychiatrists may try a combination of drugs to maximize the positive effects and concurrently minimize the side-effects. However, there are individuals (estimated at about 5%) who seem to be resistant to any drug therapy.

ILLNESS COMORBIDITY

Depressive disorders, as we've already seen, may be comorbid with a variety of other illnesses. The term 'comorbidity' does not simply mean that depression often appears after an illness or an event such as heart attack (although it might). Rather, it means that one illness is predictive of the other occurring at some time, and they potentially might involve common environmental triggers (e.g., stressors) or underlying processes (such as activation of the inflammatory immune system). We saw this when we discussed cardiovascular illness as well as inflammatory disorders, but there's a much broader range of comorbidities that ought to be considered. Figure 8.1 shows some of the conditions that have been reported to be comorbid with depression, and if nothing else, points to the need for greater attention being devoted not only to research to cure depression, but also to greater public awareness about this. In fact, we have suggested that depression ought to be considered a marker that forewarns physicians about the potential for other illnesses subsequently emerging (Anisman & Hayley, 2012a).

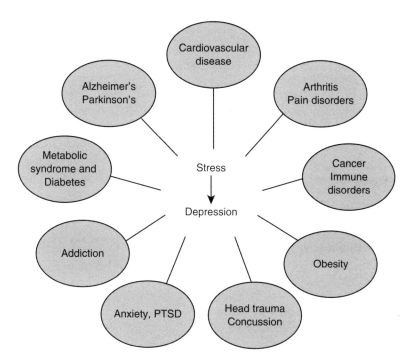

FIGURE 8.1   Depressive illness, frequently brought on by stressful experiences, is often comorbid with a large variety of other psychological and physical disorders. As well, many of these illnesses are highly comorbid with one another, such as diabetes and heart disease. Just as depression is associated with heart disease, it is often seen following stroke, and in these patients their recovery from stroke is poorer than it is among those who were not depressed. Furthermore, depression was accompanied by a poorer response to neoadjuvant chemotherapy for breast cancer (this refers to the administration of therapeutic agents prior to the primary treatment being initiated, e.g., hormone treatment administered prior to radical treatments) relative to the effectiveness evident among those individuals who were less depressed. In effect, depressive illness is not only related to the appearance of other illnesses, but also to the course of these illnesses and the response to medications.

THEORETICAL CONSTRUCTS RELATED TO DEPRESSIVE ILLNESS: COGNITIVE PERSPECTIVES

Several theoretical positions have been adopted concerning the factors that provoke and maintain depressive disorders, as well as the most appropriate treatment strategies. In a broad sense, these have included perspectives that focused on medical models (the illness is a result of disturbed biological processes and can be remedied by pharmacotherapy) and those that involved cognitive processes (depression arises as a result of disturbed ways of thinking of oneself or thinking of oneself in the context of their environment). Of course, these two are not exclusive of one another, and increasing efforts have been made to tie particular biological disturbances to aberrant cognitive processes.

HOPELESSNESS

One of the most influential views of depression was advanced by Beck (1967), who suggested that 'hopelessness' was a primary characteristic of depressed individuals. He maintained that streams of negative thoughts tended to emerge spontaneously (which he referred to as 'automatic thoughts') among depressed individuals. These individuals see the past negatively, the present as being fraught with unassailable threats, and the future as hopeless. The perspectives these individuals have of themselves often comprise themes such as inadequacy, worthlessness (poor self-esteem and self-worth), and failure, and they tend to form dysfunctional attitudes that influence how they perceive external events and their value in relation to others.

Fundamental to this cognitive model of depression is that individuals develop schemas (or perspectives) based on experiences that subsequently influence the way events are appraised and interpreted, thereby promoting biases regarding information acquisition and processing (Beck, 2008). As a result, adverse events experienced early in life (including neglect) might be involved in the development of dysfunctional self-referential schemas, which may then have repercussions that carry through to adulthood. When individuals encounter stressors at some later time, then these schemas are again activated, resulting in negative reactions being reestablished. With repeated negative experiences the schemas become more entrenched, resulting in biased information processing, memories of past events take on a more negative tone, and the individual develops pervasive negative perspectives of the future. The dysfunctional attitudes will even result in the individual selectively attending to those stimuli that are consistent with their negative perspectives, while concurrently filtering out or ignoring positive events (or evidence inconsistent with their negative perspectives), thereby strengthening their warped cognitive views, and further aggravating their depression (Beck & Dozois, 2011).

We saw earlier that individuals might cope with stressors through rumination, and often this involves negative thoughts that feed on themselves to the extent that they appear compulsive. These ruminations might arise because of a disturbance of an inhibitory process that allows for this ruminative response style to take hold (Gotlib & Joormann, 2010). That is, there is ordinarily a cognitive system that operates to keep excessive, negative rumination in check, but in those individuals (or under those conditions) in which these control systems are not operating properly, ruminative behaviors may proceed unabated. In fact, this type of negative rumination (termed 'depressive rumination') is a good predictor of later depression, as well as the deteriorating and chronic course of physical illnesses (Nolen-Hoeksema, 2000).

BRAIN PERSPECTIVE OF HOPELESSNESS

The first scent of an illness may begin with one or two disturbed thoughts or processes, which subsequently give rise to still other changes. However, the concatenation of symptoms that eventually emerge no doubt involves multiple biological and experiential factors.

Elaborating on Beck's theorizing, Disner et al. (2011) offered a cognitive model wherein the different attributes of depression engage diverse biological networks. As depressive symptoms are reinforced by negative ruminative thoughts that are associated with altered emotion and memory processing, biased self-referential cognitions, and a diminished ability to inhibit these cognitions, these investigators considered those brain regions involved in each of these elements of depression.

BRAIN IMAGING APPROACHES

There is hardly anyone left that hasn't heard of brain (or body) imaging. Two of the most common methods to assess brain dysfunction in an experimental setting are functional magnetic resonance imaging (or fMRI) and positron emission tomography (PET). The fMRI method indirectly measures brain activity by assessing changes in blood flow at two points in time (e.g., before or after a stimulus is presented). In this regard, it is of interest to assess the blood-oxygen-level-dependent (BOLD) contrast that occurs. Fundamentally, the more oxygenation detected, the greater the neuronal activity engaged. This procedure does not require the administration of chemicals or radiation, and hence has become popular. This isn't a simple procedure as there are all sorts of background noise conditions that can affect the results (e.g., artifacts of small movements), and stastical algorithms are used as correction factors. Also, one has to have sophisticated brain knowledge to evaluate what is actually happening in various brain regions. The brain activation profile is ordinarily represented by color-coding the strength of changes of activity across the brain, thereby distinguishing brain changes even a few millimeters apart.

Positron emission tomography (PET), like fMRI, provides an image of activity within the brain, but there are distinct and important differences concerning what the two procedures can tell us. Ordinarily, individuals are injected with a radioactive tracer, such as fluorodeoxyglucose (a sugar attached to a tracer that is readily taken up by neurons), that is incorporated into a molecule that is biologically active. What is then looked for is the decay of the short-lived radioactive isotope that had been incorporated into the most active cells. Essentially, the more of the radioactive tracer found, the more active a certain cell would have been in taking up the sugar attached to the isotope. The expression of the tracer can be scanned in three dimensions by having a near simultaneous CT or MRI scan. Thus, for example, tumor cells tend to be 'hungrier' than other cells, and so will take up more of the sugar (and hence the tracer), and in this way one can see where the tumor resides, and whether it has metastasized elsewhere. For neurologists or neuroscientists, PET can be especially useful, as the tracer (say O^{15} which decays over several minutes) can be attached to a substance that can combine with specific receptors (e.g, raclopride, in the case of particular dopamine receptors). Thus, this can indicate not only which neurons are activated, but also which types of receptors might be involved in this regard. Recently, PET has been combined with fMRI to show changes of activity over small time-frames, which will allow the identification of neuronal activity and receptor changes in response to specific stimuli.

The model described by Disner has two major components: one involves the limbic brain regions that regulate emotionality (bottom–up components), and the other involves the inhibition of cognitive processes through a top–down process that involves cortical regions. It is particularly important to this model that depression is most likely to occur under conditions where inhibitory control is limited, thus permitting unrestrained neuronal activation in the brain regions that govern emotional responses, including rumination. Essentially, depression might be viewed as a dysfunction in limiting the automatic responses (e.g., rumination) that propogate depression, coupled with a focus or bias on negative appraisals of events. In this regard, it was suggested that different aspects of the prefrontal cortex contribute to depressive disorders; disturbed medial prefrontal cortex functioning was important for control of self-referential schemas; the dorsolateral prefrontal cortex was important for rumination and biased processing; and the ventrolateral prefrontal cortex for biased attention. Ordinarily, the prefrontal cortex (and adjacent cortical regions) influences amygdala functioning so that disturbed prefrontal cortical activity results in the control over subcortical regions being abdicated (i.e., its influence on the amygdala will be diminished), so that the impact of disturbed bottom–up processing persists. The resulting enhanced amygdala reactivity will encourage biased attention and processing, thereby allowing for negative appraisals, attributions, and depressive rumination to progress undisturbed, and in addition, nucleus accumbens responses will be blunted, affecting the recognition of and/or the response to positive stimuli or events (Eugene et al., 2010).

PREDICTING THE RECURRENCE OF DEPRESSION

Given its high rate of recurrence, depression has sometimes been considered to be a life-long disorder. In both currently depressed patients and those in remission, a sad mood induction (in which individuals are exposed to autobiographical memory scripts) was accompanied by reduced cerebral blood flow in the medial orbitofrontal cortex, but this was not evident in never-depressed controls. In addition, in the remitted group, mood provocation decreased blood flow in the anterior cingulate cortex (Liotti et al., 2002). These investigators suggested that when patients were in remission a mood challenge 'unmasked' a depression trait marker that could potentially predict who might be most likely to fall back into depression given further stressor encounters.

When patients with recurring depression were assessed during a well period, viewing a sad film clip caused variations in activity within the medial prefrontal cortex which predicted the propensity toward rumination, and was associated with increased risk for relapse. In contrast, among patients who showed a sustained remission, the prefrontal cortical response was like that of participants who had never been depressed (Farb et al., 2011). As such, increased neuronal activity within this region in previously depressed patients, especially if it occurs with rumination, might serve as a marker for illness recurrence. Studies such as these might turn out to be useful in predicting illness recurrence, and perhaps clinically relevant as they might call for continued cognitive therapy to thwart further depressive episodes.

A key aspect of the cognitive model of depression was that individuals who were depressed (or at risk of depression) tended to react strongly to negative events and also tended to exhibit memory biases of a negative nature. As negative memories might be tied to biases related to attention (toward negative stimuli) and the negative processing of information, it was thought that the memory disturbances in depression might be related to each of these processes. Once again, as aspects of the amygdala might contribute to emotional memory (Hamilton & Gotlib, 2008), and the hippocampus seems to be involved in episodic memory (memory pertaining to autobiographical events, including times, places, and contextual knowledge), it was suggested that these regions might be involved in the memory biases associated with depression. Interestingly, just as stressors do not affect the left and right brain hemispheres in the same way (e.g., Sullivan & Gratton, 1998), it seems that this is also the case with respect to memory biases in depression. In particular, among depressed individuals, the presence of hyperactivity in the right amygdala was associated with the superior encoding of negative stimuli (i.e, the stimuli are converted into a construct, stored, and then potentially recalled later), whereas this bias was not apparent in response to either positive or neutral stimuli (Hamilton & Gotlib, 2008).

The perspective advanced by Beck was among the most influential in the development of a cognitive school of thought regarding depression. It was also instrumental in the development of cognitive behavioral therapy (CBT) as well as variants of this procedure, one of the most widely endorsed therapeutic strategies to deal with this illness. We'll be talking about CBT and other treatment strategies in Chapter 12, so we'll move on for the moment. However, as we deal with other pathologies, we'll see that beyond its use in treating depression, CBT is also used in the treatment of anxiety disorders, including PTSD, obsessive compulsive disorder (OCD), bulimia nervosa, and excessive eating, among others.

COGNITIVE APPRAISALS AND SLOW/FAST THINKING

You might have noticed that in some respects there is a remarkable similarity between the views expressed by Beck, Disner, and their associates in relation to the negative thoughts and schemas associated with depressive illness, and the involvement of System 1 and System 2 in determining the decision-making processes outlined by Kahneman. In both instances there is an automaticity of thought based on previous experiences (priming) that influences the way we see the world. In a sense, among depressed individuals, negative perspectives and appraisals associated with automatic thoughts (System 1) have hijacked the more logical System 2 processes. Ultimately, the job of cognitive behavioral therapy is to reestablish more appropriate System 1 (automatic) responses, and reshape the schemas (System 2) that have been established concerning our perceived self-worth and negative views of the future. Kahneman (2011) offers a great number of manipulations that can be useful in affecting automatic responses, including the use of priming or altering 'anchors' that individuals use in judgments and decision making. Incorporating these different perspectives might be useful in defining effective treatment strategies for behavioral disturbances.

HELPLESSNESS

In an effort to explain how depression comes about, Seligman and his associates offered a position related, to some extent, to the hopelessness view. This perspective, which came to be known as 'learned helplessness', was initially developed in animal experiments and then extended to humans. You'll recall from Chapter 1 that when animals were exposed to an escapable stressor (footshock) regimen, or had not been stressed, they subsequently exhibited proficient performance in a test where they were required to escape from a stressor. However, animals that had received an identical amount of inescapable shock subsequently exhibited profound behavioral impairments in a test where an active response would have terminated the stressor. These animals often did not make overt attempts to avoid or escape, but instead appeared to passively accept the stressor. These animals might have 'learned' to be helpless, and consequently gave up further attempts to escape.

These basic animal experiments led to studies that considered how uncontrollable events affected human behavior. Vaguely similar studies were conducted in humans: if participants were initially tested in problem-solving tasks that were rigged so they would fail, then their subsequent performance in legitimate tasks was impaired, much like that ordinarily evident among depressed college students. It appeared that the participants' expectancy regarding their performance, and their failure to meet this expectancy, were fundamental in provoking the impaired performance. It was subsequently suggested that if individuals encounter uncontrollable situations in everyday life, this could lead to feelings of helplessness that would then lead to depression among some individuals. One would think that animals exposed to uncontrollable neurogenic stressors and college students who fail in some tests in a contrived laboratory setting don't have much in common with one another. Nor does it seem that either fits with the complex cognitive disturbances associated with depressive disorders, to say nothing of some of the severe, chronic, unremitting stressors that humans might encounter. However, the idea that these students (or dogs and rats) learned to be helpless seemed to fit the zeitgeist and the helplessness perspective was thus widely accepted.

INDIVIDUAL DIFFERENCE FACTORS RELATED TO ATTRIBUTIONAL STYLE

Not all individuals who encounter a given stressor respond in the same way, and only some individuals that experienced stressful events succumb to depression. To account for these individual differences, it was suggested that attributions concerning failure were fundamental in determining the development of helplessness, and hence the ensuing depression (Abramson et al., 1978). Specifically, individuals were seen as differing on three appraisal dimensions related to *locus of control*, which in particular combinations would be more likely to favor the emergence of helplessness. It is thought that when individuals fail in reaching their goals they frequently ask themselves why this occurred. They make appraisals of the situation and then form attributions concerning their failure. These attributions can be internal ('I'm not very good at writing exams') or external ('Professors ask the dumbest questions, and so I don't do well on exams'), they can be stable or unstable ('I'm never any good at writing exams' versus. 'At times, I'm not very good at writing exams'), and they can be specific or global ('I'm not very good at writing math exams' versus 'I'm not good at writing math exams, or any other exams'). Individuals who make internal, stable, global attributions regarding their inabilities will have negative expectations of the future, and may also have broad feelings of inadequacy and poor self-esteem, which culminate in feelings of helplessness that favor the evolution of depressive disorders.

Most cognitive perspectives of depression have followed from Beck's initial considerations, and have taken the view that depressive disorder stems from negative appraisals and a general dysfunctional (maladaptive) pattern of thinking in relation to life events (Abramson et al., 1978; Beck & Dozois, 2011). The negative attributions concerning adverse or failure experiences were likewise viewed as being fundamental to the development of helplessness. Related to this, Alloy et al. (2008) provided a model describing the sequential steps leading to hopelessness and depression. Briefly, they suggested that the confluence of several psychosocial factors might shape a negative cognitive style. In particular, the evolution of this dysfunctional way of thinking might be related to (a) early experiences (e.g., a child's modeling their parents cognitive styles), (b) negative inferential feedback (i.e., the tendency to attribute negative events to stable and widespread causes), and (c) emotional maltreatment. Once present, the negative cognitive styles will influence how individuals respond to stressful events, leading to inappropriate inferences being drawn regarding the causes of events, and the consequences of these events with respect to an individual's future, as well as attributes of the self (e.g., self-worth). Ultimately, these inferences will influence the behaviors individuals engage in to deal with stressors (such as rumination), culminating in feelings of hopelessness and hence depressive illness.

Perhaps because depressed patients often describe themselves as feeling helpless and their situation as hopeless, the learned helplessness model was widely adopted in the psychological and psychiatric literature as being fundamental to the emergence of depression. The alternative, specifically that feeling helpless was a symptom of depression, but did not necessarily act as a causal agent in this regard, seemed to receive only limited attention. To be sure, it is possible that stressful events of an uncontrollable nature could lead to helplessness and hence promote depressive illness, but it is equally likely that feelings of helplessness represent one of the early symptoms associated with depression or that helplessness was more readily induced by stressors among depressed individuals or those with subclinical levels of depression.

NEUROCHEMICAL PERSPECTIVES ON STRESSOR-PROVOKED BEHAVIORAL DISTURBANCES

Depression is a complex mood state that we sometimes think of as being a uniquely human condition, and so one might wonder whether it is possible to have an animal model of such a disorder, and if so, then what are the requirements for such a model? On the one hand, it can be argued that mice and rats don't have the same feelings that humans do, and if they do, then these wouldn't necessarily be governed by attributions like those associated with depression in humans (e.g., I'm no good; I'm a failure; I can't find cheese). On the other hand, one wonders whether these complex processes are really necessary for depression to occur. Isn't it possible that certain symptoms or biological processes related to depression can readily be recapitulated in animal models? When piglets are separated from their moms they become exceptionally distressed, and they seem to show all the signs of depression; the momma pig likewise undergoes considerable distress and she too shows behavioral changes that look a lot like depression. The same thing seems to happen in rodents, but it might seem a bit less obvious as their vocalizations are ultrasonic and so we don't hear their distress. Although we can't be certain whether the behavior of these critters is really akin to our own, several animal models were developed that seemed to recapitulate many of the characteristics of human depression and were affected by antidepressant drugs.

ANIMAL MODELS OF PSYCHOPATHOLOGY

It has frequently been acknowledged that human psychological disorders are not fully captured through animal models. Do animals feel shame and humiliation as humans do? Is there self-stigma among animals with certain illnesses? Are animals ever hopeful about the future (and do they even know there is a future?)? Despite these questions, most researchers agree on the minimum criteria for an animal model to be considered valid. Of course, just because criteria have been provided to ensure a model's validity doesn't necessarily mean that the model is actually valid. In an odd sort of way, it's like a jury trial. Because a jury finds a defendant not guilty, this doesn't mean that that defendant is actually innocent. It's not perfect, but it's the best we've got.

Animal models must resemble the human condition in several respects (Anisman & Matheson, 2005): (a) there should be similarity in the symptom profile presented (face validity); (b) treatments effective in the amelioration or attenuation of symptoms in humans should be effective in animal models, and conversely those treatments that are ineffective in attenuating the human disorder should not be effective in an animal model (predictive validity); (c) those events or stimuli that provoke the pathology in humans should also be effective in eliciting the symptoms in animals (etiological validity); and finally, (d) the human and animal models ought to involve similar biological processes (construct validity).

These fundamental criteria are certainly straightforward. However, numerous obstacles need to be overcome to meet these criteria. By example, often we don't know what underlies a syndrome in humans (i.e., which brain neurochemical changes) or what treatments might be effective, and hence meeting these criteria may, in fact, be near impossible. For example, in the case of autism, we don't know the factors that promote the disorder or which brain mechanisms are responsible, and there are no simple treatments for the disorder. Thus, creating an acceptable animal model for this disorder has proven to be very difficult, and certainly having it accepted broadly is no easy task, but it can be done.

A NEUROCHEMICAL ALTERNATIVE TO LEARNED HELPLESSNESS

An alternative explanation for the behavioral interference induced by an inescapable stressor comes from studies showing that stressful events provoke several brain neurochemical changes, some of which are aligned with the processes that are thought to subserve depression. Specifically, when confronted by a stressor, animals ordinarily emit species-specific defensive responses to contend with this challenge. Concurrently, as described in Chapters 3 and 4, a sequence of neurochemical changes is provoked (e.g., including altered NE, DA, and 5-HT activity, as well as several hormones and growth factors) to facilitate adaptive behavioral responses, or maintain the integrity of the biological processes necessary for survival. Essentially, coping with stressors is shared between behavioral and neurochemical processes. However, when behavioral methods of dealing with stressors are unavailable or ineffective (i.e., in response to an uncontrollable stressor), then the burden of coping rests on neurochemical processes. This may result in excessive utilization of monoamines, ultimately provoking a decline of the levels, rendering animals less able to deal with further stressors, and favoring the emergence of behavioral disturbances. In essence, rather than relying on cognitive changes to account for the behavioral interference elicited by uncontrollable stressors, this explanation attributes the behavioral interference to brain neurochemical changes that, in turn, affect behavioral and cognitive processes.

In line with this perspective, the pharmacological treatments that reduced NE, DA, and/or 5-HT functioning mimicked the behavioral effects of inescapable shock among animals that had not been stressed (i.e., these drugs disrupted escape performance, just as inescapable shock had this effect). Furthermore, a variety of drug treatments that were effective in treating human depression (e.g., SSRIs) were also effective in attenuating the behavioral disturbances (Anisman et al., 2008). Although this is certainly consistent with an animal model, and speaks to their validity, several drugs known to be *in*effective as antidepressants (e.g., the anticholinergic, scopolamine, and the dopamine precursor, l-DOPA) diminished the adverse effects of uncontrollable stressors (Anisman et al., 2008). What these data tell us is that assessing rats or mice in an escape test after exposure to inescapable shock might, in fact, not be a valid model of depression. Instead, it might be useful as a *screen* for antidepressant agents just as the forced swim test has been used in this regard (see the box overleaf). There are other behavioral tests, however, that can be used to assess the influence of uncontrollable stressors to model depression, and some of these have fared relatively well. For instance, one can assess the anhedonic effects of stressors by evaluating whether animals will engage in rewarding behaviors after they have been stressed (consuming ordinarily preferred snacks or responding for rewarding electrical brain stimulation), and one can also evaluate an animal's cognitive abilities in different types of problem-solving tests. Thus, it seems that appropriate animal models can be developed, but this requires a fair bit of perseverance. That said, there's really no way to get around it: an approach that uses animals to discern the mechanisms responsible for human psychopathologies does have problems, and the inappropriate use of animal models may have counterproductive consequences.

SCREENING FOR ANTIDEPRESSANT DRUGS

The Porsolt forced swim test was first introduced as a model sensitive to antidepressant drugs (Porsolt et al., 1978). In this test mice or rats are placed in a cylinder of water for several minutes on either one or two days. At first the animal swims about and struggles in an effort to escape, and then as it tires it adopts a floating posture. Some investigators have suggested that these animals have given up due to helplessness, although it strikes me that a smart mouse or rat will be the one who adopts this posture more readily, thereby conserving energy.

It has been shown that those drug treatments that do not alter swim performance are not useful as antidepressant drugs, whereas some of those that attenuate passive floating turn out to be useful as therapeutic agents. It ought to be underscored that if a drug does attenuate floating in this paradigm this does not mean it 'will' be useful as an antidepressant, but that it 'might' be useful in this regard. Therefore, the test can be used to eliminate (screen) those drugs that will not be effective from those that might be effective as antidepressants. Researchers have sometimes inappropriately used the forced swim test to model depressive illness, forgetting that there are many treatments that can induce disturbed swim performance, and there are many drugs that are not antidepressants that can eliminate the impaired swim performance. The popularity of this paradigm likely stems from its simplicity rather than its validity as an animal model for depression.

We saw earlier that the effects of acute and chronic stressors yielded very different results, depending on the characteristics of the chronic stressor. When the same stressor was applied day after day, the neurochemical changes ordinarily elicited by an acute uncontrollable stressor became progressively less pronounced. However, when the stressor regimen entailed a series of different stressors applied chronically, the neurochemical changes might be more pronounced. Now, let's apply this information to the helplessness paradigm. If the behavioral interference induced by inescapable shock was due to learned helplessness, then it would be expected that repeated sessions of inescapable shock would promote more profound feelings of helplessness (i.e., the cognitive appraisal 'I have no control' or 'Nothing I do matters' should become progressively stronger) and hence greater behavioral disturbance ought to be apparent relative to that evident after a single stressor session. Contrary to this fundamental view, however, with repeated stressor experiences the interference effect was less pronounced than it was after a single stressor session (Weiss et al., 1975), paralleling the neurochemical changes induced by the chronic stressor condition. This outcome is clearly at odds with the helplessness view, unless of course it is assumed that the cognitive change (helplessness) induced by the stressor is mediated by particular neurochemical variations. This may or may not be the case; however, as we can measure neurochemical changes and isolate where in the brain they are occurring, it might be better to think in terms of such concrete changes rather than the more ephemeral 'helplessness' perspective, at least when dealing with an animal model of the disorder.

There's now considerable evidence indicating that the adapatation that develops in response to a stressor being applied repeatedly is less likely to occur when a series of different stressors is administered. Even if an adaptation-like effect develops with a chronic stressor, as indicated earlier, this doesn't mean that all is well. When a stressor persists for too long, and especially if the stressor experiences vary over days, the demands placed on adaptive biological systems may become excessive, and as a result the effectiveness of several neurobiological systems may be compromised or secondary neurobiological changes might develop that have adverse effects (allostatic overload), including the provocation of mood disorders, neurodegenerative processes, immune-related pathologies, diabetes, and cardiovascular disease (Anisman et al., 2008; McEwen, 2007).

CROSS-SITUATIONAL EFFECTS OF UNCONTROLLABLE STRESSORS

Given the numerous neurobiological effects of stressors, it isn't in the least surprising that uncontrollable stressors induce a wide array of behavioral impairments. Whereas some of these effects are elicited primarily in response to uncontrollable stressors, others are induced by both controllable and uncontrollable stressors, implying that stressor controllability is not fundamental for their occurrence. It also appears that the adverse effects of uncontrollable stressors are evident in several situations including those that are very different from that in which animals had initially been stressed. For instance, controllable and uncontrollable shock differentially influenced performance in a water-escape task and in a forced swim test (Irwin et al., 1980). Such effects, it seems, also vary over time following a stressor experience. In particular, when assessed in a forced swim test soon after an uncontrollable stressor, increased swimming was apparent, likely reflecting arousal elicited by the stressor experience. However, when animals were tested at longer intervals after the initial stressor (e.g., 24 hours), when the initial arousal/anxiety had subsided, markedly reduced active efforts were evident (Prince & Anisman, 1984). It seems that an uncontrollable stressor might promote a depressive-like state, but the arousal initially elicited by the stressor obfuscated the appearance of this effect, so that the overall profile was one characterized by biphasic variations of swim performance.

In addition to responses in aversive situations, uncontrollable stressors also affected responding for positively rewarding stimuli. For example, the stressor made animals more sensitive to learning that responses and outcomes were independent of one another in a food reinforcement situation, which in a sense is reminiscent of the negative biases that depressed individuals display when they encounter difficulty in achieving goals ('I can do what's required, but I know that it just won't work out'). Added to this, the rewarding value of positive stimuli was found to be reduced among animals that had been exposed to an uncontrollable stressor. This was apparent with respect to rewards obtained from novel situations or from favored foods (e.g., sucrose or cookies) and in terms of the positive effects of rewarding brain stimulation (Bevins & Besheer, 2005; Zacharko & Anisman, 1991). As indicated earlier, although escape tests are not optimal to understand the depressive consequences of uncontrollable stressors, behavioral disturbances are seen in other situations that might be more reflective of depression.

NEUROCHEMICAL EXPLANATIONS OF DEPRESSIVE DISORDERS

BASIC PERSPECTIVES AND DIFFICULTIES

As we've seen, stressors elicit numerous neurochemical, hormonal, and cytokine changes, any of which might contribute to pathology. Uncovering the specific neurochemical mechanisms subserving illnesses is complex, and this is particularly the case in clinical depression as it likely involves numerous brain regions and multiple biochemical factors. Furthermore, subtypes of depression may involve not only several common neurochemical features, but also several distinct differences. In fact, even among individuals diagnosed with a particular form of depression, vastly different symptoms might be present, and the efficacy of treatment strategies can vary between individuals, potentially signaling the involvement of various neurobiological processes. One gets the sense that we're actually dealing with several disorders that share common features, namely that the individual is unhappy or doesn't find life as pleasurable as it once was.

EFFECTIVENESS OF PHARMACOTHERAPY IN TREATING DEPRESSION

Even though many advances have been made in determining which factors cause depressive symptoms, we're still a long way from fully defining the disorder from a biological perspective or developing appropriate treatment strategies. In the late 1980s, with the broad introduction of the selective serotonin uptake inhibitors (SSRIs), the media were littered with reports of this new class of miracle drugs. In fact, their effectiveness hasn't been all that it was cracked up to be. At present, about 50–60% of patients are successfully treated with drugs (not all that impressive considering that there is about a 20–30% placebo response). Moreover, even when treatment is successful, it takes two to three weeks for this to occur, and usually the depression isn't entirely ameliorated as residual symptoms frequently persist, and the recurrence of illness is exceptionally high (50–70% over five years).

Admittedly, the drug treatments could be more efficacious, but the statistics cited are also a bit misleading. If patients see their GP for treatment they might, indeed, receive the favorite treatment in that clinician's arsenal. However, if they see a psychiatrist trained with pharmaceuticals (reiterating, not just any psychiatrist, but one trained with drug treatments), then they might receive combination treatments that may be much more effective. Indeed, the assiduous use of drug combinations can lead to markedly improved treatment responses (Millan, 2006), and Blier et al. (2010) indeed found that the frequency of positive outcomes in treating depression could be doubled.

DETERMINING THE BIOLOGICAL SUBSTRATES OF MENTAL ILLNESS

The research methods used to define the biological processes associated with depression have included:

1. animal models in which the biochemical effects of stressors are determined, coupled with analyses of the effects of pharmacological treatments in attenuating stressor-induced behaviors reminiscent of depression;

2. pharmacological studies in humans that assessed the effectiveness of antidepressants, or those that compared the relative effectiveness of different treatments;

3. an evaluation of the hormone and neurochemical factors in blood and cerebrospinal fluid in relation to depression;

4. imaging studies (e.g., PET, fMRI) to determine functional changes in specific brain regions in patients versus healthy controls (by assessing either blood flow indicative of cellular activity in certain brain regions, or the activity or density of particular neurotransmitter receptors);

5. analyses of brain chemicals and receptors in postmortem tissues obtained from depressed individuals who had died by suicide in comparison to those that had not been depressed and had died through causes other than suicide;

6. genetic analyses related to depression (e.g., identifications of the polymorphisms that might be uniquely associated with the illness).

Remarkable elegance has been brought to many studies, and each approach has considerable merit, especially when this body of research is considered as a whole. These studies have made it clear that several organismic variables (genetic, age, sex) and experiential factors (ongoing stressors, previous stressful experiences) contribute to the provocation and maintenance of depression, as well as its frequent recurrence following successful treatment. Likewise, stressor-provoked neurochemical changes, some of which may be aligned with depression, might vary across individuals, possibly accounting for the diversity reported concerning the efficacy of treatments.

As briefly described in Chapter 1, one approach that has been proposed to determine the process associated with mental illnesses focused on evaluating the 'endophenotypes' that comprise the disorder (e.g., genetic and biological components that link to specific characteristics of the illness) (e.g., Cryan & Slattery, 2007). This approach may be particularly useful as it permits the analysis of linkages that exist between specific genes, intermediate factors (such as specific neurobiological mechanisms including neurochemical processes), and specific features or symptoms (phenotypes) of the illness. Alternatively, instead of dealing with individual symptoms, the focus could be placed on dimensions of illness, as particular clusters of symptoms often fall together (e.g., certain neurovegetative vs cognitive features). Both approaches could also incorporate risk factors (premorbid conditions as well as stressor experiences) and the biomarkers of illness.

MONOAMINE VARIATIONS ASSOCIATED WITH DEPRESSION

At various times over the past three decades, norepinephrine (NE), dopamine (DA), and serotonin (5-HT) have been implicated as being fundamental in either the etiology of depression or the treatment of this disorder, with 5-HT functioning being the most widely studied. It seems fairly certain that this transmitter plays some sort of role in the illness given the success, albeit limited, of serotonin reuptake inhibitors (SSRIs) in ameliorating symptoms.

SEROTONIN

Stressors provoke marked changes of 5-HT levels and turnover, as well as various 5-HT receptor subtypes that seem to be linked to behavioral impairments in rodents that are thought to reflect depressive symptoms. Indeed, studies in animals have shown that SSRIs are effective in eliminating many stressor-induced behavioral disturbances in animal models. The effectiveness of SSRIs may be derived, at least in part, by the increase of 5-HT at the synapse that is promoted by reuptake being inhibited, and it also seems likely that the beneficial effects of these agents are related to effects on specific 5-HT receptor subtypes.

Despite the initial optimism concerning SSRIs after they were first introduced, things haven't worked out as well as the hype would have had us believe. The data from human pharmacological studies demonstrated the treatment efficacy of SSRIs was only moderate, although the side effects were diminished with these compounds relative to those of older antidepressants. Yet, as we'll see in Chapter 12, these agents still carry some problems that have limited treatment compliance. The limited effectiveness of these compounds and others like them does not speak well for a model of depression that focuses exclusively on 5-HT, nor on the success of 'big pharma' in bringing effective treatments to market. These limitations, coupled with the realization that depressive disorders likely involve numerous biological factors, have prompted multi-targeted approaches in the treatment of depressive disorders. Contrary to earlier approaches that focused on increasingly more 'specific' treatments, hoping to limit side effects, greater beneficial effects could be obtained from drug combinations that affected several neurotransmitters (Millan, 2006).

5-HT RECEPTORS IN HUMANS: IMAGING, BINDING AND POSTMORTEM ANALYSES

In assessing the relation between neurotransmitter and pathological states it is important not only to assess the turnover and utilization of transmitters, but also to determine receptor functioning. There have been numerous reports of 5-HT receptor changes being associated with depression, but there have been inconsistencies across studies (Stockmeier, 2003). For instance, in their review of this literature, Shrestha et al. (2011) indicated that of the eight studies that assessed 5-HT_{1A} (auto) receptor variations in depression (when stimulated, these autoreceptors have the effect of diminishing 5-HT production), four reported lower 5-HT_{1A} receptor density, two reported no change, and two reported increased 5-HT_{1A} receptor density. These variations could have been due either to methodological differences across studies or to the clinical heterogeneity in the samples assessed. Clearly, it is premature to make conclusions concerning the involvement of 5-HT_{1A} receptors in depression. In fact, although 5-HT_{1A} receptors were reduced in depressed individuals, when factors such as age and the time between death and tissue becoming available were controlled for statistically, the 5-HT_{1A} differences between controls and depressed persons were minimized. Having said this, it has been reported, based on PET analyses, that 5-HT_{1A} binding, even if it does not relate to the development of illness, effectively predicted the response to antidepressant medications (Parsey et al., 2006).

WHAT DO STUDIES OF BRAINS FROM DEPRESSED SUICIDES REALLY TELL US?

There have been a fair number of studies that assessed differences in brain chemistry or morphology in depressed individuals who died by suicide and that of nondepressed individuals who died of causes other than suicide. As impressive as these studies have been, they are difficult to conduct, and in some instances the value of the data might have been compromised by procedural factors, for example: (1) Were the depressed individuals who died by suicide really depressed or did they also (or instead) suffer from something else? Indeed, although depression and suicide have been linked, numerous other factors have been associated with suicide. These include alcohol/drug use, schizophrenia, relationship issues, financial or workplace issues, bullying at school or at work, severe loss (e.g., of a partner or child), incurable illness, and shame (related, for instance, to job loss, relationship issues). (2) What was the nature of the depression (i.e., as indicated earlier there are different types of depression)? (3) What drugs had the person been taking? (4) Were the nondepressed controls really not depressed, especially as depression often goes undiagnosed? (5) Given that an individual's stressor experiences can affect brain neuronal activity, what was the stress history, including early life experiences, of these individuals? (6) What was life like for these individuals just prior to death (was death dragged out, or painful) and could these factors have affected brain functioning? (7) What was the lag between death and obtaining the brain and freezing it? (8) Was the tissue obtained actually 'good', especially if the postmortem delay in getting tissue was lengthy? (9) Is the depressed person who commits suicide actually representative of depressed patients in general (e.g., do they exhibit impulsiveness that might not be evident in others)? (10) Could thoughts or emotions immediately preceding the actual suicide have affected neurochemical and/or receptor functioning? So, what do studies of this sort actually tell us? They do have the potential to be highly informative, but because of the problems inherent in some studies, their usefulness is often limited.

In addition to variations of 5-HT_{1A} receptors, it was reported that 5-HT_{2A} receptors were increased in the prefrontal cortex of depressed suicides (Lemonde et al., 2003), and with symptom remission following antidepressant treatment, receptor normalization was apparent (Zanardi et al., 2001). If these results were uncontested we might have a clearer picture of the processes associated with depression, but this isn't the case, as some studies indicated that there were no 5-HT_{2A} differences between controls and the depressed individuals who died by suicide (see the review in Stockmeier, 2003). Moreover, DNA microarray analyses, a technique that broadly assesses potential gene involvement, did not reveal molecular genetic differences within the prefrontal cortex of suicides and controls (Sibille et al., 2004). Likewise, imaging studies of suicide attempters did not show 5-HT_{2A} differences from those of nondepressed individuals. There have been other 5-HT receptors assessed in relation to depression, but their analyses have similarly yielded inconclusive results.

Given the inconsistent findings that have been reported, one might wonder why these studies are even being mentioned. The fact is that science is a process where incremental improvements are realized as better approaches, techniques and theorizing develop. Hence, it is particularly interesting that 5-HT receptor differences were observed when analyses were undertaken as a function of the characteristics of depressed individuals. In particular, increased 5-HT_{2A} binding was seen in the dorsolateral prefrontal cortex among those patients with particularly elevated feelings of pessimism and hopelessness (Meyer et al., 2003). Differences in receptor subtypes have also been reported in relation to other behavioral variables associated with depression, such as hostility or aggressiveness. In effect, these data are consistent with the view that individual symptoms ought to be given greater attention when assessing depression, rather than simply considering patients as being either depressed or not.

THE 5-HT TRANSPORTER

Let's now turn to yet another aspect of 5-HT functioning that might be pivotal in the depressive process. Following its release, 5-HT is taken up into the presynaptic neuron through a reuptake process that involves the 5-HT transporter (5-HTT). The serotonin reuptake inhibitors, as the name indicates, have the effect of inhibiting reuptake, thereby allowing 5-HT to remain in the synaptic cleft longer. Thus, it was considered that depression might be caused by the dysfunction of endogenous processes associated with reuptake. Although early studies were inconsistent in this regard, with more effective methods of assessing reuptake, 5-HTT was reported to be disturbed in the prefrontal cortex and amygdala of depressed individuals.

GENETIC ENGINEERING AND BEHAVIORAL IMPAIRMENTS IN ANIMAL MODELS

Animal models have increasingly focused on the analysis of stressor effects on behavioral outputs in vulnerable strains of mice or in those with a genetic deletion (knockout) or insertion (transgenic) of genes implicated as vulnerability factors for depression. Using this approach it was found that manipulations of the 5-HT transporter (5-HTT or SERT) could also affect 5-HT_{1A} receptors. Interestingly, it seemed that although 5-HTT knockout mice displayed hypoactivity, a characteristic of anxiety, they did not display signs of anhedonia (a key feature of depression). Thus, it was suggested that 5-HTT might underlie one component of the depressive profile (anxiety), whereas 5-HT_{1A} receptor variations that occur secondary to the 5-HTT deletion might be responsible for the mood disturbances (Kalueff et al., 2006). Whether this turns out to be correct remains to be seen, but it tells us once again that the analysis of the biochemical processes related to depression might need to characterize discrete aspects of neuronal processes and tie these to discrete behavioral symptoms.

GENETIC LINKS BETWEEN SEROTONIN FUNCTIONING AND DEPRESSION IN HUMANS

Having a family history of depression represents a risk factor for depression, and extensive efforts have been made to identify the specific genes associated with this disorder. While early studies focused on determining the amount of variance that could be attributed to genetic versus environmental factors in accounting for depression, more recent studies have dealt with the identification of polymorphisms or specific allelic variations. In this regard, a polymorphism was found for the gene controlling the enzyme tryptophan hydroxylase-2, which is fundamental in 5-HT synthesis. If, as a result of a genetic mutation, this enzyme isn't working properly, then the availability of 5-HT would be reduced and depression might ensue. This polymorphism was not only present at high frequencies among depressed patients, but was also predictive of diminished SSRI responsiveness. A polymorphism was similarly detected on the promoter region of the gene regulating the 5-HT$_{1A}$ receptor (the term 'promoter', as described earlier, refers to a region of DNA whose function is one of directing or orchestrating the transcription of a particular gene) that could be linked to depression. Consistent with postmortem analyses showing that depression/suicide was associated with 5-HTT disturbances, a 5-HTT gene promotor polymorphism (5-HTT-lpr) was reported in relation to depression (Arango et al., 2003).

Several studies had indicated that depression and suicidality were more frequent among individuals carrying a particular polymorphism on the alleles of the 5-HTT gene. The alleles in this case can be either short or long (a gene can be shortened because part of it has been deleted, or it can be long because nucleotides have been added). Those individuals carrying the short form of the 5-HTT promoter on one or both alleles were at greater risk of depression than those individuals who were homozygous for the long allele (i.e., they have the long form of the gene on both alleles) (Caspi et al., 2003). In addition, individuals homozygous for the long allele displayed better SSRI responsivity than did individuals with the short allele. Interestingly, those individuals homozygous for the short allele also displayed reduced postsynaptic 5-HT$_{1A}$ receptors (David et al., 2005). As these receptors may be fundamental to the effects of SSRIs, the disturbances related to 5-HTT, through actions on 5-HT$_{1A}$ receptors, may account for the blunted response to treatment that has been reported.

These findings became still more exciting with further evidence that this gene interacted with environmental factors in predicting depressive illness. Specifically, depression was especially common among individuals with the short alleles of the 5-HTT gene, provided that they had also encountered major life stressors, early life trauma, or experienced a stressful family environment (Caspi et al., 2003). Brain activity among carriers of the short allele was also found to be distinguishable from that of other individuals. Among those with the short allele, amygdala and hippocampal functioning was tonically (continuously) activated and the response to negative events was altered (Canli et al., 2006). Tonic activation, in a sense, would have effects like those associated with a chronic state of distress (hypervigilance, threat, and rumination), and hence the response to stressors would be augmented, thereby encouraging depressive disorders. In effect, genetic constitution might dispose individuals to depression because of greater sensitivity or reactivity to environmental stressors (Caspi et al., 2010), but simply having a particular gene doesn't necessarily condemn an individual to bouts of depression, unless environmental triggers are also present.

Following the initial reports of the 5-HTT gene × environment interaction, there have been many studies that evaluated this synergy. Two independent meta-analyses, to different degrees, have questioned the conclusion regarding the 5-HTT/stressor collusion with respect to depressive disorders. However, it has since been pointed out (Wankerl et al., 2010) that owing to the approach used in the meta-analyses, only a subset of the data available were included. Moreover, some of the negative results might primarily have been a consequence of relying on retrospective, self-report measures of life stress. Of those studies that relied on interviews and objective measures of stressor experiences, 13 of 19 studies replicated the findings concerning 5-HTT × stressor interactions in depression, and 5 of the 19 provided partial support (Wankerl et al., 2010). Furthermore, a meta-analysis that stratified the sample on the basis of the type of stressor individuals experienced added considerably to this conclusion (Karg et al., 2011). Specifically, childhood maltreatment as well as specific medical conditions interacted with the 5-HTT gene to increase stressor sensitivity, whereas an analysis based strictly on adult stressor experiences yielded a weaker effect. Evidently, disturbances of 5-HT receptors and 5-HTT may contribute to depression, but the influence of these genes is moderated by stressor events, particularly those encountered in early life. As interesting as these findings might be, it is essential to consider that 5-HT is only one of several neurochemical changes that operate in tandem or interact with one another to increase vulnerability to depression.

A GENE FOR DEPRESSION OR IS IT SOMETHING ELSE?

The data concerning the interaction between 5-HTT and environmental factors in predicting depression have often been taken to suggest that there's a gene for depression whose behavioral expression is moderated by environmental factors. However, there's another perspective that can be adopted. Specifically, the 5-HTT polymorphism has been associated not only with depression, but also with other conditions, such as PTSD and OCD (Kenna et al., 2012). Although these illnesses are often comorbid with depression, making it hard to tease them apart, it seems that the 5-HTT polymorphism does not have actions unique to depression. Instead, this polymorphism might influence reactions to stressors, and in this way increase vulnerability to stress-related illness, including depression. Essentially, 5-HTT functioning might be particularly important for our ability to cope with stressors (or perhaps to appraise them properly), and thus when the uptake process is altered the response to stressors is disturbed, thereby favoring the emergence of pathological outcomes.

Arguing from a similar perspective, Belsky et al. (2009) proposed that the 5-HTT gene polymophism was associated with increased plasticity, so that the presence of the gene increased the propensity for adverse events actually culminating in pathology, whereas positive experiences might have a protective effect in this regard. Essentially, 5-HTT related gene changes make us vulnerable to depression, because they increase the reactivity to environmental events, both negative and positive, and thus determine whether pathology will occur or whether, in contrast, high levels of functioning will be apparent.

DOPAMINE

As we've seen, DA plays an integral role in reward processes, and as depressive disorders are frequently characterized by anhedonia, one would have thought that DA would be intimately related to this illness. Perhaps because drugs that affect DA (e.g., l-DOPA) did not act as an effective antidepressant, or because DA was overshadowed by 5-HT as the main culprit of depression, analyses of DA in depression were sidelined. Yet, as will be seen in Chapter 12, recent therapeutic strategies have incorporated DA functioning in the treatment of this disorder. With the apparent need to go beyond 5-HT in relation to depression, the possible involvement of DA in depression has been rejuvinated in recent years based on findings, described in Chapter 3, that stressors affect DA functioning in brain regions associated with reward processes, notably those that involve the midbrain ventral tegmental (VTA) and nucleus accumbens circuitry. This focus intensified with the finding that manipulations of this DA circuit had the effect of diminishing the impact of stressors on depressive-like behaviors in animal models, and that stressor effects could potentially have epigenetic effects that affected reward pathways (e.g., Maze et al., 2010).

Yet it is somewhat paradoxical, as mentioned earlier, that both stressors and appetitive reward both increase activity in this circuit. It is possible that the nucleus accumbens responds to changes in environmental stimuli, irrespective of the valence of this change. In a sense, it might be readying other systems for something that is happening or is about to happen. Alternatively, it may be that the neuronal signatures of these different motivational forces might be distinguishable from one another. In fact, it seems that VTA dopamine neurons display either a low frequency, tonic (continuous) firing pattern or a phasic (intermittent or bursting) high frequency pattern that is involved in encoding signals with rewarding properties (Grace et al., 2007). When mice were chronically stressed by repeated social defeat, both the spontaneous firing rates and bursting events of neurons of the VTA increased, but this outcome was only evident in those mice that developed depressive-like symptoms (e.g., exhibiting social avoidance), and was absent in behaviorally resilient mice. As expected, the depressive-like behavioral effects were abolished by treating mice with an SSRI for a two-week period (Cao et al., 2010). It has since been shown using an optogentic approach (this is one in which the inhibition or activation of neurons can be achieved by shining a light on specifically 'tagged' neurons) that instigating a phasic, but not a tonic, firing pattern in DA neurons can induce a susceptible behavioral profile in response to a moderate degree of social distress. Indeed, this behavioral profile could even be induced in mice that had previously been found to be resilient in the face of social defeat. Significantly, this outcome was apparent in those VTA neurons that projected to the nucleus accumbens, which is involved in reward processes, but not those that went to the prefrontal cortex. These data raise the possibility that VTA neurons serve different functions depending on where they project. In fact, it was shown that inhibition of the VTA-nucleus accumbens network had the effect of promoting resilience in mice, whereas a similar inhibition of VTA neurons projecting to the PFC elicited behavioral susceptibility to stressor effects (Chaudhury et al., 2013). Thus, it seems that the behavioral responses of animals that were susceptible versus resilient to stressor-induced depression were related to the firing patterns of mesolimbic dopamine neurons as well as the specific neural circuits engaged.

One would think that these remarkable experiments would bring closure to the issue of DA involvement in depression, and now the difficult task would be one of finding a method of stimulating specific DA neurons in just the right way to treat depression (if that were even possible at this time). However, another kink to this story was added in a companion paper to the Chaudhury et al. (2013) report. Specifically, the findings in the Chaudhury paper were based on a stressor that comprised repeated social defeat over many days. However, Tye et al. (2013), using a different stressor paradigm (namely chronic exposure to a series of mild, unpredictable stressors over several days, that also caused behavioral indices of depression), found effects that were precisely opposite to those of Chaudhury et al. Specifically, they observed that the depressive effects of the chronic stressor could be attenuated by the induction of high firing rates of VTA neurons, whereas optogenetically inhibiting VTA neurons provoked a depression-like outcome. So what can we make of these contradictory findings? As indicated earlier, different stressors activate diverse neuronal circuits, and it might be the case that the chronic mild stressor procedure and the chronic social stressor paradigm do so as well. At this point it certainly is hard to know whether or not this is the case. Nevertheless, these data point to the importance of distinguishing between depressive states brought on by different stressor conditions, and the need to define biological and behavioral markers in order to develop proper individualized treatment strategies.

CORTICOTROPIN RELEASING HORMONE (CRH)

Depressive disorders have been associated with variations of several aspects of HPA functioning. This has included elevated cortisol levels, early escape from dexamethasone-induced cortisol suppression (see the insert), and a blunted ACTH response to CRH (Nemeroff & Vale, 2005). Of particular relevance was the finding that HPA abnormalities were present among genetic relatives of depressed patients prior to the presentation of clinical symptoms (Holsboer & Ising, 2010). As a result, basal cortisol levels could potentially serve as a biomarker for an increased risk of illness. At the same time, these endocrine disturbances might not simply be correlates or markers of depression, as drugs that act as glucocorticoid antagonists may reduce the symptoms of depression.

Aside from the potential involvement of glucocorticoids, CRH might play a prominent role in depression. In this regard, these CRH variations may be apparent in limbic and cortical regions in addition to those associated with HPA functioning (Merali, Khan et al., 2004).

Elevated CRH was observed in the cerebrospinal fluid of depressed patients, and CRH levels were elevated in the frontopolar and the dorsomedial prefrontal cortex of depressed individuals who had died by suicide. The elevated CRH levels were accompanied by reduced mRNA expression of CRH_1 receptors, possibly reflecting a compensatory down-regulation secondary to the sustained CRH elevation (i.e., following the excessive stimulation of receptors, their number or their functionality may be reduced) (Merali, Khan et al., 2004). In contrast to CRH_1, the expression of the CRH_2 receptor mRNA was not affected, supporting a primary role for the CRH_1 receptors in depression (Reul & Holsboer, 2002). However, given reports concerning the sex-dependent differences of stressors on CRH_2 receptor expression, it may be premature to dismiss a role for this receptor in depression and anxiety-related behaviors.

TESTS OF HYPOTHALAMIC–PITUITARY–ADRENAL FUNCTIONING

Two tests of HPA functioning have frequently been conducted in relation to psychological disturbances. The first relies on the administration of CRH and then assesses the changes that are observed with respect to ACTH secretion. Ordinarily CRH stimulates ACTH release from the pituitary, and thus injecting CRH should increase the presence of ACTH in circulation (i.e., in blood). If this response is blunted, it suggests that communication between CRH and its receptors on the pituitary is not operating properly or that there is a dysfunction that is preventing the ACTH release.

The second approach, the dexamethasone suppression test (DST), has been used more commonly. Dexamethasone is a synthetic corticoid which, like corticosterone, has the effect of inhibiting (suppressing) a further release of cortisol from the adrenal gland. If dexamethasone is given at 11:00PM, most individuals escape from this suppression by late in the next afternoon (4:00PM). However, many depressed individuals show an early escape from this suppression, suggesting that the feedback processes involved in the suppression of cortisol release are not fully functional. An early escape from dexamethasone suppression has been found to be fairly frequent among depressed individuals, especially if the depression is severe. However, there are other syndromes that are also subject to an early escape from suppression, and so it can't be used as an index of depression, but is nevertheless useful in assessing biological features of depression and might also be useful in predicting a relapse after successful therapy (i.e., has the reduced depression been accompanied by normalization of the DST response?). It is possible, after all, that the depressive symptoms diminished, but the biological disturbances underlying the disorder persisted (i.e., the symptoms were masked).

HPA POLYMORPHISMS RELATED TO DEPRESSIVE DISORDER

Glucocorticoid-related polymorphisms have been identified that are germane to depressive disorders. Individuals with a polymorphism related to glucocorticoid resistance (i.e., diminished responsiveness to cortisol) were at increased risk of developing a depressive disorder and a diminished clinical response to antidepressant medication (van Rossum et al., 2006). In addition, several SNPs were identified involving the CRH_1 gene that might be relevant to depression. One of these was also associated with a diminished therapeutic response to the SSRI treatment among anxious depressed patients (Liu et al., 2007). Thus, CRH and gluco-corticoid receptor gene polymorphisms seem to be risk factors for depression and might predict the response to treatment. It is uncertain whether the effects of HPA polymorphisms are moderated by stressful life experiences like those described regarding the 5-HTT genetic influence. However, given the integral role of these hormones in the stress response, it would be reasonable to predict that such interactions are intimately involved in depressive out-comes. There are, however, insufficient data available to know whether CRH involvement is generally related to depression or is more likely to occur when depression is highly comorbid with anxiety.

CRH–AVP INTERACTIONS

Arginine vasopressin (AVP), also referred to as vasopressin, is present in various brain regions in addition to the hypothalamus, where it can influence memory processes and social behaviors. The role of AVP in depression has largely been overshadowed by that of CRH, but the level of this hormone was reported to be elevated in the cerebrospinal fluid of depressed patients, in the plasma of melancholic (severe) and anxious-retarded depressed patients, and in several brain regions (e.g., the locus coeruleus and dorsomedial prefrontal cortex) of depressed individuals who died by suicide (Merali et al., 2006). Furthermore, a challenge with desmopressin (an analog of vasopressin that stimulates a fundamental AVP receptor, namely the V3 receptor) provoked greater ACTH and cortisol responses in depressed patients than in controls, supporting the possibility that AVP might be linked to depression through its effects on HPA activity (Dinan et al., 2004). There has been interest in assessing the effects of blocking AVP receptors in the treatment of depression, given that this treatment in rodents had both anti-anxiety and antidepressant-like effects, but large-scale trials of AVP antagonists in humans have yet to be reported.

A particularly interesting perspective regarding the role of AVP in depression has come from studies in animals that assessed changes of AVP which occurred in response to chronic stressors or with the passage of time following acute stressors. As described earlier, neuro-chemical systems, including HPA functioning, can become sensitized after an animal has been exposed to a stressor, so that upon further stressor exposure these stress responses (e.g., ACTH release from the pituitary) are markedly increased. One explanation regarding the processes that promote a sensitized response is especially germane to the evolution of depres-sion (Tilders & Schmidt, 1999). Specifically, the most ventral (bottom) portion of the hypo-thalamus, termed the 'external zone of the median eminence', has neuronal terminals that primarily contain CRH and a small amount of AVP. However, following a chronic stressor regimen, or with the passage of time following an acute stressor (or after cytokine chal-lenges), changes are evident within these terminals so that the storage of AVP increases greatly. As a result, in response to subsequent stressors CRH and AVP are co-released. Together, CRH and AVP synergistically stimulate ACTH release from the pituitary, which ultimately gives rise to an exaggerated increase of adrenal corticosterone secretion. In essence, neurosecretory neurons within the hypothalamus have the capacity to change (reflected by the co-occurrence of CRH and AVP) for extended periods of time, and consequently may have long-term behavioral ramifications. This could explain how stressful events (even those encountered during infancy) prime neural circuits so that later stressful experiences lead to depression. It isn't known whether the co-expression of these hormones normalizes after successful pharmacotherapy. However, if this normalization doesn't occur, it might also account for why individuals tend to fall back into their depressive state upon later stressful encounters.

PHARMACOLOGICAL STUDIES

Manipulations that affect CRH can influence behavioral outputs reminiscent of anxiety and depression in animals. However, progress regarding CRH as a pharmaceutical target for depression in humans has been limited, although efforts have been made in this respect (e.g., Holsboer & Ising, 2010). Administration of a CRH_1 antagonist reduced the symptoms of depression in a relatively small study of MDD patients, and this treatment altered the depressive EEG sleep profile, with few side effects or disturbances of neuroendocrine functioning. Several subsequent reports similarly reported that CRH_1 acting agents may have antidepressant effects (Holsboer & Ising, 2010). Not all patients showed a positive response to such treatments, and the usefulness of this type of therapy may come down to finding biomarkers that tell us about the nature of the biochemical disturbances in each individual, and then tailoring treatment strategies accordingly.

γ-AMINOBUYTRIC ACID (GABA)

$GABA_A$ functioning, as we saw in Chapter 5, is affected by stressors, and it seems that it may also be important in mediating depression and perhaps contribute to the comorbidity that exists between anxiety and depressive illness (Anisman et al., 2012). Indeed, GABA levels were lower in the dorsolateral prefrontal and occipital cortex of depressed individuals than in controls. Furthermore, variations of an enzyme involved in GABA synthesis, glutamic acid decarboxylase (GAD), were observed in the hippocampal and prefrontal cortical region of depressed suicidal patients relative to controls. As might be expected, antidepressants that influence GABA also had positive effects (Krystal et al., 2002). Not all of the data available have been consistent with the view that depression and GABA are linked, but this is not unexpected given the numerous differences between the depressed populations assessed across studies, and the various aspects of GABA functioning that were evaluated.

It was indicated earlier that GABA receptors comprise five subunits from a set of many types of subunits, and the specific combination of subunits determines how they behave and which drugs stimulate these receptors. The possibility was raised that stressors elicited anxiety and depression by affecting the presence of these subunits and hence the composition of the $GABA_A$ receptors. In line with this perspective, in some brain regions the mRNA expression of $GABA_A$ subunits may be either up or down regulated in association with major depression (Merali, Du et al., 2004; Poulter et al., 2010). Furthermore, a broad gene expression analysis revealed that GABAergic-related genes in those who died by suicide were altered in several cortical and subcortical brain regions, including the prefrontal cortex and hippocampus. As these effects were evident among individuals who died by suicide irrespective of whether or not they had been depressed, these findings likely were related to suicide (or antecedents of suicide) rather than depression per se (Sequeira et al., 2009).

Our own research, using both animal models and brain tissue from depressed individuals who died by suicide, has been consistent with that of others regarding GABA subunit expression in relation to depression. But more than just differences in the frank mRNA expression, we also observed interesting differences in the GABA$_A$ subunit expression 'patterns' (Merali, Du et al., 2004). Specifically, among nondepressed individuals who had died suddenly of causes unrelated to suicide, the expression of the different GABA$_A$ subunits in the frontopolar cortex, hippocampus, and amygdala was highly correlated; variations in a particular subunit's mRNA expression were often matched by similar changes in the expressional levels of other subunits. It seems as if there is some central conductor that gets these subunits to react in a synchronous manner. In contrast to the coordinated profile evident in controls, among the depressed individuals who died by suicide the inter-relationships between the GABA$_A$ subunits were markedly less frequent. Although it seemed reasonable to suggest that the disturbed inter-relationships between the subunits in the depressed suicide brain samples reflected a dysfunctional profile, this supposition is likely too simplistic (Poulter et al., 2010). Nevertheless, we provisionally suggested that coordination between these subunits might be essential for the behavior of neural networks and for the neuronal rhythms that ordinarily occur in various brain regions (Anisman et al., 2012; Poulter et al., 2010).

A DIFFERENT PERSPECTIVE ON DEPRESSION: THE INFLEXIBLE BRAIN

There aren't sufficient data available to explain how the coordinated patterns of GABA$_A$ subunits play out with respect to the emergence of depression or suicidality. However, in another context, a very interesting perspective was offered in which depression was associated with increased connections between many brain regions (Leuchter et al., 2012). It was similarly observed through imaging procedures that increased connectivity seemed to be present in a region of the brain important for information processing, the dorsolateral frontopolar cortex, and this was diminished following electroconvulsive treatment (ECT). It was suggested that for efficient brain functioning, including proper appraisals, decision making, coping responses, and the emergence of mood change, synchronous activity across brain regions is necessary. However, at some point this needs to be turned off, or at the least, there needs to be selectivity concerning the interconnections that are formed. What this means is that it might not always be advantageous to have too many associations in our memory circuits. Instead, it might be necessary to have circuits be selective with respect to activation patterns; otherwise our thoughts might go to places where they could be counterproductive. In a sense, this is exactly what one sees in regard to symptoms such as rumination, where the person keeps on thinking, usually negatively, and seems unable to turn off these thoughts.

The suggestion was made earlier that central to appraisal and coping was the ability to maintain flexibility and to be able to move from one strategy to another as the situation demands. What Leuchter et al. essentially demonstrated was that depressed individuals' brain networks, particularly within the prefrontal cortex, have lost their flexibility in making and eliminating connections, essentially being unable to adapt to changes that are necessary for proper functioning. Inasmuch as GABA is the most abundant neurotransmitter within the brain, and plays a pivotal role in inhibiting the messages between neurons, variations of the subunit coordination might be intricately involved in maintaining flexibility.

GROWTH FACTORS IN DEPRESSION

Structural and functional brain changes, including reduced hippocampal volume, have been associated with depressive illness. The extent of the hippocampal reduction was particularly marked in those with repeated depressive episodes or lengthy depressive episodes (MacQueen et al., 2003), and was lower in non-remitted patients than among those in remission (Frodl et al., 2004). Moreover, just as depressive illness can be influenced by early life stressful experiences, it seems that the grey matter volume (reflecting neural cell bodies) within cortical brain regions can be influenced by such events, depending on the nature of the maltreatment (physical vs emotional neglect vs both) (Edmiston et al., 2011). It is thought that factors such as genetic influences, previous distressing events, or corticoid variations in response to chronic strain contribute to this outcome, although the possibility cannot be excluded that pre-existing hippocampal disturbances act as a risk factor for depression. Significantly, as well, reduced hippocampal volume was not unique to depression, having been reported in patients with schizophrenia and posttraumatic stress disorder. Thus, the hippocampal changes might represent a risk factor for a variety of mental illnesses, which is not in the least surprising given the fundamental role that hippocampal factors play in numerous psychological processes.

BRAIN-DERIVED NEUROTROPHIC FACTOR (BDNF)

Factors that encourage the survival of neurons, and promote the growth of new neurons and synapses (neurogenesis), might be fundamental in depressive illnesses. As described in Chapter 4, growth factors, such as BDNF and Fibroblact growth factor-2 (FGF-2), were reduced in several limbic brain regions of stressed rodents. Likewise, BDNF expression and protein levels and those of its receptor (tyrosine kinase B; TrkB) were lower within the hippocampus and prefrontal cortex of individuals who died by suicide than in age- and sex-matched controls. It was therefore suggested that disturbed hippocampal neurogenesis, mediated by BDNF, was responsible for the emergence of depression (Duman & Monteggia, 2006). It is not entirely certain how these BDNF effects of stressors come about, although several suggestions have been offered. In this regard, the reduced hippocampal BDNF levels in stressed mice were linked to epigenetic changes, and in humans, major depression was similarly linked to epigenetic factors involving genes that code for BDNF (Fuchikami et al., 2011).

Consistent with the perspective linking BDNF and depression, the positive effects of several antidepressants (and electroconvulsive shock) were accompanied by elevated hippocampal neurogenesis and prevention of the down-regulation of hippocampal cell proliferation ordinarily induced by stressors (Malberg & Duman, 2003). Added to this, the antidepressant actions were diminished among mice with the targeted deletion of genes for BDNF (Monteggia et al., 2007). As a result, not only do antidepressants influence neurogenesis, but for an antidepressant to be effective, functional BDNF activity is also necessary.

In addition to the brain BDNF variations, BDNF concentrations measured in blood serum were reduced in depressed patients, and the BDNF levels were inversely related to the degree of clinical impairment (although diminished BDNF was also apparent in chronic low-grade depression, i.e., dysthymia) (Yoshimura et al., 2011). Moreover, the lower BDNF levels were particularly notable in depressed patients who also presented with anxiety, those with recurrent depressive episodes, and in patients who were the most suicidal (Lee et al., 2007). Predictably, serum BDNF levels increased with clinical improvement following antidepressant treatment, but not in patients who did not show clinical improvement (Lee & Kim, 2008). Taken together, the available data indicate that stressful events could reduce brain BDNF, which could then lead to the appearance of depressive symptoms. Antidepressants, conversely, have the effect of increasing BDNF. However, it may take several days or weeks for antidepressants to have these effects on BDNF and hence on 5-HT synapses, which could account for the lag between antidepressant treatments and the eventual decline of depressive symptoms.

As impressive as the available data might be, several findings don't fit the BDNF–depression story. Reduced BDNF in blood was not always found to be associated with depression, did not vary as a function of depression severity, and was also found to be unrelated to particular depressive symptoms (Jevtoviž et al., 2011). Moreover, BDNF levels were only diminished in patients who were depressed and suicidal, raising the possibility that BDNF was tied to suicidality as opposed to depression per se (Kim et al., 2007). As well as this, although serum BDNF levels were lower in depressed human patients than in controls, and increased following antidepressant treatment (e.g., using the SSRI sertraline), the positive effects of antidepressants were not always accompanied by elevated BDNF levels. It seemed, as well, that depressed patients with relatively high levels of BDNF were more responsive to treatment than those with low BDNF levels (Wolkowitz et al., 2011), suggesting that BDNF was not directly related to depression, but the presence of higher BDNF levels acted as a permissive factor so that the action of antidepressants was most readily elicited. Finally, although the case for hippocampal BDNF involvement in depression seems strong, in other brain regions associated with depression, such as the prefrontal cortex, the BDNF relationship to stressors and depression is less impressive. Indeed, in animal models of depression it is not uncommon for stressors to increase, rather than reduce, the levels of BDNF mRNA expression in the prefrontal cortex.

One final caveat seems to be in order at this point. Considerable theorizing concerning BDNF has come from studies in humans in which BDNF was measured in serum. It has been reported that BDNF in blood was related to brain BDNF, but it's not clear that these BDNF changes in blood are representative of what's actually happening within those brain regions that are specifically responsible for depressive symptoms. Is the BDNF in blood coming from the hippocampus or is it mingled with that coming from other brain regions that are not tied to depression? Or are perhiperal BDNF levels altered in parallel with BDNF in the brain, but the peripheral levels of BDNF aren't coming from the brain? At this point it certainly seems as if BDNF is involved in depression, but there are gaps in our understanding as to the conditions that favor BDNF changes, and how the BDNF variations are linked to the efficacy of treatment responses.

BDNF POLYMORPHISM

Interesting findings regarding depression have come from reports regarding a single nucleotide polymorphism on the BDNF gene that is associated with disrupted BDNF secretion. This polymorphism is one where the amino acid valine was substituted by methionine, and is referred to as a Val/Met polymorphism. A prospective study of at-risk adolescents indicated that depression was elevated among those with the Val/Met polymorphism who also displayed elevated morning cortisol levels (Goodyer et al., 2010). Moreover, among healthy, nondepressed individuals, those who carried either the BDNF mutation or the s/s 5-HTT allele (recall that the latter was also linked to depression) ruminated more following experiences of life stressors than did those with other genotypes (Clasen et al., 2011), and thus they might have been at an increased risk for later depression. Parenthetically, it might be significant that the presence of the Val/Met mutation not only predicted the occurrence of depression in relation to general life stressors, but was also accompanied by increased vulnerability to depression following a stroke (Kim et al., 2011). It therefore seems that the presence of genetic dispositions related to BDNF or to 5-HTT may increase the risk of depressive illness associated with a variety of challenges. Not all studies that have assessed the Val/Met polymorphism have provided support for the involvement of BDNF in depressive disorders. In fact, a case has been made that the presence of this polymorphism doesn't cause depressive disorders, but simply influences whether or not environmental factors will affect the later emergence of depressive symptoms (Caldwell et al., 2013).

BDNF AND OBESITY

Although BDNF disturbances have most often been related to depression and PTSD, it seems that BDNF can also contribute to obesity (Rios, 2013). A polymorphism for the BDNF gene has been discovered wherein only the short transcript of BDNF is formed, and BDNF is only seen in neuronal cell bodies and not at the dendrites. As a result, excessive immature synapses will be

(Continued)

(Continued)

formed that could translate into poor learning and memory. As it turns out, when present, this mutation was also accompanied by obesity in mice, and large-scale genome-wide association studies in humans revealed that BDNF gene variants were often tied to obesity.

Leptin and insulin that are fundamental in eating processes have also been found to stimulate BDNF synthesis in dendrites, thereby facilitating messages to start or stop eating. In the presence of the BDNF variant, these signals would not operate properly and could thus be associated with obesity (Liao et al., 2012). Given the link between the BDNF mutation and both depression and obesity, it will be interesting to see if this polymorphism is associated with the depressive subtype (atypical depression) where individuals eat more and express carbohydrate cravings.

LINKS BETWEEN EARLY LIFE EVENTS, SNPS AND DEPRESSION

Adverse early childhood experiences are associated with an increase in the frequency of adult depression, which might be related to BDNF variations. In fact, in female rhesus macaques, maternal deprivation was associated with reduced plasma BDNF levels, accompanied by behavioral passivity, possibly reflecting a depressive profile. These effects could be attenuated if monkeys were reared by peers, and this positive outcome was least apparent if they carried the Met allele. Consistent with these findings, the extended separation of rat pups from their mom resulted in signs of depression that were accompanied by growth factor changes, including reduced BDNF in the amygdala and the hippocampus. There is also evidence indicating that early life adverse experiences in humans, especially in the presence of the Val/Met mutation, have important implications for depression in adulthood. The negative consequences of early life adversities in relation to depression was markedly greater among individuals carrying the Met allele of the BDNF gene (Aguilera et al., 2009), as was the tendency toward a negative affectivity and biases towards recalling negative stimuli. These outcomes were still more prominent in individuals who carried both the short s/s alleles of the gene for 5-HTT, and the Val/Met polymorphism (Carver et al., 2011).

Paralleling some of the behavioral changes associated with early life abuse and the presence of the Met allele, the presence of childhood adversity, coupled with this polymorphism, was associated with low grey matter within the subgenual anterior cingulate cortex, but not in other brain regions that have been implicated in depression (the hippocampus, prefrontal cortex). From this it was suggested that this region might serve as a mechanistic link between stressful early life experiences, the BDNF polymorphism and adult depression (Gerritsen et al., 2011), yet the same interactions were also apparent among psychotic individuals, and hence it is possible that this combination is aligned with general psychological dysfunction rather than being tied uniquely to depression. Indeed, the relationship between BDNF and suicidal behavior was not exclusive to depression, but was apparent in relation to PTSD and substance abuse disorders, as well as other conditions that have been linked to suicide.

FIBROBLAST GROWTH FACTOR-2

Of the various growth factors, BDNF has been the most studied link to depression, but increasingly there has been attention given to fibroblast growth factor-2 (FGF-2). Stressors disturb FGF-2 functioning, and studies in depressed individuals indicated that FGF-2 and its receptors are reduced in limbic brain regions, including the prefrontal cortex (Evans et al., 2004). It also seems that the FGF system might contribute to the actions of SSRIs, as the reduction of FGF transcripts was attenuated in those individuals who had been receiving antidepressant medication.

In line with a role for FGF-2 in depression, studies conducted in both animals and humans indicated that antidepressant treatments effectively increased the levels of this growth factor. In addition to this, in animal models the administration of FGF-2 directly into the brain attenuated behavioral disturbances that were associated with stressors (Elsayed et al., 2012). These investigators also showed that the positive behavioral effects of antidepressant treatment in attenuating the effects of stressors were abolished by treatment with an FGF-2 antagonist. It remains to be determined how FGF-2 comes to produce its antidepressant effects, although it could involve changes in glutamate or the excitatory synapses in some brain regions. Moreover, although the reported studies pointed to the importance of FGF-2 within aspects of the prefrontal cortex, this does not exclude a role for this growth factor in other brain regions that have been implicated in depression.

TARGETING NEUROGENESIS IN THE TREATMENT OF DEPRESSION

There's been a deluge of data supporting the view that growth factors contribute to depression, and for years there's also been the knowledge that elevated cortisol is linked to depression. These might be independent processes, each contributing to depression in its own way, but there's also the possibility that cortisol might influence neurogenesis, thereby favoring the development of depression. In fact, in the presence of high cortisol concentrations stem cells may be damaged so that fewer newborn cells develop (Anacker et al., 2013). This seems to occur through a particular process called the 'Hedgehog pathway'. When these findings were extended to an animal model of depression, it was indeed found that stressors inhibited the functioning of this pathway in the brain. Going yet another step, when animals were treated with purmorphamine, a compound that ordinarily stimulates the Hedgehog pathway, the damage caused by stress hormones was antagonized. Although it may be a bit early to make this conclusion, it is possible that these findings might point to another potential target to attenuate depression in humans.

INFLAMMATORY PROCESSES ASSOCIATED WITH DEPRESSION

Stressful events profoundly affect immune functioning and may influence immune signaling molecules (cytokines). The converse seems to be true, as well, in that treatments that increase the presence of proinflammatory cytokines markedly increase HPA activity and affect the turnover of brain monoamines (Anisman et al., 2008). As the effects of these cytokines on central neuroendocrine and neurotransmitter processes are remarkably similar to those elicited by stressors, the view was advanced that the brain translates immune activation much like it interprets psychological and physical stressors (Anisman & Merali, 1999). Likewise, it was suggested that as with other stressors, activation of the inflammatory immune system may contribute to the development of depressive illness, as well as other varied neurological conditions (Dantzer et al., 2008; Maes, 1999; Raison et al., 2006).

CYTOKINES IN THE BRAIN

Cytokines released from activated immune cells are relatively large molecules, and hence don't readily gain access to the brain, although they might do so where the blood–brain barrier (BBB) is relatively permeable (i.e., at sites that surround the ventricular system within the brain and are thus called circumventricular organs). Transport mechanisms also exist that can move cytokines from the periphery into the brain, and cytokines can also indirectly influence brain processes through the stimulation of specific nerve fibers (e.g., vagal afferent fibers) that project from the periphery to the CNS. Further, the integrity of the BBB may be compromised by infectious and traumatic insults, thereby permitting greater cytokine passage into the brain where they can interact with endogenous cytokine receptors and may thus affect neuronal functioning.

Once present in the brain, cytokines can increase HPA activity and CRH activity at the central amygdala, and can also affect growth factors (e.g., BDNF). Added to this, cytokines, such as IFN-α, may stimulate the activity of an enzyme (indoleamine-2,3-dioxygenase, typically referred to as IDO) that degrades the 5-HT precursor tryptophan, thereby reducing 5-HT production and availability. As well, IDO metabolites, 3-hydroxy-kynurenine and quinolinic acid, both of which have well documented neurotoxic actions, may promote cell loss. Through either of these routes IDO could disturb 5-HT functioning and hence favor the development of depressive disorders (Dantzer et al., 2011; Maes et al., 2011).

Cytokines had primarily been thought of as signaling molecules of the immune system, and attempts to link cytokines and depression had typically considered the impact of peripheral inflammatory changes. However, cytokines and their receptors are endogenously expressed in the brain, where they are synthesized by microglia and possibly by neurons (Rivest, 2009). These brain cytokines or their mRNA expression are markedly increased in association with traumatic head injury, stroke and seizure, as well as in response to bacterial endotoxins and by stressors (see Anisman et al., 2008). It might be particularly significant that the effects of bacterial challenges and stressors may synergistically influence brain processes related to inflammation. In this regard, rats that had a bacterial endotoxin (e.g., LPS) injected directly into the prefrontal cortex exhibited a strong inflammatory response, but if rats had first been exposed to a stressor, microglial activation and the levels of TNF-α were augmented, and the loss of glial cell and neurons was more pronounced (de Pablos et al., 2006). Similarly, in rats that had been stressed on several successive days, LPS markedly activated microglia and there was a marked loss of neurons in the hippocampus. Predictably, the depressive-like behaviors elicited by a chronic stressor were augmented by cytokine (or LPS) challenges, whereas these outcomes were attenuated in mice in which the IL-1 receptor was knocked out (Goshen et al., 2008). These findings speak to the fact that stressors can interact with inflammatory factors in provoking damaging outcomes, and that these interactive effects are manifested in the brain, just as they are with respect to peripheral immune responses.

PROMOTION OF DEPRESSION IN ANIMAL MODELS

In addition to the stressor-like neurochemical changes elicited by cytokines, animals treated with pro-inflammatory cytokines or immune activating agents (LPS) display a depressive-like behavioral profile, including anhedonia and disrupted social interaction. These treatments also give rise to a constellation of symptoms, collectively referred to as 'sickness behaviors' (e.g., anorexia, fatigue, reduced motor activity, curled body posture, ptosis), that in some respects are reminiscent of the neurovegetative features comprising atypical depression, which could be attenuated by chronic antidepressant treatments (Dantzer et al., 2008). These behavioral changes can be exacerbated by stressors, raising the possibility that stressors and inflammatory immune activation synergistically promote depressive disorders (Anisman et al., 2008). It seems, however, that the sickness behavior and the depressive-like outcomes can be distinguished from one another in several respects, and antidepressants preferentially influence the affective impact of cytokines relative to the sickness symptoms. It might be the case that the sickness behaviors reflect the neurovegetative features of depression more than they reflect the cognitive or mood changes that characterize these disorders.

PROMOTION OF DEPRESSION IN HUMANS

Several lines of research have pointed to a role for the inflammatory immune system in the provocation of depressive disorders in humans. Some of the findings come from studies showing that immune-related disorders, viruses, and common parasites were associated with increased levels of depressive illness. For instance, individuals infected with Toxoplasma gondii were much more likely to attempt suicide than were uninfected individuals. Other studies have shown that depressive illness was accompanied by an inflammatory response being mounted, including the presence of elevated acute phase proteins, such as C-reactive protein, and elevated circulating and mitogen-stimulated cytokine concentrations (Maes, 1999). The data concerning brain cytokines in humans in relation to depression are limited, but it was reported that among teenaged individuals who died by suicide, mRNA and protein expression levels of IL-1β, IL-6, and TNF-α were increased in the frontopolar cortex relative to normal controls. However, not all individuals who died by suicide had been diagnosed with depression, and so the cytokine variations likely were related to suicide or the presence of a pathological condition as opposed to an outcome that was unique to depression (Pandey et al., 2011).

There have been reports that the elevated blood levels of IL-1β, IL-6, TNF-α, and IFN–γ that were associated with depression normalized with antidepressant treatment, although there have been just as many reports indicating that this did not occur. The latter studies might suggest that peripheral cytokine elevations could serve as markers for a disposition toward depressive disorder, but are not causally related to the illness. It might also be the case that sustained cytokine elevations, despite behavioral normalization after antidepressant treatment, are indicative of something still being amiss that could promote a further depressive episoode. Therefore, it would be informative to know whether those with the continued cytokine elevations were the most likely to fall back into depression once pharmacological treatment for the illness was discontinued. Further, the possibility shouldn't be ruled out that factors secondary to depressive illness (e.g., altered appraisal and coping, drug use, institutionalization, disturbed sleep and circadian rhythms, sleep, poor health-related behaviors, and changes in weight) were responsible for the cytokine alterations, but otherwise have little to do with the provocation of the disorder (Irwin, 1999).

OBESITY CAN AFFECT HEALTH THROUGH AN INFLAMMATORY PROCESS

Typically, when we think of inflammatory factors we might have in mind infection, viral insults, or various forms of head trauma. There are numerous factors that affect humans that aren't immediately seen as being relevant to inflammatory processes, but yet are fairly important in this respect. One of these is concerned with obesity. We all know that obesity may be a risk factor for such things as heart disease, but have you ever considered obesity as a factor that was related to inflammation or depressive illness? Even if you knew that overweight individuals were more likely to be depressed than average weight people, you might have attributed this relationship to heavier people having issues related to stigma/shame, bullying, but not to inflammatory factors. In fact, adipose tissue (fat) is an exceptionally rich source of several cytokines and related factors. As a result, it has been suggested that more frequent depression in overweight people might have to do with the greater release of cytokines from fat deposits. Shelton and Miller (2011) pointed out that there was indeed a vicious cycle in which adiposity contributed to depression, and this depression, in turn, promoted elevated eating. They also make the interesting point that inflammatory factors, known to be involved in heart disease as well as diabetes, might be key contributors to the high comorbidity that exists between depression and both heart disease and diabetes.

CYTOKINES ASSOCIATED WITH DEPRESSION UNDER BASAL AND CHALLENGE CONDITIONS

From what's been said to this point, the impression might have been given that elevated cytokine levels are bad for us (e.g., promoting neurotoxicity or acting like strong stressors). However, an alternative view is that cytokines are activated to promote the healing of microdamage in the brain, and depression is an unfortunate by-product of these healing processes. Specifically, in response to strong stressors or head injury, microglial responses trigger an injury repair response that comprises the release of neuroinflammatory factors that could potentially serve as growth factors to promote tissue regeneration. However, these molecules could instigate other neurochemical effects that might provoke psychological disturbances, such as depression. Often, as indicated earlier, it was concluded that in small amounts, cytokines may act in a neuroprotective capacity, but at high levels they might be neurodestructive. Moreover, the effects of cytokines on behavioral outcomes also vary as a function of background conditions (e.g., stressor presence). The conditions that lead to one outcome or another under clinical conditions, however, have yet to be established.

Beyond the data indicating a correlation between inflammatory factors and depression, several studies assessed the causal connection between immune activation and mood states. For instance, treatment with a low dose of an endotoxin (E. coli) that increased plasma TNF-α and IL-6 levels elicited a mildly depressed mood (although nowhere near the clinical levels for depression) and a feeling of 'social disconnection' (Inagaki et al., 2011). It was likewise demonstrated that triggering an inflammatory response using vaccines (e.g., typhoid) also elicited increased plasma IL-6 that was accompanied by a depressive-like mood, as well as fatigue, confusion and impaired concentration that may have been related to altered neuronal activity within the anterior cingulate cortex (Harrison et al., 2009). Although the mild depressive-like symptoms (e.g., lassitude, social anhedonia) elicited by an endotoxin were attenuated by pretreatment with the SSRI citalopram, the peripheral cytokine changes were not altered in citalopram-treated individuals, suggesting that the cytokine variations were markers of depression, but were not direct modulators of mood state (Hannestad et al., 2011).

It has also been shown that following an intravenous injection of a low dose of an endotoxin, plasma IL-6 increased as did depressed mood. When these participants were put through a test of social rejection (the computerized ball-throwing task described in Chapter 2), the females that had been exposed to endotoxin displayed still more pronounced IL-6 elevations (Eisenberger et al., 2010). The elevated IL-6, in turn, was associated with increased neural activity in the dorsal anterior cingulate cortex and anterior insula (brain regions implicated in depression), as well as the ventral striatum (associated with reward processes), which mediated the relationship between IL-6 and depressed mood. Together, these data are consistent with the view that the activation of inflammatory processes gives rise to depressive features; however, it is equally possible that inflammatory immune activation causes a broad condition, in which depression is a primary characteristic, but that other pathological conditions can emerge as well.

DEPRESSION ASSOCIATED WITH IMMUNOTHERAPY: THE CASE OF IFN-α

Some of the most telling findings concerning inflammatory effects on mood states have come from studies of patients receiving IFN-α immunotherapy in the treatment of some forms of cancer or hepatitis C. Treatment with IFN-α is often used becaue of its antiviral and anti-tumor effects, but over the course of being treated, a large percentage of patients (30–50%) develop depressive-like states that might require treatment discontinuation (Raison et al., 2006). As reviewed by Miller et al. (2009) and Capuron and Miller (2011), the severity of depression was particularly pronounced among individuals with higher levels of depressive symptoms prior to immunotherapy, among women with a history of depression, and in those individuals with poor social support. In addition, depression was elicited most readily among individuals with low levels of tryptophan, which is necessary for the production of 5-HT, those with relatively high baseline levels of IL-6, and those individuals with the greatest ACTH and cortisol elevations following IFN-α administration. These risk factors for cytokine-induced depression are very much like those usually thought of when considering stressor-related depressive states, and indeed, treatment with antidepressants reduces the depressive symptoms provoked by IFN-α (Raison et al., 2006).

As impressive as these findings might be in linking cytokine variations and depression, one ought to consider whether the actions of IFN-α are a reflection of genuine depression, or secondary to other factors. Patients treated with IFN-α not only present with the neurovegetative and mood symptoms, but also with a range of cognitive disturbances. These patients report feeling 'in a fog', they experience a fairly severe malaise, especially over the first few days of treatment, and at the higher doses used in cancer patients, patients may experience impaired concentration and memory, as well as numerous non-specific features such as a confusional state, disorientation, psychotic-like features, irritability, anxiety, disturbed vigilance, and alertness. In effect, the actions of IFN-α might reflect a nonspecific state characterized by a general malaise or toxicity engendered by the treatment, and the emergence of depression might represent all of these factors superimposed on individuals having the knowledge that they may be critically ill. Thus IFN-α certainly causes depressive-like states, but it may have effects beyond mood disturbances alone.

The finding that drugs such as IFN-α can elicit a depressive state is exceptionally relevant in regard to a cytokine model of depression, but these findings still beg the question regarding how cytokine changes actually come to elicit mood disturbances. As discussed earlier, in response to stressors or immunological insults, cytokines are released from microglia in the brain, generating a cascade of biological changes that culminate in 5-HT, CRH, and growth factor changes that could promote depressive illness (Anisman et al., 2008). However, only about half the individuals treated with IFN-α actually develop depressive features. Although there are several factors that might be fundamental in determining this vulnerability, genetic differences regarding the gene that influences IDO functioning may play a role in this regard. Specifically, an SNP was found in the promoter region of the IDO gene, which was associated with IFN-α-induced depressive symptoms measured 12–48 weeks into the IFN-α treatment regimen. As well, the odds of developing depressive symptoms were very much lower among African Americans, who are at relatively reduced risk of carrying the IDO allele (Smith et al., 2011). In essence, vulnerability to IFN-induced depression could be related to genetic make-up, and thus once again it ought to be possible to use this as a biomarker in deciding which patients to treat with antidepressant medications in advance of IFN therapy.

CYTOKINE AND STRESSOR INTERACTIONS

Most studies and theoretical reviews of IDO have focused on the neuronal changes that occur as a result of cytokine immunotherapy. However, as stressful experiences affect 5-HT processes, there have also been studies conducted to assess whether stressors might also affect IDO and hence 5-HT functioning. In fact, psychological stressors are capable of promoting cytokine-driven IDO activation, which then promotes 5-HT alterations that could potentially engender behavioral alterations (Kiank et al., 2010). This takes us back to the issue of what stressors might have to do with IFN-α immunotherapy. As already mentioned, those with subsyndromal levels of depression, a history of depression, or low levels of tryptophan may be at particular risk for more severe depression following immunotherapy. Consider, however, that patients who are given IFN-α are already pretty sick and probably very stressed, and in some cases social support systems might be absent and quality of life is likely impoverished (especially as a large number of hepatitis C patients will be drug users who contracted the illness through tainted needles; another segment of the hepatitis C population are those who were victims of tainted blood prior to testing being conducted to screen for this). Accordingly, it is possible that the cytokine treatment and stressful experiences collaborate to instigate depression. Indeed, when immune activating agents, including IFN-α, were administered to mice that had undergone a social stressor, much greater changes were apparent with respect to sickness behaviors, corticoid and central monoamine activity, and circulating cytokines, as well as cytokine production within the brain (Anisman et al., 2007; Gibb et al., 2011). Evidently, the biological repercussions of immune activation are greatly magnified if administered against the background of a stressor experience, which could promote a constellation of behavioral/cognitive changes, including depressed mood.

GUT MICROBES AND DEPRESSION: IS YOGURT THE ANSWER?

By now you might be convinced that immune-related processes influence mood states. However, it might take even more persuasiveness to convince you that microbes present in your gut are in any way significant for depressive disorders. There are trillions of immune cells in our body, most of which are situated in the intestine (amounting to about about 1.5 kg). Apparently, microbial factors present in the gut might be involved in inflammatory processes, and in stress situations bacteria may translocate (move) to lymphoid tissue where lots of lymphocytes reside (Bailey et al., 2011). In individuals with 'leaky gut' syndrome, which elicits systemic inflammatory response syndrome and may contribute to inflammatory bowel disease, and even diabetes and allergies, stressors might be particularly likely to promote depressive-like behaviors (Haroon et al., 2012).

In mice treated with antibiotics, intestinal microflora were reduced and the ability of social stressors to increase blood cytokines, such as IL-6, was concomitantly attenuated (Bailey et al., 2011). In addition to this, the depressive-like behavior observed in a forced-swim test among rats that had experienced early-life separation from their mom was attenuated following treatment with the probiotic Bifidobacterium infantis, and this treatment concurrently reduced circulating levels of IL-6 (Desbonnet et al., 2010). It was similarly observed that chronic treatment with the lactic acid bacteria Lactobacillus rhamnosus increased GABA mRNA changes that varied across

(Continued)

(Continued)

several cortical brain regions as well as in the amygdala and hippocampus (Bravo et al., 2011). Of particular interest here was that L. rhamnosus reduced stress-induced corticosterone and behaviors that reflected anxiety and depression. As the neurochemical and behavioral effects were absent in vagotomized mice, it was suggested that the vagus nerve served as the essential pathway between the action of gut bacteria and the brain.

It might be recalled that depression and heart disease are highly comorbid, as is inflammatory immune activation and heart disease. It seems that just as gut bacteria are linked to depression, they are also associated with heart disease. In rats, a treatment that reduced leptin levels was associated with smaller heart attacks than observed otherwise. This effect was reversed by the administration of leptin, suggesting a significant mediating role for this hormone (Lam et al., 2012). Another group of animals received a probiotic as part of their diet. This also reduced leptin and reduced the size of heart attacks. The authors, in an interview, pointed out that it may be premature to use yogurt for heart attack prophylaxis. Nevertheless, given the potential importance of good bacteria in the gut, it could be said of yogurt, as in the case of the chicken soup remedy, 'it couldn't hurt'.

POSTSTROKE DEPRESSION

There is another clinical venue in which depression levels are very high. One can reasonably expect that people in hospital or those who are in the midst of a severe medical illness are more likely to be depressed than are those who are well. Especially high levels of depression are seen following a stroke, and this is often accompanied by suicidal ideation. As it turns out, as indicated earlier, pro-inflammatory cytokine levels are elevated following a stroke, just as they are following other neurological challenges. These cytokines could be acting in a beneficial manner (clearing debris and reducing infection), but they might also act in a neurodestructive fashion and hence promote pathology, including depression. Studies in animals indeed indicated that middle cerebral artery occlusion (MCAO), a commonly used procedure to mimic an ischemic stroke (the type of stroke that entails diminished blood flow and hence reduced oxygen to the brain), provoked a key feature of depression, namely that of anhedonia, and this outcome could be attenuated by a treatment that antagonized IL-1β (Craft & DeVries, 2006). Thus it was suggested that poststroke depression might be due to cytokine elevations that affect IDO metabolism and the subsequent decline of serotonin in limbic brain regions, or the neuronal loss stemming from neurotoxic conditions associated with IDO elevations (Spalletta et al., 2006).

The occurrence of depression following stroke predicts a poor prognosis for functional recovery and future global functioning, and the early appearance of depressive symptoms after stroke was associated with sustained poststroke depression as well as increased mortality over the ensuing few years. It is possible that specific inflammatory cytokines could mediate functional recuperation and might constitute a clinical marker of later functional recovery, later incidence of stroke, persistence of depression, and mortality. The identification of the specific cytokine sequelae of ischemic stroke might be instrumental in the development of novel targets to treat or limit the downstream negative consequences that are typically associated with a stroke.

TREATMENTS FOR DEPRESSION BASED ON INFLAMMATORY PROCESSES

Given that inflammatory processes are relevant to depression, does this have any implications for treatment strategies? It had been reported that the TNF-α antagonist (e.g., Etanercept) reduced depressive symptoms among individuals being treated for rheumatoid arthritis or psoriasis (Kekow et al., 2011). It is premature to conclude that their improved mood was directly related to the TNF-α changes rather than being secondary to the amelioration of the symptoms of arthritis or psoriasis. Still, the findings are enticing, and it won't be long before additional data are available to clarify what might be going on.

In animals that had been pretreated with a nonstereoidal anti-inflammatory agent (NSAID) the effects of IFN-α were markedly reduced, and common agents such as ibuprofen facilitate brain repair following a stroke in rats by diminishing the adverse effects of inflammatory factors (Asnis & De La Garza, 2006). Moreover, in humans, NSAIDs enhanced the effectiveness of antidepressant medication in treating depression, and when coupled with fluoxetine, the production of pro-inflammatory cytokines was reduced and the antidepressant actions were superior to those elicited by fluoxetine alone (Akhondzadeh et al., 2010). Yet there have also been reports indicating that anti-inflammatory agents reduced the effectiveness of antidepressant agents. Reconciling these different outcomes is not simple, and at the very least, studies need to be done to evaluate the effects of these treatments in subtypes of illness, or better still, among individuals presenting with particular symptoms, together with biomarkers related to inflammation. At this point, anti-inflammatory drugs are not being suggested as treatments for depression, but they could turn out to be effective adjunctive treatments that would enhance the effects of drugs such as SSRIs.

REMEMBER ERYTHROPOIETIN (EPO)? HERE IT IS IN A NEW CONTEXT

Research concerning the cytokine–depression connection has focused on the pro-inflammatory cytokines, and numerous other immune-related factors have been sidelined, even though they might be especially significant in this regard. One of these is erythropoietin (EPO), and yes, that's the same substance that has become (in)famous because of its involvement in blood doping (e.g., among professional cyclists). EPO is a hormone that is essential for red blood cell production. It is a cytokine that stimulates the precursors of red blood cells that are present in the bone marrow, and it also acts to protect red blood cells from death that ordinarily occurs through a process

(Continued)

(Continued)

referred to as apoptosis (programmed cell death). Beyond these effects, EPO seems to have beneficial actions in traumatic brain injury and stroke (Sargin et al., 2010), and EPO or one of its analogues Carbamylerythropoietin can have positive effects when administered during a brief window following a stroke (Villa et al., 2007). Furthermore, accumulating data have also pointed to EPO as having cognitive benefits as well as antidepressant-like effects in animal models of the disorder. In addition, in humans, EPO produced brain activity changes (measured by fMRI) like those associated with antidepressant treatments (Miskowiak et al., 2012). How EPO might have such positive effects isn't fully understood as yet. But it is significant that it can serve to preserve or increase neuronal functioning, and promote anti-inflammatory, anti-apoptotic, antioxidant, and neurotrophic actions, and it has also been shown to increase the synthesis and levels of BDNF. In view of these findings, it was suggested that EPO might be useful as an adjunctive treatment for depression (Hayley, 2011).

DEPRESSION – WHAT'S IT GOOD FOR ANYWAYS?

Over the course of evolution, phenotypes that were useful and allowed for species to prop-agate should have been maintained, whereas those phenotypes that were disadvantageous should have been selected against and hence ought to have disappeared. And yet there are many phenotypes that have persisted despite their apparent uselessness. How does this come about? As mentioned earlier, a gene can be altered by mutations (e.g., polymor-phisms) and thus genes that favor depression could occur simply by chance. Likewise, epi-genetic changes could occur and the resulting gene suppression can be passed on across generations. As well, although genetic factors can be associated with phenotypic effects that are apparent all of the time, there are genetic factors that have negative consequences only under certain conditions (e.g., such as the presence of stressful experiences). Thus the selection pressure against these characteristics might be diminished, allowing for the phenotype to persist.

There are also instances in which a gene might have some sort of positive effect and hence there is selection *for* this characteristic, even though it might also have some bad conse-quences. The classic example of this is sickle cell anemia, which has the selective advantage of offering a resistance to malaria, but also has the unfortunate effect of reducing the oxygen-carrying capacity of red blood cells. In effect, inheriting the genes for sickle cell anemia might be advantageous in some parts of Africa, but it won't be of much value for individuals living in Toronto, Baltimore, or London. In addition to these processes, there are conditions in which a gene is passed on because the phenotype of the affected individual might not be apparent until much later in life, well after they might have passed on their genes. Here the classic example is Huntington's disease which doesn't show up until an individual is about forty years of age, and might already have passed on their genes. The same holds true, incidentally, for several other genetic characteristics involved in other pathologies, such as certain types of cancer and heart disease.

There are other characteristics present in humans that at first blush seem to be useless, but are exceptionally common. Nausea and vomiting are highly aversive, but they also inform us that something is amiss that needs to be looked after. Moreover, it tells us that whatever it was that you did or ate, it's best not to do this again. Earlier, we used the example of feeling pain as having positive attributes in that it lets us know when we've done something to harm ourselves and that care needs to be taken. The pain of a sprained ankle diminishes the likelihood that we will place weight on it, thus allowing for healing to occur; likewise, pain receptors on our fingers tell us to remove our hand from a hot object quickly so that greater tissue damage doesn't occur, and receptors in our mouth give us some fairly important information (even if a bit late) about the blistering that's occurring on our palate as hot cheese from your pizza sticks to it. Of course, there are severe pains that seem absolutely unnecessary, such as that associated with cancer or other diseases. Surely, nature could have been kinder and given us some other sign that might have been just as effective.

Perhaps, as in the case of nausea and pain, the presence of depression provides a signal that all isn't right and that actions need to be taken to change our situation. Most individuals who have been severely depressed will likely tell you about how bleak and horrid their lives had been, the dark dirty pool in which they had been submerged, and the endless days of rumination and thoughts of suicide. I doubt there are many scientists who would suggest that severe depression has a whole lot of positive value, but mild depression might, so long as it doesn't end up getting out of control and culminating in severe illness.

There is a school of thought (well, as there aren't a huge number in this camp, maybe we should call it a 'small class of thought' rather than a whole school) that suggests mild depression has some value. For some time there has been an interest in the topic of self-regulation and goal pursuits; this essentially refers to an individual's ability to recognize and identify goals, and then to pursue and possibly attain these goals. When I was in grade school, we were taught certain maxims as if they were absolute truths. The best known in my day was 'if at first you don't succeed, then try, try, try again'. Essentially, quitting wasn't an option, and if you failed, then you simply had to stick with it until you succeeded. In many cases this is how it should be, but is it always the case? Simply because an individual has a certain goal this doesn't mean they can attain it. Should the athletically-challenged kid be pushed to the extent that he believes he can be a professional sports figure if he just tries hard enough, or similarly the kid who can't hold a tune into believing he might become the next American Idol? These goals might simply be unattainable for them. So, should they try, try, try again to reach this unattainable goal? Or, alternatively, should they abandon the futility and move on to more productive endeavors (then again, even as I write these words, I can imagine Amalié Freud saying 'Siggy, Siggy, stop your foolishness about this psychoanalysis. Come and give muttie a nice hug and I'll make you something to eat')? It seems that mild depression might have positive effects as it was associated with goal disengagement and/or goal reengagement (finding some new more attainable goal, which was accompanied by improved health and sleep efficiency, as well as more normal diurnal cortisol variations). Conversely, individuals who had trouble disengaging from the chase of unattainable goals exhibited elevated levels of the inflammatory marker C-reactive protein, which might be predictive of later health problems. In effect, the early signs of depression might be a harbinger that things aren't going well, and might get still worse if the same path is continued (Wrosch et al., 2003). As a result, mild depression might be a signal for the individual to reexamine and perhaps regulate their goals more appropriately, thereby precluding more severe depression at a later time.

CONCLUSION

Numerous factors likely contribute to the emergence of depression, and it is highly unlikely that any one neurotransmitter, neuropeptide, inflammatory factor or hormone accounts for all of the symptoms observed. Likewise, the specific biological processes that

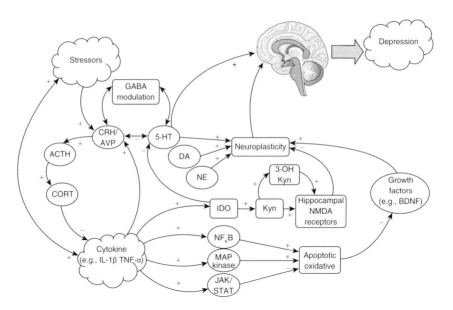

FIGURE 8.2 Schematic representation depicting potential routes by which stressors and cytokines could influence depressive state. A stressor could potentially influence major depression through several interconnected loops. Stressors and cytokines can both increase hypothalamic (and extra-hypotalamic) CRH release. In addition to activating HPA functioning, CRH may influence 5-HT processes, and GABA$_A$ activity may act as a mediator in this regard. This, in turn, may influence depression directly, or may do so by impairing neuroplastic processes. An alternative, although not necessarily mutually exclusive, pathway involves cytokine/stress activation of either NFkB, MAP kinases, or JAK/STAT signaling, which serve to transmit information derived from chemical signals outside of a cell to gene promoters on DNA within the cell's nucleus. These processes influence oxidative or apoptotic mechanisms, leading to altered growth factor expression (e.g., BDNF), hence again favoring impaired neuroplastic processes, and culminating in major depression. As well, immune activation leading to cytokine changes might then affect IDO that could either reduce 5-HT availability, or through several oxidative metabolites might disturb neuroplasticity, which would then favor the development of depression (adapted from Anisman et al., 2008 and Hayley et al., 2005).

lead to depression in one individual might differ from those that provoked depression in a second, just as the specific life events that led to this outcome differed among individuals. Figure 8.2 is a schematic representation of one neurochemical model of depression, and it is admittedly limited in the number of biochemical mechanisms proposed. You'll recognize that we have discussed each of these processes in this and in Chapters 3, 4, and 5, and at this point it is being brought up as an illustration of how biological process can be linked to one another, ultimately resulting in depressive illness.

The figure caption largely explains the sequence of events this figure portrays, but there are several other messages embedded in it that you should attend to, which might be more important for you than the actual chemical processes described.

1. Placing enough strain on a structure will likely cause it to break at its weakest point, and likewise the stressors encountered by an individual will cause the most vulnerable component of our biological defensive system to crack. For one individual this might be their 5-HT responses, for another BDNF or HPA functioning, and for still another it might involve GABA disturbances.

2. The fact that multiple routes exist in the evolution of depression might also account for why the success rates for pharmacological treatments are as low as they are and why it takes several tries, using different remedies, before success is realized in alleviating depressive symptoms. In addition, this model may help to explain why recurrence rates are as high as they are after successful treatment. For starters the treatment might not have fully 'cured' the illness, and as often as not the treated individual might still present with residual symptoms, attesting to the partial efficacy of the treatment. In addition, however, the treatment choice might not be getting to the root of the problem. By example, as illustrated in the figure, cytokine disturbances might come to affect 5-HT or BDNF functioning in a given individual. In this instance, treatment with a 5-HT targeted manipulation might be effective in attenuating symptoms. But the original problem, cytokine dysregulation in this instance, might still be present, and so the symptoms of the illness are eliminated (masked) for the moment. However, when the drug is withdrawn, the adverse effects attributable to the disrupted cytokine process will again emerge. Similarly, if the stressors experienced by an individual are responsible for the overload of neural circuits, hence leading to depression, the drug treatment might make things manageable for the moment, but once more, when the drug treatment is stopped, the system will crumble unless the root of the problem has been dealt with (i.e., the presence of the stressor or how to appraise and deal with it). This said, it is certainly possible that when symptoms are attenuated by the drug treatment, the individual, being in a better place, might be more able or ready to rearrange the way they appraise and cope with their situation, and how they deal with future stressors. Thus a combination of drug treatment and cognitive behavioral therapy, as described in Chapter 12, might be particularly efficacious.

3. In some individuals the presence of depressive illness might be due to multiple neurochemical disturbances, acting in series or in parallel. Thus, pharmacotherapy that involves multitargeting might in many cases be preferential over strategies that are restricted to simpler treatments, such as SSRIs.

More than anything, this chapter has emphasized that depression is a complex disorder involving multiple neurochemical processes and that the mechanisms governing this illness in one individual might not be identical to that apparent in a second. Increasingly, the notion is being accepted that whether it's depression, heart disease, cancer, or a variety of other illnesses, the effectiveness of treatments will improve once an individualized (personalized) treatment approach is adopted. Once illnesses are diagnosed on the basis of specific symptoms, genetic factors, etiological processes, and biomarkers, it will be possible to tailor treatments more appropriately, and ought to provide better patient care and might also limit the comorbidities often associated with depression.

SUMMARY

- Depressive disorders are linked to numerous other medical conditions, and can be elicited by stressful experiences.
- The occurrence of stressor-related depression is influenced by a broad range of factors associated with early life experiences, previous stressor experiences, appraisal and coping abilities, and genetic factors.
- This illness has been attributed to disturbed cognitive processes, such as learned helplessness and hopelessness.
- Multiple biological processes have been implicated in depressive disorders, including the classic monoamines, various hormones, several growth factors, and inflammatory immune activation.
- Several treatment strategies have been offered for depression, but to this point there haven't been any magic bullets identified.

9 ANXIETY DISORDERS

IS IT A REALITY OR AN OPINION?

In a recent episode of a television program, one of those that include the crime, the search for the bad guy, and then the trial, the defense's case was that the alleged perpetrator suffered from PTSD and as a result should not be found guilty. The prosecution lawyer, in cross-examining the expert witness, a psychiatrist, asks 'How did you diagnose this illness?'. The psychiatrist replied that he did this 'on the basis of several interviews to see whether the alleged perpetrator showed signs of PTSD', to which the prosecutor replied with something like 'So, I take it that you didn't perform any brain imaging analyses to see if there was disturbance in the brain, or any blood tests or analyses of cerebrospinal fluid that could tell us whether there were chemical imbalances? So, really, this diagnosis of yours is nothing more than an opinion, a guess. Perhaps it was an educated guess, but still just a guess'.

Although psychological disorders are thought of as diseases of the brain and so should have some biological origin, finding these underlying mechanisms hasn't been easy, and even finding the markers for these illnesses has been difficult. Unlike diabetes that can be detected on the basis of blood sugar levels, or heart problems that can be seen through different tests of varying invasiveness, to assess the presence of mental disorders we're often reliant on behavioral or cognitive symptoms. To be sure, with improved molecular, biochemical, and imaging technologies, it's just a matter of time before biological indices of various illnesses will be determined. Yet, as most illnesses represent an amalgamation of multiple disturbed processes and biological mechanisms, this won't be simple or fast. In the case of anxiety, this might be especially difficult as there are many subtypes of anxiety that differ from one another and may involve some common mechanisms and some that differ from one another.

Most of us have felt anxious at one time or another, usually in anticipation of something negative or uncertain (such as an exam, having to give an oral presentation to a group, or waiting for the results of a medical test). The anxiety most people feel is usually mild, occurs only under certain circumstances, and likely has significant adaptive value as it keeps us in a heightened state of alertness and readiness to respond. For others, it can be persistent and intense to the extent that individuals describe themselves as 'just wanting to crawl out of their skin'. Some individuals who have suffered anxiety that was comorbid with severe depression have also indicated that the anxiety was actually as bad as, or even more disturbing than, the depression. What differentiates 'normal' anxiety from anxiety that requires treatment is the degree of discomfort it creates and the extent to which it affects social and workplace functioning or family interactions. Anxiety disorders may be debilitating, chronic conditions that in some individuals first appear at a very early age, possibly among individuals with a familial history of anxiety, or they may be elicited by specific events. This chapter has several core objectives regarding what the reader should learn from it:

- anxiety can be mild, reflecting a normal response to challenging or threatening situations. Alternatively, it can come in any of several disorders that call for some sort of treatment. These comprise general anxiety disorder, panic disorder, phobias, social anxiety, obsessive-compulsive disorder, and posttraumatic stress disorder. Moreover, these anxiety-related illnesses can be comorbid with depressive disorders;
- the causes for each of these disorders can be very different, and the social and biological processes associated with them are different as well;
- although each of these disorders comprises very different symptoms, and involve several different biological processes, some of them seem to have several common underlying mechanisms;
- despite the different characteristics of these disorders, they are amenable to some of the same treatments, although their effectiveness has not been particularly strong.

SUBTYPES OF ANXIETY

'Anxiety Disorder' is actually a broad term that applies to several forms of abnormal and pathological anxieties or fears that affect 18% of individuals in Western societies. Although each of these illnesses is classified as an anxiety disorder, the course and etiological processes associated with them may differ appreciably from one another, and the various disorders are not necessarily responsive to the same treatments. As we'll see, disorders that comprise anxiety and those that involve fear (e.g., phobias) are generally placed under the rubric of 'Anxiety Disorders', although they are actually quite different and involve different biological underpinnings. Fear has been considered as an apprehension whose onset occurs rapidly in response to a threat, and then abates quickly once the threat is removed. In this sense, the 'fear' response is perfectly adaptive provided that there's an *actual* threat present. Anxiety, it seems, is more closely aligned with threats that are neither as specific nor as predictable as those that elicit fear, and because it may not be tied to specific stimuli, the course of this anxiety may be very protracted. Table 9.1 provides a summary of different types of anxiety-related disorders. We'll deal with each independently, but as we move through these it should become clear that despite profound differences between them, there are also several commonalities, including a core made up of common symptoms, and in some instances the same treatments are applicable. That said, the treatments available are not perfect, and there is certainly room for some refinement of the current therapeutic strategies.

TABLE 9.1 Anxiety disorders

Generalized anxiety disorder, the most common anxiety disorder among adults, is characterized by persistent (at least six months) anxiety or worry that is not focused on any single subject, object, or situation.

Panic disorder is characterized by discrete periods involving the sudden and unpredictable onset of intense apprehension or terror accompanied by features such as shortness of breath, chest pain and palpitations, feelings of choking or smothering, and a fear of losing control. It may result in profound behavioral changes involving worry about the implications or concern about having other attacks.

Phobias are characterized by clinically significant anxiety (fear) elicited by certain situations, activities, things, or people, in which individuals display an excessive and unreasonable desire to avoid or escape from the feared object or situation. There are several classes of phobias, and as a group these are exceptionally common.

Social anxiety disorder (social phobia) comprises an intense fear of public embarrassment or humiliation (negative public scrutiny). Most often this fear is evident across situations, but can be specific to certain venues (e.g., public speaking). The severity of symptoms can be sufficiently intense to provoke social isolation.

Obsessive-Compulsive Disorder (OCD) comprises obsessions or intrusive thoughts that provoke anxiety and compulsions (e.g., hoarding, repeated checking, repeated behavioral acts such as hand washing, or preoccupation with sexual, religious, or aggressive impulses) that serve to alleviate the anxiety (although the compulsions aren't necessarily overt).

Posttraumatic Stress Disorder (PTSD) is elicited by traumatic or chronic physical or psychological stressors. It is characterized by the re-experiencing of a traumatic event, avoidance of related stimuli, and hyperarousal. In addition, PTSD is often associated with emotional numbing and cognitive disturbances. Acute Stress Disorder (ASD) comprises similar symptoms evident soon after a traumatic event (three days). It largely differs from PTSD on the basis of the number of symptoms required for a diagnosis, and is accompanied by "dissociative" symptoms.

Separation anxiety disorder comprises excessive and inappropriate levels of anxiety in response to being separated from a person or place. Such feelings are common in children, but are considered a disorder only when these are excessive and inappropriate.

GENERALIZED ANXIETY DISORDER (GAD)

This fairly common illness, whose symptoms are provided in Table 9.2, markedly influences social functioning, and has a life-time prevalence of about 5%. The appearance of GAD can occur early in life, although the onset is most common when individuals are in their twenties or early thirties and appears twice as frequently in women as in men. The development of GAD is relatively slow, but once present it may be fairly persistent. It is frequently a comorbid feature of major depression or dysthymia, as well as other anxiety disorders (panic disorder, social phobia). The frequent comorbidity between major depression and GAD raises the possibility that they share etiological processes.

There appears to be a genetic link for this disorder as it runs in families, and concordance for the presence of GAD was more frequent in monozygotic (identical) than in dizygotic twins, although to a great extent a vulnerability to GAD was tied to contextual

TABLE 9.2 Generalized anxiety disorder (GAD) symptomatology

According to the DSM-5, GAD is characterized by:

(1) excessive, uncontrollable, and often irrational worry about day-to-day things and events; the anxiety persists for at least six months, being present on more days than not;
(2) an inability to or difficulty in controlling these thoughts.
(3) In addition, three of the following symptoms must be present: restlessness (or feeling on edge), easily fatigued, difficulty concentrating, irritability, muscle tension, sleep disturbance typically involving difficulty falling asleep or staying asleep (or restless sleep).

The excessive anxiety should not be related to the use of illicit drugs and is not limited to anxiety or worry about other psychological disorders.

Beyond these core symptoms, GAD is often accompanied by physical signs that include sweating, cold clammy hands, dry mouth, headaches, muscle tension, muscle aches, nausea or diarrhea, numbness in the hands and feet, difficulty swallowing or the feeling of a lump in the throat, occasional bouts of breathing difficulty, trembling, and twitching.

For those who might have thought that an anxiety disorder is not all that serious, and really amounts to 'just a bit of anxiety', this list of symptoms lets you know how problematic it can be.

(environmental) factors. Encountering a major life stressor (e.g., a car accident, or a breast cancer diagnosis, as well as natural disasters such as earthquakes) has been implicated in the emergence of GAD. Likewise, GAD, along with PTSD, can even occur through witnessing a trauma. For instance, these disorders appeared more frequently among individuals who knew someone at the 9/11 terrorist site than among those who did not. This is not to say that GAD occurs exclusively in those who have been traumatized. Individuals who experienced high psychological job demands (excessive workload, extreme time pressures) had a two-fold risk of depressive disorders or GAD relative to those with low job demands. And added to this, early life stressors might contribute to the emergence of GAD, just as it may be a predisposing factor for depression.

BIOLOGICAL FACTORS AND TREATMENT OF GAD

In view of the large amount of data suggesting that the amygdala and the bed nucleus of the stria terminalis are involved in anxiety and fear (Davis et al., 2010), it is thought that GAD might also involve disturbed amygdala functioning or disturbed connectivity to other brain regions that might be fundamental in processing information related to anxiety-provoking stimuli. In the latter regard, it is clear that the prefrontal cortex and hippocampus are also involved in anxiety and fear, particularly as they may contribute to an appraisal of fear-related events and also the memory of these events. For example, functional imaging studies indicated that GAD was accompanied by increased prefrontal cortical activity, which was attenuated following effective treatment of the disorder. Recent evidence concerning brain interactions has, however, put a different spin on how anxiety emerges. It was suggested that the connection that exists between the amygdala and both the prefrontal and anterior cingulate cortex, a white matter tract referred to as the uncinate fasciculus, was disturbed among GAD patients (Tromp et al., 2012). Ordinarily the anterior cingulate tells the amygdala to calm down in the face of non-threatening stimuli, but in those with GAD this might not occur and hence elevated anxiety persists.

Admittedly, the available data concerning the brain processes specifically associated with GAD are still limited, and a unitary hypothesis regarding the development of this disorder is still a way off. For the moment, the disorder is being treated, sometimes very successfully, based on knowledge of stressor effects on biological systems and on the basis of which drugs are effective in the treatment of other anxiety disorders. When people think of anti-anxiety medications, those that likely come to mind are benzodiazepines, such as diazepam (valium), alprazolam (Xanax,) or lorazepam (Atavan), each of which is fast acting and may be an effective short-term remedy. However, these drugs are not recommended for long-term use as they may be associated with the development of tolerance, physical dependence, and withdrawal symptoms. More often, GAD is treated with SSRIs as well as the serotonin-norepinephrine reuptake inhibitors (SNRIs), such as venlafaxine (Effexor) and duloxetine (Cymbalta). These agents may be more effective than benzodiazepines as they access comorbid depression that might be present, whereas benzodiazepines typically won't (Gorman, 2003). However, SSRIs may take several weeks to modify GAD, just as there is a delay in the alleviation of depression. As well as this, the remission may be incomplete, and SSRIs and SNRIs may have some unwanted side effects. Chapter 12 covers an array of antianxiety medications and so we won't repeat these in much detail here. Suffice it to say that there are several other drugs that fall out of the usual categories that have been used in the treatment of GAD. For instance, buspirone (BuSpar), a 5-HT$_{1A}$ receptor partial agonist (this means the drug only partially activates the receptor, and at some doses may actually work in an opposite fashion) that also acts as a dopamine D$_2$ and α-adrenergic antagonist, may be effective in treating moderate GAD. Pregabalin (Lyrica), which is used in the treatment of neuropathic pain, is also useful in the treatment of GAD, and the NE β-blocker propranolol (Inderal), which is primarily used for hypertension, also acts as a potent anti-anxiety treatment.

A meta-analysis conducted some years ago indicated that although pharmacological treatment and cognitive behavioral therapy (CBT) were both effective in attenuating GAD, the latter was more efficacious in several respects. Specifically, CBT was associated with having greater effects on the depression that accompanied GAD, and therapeutic gains were maintained after a discontinuation of treatment, whereas the efficacy of pharmacologic treatment diminished following medication discontinuation (Gould et al., 1997). Thus, CBT may have more long-term effects, whereas the pharmacological route appears to promote a more immediate fix. Having said this, it seems that CBT is effective to some extent in 50–60% of GAD patients (and about 30% don't gain any benefit), and other forms of behavioral therapy (e.g., relaxation or those treatments that focus on improving a tolerance for uncertainty) were about as effective.

PANIC DISORDER

Having seen the movie *Analyze This*, with Robert De Niro and Billy Crystal, it strikes me that panic disorder is now more mainstream than it had been previously. As indicated in

TABLE 9.3 Panic disorder symptomatology

According to the DSM-5 criteria, a panic attack is diagnosed when four of the following symptoms are present:

1. palpitations, heart pounding, or accelerated heart rate
2. sweating
3. trembling/shaking
4. sensations of shortness of breath/smothering
5. feeling choked
6. chest pain or discomfort
7. nausea or abdominal distress
8. feeling dizzy, unsteady, or light headed
9. depersonalization (person feels detached from themselves) or derealization (a feeling of unreality)
10. fear of losing control or going crazy
11. fear of dying
12. numbness or tingling sensations
13. hot flashes

Clearly, panic attacks can be pretty grim, and their anticipation can be understandably distressing.

Table 9.3, this is an anxiety disorder in which an individual may have brief attacks of intense terror and apprehension that peak within a few minutes and typically last for only a brief period (1–20 minutes), but can be longer lasting. It isn't certain what brings on the initial attack, and whether that experience leads to sensitized processes that might facilitate further attacks. It is thought that stressful life events, or appraisals of events that promote embellished perceptions of potentially stressful stimuli, contribute to the development of panic disorder. This assumption is based on reports that panic attacks are first seen following such events, as well as after physical illnesses or certain drug treatments (including illicit drugs that might have engendered negative effects).

Panic attacks are recurrent and in some people these attacks occur weekly or even daily. As a result, individuals often have ongoing concerns about having further attacks, particularly as the attack may cause them embarrassment and promote social stigma. Panic disorder is frequently comorbid with agoraphobia, and has also been reported to be comorbid with other illnesses such as bipolar disorder and alcoholism. Although panic disorder runs in families, individuals with no family history of the disorder may also suffer from panic attacks. Several genes have been identified that confer a susceptibility to panic disorder, but like many other genes that have been identified in relation to various disorders, translating this knowledge into treatment or predictive strategies has been slow in materializing (Smoller et al., 2008).

BEHAVIORAL AND COGNITIVE VIEWS OF PANIC DISORDER

In their review of panic disorder, Schmidt and Keough (2010) indicated that cognitively-based models have been fundamental in our conceptualization of this illness. They describe three perspectives that have been particularly influential in this regard. These models comprise an emotion-based model, a cognitive perspective, and an expectancy model. The emotion-based model has it that some individuals may be disposed to overreact to stressors. This heightened reactivity could then be related to genetic factors or adverse life events that had been encountered, including those that occurred early in life or during adolescence, and that panic will be most prominent if individuals also had the sense that events and emotions were uncontrollable and unpredictable. It was further suggested that through classical conditioning, anxiety-related arousal and panic may be associated with internal sensations (i.e., interoceptive cues), so that when these internal cues appear again, possibly as a response to reminder stimuli, a panic attack may be instigated. The second (cognitive) position also includes the perspective that feedback from the body is fundamental in the instigation of panic attacks. According to this view, certain sensations may be 'catastrophically' misinterpreted as being especially threatening (e.g., an elevated heart rate or feelings of indigestion may be misinterpreted as a heart attack), leading to high levels of arousal, which then promote further bodily changes and still greater perceived threat. This recurrent cycle ultimately results in a panic attack. Finally, according to the third model, anxiety is derived from the fear of symptoms re-emerging, and indeed the fear of the consequences of anxiety is greater in panic disorder patients than in most other anxiety disorders (Olatunji & Wolitzky-Taylor, 2009).

BIOLOGICAL FACTORS RELATED TO PANIC DISORDER

Several biological processes have been implicated in subserving panic disorder. GABA is an inhibitory transmitter that acts as a brake for neuronal activity, and it is thought that anxiety emerges when the inhibitory signaling associated with GABA activity is diminished. In fact, relative to controls, patients with panic disorder exhibited lower GABA concentrations in the anterior cingulate cortex and basal ganglia (Ham et al., 2007). Moreover, cortical GABA concentrations were diminished in patients with a family history of mood and anxiety disorders, raising the possibility that genetic factors related to GABA functioning might be at play in determining a vulnerability to panic disorder.

In addition to GABA, 5-HT might contribute to panic disorder. It has been known for some time that anxiety can be induced by drugs that stimulate certain 5-HT receptors ($5\text{-HT}_{2C}/5\text{-HT}_3$) or reduce 5-HT_{1A} receptor availability (Nash et al., 2008), whereas the opposite effect is elicited by treatments that antagonize the $5\text{-HT}_{2C}/5\text{-HT}_3$ receptors. The finding that SSRIs can be used to treat panic disorder, at least to some degree, is consistent with 5-HT involvement in panic disorder. Yet there have also been reports that SSRIs may actually elicit panic disorder symptoms, especially during the early stages of treatment. Thus, although 5-HT regulation might contribute to panic disorder, there's much more behind this illness. Indeed, NE might also be associated with panic disorder, as the drugs that block NE receptors (particularly α2 receptors) promote anxiety responses. There has also been interest in the possibility that panic disorder might be related to particular neuropeptide factors, such as CRH, AVP and one that we didn't discuss earlier, cholecystokinin (CCK). Although CCK is more often considered as one of several gut peptides involved in digestion, reports that a low dose of CCK could induce a panic attack in patients with panic disorder is consistent with a role for this peptide in this particular anxiety disorder.

One of the difficulties associated with determining the mechanisms underlying panic disorder is the wide range of brain regions that could potentially be involved in this illness.

In response to a challenge that comprised emotionally salient cues (anxiety-provoking visual stimuli or threatening words), patients exhibited particularly elevated neuronal activity in brain regions involved in appraisal and executive processes, such as the anterior cingulate cortex, posterior cingulate cortex, orbital frontal cortex and hippocampus. As expected, following psychotherapy that diminished panic disorder symptoms, the activation patterns in some brain regions normalized (Beutel et al., 2010). However, in remitted patients (patients who purportedly had been successfully treated) tested in an emotional conflict paradigm (in which they were presented with emotionally congruent and incongruent faces and words), elevated neuronal activity was still evident in the anterior cingulate cortex, dorsal medial prefrontal cortex, and amygdala (Chechko et al., 2009). Evidently, among remitted panic disorder patients, the brain responses to emotional stimuli were still exaggerated, raising the possibility that these neuronal changes were indicative of relapse potential upon exposure to particular types of events.

TREATMENT OF PANIC DISORDER

Both pharmacological and behavioral methods have been used to treat panic disorder, with moderate success being achieved in both cases. Positive effects were obtained through psychodynamic therapy, a psychoanalytic-like procedure that attempts to get at unconscious content and thus diminish tension. CBT has been found to be an effective treatment strategy in about 60% of panic disorder patients, and was especially effective when treatments focused on the perceived likelihood of panic, the perceived consequences of that panic, and panic-coping efficacy (Mitte, 2005). Furthermore, CBT and related treatment strategies have also been effective in attenuating some of the comorbid features of panic disorder, but in some cases (e.g., where PTSD was a comorbid condition) treating the panic did not affect the accompanying PTSD (Teng et al., 2008). Antidepressant drugs can also reduce panic disorder in some patients, but the doses required were well beyond those needed to treat depression, suggesting the involvement of different processes in these disorders. Despite the success of SSRIs (and SNRIs), it was suggested that CBT should still be considered the treatment of choice. One would think that a combination of CBT and drug treatment would produce still better results, but this was not the case (Schmidt & Keough, 2010). Likewise, there was little value in combining psychotherapy and benzodiazepine treatment.

PHOBIAS

A phobia refers to an intense and persistent fear of certain situations, activities, things, or people, and is typically characterized by an unreasonable avoidance of this stimulus. When the fear, which is typically seen as uncontrollable, comes to interfere with daily life, a diagnosis corresponding to this type of anxiety disorder can be applied. More people seem to know about phobias because they are relatively common, and appear more often in the media, as well as in films. Estimates of the prevalence of phobias range from 8 to 18%, and are typically more common in women than in men.

For many phobic individuals the feared object or condition is not all that frequently encountered (e.g., a fear of tarantulas if you live in Canada), and thus can be readily avoided. However, other phobias might comprise daily confrontations that need to be dealt with if a reasonable quality of life is to be maintained. For instance, people with social phobias, and especially those whose phobia becomes so strong they never leave the house, have a tremendous burden to deal with. Those with fears of public speaking, which is fairly common, know that this can become incapacitating, especially when their job demands it, and being phobic about planes certainly cuts down on the good times, and might interfere with certain business ventures.

PHOBIA SUBTYPES

Phobias come in several varieties, all of which are considered to reflect anxiety-related disturbances. Phobias that are specific to particular objects or situations, such as a fear of snakes, heights, enclosed spaces and so forth, are common. Most individuals with these phobias know that their fears are irrational, but this doesn't diminish the anxiety elicited by the feared object or situation. Another form of phobia entails those that involve a social component. Many of us have fears that are related to social situations, but once more we don't usually consider it a phobia unless it affects our daily functioning. Social phobias are related to a fear of public scrutiny (walking into a room and worrying that everyone is watching you, or making a public statement that results in attention being drawn to you). A social phobia may be broad (generalized social phobia) or specific to particular situations. Another fear that comprises the fear of leaving home or places where one feels safe is referred to as agoraphobia. Agoraphobia can also be tied to social phobia that is manifested when the comfort of a safe place is replaced by wide-open situations where we can be embarrassed or at least open to public appraisal and scrutiny.

SOCIAL ANXIETY

Social anxiety, which has been viewed as a social phobia, is the most common of the anxiety disorders. It is characterized by emotional discomfort, fear, apprehension, or worry about social situations, interactions with others, and about being evaluated or scrutinized by other people. The fact is that many of us share some of these characteristics, and social evaluative threats (e.g., in relation to public speaking or other public performances) are especially stressful and especially common. Social anxiety frequently begins during childhood, typically waning with age, but it often persists into adolescence and adulthood (Albano & Detweiler, 2001). In children, the disorder can prove fairly incapacitating, to the extent that they end up being fearful of playing with others or speaking to teachers. How the disorder comes about is uncertain, but it is not unlikely that negative experiences in social situations (e.g., public speaking in a classroom) might have contributed to the development of this form of anxiety disorder. Once the anxiety is present, individuals may experience a confirmation bias in which they look for negative reactions from others (e.g., during public speaking the individual may focus on those in the audience who appear not to be receptive, or those who appear critical of the oral presentation). There is also reason to believe that social anxiety disorder has biological underpinnings, as there is a modest genetic component. It might be the case that individuals inherit anxiety-related characteristics, but the disorder evolves given negative social experiences.

Exaggerated neuronal activity in the limbic (amygdala) regions might be associated with elevated attention to, and processing of, the social threats that accompany social anxiety (Miskovic & Schmidt, 2012). In view of the earlier discussion concerning the role of oxytocin in relation to social behaviors and social stressors, it's a fairly reasonable bet that disturbed levels of this hormone or its receptor might contribute to the disorder. Indeed, manipulations of oxytocin and arginine vasopressin are being advanced as possible novel targets for social anxiety disorder (Meyer-Lindenberg et al., 2011).

TREATMENT OF PHOBIAS

It is thought that phobias develop through simple conditioning processes. Specifically, an event or stimulus occurs in conjunction with a negative feeling or emotion or other aversive stimulus. This pairing results in a classically conditioned anxiety response, so that future presentations of the conditioned stimulus will elicit the anxiety/fear response. Thus, most therapies for phobia have focused on behavioral/emotional methods to diminish (extinguish) this conditioned response. In this regard, imagery and virtual reality treatments have been used in an effort to *desensitize* the individual, typically in small steps. Likewise, CBT has been used to help individuals come to understand their negative thought patterns, and then to modify them. Gradual desensitization treatment (reducing the distress in small steps in which the feared situation or object becomes closer and closer or progressively more real) and CBT have a high success rate, provided that the patient is willing to endure the discomfort that comes with being exposed to the feared object or situation. As in the case of other phobias, the treatment of social anxiety is not especially difficult, but it does vary with individual cases. Generally speaking, CBT is the most common treatment for the disorder, and in some cases may be given in conjunction with anti-anxiety agents or SSRIs, which have also been found useful in treating social anxiety.

FEAR OF FLYING

For years I had a fear of flying in an airplane. I don't anymore, but I think this phobia, in part, stemmed from not having control over the situation. I'm certain I would have been more comfortable if I had been actually flying the plane, even if it distressed other passengers. Actually, when I had this phobia it wasn't the plane ride that got to me, it was the days preceding the flight that were worst. In fact, once I was on the plane, and had resigned myself to certain death, an odd calmness fell over me. Of course, this didn't stop me from making deals with God (e.g., 'If I make it back alive I'm giving 10% of everything I have to charity . . . Yes, yes, yes, I know I said that before and then reneged, but this time I really, really, really mean it').

Often, when friends tried to get me to abandon the phobia (as if a person can just do so at will) they would tell me that my fear was 'irrational' and that more people died in car accidents within two miles of home, as if I would then just change my mind about the phobia (incidentally, if it's so irrational, then why did so many people stop flying after 9/11?). The second frequent comment I would hear is 'Oh, it's all in your head'. Well that was helpful, as I had thought it was in my bladder given the sensation that flying created.

Phobias aren't all that difficult to get rid of through procedures such as CBT. However, any plane phobic will tell you that desensitization and cognitive therapy only work so well, and it still takes some commitment on the part of the individual with the phobia.

OBSESSIVE-COMPULSIVE DISORDER (OCD)

Virtually everybody who's a fan of scary movies, and many who aren't, knows something about obsessive-compulsive disorder (OCD). Remember the scene in *Sleeping with the Enemy* when the woman (Julia Roberts) who runs away from her abusive husband (Patrick Bergin) opens her kitchen cabinet and sees the soup cans lined up neatly in rows facing forwards? Or do you remember your high school Lit class where you were introduced to Lady Macbeth compulsively washing her hands? However, if you had been asked to classify these OCD-like behaviors, you likely wouldn't have seen them as being an anxiety disorder.

Obsessive-compulsive disorder is considered an anxiety disorder that primarily involves repetitive obsessions (distressing, persistent, and intrusive thoughts or images) coupled with compulsions (that entail urges to perform specific acts or rituals). These components can be independent of one another, as some individuals may present with obsessions, but not the compulsive behaviors. Although OCD sounds fairly unusual, its lifetime prevalence is 2%. However, not everyone who exhibits obsessive or compulsive features should be considered to be suffering from the disorder. Some people may be just a little more obsessive or quirky (i.e., it's a personality style), but wouldn't be classified as being ill.

Obsessions refer to recurrent and persistent thoughts that are difficult to shake. Initially, obsessive thoughts present weakly or are largely unformed, creating discomfort or anxiety until the obsession has been dealt with. The relief may be transient, and when obsessive thoughts again emerge, the behaviors that diminish anxiety will again be emitted and reinforced by the reduction of anxiety. As these thoughts become more formed, individuals might become preoccupied with particular notions, such as someone close to them becoming infected by a disease or dying, or that certain objects have important characteristics that are 'meaningful'. Still other obsessive thought can take the form of conspiracies, or sexual characteristics, and in a severe form the obsessions may be delusional.

IS IT REALLY ALL THAT ODD?

At first blush obsessive-compulsive behaviors do seem rather strange. Why would anyone engage in these behaviors? Is there anything even remotely rewarding about them that might promote their frequent repetition? For that matter, does it become stranger still when the behavior involves self-injurious acts such as hair pulling (trichotillosis) or the repeated cutting of body parts? Many of us will have had the experience of being bugged by leaving something undone, and when finally we do whatever it is to get rid of what had been gnawing at us, there's a sense of relief. Can you remember as a kid playing a game in which you touched every sign on the way to school (or had to step on every sidewalk crack)? If you missed one you had to go back and 'get it', since not doing so ate away at you. The relief was tangible when it was done, even though you knew it was dopey. Perhaps the person with OCD is taking this to an extreme and it's rewarding to 'scratch that itch'. Alternatively, certain behaviors, particularly those that involve self-injury, cause the release of certain brain chemicals (e.g. dopamine, endorphins) that provide a high, thereby reinforcing the behavior. This would be all the more dramatic if, after the act is done, the initial tension that was accompanied by an elevated heart rate turned to bradycardia that might signal relief.

Self-injurious behaviors aren't all that uncommon. It's frequently seen in animals under some conditions. Dogs, for example, will repeatedly lick at themselves to the extent that they might create open wounds or infection (hotspots). Likewise, hair pulling, self-biting, or feather pulling are observed across many species. Often, these behaviors occur in animals that are kept in penned conditions, including caged zoo animals (they might also exhibit OCD-like behaviors in the form of repeated pacing back and forth). It might be that the isolation and loneliness triggered these behaviors if for no other reason than to create a degree of stimulation that was followed by a relief from boredom.

The behaviors that comprise OCD vary appreciably across individuals, and may include behaviors such as hoarding, aggressive or sexual impulses, repeated checking (e.g., whether the door is locked, the stove is off), hair pulling, or hand washing. Added to this, some individuals will display ritualistic behaviors (locking doors and checking and rechecking in a specific sequence; making sure that they take a certain number of steps between their front door and the sidewalk, and restarting the process when the number is wrong; touching certain objects when entering a room or when leaving). Such behaviors would obviously appear abnormal to others, and social alienation may then develop, aggravating an already bad situation. Moreover, the OCD-affected person will realize that their behaviors are unusual, and this too creates distress and anxiety. Perhaps for this reason, the compulsive component of OCD might not be manifested as overt compulsions, but instead individuals may go through mental compulsive rituals.

PIGEONS AND BASEBALL PLAYERS

You might recall B.F. Skinner's description of superstitious behaviors in pigeons responding to a particular schedule of reinforcement. Having been adventitiously reinforced shortly after adopting a particular posture or behavior, they continued to adopt these behaviors or postures. Next time you watch a baseball game, see whether some of the batters go through their own rituals (touch one shoulder, then the other, scrape their left foot on the ground, then the right, then the left, and the right once more, followed by three movements of the bat – no wonder the game takes so long), and when interrupted how they go through the ritual again. I'm not suggesting that baseball players are necessarily affected by OCD, but they sure remind me of pigeons.

BIOLOGICAL FACTORS RELATED TO OCD

The view was offered that OCD is produced by a complicated loop comprising the frontal cortical brain regions involved in executive functioning and decision making (i.e., the anterior cingulate cortex, ventromedial, dorsolateral, and lateral-orbital cortex) that link to those associated with reward processes (the nucleus accumbens, caudate). Neurons in these regions, in turn, activate the thalamus and the basal ganglia, which are connected to several brain regions, including the cortex. This loop has been implicated in routine behaviors and habits, as well as in decision making regarding the selection of which of several behaviors to emit when there are several options (Milad & Rauch, 2012). In recent years there have been reformulations of this view of OCD. Fundamental to this perspective has been that the lateral and medial orbitofrontal cortex (lOFC and mOFC) are responsible for processing information with a negative or a positive valence, respectively. The lOFC is viewed as essential for both responding to punishment and escaping from danger, and might contribute to the repetitive or ritualized behaviors characteristic of OCD. The importance of the mOFC comes from reports that this region is essential for the extinction of fear memories (Milad et al., 2007). Ordinarily, when a fear-producing situation is encountered repeatedly and found to be safe, the fear response may extinguish, an outcome that involves the inhibition of neuronal activity within the ventromedial PFC. It was suggested that OCD may stem from a failure of the mOFC to properly inhibit the ventromedial PFC in response to danger cues, thus resulting in the OCD-related fears being sustained. As a result, although the excessive activation of the ventromedial PFC and the OFC might contribute to OCD, the real culprit might be the mOFC which isn't doing its job of controlling (inhibiting) functioning in these other cortical regions.

As crucial as the lOFC and mOFC are for OCD, the story doesn't end there, as it seems that the anterior cingulate cortex may be involved in OCD. This brain region has been mentioned several times in the context of other disorders (such as depression), and it seems that some of its functions, namely identifying cognitive conflict, error monitoring, and decision making, also play into OCD. Ordinarily, when we are placed in a situation where dual and inconsistent messages are received, or when we must interpret messages where one signal tells us to 'go' and another tells us to 'stop', and especially when interference comes from external sources, the anterior cingulate cortex appears to be activated as it is necessary for decision making. However, hyper-activation of the anterior cingulate cortex was evident when individuals presenting with OCD were placed in decision-making situations (Page et al., 2009). Thus, it was suggested that this brain region might be having difficulty in making appropriate appraisals and decisions, so that we end up with improper feedback that might lead to repeated behavioral responses.

To some extent this formulation is reminiscent of a proposition advanced by Woody and Szechtman (2011) in which the existence of a 'security motivation system' was proposed to explain the appearance of OCD. Essentially, they suggested that we ordinarily have a 'feeling of knowing' (they use the term 'yedasentience', a combination of Hebrew and Latin) that is essential for us to end a task and move on to other activities. If this signal or its reception is not operating properly, then the OCD symptoms will persist. Have you ever had the worry after leaving home of 'Did I turn off the iron (or stove)?' or 'Did I shut the garage?'. This feeling might haunt you all day (some of us more than others), unless you go back and check. I suspect that the person with OCD might be affected in this way all or much of the time.

FINDING INFORMATION IN ODD PLACES

Parkinson's disease, which occurs owing to degeneration of DA neurons within the substantia nigra (although other factors are also involved), is typically treated with drugs that increase DA functioning. However, these drugs don't just cause DA to increase in the substantia nigra, but also affect DA in brain regions associated with reward processes. It has been reported that other disorders that fall in the impulsive-compulsive spectrum sometimes emerge following the treatment with DA acting agents. These secondary effects include compulsive shopping, binge eating, hypersexuality, compulsive hobbying, compulsive computer use, and gambling. These characteristics are most notable in patients with an early onset of the disorder, those with a history of use of recreational drugs, and novelty-seeking personality characteristics. These findings are obviously in line with suggestions that DA plays a pivotal role in reward processes, and the behaviors observed could simply be a reflection of the elevated DA in some brain regions making certain behaviors seem to be more rewarding (e.g., gambling). These findings might also suggest a role for DA in compulsive behaviors or those with impulse control disturbances.

TREATMENT OF OCD

It is difficult to determine whether there is any single best treatment of OCD as the symptoms can vary appreciably from one individual to the next, and it is possible that the mechanisms involved may also vary with features of the illness (e.g., does repeated checking involve processes akin to those involved in hoarding?). Some success has been achieved with CBT and with 'exposure and response prevention' (ERP) in which patients learn, in gradual steps, to tolerate the anxiety that occurs when they do not engage in the compulsive behavior. Yet another approach has been to alter the associations that are normally made in response to obsessive thoughts. For instance, an individual who is obsessed with not touching anything 'contaminated by germs' might be 'taught' to appraise external objects less negatively by having them pair the thought of these objects with neutral thoughts or emotions.

High doses of SSRIs have also been used to treat OCD, although it may take a relatively lengthy period for positive effects to appear. It seems that targeting glutamate, a neurotransmitter known to be involved in learning and memory, might also provide positive outcomes (Marazziti et al., 2010). As well here, studies in animals have pointed to the DA mechanism, probably involving the nucleus accumbens, in maintaining repeated checking (Dvorkin et al., 2010). Yet given the breadth of symptoms associated with OCD, the possibility was expressed that each symptom dimension might involve different mechanisms and diverse etiological processes, and that (once again) the most effective treatment strategies will necessarily be tailored for individual patients.

POSTTRAUMATIC STRESS DISORDER (PTSD)

Posttraumatic stress disorder (PTSD) has received growing levels of attention, particularly as it affects a fairly substantial portion of individuals who encounter traumatic experiences, and because we hear about it more often in relation to soldiers returning from combat missions. Most of us will encounter traumatic events at one time or another, and the incidence of PTSD is as high as 10% in the USA. The *DSM-IV* had described PTSD as occurring in response to an intense stressor that involves actual or threatened death, injury, or learning about an unexpected or violent death, and that the individual's response must comprise intense fear, helplessness, or horror. In recent years, the criteria regarding fear, helplessness and horror have been disputed, as symptoms of PTSD may emerge even in the absence of these extreme emotional responses. Thus, the *DSM-5* criteria for PTSD were recalibrated to take into consideration the factors that lead to PTSD, including nontraumatic stressors, the time-line for the appearance of PTSD, and expansion of the symptoms that comprise the disorder (see Table 9.4). In addition, within the *DSM-5* PTSD is no longer present in the section dealing with anxiety, but was instead placed in a category of 'Trauma and stressor-related disorders'. However, it's been left in this chapter on anxiety because it shares many characteristics with other disorders of this class, although as we'll see, it is also quite different from other anxiety-related disorders.

PTSD is usually considered in the context of individuals who experienced any of numerous natural disasters (earthquake, hurricane, tsunami), as well as war experiences, car accidents, rape, being held hostage, medical complications, being told about a severe medical condition, bullying and common assault, witnessing traumatic events (e.g., abuse). In addition, PTSD symptoms can be instilled by chronic stressors, such as chronic racial discrimination (Matheson & Anisman, 2012), and symptoms of PTSD even developed when the stressor was a distal one (i.e., when individuals were not directly confronted with the trauma), as occurred among US residents following the 9/11 terrorist attacks (Silver et al., 2002).

A diagnosis of PTSD is made when symptoms persist for six months or more. However, when the *DSM-IV* was first released a syndrome referred to as Acute Stress Disorder (ASD)

TABLE 9.4 Posttraumatic stress disorder (PTSD) symptomatology

The *DSM-5* diagnostic symptoms associated with PTSD include several changes from the *DSM-IV*. The section below is from www.dsm5.org/ProposedRevisions/Pages/proposedrevision.aspx?rid=165#.

A. Exposure to actual or threatened death, serious injury, or sexual violation, or witnessing others experience these traumatic event. Trauma experiences can also comprise learning of trauma experienced by a close friend/relative, or repeated exposure to details (consequences) regarding the traumatic event (e.g., first responders collecting human remains; police officers repeatedly exposed to details of child abuse), but not through exposure that occurs through electronic media, television, movies, or pictures.

B. Presence of one or more of the following intrusion symptoms:

1. intrusive distressing memories of the traumatic event(s) of an involuntary nature that occur spontaneously or in response to specific cues
2. recurrent dreams in which the content or affect is related to the traumatic event(s)
3. dissociative reactions in which individuals feel as if the traumatic event(s) are recurring (flashbacks): in its extreme form individuals may experience loss of awareness of their current surroundings
4. reminders of the trauma elicit intense or prolonged psychological distress or physiological reactions

C. Persistent avoidance of stimuli associated with the trauma. These behaviors comprise:

1. avoidance of distressing thoughts, or feelings associated with the traumatic event(s)
2. avoidance of reminders of the events (people, places, conversations, activities, objects) that promote distress

D. Disturbed cognitions and mood manifested by two or more of the following:

1. disturbed recall of an important aspect of the event(s) for reasons other than head injury or drug intake
2. exaggerated, persistent negative perspectives or expectations about oneself, others, or the world
3. persistent and distorted self- or other-blame regarding the cause or consequences of the traumatic event(s)
4. a strong, persistent negative emotional state (e.g., fear, horror, anger, guilt, or shame)
5. anhedonia
6. feelings of detachment or estrangement from others
7. persistent failure to experience positive emotions (e.g., psychic numbing)

E. Marked arousal and reactivity associated with the traumatic event(s) that began or became worse following the traumatic event. Arousal and reactivity are reflected by two or more of the following:

1. irritability or aggressiveness
2. reckless or self-destructive behavior
3. hypervigilance
4. hyperarousal or an exaggerated startle response
5. concentration difficulties
6. sleep disturbance (e.g., difficulty falling or staying asleep or restless sleep)

was introduced, which has been maintained in the *DSM-5*, but has been moved to the 'Trauma and stressor-related disorders' category. It is not unusual for symptoms such as intense emotional reactions to appear soon after a catastrophic stressor, but they typically diminish with time. If symptoms are present three days after the trauma, then it may be categorized as ASD, provided that a series of other symptoms are present as well. Although many of the symptoms of ASD and PTSD are very similar, ASD is also accompanied by 'dissociative' symptoms. Of five potential dissociative features, a diagnosis of ASD requires the presence of three of the following: (a) a sense of numbing, absence of emotional responses or detachment, (b) reduced awareness of surroundings, or feeling as if in a daze,

(c) derealization, wherein individuals experience altered perception or experience of the external world so that it seems unreal, (d) depersonalization, in which individuals have the feeling of watching themself act, but lack control over the situation – the world is dreamlike, less real, or lacking in significance, and (e) dissociative amnesia characterized by memory gaps in which individuals are unable to recall information concerning events of a traumatic or stressful nature.

As in the case of PTSD, those with ASD may repeatedly re-experience the event through either recurrent images, thoughts, dreams, illusions, flashbacks, as well as the feeling that they're reliving the traumatic experience, or distress that occurs in response to trauma reminders. They may also display avoidance of stimuli that arouse recollections of the trauma, and symptoms of anxiety and/or arousal are present, characterized by poor sleep, irritability, impaired concentration, hypervigilance, motor restlessness, and hyper-reactivity. At the time that ASD was introduced as an independent disorder, it was thought that the dissociative symptoms might predict whether or not PTSD would subsequently be present. However, it turned out that many individuals with ASD don't continue with PTSD symptoms, and conversely, it is not unusual for those without ASD to later develop PTSD (Bryant et al., 2011).

VULNERABILITY AND RESILIENCE

Although most of us will encounter a traumatic experience at some time, only a relatively small number will develop PTSD. This raises the question concerning which factors make individuals vulnerable to the effects of traumatic experiences, and which variables contribute to resilience. To a considerable extent, the vulnerability factors outlined earlier concerning other stressor-related pathologies are also pertinent to the development of PTSD. In this regard, factors related to appraisals of the trauma (i.e., perceived level of threat) and post-trauma elements (i.e., the response to the trauma) predicted the emergence of PTSD. In addition, some pretrauma features (psychiatric history, being abused, or experiencing trauma as a child, as well as being separated, divorced, or widowed) and some peritrauma variables (i.e., events that occur soon after the traumatic event) contributed to the emergence of PTSD, as did a constellation of psychosocial factors, including the coping strategies used and perceived social support (King et al., 1998). It also appeared that those people who score highly on a neuroticism scale (i.e., constant worriers who exhibit chronic anxiety and tend to over-react to daily negative experiences that most people take in their stride) were particularly likely to develop PTSD in response to trauma.

An important predictor of PTSD is that of having previously experienced multiple traumas (Suliman et al., 2009). It seems that a traumatic event may prime (sensitize) biological systems so that responses to later traumatic experiences are exaggerated. This view, however, is not universally accepted, as PTSD might be more likely to develop among individuals who encountered a previous trauma or multiple traumatic events *provided* that these experiences resulted in PTSD at that time (Breslau & Peterson, 2010). In effect, the initial trauma might be disclosing which individuals are most likely to develop PTSD, or it might be that the initial trauma increases the vulnerability to later PTSD only if it affected those circuits responsible for the emergence of PTSD. It also appears that mental health status prior to a trauma experience may be related to whether or not PTSD will emerge. By example, among soldiers returning from Afghanistan, those with prior trauma experiences or modest mental health problems prior to deployment were at elevated risk for PTSD stemming from war experiences. And further to this same point, trauma experiences, including abuse or neglect in childhood, have long-lasting effects on the ability to cope with stressors in adulthood, and might thus favor the development of PTSD. Furthermore, those individuals who experienced childhood trauma, interpersonal violence, or a secondary anxiety or affective disorder were least likely (or took longer) to remit from PTSD (Chapman et al., 2011).

The way in which individuals appraise and cope with stressors may also be related to the development of PTSD features. An avoidant strategy that favors compartmentalization of the stressor actions may be beneficial, given that the memory of an event and the cues that stimulate these memories are particularly effective in aggravating the symptoms. Furthermore, greater use of emotional avoidance and lower levels of emotional expression were accompanied by increased PTSD symptom severity. As a result, while emotional expression is often viewed as a poor coping method, encouraging this strategy might have positive effects in relation to PTSD (Hassija et al., 2011), and as well as this, the extent to which individuals separate emotional responses from the cognitive representation of the event (cognitive-emotional distinctiveness) may be related to the appearance of PTSD symptoms. In addition to these methods of coping influencing PTSD development, the negative effects of trauma events were most pronounced among individuals with low social support, and it was further observed that social support was found to be associated with a reduction in maladaptive cognitive coping methods (i.e., worry, self-punishment) and the use of avoidant coping (e.g., social and non-social avoidance coping) strategies, which might otherwise favor PTSD symptoms (Bennett et al., 2009). It was thus suggested that interventions that target maladaptive coping strategies (worry, self-punishment, and social avoidance), and those that encourage social support and understanding from others, might be effective in diminishing PTSD symptoms.

THINKING OF PTSD IN THE CONTEXT OF OTHER ILLNESSES

One of the predictors of PTSD is whether individuals had experienced a psychological disorder prior to the most recent traumatic experience. In line with these findings, it was reported that women with a history of a mood disorder were more likely to exhibit PTSD in response to a later trauma than were women without a history of mental health problems. This finding might reflect the possibility that certain people are particularly vulnerable to a range of mental health disturbances. Alternatively, it might be that mental health problems, like an earlier trauma, might result in the sensitization of biological systems, so that these individuals would be more vulnerable to a subsequent stressor-promoted pathology.

Regardless of the source of these outcomes, given that severe illnesses, such as cancer, may lead to PTSD, it might be useful for oncologists to determine an individual's previous psychiatric history before beginning therapy. Of course, the oncologist's primary duty is to treat the cancer, but if it's the case that stressful events influence disease progression, then it is possible that the treatment might be more successful if precautions were taken to deal with the mental health issues related to the trauma rather than just focusing on the cancer. In fact, in a study of women who had been surgically treated for breast cancer, in which some received psychological intervention to reduce distress, improve their moods, alter health behaviors, and adhere to cancer treatment and care, the probability of recurrence and death within an eleven-year window was appreciably reduced, relative to women who had not received the psychological intervention (Andersen et al., 2008).

NEUROANATOMICAL UNDERPINNINGS OF PTSD

As stressors give rise to multiple biological changes, any of these might potentially contribute to the evolution and maintenance of PTSD. Indeed, the primary symptoms of PTSD are fairly diverse and it is not only possible, but also very likely, that many of these behaviors involve one or more different neuronal mechanisms. In addition, PTSD is often comorbid with other pathological conditions that might be secondary to immune, HPA, or autonomic disturbances related to PTSD, making it evermore difficult to identify which processes underlie the disorder and which are related to the comorbid conditions.

PTSD AS A DISTURBANCE OF MEMORY PROCESSES

The finding that hippocampal atrophy was associated with PTSD gave rise to the view that it was the traumatic event that led to this outcome; however, it was subsequently demonstrated that a reduced hippocampal size was present in the co-twin of individuals suffering PTSD following a war experience, even though they had neither been traumatized nor suffered PTSD (Pitman et al., 2006). Thus, having a relatively small hippocampus might increase the vulnerability to PTSD rather than be a consequence of the disorder. This may well be, but reduced hippocampal volume was also associated with more chronic PTSD relative to that evident among individuals who had shown symptom remission, thereby implicating hippocampal volume in sustaining PTSD symptoms (Apfel et al., 2011).

The hippocampus is intimately related to short-term memory processes, and may be fundamental when memory is retrieved from storage. Neurons in this brain region are exceptionally plastic (interconnections are readily influenced by environmental or experiential factors), making it a potential contributor to the adverse effects of trauma. If the hippocampal disturbances are, in fact, related to PTSD, then it would be appropriate to consider whether memory processes are involved in this disorder. After all, having been traumatized by a particular event it would be perfectly understandable to react strongly to stimuli subsequently experienced that were relevant to the trauma. For example, a woman who is assaulted in a dark parking lot might subsequently be afraid of dark parking lots, which certainly might be a highly adaptive response. But what if this response generalizes to all dark places, all parking lots (even in daylight), or flat open spaces, or places where there are lots of cars, such as shopping center lots? Obviously, this over-generalization might be maladaptive, and may disturb the individual's quality of life. This also raises an odd sort of paradox concerning memory related to traumatic events. When a memory is focused and accurate, strong responses should be evident to the primary aversive stimulus, and moderate generalization should be expected. If, in contrast, the memory of an event is vague, then individuals might not respond just to the primary aversive stimulus, but might also respond to events that were modestly reminiscent of the original stressor. PTSD-affected individuals seem to react very strongly to cues highly reminiscent of the original trauma, but also react to relatively vague cues as if the memory had not been well entrenched. Given the involvement of the hippocampus in memory processes, some sort of disturbance in memory functioning might contribute to these dual responses in those with PTSD.

When an animal or human is exposed to cues associated with a previous trauma, a recollection of that event, together with biological responses, will be elicited. It also appears, however, that memory processes may be activated even when cues are stressful but also entirely distinct from the previously encountered experience (Jezek et al., 2010). Essentially, stressful stimuli might be capable of energizing the memory processes related to a previous event not because they are reminders of that event, but because they engage the same neural circuits that are activated by stressors. From this perspective, PTSD might not be related to disturbed memory as we might ordinarily think of it, but to generalized biological responses to stressors, without necessarily assuming impairments regarding the memory of the initial trauma. Alternatively, PTSD may be a disorder of forgetting in that the normal extinction of fear responses does not occur readily.

PTSD IN RELATION TO NONASSOCIATIVE PROCESSES

Yet another perspective of PTSD is that the disorder might reflect a failure of our recovery system(s). Ordinarily, most individuals ought to react strongly to traumatic events, but with the passage of time or appropriate coping responses being used, this 'damage' should heal. However, in some individuals, a failure of recovery in the biological systems may result in the PTSD syndrome emerging. As much as the data might point to memory processes being tied to PTSD, it might also be considered that these 'apparent' memory changes could involve other types of processes that were not of an associative nature, but instead involved the brain regions that govern attention or decision making. Beyond the involvement of the hippocampus, the prefrontal cortex might also be a key player in PTSD. In this regard, subtle impairments of response inhibition, and regulation of the attention mechanisms involving this brain region, may act as risk factors for PTSD (Aupperle et al., 2011). In fact, the anterior cingulate cortex, like the hippocampus, is reduced in size among patients with PTSD (Woodward et al., 2006). Based on a twin study it was suggested that this was not a genetically endowed reduction of the anterior cingulate cortex, but was dependent on PTSD being present (Kasai et al., 2008). As described earlier, the PFC, and specifically the anterior cingulate cortex, is exceptionally reactive to stressors and is important in our appraisal of events and decision making. Thus, the suggestion that this region might be involved in a syndrome such as PTSD is intuitively appealing.

Functional imaging studies indicated that among PTSD patients activation of the medial PFC response was diminished upon the presentation of aversive stimuli, such as pictures and the sound of combat, as well as in response to narratives of a negative nature that were unrelated to the trauma experience, for example, scripts containing traumatic imagery or images of fearful faces, as well as a test that elicited an emotional response unrelated to the trauma (e.g., Bremner et al., 2004; Gold et al., 2011). However, following successful treatment of the disorder, the PFC activation to stressful stimuli was found to normalize. In effect, among individuals with PTSD frontal cortical functioning was altered, not just for reminder stimuli, but for all sorts of stressor images, suggesting that aberrant behavioral responses could be expected among these individuals in response to any number of stressor events that might be encountered.

The PFC, amygdala, and hippocampus appear to be involved in the regulation of emotional memories. As such, beyond the PFC and hippocampus, aspects of the amygdala might contribute to PTSD. In fact, vague cues that were related to a traumatic experience influenced amygdala functioning (Liberzon & Sripada, 2008), suggesting that affected individuals were hyper-alert or hyper-responsive to even the mildest stimuli (at a nonconscious level) relevant to the trauma experience. In effect, the axis comprising the PFC, amygdala, and hippocampus, representing appraisals, emotional responses, and memory processes respectively, is critically involved in PTSD, and this circuitry might define re-experiencing, emotional reactivity, and fear (avoidance), which comprise the specific characteristics of the syndrome.

BIOCHEMICAL DETERMINANTS OF PTSD

Assessing the neurochemical and hormonal mechanisms underlying PTSD is fairly difficult as individuals might not only differ in the symptoms expressed, but also the neural circuitry activated may vary as a function of the specific stressor encountered. Moreover, given the limitations concerning what can be analyzed in human brain tissue, the conclusions that can be drawn regarding the biochemical underpinnings of PTSD are limited. A good deal of the evidence regarding the mechanisms subserving PTSD comes from studies assessing the effectiveness of drug treatments in attenuating the disorder, but even here it is uncertain whether the treatments are masking symptoms or actually getting at the mechanism(s) responsible for the illness. In the ensuing section we'll examine the contribution of several neurochemical and hormonal processes to PTSD. The intent isn't simply to provide a catalogue of these biological processes. However, we simply don't know to what extent each of these factors contributes to the specific symptoms that characterize PTSD, and so with the understanding that different factors might subserve the varied symptoms, we'll cover some of the main players implicated in this disorder.

In assessing the biological processes of PTSD, researchers have often relied on animal models of disorders, but as discussed earlier, it is frequently questionable whether complex human pathologies can be simulated in rodents, and this is true of PTSD. It is fairly simple to assess some behaviors that are characteristic of PTSD, such as hyperarousal (e.g., by evaluating startle responses to sudden noise) or the avoidance of particular stimuli. It is another matter to evaluate whether rodents are 're-experiencing' the trauma. In some studies attempts were made to strengthen traumatic memories by exposing rodents to cues reminiscent of an earlier trauma (Anisman, 2011). This had interesting experimental and clinical implications, but reminders of an event might be distinctly different from spontaneously 're-experiencing' that event.

A second difficulty comes from the fact that stressors, especially traumatic-like stressors, might not only elicit PTSD, but also produce general anxiety and depression, and the paradigms used to assess the behavioral changes that are thought to reflect PTSD are frequently the very same tests that are used to assess anxiety and depression. Because of this, it's uncertain whether the studies are actually tapping into PTSD, depression, anxiety-related features, or some combination of these syndromes. The predictive validity of the models is also compromised, as the treatments used to attenuate the behavioral disturbances in PTSD (e.g., SSRIs) are likewise effective for other anxiety disturbances and depression. Finally, most people who encounter traumatic events adapt to the situation through behavioral and biochemical processes. Typically, adaptation (the disappearance of symptoms) occurs within a matter of weeks; however, in about 15% of individuals adaptation does not occur, and PTSD symptoms are still present long after the trauma. In animal studies it is essential to understand what governs these individual differences, and why the pathology persists over time, and perhaps even increases in intensity in some instances.

NOREPINEPHRINE AND SEROTONIN

Despite the limitations, there have been several promising animal models of PTSD. One of these capitalizes on animals' natural responses to predators (e.g., rats' responses to a cat or even to the scent of cat urine) (Cohen et al., 2011). A second involves exposure to a single prolonged stressor comprising several different insults, followed by re-exposure to reminder stimuli every four days over the ensuing three weeks. When later tested in behavioral paradigms these mice showed an exaggerated startle response, mimicking the reactivity associated with PTSD (Olson et al., 2011). Of particular interest here was that these mice were also more resistant to extinction of the fear response, engaged in less social interaction, and were unusually aggressive toward an intruder. Moreover, these animals also exhibited increased neuronal activation, especially within brain regions such as the locus coeruleus, central amygdala, and the bed nucleus of the stria terminalis, all of which are regions in which stressors ordinarily increase the activity of NE neurons. Significantly, the effects of the traumatic stressor could be modified by a drug treatment that disrupted NE functioning, thus implicating NE in PTSD-like characteristics in mice.

Studies in humans likewise implicated NE functioning in PTSD. For instance, among individuals with PTSD, NE accumulation in urine was elevated, and increased NE receptor sensitivity was detected in the brain. Added to this, in a prospective analysis of high-risk individuals (e.g., police officers), the increased utilization of peripheral NE was predictive of those who later developed PTSD symptoms following a critical incident (Apfel et al., 2011b). Finally, treatments that attenuated NE functioning had an ameliorative effect on this disorder in some individuals.

In addition to NE, PTSD was also accompanied by variations of 5-HT functioning. In animal models the expression of the 5-HT$_{1A}$ receptor at the dorsal raphe nucleus was increased, which would have the effect of diminishing 5-HT release at the PFC and hippocampus (Luo et al., 2011). Further, as alluded to earlier, among those carrying the short allele of the 5-HTT gene, PTSD was more common if individuals had also encountered both a childhood and adult trauma (Xie et al., 2009). Essentially, these findings suggest that several risk factors might need to come together for PTSD to emerge, and for some individuals 5-HT functioning might be a critical element in this mix. Obviously, however, PTSD and depression have unique behavioral characteristics and it will be necessary to identify their unique neurochemical signatures.

CRH AND CORTICOIDS

CRH might play a role in PTSD just as it does in other anxiety-related illnesses. For instance, when a CRH$_1$ receptor antagonist was administered to rodents either before a traumatic experience comprising exposure to a predator or 30 minutes later, during the period when memory was being consolidated, the subsequent anxiety induced by the stressor (measured days later) was markedly diminished. As such, CRH$_1$ receptors might be involved in either the initiation or consolidation of traumatic memories that feed into PTSD. There is also good reason to believe that corticosterone (cortisol) plays an essential role in the development and/or manifestation of PTSD. As an example, following the retrieval of a memory (e.g., having animals respond to stressor cues to encourage a previous memory to come forward), administration of a glucocorticoid receptor antagonist diminished the memory of this test. Thus, when the memory of an aversive event was retrieved, it was susceptible to disruption by a glucocorticoid manipulation (Taubenfeld et al., 2009). It should be underscored here that for the drug to have the effect that it did, it was essential that it be administered once the memory was retrieved (we'll come back to this shortly, and the significance of this will become more apparent).

In addition to such findings, interesting corticosterone (cortisol) changes have been associated with PTSD that may be important for analyses of the processes leading to PTSD. In Chapters 3 and 4 we learned that an elevated release of cortisol from the adrenal gland is a prototypical response to stressful situations. Thus, it might be expected that PTSD would be accompanied by elevated levels of this hormone, possibly acting in an adaptive capacity. However, this might not occur in response to chronic stressors or among individuals who experienced trauma that led to PTSD. On the contrary, with the appearance of pronounced PTSD symptoms cortisol levels are comparable to, or even fall below, those of individuals who show no symptoms (Yehuda, 2002). Furthermore, PTSD is associated with a change in the diurnal pattern of cortisol secretion, so that the normal daily fluctuations become flattened (i.e., the morning cortisol levels are lower, and evening cortisol levels are elevated) (Michaud et al., 2008). This might represent a fundamental adaptive response to strong or chronic stressors, as excessive or prolonged cortisol release might promote the loss of hippocampal corticoid receptors, so that the message necessary to regulate cortisol secretion might become disturbed (hippocampal function is necessary to inform the hypothalamus to cease the release of CRH and ultimately cortisol secretion), leading to yet more adverse consequences (McEwen & Gianaros, 2011).

One might think that once HPA functioning is down-regulated, individuals might be at risk for pathology as they might not have the biological resources necessary to contend with further stressors. In a series of interesting studies Heim and Nemeroff provided important information regarding the processes related to trauma effects that have clear clinical implications (Heim et al., 2010). Specifically, when depressed women who had previously been traumatized (abused) were challenged with CRH, which ordinarily causes the release of ACTH from the anterior pituitary gland, the ACTH response was muted. These data are clearly consistent with the view that the HPA system was down-regulated. However, when these women were placed in a Trier Social Stress Test (public speaking) that was usually accompanied by feelings of shame and elevated cortisol, they exhibited a particularly exaggerated HPA response, relative to controls (Heim & Nemeroff, 2002). It was similarly observed that among women who had experienced dating abuse, high levels of PTSD were accompanied by lower cortisol levels relative to abused women who showed only moderate PTSD symptoms. However, when these women were provided with reminders of their abusive experiences, an especially marked increase of cortisol levels was instigated in those women with the highest levels of PTSD (Matheson & Anisman, 2012).

So what might be accounting for these unusual ACTH or cortisol changes? As already indicated, HPA activity might be down-regulated among traumatized individuals as an excessive cortisol release might leave those individuals at risk of adverse outcomes. However, this down-regulation might itself be maladaptive as the cortisol changes might be necessary to deal with certain stressors. Therefore, it might be advantageous for HPA functioning to be generally diminished, but when certain brain regions are activated (e.g., the prefrontal cortex, amygdala) in response to *relevant* stressor cues, this activation might serve to over-ride the otherwise down-regulated HPA system.

GABA AND NPY

As GABA has been implicated in anxiety, it's not at all surprising that it might also contribute to PTSD. GABA, it will be recalled, is an inhibitory transmitter that puts the brakes on some neuronal processes, and it is possible that when GABA levels in certain brain regions are low, the lack of inhibition allows for the persistence of the neuronal functioning that is part of a fear or PTSD-like state (i.e., the fear response does not extinguish). Support for GABA involvement in PTSD has come from findings such as those indicating that among combat veterans, PTSD was accompanied by a reduced number (or binding) of benzodiazepine receptors, which are tied to GABA functioning (Geuze et al., 2008). It was was further demonstrated that GABA levels in blood were diminished in those with PTSD, and it was suggested that its levels might be used as a biomarker to predict illness vulnerability (Vaiva et al., 2004). Unlike the effects of NE and glucocorticoid manipulations, however, administering a benzodiazepine after the trauma event did not deter the emergence of the pathology. In fact, in an animal model, treatment with a benzodiazepine shortly after trauma exacerbated the adverse effects of a later stressor (Matar et al., 2009). Hence, GABA might serve in some capacity in maintaining PTSD, but it is less likely that altered GABA functioning was directly responsible for the development of PTSD. As already indicated, it is possible that it plays some sort of role in sustaining PTSD that is already present. In this regard, a synthetic analogue of GABA, pregabalin, which is marketed as Lyrica, was found to have positive effects in animal models (e.g., Zohar et al., 2008) as well as in accident-related PTSD in humans (Pae & Patkar, 2009). This compound, which is more commonly used in the treatment of fibromyalgia and some seizure conditions, seems to have its effects by altering GABA uptake, although there are a variety of other as yet unidentified processes that might contribute to its effects.

Neuropeptide Y (NPY) might also contribute to stressor-provoked behavioral disturbances. This peptide is associated with stress responses, and studies in animals also revealed that following a predator-odor, the anxiety and hyper-reactivity elicited were accompanied by a reduction in the expression of NPY in the hippocampus and amygdala. Of particular significance was the finding that those animals that showed highly disrupted behavior were also those that exhibited symptom amelioration following the administration of NPY directly into the brain (Cohen et al., 2012). Likewise, when NPY was administered intranasally to rats prior to a prolonged stressor, the subsequent development of PTSD-like symptoms was diminished (Serova et al., 2013). Predictably, nasal spray containing NPY is currently being assessed as a method to ameliorate PTSD in humans.

Assuming that the stressor-provoked behavioral disturbances are related to PTSD, these findings are in line with the perspective that NPY plays a mediating role for PTSD, and hence NPY might serve as a therapeutic target for this disorder. A gene polymorphism on the promoter gene for NPY has been associated with exaggerated HPA responses following early adversity (Witt et al., 2011), but it is likely still too early to determine whether this polymorphism is related to PTSD.

Summarizing briefly, there is ample reason to believe that both NE and HPA functioning are associated with PTSD. However, there are other processes that need to be evaluated more thoroughly before we can assume that these systems are not tied to this disorder. Good candidates to start with are various 5-HT receptors and NPY (Krystal & Neumeister, 2009), and possibly GABA/glutamate functioning. In their very interesting review, Sah and Geracioti (2013) made an impressive case concerning the involvement of NPY in PTSD, particularly as they tied NPY to specific features that comprise this syndrome. Like GABA, it is thought that NPY acts as a brake to prevent or diminish the effects of stressors in the promotion of CRH and NE release within the amygdala, and in this way is the controller for the development of stress-related pathology, particularly fear-related symptoms, such as avoidance and hyper-reactivity.

It should also be considered that stressful events, through their actions on glucocorticoids, might promote a cascade of intraneuronal changes leading to epigenetic modifications of gene expression of the processes that serve as an access route to the hippocampus. As these epigenetic changes can persist throughout an individual's life, they may be rendered vulnerable to pathology in the future.

LEARNING FROM THE HEART

Type 2 ryanodine receptors (RyR2) comprise channels (much like those we saw when discussing the GABA receptor) that regulate calcium levels in neurons. Research conducted by Marks and his associates had indicated that stressors could result in a leakage of calcium in the heart and other muscles, culminating in heart failure and arrhythmias. It likewise seems that when mice are chronically stressed, the RyR2 receptors within the hippocampus destabilize and become leaky, just as they had in the heart. Interestingly, these mice exhibit marked behavioral disturbances that were indicative of memory and learning problems like those associated with PTSD. Significantly, in mice that had been pretreated with a drug to prevent calcium leakage, the stressor-induced behavioral disturbances were not evident. Likewise, in mice that had been genetically engineered so that leaking would not occur, behavioral impairments were prevented (Liu et al., 2012). These findings raise the possibility of a new therapeutic target for PTSD.

A skeptic would suggest that every time we think we've got a grip on things, another potential process for PTSD is offered. Maybe so, but this tells us that PTSD is a complex disorder, and the symptoms of the illness might involve many interlocking mechanisms. What struck me about this study is that it borrowed from previously investigated processes associated with heart problems and applied these to another stress-related psychological disturbance.

SENSITIZED RESPONSES AND EPIGENETIC FACTORS IN RELATION TO PTSD

There are several puzzling features regarding the temporal dynamics of PTSD. Why would the emergence of PTSD become more pronounced with the passage of time following a traumatic experience? Likewise, why would an individual who seemed to have dealt well with a traumatic event develop PTSD at some later time? These issues can be addressed from a psychodynamic perspective or one that involves brain biological processes. From the psychodynamic side it can be argued that the distress associated with trauma might, in some individuals, result in persistent rumination and replaying of events that cumulatively have disastrous consequences, much like chronic stressors can have such effects. This view is in line with the position that stressors may result in permanent changes in the characteristics of neurons so they are more readily triggered by appropriate stimuli, and especially by reminders of the adverse event. In effect, neurons might become sensitized, so that with repeated trauma or even reminders of the trauma, a progressively greater propensity toward pathology might develop. In discussing animal models of PTSD, it was pointed out that a single strong stressor followed by intermittent reminder cues resulted in anxiety-related behavioral changes, and that reminder cues were necessary for this long-lasting outcome to occur. These reminder cues might have their effects by strengthening the neuronal network associated with the emotional memories regarding the trauma, or alternatively, they might prevent the time-related dissipation of emotional trauma memories that might otherwise occur.

DANGER: BRAIN AT WORK

Individuals often make the mistake of assuming that once a traumatic or exceptionally distressing event is over, so are the distress and the accompanying biological changes, and consequently they should start to recover. We even have expressions that speak to this, such as 'Time heals all wounds'. Time might allow for some wounds to heal in some individuals, or it might remove them from the surface. For others, time moves ever so slowly, and the trauma memories linger and so do their psychological and physical consequences. Parents who have lost a child, individuals who experienced the horrors of warfare, or survivors of genocidal efforts don't simply forget. Some might never speak about their experiences (a conspiracy of silence), whereas others can't stop speaking about it. Although the majority of individuals go on with life, their traumatic memories are often just below the surface, and their effects can reemerge over time.

It's odd that so many people gain some sort of pleasure in deriding Sigmund Freud, despite the enormous contributions he made to brain sciences, including his thoughts on defense mechanisms and other processes that are still considered to be useful. He had postulated, among many other things, that early experiences might mark individuals for life, although he didn't understand how this came about from a biological perspective. After all, he didn't have the luxury of knowing about the workings of neurochemical systems. In an interesting paper, McFarlane (2010) reminded me of a notion attributed to Freud, namely that traumatic memory represents a causative 'agent still at work'. Essentially, traumatic memories can be exceedingly aversive, and replaying incidents and ruminating about these events might encourage the development of PTSD.

What makes these reports particularly interesting is that they focus on the evolution of PTSD symptoms that might occur with the passage of time and upon reexposure to relevant contextual stimuli. As discussed earlier, exposure to a strong, uncontrollable stressor may result in the sensitization of norepinephrine neuronal activity so that responses to later similar or dissimilar stressors are exaggerated and might serve to promote behavioral disturbances (Anisman et al., 2003). These sensitization effects are not limited to NE, having been observed with respect to 5-HT, GABA, and BDNF activity within regions such as the prefrontal cortex, and sensitization was reported with respect to neuroendocrine and cardiac hormone responses, as well as growth factors such as BDNF. It has been suggested that sensitized effects such as these are responsible for the recurrence of depressive illness and could contribute to PTSD, especially as the sensitized responses become progressively greater with multiple traumatic episodes (Anisman et al., 2008).

In addition to sensitized responses of this sort, stressful events may engender epigenetic changes so that the functioning of certain genes is turned off. Traumatic experiences, especially if they occur early in life, might engender epigenetic changes that will influence responses to stressors later in life (Szyf, 2009), and might thus increase vulnerability to PTSD. Although this is certainly a possibility, there are currently limited data showing that epigenetic factors are tied to PTSD in humans, but patterns of hypermethylation were seen in US service members that had previously been deployed to Afghanistan. Those inviduals who exhibited PTSD symptoms could be distinguished from controls with respect to their genetic and epigenetic profiles. It was of particular significance that individuals with PTSD could also be distinguished from one another on the basis of epigenetic differences, which seemed to depend upon whether or not they had also encountered adverse early life experiences. In effect, it is possible that events in childhood may promote epigenetic changes that result in vulnerability to PTSD and to the development of particular symptoms (Mehta et al., 2013). There have also been reports on rodents suggesting this possibility. Of particular relevance was the finding that BDNF gene methylation within the hippocampus, but not the prefrontal cortex or amygdala, was also affected by the adult stressor treatment, implicating an epigenetic process related to memory processes, but not fear/anxiety, in the provocation of a PTSD-like state (Roth et al., 2011).

TREATMENT OF PTSD

There has been an assortment of treatments used to treat PTSD, including family or interpersonal therapy, trauma management therapy, mindfulness training, imagery training (rehearsal) and virtual reality treatments, acceptance and commitment therapy, and various pharmacological approaches. We'll limit our discussions here to some of the most prominent treatments (see also Chapter 12), especially those that point to potential processes underlying PTSD. A detailed review of treatment strategies is available in Cukor et al. (2009).

Several types of psychotherapy and behavioral therapy have been used in the treatment of PTSD. One of the more useful has been individualized CBT (Bisson et al., 2007). Indeed, CBT was effective in treating PTSD (together with depression and complicated grief) that had been elicited by a terrorist attack even when ongoing threats of terrorism persisted (Bryant et al., 2011). In contrast to individual CBT, stress management/relaxation and group CBT were less successful, and still other therapies (e.g., supportive therapy/nondirective counseling, psychodynamic therapies, and hypnotherapy) were generally reported to be entirely ineffective. Although CBT has been the treatment of choice for PTSD, it may be especially pertinent that CBT was least effective in those individuals who carried the short allele for 5-HTT (Bryant et al., 2010), and so it might be useful to screen an individual's genotype, and then on this basis determine the most suitable form of treatment.

A form of behavioral therapy, namely that of prolonged exposure (PE), has been widely used in the treatment of PTSD. This approach focuses on efforts to extinguish emotional and cognitive responses to danger cues that had not been properly extinguished previously, so that individuals continued to exhibit excessive responses to cues that might signal danger. In the course of treatment, the danger cues are reintroduced (using imagery or actual exposure to cues), thereby resulting in habituation and extinction to these stimuli. Significantly, during the therapy sessions individuals also repeatedly retell their trauma experiences and engage emotionally with these. Eventually, the memories and cues that had elicited these powerful emotional and physiological responses might no longer have these strong effects.

A particular form of therapy, eye movement desensitization and reprocessing (EMDR), is at first blush a bit flaky and, predictably, has not been easily accepted as a method of treatment.

Yet there is some evidence supporting its effectiveness (Seidler & Wagner, 2006). Over the course of several sessions, patients are asked to focus on a vivid image of the traumatic event, during which the therapist has the patient conduct various eye movements (e.g., following a finger that moves across their visual field), as well as stimulating other senses. Essentially, it is thought that the memory of the trauma (which has been activated during the session) will be associated with other, less threatening stimuli, so that the traumatic memory and the emotions ordinarily elicited by these memories will be dissociated from one another. Sounds strange, but if it works, then why not use it? Besides, as we'll see shortly, there is actually a scientifically-based reason for why this treatment might work.

Given the profound neuronal changes that are elicited by stressors, and especially traumatic events, it would be expected that pharmacotherapy would be a main line for treatment to ameliorate the symptoms of PTSD. In fact, SSRIs have been widely used to treat this disorder. Indeed, the main pharmacological methods of treatment of PTSD have been certain SSRIs or SNRIs (e.g., Davis et al., 2006). Unlike depression, however, where a combination of CBT and an SSRI provoked a better outcome than either treatment alone, this did not seem to be the case regarding PTSD (Hetrick et al., 2010), although it is uncertain whether the combination therapy would have long-term benefits, particularly with respect to the impact of subsequent traumatic encounters.

As PTSD is accompanied by variations of HPA functioning, there has been an interest in determining whether the treatments that affect HPA activity might be beneficial in attenuating the disorder. It was particularly noteworthy that although the manipulation of cortisol didn't have much of an effect on individuals who presented with PTSD symptoms, a high dose cortisol treatment administered within six hours of the trauma could prevent the emergence of PTSD. Regardless of the mechanism by which glucocorticoids introduced their beneficial effects, these data point to the possibility that a 'window of opportunity' exists following a trauma experience, during which the protracted adverse effects can be diminished (Zohar et al., 2011).

Based on the findings that stressful experiences have significant autonomic effects and also influence brain NE activity, there has been considerable attention devoted to the possibility that α- and β-adrenergic antagonists might be useful in treating PTSD. In this regard, drugs that diminish NE release, such as α_2 agonists (clonidine), or block α_1 and β receptors (such as prazosin and propranolol, respectively), attenuate symptoms of PTSD (Krystal & Neumeister, 2009). For instance, the α_1 adrenergic antagonist prazosin reduced some symptoms associated with PTSD, such as trauma-related nightmares and insomnia. This contrasts with propranolol, which is said to be efficacious in alleviating the emotional content associated with traumatic memories. As a result, it was suggested that the combined use of prazosin and propranolol might be particularly effective in treating PTSD (Shad et al., 2011).

As with behavioral changes, the augmented physiological responses associated with PTSD were diminished if the β-adrenergic antagonist propranolol was administered soon after the trauma (Pitman et al., 2002). It had been suggested that when memories were already consolidated and were in long-term storage, they were fairly resistant to being altered. However, when memories were fresh (i.e., not yet thoroughly consolidated), they might be less resistant to disruption, and hence treatments that modified NE activity during the period soon after a trauma would be effective in altering the course of PTSD (McIntyre et al., 2011). It was likewise suggested that when memories were recalled, they might also be more vulnerable to being changed, so that the emotional responses associated with a memory and the recall of the events might actually be dissociated from one another and then reconsolidated in this new form (Johansen et al., 2011; Nader et al., 2000). In line with this, if a fear memory in rodents was reactivated by reminder cues, disrupting NE activity within the lateral amygdala, the animals' fear recall was subsequently impaired. Similarly, PTSD symptoms were attenuated among individuals in whom PTSD had already developed and were treated with propranolol shortly after these individuals recalled (retrieved) these memories. However, there have also been reports indicating that propranolol was ineffective in limiting the development of PTSD in either animal models or humans (e.g., Cohen et al., 2012). Thus, firm conclusions will have to await data that might be relevant to whether there are certain individuals or conditions that are more or less amenable to this treatment approach, or whether β-blockers would be effective when combined with other therapeutic treatments. Regardless of the most efficacious drug treatment in disrupting reconsolidation and hence limiting PTSD, it should be considered that the eye movement desensitization and reprocessing (EMDR) described earlier might have its beneficial effects by affecting memory during reconsolidation. Perhaps eye movements that cause brain activity changes while recalling events have the effect of confusing or dissociating memories of events from the emotional responses associated with these events.

Another promising strategy to treat PTSD has involved the manipulation of glutamate activity, which is fundamental to learning and memory processes. Studies in animals indicated that D-cycloserine (Seromycin), which acts as a partial N-methyl-D-aspartate (NMDA) glutamate receptor agonist, facilitates fear extinction (Ledgerwood et al., 2005). It turned out that D-cycloserine has promising effects in the treatment of PTSD, particularly when used in combination with CBT or exposure (extinction) therapy. Once again, however, D-cycloserine isn't effective in all patients, and, it is important to determine whether there are predictors that can be informative as to the optimal treatment strategy for any given individual.

A BROAD CAVEAT CONCERNING TEMPORAL CHANGES IN PTSD

One final point needs to be considered, which is applicable not just to PTSD, but also to anxiety disorders and depression, as well as drug addictions. The evolution of PTSD seems to involve dynamic neurochemical systems, and it is possible that those neurochemical systems activated soon after trauma might not be identical to those that are present during later phases and during chronic PTSD. Therefore, it is possible that the effectiveness of treatment strategies might similarly vary over the different phases of the disorder. Particular treatments, such as cortisol or NE antagonists, might be effective when administered during a window of opportunity soon after the traumatic experience. Other treatments or treatment combinations (e.g., cognitive behavioral therapy in combination with an SSRI or D-cycloserine), in contrast, might be most effective in ameliorating the symptoms once PTSD is established. Still other treatments might be especially useful in limiting memory reconsolidation that is otherwise strengthened by reminder cues. Finally, if sensitization of neurochemical changes is fundamental in the development and strengthening of PTSD symptoms, then it may be propitious to establish strategies that target the sensitized mechanisms. Essentially, the view being proposed here is in line with the suggestion that multi-targeted approaches may ultimately be needed to limit the emergence of PTSD or treat the disorder once it is established. More than this, however, is that the treatment or treatment combinations necessary at one phase might not be the most useful at a second phase in the disorder's development.

CONCLUSION

The various subtypes of anxiety and PTSD share several common features, although in some respects they are very different from one another (contrast, for instance, the characteristics of OCD, GAD, and PTSD). Likewise, the presumed biological processes for these disorders may be biochemically heterogeneous, and although they share some biological features there are likely several differences as well. It is similarly the case that the most efficacious treatments vary across conditions, although it should be said that in some instances the headway in developing good treatment strategies has been limited. Given the biological and behavioral complexity of anxiety disorders, as well as the frequent comorbid conditions that occur, effective treatment may have to await a broad-scale endophenotypic approach such as that advocated for other psychological conditions.

Although it is broadly acknowledged that anxiety disorders affect a large portion of individuals, other than PTSD, these disorders don't seem to be given the attention (or financial support for research) that's needed. Having champions for various causes has been extremely helpful for the support of individuals with a particular pathology. Heart disease, juvenile diabetes, immune-related disorders, cancer of one sort or another, Lou Gehrig's disease, Parkinson's disease, Alzheimer's, and others, have all received public and private support. To a great extent, GAD, OCD, and phobias are still waiting their turn. That said, anxiety-related disorders represent a tremendous burden on individuals and their families as well as the health system. As with many of the illnesses we've discussed, anxiety is highly comorbid with other conditions, and thus its toll goes well beyond that attributed to the primary anxiety condition.

SUMMARY

- Several anxiety disorders have been identified that are not only distinguishable based on their overt symptoms, but also involve different etiological processes and life-time trajectories.
- The various anxiety disorders likely involve both common and different brain processes and neural circuits.

- Diverse underlying mechanisms are likely responsible for the various anxiety disorders. Particular attention in this regard has focused on 5-HT, NE, CRH, and GABA, but depending on the specific condition being considered, the involvement of these factors may vary over the course of the illness.
- Because the symptoms of depression, PTSD, and other anxiety disorders are shared, it has been a challenge to create animal models that distinguish between these illnesses, making it that much more difficult to establish treatment strategies. However, it has become increasingly apparent that individualized treatment strategies will eventually be needed for the treatment of anxiety, just as these have been called for in the case of depressive disorders.

10 ADDICTION

WHAT'S MEANT BY ADDICTION?

Most people think of addiction as a physical and psychological dependence on particular substances (e.g., alcohol, cocaine, heroin, tobacco), and that over time the dose needed to maintain the pleasurable effects of these substances increases, whereas their discontinuation has a highly aversive impact. To an extent this is true, but not always, especially as addiction is not limited to drugs. One often hears the term 'addiction' being applied to sex, the internet, email, and pornography, but are these genuine addictions, like those that involve drugs, or are they excuses to explain away some behaviors once they come to light? In several respects, some psychological addictions (e.g., gambling) are at least as powerful as those related to cocaine and heroin, and might be even harder to shake. But do email addiction and internet addiction fall into this category, or should they more appropriately fall into categories related to compulsive behaviors?

One can view addictions as a choice that individuals make, and thus little sympathy is offered to those who are addicted. On the other side, one can see addiction as the unfortunate confluence of poor or impoverished early life experiences, stressors encountered in adulthood, some poor life choices, the wrong social influences, and a particular genetic constitution. Whatever the case, addiction is a huge problem both for the individual and society, and is among a number of pathological conditions actually encouraged by different levels of government (witness the proliferation of gambling venues, the paucity of attention given to limiting excessive alcohol consumption, and the weak response that existed for years in curtailing nicotine addiction). Addiction is a complex and multidimensional problem, but there are several core issues that the reader should come away from the chapter understanding better:

- addiction comprises a process. It can arise as a response to positive experiences that the individual might want to re-experience, or it can stem from counterproductive efforts to cope with stressors, essentially a self-medication strategy. Over the course of an addiction, changes may occur regarding its underlying processes. Factors that favor the addiction developing may be different from those involved in it being sustained, and these may differ yet again from those responsible for the recurrence of an addiction after the habit had been kicked;
- most biological perspectives on addiction have focused on the contribution of neurotransmitter processes responsible for reward processes: those thought to be involved in stress processes, and those that serve as growth factors that could affect memory or habits related to addiction. Added to this, conditioning to environmental cues might instigate these neurochemical changes, thus furthering pathology and promoting drug reinstatement;
- stressful events or reminders of stressors can have particularly potent effects in causing the reinstatement of an addiction;
- many addictions have common elements and so there are likely common processes governing them. At the same time there are clear differences between addictions, and hence treatments that have some positive effects for one addiction may have few beneficial effects in the treatment of another addiction.

The *DSM-IV* and the *DSM-5* describe the criteria to be used in defining substance-related disorders, but other definitions have been offered as well (see Table 10.1). Experts in the field often distinguish between addiction and dependence. In particular, addiction is characterized as an intense craving for a particular substance, coupled with the inability to control its use, despite negative consequences. Dependence refers to the use of a substance excessively on a regular basis, despite the knowledge that they are endangering themselves, jeopardizing relationships, or falling through on major responsibilities. However, they are at a stage where they don't yet exhibit dependence that is characterized by psychological compulsions or physical need to use the substance.

Although addiction had at one time been thought to involve tolerance and withdrawal, these are not a necessary condition for substance abuse to be diagnosed. In addition to the primary features of substance dependence, it is not uncommon for any of several secondary characteristics to be present. For instance, amphetamine and cocaine may induce symptoms that are virtually indistinguishable from those associated with schizophrenia. Likewise, alcohol has been associated with the emergence of depression, and psychedelic agents may have long-term effects on some of the symptoms related to delusions. In the absence of physical damage, however, many of these features diminish with continued abstinence. Of course, once sufficient damage has occurred, as in the case of Korsakoff's syndrome (which involves damage to neurons and glial cells following chronic alcohol abuse), the CNS problems cannot be undone.

STRESS IN RELATION TO THE ADDICTION PROCESS

There likely isn't a single factor that is responsible for different types of drug addictions, and it is not necessarily the case that the same factors responsible for one form of addiction (e.g.,

TABLE 10.1 Defining physiological 'dependence'

An individual is said to be physically dependent (note that the term 'dependent' will no longer be used to mean psychological dependence) when they experience impaired functioning or distress, reflected by at least three (or more) of the following in the preceding 12-months;

1. Tolerance should be evident, reflected by either (a) a need for greater quantities of the substance to obtain the desired outcome or for intoxication to occur; or (b) the use of a given amount (dose) of the substance induces progressively smaller effects with continued use.
2. Withdrawal occurs as reflected by (a) greater amounts of the drug being taken to limit withdrawal symptoms, or (b) substances (typically being closely related) are used to limit withdrawal.
3. The substance is taken not only in larger amounts but over longer periods than the individual had intended.
4. The individual was unable to reduce substance use despite the desire to do so.
5. The individual spends a considerable time and effort to use or obtain the substance.
6. Typical social, occupational or recreational activities are reduced owing to the substance abuse.
7. The abuse of the substance continues even though the individual is aware that the use of the substance has created physical or psychological disturbances.

amphetamine, cocaine) are responsible for a second addiction (e.g., alcohol, nicotine). However, this doesn't mean that there aren't common elements that are relevant to a variety of addictions. It has frequently been proposed that for some individuals stressful events may be a fundamental contributing factor that might encourage their initial drug intake, the subsequent development of a drug (or gambling) addiction, drug craving, and the recurrence of drug taking, even after lengthy periods of withdrawal/abstinence. It also appears that stress-related illnesses, such as depression and PTSD, are often comorbid with substance use disorders, and individuals with alcohol or drug problems frequently report antecedent traumatic experiences. Predictably, the combination of PTSD plus substance abuse disorder has been associated with greater and more frequent dysfunctions than either condition alone.

MULTIPLE STRESS-RELATED CAUSATIVE FACTORS

Several lines of evidence have supported the view that stressors and traumatic events and substance use are linked, but as we'll see, the role of stressors may vary over the course of an addiction (Cleck & Blendy, 2008; Heilig & Koob, 2007). It was suggested that addictions were related to (a) recent stressful experiences, often involving psychosocial problems (the loss of a child, unfaithfulness on the part of others, the death of a significant other, rape, being the victim of violence, or observing violent victimization); (b) early life stressors (e.g., emotional abuse or neglect, parental loss, divorce, or conflict, isolation, physical abuse by a parent or caretaker); (c) cumulative stressor experiences, irrespective of whether they occurred in childhood or as an adult; (d) particularly profound neurochemical disturbances elicited by stressful events among drug-addicted individuals that exacerbate the addiction; and (e) chronic psychiatric illnesses.

The fact that stressors might contribute to addiction isn't particularly surprising. Drug addiction might reflect a poor attempt at self-medication, wherein those who have experienced trauma might turn to alcohol or other drugs to help them deal with the emotional pain, bad memories, poor sleep, guilt, shame, anxiety, or terror (Sinha, 2008). Of course, such drug use might temporarily dampen the adverse effects of stressful or traumatic experiences, but this escape works only so well and for only so long. Individuals may find themselves in a cycle in which stressful events produce increased alcohol and drug use, which might then engender yet more stressful experiences (i.e., the drug use may act as a 'stress proliferator'), thereby encouraging further substance use, and so forth. Related to this view is the susceptibility hypothesis of addiction which suggests that individuals who use alcohol and other drugs might be more disposed to encounter trauma, and when they do, they will be more susceptible to psychopathology (such as PTSD), in part, because of poor coping. Related to this is the high-risk hypothesis, according to which experiencing traumatic events and substance abuse is actually part of a broader tendency among some individuals to engage in high-risk behaviors (e.g., Brady et al., 1998). Finally, the common factors hypothesis suggests that addiction and other pathological conditions share common antecedents, such as stressful or traumatic experiences that provoke illness. As indicated earlier, it is likely that the comorbidities that develop may do so for different reasons across individuals, and in some instances multiple factors will feed into the comorbidity between drug addiction and other psychopathological conditions.

Drug addiction may also be linked to comorbid conditions that are gender dependent. Specifically, in response to distress women can often exhibit internalizing behavior (e.g., rumination) that favors the development of mood and anxiety disorders, whereas men are more likely to display externalizing behaviors, such as impulsivity, an antisocial personality and substance use disorders. As a result, treatment protocols might also benefit from different approaches for men and women. For women, for instance, coping and cognitive skills that limit rumination might be particularly effective, whereas the treatment for men might focus on limiting impulsive behaviors.

CHANGES DURING THE COURSE OF AN ILLNESS

Although few would disagree with the views expressed concerning the relation between stressful events, PTSD/depression, and drug addiction, several pertinent questions remain. First, regardless of whether the drug intake serves as a coping mechanism or occurs owing to other factors (the rewarding feelings obtained through drug use), what are the biological underpinnings for addictive behaviors? Second, do stressor effects on neurochemical processes alter the rewarding value of self-administered drugs, thereby increasing the addiction risk? In considering these questions it should be underscored that addiction is a dynamic process, likely involving changes over the course of the addiction. The addiction process involves the original acquisition of the drug-taking behavior, the development and maintenance of an addiction, and a reinstatement of addictive behaviors following a period of cessation of drug intake. This brings us to a third essential question, namely, do these phases involve similar motivational and reward processes as well as underlying biological mechanisms?

By now you might be getting a bit tired of the recurrent theme regarding individual difference factors. Nevertheless, it warrants repetition. As in the case of anxiety and depression, the unique factors that result in one individual succumbing to an addiction (or another health problem) and other individuals not being affected in this way, likely involve many different processes and events (e.g., genetic factors or those that might dispose individuals to behave in certain ways to deal with stressors). To avoid any misunderstanding, the view is not being taken that stress is the only reason that people might start using a drug. On the contrary, anyone who went through university in the 60s (or 70s, 80s, 90s or 00s or 10s) knows that initial drug use for many was a matter of experimentation, social pressure, or simply the desire to have fun or engage in risky behaviors. Later on, drug use might have been repeated in an effort to re-experience earlier positive feelings or as a means to escape boredom. Still later, drug use for some individuals might have continued in order to prevent the distress associated with withdrawal.

BEATING THE ODDS: A HEN IN THE FOX PEN

Most researchers in the addiction field have focused on drug addictions. However, gambling addiction has also been a fairly significant problem. This state-sponsored (even encouraged) addiction has devastating effects on individuals and families. In the main, problem gamblers don't stagger down the street in a haze, aren't incoherent, don't attack others in a gambling-fueled rage, and so it's often assumed that the problem isn't as acute as that of a drug addiction. In fact, however, in several respects, a gambling addiction can be more devastating than a drug addiction. In the case of a drug, say cocaine, there's only so much that can be used before the need is sated (although this can be fairly expensive). In contrast, in the case of gambling there may not be anything like satiety. You can bet on horses, football, baseball, and any other sport; you can bet at the track, at the casino, at your buddy's house, at bars (in some cities); lottery tickets can be obtained anywhere, even at the corner store, and if all else fails there is always internet betting. In essence, gamblers suffer from a double whammy: the natural 'stop' mechanisms that apply to other forms of addiction seem not to apply to gambling (at least not in the same way), and this problem is compounded by the remarkable availability of gambling venues.

REWARD AND AVERSION IN RELATION TO ADDICTION

Most of the theoretical constructs related to addiction have included both reward and aversion processes, and typically their contribution has involved complex neural circuits whose functions vary over the course of the addiction (see Koob & Volkow, 2010). As we've already learned, the initial drug intake may occur as a result of the hedonic effects elicited by the drug (feeling good), often prompted by social factors, or it might be used as a coping response to contend with an ongoing or a previous stressful experience. In the former instance, during this early phase, drugs are thought to engage the neurochemical processes associated with reward (i.e., DA and opioid peptide activation). Things change over time, and the next phase of the addiction process may reflect an effort to attenuate the lousy feelings endured if the drug is not taken (withdrawal symptoms). Essentially, neuronal activity that involves changes in CRH, NE, and the opioid peptide dynophin, plays an integral role in mediating the poor feelings that are present when the desired drug is not obtained, and the positive effects that accrue when the drug is once again taken.

With continued drug use a preoccupation/craving stage of the addiction begins to become more pronounced. In this stage conditioned effects related to reward processes emerge and individuals exhibit a craving for the drug and are preoccupied with ways of obtaining it. These processes are thought to entail activation of the basolateral amygdala and nucleus accumbens to obtain conditioned reward effects, hippocampal functioning to process contextual information related to obtaining the drug, and the craving is determined by aspects of appraisal that involve activation of the orbital and anterior cingulate cortex, together with the amygdala. Thus, among individuals who had stopped using the drug, a relapse (also called 'reinstatement') can be promoted by a reintroduction of the cues associated with the drug (Shaham et al., 2003), or by stressors. Although the influence of reminder cues and stressors doesn't necessarily involve identical processes, both of these could elicit the cravings that encourage drug taking and hence a relapse.

DOPAMINE AND REWARD PROCESSES

To gain a better understanding of addiction processes, we ought to consider how stressors and stress-related neural circuits interact with the brain mechanism underlying reward mechanisms. As discussed earlier, several neurochemical mechanisms are involved in reward processes, but the activity of neurons within the mesolimbic DA system is particularly important (Robinson & Berridge, 2003; Wise, 2004). This system involves the ventral tegmental area (VTA), which contains cell bodies that send fibers to several forebrain cortical and limbic regions. These DA-rich regions are essential for promoting reward-seeking behaviors, as well as the formation of implicit (the ventral striatum) and explicit (hippocampus and prefrontal cortex) associations between environmental cues and reinforcing stimuli, emotions (the amygdala), and executive functions (the frontal cortex) (Robinson & Berridge, 2003)

Dopamine activity in this brain circuit is responsible for feelings of reward (Wise, 2004), and might be fundamental in determining the salience of stimuli associated with a particular reward (i.e., the cues that signal that reward will take on particular significance). Once an association has been made between environmental cues and addictive drugs, which entails synaptic remodelling, re-experiencing these cues will excite reward pathways and pose a significant challenge for recovering addicts who can readily be pushed into relapse (Bonci & Borgland, 2009). A related view has it that addiction evolves from the conjoint influence of several brain changes that occur during the addiction process (Volkow et al., 2010, 2013). From this perspective, DA is a key player in addiction, but it is not alone in this regard. The activity of DA neurons at the nucleus accumbens is seen as being fundamental in defining the salience of rewarding stimuli, and is involved in reward expectation as well as motivational and emotional processes. However, as often occurs when receptors are repeatedly stimulated, their sensitivity might decline in some brain regions, and hence larger amounts of the drug may be necessary to elicit pleasure (reward). It was suggested that the down-regulated DA functioning in frontal cortical regions, along with that of 5-HT, had yet another important action, namely that of promoting impulsivity. Thus, when impulsivity and reward processes are both altered, individuals may be particularly motivated to obtain immediate gratification through drug use, and inhibitions that might ordinarily give the individual pause are essentially absent.

NEURONAL MEMORIES RELATED TO ADDICTION

The signal through which one neuron excites an adjacent neuron can be facilitated if these neurons are activated in synchrony. This phenomenon, known as long-term potentiation (LTP), has been viewed as a model of memory wherein events that occurred in relation to one another are linked because synaptic strength is increased. We saw this in the case of PTSD in which rumination or repeated thoughts of the trauma encouraged the strengthening of synaptic connections and the related memories. The enhanced ability of a cell to receive a message from an adjacent neuron may stem from an increase in the sensitivity or the number of receptors on the postsynaptic site. It is conceivable that addiction and sensitization involve this sort of memory process, in that synaptic connections are strengthened with repeated drug consumption. It is equally possible that the network of neurons involved widens with repeated drug experiences, as well as in association with specific environmental cues. As a result, the constellation of cues that promote craving increases proportionately, and these feelings are more readily elicited in a wider set of situations.

As interesting as this perspective appears, there are other aspects of DA stimulant drugs like amphetamine that ought to be considered. Although the effects of some drugs become less profound with repeated use (tolerance), one of the most prominent features of cocaine and amphetamine is that many of their behavioral effects become more pronounced with continued intake, as do brain DA changes. Moreover, addictive behaviors are very persistent, and the recurrence of the addiction can readily be re-induced long after drug use has been eliminated simply by having animals (or humans) get another 'taste' of the compound or by exposing them to stressors or stress-related cues. The sensitization of neurochemical systems may be fundamental for the exaggerated behavioral changes that accompany repeated use of amphetamine, cocaine, opiates, and alcohol. In fact, following repeated drug treatment DA cells in the VTA (and in the prefrontal cortex) undergo long-lasting neuroanatomical, electrophysiological, and molecular changes, possibly owing to the activation of growth factors, such as BDNF and FGF-2 (Flores & Stewart, 2000).

It is similarly possible that a remodelling of DA neurons is responsible for the development of addictions. In this regard, cocaine promotes long-term potentiation involving DA neurons, and decreases the threshold for dopamine cells to be activated, possibly by facilitating the development of interconnections between neurons (Liu et al., 2005). Some drugs may also promote long-lasting changes of transcription factors involved in the expression of proteins that include receptors for dopamine and glutamate (Bibb et al., 2001; Nestler et al., 2001), as well as growth factors such as BDNF and FGF-2 (Flores & Stewart, 2000; Pu et al., 2006). These processes, together with several intracellular changes that occur, might be fundamental in accounting for the 'synaptic memory' associated with the drug and may therefore be involved in maintaining an addiction.

Perhaps not surprisingly, repeated use of drugs of abuse may affect the brain processes that are involved in executive functioning and decision making. In fact, long-term cocaine use was accompanied by reduced grey matter in the hippocampus and several cortical regions. And in addition to this, among cocaine users the normal brain electrical response to rewarding stimuli (referred to as 'an event-related potential') was disturbed (Parvaz et al., 2011). In this instance, electrophysiological responses were measured when participants had the opportunity of earning varying amounts of money for making particular responses. Ordinarily, as the monetary value increases so does the electrical response (termed 'the P300 response'), but in cocaine users the differential response to varying amounts of reward was not apparent, even though participants indicated that with greater amounts of potential winnings, the task was more interesting and exciting. Moreover, it seemed that the P300 response to reward was tied to the amount of gray matter present in the prefrontal cortex. Thus, it was suggested that the altered brain functioning in the cocaine abusers might undermine their ability to distinguish different levels of reward and to obtain pleasure, particularly in high-risk situations (e.g., in response to stressors or in the presence of cravings), leading to increased drug intake.

ADDICTION IN RELATION TO THE DOPAMINE CHANGES ASSOCIATED WITH STRESSORS

The mesolimbic DA system is not only essential in relation to natural reinforcers, such as food and social and sexual interactions, it also seems to be an essential player in recognizing and responding to threatening situations (Robinson & Berridge, 2003). Given the actions of drugs such as amphetamine and cocaine on mesolimbic DA neuronal activity, it might be particularly relevant, although a bit puzzling, that stressful events affect DA functioning in some of these same brain regions. As discussed in Chapter 4, stressors ordinarily increase the DA release at the nucleus accumbens as well as at the medial PFC. Given the similarity between biological changes elicited by aversive events and those that are rewarding, it has been suggested that the DA nucleus accumbens release might serve to enhance the *salience* of stimuli related to motivational and emotional systems, so that behaviors are influenced upon a later exposure to the cues related to stressors or rewards. In addition, this system may serve in a preparatory (or 'get ready') capacity that lets the organism know that something significant is happening or about to happen, regardless of whether the event is positive or negative, and it is equally possible that this system amplifies the effects that would otherwise be elicited in response to positive or negative stimuli, but does not determine whether something will be viewed as positive or negative.

The importance of the nucleus accumbens with respect to stressor actions has come from studies showing that aversive experiences, such as social defeat, are accompanied by the activation of an immediate early gene DeltaFosB (ΔFosB; immediately early genes are those that are rapidly activated by numerous cellular stimuli; activation of the early genes represents a transcriptional change that might be indicative of later synthesis of particular proteins in this region). For instance, chronic cocaine administration altered mRNA for ΔFosB as well as the accumulation of ΔFosB protein in the nucleus accumbens and caudate-putamen (Larson et al., 2010). Similar effects have also been observed with other substances with abuse potential (such as morphine), as well as in response to stressors, raising the possibility that ΔFosB in reward-related brain regions might be a marker for addiction or reflect the potential effects of stressors on addiction processes (Nestler, 2008). As alluded to earlier, our ultimate understanding of the neuronal processes related to addiction might hinge on determining why addiction is as persistent as it is, particularly given the assumption that many stressor actions are usually fairly brief. It is therefore particularly significant that ΔFosB was elevated for protracted periods among mice that had been repeatedly treated with any of several drugs with abuse potential.

As much as stressors and drugs such as cocaine have overlapping effects, this doesn't imply that linking these is straightforward. The activation of some genes may comprise unique aspects of the stress response (e.g., those involved in the provocation of a depressive-like state), whereas activation of other genes might govern drug addiction. Then again, there may be still other downstream factors that operate to influence both the stress and reward/addiction process. In this regard, it has been suggested that this includes a signal cascade set in motion by the activation of particular dopamine receptors (D_1 and D_2 receptors) that ultimately differentiate between the effects of stressors and reward.

EPIGENETIC FACTORS RELATED TO DOPAMINE NEURONS

Epigenetic changes stemming from some drugs have been implicated in the persistence of addictions. In this regard, for instance, two factors associated with methylation processes may be fundamental in cocaine-induced structural and behavioral plasticity: these comprise histone 3 lysine 9 (H3K9) dimethylation and the lysine dimethyltransferase G9a. Specifically, cocaine administration resulted in the repression of these substrates, both of which are ordinarily involved in the regulation of dendritic plasticity associated with elevated cocaine intake (Maze et al., 2010). Moreover, when G9a was experimentally downregulated, dendritic spine plasticity increased within the nucleus accumbens and cocaine preference was concurrently augmented. Conversely, in mice that overexpressed G9a, the behavioral impact of a stressor on drug intake was attenuated (Covington et al., 2011). As epigenetic changes can be long lasting, the effects of cocaine on these processes could be responsible for the difficulties encountered in trying to eliminate an addiction, and why stressors or cues related to cocaine might be as effective as they are in reinstating an addiction that had seemingly been kicked.

Epigenetic processes have only recently come to the foreground as a possible way by which addictions are maintained, and there has been a substantial upswing in the analyses of epigenetic factors in relation to addictions. In addition to cocaine, epigenetic factors have now been implicated in effects related to alcohol, methamphetamine, and nicotine addiction, as well as how events in early life might come to promote addiction. There has also been a surge in research that has focused on the role of epigenetic processes in determining the toxicity associated with drugs.

SENSITIZATION IN RELATION TO ADDICTION

Just as a stressor enhances the response to a later challenge, cross-sensitization effects have been demonstrated in which a stressor experience influences later responses elicited by amphetamine or cocaine (Koob, 2008). For example, stressor-related sensitization was shown with respect to mesolimbic DA activity, and was related to potentiated behavioral responses to drugs, including drug self-administration and relapse. Likewise, cocaine and amphetamine also provoked synaptic remodelling in VTA dopamine neurons that could affect the reinforcing properties of drugs, and might thus influence the propensity for its intake (Bonci & Borgland, 2009). In effect, responses to stressors and drugs such as amphetamine and cocaine involve overlapping biochemical processes and neural circuitry. As a result, experiences with stressors might enhance a later propensity for drug addiction, and conversely, drug intake may have long-term ramifications in determining subsequent stress responses.

CORTICOTROPIN HORMONE IN RELATION TO STRESS AND ADDICTION

As impressive as the findings are concerning the involvement of DA in stress and addiction processes, it is unlikely that this transmitter acts alone in the promotion of addiction. Indeed, studies in animals have indicated that 5-HT, CRH, opioid peptides, GABA, glutamate, and endocannabinoids might all contribute to the addiction process.

CRH IN RELATION TO ADDICTIONS

There has been a marked interest in determining the role of stressor-provoked CRH changes on addiction processes. As indicated in Chapters 3 and 4, CRH within the hypothalamus and at extra-hypothalamic sites (e.g., amygdala, mPFC) is markedly affected by stressors. Moreover, fear cues increased CRH mRNA expression at the central amygdala, and diffuse stimuli (that provoked general anxiety) engendered greater CRH variations at the bed nucleus of the stria terminalis. If stress responses are associated with drug addiction, then it might be expected that CRH, in some capacity, might also contribute to the addiction process. In line with this perspective, blocking CRH_1 receptors in rodents reduced the self-administration of cocaine, heroin, and alcohol and attenuated a drug relapse ordinarily provoked by stressors. Of significance, as well, CRH itself increased the activity of DA neurons in the VTA and promoted the release of DA at the nucleus accumbens, and these effects also seemed to be mediated by CRH_1 receptors. Thus, CRH might contribute to addiction directly through its responses to stressors (i.e., it might be responsible for the anxiety that occurs when individuals have not taken the desired drug for some time), and also indirectly by influencing DA-related reward processes (Koob & Le Moal, 2008).

AN OPPONENT PROCESS PERSPECTIVE

A related view, based on the 'opponent process theory' of motivation, can be incorporated with other perspectives of addiction. This view has it that consumption of a drug, even though it will elicit a state of euphoria, also provokes homeostatic changes that counteract these drug effects. Essentially, although the drug might promote a change of DA activity that promotes euphoria, a compensatory response involving CRH activation is elicited that counteracts these effects (George et al., 2012). As the drug's euphoric effects wear off with the passage of time, the opponent responses persist, and so the feelings of euphoria are replaced by dysphoria. With repeated drug use the countervailing dysphoria grows, thereby necessitating greater drug doses to promote the positive state again. Ultimately, the 'set point' responsible for the positive state is altered, so that the processes responsible for reward and those that subserve the dysphoric effects are reset. Once the set point has been lowered, it has the effect of encouraging drug intake simply to limit the negative affect that otherwise occurs more readily (Heilig & Koob, 2007). A similar view was previously offered to account for the processes involved in addiction based on the classical conditioning of compensatory responses (Siegel, 1999). This explanation was similar to that described earlier in relation to stressors (Figure 4.4), but was tied to explicit cues that had been related to drug intake. By assuming that compensatory responses were conditioned and could be instigated by situations or cues, this model offered a way to explain how a tolerance developed toward drugs, and also raised the possibility that drug overdoses could occur when addicted individuals consumed a drug in novel contexts where compensatory responses were absent or limited. Specifically, the net effect of a drug might reflect its genuine physiological action coupled with the opposing conditioned compensatory response. Thus, over time and successive drug injections, the amount of drug needed for a high increases simply because the compensatory response becomes progressively more elevated. If, on a particular occasion, the drug (at a now fairly high dose) is taken in a novel context, the classically conditioned compensatory response would not be provoked, and because of this the action to oppose the drug's physiological effect would be absent, thus leading to an overdose.

DIFFERENT DRUGS, DIFFERENT ADDICTION PROCESSES?

Drugs such as cocaine, heroin, and alcohol have some common actions and their effects are influenced by some of the same manipulations (e.g., being influenced by a CRH_1 antagonist), but the development of an addiction to different drugs might not follow the same temporal trajectory, and likely does not involve all of the same underlying processes. It follows that those treatments effective in attenuating one form of addiction might be ineffective or less effective in modifying a second type of drug addiction. For instance, DA and GABA functioning at the nucleus accumbens may play a pivotal role in the reinforcing and addictive properties of amphetamine and cocaine (e.g., Volkow et al., 2003), whereas altered DA functioning may be more germane in accounting for the dysphoria associated with abstinence as well as relapse. It also seems likely that although CRH processes may be related to alcohol dependence, its role might vary with the phase of the addictive process.

In line with the perspective that CRH plays a causal role in addiction, it was reported that a blockade of CRH_1 receptors had the effect of reducing the self-administration of cocaine, heroin, and alcohol and also attenuated relapse in response to stressors (Shaham et al., 1997; Stewart, 2000). Of significance, as well, was that CRH itself increased the activity of DA neurons in the VTA and promoted the release of DA at the nucleus accumbens, and these effects also seemed to be mediated by CRH_1 receptors (Bonci & Borgland, 2009). Essentially, through its action on DA functioning, CRH may alter reward processes, and in this way might affect addiction. In addition to these DA variations, however, CRH influences receptors present at the dorsal raphe nucleus (the site of 5-HT cell bodies), thereby increasing 5-HT release within terminal regions, including the prefrontal cortex and the dorsal hippocampus (Linthorst, 2005). Furthermore, CRH administration increased locus coeruleus NE activity (the site of NE cell bodies), whereas CRH antagonists attenuated this effect (Shimizu et al., 1994). It seems that although there is ample reason to believe that CRH–DA interactions contribute to the addiction processes, it would be premature to assume that NE and 5-HT do not contribute in this regard. For instance, social defeat in mice, which has been used to elicit depressive-like symptoms, also reliably elicited the reinstatement of cocaine preference, and as expected, the reinstatement could be prevented by disturbing the functioning of the serotonin-producing neurons of the dorsal raphe nucleus.

It will be recalled that a reinstatement of drug intake, possibly by encouraging drug craving, could be instigated by the presentation of cues that had been associated with the addictive substance, priming by administration of the abused substance, or exposure to a stressor (Koob & Le Moal, 2008). The reinstating effects of these treatments, however, might operate through distinct processes. Specifically, the reinstatement elicited by alcohol-related cues could be attenuated by naltrexone, an opioid receptor antagonist that has been used in the treatment of alcoholism, whereas this treatment did not affect a stressor-provoked reinstatement (Burattini et al., 2006). Conversely, a stressor-elicited reinstatement could be attenuated by a CRH antagonist, but this treatment did not have such an effect on cue-elicited reinstatement (Liu & Weiss, 2003). Similarly, it has been demonstrated that a relapse engendered by 'priming' injections of either cocaine or heroin involved mesolimbic DA neuronal activation, whereas a relapse provoked by a stressor seemed to involve CRH and NE neuronal activity (Stewart, 2000). It also appeared that a drug-induced reinstatement might involve a reward circuit entailing glutamine activity that is modulated by DA functioning within the prefrontal cortex and nucleus accumbens. Cue-elicited craving, in contrast, may be determined by projections between the basolateral amygdala and the nucleus accumbens, although these might also be modulated by cortical DA activity (Heilig & Koob, 2007). Evidently, even though different treatments may promote the reinstatement of addiction, they might do so through different processes or brain networks. Thus, in developing strategies to limit recurrence, it might be important to consider not only different treatments independently, but also the nature of the reinstatement stimuli that could promote recurrence.

Given the diversity of factors that might contribute to addiction, and the possibility that their involvement may vary over the course of an addiction, it won't be surprising to find that pharmacological treatments for substance abuse might also need to vary over the course of an addiction, and that it may be necessary to continue treatment even after individuals have seemingly kicked the habit. As described earlier, the biochemical processes associated with one sort of addiction might be different from another form (e.g., alcohol vs cocaine vs gambling), and likewise the influence of stress-related variables at each phase of an addiction needn't be the same. As a result, a unitary treatment for addiction hasn't been found. Perhaps there is no such thing as a unitary panacea, but it still needs to be recognized that all or most addictions might bear some common elements (e.g., the involvement of reward processes, impulsivity, stressor effects, craving) and thus treatments that affect these processes might be useful as primary or adjunctive treatments. However, if one accepts that different mechanisms are operative over the different addiction phases, it would follow that different treatments might be desirable at different times (e.g., treatments that work on cravings might be best at the later stages, whereas DA or CRH acting agents might be effective in earlier phases of the addiction).

BETTING ON GAMBLING

I think it's likely that an effective treatment will be found for most drug addictions. But what do you think the odds are that scientists will discover a cure for gambling addiction in, say, the next decade? If you say the odds are high, then I would take that bet.

Look at this from the scientist's perspective. To do the research, grant funding has to be obtained. This requires weeks or months of preparation, but only about 8–20% of grant submissions are funded, and the funds obtained are barely sufficient. Next, an ethics submission to do the research must be prepared. The evaluation of this submission may take weeks or many months, may require revisions or clarifications, and the re-evaluation might again take some time. Once ethics approval has been received, the hard part begins. This entails recruiting participants and gaining permission to test them in their natural environment (e.g., in a casino). Well, the

(Continued)

(Continued)

casino doesn't want researchers on their premises bothering the clientele, who should be gambling rather than dealing with the researcher. Besides, should a treatment strategy be found for the addiction, the casino will be the big loser. If access to the casino is eventually made possible, then the researcher is ready to round up participants. As most problem gamblers don't think that they have a problem (or don't want to be judged, or don't want to spend their time completing questionnaires when they could be spending quality time gambling), they won't participate. Eventually the study gets done, and as often as not the data aren't as clean as one would like. Editors or reviewers may (or may not) give the researchers heartache concerning the worthiness of the project. It's not uncommon for a researcher to have encountered so much frustration over the course of all of this that they decide to move on to some other topic.

On the other side are the folks who don't want the gambling to stop. These are the people who own the casinos or build the equipment that is used for gambling purposes. They too are busy doing research. But their aim is one of increasing their profits, which amounts to getting more customers, and having them bet for a longer duration and/or greater amounts. To do their experiments they don't require grants. They simply apply some of their profits to 'market research' and then pay less tax as this was a legitimate expense. In order to do their research, they don't have to receive ethics approval, and they also don't need to search for participants and then obtain their informed consent. Plenty of participants show up without even being asked to do so, but if a push is needed, their hotels can be offered as freebies, and this ought to do the trick. The outcome measures are pretty straightforward, namely how much time is spent gambling by participants, and how much money they leave behind. Ultimately, the lighting, oxygen circulation, drinks being consumed, the nature of the gaming (e.g., slots vs cards or craps), presence of hostesses, presence of restaurants, and so on, are thoroughly examined to support addictive behaviors. The biggest problem these operators have is a desire not to share the loot with their partners (no, not the mob!), namely, the government that takes a cut of the action (in the form of federal, state/province, municipal taxes; they're all in on this together, and that's not just another conspiracy theorist talking). In some places, these government guys even build casinos, operate lotteries, and provide the amenities to facilitate gambling (e.g., transportation), and even place ads for their own gambling venues. Unlike everyone else, they don't pay taxes (but if they did, it would be to themselves), and remarkably, they're not in the least bit ashamed of their behaviors.

A DIFFERENT PERSPECTIVE ON ADDICTION: EATING-RELATED PEPTIDES

OPPOSING EFFECTS OF STRESS AND EATING SYSTEMS

The biological systems that support appetitive and aversive behaviors, as described in Chapters 3 and 4, typically act in opposition to one another. The activation of stress systems suppresses those associated with feeding, whereas pharmacological treatments that reduce anxiety (e.g., benzodiazepines) have side-effects that include increased food consumption. For some individuals eating serves as a means of attenuating distress, and in emotional eaters and restrained eaters (those trying not to eat, such as dieters) stressful events are the triggers for increased eating. Among these individuals, eating might limit the negative emotions evoked by stressful experiences, essentially serving as a form of self-medication to diminish negative mood. As a matter of fact, the systems implicated in stress responses, namely DA and CRH, have also been implicated in food intake and drug abuse. Furthermore, the stimulation of CRH_2 receptors within the lateral septum had the effect of eliciting a stress (anxiety)-like response and reducing food intake (Bakshi et al., 2007). In light of these congruencies, coupled with the fact that sucrose consumption is predictive of the intake of amphetamine (DeSousa et al., 2000), it might be a good idea to examine whether eating-related systems might play some role in substance abuse.

There have been attempts to assess the brain's neurochemical changes that accompany positive and negative brain responses to stressors and food snacks, and how they interact with one another. It was shown, for instance, that providing animals with palatable snacks reduced the mRNA expression of the endogenous opioid peptide proenkephalin in the bed nucleus of the stria terminalis and the nucleus accumbens, whereas a chronic stressor increased proenkephalin mRNA in several limbic brain regions. Of particular relevance, the consumption of a palatable food prevented the stress-induced gene expression changes in these brain regions. Although it is usually thought that stressful stimuli serve to diminish the impact of positive events, these findings point to the possibility of developing treatments based on positive stimulation to attenuate the effects otherwise provoked by stressors.

SELF MEDICATING: DRUGS AND EATING AS COPING MECHANISMS

There have been some attempts to link stress responses and motivational processes to hormones associated with the regulation of energy balance that, in turn, have been tied to addiction (Abizaid et al., 2006). This linkage is supported by findings that fasting and chronic food restrictions, like traditional stressors, are associated with HPA axis activation and increased mesolimbic DA activity. In addition, chronic food restriction lowers the threshold for responding to rewarding brain stimulation, potentiates drug-seeking behaviors, engenders the behavioral sensitization to psychostimulants (e.g., cocaine and amphetamine), and increases relapse to drug self-administration. The tie between eating and drug addictions raises the possibility that hormones associated with consummatory behaviors might mediate this relation. In this regard, the hormone orexin has recently received increasing attention. Although orexin is best known for its role in arousal and increased food intake, it also affects the neural mechanisms associated with stress responses, and stressors stimulate the activity of orexin cells through CRH processes. When the receptors for orexin located at the VTA are stimulated, they provoke the release of DA at terminal sites at the prefrontal cortex and the nucleus accumbens, which then promote drug-seeking behaviors and may support addiction (Borgland et al., 2009; Winsky-Sommerer et al., 2005).

Neuropeptide Y (NPY), which was discussed earlier in relation to anxiety disorders and eating processes, has also been implicated in mediating substance use. NPY increases heroin and cocaine self-administration and facilitated a reinstatement of heroin intake in rats

(Maric et al., 2008). As well, NPY is relatively low in high alcohol-consuming rats, raising the possibility that this peptide (along with DA) is important in determining the rewarding value of alcohol. It is thought that when NPY was low and the rewarding value of alcohol was thereby diminished, rats would consume more to gain the same rewarding feelings they had previously obtained from alcohol (Koob & Le Moal, 2008). In effect, these data again indicate that a substance such as NPY, which is involved in both appetitive processes and stress responses, might be fundamentally related to voluntary drug consumption, and could thus be a suitable target for the treatment of alcoholism, or at least for the transition to alcohol dependence.

As we learned earlier, ghrelin is involved in the initiation of consummatory responses, but this hormone is a relative stranger in the stress and addiction literature despite the fact that ghrelin levels are altered in response to social stressors (Patterson et al., 2010). Of particular significance, ghrelin levels ordinarily increase in anticipation of a meal and then decline after eating. However, in stressed individuals the ghrelin levels remained elevated after food consumption (Raspopow et al., 2010). The latter findings suggest that in stressed individuals the message of 'go ahead and eat' doesn't turn off in response to eating as it normally should. In a sense, the stressor promotes continued eating, but as genuine hunger is not present, individuals will resort to feel-good foods, rather than those that fulfil their nutritional requirements. In fact, ghrelin is secreted within several brain regions and binds to receptors at sites associated with reward processes, including the VTA, where it stimulates DA cell activity (Abizaid et al., 2006). Thus, the rise of ghrelin associated with a stressor could potentiate the positive effects obtained from rewarding stimuli. Indeed, when administered directly to the VTA, ghrelin enhanced the intake of alcohol, whereas a ghrelin antagonist had the opposite effect (Davis et al., 2007; Wellman et al., 2005). At this point the available data are a bit sparse and it's premature to conclude that ghrelin and other hormones associated with eating processes underlie addictions. However, it's also premature to dismiss a role for eating circuitry in the addiction process and the data at hand are sufficiently compelling to prompt further research on this issue.

AN INTEGRATED PERSPECTIVE

In their insightful review, Koob and LeMoal (2008) offered a step-by-step perspective concerning the processes by which addiction develops. The reader is encouraged to go to this original source, but we'll recapitulate their views here in a much abbreviated form, with a few thoughts thrown in based on the work of other players in this field:

- Numerous factors influence an individual's disposition or vulnerability to addiction. These needn't be the same in all individuals with such an inclination, and they needn't be the same for all drugs. Vulnerability to addictions may be dictated by genetic factors, gender, socioeconomic class, early life stressful experiences, prenatal stressor experiences, the presence of pathologies that are comorbid with addictions (e.g., depression), disturbed self-esteem, and the age of first experience

ADDICTION **325**

of intoxication (i.e., those who experience intoxication prior to age 16 are far more likely to become addicted). Conversely, factors that promote stress resilience diminish vulnerability to drug consumption.

- Our initial consumption of a drug may occur for fun or because of peer pressure. However, for many individuals this may be a form of self-medication owing to stressful experiences. The many factors that influence the way individuals appraise or cope with stressors govern whether they will resort to self-medicating. And as well as these, those stressors that favor rumination (e.g., following a relationship break-up) will be particularly tied to drug intake.

- Drugs and stressors activate reward pathways (those involving DA) as well as those that promote CRH release, and these treatments can act synergistically, so that the euphoric effects of the drugs are enhanced. However, with continued use the sensitivity of reward circuits may be diminished so that more of the drug is needed to promote these positive effects.

- Eventually, craving for the drug evolves so that environmental stimuli (i.e., stimuli that had been paired with the drug) elicit this response. Those individuals with greater levels of impulsivity are more likely to give in to the craving despite the fact that they might be aware of the problems in doing so.

- The neurochemical changes elicited by drugs, such as alcohol, give rise to positive feelings that are countered by naturally occurring homeostatic changes in an effort to maintain a degree of balance. With continued drug use, this compensatory (anti-reward) response becomes progressively stronger. Consequently, as the euphoric effects of the drug diminish, the dysphoria becomes prevalent and more of the drug is needed to counter this.

- Among individuals who had ceased drug taking, the negative emotional state that had developed favoured the resumption of drug use. In the context of this dysphoria, the influence of cues related to the rewarding value of the drug promotes a craving that instigates the reinstatement of consumption, and this would presumably be influenced by impulsivity.

- Among individuals who had ceased drug use, stressful experiences may engender the reinstatement of drug consumption by activating the stress circuits that elicited the craving. These systems will have been sensitized previously and hence even moderate stressors are able to provoke this outcome. Essentially the 'memory circuits' associated with drug expectancy are increased, making the craving that much stronger.

- By hijacking the neural circuits that alter our reward sensitivity and expectations of the effects of drugs, addictive agents might serve to 'overwhelm' the control circuits that might ordinarily limit compulsive drug consumption (Volkow et al., 2010). In fact, long-term cocaine use has been accompanied by reduced grey matter in the orbitofrontal, dorsolateral prefrontal, and temporal cortex as well as the hippocampus, and the normal brain response to rewarding stimuli was disturbed.

- A personality trait comprising negative emotionality, especially when it occurs together with elevated sensitivity to drug-based reward, might be a perfect combination of the individual characteristics that make individuals especially vulnerable to addiction. Similarly, impaired executive functioning that leads to impaired impulsivity, especially if it is accompanied by elevated reward sensitivity, might favor drug abuse.

- Genetic factors likely exist that in one way or another might come to affect our propensity for addiction. For instance, the presence of a mutation of the Mu opioid receptor was found to predict drinking alcohol for its rewarding effects, and there have been other genes that have been associated with alcohol dependence as well. Likewise, genetic factors have been identified that are associated with nicotine dependence and cocaine addiction.

TURNING OFF BAD HABITS

Once a behavioral style is well entrenched and runs on automatic pilot, these 'habits' are hard to break even though they might indeed be harmful. These habitual behaviors are often triggered by environmental cues, such as smoking after a morning cup of coffee, or having a drink at the end of a day. It seems, however, that the brain regions involved in these habits have been identified, and that this could potentially lead the way to developing a strategy to reduce or eliminate the habits, including addiction.

Rats were trained to run down an alley, at the end of which they had to turn left or right (based on a tone they were presented with) to receive a yummy treat. Once this habit was established, rats would continue making the response even after the reward was no longer offered, and in fact, they made the response even if it led to sickness (by injecting lithium chloride that caused some nausea). What was particularly interesting was that when the cells of the infralimbic cortex (part of the prefrontal cortex) were turned off (using an optogenetic approach in which brain cells are 'tagged' with particular markers, so that light delivered by fibre-optic diode technology can alter the activity of these cells), when rats approached the choice point of the maze, they no longer turned in the direction that would result in them becoming sick. It was as if these rats switched from their automatic mode to one that was more cognitively based, essentially making judgments and decisions. It was also interesting that once these rats broke the old habit, they began turning in the other direction to receive their reward, and this behavior could also be eliminated by turning off cells in the infralimbic cortex. Surprisingly, when these cells were turned off, the rats then reverted to their initial preference (the old bad habit), indicating that the habit had not been broken, but was hiding out waiting for an opportunity to emerge, just as one sees when a previously addicted individual takes just one hit or experiences certain stressors (Smith et al., 2012).

TREATMENT FOR ADDICTIONS

Addictions aren't easy to treat, and at the moment there is no magic pill that resolves the problem. The choice of treatment will depend on the nature of the addiction and its severity, as well as a constellation of factors related to the individual, including not just their readiness for treatment, but also their belief that certain treatments will be effective. In general, there are several 'types' of treatment for addiction, including behavior therapy, 12-step programs, and residential treatments. The residential-based approach that comprises a variety of 12-step programs (e.g., Alcoholics Anonymous, Narcotics Anonymous) is particularly well known. As social support is a fundamental component of these programs, they are inherently taking advantage of one of the most important ways of coping. On the down-side, the religious aspects often associated with these approaches are a turn-off for some individuals. Another approach is to check into 'rehab' (more formally referred to as 'substance-abuse rehabilitation') that allows for individuals to be away from the cues related to their addiction, and at the same time to engage in therapy that facilitates the active elimination

TABLE 10.2 The Transtheoretical Model of Behavioral Change (TTM)

1. *Precontemplation* – During this initial stage, participants might not yet have realized or even contemplated that they have a problem. At this stage individuals are not ready to change. They need to think about the benefits of change, and the hazards of not changing.
2. *Contemplation* – At this stage there is acknowledgement that the individual has issues, but they are still assessing whether the addiction is problematic.
3. *Determination/Preparation* – Individuals complete a plan to determine how they will deal with their addiction, bearing in mind those situations that might encourage relapse.
4. *Action* – Individuals decide on and manage approaches to deal with their addiction. To this end, multiple resources can be used, including professional counseling, support from groups, or self-help. In this stage individuals are taught techniques to keep commitments (e.g., substituting activities related to the unhealthy behavior with those that are positive) and rewarding themselves for appropriate steps toward avoidance of people and situations that tempt them to engage in behaviors that are not healthy.
5. *Maintenance* – With diligence, time, and despite bouts of craving, behavioral change is realized and the individual digs in to stabilize their forward movement.
6. *Relapse* – Although not inevitable, relapse is fairly common. Interestingly, if relapse is dealt with appropriately it can have positive effects in that it can actually facilitate later cravings/temptations as individuals will have learned what not to do.
7. *Termination* – Once individuals have maintained the abstinence for a sufficient period, they can move on and continue with their life undisturbed.

of that addiction. Bear in mind that rehab will only be effective if the individual accepts that they have a problem, wants to get better, and believes that they can beat the problem. I'm reminded of Amy Winehouse singing 'They tried to make me go to rehab, but I said no, no, no'. For individuals who are at this point, rehab would not be useful.

Behavioral methods of dealing with addictions involve variations of CBT. One of these, the Transtheoretical Model of Behavior Change (TTM), also referred to as SMART (Self Management and Recovery Training), is particularly appealing to some individuals (see Table 10.2). This program considers an individual's readiness to act in order to gain new healthier behaviors, and provides strategies (or stages of a processes) that guide individuals through a series of stages from Action to Maintenance. As the individual moves through these stages it is understood that people are just people, accidents happen, and they sometimes fail in their efforts to abstain – and that the right thing to do is to continue with the program. Crucially, it is necessary to go through each stage, and as much as one would like to be able to just jump from step 1 to 7, this program is a systematic one that follows these steps closely.

This approach, not surprisingly perhaps, has not been universally accepted. In this regard, a review of many studies concluded that a stage-based intervention strategy to eliminate smoking and eating disorders was not any more effective than a non-stage-based approach. Equally predictable has been the vociferous defense of this approach by those who have used the method in clinical practice and researchers who have found positive results. The last word on this topic hasn't been uttered yet. However, once again it might be the case that it's a very effective method for treating some individuals, but not others. The approach might need to be tailored for each individual, including making a decision as to whether it is appropriate for any given person.

In addition to these programs, drug therapies may be used as adjunctive treatments. For instance, baclofen (Kemstro, Lioresal), a GABA$_B$ agonist, has been used to reduce drug cravings, and hence diminish relapse among those using amphetamines and alcohol. In fact, patients treated with baclofen may report a general indifference with respect to the drug to which they are addicted, possibly indicating that baclofen is affecting a reward/craving system (Kenna et al., 2007). Thus, this agent could be used effectively if combined with another treatment (e.g., one that targets a specific type of addictive agent). In addition, there are several other drugs, such as dilaudid, that reduce drug cravings. Similarly, methadone or buprenorphine serve as an opioid replacement therapy for the treatment of opioid dependence, benzodiazepines have been used to limit the delirium tremens associated with alcohol withdrawal, and antiepileptic medications (gabapentin, valproate) have been used to deal with barbiturate or benzodiazepine withdrawal. As well here, the combination of drugs that affect different components of certain systems, such as naltrexone and buprenorphine, may have positive effects in attenuating cocaine addiction. Remarkably, it has also been reported that opioid drugs bind to receptors within the immune system (TLR4 receptors), and it is thought that these receptors serve as amplifiers for addiction. In fact, naloxone, which can reverse the effects of opioids and shut down the need to consume these agents, might have its effects, in part, by antagonizing TLR4. In effect, these findings are consistent with the perspective that brain immune signaling plays a role in drug reward and addiction.

Another approach that has been used is that of having individuals take certain medication that when combined with the addictive substance would cause sickness. Of course, this means that the individual would have to remember to take the drug (which they might choose not to do on a regular basis, thus 'allowing' them a holiday to resume their addiction). Furthermore, in some instances patients discovered that when they took this treatment, a small amount of the problem drug (e.g., alcohol) would now give them the same high they had obtained previously following high doses. Thus, the treatment actually facilitated the addiction by reducing the amount of illicit drug required, and thereby the amount of money spent to obtain the expected outcome.

CONCLUSION

Addiction of any sort likely involves multiple processes, several of which no doubt interact to promote specific outcomes. There are likely common features to all or most forms of addiction, and it might be possible to decipher the underlying genetic contributors, or those associated with specific addictions. This would almost certainly reveal a complex heterogeneous process involving reward mechanisms, impulsivity, and multiple types of stressor responses, as well as irrational thinking. This might be complicated further by the fact that addiction goes through different phases, each of which might involve distinguishable processes. Thus the symptoms and mechanisms evident early on in an addiction may differ from those in a later phase, and then differ once again during an addiction reinstatement. Nevertheless, if addictions are promoted by stressful experiences, aberrant stressor appraisal processes, and the use of ineffective coping strategies, then a first line of defense against addiction, or as an adjunct to pharmacotherapy, might entail the use of treatments that focus on training individuals to use effective appraisal and coping methods to deal with stressors.

SUMMARY

- Multiple forms of addiction exist, some of which involve drugs, but others which do not.
- The mechanisms involved in various drug addictions, as well as other forms of addiction such as gambling, involve different processes, although they may share several common denominators.
- For some individuals, although certainly not all, stressful experiences may contribute to the development of an addiction, and in most instances that addiction can be aggravated by stressful experiences.
- Research to uncover the biological processes of addictions have focused on those involved in reward processes (dopamine), stress responses (CRH), and impulsivity (serotonin), but increasingly there has been a consideration that the growth factors involved in neuronal plasticity and learning/habits might also contribute to addictions.
- Behavioral therapies for addictions have met with limited success, and pharmacological treatments likewise have had the same outcome; hopefully this will change.

11 TRANSMISSION OF TRAUMA ACROSS GENERATIONS

A BRIEF WALK THROUGH A COLLECTIVE, HISTORICAL TRAUMA

Prior to colonization by Europeans, Aboriginal populations throughout North America had established their own political and economic institutions, and familial and educational practices were well-entrenched, as were religious beliefs and traditions. Contact between the Aboriginal peoples and Europeans occurred in the 16th century, based largely on interactions founded on the fur trade and missionary activities to save the heathen souls of the 'savages' through religious conversion (Fisher, 1977). This early period of contact was also marked by community massacres and warfare, as well as epidemics stemming from the introduction of new diseases.

Within Canada, the signing of the Royal Proclamation in 1763 resulted in the creation of Indian reserve lands and land rights (e.g., hunting and fishing rights). By the early 1800s these provisions were no longer comfortable for the European expansion, and the government gradually diminished the rights of Aboriginal peoples (Armitage, 1995; Royal Commission on Aboriginal Peoples, 1996). The period that followed involved unrelenting government and church interventions in the lives of Aboriginal peoples, that largely stemmed from the racist and assimilationist policies established by the 1867 Indian Act. Imagine the hubris involved in Europeans creating an Act that dictated who was an Indian and who was not (i.e., Status Indians), and one that forbade cultural activities and ceremonies (Armitage, 1995). One of the most egregious actions undertaken was that conducted from the mid-1800s until 1996 in which Aboriginal children were forcibly removed from their families with the goal of assimilating them into a single non-Aboriginal Christian community. Health suffered among those attending these schools (Kelm, 1998), owing to a combination of factors, including neglect and abuse, strict discipline, the loss of identity and cultural expressions, and feelings of shame and isolation, as well as marked dissociation from their families.

As bad as the Residential School experiences may have been, these events were not unique, but reflected one of many assaults against Aboriginal peoples in North America (and elsewhere), and these occurred over many generations. It has been proposed that 'Historical Trauma' or 'soul wound', which is described as cumulative emotional and psychological wounding over the lifespan and across generations, contributes profoundly to current well-being of Aboriginal peoples (Brave Heart, 2003; Duran, Duran, Brave Heart, & Yellow Horse-Davis, 1998). For them, these historical traumas act as daily reminders of the numerous indignities committed against their group, and these reminders frequently come in the form of discrimination (Evans-Campbell, 2008; Whitbeck, Adams, Hoyt, & Chen, 2004). Collectively experienced traumas have unique social and psychological trajectories, and their consequences may be aligned with collective responses and interpretations at the family and community levels that result in changes in social dynamics, processes, structures, and functioning (Bombay, Matheson, & Anisman, 2009). Community-level changes in the aftermath of mass trauma have included erosion of basic trust, silence, deterioration in social norms, morals and values, and poor leadership (Commission for Historical Clarification, 1999).

Of course, it isn't just Aboriginal groups in Canada and the US that have experienced historical, collective trauma. The same can be said of Aboriginal groups in Australia and New Zealand, as well as large parts of Africa where Black people had been, and in some places continue to be, denied basic human rights. The same holds for religious groups, such as the Baha'i, and the Jews haven't been strangers to repeated discrimination and aggression. For these groups, the latest assaults on their lives and dignity reflect just one chapter of a very long book.

Often, the effects of stressors, even if they are traumatic, are not persistent, and we generally won't dwell on them continuously. However, stressful experiences can also have powerful, enduring effects, as can stressors experienced during childhood. But more than this, traumatic events can have profound effects on ensuing generations (Yehuda & Bierer, 2008). The generational interchange from parent to child and then to their children, often termed 'intergenerational, transgenerational or multigenerational effects', like the immediate outcomes associated with a stressor, depend on a variety of psychosocial and socioeconomic factors. Although studies of intergenerational trauma effects typically consider the impact of events that are especially severe (e.g., genocide, famine, earthquake, tsunami), in some instances, stressors that are usually considered to be 'non-traumatic', such as financial problems or work-related distress, especially if these occur on a chronic basis, can have fairly disturbing consequences. Moreover, when combined with traumatic stressors, non-traumatic events can have additive or synergistic effects on health outcomes. Thus, in discussing the intergenerational transmission of health and social outcomes it would be negligent not to consider both traumatic and apparently non-traumatic stressors, and to assess their effects from varied perspectives.

As in each of the preceding chapters, there are several issues that the reader might focus on, and there are several take-home messages that this chapter offers:

- trauma may have long-lasting effects on a society or culture, but to a significant extent the long-term ramifications are dependent on what occurred after the traumatic event, including the support resources available and the individual's ability to maintain their group identity. Trauma effects are especially notable when survivors and the children of survivors are raised under toxic conditions stemming from poverty or even low socioeconomic levels;
- traumatic events, like mental illness, have been associated with poor parenting. Intergenerational transmission of trauma could reflect the imitation of poor parenting styles by the children who themselves received poor parenting from a traumatized parent;
- the effects of trauma are particularly poignant if the initial stressor was experience in childhood, and intergenerational effects are similarly evident when trauma was experienced during childhood. Added to this, trauma effects are also apparent when the initial stressor was experienced prenatally (i.e., the mother experienced the trauma, resulting in stress-provoked biological changes affecting the fetus);
- stressful experiences, especially when they occured during childhood, can lead to variations in a gene's expression, but without affecting the DNA sequence associated with that gene. Thus, behavioral phenotypes can be manifested in the individual who directly experienced the trauma, but more than this, this gene in its altered form can be passed across generations, thereby affecting subsequent generations;
- the impact of trauma should be viewed in the context of collective and historical trauma that can either promote vulnerability or resilience to further adverse experiences.

A VOYAGE ACROSS GENERATIONS

There are multiple routes, both direct and indirect, by which traumatic events can have their intergenerational consequences. It won't be surprising to be told that the trauma-elicited behaviors of a parent might directly affect their children, thereby influencing their behaviors. These effects can be still more dramatic when these parent–child interactions are superimposed on a negative environment (e.g., poverty), which might also be secondary to the trauma an individual has endured (e.g., witnessed the financial and social consequences of many recent or ongoing civil and international wars). Having experienced poor parenting themselves, the parenting skills of the next generation of children might likewise be affected, which in turn may then influence the emotional stability and behaviors of their children.

In addition to the effects brought about through disturbed parenting, stress-related biological changes that occurred in the mother during pregnancy might also affect an offspring's ability to contend with life events. It might similarly be the case that certain genetic characteristics in the offspring were silenced (epigenetic changes) owing to prenatal or early postnatal trauma, and these genetic characteristics can be passed from one generation to the next. Finally, in addition to socio-developmental and biological processes, cultural factors and collective and historical memories might play a significant role in promoting the inter-generation effects of traumatic events. In this chapter, we'll be covering each of these topics, and so the journey we'll be taking will cover a very broad range, from the situations in which stressors affect individuals and those that affect whole societies, and they might have effects across generations.

INTERGENERATIONAL EFFECTS OF TRAUMA

In her discussion related to genocide and its impact across generations, Marianne Hirsch (2001) discusses what is referred to as 'postmemory' or a 'reclaiming of memory'. She views postmemory as the relationship of children of *'survivors of cultural or collective trauma to the experiences of their parents, experiences that they "remember" only as the narratives and images with which they grew up, but that are so powerful, so monumental, as to constitute memories in their own right'* (p. 16). Over generations the consequences of trauma experiences can wane, but they might not always be far from the surface.

Let's begin our analyses of trauma consequences with a view of two (not so) hypothetical groups who were the victims of attempted genocide. After the trauma, one of these groups receives considerable intra- and intergroup support, so that they have the potential to rebuild their lives, and they and their children have the opportunity to achieve remarkable goals. Following the trauma, members of the second group, by contrast, live in the horrid conditions that are the aftermath of the trauma, have lost their ingroup social support system, receive very little intergroup support, have been robbed of their cultural values, and possess limited opportunities for education and growth (no matter which yardstick is used to define growth). Both groups might share some of the biological consequences (such as the epigenetic changes) associated with the original trauma, and hence both may be similarly affected by that trauma, at least initially. Likewise, other things being equal, cultural memories will affect both groups and could potentially affect their identity as well as their potential for illness. (You can bet your socks that the impact on a variety of health and social outcomes will be more dramatic in the latter instance.)

When we consider the influence of trauma, both within and across generations, it's clearly vital to consider aspects of the trauma itself as well as the events that constitute the posttrauma period. The influences of traumatic experiences on intergenerational behavioral processes also ought to be viewed within the context of other cultural and historical traumas. Among other things, it is important to know whether the trauma was unique to an individual or small group, or whether it was a large group or collective that was affected. Moreover, it is essential to consider the individual in the context of other members of their group (e.g., other survivors or descendents of survivors, including their broad social community that had not directly experienced the trauma), as well as the responses of outgroup members, comprising those of other religions or cultures for whom the trauma was not particularly germane. As we saw earlier, social identity and social support (and unsupportive interactions) may have crucial ramifications for dealing with stressors and in promoting personal resilience particularly, as social identity in the face of trauma may encourage a collective resilience that favors survival and recovery (Haslam et al., 2012). The impact of traumatic events might never be entirely eliminated as can be deduced from Marion Hirsch's comment. However, their adverse effects across generations might be diminished by allowing or encouraging the development of effective social networks, support from ingroup members, and importantly, by allowing individuals to develop appropriate social identities.

HAVING TO SAY I'M SORRY (AND MEANING IT) VS SAYING IT NEVER HAPPENED

There is substantial information concerning the impact of apologies from governments towards groups of individuals that had been targeted by government policies (recent examples are the apologies by the Canadian and Australian governments to their Aboriginal populations). There have also been attempts at reconciliation (as in South Africa) and expressions of wrong-doing from governments to the descendants of people no longer in that country (e.g., the attitude of the government of Germany towards descendants of the Shoah). These apologies, if sincere, could potentially allow all parties to move forward, even if the misdeeds are never forgotten.

In light of the collective memory and the postmemories among those whose forebears suffered the abuses of others, it is no wonder that the reaction toward Holocaust deniers is as great as it is. Make no mistake, however, these deniers have their following, and if the lie is repeated often enough it can become a truth, and over generations it will be as if it never happened. But it did! How many readers know about the Armenian genocide conducted by the Turks? It seems that successive Turkish governments, including the current one, have been very successful in their denial, even though some countries (e.g., France) have made a point of recognizing this genocide. A quote by Winston Churchill seems particularly appropriate here, given the denials that have so often been voiced by some individuals or groups: 'A lie gets halfway around the world before the truth has a chance to get its pants on.'

PSYCHOLOGICAL AND PHYSICAL SEQUELAE OF TRAUMA IN RELATION TO THE SHOAH

The transmission of trauma effects (both within individuals and within communities) has been evaluated in several specific populations. Data collected from Jewish survivors of the Shoah (this term, which means 'calamity', is often preferred to the more common term 'Holocaust' to distinguish it from other historical genocides) and their families have implicated biological changes, as well as the influence of parenting and attachment styles, as being fundamental in mediating the intergenerational effects of trauma. In fact, however, it is no simple matter to make sweeping statements regarding the factors that promote the effects of this trauma. There exists a marked diversity of experiences among Holocaust survivors, as well as very great differences in their general behaviors (e.g., talking about their experiences vs the 'conspiracy of silence' that was frequently the norm). Moreover, survivors display a wide range of psychological symptoms, and considerable variability regarding the emotional stress responses that emerged, such as survivor guilt, denial, agitation, mistrust, intrusive thoughts, nightmares, disorganized reasoning, difficulty in expressing emotions, anxiety, and depression, although in most instances these had been at subsyndromal levels

(Bar-On & Rottgardt, 1998). Nevertheless, as a group, the children of Holocaust survivors were more vulnerable to the negative effects of stressors and more likely than controls to develop PTSD and depression (or subthreshold symptoms) when faced with traumatic events (Yehuda & Biere, 2009). Predictably, given the frequency of collective trauma experiences across cultures, the intergenerational effects of trauma have not been unique to the children of Shoah survivors, having been documented in Japanese Americans subjected to internment during World War II, and survivors of the Armenian genocide conducted by Turks, as well as Aboriginal groups that had been torn from their families and placed in 'Indian Residential Schools' as an exercise in forced assimilation (Bombay et al., 2009). Then there's Syria, Somalia, Darfur, Bosnia, the mass killing of Tutsis by Hutus in Rwanda in 1994, and the deaths of Hutus at the hands of Tutsis in Burundai after 1973, whose intergenerational effects remain to be assessed.

Although considerable data were collected regarding the intergenerational consequences of the trauma experienced by second- and third-generation survivors of the Shoah, for a variety of reasons much less information is available regarding the intergenerational effects of trauma in other groups. The experience of survivors across different collective traumas cannot, of course, be compared to one another given the differences in the magnitude, ferocity, and duration of the events, as well as the hatreds and motivations that gave rise to these. Nevertheless, information can be drawn to understand how these experiences might come to have their intergenerational consequences.

THE CASE OF ABORIGINAL PEOPLES IN CANADA

Let's have a look at a situation that is (physically) close to home to see how an intergenerational trauma plays out and the sorts of processes that might contribute in this regard. Aboriginal people within Canada have a long history of being mistreated, as they have in other countries that were colonized by Euro-Caucasians. Among other things, following the invasion by Europeans, First Nations people were frequently kept on reserves where they experienced poverty, a poor education, and exceptionally poor health, as well as encountering corruption and unsupportive interactions with the government as well as non-Aboriginal people. To be sure, there were those who were exceptionally supportive of Aboriginal issues. However, as intimated in Chapter 2, even in the context of much positive support, the presence of unsupportive relations may have devastating effects, especially on those who are already distressed.

A particular era of poor treatment of Aboriginals was precipitated by inept attempts at assimilating them into Western ways ('taking the Indian out of the Indian') by forcibly removing children from their parents and keeping them in Indian Residential Schools (IRSs) where they experienced harsh and denigrating conditions, perpetrated not only by the administration of these IRSs, but also by other residents (inmates). The impact on Aboriginal peoples did not end when they left the IRSs, as the communities they had been taken from were often in disarray or entirely gone, families had been broken up, and poverty was rampant. Thus, the travails of IRS residents continued for an extended period (see the box overleaf).

WHAT WERE THEY THINKING?

The policy of forcing Aboriginal children to attend IRSs from the mid-1800s to 1996, as well as the 'Sixties Scoop' (the 1960s to 1990s) in which large numbers of children were forcibly taken from their homes, often placing them in distant non-Aboriginal families or in IRSs, were allegedly initiated to save and protect Aboriginal people. However, health declined and mortality rates increased among those attending these schools. Individuals experienced a regimen of strict discipline, and suffered neglect and abuse, a loss of identity, and feelings of shame and isolation. Cultural expressions through language, dress, food, or beliefs were suppressed, and children were taught to be ashamed of their culture. When students subsequently returned home they were often seen as or felt like strangers to their families and communities, and frequently displayed inappropriate behaviors, such as the abusive behaviors modeled after those who had punished them at the IRSs. Remarkably, although the alleged purpose of the schools was to 'educate' Aboriginal children, they frequently attained low educational levels, and the practical skills they acquired were typically applicable to menial jobs only.

This large-scale removal of Aboriginal children from their homes also resulted in deeply painful effects on the parents and extended families left behind. Familial bonds were disrupted and often irreparably broken, and parents were frequently beset by feelings of powerlessness, guilt, and shame, for not saving their children from being taken, and there were often feelings of no longer being needed by their children.

Aboriginal peoples in Canada have gone through many traumas since their first contact with Euro-Caucasians, including an 80% decline in their population by the early 1800s. The Residential Schools and the Sixties Scoop are recent reminders of a series of traumas. The impact of the IRSs not only affected those who were directly exposed to the trauma, having affected individual communities, and Aboriginal peoples, in general. It has also become a reminder of the relationship that existed between the government of Canada and its indigenous peoples.

The First Nations Regional Longitudinal Health Survey, which was the most extensive analysis of the impact of IRSs, revealed that Aboriginal youth who had one or both parents attend an IRS (this amounted to one-third of the Aboriginal population) experienced a relatively poor quality of parenting. In fact, even if it was their grandparents that had attended Residential Schools, the majority of adults in this survey indicated that they had experienced poor parenting. It was subsequently reported that those First Nations adults who had a parent who attended a Residential School experienced higher levels of depressive symptoms, more frequent thoughts of suicide, more frequent adverse childhood experiences and adult traumas, and also perceived higher levels of discrimination relative to First Nations adults whose parents did not attend Residential Schools (Bombay et al., 2010). Similar effects were apparent even in third generation survivors of the IRSs, and the magnitude of the transmitted effects was greater for those who had both a parent and grandparent attend IRSs than among those who had either a parent or a grandparent in this circumstance (the IRSs were in existence for a long time, and so several generations of a single family were sometimes victimized).

It is not uncommon for parents who experienced certain traumatic events to develop psychological problems that culminate in their living at or below the poverty line, and even in the absence of such psychological disturbances, trauma events often give rise to poverty. The children of survivors, who would also be living in these same poor conditions, might therefore also be at an increased risk of encountering stressful experiences. For the IRS survivors the conditions experienced in the period following their incarceration were fairly grim, and consequently a period of recuperation and healing was not possible. These effects were not restricted to those Aboriginal people who were living on reserves, but were also apparent among individuals who were living in urban centers, indicating that the second-generation consequences of IRSs were not simply a result of living on reserves.

There is little doubt that the postmemory concerning IRSs among the children of survivors is ever-present and likely influences many of the behaviors that are witnessed today. This includes not only behaviors of a dysfunctional nature in some individuals, but also those (e.g., organized protests) that are meant to reclaim not just lands, but to reclaim their identity as well, and in so doing they would no longer be 'victims'.

MONEY MAKES THE WORLD GO ROUND

There was an article in *Maclean*'s magazine (March 11, 2013) that focused on the health problems associated with living in poverty. This article, in part, was based on the findings of a study entitled 'Code Red' and initially reported by journalist Steve Buist and epidemiologist Neil Johnston who evaluated 135 communities within Hamilton, Ontario. The article makes many very interesting points, but what comes out most clearly is a quote in that article: 'Once they know where a baby is born, they can predict the outcome of the child.' Of course, this is a bit over the top and the correlation between the two certainly isn't perfect. Still, the data were telling. Those in the lowest (20%) economic rung were six times more likely to be teenage mothers and school drop-outs, and prenatal care was sought far less often than among those in high economic brackets. The children born in poverty were also likely to die 10–15 years before those of the wealthiest 20%, and the experiences between birth and death was no picnic either. A similar study conducted in Sudbury, Ontario, indicated that relative to the least deprived individuals, among the most deprived groups infant death was 139% higher, obesity was 102% higher, emergency department visits 71% higher, and emergency visits owing to mental health issues was elevated by fully 341%, while hospital visits owing to self-harm was increased by 205%.

Those numbers resulted in some pretty daunting conclusions about the link between economics and health, regardless of how and why the levels of poverty came to be what they were. Now, take this information and add one additional variable: What if these individuals aren't average citizens but survivors, and the children and grandchildren of survivors of those who experienced IRSs? How much more would their health be jeopardized?

You doubtless know that old adage about 'Money doesn't make you happy'. I think that's something rich people say to appease the poor, and what poor people say to rationalize their circumstances.

IMPACT OF TRAUMA ON LATER RESPONSES TO CHALLENGES

PERSISTENT NEGATIVE INFLUENCE OF EARLY LIFE STRESSORS

There are a number of factors that feed into the way that traumatic experiences, especially those encountered in childhood, can affect later behaviors. Just as depressive illness has been associated with stress generation (stress proliferation), adverse childhood experiences have been associated with an increased risk of encountering subsequent trauma in adulthood. For instance, adults who had experienced childhood abuse were at an increased risk of re-victimization experiences, including rape or being the victim of domestic violence. In addition, as we saw earlier, stressful events may result in the sensitization of biological systems so that the effects of later trauma experiences are amplified and sustained, making pathological outcomes more likely. In fact, among children exposed to family violence and discord, but who had normative levels of anxiety, the depiction of angry faces (but not sad faces) was accompanied by increased neuronal activity in the amygdala and anterior cortex, likely reflecting threat responses (McCrory et al., 2011). These investigators made the point that although an elevated reactivity to such threat cues might be a perfectly normal response, the extent of the excitation might represent a neurobiological marker indicative of an elevated risk for pathology. In line with the literature regarding re-victimization (re-traumatization), those First Nations adults who reported high levels of adverse childhood experiences also reported experiencing greater exposure to a variety of traumatic experiences in adulthood, and this outcome was particularly prominent among those individuals who had a parent who forcibly attended an IRS (Bombay et al., 2009).

In addition to the re-traumatization, childhood abuse may disrupt school performance, decision-making processes, and the ability to form and maintain close relationships (Pearlin et al., 2005). These disturbances might then directly and indirectly increase the risk of stressor experiences in adulthood. Therefore, in assessing the influence of childhood stressors in relation to the subsequent emergence of pathology, analyses should not be limited to particular severe stressors, but instead ought to examine the cumulative effects of multiple stressors that might be endured. Indeed, individuals who reported a large number of experiences tied to early life abuse (i.e., those related to childhood maltreatment and disturbed home environments) were at a particularly high risk for adult psychopathology, such as depression, suicidality, and drug abuse, as well as physical illnesses that are often comorbid with depression, including diabetes (Dube et al., 2003), which is particularly prominent among Aboriginals.

As indicated repeatedly, stressful encounters (e.g., childhood abuse) often don't occur in isolation from other trauma experiences, and hence the way things play out is determined by the constellation of adverse events that might be experienced. In this regard, the point has been made that victimization is not simply an 'event', but is a 'condition' that entails ongoing distress (e.g., Pratchett & Yehuda, 2011). The same holds true for the experiences of IRS survivors. The residential schools attended by Aboriginals represented just one phase of a 'condition' that frequently extended from childhood through to adulthood.

PASSAGE OF POOR APPRAISAL AND COPING METHODS WITHIN A GENERATION

Traumatic early life experiences might disturb the way individuals appraise the world around them as well as the way they interpret stressful experiences, their perceived ability to contend with these stressors, and ultimately the coping strategies that they are likely to use. As a result, individuals who had experienced trauma may not only be at risk for further stressor encounters (stress generation), but they may also be less well prepared to handle these events when they do occur. In fact, stressor experiences might be accompanied by warped internal attributions (i.e., self-blaming and self-criticizing) and other cognitive distortions, including those associated with safety or a preoccupation with danger, as well as issues related to having control over their own lives. Furthermore, a link exists between adverse childhood experiences and the development of negative cognitive styles that might be carried into adulthood. These negative appraisals might lead to exaggerated perceptions of future harm, and maintaining this sense of threat and unpredictability about the future may contribute to the development of anxiety, depression, and PTSD following a subsequent traumatic experience.

Appraisal and coping typically go hand-in-hand and individuals, especially children, who have experienced traumatic events tend to use inappropriate coping strategies to deal with ongoing challenges. These include the use of avoidant coping or strategies characterized by risk-taking, confrontation, and the release of frustration. In this regard, children and adolescents who experienced community violence, sexual abuse, or maltreatment were particularly likely to use emotion-focused and avoidant coping strategies, rather than methods that might eliminate the stressor (Bal et al., 2003). As described in Chapter 2, the coping strategies available to children are typically not well formed, and their resources to deal with stressors are limited, thus it is to be expected that traumatic events will have profound repercussions. Chronic or repeated childhood adversities may also give rise to an inferential process wherein children attempt to understand why abusive or neglectful experiences are happening to them. These children might internalize the belief that these adverse events are stable, and attributable to aspects of themselves, and indeed perhaps childhood traumas have the effect of stunting an individual's coping development and their ability to engage new and more effective strategies; these effects can then extend into adulthood so that individuals might be more apt to use ineffective coping methods.

CONSPIRACY OF SILENCE

The children of survivors of the Shoah have recounted that some parents recapitulated their experiences over and over. Conversely, many Shoah survivors were reported to have withheld any communication about their experiences, an intergenerational communication pattern that was

(Continued)

(Continued)

termed the 'conspiracy of silence' (Danieli, 1998). The messages embedded within this silence were very clear, and perhaps not surprisingly, children who experienced this silence generally seemed to be more vulnerable to an intergenerational transmission of trauma (Wiseman et al., 2002). This same profile has also been apparent in our research (with Amy Bombay and Kim Matheson) with the Aboriginal survivors of IRSs. Children often grew up in families in which there was no outright communication regarding the parents' trauma, but the trauma was still 'silently present in the home'.

In her remarkably powerful book, *After Such Knowledge*, Eva Hoffman, states 'A few survivors were determined never to talk about what they had lived through; but others wanted to give expression to the horror, or perhaps couldn't help doing so ... to their immediate intimates, to spouses and siblings, and yes, to their children. There, they spoke in the language of family – a form of expression that is both more direct and more ruthless than social and public speech ...'.

TRANSMISSION OF TRAUMA FROM PARENT TO CHILD: THE CASE OF POOR PARENTING

As we've seen, poor parenting can have marked and long-lasting repercussions on children, and may affect the way they subsequently treat their own offspring. Conversely, to a certain extent, good parenting begets future good parenting. As such, it is predictable that parental mental health problems (including drug addiction) can have enormous repercussions on a range of parenting-related issues, including disengagement and disorganization, hostility, coercion, and low positive parent–child interactions (Hammen et al., 2004). Likewise, high levels of parental stress and trauma, including stressors encountered in childhood, were related to subsequent poor parenting efficacy, as well as abusive or neglectful behaviors in relation to their own children. In fact, it has been estimated that child maltreatment occurs in about 30% of children whose parents had themselves been maltreated (Kaufman & Zigler, 1987). As adverse childhood experiences often occur in clusters, the long-term effects of childhood abuse might stem from a combination of several adverse childhood experiences. Indeed, cumulative trauma was predictive of subsequent parental abuse potential, including psychological and physical aggression, even after taking into consideration (controlling for) demographic variables and the presence of mental health disorders.

There are several routes by which poor parenting could affect offspring, including their own subsequent parenting styles. Poor parenting (as well as childhood abuse and neglect) was associated with the development of depressive symptoms, PTSD, and interpersonal difficulties, and these relations were largely mediated by negative perceptions of both the self and the future (Browne & Winkelman, 2007). In addition, traumatic experiences may influence parental coping processes, which might promote poor coping methods in their children, thereby rendering these children less well equipped to deal with the stressors that they encounter. A particularly interesting study addressed the question of whether genetic factors and parenting interacted to predict a later parenting style in offspring (Beaver & Belsky,

2012). Focusing on the contribution of four genes that were involved with monoamine functioning, these investigators found that with increasing stress, parenting quality declined, provided that a particular polymorphism was present in each of the four genes (and to a lesser extent when polymorphism was present in three of these genes). Essentially, stress doesn't always lead to poor parenting and other adverse outcomes, but does so in an interactive way with genetic factors. Evidently, genetic factors and the adverse experiences of one generation are the (im)perfect ingredients that might result in the recapitulation of negative events in the next generation.

EARLY LIFE STRESSORS INFLUENCE BIOLOGICAL PROCESSES

A parent who has encountered trauma can, through their behaviors and particularly through their child-rearing practices, affect the psychological and cognitive development of their children, ultimately affecting these children throughout their lives. It seems that the parental behaviors can also affect biological processes in the child that might influence their ability to cope with further stressors, thereby affecting their psychological development as well as their vulnerability to several physical illnesses. In the section that follows we will consider the influence of psychological stressors (particularly those related to poor parenting), as well as neurogenic and immunological insults on later psychological and physical health.

LIKE MOM SAID, 'STRESS MAKES YOU OLD BEFORE YOUR YEARS'

The DNA sequences found at the tips of chromosomes, which serve to prevent the DNA from unraveling, are referred to as 'telomeres'. With each replication of the DNA strand these telomeres become shorter, and at a certain point the cell will not be able to replicate. This is part of our aging process. Interestingly, it seems that stressful events also have the effect of reducing the length of these telomeres, effectively causing the equivalent of the aging process. In this regard, stressful experiences in children, including maternal violence, verbal or physical assaults, or even witnessing domestic disputes, resulted in the shortening of telomere length. In a sense these findings also tell us about the cumulative effects attributable to stressors, much like rings on a tree can inform us about its age and past weather conditions. How the telomere length comes to be shortened isn't known (although the activation of inflammatory processes might contribute), nor is it known whether the telomere changes are in any way responsible for the psychological disturbances associated with early life distress. Nevertheless, these data speak to the profound effects that early life abuse can have on individuals that could potentially influence their life span.

We learned earlier that stressors experienced during early life or during the juvenile period could have repercussions on several hormonal and behavioral processes. In the main, these studies indicated that these early stressors (including maternal neglect) influenced developmental trajectories that culminated in impairments in the ability to deal with stressors, resulting in more frequent adult anxiety, depression, and chronic fatigue syndrome, as well as vascular disease, autoimmune disorders, and even stroke. Essentially, stressors encountered during these times provoked the reprogramming of various types of biological signals, such as those related to hormonal and immunological processes that in turn might have influenced behavioral and cognitive functioning (e.g., high threat vigilance, a mistrust of others, disrupted social relations, disturbed self-regulation, and unhealthy choices). These emotional and behavioral changes themselves might have further fueled disturbed hormonal and immunological functioning that might eventually culminate in pathology.

The behavioral consequences of early life stressors in animals, as discussed in Chapters 1 and 3, are accompanied by altered HPA activity and CRH levels in numerous cortical and limbic brain regions. These effects may stretch into adulthood, and are particularly notable upon later stressor experiences. The early life stressors that elicit these protracted effects in animals were not restricted to those that involve maternal–pup interactions, as similar long-term outcomes were observed in rodents in response to systemic insults, such as bacterial infection during the first few days after birth (Shanks et al., 2000). Although particular attention has been devoted to the analysis of early life stressors on HPA hormones, it is clear that such events affect multiple processes. For instance, maternal separation in rodents induces social anxiety in adult mice that was accompanied by reduced 5-HT$_{1A}$ receptor expression in the dorsal raphe nucleus (Franklin et al., 2010). In addition, when mice that had been stressed in early life were exposed to a stressor in adulthood, the mRNA expression of the 5-HT transporter and for tryptophan hydroxylase (a critical enzyme in the production of 5-HT) was elevated (Gardner et al., 2009), as was DA activity within the mesolimbic brain regions that mediate reward processes (Jahng et al., 2010). Moreover, as described in the discussion of depressive disorders in Chapter 8, early life stressful events also affect growth factors (such as BDNF) and brain cytokines. Given this array of biological outcomes, it's not in the least surprising that negative early life events would have important ramifications for adult well-being.

GENE X ENVIRONMENT INTERACTIONS

As we saw in Chapter 4, 5-HTT and BDNF polymorphisms can interact with early life stressors in promoting depression. As mentioned in our discussion of the 5-HTT and BDNF polymorphisms, it might not be the case that a gene mutation invariably causes antisocial behavior, but it may be that the presence of this polymorphism would influence an individuals' malleability (or at least make their biological systems more or less plastic), so that environmental events could differentially shape behavioral outcomes, for better or for worse (Belsky et al., 2009). In effect, having certain genes might make some susceptible to the influence of environmental or experiential factors so that negative early life events may then result in a greater likelihood of bad outcomes, but equally, positive events might similarly increase the probability of positive outcomes emerging (Pluess & Belsky, 2012). The essential issue here is that adverse early life events may have profound implications for later pathology, but this might depend on the presence of other factors, the individual's genetic disposition being one of these.

IMPACT OF PRENATAL INSULTS

As we consider whether and how the effects of stressors can be passed from one generation to the next, we probably shouldn't limit ourselves to events that occurred early in childhood, but also consider what happens when a pregnant person or animal encounters a stressor. Like other teratogens, viral illnesses (e.g., rubella, sometimes called German measles) contracted during pregnancy can have profound effects on offspring. It also seems that stressors experienced by a pregnant woman may affect the physical and psychological well-being of offspring, even when measured in adulthood (Beydoun & Saftlas, 2008). We'll now take a closer look at the ramifications of psychogenic and systemic stressors in pregnancy on the well-being of the offspring across its life span.

STUDIES OF PRENATAL STRESS IN HUMANS

The best documented effects of prenatal stressors comprise reduced birth weights and shortened gestation periods (Talge et al., 2007), which have been linked to subsequent adult disturbances. The stressors that promote reduced birth weight and abbreviated gestation period are fairly ubiquitous, ranging from domestic violence and work-related psychosocial distress, through to experiences of racial discrimination and war-time conditions (e.g., the bombings in Bosnia in 1999). It was also observed that the offspring of mothers who had experienced PTSD during pregnancy had lower birth weights relative to both the offspring of non-stressed mothers and mothers who experienced trauma, but did not develop PTSD (Seng et al., 2011). Hence, it might not be the stressor itself that caused the changes in the offspring, but rather the mother's psychological or physical responses to these events that were responsible for the adverse outcomes. Similarly, it might not be the severity of a given prenatal stressor event that was responsible for negative outcomes, as multiple stressful events were more closely aligned with these outcomes (Robinson et al., 2011).

Prenatal stressors have been linked to numerous physical disturbances. Among other things, offspring of mothers who had been stressed while pregnant were at an increased risk of metabolic syndrome that often comes with chronic adult distress, and insulin resistance was evident in prenatally stressed young adults (Rinaudo & Wang, 2011), and the incidence of Type 1 diabetes was increased (Virk et al., 2010). Moreover, stressful experiences in pregnant mothers were associated with an increased risk of the child developing immune-related disorders, such as allergies and asthma, increased reactions to immunological challenges (Bellinger et al., 2008), elevated production of both pro- and anti-inflammatory cytokines, such as IL-6, IL-10 and IL-4 (Entringer et al., 2008), and an appreciable increase in the probability of contracting infectious diseases (Nielsen et al., 2011). If the stressor experienced was especially intense (e.g., the loss of a close relative during pregnancy), even the incidence of cerebral palsy was elevated (Li et al., 2009). Remarkably, prenatal stress was even associated with shorter telomere length in later adulthood, suggesting more rapid aging (Entringer et al., 2011).

OH-OH!

In a report in the *Daily Beast* (November 18, 2011), Anneli Rufus indicated that a variety of childhood disorders, including asthma, ADHD, obesity, and developmental delays, might be attributable to environmental challenges experienced by pregnant mothers. For instance, magnetic fields created by modern technology (microwave ovens, vacuum cleaners) were associated with a three-fold increase of asthma by the time children reach 13 years of age, and mothers living within 1000 feet of a freeway during pregnancy had children with a two-fold chance of autism spectrum disorder. Cell phones were associated with a 30% rise in attention deficit hyperactivity disorder (ADHD); pesticide exposure during pregnancy was accompanied by lower intelligence in offspring; and consuming SSRIs was associated with a doubling of autism spectrum disorder in offspring. Ms Rufus also indicated that among men whose mothers smoked while pregnant, a 25% lower sperm count was found relative to offspring whose mother's didn't smoke.

She also stated 'Don't look down . . . men who were exposed to smoking in utero also have testicles 1.15 milliliters smaller than men whose mothers never smoked while pregnant'. Seeing this part of the article, my first thought was 'What's the implication of that?'. My second thought was 'Who does research of this sort, and why? ... but more than that, I wondered 'Who are the people who volunteer for these studies?'.

Beyond their physical effects, stressful events experienced by pregnant women can have pronounced psychological consequences on their offspring. For instance, the distress associated with relationship strain during pregnancy predicted later mental development and fearfulness, and cognitive disturbances were evident among children whose mothers were pregnant during a severe and protracted ice storm that created considerable distress. Moreover, the children of mothers stressed during pregnancy were more likely to exhibit emotional or cognitive problems, including an increased risk of attention deficit hyperactivity, anxiety, and language delay (Glover, 2011), and epidemiological studies indicated that prenatal stressors were more likely to be associated with neurodevelopmental disorders, such as schizophrenia and autism spectrum disorders (Kinney et al., 2008).

There's some debate about the gestational stage at which stressors might have their greatest impact. It has been reported, for instance, that indices of distress during the first trimester of pregnancy, and to a lesser extent the second trimester, were associated with a reduced birth weight (Sandman et al., 2011). Several other studies, however, indicated that women stressed during late pregnancy showed the most pronounced associations with offspring psychopathology. Of course, there are multiple effects of prenatal stressors, and it is certainly possible that the effects of stressors that occurred at different ages may preferentially influence particular outcomes. Furthermore, women who experienced a moderately strong stressor either during or just prior to pregnancy had infants with reduced birth weights and shorter gestation periods than did non-stressed mothers (Talge et al., 2007). In effect, the stressor need not even have been experienced during pregnancy to cause adverse outcomes, but can still have proactive effects on the fetus. As indicated repeatedly, distress does not just occur in the moment that an aversive event occurs, but because of its ruminative effects may have negative repercussions that persist long after the initial trauma has passed. This said, the possibility also ought to be considered that even if stressful events elicit adverse outcomes regardless of the stage of pregnancy at which these events occurred, this doesn't mean that the time of the stressor experience will uniformly elicit the same negative outcome. Stressors during certain prenatal periods may favor the development of a particular pathological outcome, but at another period some other pathology may be favored.

Given the consistency of the available data, it is fairly certain that adverse prenatal experiences may have protracted effects on offspring well-being. Yet it is possible that the effects of this prenatal trauma may be confounded with other factors, including postnatal rearing conditions, particularly as prenatally stressed mothers could differ in numerous ways from those who had not been stressed. Likewise, it is possible that genetic factors may have interacted with the prenatal stressors to produce effects on offspring. To assess this possibility, Rice et al. (2010) evaluated prenatal stress where pregnant mothers were either genetically related or unrelated to their child as a result of in vitro fertilization (IVF). Using this approach, it was found that offspring birth weight and antisocial behavior associated with prenatal stressors were apparent regardless of whether the offspring were genetically related or unrelated to the mothers. In contrast, the relation between prenatal stress and offspring anxiety was more closely aligned with postnatal maternal anxiety/depression, whereas the prenatal stressor experience and subsequent attention deficit hyperactivity disorder (ADHD) in the offspring was uniquely present in mother–offspring pairs who were genetically related, pointing to the involvement of inherited factors. Evidently, genetic and environmental factors may both have effects on offspring, but their relative contributions vary with the specific phenotypes of interest.

BIOLOGICAL CORRELATES OF PRENATAL STRESS IN HUMANS

Chronic maternal distress increases circulating CRH, probably of placental origin, and together with other hormones (e.g., cortisol and the endogenous opioid met-enkephalin) that pass through the placenta might precipitate preterm labor and contribute to a reduced birth weight. As with stressors, treatments that increased endogenous glucocorticoid levels late in gestation (as well as synthetic glucocorticoids, such as betamethasone, used to promote lung maturation in fetuses at risk of preterm delivery) may have effects on neurotransmitter systems and RNA transcriptional machinery, and may also increase later corticoid responses to stressful stimuli, infant temperament (negative reactivity), and behavioral reactivity (Davis et al., 2011).

Just as early life stressors influence adult stress responses, among adults whose mothers experienced distress during pregnancy, ACTH concentrations following a Trier Social Stress Test (TSST) were higher than among individuals whose mothers had not experienced distress while pregnant. It was especially interesting that cortisol levels prior to the TSST (baseline) were lower in the prenatally stressed participants than in controls, but were higher following the TSST. In contrast, a pharmacological challenge did not give rise to the same outcome. In fact, following an ACTH challenge, which ordinarily stimulates cortisol release, the cortisol response was diminished in the prenatally stressed individuals (Entringer et al., 2009). This profile is very much like that seen among individuals who had experienced early life abuse, and was also reminiscent of that associated with PTSD. Thus, the prenatal stressor might have had its effects by influencing the same (or related) neurochemical circuits.

As much as prenatal stressors might affect later cognitive and neuroendocrine functioning, these events don't necessarily doom the offspring to disturbances in adulthood. Although depression in pregnant women can have adverse effects on their offspring (reflected by infant fear and anger, as well as their heart rate response to a stressor when they were seven months of age), these outcomes could be diminished by the mother providing an infant with a high degree of contact comfort during the initials weeks of life. It also seemed that elevated prenatal cortisol levels (measured in amniotic fluid at 17 weeks of gestation) predicted poor cognitive abilities in the presence of insecure attachment, but this was not evident in children who exhibited secure attachment (Bergman et al., 2010). Clearly, as strong as the effects of prenatal stressors might be, the expression of these effects varies with postnatal influences.

It was suggested that elevated levels of several circulating stress hormones can have multiple effects. For instance, hormones can promote delayed fetal nervous system maturation and that of neuromuscular development, as well as impaired mental development, and could potentially promote diminished grey matter volume in children (Sandman et al., 2011). In view of the breadth of biological and behavioral changes associated with prenatal stressors, these insults create a 'general susceptibility' to pathology, rather than one that is related to particular pathological states (Huizink et al., 2009).

BIOLOGICAL CORRELATES OF PRENATAL STRESS IN ANIMALS

As in humans, it seems that in several species, such as rhesus monkeys and pigs, the psychological stressors experienced by a pregnant dam can be as disruptive to the fetus as physical stressors. It is thought that when animals are stressed *in utero*, especially during the development of limbic brain regions and the HPA axis, the trajectory for neuronal development in these regions will be disturbed. Among other things, this will result in animals subsequently exhibiting high levels of anxiety and depressive-like behaviors, as well as attention disturbances. These prenatal stressor effects are persistent, being apparent during early life, the juvenile period, and in adulthood. As in the case of postnatal stressors, it has been considered that the glucocorticoid changes induced by prenatal stressors play a significant role in affecting neurodevelopmental changes. Indeed, prenatal administration of the synthetic corticoid dexamethasone had the effect of programming offspring hypertension and increasing basal plasma corticosterone levels. Such treatments also affected hippocampal glucocorticoid receptors and were proposed to contribute to some of the behavioral disturbances associated with learning appropriate responses to stressful stimuli (Welberg et al., 2001).

Consistent with the findings that prenatal stressors increase the propensity for elevated anxiety and depressive symptoms, these stressor conditions also affect neurotransmitter functioning relevant to these disorders. In mice, strong prenatal stressors that were sufficient to promote anxiety-like behavior in the offspring also disrupted the development of

5-HT neurons, and altered the response to drugs (e.g., amphetamines) that affect DA neuronal activity (Silvagni et al., 2008). Given the involvement of DA in disorders such as schizophrenia, coupled with the fact that chronic amphetamine elicits some of the characteristics of schizophrenia, these findings were consistent with the possibility that prenatal stressors contribute to the evolution of this illness.

You will doubtless recall that those individuals carrying the ss or Ss alleles for the 5-HT transporter (5-HTT) were more vulnerable to depression than those carrying the SS allele, provided that those individuals also experienced strong life stressors. Studies in animals likewise revealed that a prenatal stressor was more likely to cause depressive-like behaviors among female mice carrying the Ss genotype (i.e., heterozygotes) on the 5-HTT promoter gene relative to that seen in the wild-type mice (that did not carry the short allele) (Van den Hove et al., 2011). It also appeared that neurotrophin signaling (neurotrophins, you'll recall, are growth factors involved in the survival and development of neurons) was regulated by both the 5-HTT genotype and prenatal stressor exposure, thus implicating these factors in mediating the interaction between genes and the prenatal environment.

Earlier, BDNF was introduced as a growth factor that is reduced by stressors and one that was likely involved in depressive disorders. It was reported that stressors encountered early in life reduced BDNF levels, and chronic prenatal stressor experiences similarly impaired BDNF protein formation (Van den Hove et al., 2006). This was accompanied by decreased brain cell proliferation, and once again these effects could be aggravated further by stressors encountered during adulthood (Fumagalli et al., 2004). Prenatal stressors also promote brain-region specific variations of basic fibroblast growth factor (FGF-2), which we have seen is another key regulator of development and plasticity that is related to depression (Fumagalli et al., 2005). These data are in line with the proposition that prenatal stressors might serve as a risk factor for depression, and that these effects are related to diminished cell proliferation stemming from growth factor disturbances.

Particularly interesting data have been reported that not only speak to the profound impact of prenatal stressors, but also make us consider stressor effects in a broader context. In humans, we know that simply witnessing others experience stressors may have some fairly negative effects on the observers. The same sort of thing also happens in rodents (as well as in other species). Ordinarily, when an animal is stressed, nearby animals will exhibit stress reactions even though they are not directly stressed. Likewise, if pregnant rats are bystanders to another rat being stressed, their offspring will subsequently exhibit altered behavioral responses and an altered gene expression profile that likely stemmed from epigenetic processes. These bystander effects can be fairly dramatic, in that the offspring of rats that had witnessed another animal being stressed also displayed several brain morphological changes (Mychasiuk, Gibb, & Kolb, 2011). The complexity and extent of dendritic arborization (the branching and connections characteristic of well-formed dendrites) were diminished, reduced neuronal and glial cells were apparent in the prefrontal and hippocampus, the functional maturation of hippocampal granule cells was disturbed (a small type of neuron that is subject to neurogenesis), and these effects were accompanied by depressive-like behaviors and cognitive deficits. Of particular importance is that these outcomes persisted into adulthood. Moreover, in addition to affecting those brain regions that govern hormonal responses or anxiety/fear reactions, prenatal stressors also influenced several cortical brain regions that have been associated with attention, executive functioning, information processing, and memory (Mychasiuk, Schmold et al., 2011). These brain changes were manifested behaviorally as disturbances of memory and learning, especially when animals again encountered stressful experiences in adulthood.

Given the array of hormonal, neurotransmitter, and growth factor changes, as well as the morphological alterations that are introduced by prental stressors, it is difficult to identify the correspondence between particular behavioral disturbances and specific biological perturbations. At the same time, this also tells us how powerful the effects of prenatal stressors can be. Knowing this might not help us devise biological tools to ameliorate the damage introduced by prenatal stressors in the fetus. However, it raises the possibility of engaging in stress interventions in pregnant women, and failing this, making sure that the offspring's postnatal environment is a positive one that could potentially antagonize the adverse effects that had already been created or act against the negative trajectory that would otherwise evolve.

GENDER-DEPENDENT EFFECTS OF PRENATAL STRESSORS

A persistent question that has emerged in relation to various pathologies is why females are more prone to certain disorders, especially stress-related psychological disturbances and autoimmune disorders, relative to males. In part, this might be related to the fact that males and females exhibit markedly different biological and behavioral responses to stressors encountered postnatally, but the sexual dimorphism (i.e., sex-specific effects) also appears in response to prenatal stressors, reflected by differences in later behavioral outcomes, as well as brain morphology and gene expression profiles.

Although the effects of stressors can be realized at any phase of pregnancy, it was suggested that during a particularly sensitive period of prenatal development a surge in gonadal hormones may be elicited by stressors that might be responsible for the brain being biased in a sexually dimorphic manner. With subsequent postnatal development these gonadal hormones contribute to further neuronal changes that promote the expression of sex-specific phenotypes (Seale et al., 2005). Thus, the greater anxiety and depression evident in female offspring were attributed to estrogen changes and elevated HPA responsiveness, whereas learning disturbances that occurred preferentially in prenatally stressed males were attributed to sex-dependent reductions of hippocampal neurogenesis and dendritic spine density in the prefrontal cortex (Weinstock, 2007). In effect, prenatal stressors may have adverse effects in both genders, but the specific negative outcomes that develop might be related to the prenatal hormonal changes that occur.

CONSEQUENCES OF PRENATAL INFECTION IN ANIMALS AND HUMANS

The case was made earlier that immune challenges elicit effects that are reminiscent of those associated with psychological stressors. Given that pregnant women often contract viral or bacterially-related illness, and when stressed the occurrence of these illnesses increases, it is of particular interest to establish what effects can be elicited by such challenges. There is, of course, ample evidence that a viral infection in a pregnant woman may have implications for the psychological well-being of the offspring. Fetal exposure to syphilis, rubella, herpes simplex, toxoplasmosis, and other viruses may elicit neuropsychiatric disturbances such as learning disabilities and neuromorphological anomalies, as well as severe psychiatric disturbances such as schizophrenia (Brown, 2011).

AUTISM AND IMMUNITY

Research into autism as it relates to immunity, and particularly to vaccination, has a bit of a shady history. This is largely based on controversial reports by Andrew Wakefield suggesting that vaccination with MMR (mumps, measles, rubella) led to autism. This seedy story would make a remarkable mystery novel, with big pharma initially being painted as the bad guys, and Wakefield fighting a lonely battle against huge odds to save children from the tyranny of corporate greed. But, it seems that there was a twist in the story: Wakefield's data weren't reliable (some even alleged he 'manipulated' the findings) and it was suggested that he was motivated by conflicts of interest. The research was withdrawn from the journal *The Lancet*, where it was first published, and has been described as being the greatest scientific fraud in one hundred years. It has had enormous adverse effects as parents stopped immunizing their children, thus leaving them vulnerable to these diseases.

A more credible view of autism has emerged in relation to immune functioning, although this perspective will need to go through the usual evaluations. It was proposed that immune-related disturbances might be at the root of autism in more than a third of cases. The brains of those with autism exhibit elevated microglia and astroglia that might be due to chronic inflammation, as the genes for inflammation seem to be switched on continuously and cytokine levels are elevated. Among women who had experienced a viral infection during the first trimester of pregnancy a 300% increase of autism was later detected, and when the infection occurred in the second trimester, a 40% increase of later autism occurred. It has been suggested that it's not the virus itself that causes the problem, but the strong immune responses on the part of the mother that cause the collateral damage in offspring. Some researchers also indicated that mothers of autistic children often have antibodies of a unique nature that have the capability of binding to fetal brain proteins, thereby causing damage. Others suggested that there seems to be a parallel between the autism profile and that associated with asthma; males tend to have both illnesses more often, and males are, as it happens, more reactive to inflammation in the mom than are females. Regardless of the perspectives, the common denominator in these studies is that immune dysregulation during pregnancy can have effects on the fetus that will become apparent during their later development.

PRENATAL INFECTION AND SCHIZOPHRENIA

Attempting to link prenatal events in humans and the development of later pathologies is not easily achieved, especially when pathology may not show up (or at least might not be detected) until years after those offspring were born. Prenatal inflammation related to viral challenges has been associated with varied behavioral and physiological disturbances. We can't go through all of these at this point, so we'll limit ourselves to an instructive example. There has been an interesting hypothesis that prenatal infection might, through its effects on DA neuronal activity, serve as a vulnerability factor for the later emergence of neuropsychiatric disorders such as schizophrenia (Meyer & Feldon, 2009). Indeed, it was reported that in the case of the 1964 rubella pandemic, *in utero* exposure to the virus resulted in a 500% increase of non-affective psychosis, and that at mid-adulthood, over 20% of those individuals who had been exposed to rubella had had a diagnosis of either schizophrenia or a schizophrenia spectrum disorder (Brown, 2011). As in the case of rubella, a 700% increase in the risk of schizophrenia occurred in the offspring of mothers exposed to influenza during the first trimester of pregnancy. Likewise, exposure to Toxoplasma gondii, an intracellular parasite, was associated with various CNS abnormalities, as well as neuropsychiatric consequences, as well as being associated with a 200% increase of schizophrenia. Several reports also indicated that the Herpes simplex virus type 2 (HSV-2) may result in CNS abnormalities in the offspring, but the findings regarding the risk for schizophrenia have not been consistent, and have appeared to be less marked compared to those provoked by rubella or influenza.

Studies in animals have also supported the view that prenatal infection may influence the neurodevelopmental course that leads to behavioral dysfunctions in offspring, some of which have been used to model schizophrenia. The effects of prenatal infection, in this regard, have been observed in tests that reflect deficits in attention, social interaction, and working memory (Ozawa et al., 2006). In addition, prenatal infection was accompanied by variations in DA receptors and activity, the transmitter most often linked to schizophrenia (Meyer & Feldon, 2009), and a dysfunction in glutamate (which has also been linked to schizophrenia) was apparent in the offspring of dams exposed to infection (Meyer et al., 2008).

It is of particular significance that many of the effects of prenatal infection were not evident in offspring when they were assessed soon after birth, but emerged during the post-pubertal period (Meyer et al., 2008), just as schizophrenia in humans typically emerges during a similar period (i.e., during the late teens). Several of the DA changes elicited by prenatal infection were apparent regardless of whether pups were raised (postnatally) by a dam that had experienced the infection or a surrogate dam that had not had this experience, thereby ruling out a role for postnatal factors in these studies. Moreover, some of these outcomes were attenuated by antipsychotic medication, and when applied prior to symptoms being apparent (i.e., when animals were still immature) the subsequent development of behavioral disturbances was prevented (Ozawa et al., 2006).

Data from animal studies that involved the viral infection of pregnant rodent dams resulted in disturbed social interaction in pups, as well as problems of attention, open field activity, and their exploration of novel objects, which were thought to model human schizophrenia. It was also found that prenatal viral infection was associated with various histological disturbances that had been linked to schizophrenia, such as diminished size of the cortical and hippocampal regions, coupled with an increase in cortical pyramidal cell density and more tightly packed pyramidal cells (Fatemi et al., 2002).

The proposition that cytokines contribute to schizophrenia is an attractive one, but as indicated by Brown (2011), there are other processes that might contribute to the effects of prenatal infection. For instance, febrile responses, malnutrition, and fetal/neonatal hypoxia secondary to infection are all possible contenders in this respect. Schizophrenia is a complex disorder and it could be argued that it is actually a term that applies to a constellation of illnesses that bear common features. Thus, even if cytokines (or other related factors) were involved in schizophrenia, it needs to be explained how the different symptom constellations come about (e.g., schizophrenia may be associated with positive or negative symptoms). In an interesting and provocative review of this literature, Harvey and Boksa (2012) point out that prenatal infection has been associated with numerous pathological conditions, including not only schizophrenia, but also autism, cerebral palsy, epilepsy, and Parkinson's disease. Thus, they suggest that prenatal and early postnatal infection might reflect a general vulnerability factor for neurodevelopmental disorders.

EPIGENETIC CHANGES

Early life stressful events can instigate the reprogramming of neuroendocrine or neurochemical stress responses, and might then give rise to long-term repercussions. Of particular significance, it was shown using a cross-fostering procedure (i.e., pups were transferred from their biological mother to one that displayed either high or low maternal care) and other paradigms that offspring can 'inherit' some of their behaviors from their nursing mother, rather than from just their biological mother (Anisman et al., 1998). Having a good attentive mom leads to positive outcomes, whereas having a poor mom leads to negative outcomes, although these outcomes interact with the contribution of genetic factors. These relatively long-term effects might be related to the particular stress hormone changes that are induced (e.g., the activation of CRH) or those that are associated with attachment, such as oxytocin. However, what was especially interesting from the perspective of the current discussion is that stress reactivity and health outcomes that stemmed from early life stimulation (or neglect) also influenced the behavior of these mice when they subsequently became mothers. It was similarly reported that in humans poverty during early life, and all that comes with it, can produce epigenetic effects that influence neuroendocrine and immune functioning in adulthood. Thus, in order to fully appreciate the factors that favor stress vulnerability (or resilience), the family unit (grandparents, parents, children), early life stress and poverty, in addition to the individual's later experiences, are all important levels of analyses. It is interesting that this view, based primarily on studies on animals, maps precisely onto studies on humans indicating that parental behaviors provide the basis for relatively stable characteristics (e.g., self-esteem, self-efficacy, and self-reliance) that buffer against the negative consequences of stressful experiences, and also serve to facilitate the development of skills that enable effective coping.

RESILIENCE MIGHT START IN THE SANDBOX

It's rarely talked about, but it is possible that a certain amount of childhood stress might have positive repercussions. Most of us have heard that keeping kids at home during their early development, rather than having them attend day care, might not be a great idea, as they wouldn't be exposed to the assorted viruses and bacteria that would ordinarily result in their immune systems learning about what is a threat to their health. It might similarly be the case that a certain amount of stress during the course of development might be advantageous, in that it could encourage the development of adaptive behavioral strategies and biological processes to deal with stressors that might be encountered throughout life. The suggestion here is not that anyone ought to go and distress little kids, but instead that we should not be overly protective and allow them, at least occasionally, to pick themselves up when they fall over in the playground.

INTERGENERATIONAL TRANSMISSION

There is reason to believe that the adverse effects of early life stressors (including environmental factors, maternal stressors, endocrine challenges, and diet) could be transmitted across generations through epigenetic processes (e.g., the suppression of certain genes) (Franklin et al., 2010; Lillycrop, 2011). In fact, it's been known for some time that environmental factors, including toxicants (e.g., pesticides and fungicides, dioxin, jet fuel, plastics), have epigenetic effects that can be transmitted across generations. We had discussed earlier that epigenetic processes might result in phenotypic changes, including biological and behavioral alterations. Since the gene itself is not altered, but its action is suppressed (or turned down), the altered form of the gene could be passed from parent to offspring and in this way have behavioral or physiological effects on the next generation. In fact, the behaviors of the parent can result in epigenetic changes in the offspring (termed 'experience-dependent inheritance'), which may then result in their later maternal behaviors changing. This, in turn, might result in their offspring being affected in precisely the same way. Thus, over generations, the same epigenetic changes and resulting behaviors can appear repeatedly (Danchin et al., 2011).

Epigenetic changes, as we saw in Chapter 1, can occur in DNA through a process in which certain portions of DNA become methylated, so that a section of DNA is less likely to be transcribed (i.e., referring to the process wherein RNA is formed on the basis of a sequence of DNA). In addition, the expression of genes on the DNA strand can be affected by 'chromatin remodeling'. Chromatin refers to the complex of DNA together with associated histone proteins: the latter are small spheres around which DNA is wrapped, and changes in the wrapping can alter gene expression. Ordinarily the histone proteins are separated by acetyl groups, and when these are broken down (through deacetylation), the DNA may be disturbed so that epigenetic variations occur. The essential point here is that environmental events can influence the expression of genes present on a DNA strand, and thus have phenotypic consequences; more than this, if the epigenetic changes occur in germ cells (sperm or ova) these altered genes can be transmitted from one generation to the next.

Epigenetic changes have become one of the hot topics in neuroscience during the past few years, although it has been on the radar for many years among scientists studying cancer and toxicology as well as plant biology. Increasingly frequent reports that a prenatal or early life stressor may have effects that extend beyond a single generation have been fundamental in changing our views about genomic transmission (Matthews & Phillips, 2010), as well as the processes that are linked to trauma-related pathologies. Moreover, epigenetic alterations are potentially reversible (McGowan & Szyf, 2010), and several drugs that expressly target DNA methylation and the enzymes involved in this process have been tested in clinical trials (Szyf, 2009).

EPIGENETIC MODIFICATION OF MULTIPLE BIOLOGICAL PROCESSES

The pronounced cellular proliferation and differentiation that occurs during fetal development makes it an especially sensitive period for genes to be turned on or off in response to a variety of environmental toxins and social experiences (Champagne, 2010). Indeed, several *in utero* challenges (e.g., methyl mercury, diesel fumes, the androgenic fungicide vivclozolin, the estrogenic peptide methoxychlor, and the endocrine disruptor bisphenol-A) have been associated with epigenetic changes in the genes associated with BDNF, and several immune factors (IgE and IFN-γ and IL-4) that could be related to psychological and physical illnesses (Anway et al., 2005; Champagne, 2010). It may be especially significant from an intervention perspective that the effects of toxins can be reversed by increasing the presence of folate in the dam's diet (Dolinoy et al., 2007), which has the effect of increasing the availability of methyl donors that would act against the methylation that had already occurred.

EPIGENETIC CHANGES IN RODENTS RELATED TO MATERNAL BEHAVIORS

A strong case has been made that in addition to the effects of toxins, the behavior of a dam toward her pups during early development (does she exhibit good parenting or is she neglectful?) may cause the silencing of particular genes, notably those that regulate HPA functioning, so that as adults these pups will be more likely to exhibit poor social behavior, increased stress responses, and poor parenting (Champagne, 2010). There have, in fact, been several reports showing that poor maternal care during early postnatal development may influence the methylation of the promoter for the gene regulating glucocorticoid receptors, thereby leading to altered hippocampal glucocorticoid receptor expression and elevated stressor reactivity that persists into adulthood (Szyf, 2009). If epigenetic changes can be induced by early postnatal experiences, it isn't a huge leap to expect that prenatal stressors might also induce such effects. In fact, a prenatal stressor administered repeatedly over the first trimester of pregnancy in mice reduced the DNA methylation of the gene promoter for CRH and increased the methylation of the promoter gene for glucocorticoid receptors (Mueller & Bale, 2008). Once more, as in the case of toxin-elicited epigenetic effects, the effects of an early life stressor are reversible by treating rats with a methyl donor (methionine) or a histone deacetylase inhibitor (trichostatin A) (Weaver et al., 2005).

Although considerable research has pointed to early life events influencing the epigenetic processes associated with the promoter gene controlling glucocorticoid receptors, the available data have not been uniformly consistent with this perspective. For instance, pups that had undergone periodic maternal deprivation exhibited a change in behavior that was accompanied by increased plasma corticosterone and elevated hippocampal nerve growth factor, but not the methylation status of the gene for the glucocorticoid receptor. It was suggested that the increased neurotrophin levels associated with maternal deprivation might have acted as a compensatory mechanism to diminish the long-term deleterious consequences that may otherwise have arisen (Daniels et al., 2009).

A considerable problem for this field is that of defining the specific epigenetic changes that are responsible for the negative effects of early life or prenatal experiences. Numerous epigenetic changes occur more or less concurrently, any of which could potentially be responsible for the behavioral outcomes. Some investigators placed their bets on the glucocorticoid receptor, but this by no means negates the potential involvement of other epigenetic modifications in determining later stressor reactivity. In fact, in monkeys, life events influence the DNA methylation of the 5-HTT gene, which might be particularly significant given the potential role for 5-HTT in depression (Kinnally et al., 2010). Moreover, poor maternal care also resulted in the methylation of the gene promoter of estrogen receptor alpha (ERα) in the hypothalamus of female rodents (Champagne, 2010). As ERα is important for the functioning of estrogen and oxytocin, both of which contribute to maternal behaviors, the silencing of this gene might be responsible for the poor maternal behaviors associated with impoverished early life care.

It will be recalled that prenatal stressors might affect the developmental trajectory by epigenetically altering the genes controlling sex steroids (Morgan & Bale, 2011). Stressors encountered early in prenatal development promoted dysmasculanization and enhanced stressor sensitivity in males, and in the male descendants of prenatally stressed mice, genes important for neurodevelopment likewise showed a female-like pattern. Thus, a sensitive period in early gestation might exist during which epigenetic programming of the male germ line occurs so that particular phenotypes can appear across subsequent generations.

Beyond the glucocorticoid and estrogen receptor changes, it seems that BDNF may also be subject to epigenetic changes. In an effort to simulate the experiences of abuse or neglect among children from poor homes, Roth et al. (2009) raised rat pups for the first postnatal week with adult caretakers that had been stressed, and thus displayed abusive behaviors. When the abused pups were subsequently assessed in adulthood, methylation of BDNF DNA was apparent, leading to altered BDNF gene expression in the prefrontal cortex. When this generation of rats had their own litters, this profile of BDNF methylation was also apparent in the offspring. These data not only point to epigenetic changes in this trophic factor, but also implicate it in the transgenerational effects of early life stressors (Roth & Sweatt, 2010; Roth et al., 2009).

Ordinarily, rodents stressed during the juvenile period subsequently displayed increased reactivity and anxiety, and this effect was apparent in their offspring, possibly reflecting an epigenetic change. However, if rats exposed to a juvenile stressor were subsequently raised in an enriched environment, a manipulation that itself increases BDNF (Chourbaji et al.,

2011), then the negative transgenerational stress effect was attenuated (Leshem & Schulkin, 2011). It was similarly reported that enrichment during the juvenile period could undo the negative behavioral effects otherwise provoked by poor early life maternal care (Champagne & Meaney, 2007).

As with events that occur during the juvenile period, strong stressors in adulthood that elicit depressive-like characteristics have been associated with a diminished transcription of BDNF (Tsankova et al., 2006), as well as evidence of epigenetic effects and the emergence of depressive-like features (e.g., Covington et al., 2009; Fuchikami et al., 2010). A histone deacetylase inhibitor applied directly into the nucleus accumbens shell where these histone deacetylase changes were particularly notable had the effect of precluding the epigenetic consequences, and acted like an antidepressant agent with respect to the behavioral disturbances (Covington et al., 2009). Furthermore, in adult rats, exposure to a strong stressor comprising exposure to a cat plus social instability over 31 days (a treatment that elicited PTSD-like effects), increased BDNF methylation occurred in the dorsal hippocampus, while reducing methylation in the ventral hippocampus. Evidently, epigenetic changes could occur in adulthood, and might potentially be responsible for the cognitive disturbances that have been associated with PTSD (Roth et al., 2011).

When stressor effects are transmitted from mother to daughter/son, there is the possibility that the outcomes reflect either non-Mendelian genetic changes (e.g., epigenetic effects), factors related to the uterine environment, or the transmission may simply be one related to the anxiety of the dam being transmitted through her behaviors, independent of any genetic influence. However, if it's found that a given phenotype is passed on to the offspring through paternal lineage (where the male plays no part in raising the offspring), then we can pretty well rule out a role for either a stressed prenatal environment or parent–pup interactions in determining the observed outcomes (Youngson & Whitelaw, 2008). In line with the transmission of stressor effects through epigenetic processes, male pups that experienced chronic maternal separation later exhibited depressive-like behaviors and altered behavioral responses to aversive stimuli when subsequently assessed as adults. In the offspring of males that had experienced the extended maternal separation, behavioral and neuroendocrine disturbances were also apparent even though these animals had not been subjected to any particular stressor (i.e., they were reared normally) (Franklin et al., 2010). Similarly, male mice that had been stressed through social defeat transmitted their anxiety- and depressive-like responses to their male and female offspring even though they weren't present after the dam was impregnated (Dietz et al., 2011). These effects were independent of the behavioral characteristics these males exhibited prior to being defeated, suggesting that the intergenerational transmission was related to the stressor they encountered as opposed to the general anxiety that might have been characteristic of the sires.

The possibility existed that stressed male mice might have caused the females to become distressed, which would have resulted in their behavior towards the pups being altered. To assess this, females were impregnated through *in vitro* fertilization using sperm from a stressed mouse. When this was done, the behavioral effects otherwise passed down from parent to offspring were largely absent. Hence, it seems as if the transmission might not actually be linked to epigenetic changes in the sire being passed on to the offspring. However, the possibility exists that stressors experienced by a male might affect sperm quality, including sperm motility, so that those affected by stressors are least likely to fertilize an egg, and hence limit the transgenerational effects that might otherwise occur. This explanation still begs the question as to what processes might be responsible for the effects on the offspring when a stressed male directly breeds with a female.

EPIGENETIC CHANGES ASSOCIATED WITH STRESSORS IN HUMANS

There have been relatively few studies in humans that assessed the relationship between stressful events and behavioral disturbances and the role of epigenetic factors in mediating these effects. That said, elevated maternal depressed/anxious mood during the third trimester of pregnancy was accompanied by increased methylation of the genes for glucocorticoid receptors and with increased salivary cortisol stress responses assessed in infants at three months of age. This outcome was apparent even after controlling for antidepressant use among mothers as well as their postnatal maternal mood (Oberlander et al., 2008).

It is particularly interesting that among individuals who died by suicide and had a history of early childhood neglect/abuse, hippocampal ribosomal RNA expression (this refers to the form of RNA that is involved in protein production) was hypermethylated throughout the promoter region of the gene for the glucocorticoid receptor (McGowan et al., 2009). These data are consistent with the view that early experiences contribute to glucocorticoid receptor functioning; however, causal conclusions between the epigenetic differences and suicidality or early experiences are unwarranted. Indeed, epigenetic factors have been associated with $GABA_A$ subunit expression among depressed individuals who died by suicide, pointing to non-selectivity concerning epigenetic involvement in depression/suicide (Poulter et al., 2008). It is likely that there are other epigenetic variations that correspond to suicide and depression (e.g., BDNF) that might similarly have been affected by early life adverse parenting. It is uncertain which relationships might simply be correlational and which, if any, causally contribute to pathological outcomes. Ultimately, strong inferential conclusions will be possible when studies are conducted using a larger number of participants, when more detailed analyses of early experiences are undertaken, and statistical analyses are performed that are more cogent in drawing relationships between multiple factors that likely go into the effects of early life stressor actions.

THE CAT CAME BACK THE VERY NEXT DAY

Before Darwinian theory made its mark, one way that evolution was thought to occur was by Lamarckian inheritance. The view proposed by Lamarck was that an organism could pass on to its offspring those characteristics that it had acquired during its lifetime (known as the 'heritability of acquired characteristics'). Essentially, if a person was a blacksmith and developed huge muscles, then his children would inherit these large muscles and might themselves become blacksmiths. As a result, instead of inheritance based on genes being passed on that had been selected on the basis of environmental pressures, traits were inherited simply because a parent acquired them through experience.

The Darwinian perspective was eventually adopted because it had greater explanatory power, but there still existed die-hards who were reluctant to abandon the Lamarkian perspective. Lysenko, a Russian agronomist and politician, drove the agricultural productivity of the Soviet Union into the ground, literally and figuratively, based on counterfactual thinking and a nonscientific basis for his views (largely reflecting the heritability of acquired characteristics). The story of Lysenko highlights how the ignorance of one individual can have remarkably wide-ranging consequences. More relevant to the present point is that the Lamarckian view, which was largely thrown out, might not have been entirely wrong. We might not inherit genes based on what dad does or what's happened to dad in the past, but from an epigenetic perspective, experiences in one's lifetime can influence which genes are turned off or on, and there is reason to suppose that these features can be transmitted to the next generation. Multigenerational transmission through epigenetic processes is certainly a possibility, but it is still early in the game, and as indicated in the text, there are still several odd but intriguing findings that need to be sorted out.

COLLECTIVE AND HISTORIC TRAUMA

As indicated at the outset of this chapter, there are many instances where individuals as a group are affected by a single or multiple traumatic events (collective trauma). As well, there are instances where cumulative emotional and psychological wounding is experienced by groups over generations. To understand the impact of collective assaults, it is necessary to first understand certain characteristics of a group. As indicated earlier, according to social identity theory, a sense of self, or identity, is derived from group memberships. Having a particular identity and affiliation with a group (whether it is one that comprises race, religion, or gender, or one that entails an occupation, university affiliation, or being a breast cancer survivor) serves multiple functions, including support from ingroup members, and markedly influences well-being in numerous domains (Jetten et al., 2012). These identities often take on considerable importance for an individual's and the group's well-being, particularly when the group is challenged. When this challenge essentially comprises one that threatens the viability of the group (i.e., the threat entails the group's extinction), then a common anxiety or collective angst may be instigated (Wohl et al., 2010). The nature of the threat, as well as the contextual factors surrounding it, largely influence the emotions elicited (e.g., collective shame or guilt vs collective anger), and will determine individual or group behaviors that can be either constructive (i.e., pro-social) or destructive (i.e., anti-social) (Branscombe & Doosje, 2004).

Members of a group (e.g., a religious group) might view their own lives as being impermanent, but they might also believe that the values, morals, beliefs, traditions, and symbols representing the group itself will be passed on from one generation to the next. The more group members invest themselves in the group, or the more they identify with it, the greater their cognitive dissonance will become regarding this group, and hence threats to it will yield a greater individual and collective angst (Wohl et al., 2010). In the same fashion, if the group had experienced previous (historical) traumatic incidents that threatened their survival, then a greater collective angst will be engendered by threats to generations of descendants that had not directly experienced the trauma. Indeed, such attitudes and the accompanying behaviors may even be apparent in those individuals who simply feel a connection to the victimized group as opposed to being part of the group itself. Given a history of collective abuse and threats of extermination, group members might well become especially sensitive or vigilant regarding threats to the group, manifested as exceptional caution with respect to the perceived evil or malign intent of others (Paez & Liu, 2011). (Incidentally, heightened vigilance towards potential threats should not be misconstrued as reflecting heightened paranoia: if history is any teacher, then this elevated vigilance might be perfectly reasonable and adaptive.)

It should be obvious that when considering the intergenerational transmission of trauma, it would be profitable to evaluate current challenges in the context of historical and collective traumas endured by that group. The children and grandchildren of survivors of Residential Schools recognize that these survivors were not the victims of an historically isolated event, as numerous assaults against Aboriginal peoples in North America as well as in numerous other countries had persisted for generations. These events were expressed as assaults on their culture, language, and identity, and many current events, especially experiences of discrimination and disputed land claims, act as reminders of the numerous indignities committed against their group that were part of an historical pattern of abuse (Whitbeck et al., 2004). Shoah survivors and their children likewise recognize that this event was one of a series of cumulative traumas that dated back to the pre-Christian era. Thus, when subsequent stressors are encountered, the behaviors of members of these groups will be influenced by their collective historical experiences. In fact, collectively experienced traumas might instigate unique social and psychological trajectories, and their consequences may be aligned with collective responses and interpretations of past indignities, as well as biological sequelae of those experiences. For instance, the current upswing in anti-Semitism that one sees not just in the Middle East, but also in large parts of Europe and elsewhere, has had the predictable effect of enhancing group identity in many individuals (reminding them of an historical collective trauma), while causing others to disidentify, possibly owing to their desire to assimilate with or join the outgroup.

It is essential to underscore once again that it is likely inappropriate to draw parallels between the collective, historical trauma experienced by different groups. Each is unique, each involves its own series of events, and each has its own consequences. To be sure, the experiences of Jews at the hands of the Nazis and the collaborators that sang their praises are beyond imagination. However, the survivors of the Shoah eventually experienced acceptance across countries (despite being turned away, again and again, by country after country, when it really counted, i.e., *during* the Shoah). This contrasts sharply with the experiences of Aboriginal peoples, whose communities and culture were severely undermined ('undermined' is a euphemism that in this context really means 'screwed beyond recognition'), their pride demolished, and they realized exceptionally slow improvements in their lives. In fact, it wasn't until 2008 and 2009, respectively, that the government of Australia and that of Canada offered an apology for the behavior of their forebeares. In Australia, the placement of children in Residential Schools is often referred to as the 'Stolen Generation'. It is increasingly obvious that the apologies should be made to the 'Stolen *Generations*', not only because several generations of children were placed in these schools, but also because this action has had so many profound and persistent effects over successive generations.

The consequences of trauma experiences in these populations have been very different in several respects. As described in our hypothetical example earlier in this chapter, both groups might have been at an increased risk for certain pathological conditions, possibly owing to epigenetic changes that might have occurred. However, the posttrauma environments experienced by Shoah survivors might have precluded the trajectory that could have otherwise occurred, whereas the low socio-economic and toxic conditions among Aboriginals might have exacerbated the downward course that would have been favored by the earlier trauma.

With these considerations in mind we can better understand some of the consequences of collective and historical abuses. Beyond the effects of individual traumas, there are multiple effects of collective trauma witnessed at the family and community levels that result in changes in social dynamics, processes, structures, and functioning. We suggested (Bombay et al., 2009, 2011), as have others, that changes in the aftermath of mass trauma include an erosion of basic trust, the deterioration of social norms, morals, and values, and shared collective experiences, and the retelling of these experiences over generations may result in sensitized responses to subsequently encountered stressful events. As Brave Heart (2003) suggested, the cumulative consequences of the many traumas experienced by Aboriginal peoples engendered a 'soul wound', which profoundly affects individuals across generations.

Indian Residential Schools were not unique to Canada and Australia, but were also established in the United States, and the effects of these IRSs, like those of other historical abuses, have also been dramatic. Whitbeck et al. (2004) indicated that for contemporary American Indians, historical loss is part of a schema or cognitive framework that was linked to psychopathology. In the studies conducted by Whitbeck, most participants were typically one generation removed from the IRS era, and several generations removed from the many earlier collective traumas experienced by American Indians. Nonetheless, the majority of participants indicated that they had thought about these historical losses, including the loss of language and culture, the loss of respect for traditional ways, and the loss of land. In addition, more than half the individuals had thought about the negative treatment meted out by the government, and 30% also reported frequent feelings of loss stemming from Residential Schools and broken promises. These feelings were frequently accompanied by emotional responses such as anxiety or nervousness and anger/avoidance (e.g., anger, rage, shame, fear/distrust of white people, and avoidance of places that served as reminders of losses), as well as disturbed concentration, feeling isolated, a loss of sleep, and greater experiences of discrimination (Whitbeck et al., 2004). Clearly, the numerous assaults against Aboriginal peoples did not only affect those who directly experienced the transgressions, but also continue to affect the perceptions of current group members and influence their psychological and physical health.

JUST GET OVER IT?!

In discussions dealing with collective trauma it is not unusual to have some individuals feel negatively toward this notion as they might have the desire to not be seen as a victim. This is perfectly reasonable, as those that directly experienced the cruelties of others might have been shamed by their victimization. But what about attitudes adopted in ensuing generations? Should they or do they experience feelings of shame? To some extent they might, but when they think of past egregious behaviors towards their forebears, they might also feel considerable anger, and take on what outgroup members will perceive as 'militant' behaviors when they say loudly 'Never again'. We've seen exactly this attitude from survivors of Indian Residential Schools and of the Shoah, and Blacks in the United States and in European countries, as well as numerous other groups. This anger catalyzes active resistance, and unifies the group to take strong actions. So when Aboriginals block a road because it traverses ancestral lands, consider that this behavior is coming from a history of abusive behaviors, and they're simply saying 'Enough' or 'Never again'. Unfortunately, time and again we've seen that the response of the outgroup is often unsupportive: 'Here we go again', 'Now what do they want?', or 'Playing the race card' are comments that are not uncommon from outgroup members. Perhaps it would be useful for outgroup individuals to consider the behaviors they witness as a response to collective injustices. Collective emotions, such as collective shame or anger, can be a powerful motivating force, and it's not likely that they'll 'just get over it'. The very events and ensuing behaviors that one would like them 'to just get over' have imbued them with considerable resilience in the face of future threats.

CONCLUSION

It never struck me as surprising that the collective trauma experienced by individuals of a particular generation would influence the behavior and attitudes of the next generation. In fact, it was hard to imagine that it wouldn't, at least if the traumatic event was an especially grievous one, and most particularly if it were part of a cumulative historical trauma. Imagine the 9/11 deaths occurring every single day for 2000 successive days (for five and half years): that's the toll that the Shoah had on the Jewish population of Europe, but the deaths were often slow and reflected the ultimate in psychological cruelty. However, this was only one of numerous and pervasive pogroms that had occurred world-wide over centuries. The toll of IRSs on Aboriginal peoples might not have been as great in terms of the numbers killed, but their substandard living conditions persisted for years afterward. Would it be surprising to find that such experiences influenced their collective conscious and unconscious, and that parents would pass such experiences on to their children?

You can bet that the reminders of trauma to an individual's group will be potent in eliciting emotional responses such as shame, depression, and despair in those who highly identify with the group, but as the injustice of the situation becomes more pronounced, anger and social activism may become prominent. Those who are now dealing with collective trauma might not be inclined to once again be herded into IRSs or remain silent in the face of blatant discrimination. But generations pass quickly and so might ancestral memories, unless symbols are provided to remind us not to become complacent (e.g., Veterans' Day, Armistice Day, Passover), and even then the emotions might simply be replaced by cognitions.

Past egregious actions do not only affect individuals through collective memories, but also through biological processes, such as epigenetic mechanisms, whereby the response to stressors may be altered over successive generations. The epigenome is dynamic, and epigenetic changes are alterable. Indeed, in the case of prenatal and postnatal stressor effects, the behavioral disturbances can be attenuated to some extent by pharmacological or environmental manipulations (e.g., environmental enrichment, antidepressant and neurotrophic treatments). If the environment is improved, and good social supports are available, then the sequence leading to adverse outcomes might be interrupted. Essentially, it seems that in the case of epigenetic changes the 'bell can be unrung', provided that appropriate postnatal actions are taken.

SUMMARY

- Beyond their immediate effects, stressors can have persistent neurochemical and behavioral actions, especially if individuals once again encounter stressful experiences.
- Stressors have particularly marked effects if they were encountered during early life (e.g., neglect), as can prenatal stressors and those encountered during other transition phases (e.g., adolescence).
- The effects of stressors can be passed across generations so that trauma in one generation can affect stress reactivity in subsequent generations. This can occur through different processes. Traumatic events can affect child rearing, so that the children of traumatized individuals are adversely affected, and their own child-rearing practices may affect the next generation. As well, traumatic events (and neglect) may cause epigenetic changes so that the expression of genes is altered, without affecting DNA and thus the altered responses to stressors can be transmitted across generations.
- Among minorities, the impact of collective trauma experiences can be influenced by collective, historical traumas that had been experienced by the group.

12 STRESS BUSTING: TREATMENT STRATEGIES

SNAKE OIL

There's a huge industry offering new approaches to dealing with stressors. Magazine articles that I've read while waiting for my doctor to see me relentlessly promote 'Eleven ways to beat stress', 'The five most important lessons to avoid stress', 'The ten most stressful jobs', or 'Getting rid of bad karma in 74 easy steps'. Recently, I came across two different tea companies advertising their wares (green tea or green tea plus other stuff added) to help you become mellow or to reduce stress. As these are natural products, as opposed to drugs, they don't need any federal government approvals for their claims, and hence don't require intensive research. This, of course, doesn't mean that these teas are ineffective, but they haven't gone through rigorous experimental testing.

Given the apparently widespread expertise about stress and how to de-stress, I checked-out stress management through the internet. Among other things, I found that in the city in which I live there are more stress management centres than there are shoe stores. One very well-known website provided the following de-stressing methods: cognitive therapy, autogenic training (a relaxation technique that involves a set of visualizations to induce calmness), conflict resolution, exercise, taking up a hobby, meditation, deep breathing, Yoga Nidra (a sleep-like state experienced during meditation), nootropics, nutraceuticals, and foods that improve mental functions, reading novels, prayer, relaxation techniques, artistic expression, fractional relaxation, progressive relaxation, spas, somatic training, spending time in nature, stress balls (those are the squishy rubber things), natural medicine, clinically validated alternative treatments, time management, listening to certain types of relaxing music (e.g., new age music, classical music, psychedelic music, sleep music), and spending quality time with pets. Some of these methods are pretty loopy, but some are on target. The loopy items, incidentally, are in line with all the stuff in magazine and newspaper articles found in the doctor's waiting room.

As you read through the list, some of you will notice that there are methods you'd never even consider using, whereas others seem reasonable. For instance, for some of us meditation simply isn't in the cards, whereas for others it sounds ideal. Likewise, to some people spending quality time with a pet sounds, well, goofy (what a horrible pun). However, if you're a dog (or cat) lover, then you'll appreciate what your pet can do for you.

Earlier chapters outlined the influence of stressors on pathology and the many factors that moderated the impact of stressors. So, the obvious question now is this: What can we do to diminish the negative impact of stressors? To a certain extent there isn't always an easy solution. In some instances, the stressor might be fairly mild to which we might be over-reacting because that's just part of our personality, or because we simply don't know how to deal with it in any better way. In other instances it might not be a simple matter to rid ourselves of a stressor as it may be outside of our control. Even in the worst scenario, where it seems that there's not a thing that can be done and coping might feel near impossible (and we accept that 'it just is what it is'), there may be ways of diminishing our distress, even if just a little. The main focus of this chapter is detailing some of the methods available to deal with stressors, but there are several important elements that the reader should focus on when learning about the efficacy of treatment and intervention strategies to deal with stressors and stressor-related psychopathology:

- individuals react differently to stressors, and other things being equal, they might not respond in the same way to a particular stress-reducing technique. Furthermore, the effectiveness of any particular way of dealing with distress varies across situations and over time;
- it's not all that simple to determine the best strategy for an individual to deal with distress, and even if the best strategy were identified, implementing it efficiently might be yet another issue, particularly as it might take a fair bit of effort on the part of the stressed individual, who might not be in a state to do things for themselves;
- there are numerous methods that have been advocated for reducing distress and diminishing stressor-induced psychological and some physical disturbances. These range from progressive relaxation therapy through to cognitive behavioral therapy, meditation, mindfulness training, and acceptance and commitment therapy. For some individuals each of these therapies has something to offer, particularly cognitive behavioral therapy and mindfulness, but they're not for everybody;
- drug therapies have been used extensively to diminish distress. There's a very potent placebo effect that goes with each of the drug treatments, and there's little question that some drugs can have further effects on stress processes and stressor-related illness. These include a variety of antidepressants that affect serotonin and/or norepinephrine, as well as those that affect glutamate or growth factors. Traditional antianxiety medications, such as benzodiazepines, can be very effective, but their long-term use isn't recommended;
- ultimately, treatments to reduce distress, like treatments to treat mental illness, might best be served by an individualized treatment approach based on the symptoms expressed and the presence of biomarkers related to underlying processes.

Although these various methods of coping with stressors are widely available, it seems that only a small portion of individuals experiencing signs of distress actually seek professional treatment. The sections that follow offer some methods that are commonly-used stress busters. However, if you don't like any of these methods, you can always take your chances and resort to those listed in the magazines in your doctor's office, although if it got to that point, you might be better off having some chocolate chip ice cream as a coping method.

RELAXATION TRAINING

Relaxation training encompasses a variety of methods that have the effect, as indicated by the name, of getting a person to relax (i.e. 'destress'). There's nothing inherently wrong with this, although it needs to be put into a proper perspective. A minor treatment strategy, as this is, won't go all that far if it is used in isolation from other methods. Let's face it, to obtain a genuine positive response in dealing with stressors, the actual problem needs to be tackled rather than simply masking a couple of symptoms. At the same time, some individuals are wired so that they are in a perpetual reactive state (high-strung or a tad neurotic), and so they need to relax before they can adequately tackle tough problems. Thus, for a subset of individuals a simple relaxation protocol can have some positive effects.

PROGRESSIVE MUSCLE RELAXATION

This widely-used technique to diminish anxiety has often been included in broad relaxation programs to diminish the effects of stressors. The procedure essentially involves the alternate tensing and relaxation of muscles. As anxiety and muscle tension often go together, it has been thought that relaxing muscle tension might have the effect of reducing anxiety. As well, feedback between muscles and the brain might be involved in delivering the message that the individual is anxious, and thus relaxing muscles might disturb this feedback process. Progressive muscle relaxation procedure also involves a mental component in which one focuses and feels the difference between the sensations associated with tension and relaxation, respectively. This feedback helps the individual distinguish between these states, and facilitates achieving somatic calmness. In the long run, however, especially when we're dealing with strong stressful experiences and their consequences, progressive muscle relaxation might have only very limited positive effects.

COGNITIVE BEHAVIORAL THERAPY (CBT)

It has long been known (even before Thorndike formalized this as instrumental conditioning) that particular behaviors could be elicited through positive reinforcement, and that learned responses could be extinguished by withholding reward. In the case of stress responses, such as fear, it's not quite as simple, although forced exposure to the fear-eliciting stimulus (in graded steps), a procedure referred to as 'desensitization', was found to be effective. Dealing with cognitive disturbances, such as those that lead to depression, can be a bit more difficult than fear responses, but when instrumental conditioning and cognitively-based approaches were combined positive outcomes could be achieved.

The goal of CBT, which comes from Beck's theorizing, is to diminish dysfunctional behaviors, cognitions, and emotions through a goal-oriented, systematic procedure that employs behavioral and cognitive approaches to change maladaptive thinking. To this end, CBT techniques help individuals challenge inappropriate and counterproductive patterns and beliefs, and replace cognitive errors (e.g., overgeneralizing, magnification of negatives, minimization of positives, and catastrophizing) with thoughts that are both realistic and effective, thereby limiting self-defeating behavior and emotional distress. Replacing inappropriate appraisals, coping, cognitions, emotions, and behaviors occurs through a series of steps that challenge an individual's way of thinking and their reactions to entrenched habits and behaviors.

Cognitive behavioral therapy or variants of the basic procedure that are tailored for specific conditions can be highly effective in the treatment of numerous disorders, including depression, anxiety, eating disorders, obsessive-compulsive disorder, and substance abuse, as well as psychotic disorders. It is effective when applied on a one-on-one basis and for some illnesses a group therapy approach can be used. It has also been used in a guided self-help approach, although the usefulness of this method has been questioned (Coull & Morris, 2011). It is of practical significance that in some illnesses (but not all) CBT acts additively with standard antidepressant medications as well as with other exposure techniques (Foa et al., 2011). Different pathological states call for variants of the CBT procedure, but regardless of the disturbance considered, a degree of flexibility is often needed in applying the treatment, and the odds are that a clinician's preferences and experiences influence where the greatest emphasis is placed over the course of therapy (e.g., on cognitive vs behavior modification approaches).

There is no question that CBT treatment programs have often been viewed positively for PTSD, OCD, bulimia nervosa, and clinical depression, as well as an adjunct treatment to diminish the distress associated with multiple sclerosis, breast cancer rehabilitation, epilepsy, HIV, and cancer. Despite its demonstrated effectiveness across situations, CBT is, however, sometimes rejected as a mode of treatment. In part, this might stem from the length of the therapy and the concentrated efforts that need to be expended by the therapist, and proponents of therapies such as CBT have indeed been critical of alternative procedures for devoting insufficient attention to the therapeutic relationship or alliance between patient and therapist. Some therapists have rejected CBT because of purported high non-response and high drop-out rates. Moreover, a potential limitation of CBT, in the view of some therapists, is that it works primarily in those individuals who have the belief that CBT can help them and thus are prepared to invest themselves in this approach.

PATIENT INPUT REGARDING TREATMENT OPTIONS

There are times, more often than we'd like, when our intuitions, even when based on considerable experience, don't meet the test of empirical analysis. In the previous text above, you have just learned that some therapists believe that CBT is most effective for those individuals that prefer this approach. In fact, in the case of some illnesses, when the treatment and the individual's preferences were aligned with one another the initiation of treatment, adherence rates, and attrition were improved, and in some pathological conditions somewhat superior effects of the preferred treatments were also observed (Kwan et al., 2010). In the case of depression, however, the results are less clear. There have been reports supporting the hypothesis that optimal results are obtained when the treatment preference and the treatment delivered were congruent with one another (Mergl et al., 2011), but there have also been studies that failed to observe such a relationship (Dunlop et al., 2011). The preferences that individuals have might reflect aspects of their personality, their beliefs about treatments, and their views as to what brought on the depression (biological vs experience-related factors), but none of these actually have much bearing on whether one or another treatment will actually work.

However, let's look at this from another perspective. In most studies patients were asked about treatment preferences, but they were not often asked about previous experiences (positive or negative) with medications or with any other form of treatment that could have influenced their expectancies about treatment efficacy. Significantly, as well, they typically were not consulted about treatments that they did not want. Although it seemed that a preferred treatment didn't necessarily work better than its alternatives, this doesn't speak to whether the positive effects of treatment are equally likely to occur when patients are given a treatment that they would prefer not to receive as opposed to one that they are neutral or positive about.

BEHAVIORAL AND BIOLOGICAL CHANGES

Beck (1970) viewed the cognitive system as comprising components that are primitive and those that are mature. Primitive systems are those that are idiosyncratic and unrealistic and exert a limited influence under basal conditions; however, this primitive system might predominate in the presence of psychopathology. The ways in which these primitive cognitions are expressed vary across pathologies. For example, depressed individuals may report cognitive distortions, as well as automatic thoughts or images concerned with deprivation, hopelessness, or self-debasement; anxious individuals, in contrast, may report cognitions or imagery concerned with imminent danger related to a specific or generalized stimulus.

COGNITIVE DISTORTIONS

Negative cognitions are frequently experienced automatically and do not seem to arise through reasoning, but instead automatic thoughts have an involuntary quality such that they invade the conscious experience of the depressed or anxious individual, and too often

TABLE 12.1

Common cognitive distortions

Arbitrary inference, in which the individual arrives at a particular conclusion when there is, in fact, limited (or opposite) evidence that would predict a particular outcome.

Dichotomous thinking, in which the individual considers one or both of two extreme positions without consideration of the multiple shades of grey that exist in between.

Selective abstraction, where only certain aspects of a situation (typically negative) are recalled or emphasized, and positive aspects are omitted.

Mind reading, where inferences are made regarding another individual's state of mind or thoughts without having evidence to support the conclusions.

Overgeneralization is characteristic of situations in which the individual applies the negative results of an event to a broader set of events or to all events.

Magnification refers to a situation in which the individual exaggerates the importance or meaning of a particular event.

Cognitive deficiency comprises a global pattern of thinking in which individuals fail to integrate pieces of information or when they ignore bits of information about a given situation that could inform them about the likelihood of particular outcomes.

---

these thoughts reflect that individual's negative appraisal style rather than an objective determination. Individuals frequently see the world in idiosyncratic ways, often displaying cognitive distortions that govern appraisals and hence the coping methods used (described in Table 12.1). The conceptualizations offered by Kahneman and Tversky (Kahneman, 2011) regarding decision making and appraisals that were described earlier are similar in many ways to the conceptualizations regarding CBT (e.g., the influence of priming in eliciting automatic thoughts or fast thinking). It is fascinating that work done in fairly disparate fields more or less come to the same conclusions, but arrive at these via very different avenues.

THERAPEUTIC CHANGE AND COGNITIVE THERAPY

As negative automatic thoughts are considered fundamental to the poor appraisals and coping methods that promote pathology, a primary goal of cognitive therapy is to have patients gain symptomatic relief by becoming aware and challenging these automatic thoughts (Beck et al., 1979). Later, the attitudes and dysfunctional belief systems (i.e., termed 'schemas') that generate automatic thoughts can be dealt with systematically. Among other things, a therapeutic change may arise by providing an opportunity for 'quieting' the hyperactive primitive (automatic) cognitive system. This can be achieved, in part, through Socratic questioning, wherein the therapist helps the patient identify these thoughts and then generate alternatives that are more likely and more favorable. Along with this, it might be helpful to have the patient practice identifying cognitive distortions in their thinking. Using these methods, changes in thoughts might precipitate a change in both feelings (affect) and actions, and fundamentally alter the individual's beliefs surrounding the situations in which they find themselves. Added to this, the therapeutic environment also affords the individual the opportunity to 'reality-test' their verbal and visual automatic thoughts. That is, do these automatic thoughts have some validity in fact? This reality testing can be a central component of systemic desensitization (e.g., in treating phobias) as patients may come to believe that their idiosyncratic ideas are irrational. Although 'exposure' to the irrational ideas or objects might first take place only cognitively, the patient is able to practice counteracting the irrational ideas before confronting the actual phobic stimulus.

Cognitive behavioral therapy may take weeks to complete, usually amounting to weekly sessions of one hour over about 12 to 16 weeks. Thus, this treatment requires a strong commitment to engage and follow the procedures outlined. Early in the treatment patients might recognize that their appraisals of threats are generally impractical and counter-productive, but knowing such things is only a first step. Replacing disturbed processes with those that are functionally effective is the more difficult job, and this may take weeks to achieve. As mentioned earlier, the specific therapeutic technique used will vary with the nature of the problem being addressed, but common to most approaches is that of maintaining a diary of significant events, and the related feelings, thoughts, and behaviors that were present. Furthermore, individuals are encouraged to question and test their appraisals (assumptions, evaluations, and beliefs) that might be counterproductive and likely incorrect. Finally, they are encouraged to deal directly with uncomfortable issues and find new approaches to dealing with them. Generally, the procedures used are not set in stone, and it is not uncommon for other methods to be incorporated into a CBT program, including distraction techniques and relaxation training, as will be discussed shortly.

NUTS FOR ADOLESCENTS

Young people are likely to encounter a great number of stressors, and often they have limited control over their own destinies. Finding effective treatment strategies to limit stress responses among adolescents has been difficult, although there have been some interesting programs established. One of these, the 'DeStress for Success Program' developed by Sonia Lupien at the Research Center of the Mental Health Institute at Louis-H. Lafontaine Hospital in Montreal, follows a multistep process. Adolescents are first taught about what stressors comprise (including what she calls the NUTS model of stress – novelty, unpredictability, threat to personality, sense of low control), after which they learn how to appraise stressors and recognize when they are stressed, which entails an understanding of the body's response to stress. Having gone through these steps, they then learn about different ways of coping, and how to use the NUTS model to deconstruct real-life stressors and diminish their impact. This is a fairly new program, but early signs speak to its usefulness in diminishing clinical and subclinical depressive symptoms among adolescents transitioning to high school (Lupien et al., 2013).

MEDITATION

Meditation refers to a practice wherein individuals train their mind or body so that they reach an alternative level of consciousness that would hopefully bring them a sense of calmness. Although we usually think of meditation as coming from Buddhism and Hinduism, forms of meditation are, in fact, evident in numerous religions. Whether the individual uses prayer beads, repetitive sounds or body movements, or attends to a focal point, these are, in a sense, related to meditation, and ought to have the effect of creating a positive internal state.

There is a vast amount of information available concerning different types of meditation, and data have been reported indicating that meditative practices can have physiological repercussions associated with calmness or low stress levels. The broadness of the topic, unfortunately, precludes a proper review of the literature. Suffice it that meditation practices have been associated with diminished cortisol levels, as well as variations in cognitions, brain electrophysiological (EEG) responses, and even brain activity changes assessed through neuroimaging (Rubia, 2009). For instance, following transcendental meditation, participants in a controlled study showed reduced stress responses while engaged in a stressful videogame (Mohan et al., 2011). There have also been reports that meditation was accompanied by altered psychological distress and reduced blood pressure and attenuation of the inflammatory immune response that was ordinarily evident in caregivers. Unfortunately, not all studies have been well controlled, and many have been affected by confounding variables that were not adequately considered. For example, meditation practices are often accompanied by other lifestyle factors (in relation to sleep, eating, smoking, and exercise) that also affect well-being, and the personality of individuals who seek out meditation might be distinguishable from those who don't, which also may influence well-being. As with some other approaches, meditation might be useful for some people, but definitely not for others.

MINDFULNESS

THE FUNDAMENTALS OF MINDFULNESS

Mindfulness as a way of coping was derived from both meditation-centered practices and traditions and cognitive behavior therapy (Brown & Ryan, 2003; Kabat-Zinn, 1990). Within some Eastern traditions, meditation can be used to draw attention away from unpleasant external thoughts and distractions (i.e., recent stresses, conflicts, etc.) and redirect the individual's focus towards moment-to-moment internal processes (Kabat-Zinn, 1990). To an extent, mindfulness adopts this strategy, at least insofar as it involves a focus on being attentive, aware, and non-judgmental regarding events in the present moment. Basically, if individuals are receptive to and non-judgmental of various situations, they will be less likely to ruminate or fixate on thoughts that are non-productive or even counter-productive. This permits the individual to observe events as they are unfolding, and to experience physical and emotional responses to these situations without attributing blame, judgment, or motivation to these responses (Brown & Ryan, 2003; Segal et al., 2002).

You will recall that sadness and negative rumination form a loop whereby one feeds into the other. Thinking in the moment in a non-judgmental manner may disturb the loop through which negative appraisals come to affect poor well-being, including anxiety and depressive symptoms. Hence, mindfulness has positive effects through a process that has been described as 'reperceiving'. This essentially reflects a shift in perspective that occurs through self-regulation, cognitive and behavioral flexibility, and a clarification of values. Kabat-Zinn (1990) has expressed this as follows: 'By watching your thoughts without being drawn into them, you can learn something profoundly liberating . . . which may help you to be less of a prisoner of those thought patterns – often so strong in us – which are narrow, inaccurate, self-involved, [and] habitual to the point of being imprisoning . . . .'.

Although mindfulness in a clinical context is considered as a method for dealing with stressors (or particular moods) that is taught to individuals, there are fairly pronounced differences in the degree of mindfulness that individuals exhibit in the absence of training. Just as some people are described as having one trait or another that can influence the way in which stressors affect them (or are dealt with), individuals may exhibit high (or low) trait mindfulness characteristics. The degree of mindfulness an individual has can be measured through the Mindful Attention Awareness Scale (MAAS; Brown & Ryan, 2003). This is an 11-item scale (e.g., 'I do jobs or tasks automatically, without being aware of what I'm doing', 'I rush through things without really being attentive to them'), and by using such an instrument, trait mindfulness was found to be associated with optimism, the endorsement of positive self-views, and engagement in effective problem-oriented coping strategies. An alternative to this scale is the Five Facet Mindfulness Questionnaire (FFMQ), which divides mindfulness into several components and thus is sometimes preferred as a research tool (Baer et al., 2006).

MBSR AND MBCT

The extent to which mindfulness has caught on as a therapeutic strategy to deal with stress and stress-related illness has been remarkable. It has been incorporated, with success, into treatment programs such as mindfulness-based stress reduction (MBSR, Kabat-Zinn, 1990) and mindfulness-based cognitive therapy (MBCT; Segal et al., 2002). This training reduces distress and increases general well-being, and produces positive effects among individuals with any of a number of conditions, such as substance abuse, chronic pain, binge eating, anxiety, loneliness in the elderly, recurrent depression, OCD, and distress related to cancer, and has been found to improve cardiovascular health and diminish anxiety among women in late stages of pregnancy.

Some of the positive effects of mindfulness may also develop by increasing attention control, self acceptance, and mood regulation that facilitate an appraisal of stressors in a focused and objective manner (Anderson et al., 2007). Moreover, by promoting acceptance, mindfulness might also come to diminish feelings of guilt and self-criticism that might otherwise evolve in association with some stressors or pathological conditions. Besides terminating the cycle of negative appraisals, mindfulness might also have the benefit of individuals becoming more aware of the positive events that they experience.

In addition to influencing appraisal processes, mindfulness may reduce dysfunctional coping strategies and encourage effective coping methods. As we already know, certain coping methods are automatic, reflexive-like responses that simply don't meet the needs that certain stressors create. It is thought that current moment awareness associated with mindfulness might facilitate the individual's focus on pertinent aspects of a stressful situation, rather than being overwhelmed by extraneous factors, including past or future concerns. In a sense, mindfulness might produce its effects through a process of 'disidentification', which limits habitual thoughts and behavioral patterns. This essentially entails the banishment of automatic thoughts and the replacement of them with momentary events without judgment or cognitive elaboration. This might result in diminished dysfunctional thinking patterns that lead to maladaptive appraisals and hence ineffective coping methods, replacing them with those derived on the basis of greater thought. Indeed, because mindfulness may diminish perceptions regarding uncomfortable thoughts and the resultant emotions, it could enable individuals to deal with stressors through the use of problem-focused coping. Essentially, awareness of thoughts and emotions, in concert with the appraisals of stressors as they unfold, might help individuals tailor their coping strategies to suit specific situations. In this regard, mindfulness was associated with creative problem solving, persistence in dealing with difficult tasks (Evans et al., 2009), and maintaining flexible coping strategies (Sugiura, 2004).

NEUROBIOLOGICAL CORRELATES OF MINDFULNESS

The impact of mindfulness is not only evident in its effects on psychological well-being, but has also been reported in relation to physiological indices associated with diminished distress. For instance, in a study assessing brain changes before and after MBSR (relative to a waiting-list group of control participants), the treatment promoted increased gray matter within several brain regions involved in learning and memory processes, emotion regulation, and perspective taking (Hölzel et al., 2011). As well, MBSR attenuated the changes of IL-6 elicited by stressors (Pace et al., 2009), reduced indications of inflammation, increased the antibody titer to the influenza vaccine (Davidson et al., 2003), and increased cytokine levels and NK cell activity in patients being treated for cancer (Witek-Janusek et al., 2008). Further, mindfulness can diminish the increased inflammation that has been associated with a stressful laboratory procedure comprising the Trier Social Stress Test, and might thus have implications for enhancing well-being among those affected by inflammatory conditions (Rosenkranz et al., 2013). Likewise, MBSR that diminished loneliness was accompanied by reduced levels of C-reactive protein and the transcription factor NFkB that is associated with cytokine production (Creswell et al., 2012). Clearly, mindfulness training has positive effects that go beyond psychological well-being, affecting biological processes that are ordinarily affected by stressors.

THE DEFAULT MODE NETWORK

We might often think, incorrectly, that when we're at rest, or seemingly not thinking purposefully (mind wandering), our brain might be relatively quiescent, but this certainly isn't the case. Neuroimaging studies indicated that during rest periods (quiet states) when attention was not focused on environmental stimuli, a particular neural network was active (Raichle et al., 2001). This network, which includes several cortical regions (the medial prefrontal cortex, posterior cingulate cortex and precuneus, posterior inferior parietal regions, lateral temporal cortex) and the hippocampal formation, came to be known as a default mode network (DMN). It seems that this network is active during passive thinking or what is referred to as stimulus-independent thought (Raichle et al., 2001), may be involved in mind wandering (Hasenkamp et al., 2011), and has been suggested to be a component of creativity (Buckner et al., 2008; Mason et al., 2007). Indeed, it has been suggested that analyses of DMN may be fundamental for our understanding of the mechanisms associated with consciousness (Northoff et al., 2010).

In contrast to the brain activity pattern seen at rest, the DMN is deactivated during goal-oriented activity (during tasks that are attention-demanding and involve a focus on external stimuli), and neuronal activity predominates in a different network (comprising the lateral PFC, premotor cortex, lateral parietal regions, anterior cingulate cortex, insula and occipital regions), dubbed the 'task-positive network' (TPN). As we've already seen, aspects of the brain are involved in several interesting balancing acts to maintain proper function. The TPN and the DMN, to some degree, act in an opposing fashion (Fox et al., 2005; Northoff et al., 2007). Thus, whereas the default network corresponds to task-independent self-referential thought or introspection, the TPN corresponds with action.

For cognitive tasks it is not only necessary that the TPN become engaged, it is also important for the DMN to be deactivated or tuned down (Anticevic et al., 2012). The absence of this tuning has, in fact, been associated with several pathological conditions. For instance, neurocognitive disturbances, such as schizophrenia, are accompanied by the failure of DMN suppression when individuals are performing complex tasks. Variations within the DMN have also been associated with dementia, epilepsy, anxiety and depression, autism, and attention deficit/hyperactivity disorder (Broyd et al., 2009). Disturbances of the default network were also evident in PTSD that was related to acute or early life trauma (Bluhm et al., 2009) and predicted the development of PTSD in acutely traumatized individuals (Lanius et al., 2010).

The presence of depressive symptoms has been associated with increased dominance of the DMN together with greater maladaptive, depressive rumination and lower levels of more adaptive, reflective rumination. Interestingly, as well, the neural networks associated with the two forms of rumination may also be differentially engaged in depressed and nondepressed individuals. Whereas the DMN is associated with 'bad' rumination among depressed individuals, activation of the fronto-insular cortex might engage the more adaptive TPN in those who are not depressed (Hamilton et al., 2011). Furthermore, among patients diagnosed with major depressive disorder, emotional-cognitive disturbances and an increase in self-focus were associated with DMN alterations.

If mindfulness is able to modify the networks engaged in relation to rumination and self-focus, and this becomes part of an individual's method of appraising and coping with stressors, then mindfulness training might turn out to be a useful long-term strategy to deal with stressors that might otherwise encourage depressive states. Success at mindfulness, at least insofar as brain functioning is concerned, tends not to happen just like that. In particular, mindfulness was accompanied by reduced emotional intensity in response to a series of pictures that should have elicited emotional responses, but the neural systems activated were different among experienced and novice mindfulness practitioners (Taylor et al., 2011). Among those who have had a good deal of experience meditating, but not among novices, mindfulness was associated with the deactivation of DMN areas and was not associated with changes of response in the brain regions involved in reactivity during emotional processing. It seemed that although mindfulness practice had positive effects both among novices and experts, the experience and practice in these groups were associated with different neural processes being engaged. This is not to say that mindfulness doesn't activate the 'right' regions in beginners, rather that mindfulness takes practice, just as playing a violin does. One can't reasonably expect instant success, and it may take time and practice to gain the full benefits of mindfulness training.

SLEEP: BORING BUT NECESSARY

There are some people who love to go to sleep and are ecstatic about sleeping-in. Others, however, find it a waste of time. Lying there in a state of apparent oblivion is simply seen as lost time. An acquaintance who really doesn't care for sleep described it as 'a practice run for being dead'.

Not much has been said in this book about what sleep entails, why we sleep, and how important it is for our health and ability to cope with stressors. However, it's long been known that it's as essential for our well-being as eating and drinking, and is driven by internal mechanisms, possibly being signaled by a build-up of adenosine, an endogenous substance involved in energy transfer. Much as hunger and thirst promote eating and drinking, sleepiness promotes sleep, and the biological consequences of sleeping quench the needs that otherwise drive us.

Sleep has been proposed as helping us in many ways: it can reduce our energy needs, especially when the search for food might be pointless or dangerous (i.e., at night), or it might have restorative functions so that the wear and tear that was incurred can be healed. By example, sleep may be essential for repair of cells that were damaged by free radicals that were created during very active periods. Sleep might also be necessary so that other aspects of our systems can be rejuvenated, as in the case of hormonal and immune functions that can go awry as a result of sleep deprivation. In fact, many of our biological functions, including protein synthesis and hence muscle and tissue repair, occur while we're asleep. It is particularly significant that sleep may also be fundamental for brain plasticity, and hence for appropriate brain development. The lengthy sleep periods in babies and young children might be necessary for plasticity, and as we've seen, neuronal plasticity is essential for learning and memory processes as well as being able to make accurate stressor appraisals and to cope effectively. Proper sleep won't get rid of your problems, but you likely won't deal with them effectively without proper sleep.

THE THIRD WAVE OF BEHAVIORAL THERAPIES

As with most scientific endeavors, including those that attempt to define human behaviors and modify those that are considered undesirable, change is common and typically welcomed. Newer approaches tend to adopt the best of earlier conceptualizations and add improvements. Behavior therapy has undergone three waves of change. In part, owing to the perceived shortcomings of psychodynamic approaches and cognitive behavioral therapy, a third wave of behavioral therapies emerged. Research that assessed the mechanism of exposure-based therapies (e.g., exposure to a feared object or context to diminish the affective responses ordinarily elicited) suggested that the *function* of internal events or thoughts was more important than their actual content or severity, and that notions of acceptance, change, and cognitive flexibility may have considerable utility in clinical practice, especially when treatment strategies entailed the development of broad, flexible, and effective responses.

One of these third wave approaches, Acceptance and Commitment Therapy (ACT; Hayes & Wilson, 1994), takes the perspective that psychopathology arises when long-standing beliefs or views that an individual holds limit or preclude behavioral flexibility because of an inability to distinguish between the on-going *process* of thinking as being distinct from the *products* of thinking (Hayes et al., 2006). Simply put, for some individuals thoughts become functionally equivalent to actual events. For example, in depressed individuals, the thought 'I am worthless' is not simply evaluated as a thought, but instead *cognitive fusion* may occur so that thoughts become functionally equal to actual experiences reflecting that of worthlessness. This fundamentally means that a negative process and the negative products of thinking become part of the same thing.

ACT differs from CBT in that it does not attempt to train individuals to better control their thoughts, feelings, sensations, memories, and other private events. Instead, ACT attempts to have individuals 'just notice', accept, and embrace their private events, especially those that had previously been unwanted. ACT helps people get in contact with a 'transcendent' sense of self (the person who is always there, observing and experiencing, and yet distinct from thoughts, feelings, sensations, and memories). Earlier, it was suggested that one of the most important considerations for good coping entails flexibility in changing strategies as situations require. Likewise, from an ACT perspective, cognitive inflexibility and experiential avoidance impede movement toward valued goals, and thus the function of ACT is to develop a psychological flexibility that will facilitate this movement. This entails six core constructs and processes: acceptance, defusion, mindfulness, self-as-context (observing the self), values, and committed action.

Acceptance comprises the active embrace of feelings such as anxiety, distress, and sadness, as well as the uncomfortable bodily sensations (e.g., sweating) that might accompany these states (Hayes et al., 2006). Having accepted this feature of the self, the second component, cognitive diffusion, encourages the reduction of the negative impact of certain thoughts and sensations. This entails the facilitation of processes that promote a critical analysis of the content of thoughts relative to actual experience, with the goal of the individual being able to reduce their attachment to their thoughts as reflecting reality. The third component, mindfulness, involves an on-going, non-judgmental perception of both internal (e.g., psychological) and external (e.g., environmental) events as they occur. By non-judgmentally evaluating internal and external events, the aim is to reduce the extent to which *cognitive fusion* limits psychological and behavioral flexibility and induces a failure to move toward valued goals. A central component of ACT is that we, as individuals, are not our thoughts, worries, and bodily sensations. These experiences come and go, but there is a self that remains and transcends these moment-to-moment experiences (Eifert & Forsyth, 2005). Portraying the self in this way de-emphasizes the importance or attachment to internal and external events, thereby allowing cognitive *defusion* to occur.

Finally, and this is of particular significance, ACT promotes committed *action* that moves the individual towards identified values. For this to occur, the individual's *values* must first be defined, and then committed action can be undertaken through activities, such as exposure to particular events, skills acquisition, shaping methods, and goal setting. Through committed action, the individual is able to build a larger and more flexible repertoire of psychological and behavioral responses, and simultaneously mitigate the ability of cognitive fusion and experiential avoidance to promote poor well-being. Therapeutic change can occur quickly because ACT focuses on the purpose of the actions or feelings that are the individual's central difficulty. For example, anxiety or depression is not viewed to be the problematic aspect of these disorders, but instead it is the actions undertaken to manage feelings of anxiety and depression that are problematic, especially as these limit the time and energy needed to pursue appropriate actions that are aligned with their identified goals.

Although ACT is not especially new, it has only recently been gaining a substantial number of adherents, and there have been few empirical studies thus far that have assessed its effectiveness. A meta-analysis revealed that relative to treatment as usual, a wait-list, or placebo, those in an ACT condition fared considerably better (Powers et al., 2009). However, there is no reason to assume that ACT is better than other cognitively-based approaches. Moreover, ACT is not without its own shortcomings. Among other things, it implicitly requires individuals to be psychologically minded, able to think abstractly, and to have strong verbal abilities in order for the various metaphors and demonstrations employed to be effective. Thus, it is not certain whether this particular treatment is suitable for children, elderly individuals experiencing a normal cognitive decline, or individuals with language difficulties.

SHARING THOSE EMOTIONS

Some therapeutic approaches involve patients sharing their emotions with others, including the therapist. However, for some people this is a difficult thing to do either because it's just too personal or because (in some men) it's not the macho thing to do. Recent studies assessing the influence of the hormone oxytocin revealed that following its administration numerous prosocial behaviors (e.g., increased trust) could be elicited. It was also observed that although the hormone

(Continued)

(Continued)

didn't make individuals more talkative when asked to recall a past negative experience, participants (even men) indicated an increased willingness to share that experience and the emotions it elicited with another person. It's possible that oxytocin treatments could eventually come into use to facilitate cognitive behavioral strategies to deal with stressor-provoked psychopathology. As well, oxytocin might also facilitate a person's disposition to reach out to others to gain social support that may serve to diminish feelings of distress that may otherwise feed into depressive disorders.

PHARMACOTHERAPY

In the sections that follow we'll consider the influence of a variety of drug treatments to ameliorate distress and some of the psychological problems associated with stressful events. As we've already seen, to a considerable degree our responses to stressors are governed by how we appraise the events that come about. These appraisals set up expectancies that have the effect of moving us in one direction or another. It seems that this also applies to our responses to medications to deal with pain, and there is reason to suppose that this might also be relevant to our responses to medications that ought to alleviate distress. If we are primed with the belief (expectation) that we'll get better, then it's more likely that we will. So, before we deal with the efficacy of various pharmacological treatments on stress-related psychological disturbances, we'll first have a look at how expectancies can affect illness amelioration. In this context, we'll be talking about the 'placebo response'.

THE PLACEBO RESPONSE

Placebo effects usually refer to the positive outcomes that are obtained in response to a treatment that cannot have direct effects on the physiological processes associated with a disorder (i.e., the treatment is an inert one that should, from a physiological perspective, have no effect on the pathology). It is generally thought that placebo effects arise as a result of verbal and observational cues, and classical conditioned responses, that give rise to expectancies, which then promote behavioral and clinical changes (Meissner et al., 2011). In fact, potent placebo responses can be induced even when participants are not consciously registering that they are being affected in this way.

Placebo treatments, as most everyone knows, are used in some drug studies to distinguish between the 'real' effect of the drug being tested versus the effects that are due to the patient's expectancies. The very fact that a placebo control is included in studies speaks to how frequent or how strong the placebo effect can be. Hence, it is a bit surprising to find that there are those who view patients who show a placebo response as either being a bit 'off', malingerers, or individuals who hadn't really been ill from the start. The fact is, however, that placebo treatments do actually influence biological processes and might thereby affect a variety of illnesses (Hróbjartsson & Gøtzsche, 2010), or at least the perception of their symptoms. In fact, placebo effects are so common, and expectancies of health improvement so dramatic, the case was made forty years ago that placebos ought to be considered as a part of the efficacy of many drug treatments (Cochrane, 1972). It has been shown, for instance, that patients who are told that they will receive morphine treatment through an automated infusion pump to alleviate the pain associated with a surgical procedure reported greater pain relief than did patients who weren't told when the treatment began (Colloca et al., 2004). Conversely, when patients receiving analgesic treatments were led to believe that their pain medication had been stopped, they reported increased pain perception (Bingel et al., 2011). The motivation and expectancies of the patient are so fundamental in producing a positive response that when a patient sees another person receiving pain medicine that works, they too will be more likely to show a similar response. The positive effects of placebos have most often been seen with respect to pain relief, but have also been evident in cases where patients are told they're receiving muscle relaxants or drugs that affect cardiac functioning (e.g., blood pressure), and in programs to quit smoking. Just as the expectancy of positive responses can assist the healing process, it also appears that patients who believe that a treatment will be ineffective may experience no benefits. This is referred to as a *nocebo* effect.

Placebos come in a variety of guises. They usually refer to inert medications, but they can also comprise mechanical or electrical devices to reduce pain or muscle aches, acupuncture needles inserted into inappropriate locations, or even faith healing. The key element here is that the patient believes that the treatment will work. Thus, it is understandable that physicians themselves are part of the placebo treatment, and trust in a physician may contribute to whether a prescribed treatment will be followed and whether positive effects will be realized (Stewart-Williams & Podd, 2004).

It is not unusual for depressed patients treated with antidepressants to show a positive response within a few days, after which the depression resumes until (and if) the full effects of the drug develop over the ensuing two to four weeks. Ordinarily, antidepressants require several weeks before their positive effects are significant, but the early response might be predictive of later treatment effects, perhaps because these patients are the 'true believers'. In fact, it has been suggested that a good portion of the positive effects attributable to antidepressants drugs actually come from the placebo effect that accompanies the treatment (Fournier et al., 2010), and that the added value of the drug treatments is modest (Khan et al., 2000).

As powerful as placebos might be, only a minority of patients show a sustained positive response to these treatments. As a result, there is interest in predicting which individuals will or will not display this response to treatment. It was recently reported that the presence of a particular polymorphism related to DA functioning (in this instance on the gene controlling the production of an enzyme catechol-O-methyl transferee that ordinarily degrades DA) could predict whether and to what extent an individual would exhibit a placebo response (Hall et al., 2012). Obviously, this could be of considerable clinical benefit in designing individual treatment strategies. Beyond this, however, placebo responses vary with the nature of the condition being treated. In the case of pain relief, where placebo effects are fairly high (ranging from 25 to 56%, again depending on the nature of the condition associated with the pain), the effectiveness of the treatments may approach that of low doses of morphine. Furthermore, personality factors, such as optimism and altruism, also contribute to whether and to what extent a placebo treatment will be associated with diminished pain perception (Geers et al., 2010; Morton et al., 2010). There are, to be sure, limits to the effects of placebo treatments, generally being absent when the illness involves severe physical diseases or viral illnesses, but they nevertheless might diminish the anxiety that accompanies these conditions.

It's all very well to say that the placebo response emerges as a result of expectancies, and that factors that influence these expectancies will affect the strength of this response, but what are the brain processes that govern these effects? Placebo analgesic treatments are accompanied by the activation of sub-cortical structures associated with pain and stress processes, such as the hypothalamus, amygdala, and midbrain periaqueductal gray (the latter refers to the gray matter around the cerebral aqueduct present in the midbrain; this brain region plays a fundamental role in pain perception and the elicitation of defensive behaviors) (Wager et al., 2007). Moreover, placebo analgesia is accompanied by the activation of brain regions that support emotional and varied cognitive processes as well as those associated with executive functioning, and reward processes, including the anterior cingulate, prefrontal, orbitofrontal and insular cortices, nucleus accumbens, and amygdala (Lidstone & Stoessl, 2007; Petrovic et al., 2002). As might be expected, it also appears that in several respects placebo and nocebo responses are accompanied by opposite brain outcomes (Scott et al., 2008).

WALKS LIKE A DUCK

Like many people, when I see television clips of faith healers placing their hands on the forehead of a person wishing to become well, I usually perform an eye roll and mutter something about village idiots; yet if this isn't preventing them from seeking more traditional methods of healing that could actually have some benefit, then there's really nothing wrong with it. It might be 'just' a placebo effect, but do we really care if it is? There are all sorts of plants that are said to have medicinal properties, even though these may not have been properly tested, yet few of us would roll our eyes when someone mentions these. Likewise, who among us would challenge chicken soup in helping to deal with a cold?

Deng Xiaoping, who served as the leader of the People's Republic of China from 1978 to 1992, in attempting to alter the course of China's development by dragging it into a market economy, famously stated 'No matter if it is a white cat or a black cat; as long as it can catch mice, it is a good cat'. Such beliefs caused him immense problems and as a result he was sent off for rehabilitation. After Mao died in 1976, however, he was able to attain the position of de facto head of state.

The comments Deng Xiaoping made regarding white and black cats also apply to placebo effects. It might not matter why placebos work, if they do the job then they are a good treatment.

In describing Mao (in relation to his policies), Deng diplomatically stated that he was 'seven parts good, three parts bad'. I suppose the same can be said about placebos.

CAVEATS CONCERNING DRUG TREATMENTS

Several fundamental issues ought to be resolved, or at least mentioned, before we get into the specific treatments that are used to deal with anxiety and depression. Psychiatric illnesses such as these are known to be biochemically and behaviorally heterogeneous, and it might not be appropriate to consider them as reflecting a disturbance of one neurochemical or another. Instead, these illnesses are system disorders that involve complex neural circuits. Thus, in developing a pharmacological approach to dealing with these illnesses, magic bullets might be hard to find, and even the target for these bullets will be elusive.

A second caveat concerns what the drugs are actually doing. It is often said that drugs might not be treating the disorder, but might simply be 'masking' the symptoms. Essentially, the drug treatment might not be getting to the processes underlying the disorder, only affecting specific symptoms. We certainly hear about people who were doing well in treatment, but then stopped taking their meds and fell back into the schizophrenic, bipolar, or depressed condition. Of course, it would be preferable to get to the specific processes that are messed up and fix them. Unfortunately, in most instances we aren't certain what mechanisms are responsible for a disorder, let alone what would get to those mechanisms and then fix them using some yet to be discovered tools. The mechanisms associated with mental disorders will eventually be identified, and techniques will be discovered that can fix the problem. For the moment, however, we have what we have.

Mental illnesses are often considered to be 'life-long disorders' and hence current drug treatments often need to be continued for protracted periods. I think that depressed or schizophrenic patients, as well as their families, are relieved to have the abnormal behaviors vanquished even if they are dependent on drug continuation. No doubt they would like a more complete fix so that all of the residual symptoms would be eliminated (even after a person is treated, they might not be the way they had been prior to the mental disorder emerging, and some symptoms may still remain). Think about it this way. An individual who gets a migraine headache is relieved that he or she has a drug that alleviates the pain. They likely will get a migraine headache again at some later time as the painkiller didn't fix the underlying problem, but the person is happy to have gained some relief, at least for the moment. Unfortunately, even temporary fixes aren't without their problems. Often the treatments have a variety of side-effects. Some may last for only a few days, or continue for as long as the drugs are on board, and others can appear following continued use over protracted periods.

There are several other issues that have limited the use of antidepressant medications. Soon after the commencement of treatment, some agents have been associated with increased suicidality, particularly among younger patients. This said, among severely depressed patients the period of recovery might also be accompanied by increased suicide attempts, as the depressed state has not yet been sufficiently reduced, but patients may have gained sufficient energy to initiate the active responses necessary for suicide.

Added to this, the sad fact remains that antidepressants are not as effective as one would like, and the efficacy of treatments varies on the basis of whom you believe (e.g., see Nutt & Malizia, 2008 vs Kirsch et al., 2008). In published studies the positive response rates are usually moderate or even high, whereas in the unpublished studies the efficacy hovers just above placebo rates – that in the case of depression can be as low as 20 to 35%. Moreover, as indicated earlier, even when effective, some symptoms persist and the relapse rate is high. As this information becomes more widely disseminated, trust in the treatments and those who administer them will decline. Unfortunately, with this decline the effectiveness of these treatments will also fall, as a crucial component of the treatments' effectiveness involves the belief by patients that their mental state will improve (i.e., the placebo component).

SOMETIMES DRUGS DON'T WORK FOR OTHER REASONS

There are times when a drug doesn't have a desired effect, and it is generally assumed that the drug, for whatever reason, isn't effective. In fact, sometimes the drug is very good, but the patient isn't. The patient might simply forget to take the drug, choose not to have these 'foreign' substances in their bodies, don't like feeling out of control, and in the end don't take the medication. Sometimes, patients might also not like the side-effects of the drug (in the case of SSRIs they might be discouraged by the sexual side-effects: diminished libido and difficulty reaching orgasm) and thus choose to go on drug holidays. So sometimes the culprit is not the treatment at all, it's a noncompliant patient.

When my mom was about seventy she had some bad side-effects after taking some prescription drugs. It seems that she took a few too many. When I asked her whether she was confused about the number of pills she was supposed to take, she said 'No, the bottle said take two pills every four hours. You think I'm an idiot? You think I need a PhD to read a pill bottle?'.

'So, ma, how did you end up taking too many pills?'

'Well' she said, 'I thought that if two pills every four hours would work, then four pills every two hours would work still better. I'm an old woman; you think I can just sit around forever waiting to get better?'

There's no doubt that the position offered by Kirsch et al. (2008) regarding the ineffectiveness of newer antidepressants may be partially correct, but the opposite perspective offered by Nutt and Malizia (2008) is also partially correct. Let's come at this issue of effective versus ineffective from another angle. Given the number of treatment choices that are available, how should a physician decide which drugs to administer? There are some physicians who understand what certain drugs and drug combinations do to particular symptoms, taking into account a host of variables. For these physicians their success rates are likely well above the average. There are others who have their favorite drug (based on various criteria or inclinations) and hence prescribe this particular treatment to anyone who seems depressed or anxious, as the case may be. This sounds pretty crude and doesn't inspire confidence, but the fact is that in most randomized controlled trials (RCTs) used to evaluate drug efficacy, which is what the Kirsch et al.'s (2008) report is based on, this is exactly what happens.

Patients who meet certain criteria (regarding their basic health and particular symptoms) enrol in a trial in which they receive one or another drug or a placebo treatment, sometimes in a single or a double blind protocol (or in an open-label trial comparing different drugs), and then their symptoms and outcomes are monitored over a set period of time. Even though the symptoms of a particular illness may vary across individuals, they still might appear in the same study having been conscripted based on a syndrome rather than the specific constellation of symptoms. The same theme has been recurring in this book, namely that treatments ought to be administered based on an individual's symptoms and biomarker profile, rather than on the basis of their meeting *DSM-IV* or *DSM-5* criteria for a particular disorder. Furthermore, appropriate drug combinations may have benefits well beyond those of monotherapies (e.g., Blier et al., 2010). Thus, strictly speaking the Kirsch et al. (2008) view is correct in suggesting that the effects of antidepressant drugs border on placebo response rates, but that doesn't mean the potential isn't there.

SELECTING THE RIGHT TREATMENT

Although there are numerous drugs that are more or less equally effective in the treatment of depression, at least when considering broad populations, there are differences that need to be considered. For starters, patients may not be responsive to one particular drug, and a second or third drug may be tried before some success is achieved (a subset of patients might be deemed to be 'treatment resistant' as three or more drugs were found not to be effective). Further, what are the side-effects of the treatments? Some drugs cause weight gain or sexual dysfunction and there are patients who will not stay on the treatment regimen if these side-effects occur. Indeed, sexual dysfunction is a fairly common side effect of SSRI treatment, affecting up to 80% of patients, depending on the drug, and has been reported to be the most bothersome side-effect of treatment. The sexual side effects of the SSRIs might come about owing to several biological changes exerted by the drugs, such as altered 5-HT activity or that of its receptors, DA changes, as well as through the gaseous neurotransmitter enzyme, nitric oxide synthase. In an effort to maintain the effects of the SSRIs and yet diminish the sexual side-effects, several therapeutic strategies have been used with varying levels of success. Increasing DA ordinarily enhances sexual responses, and some DA acting agents improved sexual functioning among individuals taking SSRIs. There has also been success in this regard by prescribing adjunctive treatments that affect 5-HT receptors. Most of these treatments have their own side-effects (e.g., sedation) or provide only limited diminution of the side effects of the SSRIs. The good news, however, is that there are drugs, such as bupropion, moclobemide, mirtazapine and a few others, which have little, if any, sexual side-effects, and thus might be the preferred treatments for some individuals.

Often, when one drug isn't successful in reducing depression, a second drug can be included as an adjunct. For instance, it isn't unusual for patients to receive a particular antidepressant together with trazodone (sold as Desyrel, Oleptro, Beneficat, Deprax, Desirel, Molipaxin, Thombran, Trazorel), which is a 5-HT acting antidepressant that also has strong anxiolytic and sedative effects. Likewise, quetiapine (Seroquel) and risperidone (Risperidal) are often administered with an antidepressant, especially when the depression is accompanied by high anxiety or high levels of irritability. As well as this, some antidepressant agents are used in conjunction with augmenter drugs that, as the name implies, have an augmenting action, such as buspirone (Buspar), bupropion (Wellbutrin, Zyban), gepirone (Ariza), and tandospirone (Sediel). Beyond these factors, consideration in prescribing drug treatments includes the gender and age of patients, and the presence of other illnesses, as well as any other drugs being taken. There is also reason to believe that ethnic and cultural differences exist regarding the effects of drug treatments, but these are not typically considered when drugs are prescribed, even though it is well known that polymorphisms related to depression vary appreciabley across ethnic and cultural groups. Eventually, still greater specificity will be developed to determine the most efficacious treatments, including individual data comprising the presence of genetic and other biological markers associated with illnesses.

TRANSCRANIAL MAGNETIC STIMULATION (TMS)

As electroconvulsive shock had positive effects in reducing depression, about thirty years ago attention began to focus on the possibility that magnetic stimulation of the brain could also have positive effects, although this procedure was first used to study the human motor system. In its more recent form transcranial magnetic stimulation (TMS) is a noninvasive method using electromagnetic induction to elicit weak electric currents through a rapidly changing magnetic field, thereby altering brain neural activity. A meta-analysis indicated that repeated TMS (rTMS) elicited positive effects comparable to that of antidepressant drugs, but poorer than that of electroconvulsive therapy (ECT). Moreover, it has frequently been effective in treatment-resistant patients, and was found useful in both young and older individuals. Because animal-based models aren't easily amenable to TMS, there is a paucity of information available concerning the neuronal processes by which it comes to have positive effects. However, it has been proposed that TMS might have its positive effects by stimulation of the anterior cingulate cortex. In addition to its increasing use in treating depression, TMS has also found a berth in the treatment of anxiety disorders, neurodegenerative diseases, pain syndromes, tinnitus, and the auditory hallucinations associated with schizophrenia.

ANTIDEPRESSANT AGENTS

It is not uncommon for people to think that antidepressant agents should be used only to treat depression and anti-anxiety drugs should be used exclusively to treat anxiety. However, as indicated earlier, because of their addiction potential anti-anxiety drugs are only recommended on a short-term basis, and antidepressants actually have potent effects on anxiety.

SELECTIVE SEROTONIN REUPTAKE INHIBITORS (SSRIS)

The class of drugs that had become especially popular in combating depression, known as 'selective serotonin reuptake inhibitors' (SSRIs) (Millan, 2006), was at first thought to have its beneficial effects by increasing the availability of serotonin (5-HT). You'll no doubt remember that once a neurotransmitter is released into the synaptic cleft, it is eliminated by degrading enzymes or by a process called reuptake (the latter doing most of the job). The SSRIs, as the name implies, hinder the reuptake process, leaving 5-HT in the synaptic cleft for a longer period, thus allowing greater stimulation of the post-synaptic receptors.

Fluoxetine (Prozac) and paroxetine (Paxil) had at one time been the best known of the SSRIs, but most individuals will also have heard of citalopram (Celexa, Cipramil), escitalopram (Lexapro, Cipralex), fluvoxamine (Luvox), and sertraline (Zoloft). These SSRIs have been moderately effective in diminishing psychopathology once present. However, they are not used to help individuals deal with day-to-day stressors or even moderately stressful events, and likely should not be used to deal with impending stressors (i.e., in a prophylactic capacity). The SSRIs never lived up to the hype that first accompanied their development, at least not in terms of the degree of relief obtained or the proportion of people that experienced diminished depressive symptoms. Nevertheless, in the right combinations the treatments can be fairly useful for some depressed patients, and they have been effective in treating illnesses such as OCD, GAD, PTSD, and other anxiety disorders. In fact, their relative effectiveness in dealing with certain forms of anxiety has made them front-line agents for these anxiety-related illnesses.

Although the efficacy of SSRIs isn't much better than the older tricyclic antidepressants, they are preferred because their side-effects are less pronounced. Still, as described earlier, there may be unpleasant consequences to these treatments, such as a loss of appetite, nausea, weight loss (or gain), sleep disturbance, and reduced libido or ability to reach orgasm, and in some instances coming off the drug needs to proceed in small steps since too fast a reduction of blood levels of the drug can be a bit of a bummer.

One of the shortcomings of SSRI treatments, like those of other 5-HT acting antidepressants, is that it usually takes several weeks (usually between two and four) before effects of SSRIs are evident. This itself leads to the possibility that the effectiveness of these drugs is not simply due to increasing the availability of 5-HT, but may require changes in one or more processes downstream of altered 5-HT levels. As we've already seen, these could entail gradual changes of certain receptors, changes of second messenger systems (these comprise molecules that are responsible for relaying signals from cell surface receptors to targets that reside within the cell), or cumulative indirect effects on other systems (e.g., growth factors). However, combination drug treatments may have beneficial effects in promoting the earlier onset of antidepressant actions. For instance, when SSRIs are combined with pindolol, which acts as a β-NE blocker, the antidepressant effects of these agents appear sooner (Blier, 2003).

COMBINATION DRUG AND CBT TREATMENT

There have been several reports indicating that treatment with an SSRI plus CBT yields better results than either treatment alone. Why is this? Is it a matter of the simple additive effects of the two treatments or is some other process at work here? A recent report (Karpova et al., 2011) has shed new light on this. Using mice, these investigators found that after a three-week fluoxetine regime there was no effect on responses associated with fear conditioning. That is, these animals were as likely as the controls to develop fear of a stimulus paired with an aversive event. However, when these animals received extinction training (the fear-provoking stimulus was presented in the absence of an aversive stimulus) the reduction of fear was more pronounced than in animals that had the fear extinction experience without the SSRI on board. Further experiments that assessed neural plasticity and BDNF variations indicated that fluoxetine treatment might have made the brain more plastic (more malleable) so that subsequent extinction training was more likely to engender the reshaping of maladaptive neural networks.

SEROTONIN-NOREPINEPHRINE REUPTAKE INHIBITORS (SNRIS)

The serotonin-norepinephrine reuptake inhibitors (SNRIs), a newer class of antidepressant drug, have their effect by inhibiting the reuptake of both 5-HT and NE. In addition to being used in the treatment of depression, these agents are also used to treat generalized anxiety disorder, social anxiety disorder, OCD, attention deficit hyperactivity disorder (ADHD), chronic neuropathic pain, fibromyalgia, and the relief of menopausal symptoms (e.g., Van Ameringen et al., 2009). To a considerable extent these agents have side-effects that are similar to those elicited by the SSRIs, and similarly, upon withdrawal some symptoms can potentially worsen (e.g., anxiety) and thus their discontinuation should usually be done by tapering the daily dosage. However, the sexual side-effects associated with SNRIs are usually diminished and some patients report effects opposite to those elicited by the SSRIs.

Venlafaxine (Effexor), the first agent of this class to be developed, tends to affect 5-HT at relatively low doses, and as the dose increases, effects on both 5-HT and NE occur. A second agent, duloxetine (Cymbalta, Yentreve), has also proven to be effective in the treatment of depression, but may have some pretty nasty side-effects among alcoholics and those with liver problems. In addition to being approved for major depression, it is also used for GAD and chronic musculoskeletal pain, including chronic osteoarthritis pain and chronic low back pain, as well as fibromyalgia. Other SNRIs that are available include desvenlafaxine (Pristiq), which is the active metabolite of venlafaxine, as well as milnacipran (Dalcipran, Ixel, Savella) and sibutramine (Meridia, Reductil), which was initially developed as an appetite suppressant, but found its way into the antidepressant arsenal.

MIGRATION OF DRUGS ACROSS VENUES

Many compounds that were developed for one purpose are subsequently found to be effective in other conditions. Warfarin, which was initially developed as a rat poison, has been used since the 1950s as an anticoagulant, and has proved essential for many patients (Coumadin is one of the brand names under which it is marketed). Likewise, thalidomide, which was initially used to quell morning sickness during early pregnancy, induced a vast number of birth deformities before it was removed from the market. Since then, it has resurfaced (administered together with the synthetic corticoid dexamethasone) in the treatment of multiple myeloma, a cancer of plasma cells (Singhal et al., 1999). Trials had also been undertaken to determine whether it would be effective in the treatment of leprosy, but these have since been dropped. There is also reason to believe that the antidepressant drug paroxetine may have beneficial effects for diabetes, but it does not involve effects on depression, as other antidepressants didn't have this effect.

Given the complex set of changes introduced by antidepressants, they have also found uses in the treatment of a variety of conditions other than those for which they were first developed. These have included the treatment of anxiety, PTSD, eating disorders, and even migraine headaches. This not only reduces the cost and time of bringing drugs to market, but as these agents have already been around the block, their side-effects (even potential long-term adverse actions) might also be well known already.

NOREPINEPHRINE-DOPAMINE REUPTAKE INHIBITORS

As described earlier, DA has been implicated in reward processes, and is thus thought to play a role in the anhedonia that is frequently a primary symptom of depression. However, as described in Chapter 8, the involvement of DA in depression may involve specific DA pathways, and it might prove challenging to alter these DA neuronal processes while leaving others unaffected. Nevertheless, the data concerning a potential role for DA in depressive disorders have been sufficiently compelling to warrant further research.

Years ago the involvement of DA in depression was more or less abandoned as drugs that affected DA (e.g., l-DOPA) did not act as an antidepressant. Since then, there has been evidence of DA involvement in depression. As with the other reuptake inhibitors that affect more than a single system, bupropion (Wellbutrin, Zyban) inhibits the reuptake of both DA and NE, although it may indirectly affect 5-HT activity as well. In general, bupropion is about as effective as the SSRIs (Clayton et al., 2006; Fava et al., 2005), but is not accompanied by sexually-related side-effects or weight gain, although it has been associated with increased blood pressure and the provocation of seizure. As a result it is not prescribed for individuals with risk factors for seizure, such as those withdrawing from alcohol or benzodiazepines, anorexia nervosa, bulimia, or those with brain tumors.

Although bupropion was established as an antidepressant, under the name Zyban, it has been used as an anti-smoking (cigarette) treatment, although other antidepressants can also act in this way. In addition, bupropion has also been used in the treatment of social phobia and anxiety comorbid with depression, as well as hyposexuality, obesity, and adult attention deficit disorder. Furthermore, bupropion reduces the inflammatory mediators TNF-α and IFN-γ, and thus could potentially be used in autoinflammatory conditions such as Crohn's disease and psoriasis, both of which can be aggravated by stressors.

NOREPINEPHRINE AND SPECIFIC SEROTONERGIC ANTIDEPRESSANTS (NASSAS)

These agents, also referred to as 'tetracyclic antidepressants', comprise a fairly new class of antidepressants that influence mood disturbances by increasing NE and 5-HT neurotransmission. However, unlike the SNRIs, these agents do so by blocking presynaptic α2-adrenergic receptors, which results in a greater synthesis of NE, while the drug concurrently blocks certain 5-HT receptors. Included in this group of drugs are mianserin (Bolvidon, Norval, Tolvon), mirtazapine (Remeron, Avanza, Zispin), and setiptiline (Tecipul). As with many drugs that affect mood state, these agents have side-effects such as drowsiness, increased appetite, and weight gain.

MONOAMINE OXIDASE INHIBITORS (MAOIs)

One route for the degradation of 5-HT, NE, and DA is through the enzyme monoamine oxidase (MAO). Inhibiting this enzyme increases the levels of these monoamines and hence should provide antidepressant effects, but this class of drug seemed to have only modest effects when administered by itself. Although the use of older forms of the MAOIs is relatively infrequent, a new generation of MAOIs has seen increased use. This includes moclobemide (Manerix), which is known as a reversible inhibitor of monoamine oxidase A (RIMA) that serves in a relatively short-lived and selective manner, and unlike the older MAOIs does not require a special diet. Other drugs in this group include isocarboxazid (Marplan), phenelzine (Nardil), selegiline (Eldepryl, Emsam), and tranylcypromine (Parnate).

NMDA ANTAGONISTS

Glutamate, a substance that we have only touched upon to this point, has been implicated in depressive illness, and the focus on this substance has increased dramatically in the past few years, particularly given the findings that drugs that antagonize receptors relevant to glutamate, and N-methyl-D-aspartate (NMDA) receptors in particular, may have antidepressant actions (Skolnick et al., 2009). In fact, one of the common effects of SSRI and SNRIs, as well as of electroconvulsive shock treatments, is that they influence the NMDA receptor, which could potentially account for why these treatments have their positive effects.

Ordinarily, glutamate has an excitatory action through its effects on the postsynaptic activation of NMDA receptors. Once released, and having done its work of stimulating the receptor, glutamate is taken back up into the neuron through a reuptake process. However, under certain conditions, as in response to brain injury, stroke, or other brain illnesses, a reverse process can be provoked so that glutamate levels increase outside of the neuron (or glial cell), then enter the cell through NMDA receptor channels, ultimately leading to excito-toxicity (i.e., damage to or the death of neurons). In effect, under one set of conditions NMDA manipulations can have positive effects, but under another set of conditions these can induce the opposite outcome.

Although several drugs in this class promote antidepressant-like actions, the effects of ketamine have received particular attention. Ketamine was best known as a general anaesthetic (in veterinary practice) and was typically used in conjunction with a sedative, but it has found its way into the street drug culture (where it is known as Special K) because it produces a dissociative and hallucinogenic-like effect that persists for about an hour. It has also served as an analgesic, where it was informally observed that when patients were treated with ketamine for chronic pain, the frequent comorbid symptoms of depression also disappeared, although this occurred very soon after treatment, rather than the two to three weeks usually required for antidepressants to have positive effects. Subsequent clinical trials confirmed that ketamine could, indeed, be effective as an anti-depressant (Berman et al., 2000; Zarate et al., 2006). In the first of these studies (Berman et al., 2000), which for obvious reasons involved only a small number of participants, the effect of the ketamine was dramatic, with depression scores dropping markedly within three hours of the drug being administered. However, the effect lasted for three days, and the poor mood fully returned within one to two weeks. Subsequent studies produced equally impressive results, and a rapid response was even obtained in patients who had not responded positively to standard antidepressant agents (i.e., in treatment-resistant patients) (Zarate et al., 2006). Later studies also indicated that the drug rapidly reduced suicidal ideation, and with several administrations could also have effects that lasted longer (e.g., Price et al., 2009). Other compounds, such as traxoprodil (CP 101 606), that affect certain types of NMDA receptors, also appeared to have rapid and potent effects that dissipated with the passage of a week or two (Preskorn et al., 2008). It seems that drug companies have financial faith in the promise of NMDA ant-agonists in the treatment of depression, as several plan to develop NMDA receptor antagonists for treatment-resistant depression. For instance, a new compound, tentatively called GLYX-13, which acts as an NMDA receptor antagonist, was found to have a positive effect within 24 hours among treatment-resistant patients, without the negative side effects that other treatments might have (Burgdorf et al., 2012). Still, the positive effects of the compound lasted only seven days, and further studies will determine whether it can be used repeatedly.

It's still a bit early to know precisely how ketamine comes to have the positive effects that it does, and why these effects are relatively transient. Nevertheless, it was shown that ketamine provokes an increase of BDNF, and rapidly engenders synaptogenesis and spine formation in frontal cortical regions by stimulation of the 'mammalian target of rapamycin' (mTOR; the protein that regulates cell growth, cell proliferation, cell survival, protein synthesis, and transcription), and increased levels of synaptic proteins. It has been shown that through these processes ketamine is able to reverse the atrophy of PFC neurons ordinarily produced by chronic stressors (Duman & Aghajanian, 2012). It has also been reported that ketamine affected the default mode network that accompanied depression, and it is possible that it had this effect by altering the inflexible ruminative features of depression. In effect, ketamine might have allowed individuals to break out of the negative cognitive rut that is characteristic of depressive disorders.

DEEP BRAIN STIMULATION: A RECENT FRONTIER

Given that neuronal activity involves the electrical stimulation of neural circuits, several investigators assessed whether electrical stimulation of neurons deep in the brain (this procedure is referred to as deep brain stimulation or DBS) would attenuate the symptoms of Parkinson's disease that are due to a loss of neurons within the substantia nigra, the site of cell bodies for a major dopamine pathway (Lang & Lozano, 1998). Given the success achieved with this procedure in Parkinson's patients, clinical studies were done to assess whether a similar procedure would be effective in alleviating depression in those patients for whom no other treatment seemed to work. But which brain regions should be targeted? Depression seems to involve complex neural circuits, but it appeared that activity of the subgenual cingulate cortex (CG25 or area 25) was associated with a sad mood, and this was reversed by antidepressant drugs as well as electroconvulsive therapy (ECT). Importantly as well, the CG25 has been reciprocally linked to other sites deemed significant for depression, such as the medial prefrontal, orbital, and aspects of the anterior and posterior cingulate cortices.

Mayberg et al. (2005) observed that DBS of the CG25 had marked and lasting effects in four out of six patients who had been treatment resistant, and this outcome was also seen in related brain regions. The efficacy of the treatment declined over time, but, when lasting stimulation was provided by a battery pack implanted just beneath the collar bone, more than half the patients reported a symptom reduction (and 36% reported complete relief) even after two years. In a recent interview (Sharon Kirkey, *Postmedia News*), Dr Mayberg was reported as saying that most patients reported a response immediately upon the implanted electrodes being turned on (patients are awake while the correct site for electrode placements is determined). They indicated that '... they feel lighter, they feel more connected ... The mental churning or mental pain is gone'. Dr Mayberg further stated that deep brain stimulation wasn't making people happy, but was effective in 'removing that deep, dark negative empty sadness, that interference that is so profound that it totally hijacks your brain from doing anything else'. Interestingly, she also indicated that when patients were first treated they also came to the realization that the mental pain they had been experiencing was gone, and they could think about what they should do to avoid its recurrence. Ultimately patients need some form of rehabilitation, possibly involving additional methods (e.g., CBT), to realize a full recovery.

Surgery is obviously a last resort, and although it is a relatively safe and effective procedure, as with any other surgery, it involves a risk of infection, hemorrhage, stroke, seizures, and in rare cases, death from the general anesthesia.

ANTI-ANXIETY AGENTS

BENZODIAZEPINES

There's a fairly large arsenal of anti-anxiety medications available. The anti-anxiety medications that likely come to mind are those such as diazepam (Valium), alprazolam (Xanax), chlordiazepoxide (Librium), clonazepam (Klonopin), lorazepam (Atavan), and maybe even clorazepate (Tranxene) or etizolam (Etilaam), each of which is fast acting and may be an effective short-term remedy. These drugs belong to a class known as benzodiazepines that have their effects by influencing GABA receptor activity. They are also used as anticonvulsants and muscle relaxants. As effective as they might be, benzodiazepines are not recommended for long-term use as they are associated with the development of tolerance, physical dependence, and withdrawal symptoms (Cloos & Ferreira, 2009). It is known that benzodiazepines influence DA neuronal activity, and like other addictive agents might ultimately hijack the mesolimbic reward system (Tan et al., 2011). The addiction potential of these drugs limits their use in the treatment of chronic illnesses, and SSRIs have generally become the first-line choice of drug treatment in this regard, whereas benzodiazepines are primarily prescribed for their short-term actions on anxiety and sleep problems, as well as to induce muscle relaxation and control epileptic seizures.

A treatment related to benzodiazepines (but actually quite distinct) is that of pregabalin, a structural analogue of GABA (Owen, 2007). Pregabalin is effective as an anxiolytic and is most often used among patients with moderate/severe baseline anxiety, in those with subsyndromal depression, and in older people. This compound is tolerated well, having fewer cognitive and psychomotor effects than benzodiazepines, and the most common adverse events comprise dizziness and sleepiness. Some degree of tolerance develops with several weeks of treatment, but withdrawal symptoms are moderate over a one-week period of stepped dose reductions. Consequently, this compound might be preferable to benzodiazepines in the treatment of GAD.

AZAPIRONES

These compounds, including buspirone (Buspar) and tandospirone (Sediel), are characterized by their agonistic (stimulating) action on 5-HT$_{1A}$ receptors. They do not have the addiction potential or sedation associated with benzodiazepines, but they are somewhat less effective. Azapirones may also be less effective among patients that had previously received benzodiazepine treatment, possibly because these patients might have expected the sedation ordinarily associated with the latter agents.

NOREPINEPHRINE β-BLOCKERS

As the activity of NE in several brain regions is markedly influenced by stressors, it is no surprise that NE might be involved in some of the behavioral effects of stressors, including anxiety and depression. Although used less frequently than benzodiazepines in controlling anxiety, the β-adrenergic antagonist propranolol has been used to diminish anxiety. As described in Chapter 9, in recent years it has seen a revival of sorts in that is has been used increasingly to treat PTSD, as it may be especially effective in reducing the fear memory associated with a traumatic event. Reiterating what was said earlier, the drug is used either soon after the trauma experience, or alternatively, when patients are asked to recall the traumatic event in an effort to alter reconsolidation of the trauma memory.

HERBAL (NATUROPATHIC) TREATMENTS

The array of treatments for a variety of ailments has included natural products or those developed on the basis of known effects of natural products. There is a scientific journal devoted specifically to this topic (*Planta Medica*), although one can find numerous relevant experimental papers in mainstream journals specific to particular illnesses or biological systems. Complementary or alternative medicines have ranged from treatments for breast cancer (tamoxifen) through to aloe vera for the treatment of burns, opium to reduce pain, digitalis as a heart stimulant, and aspirin as an anti-inflammatory and pain suppressant. Moreover, the hallucinogenic agent psilocybine, which is obtained from a number of different mushrooms, has in the past two decades been used in an effort to treat conditions such as OCD and cluster headaches, and to bring a reduction of anxiety and new life perspectives to those with terminal cancer.

In the case of depressive illness, the natural product that stirred the greatest attention for a while was St John's Wort. A review of the literature indicated that it was superior to placebo and had fewer side-effects than SSRIs (Linde et al., 2008), although it seemed that the effects were most notable in Germany where it has been used for some time, and where there seems to be a great deal of confidence in its effectiveness (is this a culturally-dependent placebo effect?). Subsequent studies indicated that it was not effective in the treatment of chronic low-grade depression, i.e., dysthymia, and a study conducted through the National Center for Complementary and Alternative Medicine (NCCAM) indicated that in the treatment of depression its effects were no greater than that of placebo. Not unexpectedly, supporters of St John's Wort have been critical of these negative studies, and at the moment it seems that we've reached a stalemate of sorts.

As with herbal medicines, nutritional factors have long been recognized as important to our psychological well-being. Fish oils (omega 3 fatty acids) have been suggested as a prophylactic and therapeutic treatment for depressive illness, and there has been evidence that polyunsaturated fatty acids (PUFAs) have a protective role in depressive illness, but subsequent reviews have been less inclined towards reaching the same conclusion. To be sure, PUFAs have been implicated in a variety of diseases, including those related to neuronal degeneration and immunological disturbances, and it's hard to know what's hype and what's real. At this point, a safe presumption might be that eating certain foods won't necessarily make you smarter or happier, but poor nutrition will have negative effects on these and many other states.

CONCLUSION

One message that has been set out repeatedly in this book has been that appreciable differences exist across individuals with respect to the behavioral and neurochemical changes that are induced by stressors. It is reasonable to expect that there will also be differences in the efficacy of various treatments in diminishing these effects and in attenuating pathological states. Not all individuals are equally responsive to various SSRIs or SNRIs: one individual may be most responsive to venlafaxine, whereas another might respond best to fluoxetine. Often, it's a hit-and-miss process. Likewise, there are some individuals who respond well to CBT or mindfulness training, whereas others seem not to respond well at all. Furthermore, for some depressive disorders combined drug and cognitive therapy may have positive effects beyond those of a single treatment.

For therapists, after being certain of a diagnosis, the big trick is to decide on the proper treatment. As indicated earlier, the specific symptoms presented will often guide the way, but this is not always the case. Clearly, just as there is a need for 'biomarkers' (measurable biological substrates that are tied to disease states) to predict who is vulnerable to an illness (or already has the first elements of a disease), it would be enormously profitable to discover behavioral markers that could inform which treatment will be most effective for a particular patient. This is especially the case when the treatment has a relatively low success rate, and it takes weeks to find out whether or not the drug is actually doing the job. As indicated repeatedly, and indeed it can't be said often enough, individualized treatments will ultimately be necessary wherein treatments are determined by genetic factors, the presence of certain blood or cerebrospinal fluid (CSF) markers, the individual symptoms presented, and psychosocial factors, such as the way individuals deal with stressors. Unlike the simplicity inherent in buying new socks, in the treatment of stress-related illness, there's currently no such thing as 'one size fits all'.

SUMMARY

- The way we handle stressors and the emotional/physical reactions to stressors can be modified through behavioral, cognitive, or pharmacological approaches.
- Of the cognitive approaches, CBT has enjoyed the greatest reputation and has been used across a wide range of conditions. Mindfulness training has been receiving increasing attention, and its usefulness has also been fairly impressive.
- Pharmacological treatments have clearly been effective for some individuals, but a substantial portion of individuals demonstrated little gain from drug remedies. These drugs have nevertheless been used very widely, probably owing to the ease of treatment relative to the more sustained and difficult efforts that go into cognitively-based therapies.
- As more is learned about the use of drugs in combination, and basing treatments on specific symptoms and particular biomarkers, enhanced treatment outcomes might be realized.

13 NAVIGATING STIGMA AND DISCRIMINATION AND SEEKING HELP

ONE TOO MANY

By all accounts, Susan was a typical young woman who moved from home to attend university in a city about 400 km away. Although she was excited at finally taking this big step, she was also fairly distressed, experienced a fair bit of homesickness, and seemed to have trouble with the transition to university. She met many other kids in university; happy kids, friends with each other, partying, going out, and studying. However, she didn't feel like one of them, even though they always came by and invited her to all sorts of events. Instead, she felt at the margins of the group, largely isolated and lonely. Her distress became progressively more pronounced as the term continued, and she had a great deal of trouble studying. Reading her class texts and notes through the tears, it seemed that nothing sank in. She read the same paragraph over and over, usually in automatic mode, but each time nothing seemed to stick in her head. Often, she ruminated between sentences, ruminated as she fell asleep, and ruminated still more in the mornings. She read sad books and listened to sadder music. She had lost her appetite, her weight had plummeted, her shoulders had become boney, and she hated looking at herself in the mirror; she especially hated her sallow, pale, tired-looking skin. Finally, the Christmas break came and she went home. Her family knew something was wrong with her, but she wouldn't speak to them about it. Instead, she hid away in her room. She didn't interact with her parents or her younger sister, and avoided all her high school friends. Following the Christmas break, her symptoms and social withdrawal became more profound, and she felt guilty for being such a wretch toward her family during the break. She felt that she was just a loser, and that nothing would ever change.

Several weeks later Susan disappeared from her residence. It was not until the spring ice had broken that her body was found along the shore of a nearby lake. It seems she had walked out on the lake, and eventually the ice gave way. Her friends and family were devastated, wondering why she hadn't turned to them for her help. Her friends described her behavior prior to her disappearance as stressed and withdrawn, but not desperate or extreme. She presented no extraordinary signs that she had reached the depths of hopelessness and depression. She had not relied on the caring and concerned support of those around her. It was revealed that she had shared her distress with an online 'friend', who turned out to be a viperous predator that over several weeks had encouraged her to take her life, even offering to join her in a shared suicide. Those who loved her are still trying to comprehend how such a thing could have happened, how they missed all the signs, whether anything could have been done to prevent it, and why in the world she reached out to an internet stranger while shutting them out.

Perhaps the question shouldn't be one of why *didn't* she reach out for help, but more aptly, why *couldn't* she reach out for help?

Of the stressors we encounter, there are many that have effects so strong as to scorch us permanently. Some affect us personally and some collectively, giving rise to individual or collective guilt, or to individual or collective shame. Some of these stressors are so far beyond our range of coping abilities as to make any efforts to eliminate the stressor seem entirely pointless. In these cases, as we've seen earlier, we often turn to one of our strongest coping resources, namely seeking and using our social support networks. However, as we've already seen, the act of seeking support might have repercussions that cut both ways. What happens when you seek support and don't receive it, or when supportive gestures are interpreted as being inadequate or counterproductive? Such responses coming from friends may cause immense distress and promote poor well-being, and may be sufficiently powerful as to undermine the positive effects obtained from otherwise effective social support resources.

Most books that deal with stress or treatments to alleviate it typically don't include much on the topic of seeking help, even though this is likely the primary obstacle to being healed, and the distress related to stigma and discrimination is likely the primary obstacle for people to seek and obtain help. In considering the distress associated with discrimination and stigma, there are several fundamental issues that might drive your thinking, determine how you frame this issue, and should be foremost in what you get from this chapter:

- discrimination against other groups can be manifested in various subtle or gross ways, and can have psychologically and physically damaging effects on the recipients of this abuse;
- through our social identities and with the support of our group we are able to deal with some of the potential adverse effects of discrimination, and as described in Chapter 11 in reference to the inter-generational effects of stressors, challenges of this sort can actually strengthen us;
- stigma related to mental health targets an individual for something over which they have no control, but is nonetheless often viewed as a personal shortcoming. Thus, it has many effects like that

of discrimination, but creates even more intense feelings of shame, and often there is no source for ingroup social support;

- there is a great need to bring the mentally ill out of the shadows at last (as indicated in the report by Kirby and Keon in their Canadian Senate report in 2006), create a positive social environment for the affected individuals, enhance trust in our medical and social systems, and provide the resources necessary to facilitate help seeking.

DISCRIMINATION AND STIGMATIZATION

Discrimination in its many guises (racial, religious, gender, or in relation to mental illness, physical characteristics, or deformities) has been around for ages, and often represents an exceptionally powerful stressor. At its most severe it comes in the form of genocide, which occurs across countries even today (witness the situation in Darfur that has festered for years without outside intervention, and now South Sudan is being further challenged, and Catholics in Nigeria are apparently suffering from it, as are Copts in Egypt), and those with mental illness or disabilities have suffered in a similar way (e.g., the Nazi regime's policy was exactly this). With discrimination comes something that is just as odious, namely stigmatization. The term means marking individuals (or groups) so that they might be singled out, but not in any good way. They stand apart, they're different, and they're not one of us. Typically, even if this isn't overt, they suffer the slings and arrows or glares and smirks of others, and must go through life branded.

BLATANT DISCRIMINATION AND MICROAGGRESSION

Sometimes discrimination is brutal and unmistakable, but there are times when it is manifested as microaggressions that comprise subtle remarks. In a politically correct society, individuals have learned how to express discriminatory attitudes without appearing bigoted or insensitive. Thus, when subtle discriminatory remarks are made, the recipient might be unsure whether they are over-interpreting the meaning intended: 'Was that a racist remark? Were they joking? Was the remark aimed at me personally, or at my group, or was it aimed at me as a member of my group? How do I respond? Should I challenge them and assert my rights as an individual (possibly appearing aggressive or foolish in the eyes of others), or do I "just let it go" and ruminate for days afterward (sky-high levels of stress hormones notwithstanding)?' Although discrimination is typically not considered as 'a stressor you've recently experienced' in most stress questionnaires, it is tied to anxiety and depression, and it might be associated with PTSD symptoms (Matheson & Anisman, 2012). Even in a laboratory context where social interactions were examined through the use of on-line communication, rejection by another participant (actually a stooge in the experiment) from a different race created more anger, increased blood flow, elevated vigilance, and disturbed cortisol reactivity relative to that seen among individuals who experienced rejection by a same-race participant. Interestingly, those individuals rejected by a partner of a different race also showed elevated responses to rewarding stimuli, which might have made them more likely to engage in high-risk behaviors (gambling), and they tended to be more reactive (or vigilant) to potential racism in response to ambiguous cues. Clearly, rejection and discrimination can have powerful effects, and when these occur on a systematic basis they represent a strong precipitating factor for the development of illness.

THOSE LITTLE COMMENTS

Microaggressions are common daily events that transmit, often unintentionally, a derogatory attitude toward other groups. These microaggressions have replaced outright discrimination as people have become more politically or socially correct (Sue et al., 2007): 'You're a credit to your people', which means 'Your group is generally useless/despicable/perverted/dishonest/filthy (choose the adjective), but you're . . . '. Or how does the Aboriginal kid feel who's called on in class to give their view of 'the Aboriginal experience' (as if they could possibly speak for all the members of their group)?

If you're not part of a minority group you might not notice it, and when its brought to your attention you might react with either 'Oh brother, here we go again' or 'Don't you think you're being a bit too sensitive?'. Predictably, this makes things worse. Eventually, you might get it, at least at an intellectual level, but (excuse the cliché) you won't understand it emotionally until you've walked in the other person's shoes. I get the feeling that some individuals who've never been the victims of discrimination sometimes react like alexithymic individuals who know what they're supposed to feel, and can mimic the appropriate emotions, but don't really understand their own emotions or those of others.

Occasionally we will witness the outrage that is elicited by overt racism or discrimination of any sort, but rarely will we witness the outrage elicited by subtler forms of these ideologies, including microaggressions. Recently, I was made aware of exceptional poetry by Vanessa Hidary that expresses this perfectly, but more eloquently than most of us ever could. I'll bet anything that you'll listen to it more than once (www.youtube.com/watch?v=yAeWyGGTdEE).

SOCIAL IDENTITY

Identification with a group can serve several functions, and positive effects may emerge even when one's group is socially devalued. Among other things, identifying with a group can play a buffering or protective role against stigma and the rejection associated with discrimination. Moreover, when this discrimination is targeted at a group it may facilitate collective actions being endorsed (Jetten et al., 2012). That said, being a member of a stigmatized group can be exceedingly stressful, and when injustices are perceived, this affects an individual's view concerning the notion that status in society is earned, and prejudice against the group is perceived as a profound threat against the self.

Discrimination experiences may be associated with disturbed health, particularly when the discriminatory actions occur frequently and on an unpredictable basis. However, members of groups under threat don't necessarily demonstrate disturbed psychological or other health outcomes. In fact, individuals who highly identified with their devalued social group were least likely to fall into depression or experience a loss of esteem when their identity was threatened. Essentially, group identification may serve as the basis of a cognitive framework that diminishes appraisals of threat and encourages effective coping with discrimination (Haslam et al., 2009). Individuals who identify strongly with the challenged group might acknowledge discrimination when it occurs, but at the same time they may also be the most likely to perceive that they have appreciable coping resources in the form of ingroup support. Those who have a strong sense of shared identity are especially likely to perceive social support from their group, which might act as a buffer so that individuals will not perceive themselves as the distinct target of negative stereotypes, and hence prevent feelings of rejection. In fact, with the support of other group members, discrimination may actually enhance features of identity, including self-concept (centrality), ingroup affect or pride, and a sense of emotional involvement or attachment with other group members (ingroup ties) (Cameron, 2004). In effect, adversity might create greater group cohesion, give the individuals purpose, enhance social support, and engender collective action that encourages resilience to the insidious effects of discrimination.

Even though we might have our own group to fall back on when facing discrimination, and collective action can act as a buffer to diminish feelings of helplessness, it seems that sustained, unrelenting discrimination can negatively affect our self-identity, especially if the attitudes of others are incorporated into victims' own self schema. Among other things, discrimination can elicit feelings of shame and humiliation, and might make people want to play turtle and withdraw into whatever shell they carry. To be sure, even after adjusting for age or socioeconomic status, members of socially-devalued groups (e.g., women, blacks, gays, Aboriginals) express disproportionately high levels of psychological disturbances (depression, anxiety disorders) and physiological disruptions (e.g., immune disturbances, oxidative stress in red blood cells, diabetes, cardiovascular problems, physical disabilities, infant mortality). The specific health disturbances that are associated with discrimination may vary as a function of the specific group being examined, likely stemming from a combination of genetic, cultural, and environmental contributions (e.g., diet, activity). For example, suicide is particularly high among Aboriginals, but low among African-Americans (Gibbs, 1997), who are at a greater risk of cardiovascular illness (Wyatt et al., 2003). Clearly, predisposing risk factors exist for certain pathologies, and it is possible that discrimination (as with other life stressors) contributes to their emergence. Identifying the extent to which discrimination contributes to disease is made difficult by the fact that there are strong social pressures that discourage individuals from recognizing (or discussing) discrimination.

THE LAST OF THE JUST

What is the effect of severe discrimination and bullying? As bad as this is in adults, think of how it affects children, who don't yet have the resources or coping skills to deal with these insults, and who day after day have to face their oppressor's smirk. There is a quote in *The Last of the Just* (Andre Schwarz-Bart, 1959) that struck a note with me and so I thought I'd share it. His comment refers to events in Germany in 1934, which was soon after the campaign against the Jews began, and was prevalent in schools, but preceded the mass killings that occurred subsequently. I've selected this quote because Schwarz-Bart so effectively expressed the extent of the discrimination and bullying and its consequences.

> Statistics show that the percentage of suicides among the German Jews was practically nil during the years before the end. So it was in the prisons, in the ghettos, in all the caves of darkness where the beast's muzzle sniffed up from the abyss, and even at the entrance of the crematoriums – 'anus of the world' in the words of a learned Nazi eyewitness. But back in 1934, hundreds and hundreds of little German-Jewish schoolboys came up for their examinations in suicide, and hundreds of them passed. (p. 255)

Of course, the situation today, at least in the West, is unlike the situation in 1934, yet we still hear of the distress and the most severe consequences of stigmatization and bullying across the world.

COPING WITH DISCRIMINATION

In a Canadian national survey that we conducted to examine the coping styles of women as well as several visible minorities (Matheson & Anisman, 2012), group members who experienced discrimination, but did not feel distress, often coped through cognitive restructuring that was associated with emotional expression ('This was upsetting, but I'll know better next time'). In contrast, among group members who acknowledged discrimination and were distressed by it, cognitive restructuring was highly related to self-blame. These group members were construing the experience as one that they should have been able to control, but had failed to do so ('If only I had taken precautions, this might not have happened'). Based on these findings, we suggested that the combination of coping strategies that individuals adopt was linked to how they interpreted the situation, and the levels of psychological distress they experienced.

Mood was also related to the specific combination of coping methods endorsed. When women were angered by a discriminatory situation, a broader range of coping responses was provoked. The inclination to use problem-focused coping was associated with a greater propensity to want to confront the perpetrator. As well, both problem-focused and avoidant coping styles were associated with lower feelings of shame and diminished cortisol reactions following discrimination. Thus, although anger is usually frowned upon as being 'inappropriate', it had the effect of promoting a greater range of coping methods and diminished self-derogatory feelings and fostered action-oriented methods for dealing with the challenge.

It is not only the support from ingroup members that is crucial for coping, but under some conditions outgroup support may also be equally (or more) important. Outgroup support may be particularly effective when social categories are highly integrated and overlapping (as in the case of groups based on sex or age). For example, males and females often work together, and may be in intimate relationships. Thus, male support may often be forthcoming, but because women also represent the victims of gender discrimination (by men) the dynamic in this regard may be altered. Of course, outgroup support in politically sensitive situations is almost always appreciated, especially as it might be used as confirmation of the individual's position on a given issue. In fact, support from the outgroup often has more credibility and impact than support from ingroup members ('See, *even* outgroup members agree with our position').

The coping strategies used in relation to discrimination have implications for biological responses to stressors that, as noted earlier, may render individuals more vulnerable to health problems. For example, sexism in a laboratory context where females were rejected for a position (by a male) in preference for another male, elicited elevated cortisol levels. However, when discriminated against in a laboratory context, those participants with a propensity to problem solve reported greater appraisals of control, a more optimistic mood, and limited cortisol reactivity following the discrimination challenge. In contrast, those individuals who distanced themselves from their group identity following discrimination showed increased cortisol reactivity. It might be that in the latter instance, individuals found the situation especially aversive, and thus engaged in distancing themselves in an effort to alleviate such feelings.

Thoits (2010) summarized some of the main findings of stress-discrimination research and offered implications of this research for public policy. Among the key points, it was indicated that gender, racial/ethnic, and social class differences in physical and mental health may be linked to the differential stressor experiences of groups, and minority group members were particularly harmed by discrimination. Moreover, because stressors proliferate over an individual's life and across generations, health gaps between the advantaged and disadvantaged groups might widen. Thus, to deal with health inequalities, it is necessary to consider that structural conditions can place various groups and individuals at risk. Ultimately, greater attention needs to be placed on programs and policies to diminish psychosocial and economic stressors, and programs ought to target children who, because of poverty and other factors that promote stressful family occurrences, may be at particular risk of poor well-being. Suggestions such as these are important and on target, but it might mean a lengthy wait for structural changes to occur.

WHEN IT BECOMES OKAY TO BE A RACIST!

Reflections on history make us wonder how large groups of people might come to take on hatreds of others, and then behave in unspeakable ways toward them. Why, for instance, were so many people (not all, but certainly very many) seduced by the attitudes of the Nazi regime? Okay, they were ticked at the poor treatment they received at the Treaty of Versailles after World War I. But why was it taken out on Jews, Roma, gays, and others? Times were tough and a scapegoat might have been needed so that individuals would coalesce around a common cause (as the saying goes, if the Jews hadn't existed, Hitler would have needed to invent them). However, the people of Germany and Austria were intelligent, civilized, understanding; so one wonders, how did it become okay to become a racist? Perhaps it's a matter of individuals being highly identified with their group so that they are more vulnerable to propaganda that suggests that a particular line of thought and action is better for the homeland (i.e., for the group itself). Himmler, in defending the actions against gays, commented that these were for the common good: 'That wasn't a punishment, but simply the extinguishing of abnormal life. It had to be got rid of, just as we pull out weeds, throw them on a heap, and burn them.'

Years ago there were studies that suggested that most people will engage in deplorable acts because humans have a tendency to obey authority. In recent years another view has evolved in this regard. Specifically, Haslam and his associates (e.g., Haslam & Reicher, 2012) demonstrated that when people identify with an experimenter in an experimental situation, they're more apt to engage in seemingly immoral acts when asked to do so. In effect, the horrid behavior seen in numerous contexts is not simply a matter of 'following orders', but, as these researchers say, 'it is the endeavor of a committed subject'. If participants behave this way in a contrived context, then how much more powerful will the influence be on an individual when a whole society appears to be marching in the same footfalls? When everyone else in your group is a racist, you might develop cognitions, attitudes, and emotions that could otherwise have stayed dormant. When everyone else in your group is a racist, you might say or do things that would otherwise have been suppressed. And when everyone else in your group is a racist, is it then okay for you to engage in despicable, repugnant, and immoral acts?

STIGMA RELATED TO MENTAL ILLNESS

This brings us to the main focus of this chapter, namely the stigma associated with mental health difficulties. As you read this section consider one key ingredient that too often is not thought about. In the case of racial, religious, and gender discrimination, individuals often receive support from their ingroup, and as mentioned in the preceding section, instances of discrimination can actually enhance group cohesion. However, if the ingroup comprises those with mental health problems it might be less likely that they would receive or value social support in the same way. To be sure, there have been many patient advocate groups that have been established that specifically focus on mental health, and there has been increasing recognition of the societal importance of dealing properly with individuals with such problems. Nevertheless, there's just no question that the stigma associated with mental health problems continues to be enormous, and the buffers that protect individuals from other forms of discrimination aren't there when it comes to mental illness.

The case of Susan outlined at the beginning of this chapter, which has obvious implications for help-seeking and stigmatization, is only partially fictitious, as the scenes are an amalgam of several real events. Unfortunately, this scenario represents one of the many instances and consequences of depressive disorders that occur in university-age students, although of course, depression is not restricted to university students. Depression isn't confined to particular sets within society. It appears in males and females across cultures, in rich and poor, in actors, sports figures, children, adolescents, and in older folks.

About 20% of all people will experience a mental health disorder at some point in their life, with almost 75% of cases first appearing by age 24. Indeed, the incidence of depression in the 15–25 year-old age group is exceedingly high, and has been increasing over the past decades: estimates of depression in this age cohort range from 2 to 8%; more than 50% of these individuals reported suicidal ideation; and 15% fully acted on these ideations (Rihmer, 2007). In the USA, 30,000 people die by suicide yearly and in Canada, ~3600 individuals died by suicide each year from 2002–2006, with ~750 being under the age of 29. To put those numbers in perspective, those yearly tolls exceed the combined death toll for all allied soldiers in Iraq and Afghanistan since the beginning of those wars, and suicide accounts for more deaths than does death by injury (e.g., automobile accidents).

Given these statistics, you might consider that there's a high likelihood that your mother, father, brother or sister, or perhaps your children and grandchildren, or even you yourself, might suffer from some sort of mental health disturbance at some time, and thus might experience the stigma that goes along with it. Yet very few people talk about it. It's almost as if there's an ongoing conspiracy of silence. What is particularly alarming as well is the large number of individuals with a full set of symptoms of depressive disorders (or dysthymia or other mental health disorders) who fail to seek help and even reject help when it is offered (Wang et al., 2005). Remarkably, only 15 to 30% of affected individuals seek help, and help seeking is particularly low among those with suicidal ideation (Wilson & Deane, 2010).

In studies conducted in collaboration with Kim Matheson, based on several cohorts comprising more than 2400 first-year students, we encountered a bleak situation. Specifically, in the first month of their university experience, approximately 17% of students presented with symptoms of depression that merited a clinical review, and a further 37% displayed subclinical symptoms that could be of concern, especially as these symptoms can be a forerunner of major depressive disorder. However, fewer than 15% of those with clinical levels of symptomatology were receiving professional attention for their depression and/or anxiety. One hears from these students 'I don't need help (denial)', 'I don't believe in psychiatrists', or 'I don't want foreign substances in my body' (a very odd statement given that individuals of this age group readily consume alcohol, marijuana, hashish, meth, ecstasy, and 50% of those with depression smoked tobacco, or chose to use illicit drugs to self-medicate). Left untreated these symptoms may worsen, and possibly culminate in a more severe illness.

So why don't people with problems seek help? There are likely several factors that are important in this regard: individuals might not recognize or appraise their distress appropriately, thinking that their mood was simply a transient 'down' that everybody goes through.

Alternatively, they may recognize their situation for what it is, but are unable to mobilize personal coping or social support resources in order to seek help, or they might fear that if they do seek help, then this would be a sign of weakness and they will be diminished in the eyes of others. The Kirby report (2006) on the status of mental health treatment in Canada pointed to stigma as being *the* fundamental barrier to mental health. Stigma not only impacts on those with mental health issues, it can also mark families across generations. There is little question that the stigma of mental illness, and the potential life-time labeling that is established, may have much to do with the reluctance to acknowledge mental health difficulties and seek help. In addition, stigma may be accompanied by a mistrust of the medical system ('They can't help me'), a fear of being exposed ('People will find out I'm seeing a shrink'), or identifying as a 'sick person'.

Stigma can be expressed by other people (public stigma), can be internalized by the individual (self-stigma), and can involve the desire to avoid being labeled (Ben Zeev et al., 2010). Not surprisingly, stigma in the form of social rejection or discrimination on the basis of mental illness constitutes a significant stressor in itself, and stigmatized individuals often feel devalued and unable to cope with these events (Rüsch et al., 2010). Having repeatedly been the target of stigma, these beliefs and attitudes might be internalized and integrated into the individual's self-concept, such that those with mental health problems may feel shame, self-blame, fear the judgment of others, and hence feel a 'need' to cope with secrecy (Corrigan et al., 2011; Kelly & Jorm, 2007).

For the depressed individual who carries shame as part of their identity, having to 'out themselves' may simply be too difficult. Even when help was sought, self-stigma was reported to erode morale and undermine the commitment to treatment, and both public and self-stigma were associated with increased depressive symptoms, and diminished feelings of personal efficacy and empowerment (Ritsher & Phelan, 2004; Rüsch et al., 2005). Predictably, under these conditions, individuals might prematurely discontinue the treatment that they might be receiving and turn to inappropriate help sources (e.g., internet chatrooms) where they may perhaps receive inadequate or counterproductive advice.

The stigma of obtaining mental health treatment as a child continues to have negative ramifications into adulthood (Barney et al., 2006), and predictably, young people who experience psychological distress were especially unlikely to turn to others out of a concern of being labeled and marginalized (Moses, 2009). This is particularly relevant given that mental disorders frequently begin to appear during adolescence. The stigma associated with mental illness may be so powerful as to cause families to conspire to 'protect' their loved ones by not acknowledging the problem or a need for help, both out of a sincere concern for the individual, and also to avoid the stigma and blame that generalize from the individual to the family (Larson & Corrigan, 2008). Perceived parental disapproval of seeking help from professional services, at least in some families or cultures, further promotes young people's perceptions of stigma associated with emotional problems and the need to seek help. In large measure, these familial responses unintentionally serve as a potent form of unsupport that may be more damaging than helpful to the interests of the young person experiencing distress.

SHAME AND ANGER

One of the most cogent and destructive attributes of stigma is that it leads to negative emotions, such as shame (Rüsch et al., 2009). Shame is a particularly powerful emotion that makes people shrink into themselves, and feel diminished and worthless in the eyes of others and even in their own eyes (Tangney, 1996). Given its profound brain neurochemical effects, the shame associated with stigma might exacerbate illness and limit recovery, and increase vulnerability to the impact of further stressor encounters (Matheson & Anisman, 2012). Added to this, the pervasive stigma and constant efforts to remain invisible might be traumatizing and hence serve to exacerbate mental health problems. The Czech novelist, playwright, and poet Milan Kundera made a statement that is especially pertinent in the present context: *'The basis of shame is not some personal mistake of ours, but the ignominy, the humiliation we feel that we must be what we are without any choice in the matter, and that this humiliation is seen by everyone.'*

CAN STIGMATIZING ATTITUDES BE ALTERED?

The stigmas associated with various disorders can be distinguished from one another. There's stigma associated with epilepsy, but the affected individual isn't blamed for the illness. Often, individuals with depression or anxiety disorders are perceived to be at fault for their illness (Webb et al., 2008), as if they could change if they chose to ('Come on, just snap out of it'). Thus, it had been suggested that changing attitudes within the general population might be instrumental in diminishing stigma and enhancing help-seeking behaviors, and that this could be done through education (Barney et al., 2009). If people understood that mental illness had a biological basis, like heart disease or cancer, then they might not engage in stigmatizing behaviors. Yet educating people about the biological basis for these disorders did not reduce avoidant behaviors toward those with mental disorders (Angermeyer et al., 2009; Nieuwsma & Pepper, 2010). In general, people have become more accepting, or at least more tolerant, of the social diversity surrounding them, and many people embrace this diversity. Thus, it is surprising that this same acceptance is not present in regard to mental illness. In fact, stigma can also be reflected within the processes and operations of institutions (structural stigma) that misinterpret, ignore, or relegate symptoms as unimportant or as indices of failure, rather than deserving of intervention.

THE DIRTY LITTLE SECRET

Health professionals are as likely to hold stigmatizing attitudes regarding mental illness as anyone in the general population, suggesting that education alone is not an effective route to eradicating stigma (Adams et al., 2010; Chew-Graham et al., 2003).

Health professionals are also likely to self-stigmatize when they experience symptoms, and combined with their concerns about exposing themselves to the judgment of their peers, it is likely that they might also avoid self-disclosure and treatment seeking (Chew-Graham et al.,

2003; Givens & Tjia, 2002). Clearly, if they apply such judgments to their own situations, the capacity for these health professionals to overcome the stigma associated with mental illness with their patients is going to be less than ideal.

To limit any misinterpretations, most psychiatrists, doctors, and others professionals likely do not hold the stigmatizing views just described. But there are those who do, and this has the unfortunate effect of poisoning the well.

RESPONSES TO STIGMA AND SOCIAL SUPPORT

Distinctions need to be made when assessing the effectiveness of social support, including the source of that support, whether it is enacted or rather individuals simply trust that it will be enacted (perceived availability), and the quality of the support received. Having social support available should be distinguished, yet again, from social support seeking: nothing can come of this potential in the absence of an individual sharing or divulging the problem to others. Furthermore, even though support may have multiple benefits in regard to coping with stressors, receiving support might also have counterproductive effects. In meritocratic competitive societies such as ours, a high value is placed on self-determinism and self-sufficiency. It is not unusual for individuals to feel that they are being discouraged from seeking help for problems, and hence might experience increased distress and diminished well-being. In fact, individuals might go to great lengths to avoid relying on the assistance of their social network to circumvent feeling dependent on others. Worse still, as we've seen, is when an individual finally does seek support, but is rebuffed or offered ineffective support (unsupportive interactions). For depressed individuals, who typically also have low self-esteem, unsupport may represent an especially potent stressor that exacerbates feelings of depression, and limits or re-orients help-seeking behaviors.

These caveats concerning social support notwithstanding, mutual help programs (social support networks) may be effective in attenuating the distress associated with mental illness and with stigma (Corrigan et al., 2011). Indeed, acceptance and working with others facilitated improvement with respect to the most fundamental negative aspects stemming from stigma. It is especially encouraging that there are groups, led by some very courageous people, who have come out to indicate that they have suffered a mental illness, and they have made efforts to organize others to work toward destigmatizing mental illness. Taking a stand in the face of discrimination and stigmatization may have multiple positive outcomes. Even if it has limited effects in educating the rest of the public, the individual taking action might find that this diminishes self-stigma and all that goes with it, and they might discover a social support network they might not otherwise have known.

TRUST IN THE HEALTH SYSTEM

The third component of stigma related to mental health, namely that of structural stigma, is manifested in (a) the very long waits for treatment for mental illness, (b) lower quality treatment for concurrent physical illnesses, (c) professional biases when patients seek help, and (d) an over-attribution of mental illness as a causal factor among patients presenting with other health problems (Barney et al., 2009; Wilmink et al., 1989). In fact, the life span of those with mental illness is reduced by several years because their physical illnesses are often misattributed to being a manifestation of their mental illness.

Even as mental health professionals advocate for the eradication of stigma, many of them may share these stigmatizing views. The unfortunate communication by health-care professionals (by a word, facial expression, or gesture) of low expectations of those with a mental health issue figures prominently in a reluctance to seek mental health services (Lyons et al., 2009; Wilmink et al., 1989). Predictably, such biases do little to engender trust in key potential sources of help for mental distress. When those representing the health system respond to the distressed individual in a less-than-effective manner, that individual may be even less likely to seek professional help. Regardless of whether trust is considered in the context of an individual relationship (patient–physician) or at a system level, it entails the belief that the object of trust will have one's best interests at heart. Trust in the health system may be particularly relevant with respect to mental health issues, especially given that the need for confidentiality may be essential. Indeed, reaching out to a psychiatrist or mental health counselor means exposing some of the individual's most private issues at a time when they are most vulnerable. Thus, when individuals or agencies entrusted with one's mental health well-being are perceived as letting an individual down, regaining this trust may be especially difficult.

SHARING INTIMATE SECRETS

An acquaintance once confided that he had suffered with severe depression a few years earlier, but had absolutely refused to seek help. Instead, he hoped that this dark period would simply pass, although he says that it went on forever. When I remarked that he could have saved himself a lot of grief by seeking help, his response was enlightening. He described the embarrassment and humiliation he experienced having to go for a colonoscopy. He said, in the end 'Okay, so the doctor got to see my bum, and got to look around my intestine to see what he could see. But, once you've seen one fat 60 year-old bum and one intestine from the inside, then you've seen them all. Telling my problems to a shrink would be a whole other thing. Seeing my soul, sharing my most intimate thoughts and passions, my insecurities and heartaches . . . well, there was no way I could bring myself to do that. If I wouldn't confide in friends I trust, why would I confide in a stranger? I'd rather have shown him my bum'.

TURNING TO THE INTERNET

For some young people in distress the internet presents an attractive alternative when anonymity is desired (Gilat & Shahar, 2009). Given that this has become a natural forum for establishing and maintaining social networks among young people, it is not surprising that they are likely to seek online help for personal issues, including loneliness, depression, anxiety, and suicidal thoughts. Internet support groups provide a forum that is anonymous, where non-verbal rejection is less evident, and where individuals can feel relatively comfortable disclosing their innermost feelings. Indeed, compared with face-to-face communications, online interactions demonstrate higher levels of self-disclosure and intimacy, and greater openness about personal trauma (Tidwell & Walther, 2002). Online social networks have become prominent in the day-to-day lives of many people, and there has been a proliferation of internet support groups, many of which are unsupervised by trained professionals (Webb et al., 2008).

In general, individuals reluctant to seek help from mental health professionals appeared to be particularly likely to turn to internet support in dealing with suicidal ideation. In addition, increased social isolation and loneliness as well as increased stress experiences were linked to using the internet for emotional support (Morahan-Martin & Schumacher, 2003), and these interactions were reported to diminish loneliness and depression, as well as increase perceived social support and social inclusion (Notley, 2009). Of particular note was that the internet may provide a forum wherein self-disclosure is high, and there exists a potential for shared ruminations of grief and distress, as well as providing a valuable source of information and resources that may enable people to take a more problem-solving and healthy approach to their lives. In addition, although young people may turn to the internet seeking support, they frequently also act as support providers. Such reciprocity may have positive benefits, but it has also been suggested that such interactions can reinforce pre-existing emotional difficulties (Morahan-Martin & Schumacher, 2003). Because of this, shared feelings and behaviors among like-minded individuals can then become the norm, including the encouragement of self-injurious behaviors (Webb et al., 2008). Vulnerability to exploitation or the ill effects of online relationships may be especially high for young people who have troubled offline lives (Wolak et al., 2003).

Much of the research assessing the content of online interactions has been in comparison to face-to-face communication. The primary differences between the two is that the former are generally asynchronous (enabling more time to express oneself) and lacking in social cues (increasing feelings of privacy, anonymity, and a focus on message content). Although there has been research assessing satisfaction and the effectiveness of online help (e.g., the presence of a moderator in self-help groups, reciprocity in personal disclosures), the influence of the content of online messages, and from whom support is obtained, has not been thoroughly evaluated. Nevertheless, the online medium establishes a 'detattachment' context, wherein relationships reflect a unique balance of detachment and attachment so that communicators are neither close nor intimate, nor are they complete strangers. As such, the nature of disclosure might vary as a function of the helper's ability to interact with the distressed individual in a skilled and thoughtful manner. At the same time, however, individuals' pre-existing stereotypes and images of the 'other' will influence how they communicate (Matheson, 1991). In this regard, fear of rejection from a close other, mistrust of medical professionals, or projections of their own thoughts and feelings onto a stranger with a shared experience, could influence the intimacy and level of disclosure in the communications

(Sassenberg, 2002). Together, these factors might contribute to depressed individuals' preference to seek online support from a stranger who they perceive to share their experience, and to be more willing to self-disclose in this context.

When individuals become acquainted over the internet, particularly when the goal is to obtain help related to a shared experience, they are likely to project the qualities of an ideal friend onto the other (McKenna et al., 2002). Projection like this would be less evident when the other is already known offline (and less prone to be idealized), or when there exists a stereotyped expectation (e.g., based on profession). Under conditions where the internet partners are unknown to one another, self-disclosure would be expected to be high, and when unsupportive responses are received, feelings of rejection may be less intense, as there may be a greater willingness to give a stranger the benefit of the doubt by forgiving unsupportive statements.

In the absence of having met the individual with whom one is communicating, the lack of stereotypes and feelings of shame may contribute to the willingness to disclose personal information and interpretations of the responses of other. Yet, as we all know by now, anonymity can also bring out the worst in some situations. As we saw at the beginning of this chapter, there are vipers who trawl the internet with the aim of causing harm. Moreover, a vulnerability to exploitation or the ill effects of online relationships may be especially high for those who have troubled offline lives.

CONCLUSION

In this brief chapter we've been concerned with discrimination and stigma related to our group, as well as stigma associated with mental health issues, but there are other forms of stigma that exist. How do people react to those with physical disfigurements (e.g., burn victims or those born with congenital deformities), those with chronic or fatal illnesses, and those with epilepsy, obesity, and a variety of other factors? Often, it's not a matter of ill intent that causes people to act awkwardly or inappropriately to others. Sometimes, it's simply a matter of not knowing what to say to them, so it's easier to just actively avoid them. Unfortunately, in the eyes of the person carrying some burden, this avoidance behavior can be interpreted as unsupport and can have some fairly profound negative effects. I can only repeat what I tell my students (although it makes me sound like 'Dear Abby' or one of her clones): 'Okay, it's uncomfortable. I get it. Now, just suck it up and go see the person in distress, be understanding, but without being patronizing. Talk about it.'

Historically, an issue that keeps coming up across religions, perhaps phrased differently for each, but having the same meaning, is what is called *The Golden Rule* (also referred to as the *ethic of reciprocity*). Simply stated, this ethic or rule is (a) treat others as you would like others to treat you, and (b) do not not treat others in ways that you wouldn't want them to treat you. In biblical terms it amounts to 'Do unto others . . .' or 'Love thy neighbor . . .', and indeed 5 of the 10 commandments brought down from the mountain by Moses (and not by Charlton Heston) focused on relations with thy neighbor. (Incidentally, the Bible is also replete with the importance of kindness to animals: for example, 'A righteous man knows the soul of his animal'; *Proverbs*, 12:10.) It has been suggested that The Golden Rule forms our current concepts of human rights, and might be fundamental in defining how countries and people of different cultures get along and how conflicts are resolved. The Golden Rule, clearly, applies to those in our society who are most disadvantaged, including people with disabilities or mental disorders who have 'a flaw in brain circuitry and not a flaw in character'.

SUMMARY

- Of the many stressors that can be encountered, indeed one of the most insidious is that of discrimination and stigmatization.
- Social support and having a proper ingroup identity (e.g., centrality, pride, and ties) may go a long way in diminishing the potential negative consequences of discrimination. These support resources, however, may be less available for those with mental illness.
- The stigma associated with mental illness, despite many educational campaigns aimed at reducing negative attitudes, has not diminished appreciably, and it is widely acknowledged that stigma may represent the greatest deterrent for seeking help despite the desperate need for it.

REFERENCES

Abizaid, A. (2009). Ghrelin and dopamine: New insights on the peripheral regulation of appetite. *Journal of Neuroendocrinology*, *21*, 787–793.

Abizaid, A., et al. (2006). Ghrelin modulates the activity and synaptic input organization of midbrain dopamine neurons while promoting appetite. *Journal of Clinical Investigation*, *116*, 3229–3239.

Abizaid, A., & Horvath, T. L. (2008). Brain circuits regulating energy homeostasis. *Regulatory Peptides*, *149*, 3–10.

Abizaid, A., Luheshi, G., & Woodside, B. C. (2013). Interaction between immune and energy balance signals in the regulation of feeding and metabolism. In A. Kusnecov and H. Anisman (eds), *Handbook of Psychoneuroimmunology*. London: Wiley-Blackwell.

Abramson, L. Y., Seligman, M. E., & Teasdale, J. D. (1978). Learned helplessness in humans: Critique and reformulation. *Journal of Abnormal Psychology*, *87*, 49–74.

Ackerman, K. D., Heyman, R., Rabin, B. S., Anderson, B. P., Houck, P. R., Frank, E., & Baum, A. (2002). Stressful life events precede exacerbations of multiple sclerosis. *Psychosomatic Medicine*, *64*, 916–920.

Ackerman, K. D., Stover, A., Heyman, R., Anderson, B. P., Houck, P. R., & Baum, A. (2002). Robert Ader New Investigator Award: Relationship of cardiovascular reactivity, stressful life events, and multiple sclerosis disease activity. *Brain, Behavior, and Immunity*, *17*, 141–151.

Adams, E. F., Lee, A. J., Pritchard, C. W., & White, R. J. (2010). What stops us from healing the healers? A survey of help-seeking behaviour, stigmatisation and depression within the medical profession. *International Journal of Social Psychiatry*, *56*, 359–370.

Affleck, G., Pfeiffer, C., Tennen, H., & Fifield, J. (1987). Attributional processes in rheumatoid arthritis patients. *Arthritis & Rheumatism*, *30*, 927–931.

Aguilera, M., et al. (2009). Early adversity and 5-HTT/BDNF genes: New evidence of gene–environment interactions on depressive symptoms in a general population. *Psychological Medicine*, *39*, 1425–1432.

Akhondzadeh, S., et al. (2009). Clinical trial of adjunctive celecoxib treatment in patients with major depression: A double blind and placebo controlled trial. *Depression and Anxiety*, *26*, 607–611.

Albano, A. M., & Detweiler, M. F. (2001). The developmental and clinical impact of social anxiety and social phobia in children and adolescents. In S. G. Hofmann and P. M. DiBartolo (eds),

From Social Anxiety to Social Phobia: Multiple Perspectives (pp. 162–178). Boston, MA: Allyn & Bacon.

Alloy, L. B, Abramson, K. Y., Keyser, J., Gerstein, R. K., & Sylvia, L. G. (2008). Negative cognitive style. In K. S. Dobson and D. J. A. Dozois (eds), *Risk Factors in Depression* (pp. 237–263). New York: Academic.

Amar, A., et al. (2012) Identity and function of a large gene network underlying mutagenic repair of DNA breaks. *Science*, *338*(6112), 1344–1348. doi: 10.1126/science.1226683.

Anacker, C., et al. (2013). Glucocorticoid-related molecular signaling pathways regulating hippocampal neurogenesis. *Neuropsychopharmacology*, 38, 872–873.

Andersen, B. L., et al. (2008). Psychologic intervention improves survival for breast cancer patients: A randomized clinical trial. *Cancer*, 113, 3450–3458.

Anderson, N. D., Lau, M. A., Segal, Z. V., & Bishop, S. R. (2007). Mechanisms of mindfulness: Attentional control. *Clinical Psychology and Psychotherapy*, 14, 449–463.

Angermeyer, M. C., Holzinger, A., & Matschinger, H. (2009). Mental health literacy and attitude towards people with mental illness: A trend analysis based on population surveys in the eastern part of Germany. *European Psychiatry*, 24, 225–232.

Anisman, H. (2011). Sensitization in relation to posttraumatic stress disorder. *Biological Psychiatry*, *70*, 404–405.

Anisman, H., deCatanzaro, D., & Remington, G. (1978). Escape performance following exposure to inescapable shock: Deficits in response initiation and maintenance. *Journal of Experimental Psycholology: Animal Behavior Processes*, 4, 197–218.

Anisman, H., & Hayley, S. (2012a). Illness comorbidity as a biomarker? *Journal of Psychiatry & Neuroscience*, 37, 221–223.

Anisman, H., Hayley, S., & Merali, Z. (2003). Cytokines and stress: Sensitization and cross-sensitization. *Brain, Behavior, and Immunity*, 17, 86–93.

Anisman, H., & Matheson, K. (2005). Stress, anhedonia and depression: Caveats concerning animal models. *Neuroscience & Biobehavioral Reviews*, 29, 525–546.

Anisman, H., & Merali, Z. (1999). Anhedonic and anxiogenic effects of cytokine exposure. *Advances in Experimental Medicine and Biology*, 461, 199–233.

Anisman, H., Merali, Z., & Hayley, S. (2008). Neurotransmitter, peptide and cytokine processes in relation to depressive disorder: Comorbidity of depression with neurodegenerative disorders. *Progress in Neurobiology*, 85, 1–74.

Anisman, H., Merali, Z., & Poulter, M. (2012). Gamma-aminobutyric acid involvement in depressive illness: Interactions with corticotropin releasing hormone and serotonin. In Y. Dwivedi (ed.), *The Neurobiological Basis of Suicide*. New York: Taylor & Francis.

Anisman, H., Poulter, M. O., Gandhi, R., Merali, Z., & Hayley, S. (2007). Interferon-alpha effects are exaggerated when administered on a psychosocial stressor backdrop: Cytokine, corticosterone and brain monoamine variations. *Journal of Neuroimmunology*, *186*, 45–53.

Anisman, H., Zaharia, M. D., Meaney, M. J., & Merali, Z. (1998). Do early-life events permanently alter behavioral and hormonal responses to stressors? *International Journal of Developmental Neuroscience*, 16, 149–164.

Anticevic, A., Cole, M. W., Murray, J. D., Corlett, P. R., Wang, X. J., & Krystal, J. H. (2012). The role of default network deactivation in cognition and disease. *Trends in Cognitive Sciences*, 16, 584–592.

Antoni, M. H., Lutgendorf, S. K., Cole, S. W., Dhabhar, F. S., Sephton, S. E., McDonald, P. G., Stefanek, M., & Sood, A. K. (1993). The influence of bio-behavioural factors on tumour biology: Pathways and mechanisms. *Nature Reviews Cancer*, 6, 240–248.

Anway, M. D., Cupp, A. S., Uzumcu, M., & Skinner, M. K. (2005). Epigenetic transgenerational actions of endocrine disruptors and male fertility. *Science*, 308, 1466–1469.

Apfel, B. A., et al. (2011a). Hippocampal volume differences in Gulf War veterans with current versus lifetime posttraumatic stress disorder symptoms. *Biological Psychiatry*, 69, 541–548.

Apfel, B. A., et al. (2011b). Pretraumatic prolonged elevation of salivary MHPG predicts peri-traumatic distress and symptoms of post-traumatic stress disorder. *Journal of Psychiatric Research*, 45, 735–741.

Appels, A., & Mulder, P. (1988) Excess fatigue as a precursor of myocardial infarction. *European Heart Journal*, 9, 758–764.

Arango, V., Huang, Y. Y., Underwood, M. D., & Mann, J. J. (2003). Genetics of the serotonergic system in suicidal behavior. *Journal of Psychiatric Research*, 37, 375–386.

Armitage, A. (1995). *Comparing the Policy of Aboriginal Assimilation: Australia, Canada, and New Zealand*. Vancouver, BC: University of British Columbia Press.

Asnis, G. M., & De La Garza, R. (2006). Interferon-induced depression in chronic hepatitis C: A review of its prevalence, risk factors, biology, and treatment approaches. *Journal of Clinical Gastroenterology*, 40, 322–335.

Audet, M. C., Jacobson-Pick, S., Wann, B. P., & Anisman, H. (2011). Social defeat promotes specific cytokine variations within the prefrontal cortex upon subsequent aggressive or endotoxin challenges. *Brain, Behavior, and Immunity*, 25, 1197–1205.

Aupperle, R. L., Melrose, A. J., Stein, M. B., & Paulus, M. P. (2011). Executive function and PTSD: Disengaging from trauma. *Neuropharmacology*, 62, 686–694.

Bach, D. R., Seymour, B., & Dolan, R. J. (2009). Neural activity associated with the passive prediction of ambiguity and risk for aversive events. *Journal of Neuroscience*, 29, 1648–1656.

Baer, R., Smith, G., Hopkins, J., Krietemeyer, J., & Toney, L. (2006). Using self-report assessment methods to explore facets of mindfulness. *Assessment*, 13, 27–45.

Bailey, M., Engler, H., Hunzeker, J., & Sheridan, J. F. (2003). The hypothalamic-pituitary-adrenal axis and viral infection. *Viral Immunology*, 16, 141–157.

Bailey, M. T., Dowd, S. E., Galley, J. D., Hufnagle, A. R., Allen, R. G., & Lyte, M. (2011). Exposure to a social stressor alters the structure of the intestinal microbiota: Implications for stressor-induced immunomodulation. *Brain, Behavior, and Immunity*, 25, 397–407.

Bailey, M. T., Padgett, D. A., & Sheridan, J. F. (2007). Stress-induced modulation of innate resistance and adaptive immunity to influenza viral infection. In R. Ader (ed.), *Psychoneuroimmunology* (pp. 1097–1124). San Diego, CA: Academic Press.

Baker, L. D., Barsness, S. M., Borson, S., Merriam, G. R., Friedman, S. D., Craft, S., & Vitiello, M. V. (2012). Effects of growth hormone–releasing hormone on cognitive function in adults with mild cognitive impairment and healthy older adults: Results of a controlled trial. *Archives of Neurology*, 69, 1420–1429.

Baker, S. R., & Stephenson, D. (2000). Prediction and control as determinants of behavioural uncertainty: Effects on task performance and heart rate reactivity. *Integrative Physiological and Behavioral Science*, 35, 235–250.

Bakshi, V. P., Newman, S. M., Smith-Roe, S., Jochman, K. A., & Kalin, N. H. (2007). Stimulation of lateral septum CRF2 receptors promotes anorexia and stress-like behaviors: Functional homology to CRF1 receptors in basolateral amygdala. *Journal of Neuroscience*, 27, 10568–10577.

Bal, S., Crombez, G., Van Oost, P., & Debourdeaudhuij, I. (2003). The role of social support in well-being and coping with self-reported stressful events in adolescents. *Child Abuse & Neglect*, 27, 1377–1395.

Bale, T. L., & Vale, W. W. (2003). Increased depression-like behaviors in corticotropin-releasing factor receptor-2-deficient mice: Sexually dichotomous responses. *Journal of Neuroscience*, 23, 5295–5301.

Barefoot, J. C., Dahlstrom, W. G., & Williams, R. B. (1983). Hostility, CHD incidence, and total mortality: A 25-year follow-up study of 255 physicians. *Psychosomatic Medicine*, 45, 59–63.

Barney, L. J., Griffiths, K. M., Christensen, H., & Jorm, A. F. (2009). Exploring the nature of stigmatising beliefs about depression and help-seeking: Implications for reducing stigma. *BMC Public Health*, 9, 61–71.

Barney, L. J., Griffiths, K. M., Jorm, A. F., & Christensen, H. (2006). Stigma about depression and its impact on help-seeking intentions. *Australian and New Zealand Journal of Psychiatry*, 40, 51–54.

Bar-On, D., & Rottgardt, E. (1998). Reconstructing silenced biographical issues through feeling-facts. *Psychiatry*, 61, 61–83.

Barr, A. M., Hofmann, C. E., Weinberg, J., & Phillips, A. G. (2002). Exposure to repeated, intermittent d-amphetamine induces sensitization of HPA axis to a subsequent stressor. *Neuropsychopharmacology*, 26, 286–294.

Barsegyan, A., Mackenzie, S. M., Kurose, B. D., McGaugh, J. L., & Roozendaal, B. (2010). Glucocorticoids in the prefrontal cortex enhance memory consolidation and impair working memory by a common neural mechanism. *Proceedings of the National Academy of Sciences*, 107, 16655–16660.

Baumgartner, T., Heinrichs, M., Vonlanthen, A., Fischbacher, U., & Fehr, E. (2008). Oxytocin shapes the neural circuitry of trust and trust adaptation in humans. *Neuron*, 58, 639–650.

Beaver, K. M., & Belsky, J. (2012). Gene–environment interaction and the intergenerational transmission of parenting: Testing the differential-susceptibility hypothesis. *Psychiatric Quarterly*, 83, 29–40.

Beck, A. T. (1967). *Depression: Clinical, Experimental, and Theoretical Aspects*. New York: Harper & Row.

Beck, A. T. (1970). Cognitive therapy: Nature and relation to behavior therapy. *Behavior Therapy*, 1, 184–200.

Beck, A. T. (2008). The evolution of the cognitive model of depression and its neurobiological correlates. *American Journal of Psychiatry*, 165, 969–977.

Beck, A. T., & Dozois, D. J. (2011). Cognitive therapy: Current status and future directions. *Annual Review of Medicine, 62*, 397–409.

Beck, A. T., Rush, A. J., Shaw, B. F., & Emery, G. (1979). *Cognitive Therapy of Depression*. New York: Guilford.

Beitia, G., Garmendia, L., Azpiroz, A., Vegas, O., Brain, P. F., & Arregi, A. (2005). Time-dependent behavioral, neurochemical, and immune consequences of repeated experiences of social defeat stress in male mice and the ameliorative effects of fluoxetine. *Brain, Behaviour, and Immunity, 19*, 530–539.

Bellinger, D. L., Lubahn, C., & Lorton, D. (2008). Maternal and early life stress effects on immune function: Relevance to immunotoxicology. *Journal of Immunotoxicology, 5*, 419–444.

Belsky, J., Jonassaint, C., Pluess, M., Stanton, M., Brummett, B., & Williams, R. (2009). Vulnerability genes or plasticity genes? *Molecular Psychiatry, 14*, 746–754.

Bennett, S. A., Beck, J. G., & Clapp, J. D. (2009). Understanding the relationship between post-traumatic stress disorder and trauma cognitions: The impact of thought control strategies. *Behaviour Research and Therapy, 47*, 1018–1023.

Ben-Zeev, D., Young, M. A., & Corrigan, P. W. (2010). DSM-V and the stigma of mental illness. *Journal of Mental Health, 19*, 318–327.

Bergman, K., Sarkar, P., O'Connor, T. G., Modi, N., & Glover, V. (2007). Maternal stress during pregnancy predicts cognitive ability and fearfulness in infancy. *Journal of the American Academy of Child & Adolescent Psychiatry, 46*, 1454–1463.

Berman, R. M., Cappiello, A., Anand, A., Oren, D. A., Heninger, G. R., Charney, D. S., & Krystal, J. H.(2000). Antidepressant effects of ketamine in depressed patients. *Biological Psychiatry, 47*, 351–354.

Beutel, M. E., Stark, R., Pan, H., Silbersweig, D., & Dietrich, S. (2010). Changes of brain activation pre- post short-term psychodynamic inpatient psychotherapy: An fMRI study of panic disorder patients. *Psychiatry Research, 184*, 96–104.

Bevins, R. A., & Besheer, J. (2005). Novelty reward as a measure of anhedonia. *Neuroscience & Biobehavioral Reviews, 29*, 707–714.

Beydoun, H., & Saftlas, A. F. (2008). Physical and mental health outcomes of prenatal maternal stress in human and animal studies: A review of recent evidence. *Paediatric and Perinatal Epidemiology, 22*, 438–466.

Bibb, J. A., et al. (2001). Effects of chronic exposure to cocaine are regulated by the neuronal protein Cdk5. *Nature, 410*, 376–380.

Bingel, U., Wanigasekera, V., Wiech, K., Mhuircheartaigh, R. N., Lee, M. C., Ploner, M., & Tracey, I. (2011). The effect of treatment expectation on drug efficacy: Imaging the analgesic benefit of the opioid remifentanil. *Science Translational Medicine, 3*, 70ra14.

Bird, A. P. (2007). Perceptions of epigenetics. *Nature, 447*, 396–398.

Birmingham, D. J., et al. (2006). Fluctuation in self-perceived stress and increased risk of flare in patients with lupus nephritis carrying the serotonin receptor 1A-1019 G allele. *Arthritis & Rheumatism, 54*, 3291–3299.

Bisson, J. I., Ehlers, A., Matthews, R., Pilling, S., Richards, D., & Turner, S. (2007). Psychological treatments for chronic post-traumatic stress disorder: Systematic review and meta-analysis. *British Journal of Psychiatry, 190*, 97–104.

Black, P. H. (2006). The inflammatory consequences of psychologic stress: Relationship to insulin resistance, obesity, atherosclerosis and diabetes mellitus, type II. *Medical Hypotheses, 67,* 879–891.

Blackhart, G. C., Eckel, L. A., & Tice, D. M. (2007). Salivary cortisol in response to acute social rejection and acceptance by peers. *Biological Psychology, 75,* 267–276.

Blalock, J. E. (1994). The syntax of immune–neuroendocrine communication. *Immunology Today, 15,* 504–511.

Blanchard, E. B., et al.(2008). The role of stress in symptom exacerbation among IBS patients. *Journal of Psychosomatic Research, 64,* 119–128.

Bland, S. T., Tamlyn, J. P., Barrientos, R. M., Greenwood, B. N., Watkins, L. R., Campeau, S., & Maier, S. F. (2007). Expression of fibroblast growth factor-2 and brain-derived neurotrophic factor mRNA in the medial prefrontal cortex and hippocampus after uncontrollable or controllable stress. *Neuroscience, 144,* 1219–1228.

Bland, S. T., Twining, C., Watkins, L. R., & Maier, S. F. (2003). Stressor controllability modulates stress-induced serotonin but not dopamine efflux in the nucleus accumbens shell. *Synapse, 49,* 206–208.

Blier, P. (2003). The pharmacology of putative early-onset antidepressant strategies. *European Neuropsychopharmacology, 13,* 57–66.

Blier, P., Ward, H. E., Tremblay, P., Laberge, L., Hébert, C., & Bergeron, R. (2010). Combination of antidepressant medications from treatment initiation for major depressive disorder: A double-blind randomized study. *American Journal of Psychiatry, 167,* 281–288.

Bluhm, R. L., et al. (2009). Alterations in default network connectivity in posttraumatic stress disorder related to early-life trauma. *Journal of Psychiatry and Neuroscience, 34,* 187–194.

Boksem, M. A., & De Cremer, D. (2010). Fairness concerns predict medial frontal negativity amplitude in ultimatum bargaining. *Social Neuroscience, 5,* 118–128.

Bombay, A., Matheson, K., & Anisman, H. (2009). Intergenerational trauma among First Nations: Communities in crisis. *Journal of Aboriginal Health, 5,* 6–47.

Bombay, A., Matheson, K., & Anisman, H. (2010). Decomposing identity: Differential relationships between several aspects of ethnic identity and the negative effects of perceived discrimination among First Nations adults in Canada. *Cultural Diversity and Ethnic Minority Psychology, 16,* 507–516.

Bombay, A., Matheson, K., & Anisman, H. (2011). The impact of stressors on second generation Indian Residential School survivors. *Transcultural Psychiatry, 48,* 367–391.

Bonci, A., & Borgland, S. (2009). Role of orexin/hypocretin and CRF in the formation of drug-dependent synaptic plasticity in the mesolimbic system. *Neuropharmacology, 56,* 107–111.

Borgland, S. L., et al. (2009). Orexin A/hypocretin-1 selectively promotes motivation for positive reinforcers. *Journal of Neuroscience, 29,* 11215–11225.

Brady, J. V. (1958). Ulcers in 'executive' monkeys. *Scientific American, 199,* 95–104.

Brady, K. T., Dansky, B. S., Sonne, S. C., & Saladin, M. E. (1998). Posttraumatic stress disorder and cocaine dependence – order of onset. *American Journal on Addictions, 7,* 128–135.

Branscombe, N., & Doosje, B. (2004). International perspectives on the experience of collective guilt. In N. Branscombe and B. Doosje (eds), *Collective Guilt: International Persepectives.* Cambridge: Cambridge University Press.

Branscombe, N. R., & Ellemers, N. (1998). Coping with group-based discrimination: Individualistic versus group-level strategies. In J. K. Swim and C. Stangor (eds), *Prejudice: The Target's Perspective* (pp. 243–266). California: Academic Press.

Brave Heart, M. Y. (2003). The historical trauma response among natives and its relationship with substance abuse: A Lakota illustration. *Journal of Psychoactive Drugs, 35*, 7–13.

Bravo, J. A., et al. (2011). Ingestion of Lactobacillus strain regulates emotional behavior and central GABA receptor expression in a mouse via the vagus nerve. *Proceedings of the National Academy of Sciences, 108*, 16050–16055.

Bremner, J. D., Vermetten, E., Vythilingam, M., Afzal, N., Schmahl, C., Elzinga, B., & Charney, D. S. (2004). Neural correlates of the classic color and emotional stroop in women with abuse-related posttraumatic stress disorder. *Biological Psychiatry, 55*, 612–620.

Breslau, N., & Peterson, E. L. (2010). Assaultive violence and the risk of posttraumatic stress disorder following a subsequent trauma. *Behaviour Research and Therapy, 48*, 1063–1066.

Bricou, O., Taïeb, O., Baubet, T., Gal, B., Guillevin, L., & Moro, M. R. (2006). Stress and coping strategies in systemic lupus erythematosus: A review. *Neuroimmunomodulation, 13*, 283–293.

Brodov, Y., Sandach, A., Boyko, V., Matetzky, S., Guetta, V., Mandelzweig, L., & Behar, S. (2008). Acute myocardial infarction preceded by potential triggering activities: Angiographic and clinical characteristics. *International Journal of Cardiology, 130*, 180–184.

Brown, A. S. (2011). The environment and susceptibility to schizophrenia. *Progress in Neurobiology, 93*, 23–58.

Brown, A. S., Davis, J. M., Murphy, E. A., Carmichael, M. D., Carson, J. A., Ghaffar, A., & Mayer, E. P. (2007). Susceptibility to HSV-1 infection and exercise stress in female mice: Role of estrogen. *Journal of Applied Physiology, 103*, 1592–1597.

Brown, K. W., & Ryan, R. (2003). The benefits of being present: Mindfulness and its role in psychological well-being. *Journal of Personality and Social Psychology, 84*, 822–848.

Brown, R. P., & Phillips, A. (2005). Letting bygones be bygones: Further evidence for the validity of the Tendency to Forgive scale. *Personality and Individual Differences, 38*, 627–638.

Browne, C., & Winkelman, C. (2007). The effect of childhood trauma on later psychological adjustment. *Journal of Interpersonal Violence, 22*, 684–697.

Broyd, S. J., Demanuele, C., Debener, S., Helps, S. K., James, C. J., & Sonuga-Barke, E. J. (2009). Default-mode brain dysfunction in mental disorders: A systematic review. *Neuroscience & Biobehavioral Reviews, 33*, 279–296.

Bryant, R. A., Ekasawin, S., Chakrabhand, S., Suwanmitri, S., Duangchun, O., & Chantaluckwong, T. A. (2011). Randomized controlled effectiveness trial of cognitive behavior therapy for post-traumatic stress disorder in terrorist-affected people in Thailand. *World Psychiatry, 10*, 205–209.

Bryant, R. A., Felmingham, K. L., Falconer, E. M., Pe Benito, L., Dobson-Stone, C., Pierce, K. D., & Schofield, P. R. (2010). Preliminary evidence of the short allele of the serotonin transporter gene predicting poor response to cognitive behavior therapy in posttraumatic stress disorder. *Biological Psychiatry, 67*, 1217–1219.

Bryant, R. A., Friedman, M. J., Spiegel, D., Ursano, R., & Strain J. (2011). A review of acute stress disorder in DSM-5. *Depression and Anxiety, 28*, 802–817.

Brydon, L., Walker, C., Wawrzyniak, A. J., Chart, H., & Steptoe, A. (2009). Dispositional optimism and stress-induced changes in immunity and negative mood. *Brain, Behavior, and Immunity*, *23*, 810–816.

Buckner, R. L., Andrews-Hanna, J. R., & Schacter, D. L. (2008). The brain's default network: Anatomy, function, and relevance to disease. *Annals of the New York Academy of Sciences*, *1124*, 1–38.

Burattini, C., Gill, T. M., Aicardi, G., & Janak, P. H. (2006). The ethanol self-administration context as a reinstatement cue: Acute effects of naltrexone. *Neuroscience*, *139*, 877–887.

Burgdorf, J., et al. (2012). GLYX-13, an NMDA Receptor Glycine-Site Functional Partial Agonist, induces antidepressant-like effects without ketamine-like side effects. *Neuropsychopharmacology*, 5 December. DOI: 10.1038/npp.2012.246. (Epub ahead of print.)

Cacciapaglia, F., Navarini, L., Menna, P., Salvatorelli, E., Minotti, G., & Afeltra, A. (2011). Cardiovascular safety of anti-TNF-alpha therapies: Facts and unsettled issues. *Autoimmunity Reviews*, *10*, 631–635.

Caldwell, W., McInnis, O. A., McQuaid, R. J., Liu, G., Stead, J. D., Anisman, H. & Hayley, S. (2013). The role of the Val66Met polymorphism of the Brain Derived Neurotrophic Factor gene in coping strategies relevant to depressive symptoms. *PLoS One*, *8(6)*, e65547.

Callaghan, B. L., & Richardson, R. (2011). Maternal separation results in early emergence of adult-like fear and extinction learning in infant rats. *Behavioral Neuroscience*, *125*, 20–28.

Cameron, J. E. (2004). A three-factor model of social identity. *Self and Identity*, *3*, 239–262.

Campanhã, C., Minati, L., Fregnim, F., & Boggio, P. S. (2011). Responding to unfair offers made by a friend: Neuroelectrical activity changes in the anterior medial prefrontal cortex. *Journal of Neuroscience*, *31*, 15569–15574.

Campbell, A. (2010). Oxytocin and human social behavior. *Personality and Social Psychology Review*, *14*, 281–295.

Canli, T., et al. (2006). Neural corrclates of epigenesis. *Proceedings of the National Academy of Sciences*, *103*, 16033–16038.

Cao, J. L., Covington, H. E., Friedman, A. K., Wilkinson, M. B., Walsh, J. J., Cooper, D. C., Nestler, E. J., & Han, M. H. (2010). Mesolimbic dopamine neurons in the brain reward circuit mediate susceptibility to social defeat and antidepressant action. *Journal of Neuroscience*, *30*, 16453–16458.

Capistrant, B. D., Moon, J. R., Berkman, L. F., & Glymour, M. M. (2012). Current and long-term spousal caregiving and onset of cardiovascular disease. *Journal of Epidemiology and Community Health*, *66*, 951–956.

Capuron, L., & Miller, A. H. (2011). Immune system to brain signaling: Neuropsychopharmacological implications. *Pharmacology & Therapeutics*, *130*, 226–238.

Cardoso, C., Linnen, A. M., Joober, R., & Ellenbogen, M. A. (2012). Coping style moderates the effect of intranasal oxytocin on the mood response to interpersonal stress. *Experimental and Clinical Psychopharmacology*, *20*, 84–91.

Carod-Artal, F. J., & Egido, J. A. (2009). Quality of life after stroke: The importance of a good recovery. *Cerebrovascular Disease*, *27*, 204–214.

Carter, S. (1992). Hormonal influences on human sexual behavior. In J. Becker, S. Breedlove, & D. Crews (eds), *Behavioral Endocrinology* (pp. 131–142). Cambridge, MA: MIT Press.

Carver, C. S., et al. (1993). How coping mediates the effect of optimism on distress: A study of women with early stage breast cancer. *Journal of Personality and Social Psychology*, *65*, 375–390.

Carver, C. S., & Connor-Smith, J. (2010). Personality and coping. *Annual Review of Psychology*, *61*, 679–704.

Carver, C. S., Johnson, S. L., Joormann, J., Lemoult, J., & Cuccaro, M. L. (2011). Childhood adversity interacts separately with 5-HTTLPR and BDNF to predict lifetime depression diagnosis. *Journal of Affective Disorders*, *132*, 89–93.

Carver, C. S., Scheier, M. F., & Weintraub, J. K. (1989). Assessing coping strategies: A theoretically based approach. *Journal of Personality and Social Psychology*, *56*, 267–283.

Caspi, A., et al. (2003). Influence of life stress on depression: Moderation by a polymorphism in the 5-HTT gene. *Science*, *301*, 386–389.

Caspi, A., Hariri, A. R., Holmes, A., Uher, R., & Moffitt, T. E. (2010). Genetic sensitivity to the environment: The case of the serotonin transporter gene and its implications for studying complex diseases and traits. *American Journal of Psychiatry*, *167*, 509–527.

Champagne, F. A. (2010). Epigenetic influence of social experiences across the lifespan. *Developmental Psychobiology*, *52*, 299–311.

Champagne, F. A., & Meaney, M. J. (2007). Transgenerational effects of social environment on variations in maternal care and behavioral response to novelty. *Behavioral Neuroscience*, *121*, 1353–1363.

Chapman, C., et al. (2011). Remission from post-traumatic stress disorder in the general population. *Psychological Medicine*, *14*, 1–9.

Charil, A., Laplante, D. P., Vaillancourt, C., & King, S. (2010) Prenatal stress and brain development. *Brain Research Reviews*, *65*(1): 56–79. doi: 10.1016/j.brainresrev.2010.06.002. (Epub 13 June 2010.)

Charney, D. S. (2004). Psychobiological mechanisms of resilience and vulnerability: Implications for successful adaptation to extreme stress. *American Journal of Psychiatry*, *161*, 195–216.

Chaudhury, D., et al. (2013). Rapid regulation of depression-related behaviours by control of midbrain dopamine neurons. *Nature*, *493*, 532–536.

Chechko, N., Wehrle, R., Erhardt, A., Holsboer, F., Czisch, M., & Sämann, P. G. (2009). Unstable prefrontal response to emotional conflict and activation of lower limbic structures and brainstem in remitted panic disorder. *PLoS One*, *4*, e5537.

Chew-Graham, C. A., Rogers, A., & Yassin, N. (2003). 'I wouldn't want it on my CV or their records': Medical students' experiences of help-seeking for mental health problems. *Medical Education*, *37*, 873–880.

Chida, Y., Hamer, M., Wardle, J., & Steptoe, A. (2008). Do stress-related psychosocial factors contribute to cancer incidence and survival? *Nature Clinical Practice Oncology*, *5*, 466–475.

Chida, Y., & Mao, X. (2009). Does psychosocial stress predict symptomatic herpes simplex virus recurrence? A meta-analytic investigation on prospective studies. *Brain, Behavior, and Immunity*, *23*, 917–925.

Chida, Y., & Steptoe, A. (2008). Positive psychological well-being and mortality: A quantitative review of prospective observational studies. *Psychosomatic. Medicine*, *70*, 741–756.

Chida, Y., & Steptoe, A. (2010). The association of anger and hostility with future coronary heart disease: A meta-analytic review of prospective evidence. *Journal of the American College of Cardiology, 53*, 936–946.

Chourbaji, S., Brandwein, C., & Gass, P. (2011). Altering BDNF expression by genetics and/or environment: Impact for emotional and depression-like behaviour in laboratory mice. *Neuroscience & Biobehavioral Reviews, 35*, 599–611.

Clasen, P. C., Wells, T. T., Knopik, V. S., McGeary, J. E., & Beevers, C. G. (2011). 5-HTTLPR and BDNF Val66Met polymorphisms moderate effects of stress on rumination. *Genes, Brain, and Behavior, 10*, 740–746.

Clayton, A. H., Croft, H. A., Horrigan, J. P., Wightman, D. S., Krishen, A., Richard, N. E., & Modell, J. G. (2006). Bupropion extended release compared with escitalopram: Effects on sexual functioning and antidepressant efficacy in 2 randomized, double-blind, placebo-controlled studies. *Journal of Clinical Psychiatry, 67*, 736–746.

Cleck, J. N., & Blendy, J. A. (2008). Making a bad thing worse: Adverse effects of stress on drug addiction. *Journal of Clinical Investigation, 118*, 454–461.

Cloos, J. M., & Ferreira, V. (2009). Current use of benzodiazepines in anxiety disorders. *Current Opinion in Psychiatry, 22*, 90–95.

Cochrane, A. L. (1972). *Effectiveness and Efficiency: Random Reflections on Health Services.* London: Nuffield Provincial Hospitals Trust.

Coggins, M., & Rosenzweig, A. (2012). The fire within: Cardiac inflammatory signaling in health and disease. *Circulation Research, 110*, 116–125.

Cohen, H., Kozlovsky, N., Alona, C., Matar, M. A., & Joseph, Z. (2011). Animal model for PTSD: From clinical concept to translational research. *Neuropharmacology, 62*, 715–724.

Cohen, H., Liu, T., Kozlovsky, N., Kaplan, Z., Zohar, J., & Mathé, A. A. (2012). The Neuropeptide Y (NPY)-ergic system is associated with behavioral resilience to stress exposure in an animal model of post-traumatic stress disorder. *Neuropsychopharmacology, 37*, 350–363.

Cohen, M., & Numa, M. (2011). Posttraumatic growth in breast cancer survivors: A comparison of volunteers and non-volunteers. *Psycho-Oncology, 20*, 69–76.

Cohen, S., Evans, G. W., Stokols, D., & Krantz, D. S. (1986). *Behavior, Health, and Environmental Stress.* New York: Plenum.

Cohen, S., Miller, G. E., & Rabin, B. S. (2001). Psychological stress and antibody response to immunization: A critical review of the human literature. *Psychosomatic Medicine, 63*, 7–18.

Cohen, S., Tyrrel, D. A. G., & Smith, A. P. (1991). Psychological stress and susceptibility to the common cold. *New England Journal of Medicine, 325*, 606–612.

Colloca, L., Lopiano, L., Lanotte, M., & Benedetti, F. (2004). Overt versus covert treatment for pain, anxiety, and Parkinson's disease. *The Lancet Neurology, 3*, 679–684.

Comisión de Esclarecimiento Histórico (CEH) [Commission for Historical Clarification] (1999). *Memoria del silencio* [Memory of silence]. Guatemala: CEH.

Compas, B. E., Connor-Smith, J. K., Saltzman, H., Thomsen, A. H., & Wadsworth, M. E. (2001). Coping with stress during childhood and adolescence: Problems, Progress, and Potential in theory and research. *Psychological Bulletin, 127*, 87–127.

Compston, A., & Coles, A. (2008). Multiple sclerosis. *The Lancet*, *372*, 1502–1517.

Corrigan, P. W., Rafacz, J., & Rüsch, N. (2011). Examining a progressive model of self-stigma and its impact on people with serious mental illness. *Psychiatry Research*, *189*, 339–343.

Costa, P., & McCrae, R. (1992). *Revised NEO Personality Inventory (NEO-PI-R) and NEO Five-Factor Inventory (NEO-FFI) manual*. Odessa, FL: Psychological Assessment Resources.

Costanzo, E. S., Sood, A. K., & Lutgendorf, S. K. (2011). Biobehavioral influences on cancer progression. *Immunology and Allergy Clinics of North America*, *31*, 109–132.

Coull, G., & Morris, P. G. (2011) The clinical effectiveness of CBT-based guided self-help interventions for anxiety and depressive disorders: A systematic review. *Psychological Medicine*, *41*, 1–14.

Covington, H. E., et al. (2009). Antidepressant actions of histone deacetylase inhibitors. *The Journal of Neuroscience*, *29*, 11451–11460.

Covington, H. E., et al. (2011). A role for repressive histone methylation in cocaine-induced vulnerability to stress. *Neuron*, *71*, 656–670.

Craft, T. K., & DeVries, A. C. (2006). Role of IL-1 in poststroke depressive-like behavior in mice. *Biological Psychiatry*, *60*, 812–818.

Crawley, J. N., et al. (1997). Behavioral phenotypes of inbred mouse strains: Implications and recommendations for molecular studies. *Psychopharmacology*, *132*, 107–124.

Creswell, J. D., et al. (2012). Mindfulness-Based Stress Reduction training reduces loneliness and pro-inflammatory gene expression in older adults: A small randomized controlled trial. *Brain, Behavior, and Immunity*, *26*, 1095–1101.

Cryan, J. F., & Slattery, D. A. (2007). Animal models of mood disorders: Recent developments. *Current Opinion in Psychiatry*, *20*, 1–7.

Cukor, J., Spitalnick, J., Difede, J., Rizzo, A., & Rothbaum, B.O. (2009). Emerging treatments for PTSD. *Clinical Psychology Review*, *29*, 715–726.

Daley, S. E., Hammen, C., Burge, D., Davila, J., Paley, B., Lindberg, N., & Herzberg, D. S. (1997). Predictors of the generation of episodic stress: A longitudinal study of late adolescent women. *Journal of Abnormal Psychology*, *106*, 251–259.

Dallman, M. F. (2010). Stress-induced obesity and the emotional nervous system. *Trends in Endocrinology and Metabolism*, *21*, 159–165.

Damasio, A. (1999). *The Feeling of What Happens: Body, Emotion and the Making of Consciousness*. Florida: Harcourt.

Danchin, É., Charmantier, A., Champagne, F. A., Mesoudi, A., Pujol, B., & Blanchet, S. (2011). Beyond DNA: Integrating inclusive inheritance into an extended theory of evolution. *Nature Reviews Genetics*, *12*, 475–486.

Dane, E., Rockmann, K. W., & Pratt, M. G. (2012). When should I trust my gut? Linking domain expertise to intuitive decision-making effectiveness. *Organizational Behavior and Human Decision Processes*, *119*, 187–194.

Danesh, J., et al. (2004). C-reactive protein and other circulating markers of inflammation in the prediction of coronary heart disease. *New England Journal of Medicine*, *350*, 1387–1397.

Danieli, Y. (1998). *International Handbook of Multigenerational Legacies of Trauma*. New York: Plenum.

Daniels, W. M., Fairbairn, L. R., van Tilburg, G., McEvoy, C. R., Zigmond, M. J., Russell, V. A., & Stein, D. J. (2009). Maternal separation alters nerve growth factor and corticosterone levels but not the DNA methylation status of the exon 1(7) glucocorticoid receptor promoter region. *Metabolic Brain Disease, 24*, 615–627.

Danielson, A. M., Matheson, K., & Anisman, H. (2011). Cytokine levels at a single time point following a reminder stimulus among women in abusive dating relationships: Relationship to emotional states. *Psychoneuroendocrinology, 36*, 40–50.

Dantzer, R., et al. (2007). Cytokines, sickness behavior, and depression. In R. Ader (ed.), *Psychoneuroimmunology* (pp. 281–318). New York: Elsevier.

Dantzer, R., O'Connor, J. C., Lawson, M. A., & Kelley, K. W. (2011). Inflammation-associated depression: From serotonin to kynurenine. *Psychoneuroendocrinology, 36*, 426–436.

David, S. P., et al. (2005). A functional genetic variation of the serotonin (5-HT) transporter affects 5-HT1A receptor binding in humans. *Journal of Neuroscience, 25*, 2586–2590.

Davidson, R. J., et al. (2003). Alterations in brain and immune function produced by mindfulness meditation. *Psychosomatic Medicine, 65*, 564–570.

Davis, C. G., Nolen-Hoeksema, S., & Larson, J. (1998). Making sense of loss and benefiting from the experience: Two construals of meaning. *Journal of Personality and Social Psychology, 75*, 561–574.

Davis, E. P., Waffarn, F., & Sandman, C. A. (2011). Prenatal treatment with glucocorticoids sensitizes the HPA axis response to stress among full-term infants. *Developmental Psychobiology, 53*, 175–183.

Davis, K. W., Wellman, P. J., & Clifford, P. S. (2007). Augmented cocaine conditioned place preference in rats pretreated with systemic ghrelin. *Regulatory Peptides, 140*, 148–152.

Davis, L. L., Frazier, E. C., Williford, R. B., & Newell, J. M. (2006). Long-term pharmacotherapy for post-traumatic stress disorder. *CNS Drugs, 20*, 465–476.

Davis, M. (1992). The role of the amygdala in fear and anxiety. *Annual Review of Neuroscience, 15*, 353–375.

Davis, M., Walker, D. L., Miles, L., & Grillon, C. (2010). Phasic vs sustained fear in rats and humans: Role of the extended amygdala in fear vs anxiety. *Neuropsychopharmacology, 35*, 105–135.

de Groote, L., & Linthorst, A. C. (2007). Exposure to novelty and forced swimming evoke stressor-dependent changes in extracellular GABA in the rat hippocampus. *Neuroscience, 148*, 794–805.

de Kloet, E. R., Karst, H., & Joëls, M. (2008). Corticosteroid hormones in the central stress response: Quick-and-slow. *Frontiers in Neuroendocrinology, 29*, 268–272.

de Pablos, R. M., et al. (2006). Stress increases vulnerability to inflammation in the rat prefrontal cortex. *Journal of Neuroscience, 26*, 5709–5719.

DeLongis, A., & Holtzman, S. (2005). Coping in context: The role of stress, social support, and personality in coping. *Journal of Personality, 73*, 1633–1656.

Denollet, J. (2000). Type D personality: A potential risk factor defined. *Journal of Psychosomatic Research, 49*, 255–266.

Denollet, J., Schiffer, A. A., & Spek, V. (2010). A general propensity to psychological distress affects cardiovascular outcomes: Evidence from research on the type D (distressed) personality profile. *Circulation: Cardiovascular Quality and Outcomes, 3*, 546–557.

Desbonnet, L., Garrett, L., Clarke, G., Kiely, B., Cryan, J. F., & Dinan, T. G. (2010). Effects of the probiotic Bifidobacterium infantis in the maternal separation model of depression. *Neuroscience*, *170*, 1179–1188.

DeSousa, N. J., Bush, D. E., & Vaccarino, F. J. (2000). Self-administration of intravenous amphetamine is predicted by individual differences in sucrose feeding in rats. *Psychopharmacology*, *148*, 52–58.

Dewall, C. N., et al. (2010). Acetaminophen reduces social pain: Behavioral and neural evidence. *Psychological Science*, *21*, 931–937.

Dhabhar, F. S. (2009). Enhancing versus suppressive effects of stress on immune function: Implications for immunoprotection and immunopathology. *Neuroimmunomodulation*, *16*, 300–317.

Dickerson, S., & Kemeny, M. (2004). Acute stressors and cortisol responses: A theoretical integration and synthesis of laboratory research. *Psychological Bulletin*, *130*, 355–391.

Dietz, D. M., et al. (2011). Paternal transmission of stress-induced pathologies. *Biological Psychiatry*, *70*, 408–414.

Dinan, T. G., O'Brien, S., Lavelle, E., & Scott, L. V. (2004). Further neuroendocrine evidence of enhanced vasopressin V3 receptor responses in melancholic depression. *Psychological Medicine*, *34*, 169–172.

Disner, S. G., Beevers, C. G., Haigh, E. A., & Beck, A. T. (2011). Neural mechanisms of the cognitive model of depression. *Nature Reviews Neuroscience*, *12*, 467–477.

Dockray, S., & Steptoe, A. (2010). Positive affect and psychobiological processes. *Neuroscience and Behavioral Reviews*, *35*, 69–75.

Dolinoy, D. C., Huang, D., & Jirtle, R. L. (2007). Maternal nutrient supplementation counteracts bisphenol A-induced DNA hypomethylation in early development. *Proceedings of the National Academy of Sciences*, *104*, 13056–13061.

Dube, S. R., Felitti, V. J., Dong, M., Giles, W. H., & Anda, R. F. (2003). The impact of adverse childhood experiences on health problems: Evidence from four birth cohorts dating back to 1900. *Preventative Medicine*, *37*, 268–277.

Duijts, S. F., Zeegers, M. P., & Borne, B. V. (2003). The association between stressful life events and breast cancer risk: A meta-analysis. *International Journal of Cancer*, *107*, 1023–1029.

Duman, R. S., & Aghajanian, G. K. (2012) Synaptic dysfunction in depression: Potential therapeutic targets. *Science*, *338*, 68–72.

Duman, R. S., & Monteggia, L. M. (2006). A neurotrophic model for stress-related mood disorders. *Biological Psychiatry*, *59*, 1116–1127.

Dunlop, B. W., Kelley, M. E., Mletzko, T. C., Velasquez, C. M., Craighead, W. E., & Mayberg, H. S. (2011). Depression beliefs, treatment preference, and outcomes in a randomized trial for major depressive disorder. *Journal of Psychiatric Research*, *46*, 375–381.

Duran, E., Duran, B., Brave Heart, M. Y. H., & Yellow Horse-Davis, S. (1998). Healing the American Indian Soul Wound. In Y. Danieli (ed.), *International Handbook of Multigenerational Legacies of Trauma* (pp. 341–354). New York: Plenum.

Dvorkin, A., Silva, C., McMurran, T., Bisnaire, L., Foster, J., & Szechtman, H. (2010). Features of compulsive checking behavior mediated by nucleus accumbens and orbital frontal cortex. *European Journal of Neuroscience*, *32*, 1552–1563.

Edmiston, E. E., Wang, F., Mazure, C. M., Guiney, J., Sinha, R., Mayes, L. C., & Blumberg, H. P. (2011). Corticostriatal-limbic gray matter morphology in adolescents with self-reported exposure to childhood maltreatment. *Archives of Pediatrics & Adolescent Medicine*, *165*, 1069–1077.

Egecioglu, E., et al. (2011). Hedonic and incentive signals for body weight control. *Reviews in Endocrine and Metabolic Disorders*, *12*, 141–151.

Eidelman, S., & Biernat, M. (2003). Derogating black sheep: Individual or group protection? *Journal of Experimental Social Psychology*, *39*, 602–609.

Eifert, G. H., & Forsyth, J. P. (2005). *Acceptance & Commitment Therapy for Anxiety Disorders: A Practitioner's Treatment Guide to using Mindfulness, Acceptance, and Values-based Behavior Change Strategies*. Oakland, CA: New Harbinger.

Eisenberger, N. I., Inagaki, T. K., Mashal, N. M., & Irwin, M. R. (2010). Inflammation and social experience: An inflammatory challenge induces feelings of social disconnection in addition to depressed mood. *Brain, Behavior, and Immunity*, *24*, 558–563.

Eisenberger, N. I., & Lieberman, M. D. (2004). Why rejection hurts: A common neural alarm system for physical and social pain. *Trends in Cognitive Sciences*, *8*, 294–300.

Eisenberger, N. I., Lieberman, M. D., & Williams, K. D. (2003). Does rejection hurt? An FMRI study of social exclusion. *Science*, *302*, 290–292.

Eisenberger, N. I., Taylor, S. E., Gable, S. L., Hilmert, C. J., & Lieberman, M.D. (2007). Neural pathways link social support to attenuated neuroendocrine stress responses. *NeuroImage*, *35*, 1601–1612.

Elftman, M. D., Hunzeker, J. T., Mellinger, J. C., Bonneau, R. H., Norbury, C. C., & Truckenmiller, M. E. (2010). Stress-induced glucocorticoids at the earliest stages of herpes simplex virus-1 infection suppress subsequent antiviral immunity, implicating impaired dendritic cell function. *Journal of Immunology*, *184*, 1867–1875.

Elsayed, M., Banasr, M., Duric, V., Fournier, N. M., Licznerski, P., & Duman, R. S. (2012). Antidepressant effects of fibroblast growth factor-2 in behavioral and cellular models of depression. *Biological Psychiatry*, *72*, 258–265.

Endler, N. S., & Parker, J. D. A. (1994). Assessment of multidimensional coping: Task, emotion and avoidance strategies. *Psychological Assessment*, *6*, 50–60.

Entringer, S., et al.(2011). Stress exposure in intrauterine life is associated with shorter telomere length in young adulthood. *Proceedings of the National Academy of Sciences*, *108*, E513–E518.

Entringer, S., Kumsta, R., Hellhammer, D. H., Wadhwa, P. D., & Wüst, S. (2009). Prenatal exposure to maternal psychosocial stress and HPA axis regulation in young adults. *Hormones and Behavior*, *55*, 292–298.

Entringer, S., Kumsta, R., Nelson, E. L., Hellhammer, D. H., Wadhwa, P. D., & Wüst, S. (2008). Influence of prenatal psychosocial stress on cytokine production in adult women. *Developmental Psychobiology*, *50*, 579–587.

Eugene, F., Joormann, J., Cooney, R. E., Atlas, L. Y., & Gotlib, I. H. (2010). Neural correlates of inhibitory deficits in depression. *Psychiatry Research*, *181*, 30–35.

Evans, D. R., Baer, R. A., & Segerstrom, S. C. (2009). The effects of mindfulness and self-consciousness on persistence. *Personality and Individual Differences*, *47*, 379–382.

Evans, S. J., et al. (2004). Dysregulation of the fibroblast growth factor system in major depression. *Proceedings of the National Academy of Sciences of the United States of America, 101,* 15506–15511.

Evans-Campbell, T. (2008). Historical trauma in American Indian/Native Alaska communities: A multilevel framework for exploring impacts on individuals, families, and communities. *Journal of Interpersonal Violence, 23,* 316–338.

Falagas, M. E., Mourtzoukou, E. G., & Vardakas, K. Z. (2007). Sex differences in the incidence and severity of respiratory tract infections. *Respiratory Medicine, 101,* 1845–1863.

Fanous, S., Hammer, R. P., Jr., & Nikulina, E. M. (2010). Short- and long-term effects of intermittent social defeat stress on brain-derived neurotrophic factor expression in mesocorticolimbic brain regions. *Neuroscience, 167,* 598–607.

Farb, N. A., Anderson, A. K., Bloch, R. T., & Segal, Z. V. (2011). Mood-linked responses in medial prefrontal cortex predict relapse in patients with recurrent unipolar depression. *Biological Psychiatry, 70,* 366–372.

Fatemi, S. H., Emamian, E. S., Sidwell, R. W., Kist, D. A., Stary, J. M., Earle, J. A., & Thuras, P. (2002). Human influenza viral infection in utero alters glial fibrillary acidic protein immunoreactivity in the developing brains of neonatal mice. *Molecular Psychiatry, 7,* 633–640.

Faust, T. W., et al. (2010). Neurotoxic lupus autoantibodies alter brain function through two distinct mechanisms. *Proceedings of the National Academy of Sciences, 107,* 18569–18574.

Fava, M., Rush, A. J., Thase, M. E., Clayton, A., Stahl, S. M., Pradko, J. F., & Johnston, J. A. (2005). 15 years of clinical experience with bupropion HCl: From bupropion to bupropion SR to bupropion XL. *Primary Care Companion to the Journal of Clinical Psychiatry, 7,* 106–113.

Fawzy, F. I., Fawzy, N. W., Hyun, C. S., Elashoff, R., Guthrie, D., Fahey, J. L., & Morton, D. L. (1993). Malignant melanoma: Effects of an early structured psychiatric intervention, coping, and affective state on recurrence and survival 6 years later. *Archives of General Psychiatry, 50,* 681–689.

Figueiredo, H. F., Dolgas, C. M., & Herman, J. P. (2002). Stress activation of cortex and hippocampus is modulated by sex and stage of estrus. *Endocrinology, 143,* 2534–2540.

Fisher, R. (1992). *Contact and Conflict: Indian-European Relations in British Columbia, 1774–1890* (2nd edn). Vancouver, BC: University of British Columbia Press.

Fleshner, M. (2013). Stress-evoked sterile inflammation, danger associated molecular patterns (DAMPs), microbial associated molecular patterns (MAMPs) and the inflammasome. *Brain, Behavior, and Immunity, 27,* 1–7.

Flett, G. L., Hewitt, P. L., Blankstein, K. R., Solnik, M., & Van Brunschot, M. (1996). Perfectionism, social problem-solving ability, and psychological distress. *Journal of Rational-Emotive and Cognitive-Behaviour Therapy, 14,* 245–274.

Flores, C., & Stewart, J. (2000). Basic fibroblast growth factor as a mediator of the effects of glutamate in the development of long-lasting sensitization to stimulant drugs: Studies in the rat. *Psychopharmacology (Berl), 151,* 152–165.

Foa, E., Rothbaum, B., & Furr, J. (2011). Augmenting exposure therapy with other CBT procedures. *Psychiatric Annals, 33,* 47–56.

Foley, P., & Kirschbaum, C. (2010). Human hypothalamus-pituitary-adrenal axis responses to acute psychosocial stress in laboratory settings. *Neuroscience and Biobehavioral Reviews*, *35*, 91–96.

Folkman, S., & Lazarus, R. S. (1988). *Manual of the Ways of Coping Questionnaire*. Palo Alto, CA: Consulting Psychologists Press.

Fournier, J. C., DeRubeis, R. J., Hollon, S. D., Dimidjian, S., Amsterdam, J. D., Shelton, R. C., & Fawcett, J. (2010). Antidepressant drug effects and depression severity: A patient-level meta-analysis. *Journal of the American Medical Association*, *303*, 47–53.

Fox, M. D., Snyder, A. Z., Vincent, J. L., Corbetta, M., Van Essen, D. C., & Raichle, M. E. (2005). The human brain is intrinsically organized into dynamic, anticorrelated functional networks. *Proceedings of the National Academy of Sciences*, *102*, 9673–9678.

Francis, D. D., Young, L. J., Meaney, M. J., & Insel, T. R. (2002). Naturally occurring differences in maternal care are associated with the expression of oxytocin and vasopressin (V1a) receptors: Gender differences. *Journal of Neuroendocrinology*, *14*, 349–353.

Franklin, T. B., et al. (2010). Epigenetic transmission of the impact of early stress across generations. *Biological Psychiatry*, *68*, 408–415.

Frodl, T., et al. (2004). Hippocampal and amygdala changes in patients with major depressive disorder and healthy controls during a 1-year follow-up. *Journal of Clinical Psychiatry*, *65*, 492–499.

Fuchikami, M., et al. (2011). DNA methylation profiles of the brain-derived neurotrophic factor (BDNF) gene as a potent diagnostic biomarker in major depression. *PLoS One*, *6*, e23881.

Fuchikami, M., Yamamoto, S., Morinobu, S., Takei, S., & Yamawaki, S. (2010). Epigenetic regulation of BDNF gene in response to stress. *Psychiatry Investigation*, *7*, 251–256.

Fulton, S., et al. (2006). Leptin regulation of the mesoaccumbens dopamine pathway. *Neuron*, *51*, 811–822.

Fumagalli, F., Bedogni, F., Perez, J., Racagni, G., & Riva, M. A. (2004). Corticostriatal brain-derived neurotrophic factor dysregulation in adult rats following prenatal stress. *European Journal of Neuroscience*, *20*, 1348–1354.

Fumagalli, F., Bedogni, F., Slotkin, T. A., Racagni, G., & Riva, M. A. (2005). Prenatal stress elicits regionally selective changes in basal FGF-2 gene expression in adulthood and alters the adult response to acute or chronic stress. *Neurobiology of Disease*, *20*, 731–737.

Gallagher, D. J. (1990). Extraversion, neuroticism and appraisal of stressful academic events. *Personality and Individual Differences*, *11*, 1053–1057.

Garcia Pelosi, G., Fiacadori Tavares, R., Barros Parron Fernandes, K., & Morgan Aguiar Corrêa, F. (2009). Cardiovascular effects of noradrenaline microinjection into the medial part of the superior colliculus of unanesthetized rats. *Brain Research*, *1290*, 21–27.

Gardner, K. L., Hale, M. W., Lightman, S. L., Plotsky, P. M., & Lowry, C. A. (2009). Adverse early life experience and social stress during adulthood interact to increase serotonin transporter mRNA expression. *Brain Research*, *1305*, 47–63.

Geers, A. L., Wellman, J. A., Fowler, S. L., Helfer, S. G., & France, C. R. (2010). Dispositional optimism predicts placebo analgesia. *Journal of Pain*, *11*, 1165–1171.

Geliebter, A., Gluck, M. E., & Hashim, S. A. (2005). Plasma ghrelin concentrations are lower in binge-eating disorder. *Journal of Nutrition*, *135*, 1326–1330.

George, O., Le Moal, M., & Koob, G. F. (2012). Allostasis and addiction: Role of the dopamine and corticotropin-releasing factor systems. *Physiology & Behavior, 106,* 58–64.

Gerritsen, L., et al. (2011). BDNF Val66Met genotype modulates the effect of childhood adversity on subgenual anterior cingulate cortex volume in healthy subjects. *Molecular Psychiatry, 17,* 597–603.

Geuze, E., van Berckel, B. N., Lammertsma, A. A., Boellaard, R., de Kloet, C. S., Vermetten, E., & Westenberg, H. G. M. (2008). Reduced GABA_A benzodiazepine receptor binding in veterans with post-traumatic stress disorder. *Molecular Psychiatry, 13,* 74–83.

Gibb, J., Al-Yawer, F., & Anisman, H. (2013). Synergistic and antagonistic actions of acute or chronic social stressors and an endotoxin challenge vary over time following the challenge. *Brain, Behavior, and Immunity, 28,* 149–158.

Gibb, J., Hayley, S., Poulter, M. O., & Anisman, H. (2011). Effects of stressors and immune activating agents on peripheral and central cytokines in mouse strains that differ in stressor responsivity. *Brain, Behavior, and Immunity, 25,* 468–482.

Gibbs, J. T. (1997). African-American suicide: A cultural paradox. *Suicide and Life Threatening Behavior, 27,* 68–79.

Gilat, I., & Shahar, G. (2009). Suicide prevention by online support groups: An action theory-based model of emotional first aid. *Archives of Suicide Research, 13,* 52–63.

Givens, J. L., & Tjia, J. (2002). Depressed medical students' use of mental health services and barriers to use. *Academic Medicine, 77,* 918–921.

Glaser, R. (2005). Stress-associated immune dysregulation and its importance for human health: A personal history of psychoneuroimmunology. *Brain, Behavior, and Immunology, 17,* 321–328.

Glaser, R., MacCallum, R. C., Laskowski, B. F., Malarkey, W. B., Sheridan, J. F., & Kiecolt-Glaser, J. K. (2001). Evidence for a shift in the Th-1 to Th-2 cytokine response associated with chronic stress and aging. *Journals of Gerontology Series A: Biological Sciences and Medical Sciences, 56,* M477–M482.

Glazer, H. I., & Weiss, J. M. (1976). Long-term interference effect: An alternative to learned helplessness. *Journal of Experimental Psychology: Animal Behavior Processes, 2,* 202–213.

Glover, V. (2011). Annual Research Review: Prenatal stress and the origins of psychopathology: An evolutionary perspective. *Journal of Child Psychology and Psychiatry, 52,* 356–367.

Gold, A. L., et al. (2011). Decreased regional cerebral blood flow in medial prefrontal cortex during trauma-unrelated stressful imagery in Vietnam veterans with post-traumatic stress disorder. *Psychological Medicine, 13,* 1–10.

Goldstein, D. S. (2011). Stress, allostatic load, catecholamines, and other neurotransmitters in neurodegenerative diseases. *Endocrine Regulations, 45,* 91–98.

Gonçalves, V., Jayson, G., & Tarrier, N. (2011). A longitudinal investigation of posttraumatic stress disorder in patients with ovarian cancer. *Journal of Psychosomatic Research, 70,* 422–431.

Goodyer, I. M., Croudace, T., Dudbridge, F., Ban, M., & Herbert, J. (2010). Polymorphisms in BDNF (Val66Met) and 5-HTTLPR, morning cortisol and subsequent depression in at-risk adolescents. *British Journal of Psychiatry, 197,* 365–371.

Gorman, J. M. (2003). Treating generalized anxiety disorder. *Journal of Clinical Psychiatry, 64,* Supplement 2, 24–29.

Goshen, I., Kreisel, T., Ben-Menachem-Zidon, O., Licht, T., Weidenfeld, J., Ben-Hur, T., & Yirmiya, R. (2008). Brain interleukin-1 mediates chronic stress-induced depression in mice via adrenocortical activation and hippocampal neurogenesis suppression. *Molecular Psychiatry*, *13*, 717–728.

Gotlib, I. H., & Joormann, J. (2010). Cognition and depression: Current status and future directions. *Annual Review of Clinical Psychology*, *6*, 285–312.

Gottesman, I. I., & Gould, T. D. (2003). The endophenotype concept in psychiatry: Etymology and strategic intentions. *American Journal of Psychiatry*, *160*, 636–645.

Gould, R. A., Otto, M. W., Pollack, M. H., & Yap, L. (1997). Cognitive behavioral and pharmacological treatment of generalized anxiety disorder: A preliminary meta-analysis. *Behavior Therapy*, *28*, 285–305.

Grace, A. A., Floresco, S. B., Goto, Y., & Lodge, D. J. (2007). Regulation of firing of dopaminergic neurons and control of goal-directed behaviors. *Trends in Neuroscience*, *30*, 220–227.

Grande, G., Romppel, M., & Barth, J. (2012). Association between Type D personality and prognosis in patients with cardiovascular diseases: A systematic review and meta-analysis. *Annals of Behavioral Medicine*, *43*, 299–310.

Griffin, A. C., Lo, W. D., Wolny, A. C., & Whitacre, C. C. (1993). Suppression of experimental autoimmune encephalomyelitis by restraint stress: Sex differences. *Journal of Neuroimmunology*, *44*, 103–116.

Groeneweg, F. L., Karst, H., de Kloet, E. R., & Joëls, M. (2011). Rapid non-genomic effects of corticosteroids and their role in the central stress response. *Journal of Endocrinology*, *209*, 153–167.

Grønli, J., et al. (2006). Chronic mild stress inhibits BDNF protein expression and CREB activation in the dentate gyrus but not in the hippocampus proper. *Pharmacology Biochemistry and Behavior*, *85*, 842–849.

Guillin, O., Diaz, J., Carroll, P., Griffon, N., Schwartz, J. C., & Sokoloff, P. (2001). BDNF controls dopamine D3 receptor expression and triggers behavioural sensitization. *Nature*, *411*, 86–89.

Gustafsson, J. K., & Greenwood-Van Meerveld, B. (2011). Amygdala activation by corticosterone alters visceral and somatic pain in cycling female rats. *American Journal of Physiology – Gastrointestinal and Liver Physiology*, *300*, G1080–G1085.

Hackett, R. A., Hamer, M., Endrighi, R., Brydon, L., & Steptoe, A. (2012). Loneliness and stress-related inflammatory and neuroendocrine responses in older men and women. *Psychoneuroendocrinology*, *37*, 1801–1809.

Hall, K. T., et al. (2012). Catechol-O-methyltransferase val158met polymorphism predicts placebo effect in irritable bowel syndrome. *PLoS One*, *7*, e48135.

Ham, B. J., et al. (2007). Decreased GABA levels in anterior cingulate and basal ganglia in medicated subjects with panic disorder: A proton magnetic resonance spectroscopy (1H-MRS) study. *Progress in Neuropsychopharmacology and Biological Psychiatry*, *31*, 403–411.

Hamer, M., Chida, Y., & Molloy, G. J. (2009). Psychological distress and cancer mortality. *Journal of Psychosomatic Research*, *66*, 255–258.

Hamilton, J. P., Furman, D. J., Chang, C., Thomason, M. E., Dennis, E., & Gotlib, I. H. (2011). Default-mode and task-positive network activity in major depressive disorder: Implications for adaptive and maladaptive rumination. *Biological Psychiatry*, *70*, 327–333.

Hamilton, J. P., & Gotlib, I. H. (2008). Neural substrates of increased memory sensitivity for negative stimuli in major depression. *Biological Psychiatry*, 63, 1155–1162.

Hammack, S. E., Schmid, M. J., LoPresti, M. L., Der-Avakian, A., Pellymounter, M. A., Foster, A. C., Watkins, L. R., & Maier, S. F. (2003). Corticotropin releasing hormone type 2 receptors in the dorsal raphe nucleus mediate the behavioral consequences of uncontrollable stress. *Journal of Neuroscience*, 23, 1019–1025.

Hammen, C., Shih, J. H., & Brennan, P. A. (2004). Intergenerational transmission of depression: Test of an interpersonal stress model in a community sample. *Journal of Consulting and Clinical Psychology*, 72, 511–522.

Hannestad, J., DellaGioia, N., Ortiz, N., Pittman, B., & Bhagwagar, Z. (2011). Citalopram reduces endotoxin-induced fatigue. *Brain, Behavior, and Immunity*, 25, 256–259.

Hansson, G. K. (2005). Inflammation, atherosclerosis, and coronary artery disease. *New England Journal of Medicine*, 352, 1685–1695.

Harkness, K. L. (2008). Life events and hassles. In K. S. Dobson and D. Dozois (eds), *Risk Factors in Depression* (pp. 317–342). New York: Elsevier Science.

Harkness, K. L., Bruce, A. E., & Lumley, M. N. (2006). The role of childhood abuse and neglect in the sensitization to stressful life events in adolescent depression. *Journal of Abnormal Psychology*, 115, 730–741.

Haroon, E., Raison, C. L., & Miller, A. H. (2012). Psychoneuroimmunology meets neuropsychopharmacology: Translational implications of the impact of inflammation on behavior. *Neuropsychopharmacology*, 37, 137–162.

Harrison, N. A., Brydon, L., Walker, C., Gray, M. A., Steptoe, A., & Critchley, H. D. (2009). Inflammation causes mood changes through alterations in subgenual cingulated activity and mesolimbic connectivity. *Biological Psychiatry*, 66, 407–414.

Harvey, L., & Boksa, P. (2012). Prenatal and postnatal animal models of immune activation: relevance to a range of neurodevelopmental disorders. *Developmental Neurobiology*, 72, 1335–1348.

Hasenkamp, W., Wilson-Mendenhall, C. D., Duncan, E., & Barsalou, L. W. (2011). Mind wandering and attention during focused meditation: A fine-grained temporal analysis of fluctuating cognitive states. *NeuroImage*, 59, 750–760.

Haslam, S. A., Jetten, J., Postmes, T., & Haslam, C. (2009). Social identity health and well-being: An emerging agenda for applied psychology. *Applied Psychology: An International Review*, 58, 1–23.

Haslam, S. A., O'Brien, A., Jetten, J., Vormedal, K., & Penna, S. (2005). Taking the strain: Social identity, social support, and the experience of stress. *British Journal of Social Psychology*, 44, 355–370.

Haslam, S. A., & Reicher, S. D. (2012). Contesting the 'nature' of conformity: What Milgram and Zimbardo's studies really show. *PLoS Biology*, 10, e1001426.

Haslam, S. A., Reicher, S. D., & Levine, M. (2012). When other people are heaven, when other people are hell: How social identity determines the nature and impact of social support. In J. Jetten, C. Haslam, & S. A. Haslam (eds), *The Social Cure: Identity, Health and Well-Being* (pp. 157–174). New York: Psychology Press.

Hasler, G., van der Veen, J. W., Grillon, C., Drevets, W. C., & Shen, J. (2010). Effect of acute psychological stress on prefrontal GABA concentration determined by proton magnetic resonance spectroscopy. *American Journal of Psychiatry*, 167, 1226–1231.

Hassija, C. M., Luterek, J. A., Naragon-Gainey, K., Moore, S. A., & Simpson, T. (2011). Impact of emotional approach coping and hope on PTSD and depression symptoms in a trauma exposed sample of veterans receiving outpatient VA mental health care services. *Anxiety, Stress & Coping*, 25, 559–573.

Hayes, S. C., Luoma, J., Bond, F., Masuda, A., & Lillis, J. (2006). Acceptance and commitment therapy: Model, processes, and outcomes. *Behaviour Research and Therapy*, 44, 1–25.

Hayes, S. C., & Wilson, K. G. (1994). Acceptance and commitment therapy: Altering the verbal support for experiential avoidance. *The Behavior Analyst*, 17, 289–303.

Hayley, S. (2011). Toward an anti-inflammatory strategy for depression. *Frontiers in Behavioral Neuroscience*, 13, 19–24.

Hebb, D. O. (1955). Drives and the C.N.S. (conceptual nervous system). *Psychological Review*, 62, 243–254.

Heilig, M., & Koob, G. F. (2007). A key role for corticotropin-releasing factor in alcohol dependence. *Trends in Neuroscience*, 30, 399–406.

Heim, C., & Nemeroff, C. B. (2002). Neurobiology of early life stress: Clinical studies. *Seminars in Clinical Neuropsychiatry*, 7, 147–159.

Heim, C., Newport, D. J., Mletzko, T., Miller, A. H., & Nemeroff, C. B. (2008). The link between childhood trauma and depression: Insights from HPA axis studies in humans. *Psychoneuroendocrinology*, 33, 693–710.

Heim, C., Shugart, M., Craighead, W. E., & Nemeroff, C. B. (2010). Neurobiological and psychiatric consequences of child abuse and neglect. *Developmental Psychobiology*, 52, 671–690.

Heinrichs, M., Baumgartner, T., Kirschbaum, C., & Ehlert, U. (2003). Social support and oxytocin interact to suppress cortisol and subjective responses to psychosocial stress. *Biological Psychiatry*, 54, 1389–1398.

Helliwell, J. F., Huang, H., & Putnam, R. D. (2009). How's the job? Are trust and social capital neglected workplace investments? In V. O. Bartkus and J. H. Davis (eds), *Social Capital: Reaching Out, Reaching In* (pp. 87–144). Massachussetts: Elgar.

Hemenover, S. H., & Dienstbier, R. A. (1996). Prediction of stress appraisals from mastery, extraversion, neuroticism, and general appraisal tendencies. *Motivation and Emotion*, 20, 299–331.

Herman, J. P. & Cullinan, W. E. (1997) Neurocircuitry of stress: Central control of hypothalamo-pituitary-adrenocortical axis. *Trends in Neuroscience*, 20, 78–84.

Herrmann, M., Scholmerich, J., & Straub, R. H. (2000). Stress and rheumatic diseases. *Rheumatic Disease Clinics of North America*, 26, 737–763.

Hetrick, S. E., Purcell, R., Garner, B., & Parslow, R. (2010). Combined pharmacotherapy and psychological therapies for post traumatic stress disorder (PTSD). *Cochrane Database of Systematic Reviews*, 7, CD007316.

Hill, M. N., & McEwen, B. S. (2010). Involvement of the endocannabinoid system in the neurobehavioural effects of stress and glucocorticoids. *Progress in Neuropsychopharmacology & Biological Psychiatry*, 34, 791–797.

Hill, M. N., Patel, S., Campolongo, P., Tasker, J. G., Wotjak, C. T., & Bains, J. S. (2010). Functional interactions between stress and the endocannabinoid system: From synaptic signaling to behavioral output. *Journal of Neuroscience, 30,* 14980–14986.

Hill, M. N., & Tasker, J. G. (2012). Endocannabinoid signaling, glucocorticoid-mediated negative feedback, and regulation of the hypothalamic-pituitary-adrenal axis. *Neuroscience, 204,* 5–16.

Hirsch, M. (2001) Surviving images: Holocaust photographs and the work of postmemory. *Yale Journal of Criticism, 14,* 5–37.

Hodgkinson, C. P., & Ye, S. (2011). Toll-like receptors, their ligands, and atherosclerosis. *Scientific World Journal, 11,* 437–453.

Hoffman-Goetz, L., & Quadrilatero, J. (2003). Treadmill exercise in mice increases intestinal lymphocyte loss via apoptosis. *Acta Physiologica Scandinavica, 179,* 289–297.

Hogan, B. V., Peter, M. B., Shenoy, H. G., Horgan, K., & Hughes, T. A. (2011). Surgery induced immunosuppression. *Surgeon, 9,* 38–43.

Holmes, T. H., & Rahe, R. H. (1967). The social readjustment rating scale. *Journal of Psychosomatic Research, 11,* 213–218.

Holsboer, F., & Ising, M. (2010) Stress hormone regulation: Biological role and translation into therapy. *Annual Review of Psychology, 61,* 81–109.

Holtzman, S., Newth, S., & DeLongis, A. (2004). The role of social support in coping with daily pain among patients with Rheumatoid Arthritis. *Journal of Health Psychology, 9,* 677–695.

Hölzel, B. K., Carmody, J., Vangel, M., Congleton, C., Yerramsetti, S. M., Gard, T., & Lazar, S. W. (2011). Mindfulness practice leads to increases in regional brain gray matter density. *Psychiatry Research, 191,* 36–43.

Hróbjartsson, A., & Gøtzsche, P. C. (2010). Placebo interventions for all clinical conditions. *Cochrane Database Systematic Reviews, 106,* CD003974.

Huizink, A. C., Mulder, E. J. H., & Buitelaar, J. K. (2004). Prenatal stress and risk for psychopathology: Specific effects or induction of general susceptibility? *Psychological Bulletin, 130,* 115–142.

Hyphantis, T., Palieraki, K., Voulgari, P. V., Tsifetaki, N., & Drosos, A. A. (2011). Coping with health-stressors and defense styles associated with health-related quality of life in patients with systemic lupus erythematosus. *Lupus, 20,* 893–903.

Inagaki, T. K., Muscatell, K. A., Irwin, M. R., Cole, S. W., & Eisenberger, N. I. (2011). Inflammation selectively enhances amygdala activity to socially threatening images. *Neuroimage, 59,* 3222–3226.

Ingram, K. M., Betz, N. E., Mindes, E. J., Schmitt, M. M., & Smith, N. G. (2001). Unsupportive responses from others concerning a stressful life event: Development of the unsupportive social interactions inventory. *Journal of Social and Clinical Psychology, 20,* 173–207.

Ingram, R. E., Kendall, P. C., Siegle, G., McLaughlin, S., & Guarino, J. (1995). Psychometric properties of the positive automatic thoughts questionnaire. *Psychological Assessment, 7,* 495–507.

Insel, T. R., & Young, L. J. (2001). The neurobiology of attachment. *Nature Reviews Neuroscience, 2,* 129–136.

Irwin, J., Suissa, A., & Anisman, H. (1980). Differential effects of inescapable shock on escape performance and discrimination learning in a water escape task. *Journal of Experimental Psychology: Animal Behavioral Processes*, 6, 21–40.

Irwin, M. (1999). Immune correlates of depression. *Advances in Experimental Medicine and Biology*, 461, 1–24.

Ismail, N., Garas, P., & Blaustein, J. D. (2011). Long-term effects of pubertal stressors on female sexual receptivity and estrogen receptor-α expression in CD-1 female mice. *Hormones and Behavior*, 59, 565–571.

Israel, S., Weisel, O., Ebstein, R. P., & Bornstein, G. (2012). Oxytocin, but not vasopressin, increases both parochial and universal altruism. *Psychoneuroendocrinology*, 37, 1341–1344.

Jacobs, R., et al. (2001). Systemic lupus erythematosus and rheumatoid arthritis patients differ from healthy controls in their cytokine pattern after stress exposure. *Rheumatology*, 40, 868–875.

Jacobson-Pick, S., Elkobi, A., Vander, S., Rosenblum, K., & Richter-Levin, G. (2008). Juvenile stress-induced alteration of maturation of the GABA$_A$ receptor alpha subunit in the rat. *International Journal of Neuropsychopharmacology*, 11, 891–903.

Jahng, J. W., Ryu, V., Yoo, S. B., Noh, S. J., Kim, J. Y., & Lee, J. H. (2010). Mesolimbic dopaminergic activity responding to acute stress is blunted in adolescent rats that experienced neonatal maternal separation. *Neuroscience*, 171, 144–152.

Janeway, C., & Travers, P. (2001). *Immunobiology*, (5th ed.). New York: Garland.

Jetten, J., Haslam, C., & Haslam, S. A. (2012). *The Social Cure: Identity, Health and Well-being*. New York: Psychology Press, Taylor & Francis.

Jevtoviž, S., Karlović, D., Mihaljević-Peleš, A., Seriš, V., Vrkić, N., & Jakšić, N. (2011). Serum brain-derived neurotrophic factor (BDNF): The severity and symptomatic dimensions of depression. *Psychiatria Danubia*, 23, 363–369.

Ježek, K., Lee, B. B., Kelemen, E., McCarthy, K. M., McEwen, B. S., & Fenton, A. A. (2010). Stress-induced out-of-context activation of memory. *PLoS Biology*, 8, e1000570.

Johansen, J. P., Cain, C. K., Ostroff, L. E., & LeDoux, J. E. (2011). Molecular mechanisms of fear learning and memory. *Cell*, 147, 509–524.

Johnstone, T., van Reekum, C. M., Urry, H. L., Kalin, N. H., & Davidson, R. J. (2007). Failure to regulate: Counterproductive recruitment of top-down prefrontal-subcortical circuitry in major depression. *Journal of Neuroscience*, 27, 8877–8884.

Jones, J. L., Esber, G. R., McDannald, M. A., Gruber, A. J., Hernandez, A., Mirenzi, A., & Schoenbaum, G. (2012). Orbitofrontal cortex supports behavior and learning using inferred but not cached values. *Science*, 338, 953–956.

Kabat-Zinn, J. (1990). *Full Catastrophe Living: Using the Wisdom of Your Body and Mind to Face Stress, Pain, and Illness*. New York, NY: Delacorte.

Kaffman, A., & Meaney, M. J. (2007). Neurodevelopmental sequelae of postnatal maternal care in rodents: Clinical and research implications of molecular insights. *Journal of Child Psychology and Psychiatry*, 48, 224–244.

Kahlenberg, J. M., & Kaplan, M. J. (2011). The interplay of inflammation and cardiovascular disease in systemic lupus erythematosus. *Arthritis Research & Therapy*, 13, 203–212.

Kahneman, D. (2011). *Thinking, Fast and Slow*. New York: Farrar, Straus and Giroux.

Kahneman, D., & Tversky, A. (1979). Prospect theory: An analysis of decision under risk. *Econometrica, 47,* 263–292.

Kajantie, E., & Phillips, D. I. (2006). The effects of sex and hormonal status on the physiological response to acute psychosocial stress. *Psychoneuroendocrinology, 31,* 151–178.

Kallen, A. N., & Pal, L. (2011). Cardiovascular disease and ovarian function. *Current Opinion in Obstetrics and Gynecology, 23,* 258–267.

Kalueff, A. V., Gallagher, P. S., & Murphy, D. L. (2006). Are serotonin transporter knockout mice 'depressed'? Hypoactivity but no anhedonia. *NeuroReport, 17,* 1347–1351.

Kanner, A. D., Coyne, J. C., Schaefer, C., & Lazarus, R. S. (1981). Comparison of two modes of stress measurement: Daily hassles and uplifts versus major life events. *Journal of Behavioral Medicine, 4,* 239–249.

Karg, K., Burmeister, M., Shedden, K., & Sen, S. (2011). The serotonin transporter promoter variant (5-HTTLPR), stress, and depression meta-analysis revisited: Evidence of genetic moderation. *Archives of General Psychiatry, 68,* 444–454.

Karpova N. N., et al. (2011). Fear erasure in mice requires synergy between antidepressant drugs and extinction training. *Science, 334,* 1731–1734.

Kasai, K., Yamasue, H., Gilbertson, M. W., Shenton, M. E., Rauch, S. L., & Pitman, R. K. (2008). Evidence for acquired pregenual anterior cingulate gray matter loss from a twin study of combat-related posttraumatic stress disorder. *Biological Psychiatry, 63,* 550–556.

Kaufman, J., & Zigler, E. (1987). Do abused children become abusive parents? *American Journal of Orthopsychiatry, 57,* 186–192.

Keck, M. E., & Muller, M. B. (2005). Mutagenesis and knockout models: Hypothalamic-pituitary-adrenocortical system. *Anxiety and Anxiolytic Drugs, 169,* 113–141.

Kekow, J., Moots, R., Khandker, R., Melin, J., Freundlich, B., & Singh, A. (2011). Improvements in patient-reported outcomes, symptoms of depression and anxiety, and their association with clinical remission among patients with moderate-to-severe active early rheumatoid arthritis. *Rheumatology, 50,* 401–409.

Kelly, C. M., & Jorm, A. F. (2007). Stigma and mood disorders. *Current Opinion in Psychiatry, 20,* 13–16.

Kelly, O., Matheson, K., Ravindran, A., Merali, Z., & Anisman, H. (2007). Ruminative coping among patients with dysthymia before and after pharmacotherapy. *Depression and Anxiety, 24,* 233–243.

Kelm, M. E. (1998). *Colonizing Bodies: Aboriginal Health and Healing in British Columbia 1900–1950.* Vancouver, BC: University of British Columbia Press.

Kemeny, M. E., & Schedlowski, M. (2007). Understanding the interaction between psychosocial stress and immune-related diseases: A stepwise progression. *Brain, Behavior, and Immunity, 21,* 1009–1018.

Kendler, K. S., Kuhn, J. W., & Prescott, C. A. (2004). Childhood sexual abuse, stressful life events and risk for major depression in women. *Psychological Medicine, 34,* 1475–1482.

Kendler, K. S., Thornton, L. M., & Prescott, C. A. (2001). Gender differences in the rates of exposure to stressful life events and sensitivity to their depressogenic effects. *American Journal of Psychiatry, 158,* 587–593.

Kendler, K. S., Walters, E. E., Neale, M. C., Kessler, R. C., Heath, A. C., & Eaves, L. J. (1995). The structure of the genetic and environmental risk factors for six major psychiatric disorders in women: Phobia, generalized anxiety disorder, panic disorder, bulimia, major depression and alcoholism. *Archives of General Psychiatry, 52*, 374–383.

Kenna, G. A., et al. (2012). Association of the 5-HTT gene-linked promoter region (5-HTTLPR) polymorphism with psychiatric disorders: Review of psychopathology and pharmacotherapy. *Pharmacogenomics and Personalized Medicine, 5*, 19–35.

Kenna, G. A., Nielsen, D. M., Mello, P., Schiesl, A., & Swift, R. M. (2007). Pharmacotherapy of dual substance abuse and dependence. *CNS Drugs, 21*, 213–237.

Kent, P., Anisman, H., & Merali, Z. (2001). Central bombesin activates the hypothalamic-pituitary-adrenal axis: Effects on regional levels and release of corticotropin-releasing hormone and arginine vasopressin. *Neuroendocrinology, 73*, 203–214.

Khan, A., Warner, H. A., & Brown, W. A. (2000). Symptom reduction and suicide risk in patients treated with placebo in antidepressant clinical trials: An analysis of the Food and Drug Administration database. *Archives of General Psychiatry, 57*, 311–317.

Kiank, C., Zeden, J. P., Drude, S., Domanska, G., Fusch, G., Otten, W., & Schuett, C. (2010). Psychological stress-induced, IDO1-dependent tryptophan catabolism: Implications on immunosuppression in mice and humans. *PLoS One, 5*, e11825.

Kiecolt-Glaser, J. K., McGuire, L., Robles, T. F., & Glaser, R. (2002). Psychoneuroimmunology: Psychological influences on immune function and health. *Journal of Consulting and Clinical Psychology, 70*, 537–547.

Kim, J. M., et al. (2011). Serotonergic and BDNF genes and risk of depression after stroke. *Journal of Affective Disorders, 136*, 833–840.

Kim, Y. K., et al. (2007). Low plasma BDNF is associated with suicidal behavior in major depression. *Progess in Neuropsychopharmacology and Biological Psychiatry, 31*, 78–85.

King, L. A., King, D. W., Fairbank, J. A., Keane, T. M., & Adams, G. A. (1998). Resilience–recovery factors in post-traumatic stress disorder among female and male Vietnam veterans: Hardiness, postwar social support, and additional stressful life events. *Journal of Personality and Social Psychology, 74*, 420–434.

Kinnally, E. L., Capitanio, J. P., Leibel, R., Deng, L., LeDuc, C., Haghighi, F., & Mann, J. J. (2010). Epigenetic regulation of serotonin transporter expression and behavior in infant rhesus macaques. *Genes, Brain, and Behavior, 9*, 575–582.

Kinney, D. K., Munir, K. M., Crowley, D. J., & Miller, A. M., (2008). Prenatal stress and risk for autism. *Neuroscience and Biobehavioral Reviews, 32*, 1519–1532.

Kirby (2006) Standing Senate Committee On Social Affairs, Science And Technology (May 2006) *Out of the Shadows at Last: Transforming Mental Health, Mental Illness and Addiction Services in Canada. Final Report of The Standing Senate Committee on Social Affairs, Science and Technology*. Ottawa.

Kirsch, I., Deacon, B. J., Huedo-Medina, T. B., Scoboria, A., Moore, T. J., & Johnson, B. T. (2008). Initial severity and antidepressant benefits: A meta-analysis of data submitted to the Food and Drug Administration. *PLoS Medicine, 5*, e45. doi: 10.1371/journal.pmed.0050045.

Kirschbaum, C., Pirke, K.-M., & Hellhammer, D. H. (1993) The "Trier Social Stress Test" – a tool for investigating psychobiological stress responses in a laboratory setting. *Neuropsychobiology, 28*, 76–81.

Kivimäki, M., et al. (2012). Job strain as a risk factor for coronary heart disease: A collaborative meta-analysis of individual participant data. *The Lancet, 380*, 1491–1497.

Kivimäki, M., Virtanen, M., Elovainio, M., Kouvonen, A., Väänänen, A., & Vahtera, J. (2006). Work stress in the etiology of coronary heart disease – a meta-analysis. *Scandinavian Journal of Work, Environment & Health, 32*, 431–442.

Könner, A. C., et al. (2011). Role for insulin signaling in catecholaminergic neurons in control of energy homeostasis. *Cell Metabolism, 13*, 720–728.

Koob, G. F. (2008). A role for brain stress systems in addiction. *Neuron, 59*, 11–34.

Koob, G. F., & Le Moal, M. (2008a). Addiction and the brain antireward system. *Annual Review of Psychology, 59*, 29–53.

Koob, G. F., & Le Moal, M. (2008b). Review: Neurobiological mechanisms for opponent motivational processes in addiction. *Philosophical Transactions of the Royal Society B: Biological Sciences, 363*, 3113–3123.

Koob, G. F., & Volkow, N. D. (2010). Neurocircuitry of addiction. *Neuropsychopharmacology, 35*, 217–238.

Kop, W. J. (1999). Chronic and acute psychological risk factors for clinical manifestations of coronary artery disease. *Psychosomatic Medicine, 61*, 476–487.

Kop, W. J., & Cohen, N. (2007). Psychoneuroimmunological pathways involved in acute coronary syndromes. In R. Ader (ed.), *Psychoneuroimmunology*, (4th ed., pp. 921–943). Amsterdam, Boston: Academic Press.

Kop, W. J., & Mommersteeg, P. M. C. (2013). Psychoneuroimmunological processes in coronary artery disease and heart failure. In A. Kusnecov and H. Anisman (eds), *Handbook of Psychoneuroimmunology*. London: Wiley-Blackwell.

Kosfeld, M., Heinrichs, M., Zak, P. J., Fischbacher, U., & Fehr, E. (2005). Oxytocin increases trust in humans. *Nature, 435*, 673–676.

Kowal, C., Degiorgio, L. A., Lee, J. Y., Edgar, M. A., Huerta, P. T., Volpe, B. T., & Diamond, B. (2006). Human lupus autoantibodies against NMDA receptors mediate cognitive impairment. *Proceedings of the National Academy of Sciences, 103*, 19854–19859.

Krantz, D. S., Kop, W. J., Santiago, H. T., & Gottdiener, J. S. (1996). Mental stress as a trigger of myocardial ischemia and infarction. *Cardiology Clinics, 14*, 271–287.

Krystal, J. H., et al. (2002). Glutamate and GABA systems as targets for novel antidepressant and mood-stabilizing treatments. *Molecular Psychiatry, 1*, S71–S80.

Krystal, J. H., & Neumeister, A. (2009). Noradrenergic and serotonergic mechanisms in the neurobiology of posttraumatic stress disorder and resilience. *Brain Research, 1293*, 13–23.

Kubany, E. S., et al. (2000). Development and preliminary validation of a brief broad-spectrum measure of trauma exposure: The traumatic life events questionnaire. *Psychological Assessment, 12*, 210–224.

Kwan, B. M., Dimidjian, S., & Rizvi, S. L. (2010). Treatment preference, engagement, and clinical improvement in pharmacotherapy versus psychotherapy for depression. *Behavioral Research and Therapy, 48*, 799–804.

Lakey, B., & Cronin, A. (2008). Low social support and major depression: Research, theory and methodological issues. In K. S. Dobson & D. J. A. Dozois (eds), *Risk Factors in Depression* (pp. 385–408). San Diego, CA: Academic.

Lam, V., et al. (2012) Intestinal microbiota determine severity of myocardial infarction in rats. *Journal of the Federation of American Societies for Experimental Biology, 26*, 1727–1735.

Landsberg, L. (2001). Insulin-mediated sympathetic stimulation: Role in the pathogenesis of obesity-related hypertension (or, how insulin affects blood pressure, and why). *Journal of Hypertension, 19*, 523–528.

Lang, A. E., & Lozano, A. M. (1998). Parkinson's disease: First of two parts. *New England Journal of Medicine, 339*, 1044–1053.

Langford, D. J., et al. (2010). Coding of facial expressions of pain in the laboratory mouse. *Nature Methods, 7*, 447–449.

Lanius, R. A., et al. (2010). Default mode network connectivity as a predictor of post-traumatic stress disorder symptom severity in acutely traumatized subjects. *Acta Psychiatrica Scandinavica, 121*, 33–40.

Larson, E. B., et al. (2010). Striatal regulation of ΔFosB, FosB, and cFos during cocaine self-administration and withdrawal. *Journal of Neurochemistry, 115*, 112–122.

Larson, J. E., & Corrigan, P. (2008). The stigma of families with mental illness. *Academic Psychiatry, 32*, 87–91.

Lazarus, R. S. (1966). Psychological stress and the coping process. New York: McGraw-Hill.

Lazarus, R. S., & Folkman, S. (1984). *Stress, Appraisal, and Coping*. New York: Springer.

Ledgerwood, L., Richardson, R., & Cranney, J. (2005). D-cycloserine facilitates extinction of learned fear: Effects on reacquisition and generalized extinction. *Biological Psychiatry, 57*, 841–847.

LeDoux, J. E. (2000). Emotion circuits in the brain. *Annual Review of Neuroscience, 23*, 155–184.

Lee, B. H., Kim, H., Park, S. H., & Kim, Y. K. (2007). Decreased plasma BDNF level in depressive patients. *Journal of Affective Disorders, 101*, 239–244.

Lee, H. Y., & Kim, Y. K. (2008). Plasma brain-derived neurotrophic factor as a peripheral marker for the action mechanism of antidepressants. *Neuropsychobiology, 57*, 194–199.

Lee, P. R., Brady, D. L., Shapiro, R. A., Dorsa, D. M., & Koenig, J. I. (2007). Prenatal stress generates deficits in rat social behavior: Reversal by oxytocin. *Brain Research, 1156*, 152–167.

Lee, Y., & Davis, M. (1997). Role of the hippocampus, the bed nucleus of the stria terminalis, and the amygdala in the excitatory effect of corticotropin-releasing hormone on the acoustic startle reflex. *Journal of Neuroscience, 17*, 6434–6446.

Lemonde, S., et al. (2003). Impaired repression at a 5-hydroxytryptamine 1A receptor gene polymorphism associated with major depression and suicide. *Journal of Neuroscience, 24*, 8788–8799.

Lemos, J. C., Wanat, M. J., Smith, J. S., Reyes, B. A., Hollon, N. G., Van Bockstaele, E. J., Chavkin, C. & Phillips, P. E. (2012) Severe stress switches CRF action in the nucleus accumbens from appetitive to aversive. *Nature*. (Epub ahead of print.)

Leor, J., Poole, W. K., & Kloner, R. A. (1996). Sudden cardiac death triggered by an earthquake. *New England Journal of Medicine, 334*, 413–419.

Lerner, J. S., & Tiedens, L. Z. (2006). Portrait of the angry decision maker: How appraisal tendencies shape anger's influence on cognition. *Journal of Behavioural Decision Making, 19*, 115–137.

Leshem, M., & Schulkin, J. (2011). Transgenerational effects of infantile adversity and enrichment in male and female rats. *Developmental Psychobiology, 54*, 169–186.

Leuchter, A. F., Cook, I. A., Hunter, A. M., Cai, C., & Horvath, S. (2012). Resting-state quantitative electroencephalography reveals increased neurophysiologic connectivity in depression. *Public Library of Science One, 7*, e32508.

Levine, S., & Saltzman, A. (1987). Nonspecific stress prevents relapses of experimental allergic encephalomyelitis in rats. *Brain, Behavior, and Immunity, 1*, 336–341.

Lewis, A. C., & Sherman, S. J. (2010). Perceived entitativity and the black-sheep effect: When will we denigrate negative ingroup members? *Journal of Social Psychology, 150*, 211–225.

Li, J., Vestergaard, M., Obel, C., Precht, D. H., Christensen, J., Lu, M., & Olsen, J. (2009). Prenatal stress and cerebral palsy: A nationwide cohort study in Denmark. *Psychosomatic Medicine, 71*, 615–618.

Liao, G. Y., An, J. J., Gharami, K., Waterhouse, E. G., Vanevski, F., Jones, K. R., & Xu, B. (2012). Dendritically targeted Bdnf mRNA is essential for energy balance and response to leptin. *Nature Medicine, 18*, 564–571. doi: 10.1038/nm.2687.

Libby, P., & Theroux, P. (2005). Pathophysiology of coronary artery disease. *Circulation, 111*, 3481–3488.

Liberzon, I., & Sripada, C. S. (2008). The functional neuroanatomy of PTSD: A critical review. *Progress in Brain Research, 167*, 151–169.

Lidstone, S. C., & Stoessl, A. J. (2007). Understanding the placebo effect: Contributions from neuroimaging. *Molecular Imaging and Biology, 9*, 176–185.

Liebsch, G., Landgraf, R., Engelmann, M., Lörscher, P., & Holsboer, F. (1999). Differential behavioural effects of chronic infusion of CRH 1 and CRH 2 receptor antisense oligonucleotides into the rat brain. *Journal of Psychiatric Research, 33*, 153–163.

Lightman, S. L., et al. (2000). Significance of pulsatility in the HPA axis. *Novartis Foundation Symposia, 227*, 244–257.

Lillycrop, K. A. (2011). Effect of maternal diet on the epigenome: Implications for human metabolic disease. *Proceedings of the Nutrition Society, 70*, 64–72.

Lin, S. H. (2008). Prolactin-releasing peptide. *Results and Problems in Cell Differentiation, 46*, 57–88.

Linde, K., Berner, M. M., & Kriston, L. (2008). St John's wort for major depression. *Cochrane Database Systematic Reviews, 4*, CD000448.

Linthorst, A. C. (2005). Interactions between corticotropin-releasing hormone and serotonin: Implications for the aetiology and treatment of anxiety disorders. *Handbook of Experimental Pharmacology, 169*, 181–204.

Liotti, M., Mayberg, H. S., McGinnis, S., Brannan, S. L., Jerabek, P. (2002). Unmasking disease-specific cerebral blood flow abnormalities: Mood challenge in patients with remitted unipolar depression. *American Journal of Psychiatry, 159*, 1830–1840.

Lipstein, E. A., Brinkman, W. B., & Britto, M. T. (2012). What is known about parents' treatment decisions? A narrative review of pediatric decision making. *Medical Decision Making, 32*, 246–258.

Litteljohn, D., & Hayley, S. (2012). Cytokines as potential biomarkers for Parkinson's disease: A multiplex approach. *Methods in Molecular Biology, 934*, 121–144.

Liu, Q. S., Pu, L., & Poo, M. M. (2005). Repeated cocaine exposure in vivo facilitates LTP induction in midbrain dopamine neurons. *Nature*, *437*, 1027–1031.

Liu, R. T., & Alloy, L. B. (2010). Stress generation in depression: A systematic review of the empirical literature and recommendations for future study. *Clinical Psychology Review*, *30*, 582–593.

Liu, X., et al. (2012). Role of leaky neuronal ryanodine receptors in stress-induced cognitive dysfunction. *Cell*, *150*, 1055–1067.

Liu, X., & Weiss, F. (2003). Stimulus conditioned to foot-shock stress reinstates alcohol-seeking behavior in an animal model of relapse. *Psychopharmacology*, *168*, 184–191.

Liu, Z., et al. (2007). Association study of corticotropin-releasing hormone receptor 1 gene polymorphisms and antidepressant response in major depressive disorders. *Neuroscience Letters*, *414*, 155–158.

Loftus, E. (2003). Our changeable memories: Legal and practical implications. *Nature Reviews Neuroscience*, *4*, 231–234.

Luby, J. L., et al. (2012). Maternal support in early childhood predicts larger hippocampal volumes at school age. *Proceedings of the National Academy of Sciences*, 30 January. (Epub ahead of print.)

Luo, F. F., Han, F., & Shi, Y. X. (2011). Changes in 5-HT1A receptor in the dorsal raphe nucleus in a rat model of post-traumatic stress disorder. *Molecular Medicine Reports*, *4*, 843–847.

Lupien, S. J., McEwen, B. S., Gunnar, M. R., & Heim, C. (2009), Effects of stress throughout the lifespan on the brain, behaviour and cognition. *Nature Reviews Neuroscience*, *10*, 434–445.

Lupien, S. J., et al. (2013). The DeStress for Success Program: Effects of a stress education program on cortisol levels and depressive symptomatology in adolescents making the transition to high school. *Neuroscience*. doi: 10.1016/j.neuroscience.2013.01.057.

Lutgendorf, S. K., et al. (2008). Interleukin-6, cortisol, and depressive symptoms in ovarian cancer patients. *Journal of Clinical Oncology*, *26*, 4820–4827.

Lyons, C., Hopley, P., & Horrocks, J. (2009). A decade of stigma and discrimination in mental health: *plus ça change, plus c'est la même chose* (the more things change, the more they stay the same). *Journal of Psychiatric and Mental Health Nursing*, *16*, 501–507.

Mackenzie, S., et al. (2011) Depression and suicide ideation among students accessing campus health care. *American Journal of Orthopsychiatry*, *81*, 101–107.

MacQueen, G. M., et al. (2003). Course of illness, hippocampal function, and hippocampal volume in major depression. *Proceedings of the National Academy of Sciences*, *100*, 1387–1392.

Maes, M. (1999). Major depression and activation of the inflammatory response system. *Advances in Experimental Medicine and Biology*, *461*, 25–45.

Maes, M., Leonard, B. E., Myint, A. M., Kubera, M., & Verkerk, R. (2011). The new '5-HT' hypothesis of depression: Cell-mediated immune activation induces indoleamine 2,3-dioxygenase, which leads to lower plasma tryptophan and an increased synthesis of detrimental tryptophan catabolites (TRYCATs), both of which contribute to the onset of depression. *Progress in Neuropsychopharmacology and Biological Psychiatry*, *35*, 702–721.

Maes, M., Song, C., Lin, A., De Jongh, R., Van Gastel, A., Kenis, G., & Smith, R. S. (1998). The effects of psychological stress on humans: Increased production of pro-inflammatory cytokines and a Th1-like response in stress-induced anxiety. *Cytokine*, *10*, 313–318.

Magalhaes, A. C., et al. (2010). CRF receptor 1 regulates anxiety behavior via sensitization of 5-HT2 receptor signaling. *Nature Neuroscience*, *13*, 622–629.

Maguire, J., & Mody, I. (2007). Neurosteroid synthesis-mediated regulation of GABA(A) receptors: Relevance to the ovarian cycle and stress. *Journal of Neuroscience*, *27*, 2155–2162.

Malberg, J. E., & Duman, R. S. (2003). Cell proliferation in adult hippocampus is decreased by inescapable stress: Reversal by fluoxetine treatment. *Neuropsychopharmacology*, *28*, 1562–1671.

Mansbach, R. S., Brooks, E. N., & Chen, Y. L. (1997). Antidepressant-like effects of CP-154,526, a selective CRF1 receptor antagonist. *European Journal of Pharmacology*, *323*, 21–26.

Marazziti, D., Consoli, G., Baroni, S., & Dell'Osso, M. C. (2010). Past, present and future drugs for the treatment of obsessive-compulsive disorder. *Current Medicinal Chemistry*, *17*, 3410–3421.

Maric, T., Tobin, S., Quinn, T., & Shalev, U. (2008). Food deprivation-like effects of neuropeptide Y on heroin self-administration and reinstatement of heroin seeking in rats. *Behavioural Brain Research*, *194*, 39–43.

Marmot, M. G., Rose, G., Shipley, M., & Hamilton, P. J. (1978). Employment grade and coronary heart disease in British civil servants. *Journal of Epidemiology and Community Health*, *32*, 244–249.

Marshall, B. J., & Warren, J. R. (1984). Unidentified curved bacilli in the stomach of patients with gastritis and peptic ulceration. *Lancet*, *323*, 1311–1315.

Marshall, G. D., Jr., Agarwal, S. K., Lloyd, C., Cohen, L., Henninger, E. M., & Morris, G. J. (1998). Cytokine dysregulation associated with exam stress in healthy medical students. *Brain, Behavior and Immunity*, *12*, 297–307.

Mason, M. F., Norton, M. I., Van Horn, J. D., Wegner, D. M., Grafton, S. T., & Macrae, C. N. (2007). Wandering minds: The default network and stimulus-independent thought. *Science*, *315*, 393–395.

Masten, C. L., Eisenberger, N. I., Borofsky, L. A., Pfeifer, J. H., McNealy, K., Mazziotta, J. C., & Dapretto, M. (2009). Neural correlates of social exclusion during adolescence: Understanding the distress of peer rejection. *Social Cognition and Affective Neuroscience*, *4*, 143–157.

Masten, C. L., Telzer, E. H., Fuligni, A. J., Lieberman, M. D., & Eisenberger, N. I. (2011). Time spent with friends in adolescence relates to less neural sensitivity to later peer rejection. *Social Cognition and Affective Neuroscience*, *7*, 106–114.

Matar, M. A., Zohar, J., Kaplan, Z., & Cohen, H. (2009). Alprazolam treatment immediately after stress exposure interferes with the normal HPA-stress response and increases vulnerability to subsequent stress in an animal model of PTSD. *European Neuropsychopharmacology*, *19*, 283–295.

Matchim, Y., Armer, J. M., & Stewart, B. R. (2010). Effects of mindfulness-based stress reduction (MBSR) on health among breast cancer survivors. *Western Journal of Nursing Research*, *33*, 996–1016.

Matheson, K. (1991). Social cues in computer-mediated negotiations: Gender makes a difference. *Computers in Human Behavior*, *7*, 137–145.

Matheson, K., & Anisman, H. (2003). Systems of coping associated with dysphoria, anxiety and depressive illness: A multivariate profile perspective. *Stress*, *6*, 223–234.

Matheson, K., & Anisman, H. (2012). Biological and psychosocial responses to discrimination. In J. Jetten, C. Haslam and S. A. Haslam (eds), *The Social Cure* (pp. 133–154). New York: Psychology Press.

Matheson, K., Skomorovsky, A., Fiocco, A., & Anisman, H. (2007). The limits of 'adaptive' coping: Well-being and affective reactions to stressors among women in abusive dating relationships. *Stress*, *10*, 75–92.

Matthews, S. G., & Phillips, D. I. (2010). Minireview: Transgenerational inheritance of the stress response: A new frontier in stress research. *Endocrinology*, *151*, 7–13.

Mauck, B., Lucot, J. B., Paton, S., & Grubbs, R. D. (2010). Cholinesterase inhibitors and stress: Effects on brain muscarinic receptor density in mice. *Neurotoxicology*, *31*, 461–467.

Mayberg, H. S., Lozano, A. M., Voon, V., McNeely, H. E., Seminowicz, D., Hamani, C., & Kennedy, S. H. (2005). Deep brain stimulation for depression. *Neuron*, *45*, 651–660.

Mays, J. W., et al. (2010). Influenza virus-specific immunological memory is enhanced by repeated social defeat. *Journal of Immunology*, *184*, 2014–2025.

Maze, I., et al. (2010) Essential role of the histone methyltransferase G9a in cocaine-induced plasticity. *Science*, *327*, 213–216.

Mazure, C. M., Bruce, M. L., Maciejewski, P. K., & Jacobs, S. C. (2000). Adverse life events and cognitive-personality characteristics in the prediction of major depression and antidepressant response. *American Journal of Psychiatry*, *157*, 896–903.

McCormick, C. M., Thomas, C. M., Sheridan, C. S., Nixon, F., Flynn, J. A., & Mathews, I. Z. (2011). Social instability stress in adolescent male rats alters hippocampal neurogenesis and produces deficits in spatial location memory in adulthood. *Hippocampus*, *22*, 1300–1312.

McCrory, E. J., De Brito, S. A., Sebastian, C. L., Mechelli, A., Bird, G., Kelly, P. A., & Viding, E. (2011). Heightened neural reactivity to threat in child victims of family violence. *Current Biology*, *21*, R947–R948.

McCullough, M. E. (2000). Forgiveness as human strength: Theory, measurement, and links to well-being. *Journal of Social and Clinical Psychology*, *19*, 43–55.

McCullough, M. E., Rachal, K. C., Sandage, S. J., Worthington, E. L., Jr., Brown, S. W., & Hight, T. L. (1998). Interpersonal forgiving in close relations II: Theoretical elaboration and measurement. *Journal of Personality and Social Psychology*, *75*, 1586–1603.

McEwen, B. S. (2000). Allostasis and allostatic load: Implications for neuropsychopharmacology. *Neuropsychopharmacology*, *22*, 108–124.

McEwen, B. S. (2007). Physiology and neurobiology of stress and adaptation: Central role of the brain. *Physiological Reviews*, *87*, 873–904.

McEwen, B. S., & Gianaros, P. J. (2011). Stress- and allostasis-induced brain plasticity. *Annual Review of Medicine*, *62*, 431–445.

McEwen, B. S., & Wingfield, J. C. (2003). The concept of allostasis in biology and biomedicine. *Hormones and Behavior*, *43*, 2–15.

McFarlane, A. C. (2010). The long-term costs of traumatic stress: Intertwined physical and psychological consequences. *World Psychiatry*, 9, 3–10.

McGowan, P. O., et al. (2009). Epigenetic regulation of the glucocorticoid receptor in human brain associates with childhood abuse. *Nature Neuroscience*, 12, 342–348.

McGowan, P. O., & Szyf, M. (2010). The epigenetics of social adversity in early life: Implications for mental health outcomes. *Neurobiology of Disease*, 39, 66–72.

McGregor, B. A., & Antoni, M. H. (2009). Psychological intervention and health outcomes among women treated for breast cancer: A review of stress pathways and biological mediators. *Brain, Behavior, and Immunity*, 23, 159–166.

McInnes, I. B., & Schett, G. (2007). Cytokines in the pathogenesis of rheumatoid arthritis. *Nature Reviews Immunology*, 7, 429–442.

McIntyre, C. K., McGaugh, J. L., & Williams, C. L. (2011). Interacting brain systems modulate memory consolidation. *Neuroscience & Biobehavioral Reviews*, 36, 1750–1762.

McKenna, K., Green, A., & Gleason, J. (2002). Relationship formation in the Internet: What's the big attraction? *Journal of Social Issues*, 58, 9–31.

Meagher, M. W., et al. (2007). Interleukin-6 as a mechanism for the adverse effects of social stress on acute Theiler's virus infection. *Brain, Behavior, and Immunity*, 21, 1083–1095.

Mehta, D., Klengel, T., Conneely, K. N., Smith, A. K., Altmann, A., Pace, T. W., et al. (2013). Childhood maltreatment is associated with distinct genomic and epigenetic profiles in post-traumatic stress disorder. *Proceedings of the National Academy of Sciences*, 110, 8302–8307.

Meissner, K., Distel, H., & Mitzdorf, U. (2007). Evidence for placebo effects on physical but not on biochemical outcome parameters: A review of clinical trials. *BMC Medicine*, 5, 3.

Merali, Z., et al. (2006). Corticotropin-releasing hormone, arginine vasopressin, gastrin-releasing peptide, and neuromedin B alterations in stress-relevant brain regions of suicides and control subjects. *Biological Psychiatry*, 59, 594–602.

Merali, Z., Anisman, H., James, J. S., Kent, P., & Schulkin, J. (2008). Effects of corticosterone on corticotrophin-releasing hormone and gastrin-releasing peptide release in response to an aversive stimulus in two regions of the forebrain (central nucleus of the amygdala and prefrontal cortex). *European Journal of Neuroscience*, 28, 165–172.

Merali, Z., Du, L., Hrdina, P., Palkovits, M., Faludi, G., Poulter, M. O., & Anisman, H. (2004). Dysregulation in the suicide brain: mRNA expression of corticotropin releasing hormone receptors and GABAA receptor subunits in frontal cortical brain region. *Journal of Neuroscience*, 24, 1478–1485.

Merali, Z., Khan, S., Michaud, D. S., Shippy, S. A., & Anisman, H. (2004). Does amygdaloid corticotropin-releasing hormone (CRH) mediate anxiety-like behaviors? Dissociation of anxiogenic effects and CRH release. *European Journal of Neuroscience*, 20, 229–239.

Merali, Z., McIntosh, J., Kent, P., Michaud, D., & Anisman, H. (1998). Aversive and appetitive events evoke the release of corticotropin-releasing hormone and bombesin-like peptides at the central nucleus of the amygdala. *Journal of Neuroscience*, 18, 4758–4766.

Mergl, R., et al. (2011). Are treatment preferences relevant in response to serotonergic antidepressants and cognitive-behavioral therapy in depressed primary care patients? Results from a randomized controlled trial including a patients' choice arm. *Psychotherapy and Psychosomatics*, 80, 39–47.

Merkle, S., et al. (2007). A role for caspase-1 in heart failure. *Circulation Research*, *100*, 645–653.

Merlo, L. M., Pepper, J. W., Reid, B. J., & Maley, C. C. (2006). Cancer as an evolutionary and ecological process. *Nature Reviews Cancer*, 6, 924–935.

Meyer, J. H., et al. (2003) Dysfunctional attitudes and 5-HT2 receptors during depression and self-harm. *American Journal of Psychiatry*, *160*, 90–99.

Meyer, U., & Feldon, J. (2009). Prenatal exposure to infection: A primary mechanism for abnormal dopaminergic development in schizophrenia. *Psychopharmacology*, *206*, 587–602.

Meyer, U., Nyffeler, M., Yee, B. K., Knuesel, I., & Feldon, J. (2008). Adult brain and behavioral pathological markers of prenatal immune challenge during early/middle and late fetal development in mice. *Brain, Behavior, and Immunity*, *22*, 469–486.

Meyer-Lindenberg, A., Domes, G., Kirsch, P., & Heinrichs, M. (2011). Oxytocin and vasopressin in the human brain: Social neuropeptides for translational medicine. *Nature Reviews Neuroscience*, *12*, 524–538.

Michaud, K., Matheson, K., Kelly, O., & Anisman, H. (2008). Impact of stressors in a natural context on release of cortisol in healthy adult humans: A meta-analysis. *Stress*, *11*, 177–197.

Milad, M. R., & Rauch, S. L. (2011) Obsessive-compulsive disorder: Beyond segregated cortico-striatal pathways. *Trends in Cognitive Sciences*, *16*, 43–51.

Milad, M. R., Wright, C. I., Orr, S. P., Pitman, R. K., Quirk, G. J., & Rauch, S. L. (2007). Recall of fear extinction in humans activates the ventromedial prefrontal cortex and hippocampus in concert. *Biological Psychiatry*, *62*, 446–454.

Millan, M. J. (2006). Multi-target strategies for the improved treatment of depressive states: Conceptual foundations and neuronal substrates, drug discovery and therapeutic application. *Pharmacology & Therapeutics*, *110*, 135–370.

Miller, A. H., Maletic, V., & Raison, C. L. (2009). Inflammation and its discontents: The role of cytokines in the pathophysiology of major depression. *Biological Psychiatry*, *65*, 732–741.

Miller, G. E., Chen, E., & Parker, K. J. (2011). Psychological stress in childhood and susceptibility to the chronic diseases of aging: Moving toward a model of behavioural and biological mechanisms. *Psychological Bulletin*, *137*, 959–997.

Miller, G. E., Cohen, S., & Ritchey, A. K. (2002). Chronic psychological stress and the regulation of pro-inflammatory cytokines: A glucocorticoid-resistance model. *Health Psychology*, *21*, 531–541.

Mishel, M. H. (1999). Uncertainty in acute illness. *Annual Review of Nursing Research*, *17*, 269–294.

Miskovic, V., & Schmidt, L. A. (2011). Social fearfulness in the human brain. *Neuroscience & Biobehavioral Reviews*, *36*, 459–478.

Miskowiak, K. W., Vinberg, M., Harmer, C. J., Ehrenreich, H., & Kessing, L. V. (2012). Erythropoietin: A candidate treatment for mood symptoms and memory dysfunction in depression. *Psychopharmacology*, *219*, 687–698.

Mitte, K. (2005). A meta-analysis of the efficacy of psycho- and pharmacotherapy in panic disorder with and without agoraphobia. *Journal of Affective Disorders*, *88*, 27–45.

Mohan, A., Sharma, R., & Bijlani, R. L. (2011). Effect of meditation on stress-induced changes in cognitive functions. *Journal of Alternative and Complementary Medicine*, *17*, 207–212.

Mohr, D. C., Goodkin, D. E., Nelson, S., Cox, D., & Weiner, M. (2002). Moderating effects of coping on the relationship between stress and the development of new brain lesions in multiple sclerosis. *Psychosomatic Medicine, 64*, 803–809.

Mohr, D. C., Hart, S. L., Julian, L., Cox, D., & Pelletier, D. (2004). Association between stressful life events and exacerbation in multiple sclerosis: A meta-analysis. *British Medical Journal, 328*, 731.

Mollace, V., Muscoli, C., Palma, E., Iannone, M., Granato, T., Nistico, R., & Rotiroti, D. (2001). Central cardiovascular responses induced by interleukin 1 beta and tumor necrosis factor alpha infused into nucleus tractus solitarii, nucleus parabrachialis medialis and third cerebral ventricle of normotensive rats. *Neuroscience Letters, 314*, 53–56.

Molteni, R., et al. (2001). Modulation of fibroblast growth factor-2 by stress and corticosteroids: From developmental events to adult brain plasticity. *Brain Research Reviews, 37*, 249–258.

Monroe, S. M., & Harkness, K. L. (2005). Life stress, the 'kindling' hypothesis, and the recurrence of depression: Considerations from a life stress perspective. *Psychological Review, 112*, 417–445.

Monteggia, L. M., et al. (2007). Brain-derived neurotrophic factor conditional knockouts show gender differences in depression-related behaviors. *Biological Psychiatry, 61*, 187–197.

Moody, T. W., & Merali, Z. (2004). Bombesin-like peptides and associated receptors within the brain: Distribution and behavioral implications. *Peptides, 25*, 511–520.

Moons, W. G., Eisenberger, N. I., & Taylor, S. E. (2010). Anger and fear responses to stress have different biological profiles. *Brain, Behavior, and Immunity, 24*, 215–219.

Moos, R. H., Brennan, P. L., Fondacaro, M. R., & Moos, B. S. (1990). Approach and avoidance coping responses among older problem and nonproblem drinkers. *Psychology and Aging, 5*, 31–40.

Morahan-Martin, J., & Schumacher, P. (2003). Loneliness and social uses of the Internet. *Computers in Human Behavior, 19*, 659–671.

Moreno-Smith, M., Lutgendorf, S. K., & Sood, A. K. (2010). Impact of stress on cancer metastasis. *Future Oncology, 6*, 1863–1881.

Morewedge, C. K., & Kahneman, D. (2010). Associative processes in intuitive judgment. *Trends in Cognitive Sciences, 14*, 435–440.

Morgan, C. P., & Bale, T. L. (2011). Early prenatal stress epigenetically programs dysmasculinization in second-generation offspring via the paternal lineage. *Journal of Neuroscience, 31*, 11748–11755.

Morrissey, M. D., Mathews, I. Z., & McCormick, C. M. (2011). Enduring deficits in contextual and auditory fear conditioning after adolescent, not adult, social instability stress in male rats. *Neurobiology of Learning and Memory, 95*, 46–56.

Morton, D. L., El-Deredy, W., Watson, A., & Jones, A. K. P. (2010). Placebo analgesia as a case of a cognitive style driven by prior expectation. *Brain Research, 1359*, 137–141.

Moses, T. (2009). Stigma and self-concept among adolescents receiving mental health treatment. *American Journal of Orthopsychiatry, 79*, 261–274.

Mueller, B. R., & Bale, T. L. (2008). Sex-specific programming of offspring emotionality after stress early in pregnancy. *Journal of Neuroscience, 28*, 9055–9065.

Muller, M. B., et al. (2003). Limbic corticotropin-releasing hormone receptor 1 mediates anxiety-related behavior and hormonal adaptation to stress. *Nature Neuroscience, 6*, 1100–1107.

Mychasiuk, R., Gibb, R., & Kolb, B. (2011). Prenatal bystander stress induces neuroanatomical changes in the prefrontal cortex and hippocampus of developing rat offspring. *Brain Research*, *1412*, 55–62.

Mychasiuk, R., Schmold, N., Ilnytskyy, S., Kovalchuk, O., Kolb, B., & Gibb, R. (2011). Prenatal bystander stress alters brain, behavior, and the epigenome of developing rat offspring. *Developmental Neuroscience*, *33*, 159–169.

Nadeau, S., & Rivest, S. (1999). Effects of circulating tumor necrosis factor on the neuronal activity and expression of the genes encoding the tumor necrosis factor in the rat brain: A view from the blood-brain barrier. *Neuroscience*, *93*, 1449–1464.

Nader, K., Schafe, G. E., & LeDoux, J. E. (2000). The labile nature of consolidation theory. *Nature Reviews Neuroscience*, *1*, 216–219.

Naghavi, M., et al. (2003). From vulnerable plaque to vulnerable patient: A call for new definitions and risk assessment strategies: Part II. *Circulation*, *108*, 1772–1778.

Nash, J. R., et al. (2008). Serotonin 5-HT1A receptor binding in people with panic disorder: Positron emission tomography study. *British Journal of Psychiatry*, *193*, 229–234.

Natterson-Horowitz, B., & Bowers, K. (2012). *Zoobiquity: What Animals Can Teach Us about Health and the Science of Healing*. New York: Knopf.

Nemeroff, C. B., & Vale, W. (2005). The neurobiology of depression: Inroads to treatment and new drug discovery. *Journal of Clinical Psychiatry*, *66*, 5–13.

Nestler, E. J. (2008). Transcriptional mechanisms of addiction: Role of DeltaFosB. *Philosophical Transactions of the Royal Society of London, Series B: Biological Sciences*, *363*, 3245–3255.

Nestler, E. J., Barrot, M., & Self, D. W. (2001). DeltaFosB: A sustained molecular switch for addiction. *Proceedings of the National Academy of Sciences*, *98*, 11042–11046.

Nicholson, A., Kuper, H., & Hemingway, H. (2006). Depression as an aetiologic and prognostic factor in coronary heart disease: A meta-analysis of 6,362 events among 146,538 participants in 54 observational studies. *European Heart Journal*, *27*, 2763–2774.

Nielsen, N. M., Hansen, A. V., Simonsen, J., & Hviid, A. (2011). Prenatal stress and risk of infectious diseases in offspring. *American Journal of Epidemiology*, *173*, 990–997.

Nieuwsma, J. A., & Pepper, C. M. (2010). How etiological explanations for depression impact perceptions of stigma, treatment effectiveness, and controllability of depression. *Journal of Mental Health*, *19*, 52–61.

Nolen-Hoeksema, S. (1998). Ruminative coping with depression. In J. Heckhausen & C. S. Dweck (eds), *Motivation and Self-Regulation Across the Life Span* (pp. 237–256). Cambridge: Cambridge University Press.

Nolen-Hoeksema, S. (2000). The role of rumination in depressive disorders and mixed anxiety/depressive symptoms. *Journal of Abnormal Psychology*, *109*, 504–511.

Northoff, G., Qin, P., & Nakao, T. (2010). Rest–stimulus interaction in the brain: A review. *Trends in Neuroscience*, *33*, 277–284.

Northoff, G., et al. (2007). GABA concentrations in the human anterior cingulate cortex predict negative BOLD responses in fMRI. *Nature Neuroscience*, *10*, 1515–1517.

Notley, T. (2009). Young people, online networks, and social inclusion. *Journal of Computer-Mediated Communication*, *14*, 1208–1227.

Nutt, D. J., & Malizia, A. L. (2008). Why does the world have such a 'down' on antidepressants? *Journal of Psychopharmacology*, *22*, 223–226.

Oberlander, T. F., Weinberg, J., Papsdorf, M., Grunau, R., Misri, S., & Devlin, A. M. (2008). Prenatal exposure to maternal depression, neonatal methylation of human glucocorticoid receptor gene (NR3C1) and infant cortisol stress responses. *Epigenetics*, *3*, 97–106.

O'Donnell, K., Brydon, L., Wright, C. E., & Steptoe, A. (2008). Self-esteem levels and cardiovascular and inflammatory responses to acute stress. *Brain, Behavior, and Immunity*, *22*, 1241–1247.

Offer, D., & Spiro, R. P. (1987). The disturbed adolescent goes to college. *Journal of American College Health*, *35*, 209–214.

Olatunji, B. O., & Wolitzky-Taylor, K. B. (2009). Anxiety sensitivity and the anxiety disorders: A meta-analytic review and synthesis. *Psychological Bulletin*, *135*, 974–979.

Olson, V. G., et al. (2011). The role of norepinephrine in differential response to stress in an animal model of posttraumatic stress disorder. *Biological Psychiatry*, *70*, 441–448.

Ong, A. D., Rothstein, J. D., & Uchino, B. N. (2011). Loneliness accentuates age differences in cardiovascular responses to social evaluative threat. *Psychology and Aging*, *27*, 190–198.

Opacka-Juffry, J., & Mohiyeddini, C. (2012). Experience of stress in childhood negatively correlates with plasma oxytocin concentration in adult men. *Stress*, *15*, 1–10.

Osuna, E. E. (1985). The psychological cost of waiting. *Journal of Mathematical Psychology*, *29*, 82–105.

Owen, R. T. (2007). Pregabalin: Its efficacy, safety and tolerability profile in generalized anxiety. *Drugs Today*, *43*, 601–610.

Ozawa, K., Hashimoto, K., Kishimoto, T., Shimizu, E., Ishikura, H., & Iyo, M. (2006). Immune activation during pregnancy in mice leads to dopaminergic hyperfunction and cognitive impairment in the offspring: A neurodevelopmental animal model of schizophrenia. *Biological Psychiatry*, *59*, 546–554.

Pace, T. W., Mletzko, T. C., Alagbe, O., Musselman, D. L., Nemeroff, C. B., Miller, A. H., & Heim, C. M. (2006). Increased stress-induced inflammatory responses in male patients with major depression and increased early life stress. *American Journal of Psychiatry*, *163*, 1630–1633.

Pace, T. W., et al. (2009). Effect of compassion meditation on neuroendocrine, innate immune and behavioral responses to psychosocial stress. *Psychoneuroendocrinology*, *34*, 87–98.

Pae, C. U. & Patkar, A. A. (2007). Paroxetine: Current status in psychiatry. *Expert Reviews in Neurotherapy*, *7*, 107–120.

Paez, D. R., & Liu, J. H.-F. (2011). Collective memory of conflicts. In D. Bar-Tal (ed.), *Intergroup Conflicts and their Resolution: A Social Psychological Perspective* (pp. 105–124). New York: Psychology Press.

Pagano, J. S., Blaser, M., Buendia, M. A., Damania, B., Khalili, K., Raab-Traub, N., & Roizman, B. (2004). Infectious agents and cancer: Criteria for a causal relation. *Seminars in Cancer Biology*, *14*, 453–471.

Page, L. A., et al. (2009). A functional magnetic resonance imaging study of inhibitory control in obsessive-compulsive disorder. *Psychiatry Research*, *174*, 202–209.

Paik, I. H., Toh, K. Y., Lee, C., Kim, J. J., & Lee, S. J. (2000). Psychological stress may induce increased humoral and decreased cellular immunity. *Behavioral Medicine*, 26, 139–141.

Pandey, G. N., et al. (2011). Proinflammatory cytokines in the prefrontal cortex of teenage suicide victims. *Journal of Psychiatric Research*, 46, 57–63.

Park, C. L. (2010). Making sense of the meaning literature: An integrative review of meaning making and its effects on adjustment to stressful life events. *Psychological Bulletin*, 136, 257–301.

Park, J. E., et al. (2010). Psychological distress as a negative survival factor for patients with hematologic malignancies who underwent allogeneic hematopoietic stem cell transplantation. *Pharmacotherapy*, 30, 1239–1246.

Park, S., Bae, J., Nam, B. H., & Yoo, K. Y. (2008). Aetiology of cancer in Asia. *Asian Pacific Journal of Cancer Prevention*, 9, 371–380.

Parsey, R. V., Oquendo, M. A., Ogden, R. T., Olvet, D. M., Simpson, N., & Huang, Y. Y. (2006). Altered serotonin 1A binding in major depression: A [carbonyl-C-11] WAY100635 positron emission tomography study. *Biological Psychiatry*, 59, 106–113.

Parvaz, M. A., Konova, A. B., Tomasi, D., Volkow, N. D., & Goldstein, R. Z. (2011). Structural integrity of the prefrontal cortex modulates electrocortical sensitivity to reward. *Journal of Cognitive Neuroscience*, 24, 1560–1570.

Pasic, J., Levy, W. C., & Sullivan, M. D. (2003). Cytokines in depression and heart failure. *Psychosomatic Medicine*, 65, 181–193.

Patterson, Z. R., Ducharme, R., Anisman, H., & Abizaid, A. (2010). Altered metabolic and neurochemical responses to chronic unpredictable stressors in ghrelin receptor-deficient mice. *European Journal of Neuroscience*, 32, 632–639.

Paykel, E. S., Prusoff, B. A., & Uhlenhuth, E. H. (1971). Scaling of life events. *Archives of General Psychiatry*, 25, 340–347.

Peacock, E. J., & Wong, P. T. (1990). The Stress Appraisal Measure (SAM): A multidimensional approach to cognitive appraisal. *Stress Medicine*, 6, 227–236.

Pearlin, L. I., Schieman, S., Fazio, E. M., & Meersman, S. C. (2005). Stress, health, and the life course: Some conceptual perspectives. *Journal of Health and Social Behavior*, 46, 205–219.

Pepeu, G., & Blandina, P. (1998). The acetylcholine, GABA, glutamate triangle in the rat forebrain. *Journal of Physiology – Paris*, 92, 351–355.

Peralta-Ramírez, M. I., Jiménez-Alonso, J., Godoy-García, J. F., & Pérez-García, M. (2004). The effects of daily stress and stressful life events on the clinical symptomatology of patients with lupus erythematosus. *Psychosomatic Medicine*, 66, 788–794.

Pereg, D., Gow, R., Mosseri, M., Lishner, M., Rieder, M., Van Uum, S., & Koren, G. (2011). Hair cortisol and the risk for acute myocardial infarction in adult men. *Stress*, 14, 73–81.

Pereira, O. C., Bernardi, M. M., & Gerardin, D. C. (2006). Could neonatal testosterone replacement prevent alterations induced by prenatal stress in male rats? *Life Sciences*, 78, 2767–2771.

Petrovic, P., Kalso, E., Petersson, K. M., & Ingvar, M. (2002). Placebo and opioid analgesia – imaging a shared neuronal network. *Science*, 295, 1737–1740.

Philbin, E. F., Dec, G. W., Jenkins, P. L., & DiSalvo, T. G. (2001). Socioeconomic status as an independent risk factor for hospital readmission for heart failure. *American Journal of Cardiology*, 87, 1367–1371.

Pierrehumbert, B., Torrisi, R., Laufer, D., Halfon, O., Ansermet, F., & Beck Popovic, M. (2010). Oxytocin response to an experimental psychosocial challenge in adults exposed to traumatic experiences during childhood or adolescence. *Neuroscience*, *166*, 168–177.

Pitman, D. L., Natelson, B. H., Ottenweller, J. E., McCarty, R., Pritzel, T., & Tapp, W. N. (1995). Effects of exposure to stressors of varying predictability on adrenal function in rats. *Behavioral Neuroscience*, *109*, 767–776.

Pitman, R. K., Gilbertson, M. W., Gurvits, T. V., May, F. S., Lasko, N. B., & Orr, S. P. (2006). Harvard/VA PTSD twin study investigators. *Annals of the New York Academicy of Sciences*, *1071*, 242–254.

Pitman, R. K., Sanders, K. M., Zusman, R. M., Healy, A. R., Cheema, F., & Orr, S. P. (2002). Pilot study of secondary prevention of posttraumatic stress disorder with propranolol. *Biological Psychiatry*, *51*, 189–192.

Pluess, M., & Belsky, J. (2012) Vantage sensitivity: Individual differences in response to positive experiences. *Psychological Bulletin*. (Epub ahead of print.)

Polido-Pereira, J., Vieira-Sousa, E., & Fonseca, J. E. (2011). Rheumatoid arthritis: What is refractory disease and how to manage it? *Autoimmunity Reviews*, *10*, 707–713.

Popoli, M., Yan, Z., McEwen, B. S., & Sanacora, G. (2011). The stressed synapse: The impact of stress and glucocorticoids on glutamate transmission. *Nature Reviews Neuroscience*, *13*, 22–37.

Porsolt, R. D., Anton, G., Blavet, N., & Jalfre, M. (1978). Behavioural despair in rats: A new model sensitive to antidepressant treatments. *European Journal of Pharmacology*, *47*, 379–391.

Post, R. M. (1992). Transduction of psychosocial stress into the neurobiology of recurrent affective disorder. *American Journal of Psychiatry*, *149*, 999–1010.

Poulter, M. O., et al. (2008). GABAA receptor promoter hypermethylation in suicide brain: Implications for the involvement of epigenetic processes. *Biological Psychiatry*, *64*, 645–652.

Poulter, M. O., Du, L., Zhurov, V., Merali, Z., & Anisman, H. (2010). Plasticity of the $GABA_A$ receptor subunit cassette in response to stressors in reactive versus resilient mice. *Neuroscience*, *165*, 1039–1051.

Poulter, M. O., Du, L., Zhurov, V., Palkovits, M., Faludi, G., Merali, Z., & Anisman, H. (2010). Altered organization of GABAA receptor mRNA expression in the depressed suicide brain. *Frontiers in Neuroscience*, *3*, 3–11.

Poulton, R. G., & Andrews, G. (1992). Personality as a cause of adverse life events. *Acta Psychiatrica Scandinavica*, *85*, 35–38.

Powell, N. D., Mays, J. W., Bailey, M. T., Hanke, M. L., & Sheridan, J. F. (2011). Immunogenic dendritic cells primed by social defeat enhance adaptive immunity to influenza A virus. *Brain, Behavior, and Immunity*, *25*, 46–52.

Power, T. G., & Hill, L. G. (2010). Individual differences in appraisal of minor, potentially stressful events: A cluster analytic approach. *Cognition & Emotion*, *24*, 1081–1109.

Powers, M. B., Zum Vorde Sive Vording M. B., & Emmelkamp, P. M. (2009). Acceptance and commitment therapy: A meta-analytic review. *Psychotherapy and Psychosomatics*, *78*, 73–80.

Pratchett, L. C., & Yehuda, R. (2011). Foundations of posttraumatic stress disorder: Does early life trauma lead to adult posttraumatic stress disorder? *Development and Psychopathology*, *23*, 477–491.

Preskorn, S., Baker, B., Kolluri, S., Menniti, F. S., Krams, M., & Landen, J. W. (2008). An innovative design to establish proof of concept of the antidepressant effects of the NR2B subunit selective N-methyl-D-aspartate antagonist, CP-101,606, in patients with treatment-refractory major depressive disorder. *Journal of Clinical Psychopharmacology*, 28, 631–637.

Price, R. B., Nock, M. K., Charney, D. S., & Mathew, S. J. (2009). Effects of intravenous ketamine on explicit and implicit measures of suicidality in treatment-resistant depression. *Biological Psychiatry*, 66, 522–526.

Prince, C. R., & Anisman, H. (1984). Acute and chronic stress effects on performance in a forced swim task. *Behavioral and Neural Biology*, 42, 99–119.

Pu, L., Liu, Q. S., & Poo, M. M. (2006). BDNF-dependent synaptic sensitization in midbrain dopamine neurons after cocaine withdrawal. *Nature Neuroscience*, 9, 605–607.

Qian, J., Hospodsky, D., Yamamoto, N., Nazaroff, W. W., & Peccia, J. (2012). Size-resolved emission rates of airborne bacteria and fungi in an occupied classroom. *Indoor Air*, 22, 339–351.

Quirin, M., Kuhl, J., & Düsing, R. (2011). Oxytocin buffers cortisol responses to stress in individuals with impaired emotion regulation abilities. *Psychoneuroendocrinology*, 36, 898–904.

Raichle, M. E., MacLeod, A. M., Snyder, A. Z., Powers, W. J., Gusnard, D. A., & Shulman, G. L. (2001). A default mode of brain function. *Proceedings of the National Academy of Sciences*, 98, 676–682.

Rainville, P., Bechara, A., Naqvi, N., & Damasio, A. R. (2006). Basic emotions are associated with distinct patterns of cardiorespiratory activity. *International Journal of Psychophysiology*, 61, 5–18.

Raison, C. L., Capuron, L., & Miller, A. H. (2006). Cytokines sing the blues: Inflammation and the pathogenesis of depression. *Trends in Immunology*, 27, 24–31.

Ranchor, A. V., Wardle, J., Steptoe, A., Henselmans, I., Ormel, J., & Sanderman, R. (2010). The adaptive role of perceived control before and after cancer diagnosis: A prospective study. *Social Science & Medicine*, 70, 1825–1831.

Rasmusson, A. M., Shi, L., & Duman, R. (2002). Downregulation of BDNF mRNA in the hippocampal dentate gyrus after re-exposure to cues previously associated with footshock. *Neuropsychopharmacology*, 27, 133–142.

Raspopow, K., Abizaid, A., Matheson, K., & Anisman, H. (2010). Psychosocial stressor effects on cortisol and ghrelin in emotional and non-emotional eaters: Influence of anger and shame. *Hormones and Behavior*, 58, 677–684.

Ravindran, A. V., et al. (1999). Treatment of primary dysthymia with cognitive therapy and pharmacotherapy: Clinical symptoms and functional impairments. *American Journal of Psychiatry*, 156, 1608–1617.

Reddy, V. S., et al. (2010). Interleukin-18 induces EMMPRIN expression in primary cardiomyocytes via JNK/Sp1 signaling and MMP-9 in part via EMMPRIN and through AP-1 and NF-kappaB activation. *American Journal of Physiology – Heart and Circulatory Physiology*, 299, H1242–H1254.

Reiche, E. M., Nunes, S. O., & Morimoto, H. K. (2004). Stress, depression, the immune system, and cancer. *The Lancet Oncology*, 5, 617–625.

Reul, M. H. M., & Holsboer, F. (2002). Corticotropin-releasing factor receptors 1 and 2 in anxiety and depression. *Current Opinion in Pharmacology*, 2, 23–33.

Rice, F., Harold, G. T., Boivin, J., van den Bree, M., Hay, D. F., & Thapar, A. (2010). The links between prenatal stress and offspring development and psychopathology: Disentangling environmental and inherited influences. *Psychological Medicine, 40,* 335–345.

Rihmer, Z. (2007). Suicide risk in mood disorders. *Current Opinion in Psychiatry, 20,* 17–22.

Riley, V. (1981). Psychoneuroendocrine influences on immunocompetence and neoplasia. *Science, 212,* 1100–1109.

Rinaldi, S., et al. (2006). Influence of coping skills on health-related quality of life in patients with systemic lupus erythematosus. *Arthritis Care & Research, 55,* 427–433.

Rinaudo, P., & Wang, E. (2011). Fetal programming and metabolic syndrome. *Annual Review of Physiology, 74,* 107–130.

Rios, M. (2013). BDNF and the central control of feeding: Accidental bystander or essential player? *Trends in Neuroscience, 36,* 83–90.

Ritsher, J., & Phelan, J. (2004). Internalized stigma predicts erosion of morale among psychiatric outpatients. *Psychiatry Research, 129,* 257–265.

Rivest, S. (2009). Regulation of innate immune responses in the brain. *Nature Reviews Immunology, 9,* 429–439.

Rivier, C. (1999). Gender, sex steroids, corticotropin-releasing factor, nitric oxide, and the HPA response to stress. *Pharmacology Biochemistry and Behavior, 64,* 739–751.

Robinaugh, D. J., & McNally, R. J. (2010). Autobiographical memory for shame or guilt provoking events: Association with psychological symptoms. *Behavior Research and Therapy, 48,* 646–652.

Robinson, M., et al. (2011). Prenatal stress and risk of behavioral morbidity from age 2 to 14 years: The influence of the number, type, and timing of stressful life events. *Development and Psychopathology, 23,* 155–168.

Robinson, T. E., & Berridge, K. C. (2003). Addiction. *Annual Review of Psychology, 54,* 25–53.

Rosas-Jorquera, C. E., Sardinha, L. R., Pretel, F. D., Bombeiro, A. L., D'Império Lima, M. R., & Alvarez, J. M. (2013). Challenge of chronically infected mice with homologous trypanosoma cruzi parasites enhances the immune response but does not modify cardiopathy: Implications for the design of a therapeutic vaccine. *Clinical and Vaccine Immunology, 20,* 248–254.

Rosen, N., Knäuper, B., & Sammut, J. (2007). Do individual differences in intolerance of uncertainty affect health monitoring? *Psychology and Health, 22,* 413–430.

Rosenkranz, M. A., Davidson, R. J., Maccoon, D. G., Sheridan, J. F., Kalin, N. H., & Lutz, A. (2013). A comparison of mindfulness-based stress reduction and an active control in modulation of neurogenic inflammation. *Brain, Behavior, and Immunity, 27,* 174–184.

Rosenman, R. H., Brand, R. J., Jenkins, D., Friedman, M., Straus, R., & Wurm, M. (1975). Coronary heart disease in Western Collaborative Group Study: Final follow-up experience of 8 1/2 years. *Journal of the American Medical Association, 233,* 872–877.

Roth, T. L., Lubin, F. D., Funk, A. J., & Sweatt, J. D. (2009). Lasting epigenetic influence of early-life adversity on the BDNF gene. *Biological Psychiatry, 65,* 760–769.

Roth, T. L., & Sweatt, J. D. (2010). Epigenetic marking of the BDNF gene by early-life adverse experiences. *Hormones and Behavior, 59,* 315–320.

Roth, T. L., Zoladz, P. R., Sweatt, J. D., & Diamond, D. M. (2011). Epigenetic modification of hippocampal Bdnf DNA in adult rats in an animal model of post-traumatic stress disorder. *Journal of Psychiatric Research*, 45, 919–926.

Rothwell, N. J., & Luheshi, G. N. (2000). Interleukin 1 in the brain: Biology, pathology and therapeutic target. *Trends in Neurosciences*, 23, 618–625.

Royal Commission on Aboriginal Peoples. (1996). *Looking Forward, Looking Back – Report of the Royal Commission on Aboriginal Peoples, Volume 1*. Ottawa: Communication Group Publishing.

Rubia, K. (2009). The neurobiology of meditation and its clinical effectiveness in psychiatric disorders. *Biological Psychology*, 82, 1–11.

Rubio-Perez, J. M., & Morillas-Ruiz, J. M. (2012). A review: Inflammatory process in Alzheimer's disease, role of cytokines. *Scientific World Journal*, 2012, 756357.

Rüsch, N., Angermeyer, M., & Corrigan, P. (2005). Mental illness stigma: Concepts, consequences, and initiatives to reduce stigma. *European Psychiatry*, 20, 529–539.

Rüsch, N., Corrigan, P. W., Powell, K., Rajah, A., Olschewski, M., Wilkniss, S., & Batia, K. (2009). A stress-coping model of mental illness stigma: II. Emotional stress responses, coping behavior and outcome. *Schizophrenia Research*, 110, 65–71.

Rüsch, N., Corrigan, P., Todd, A., & Bodenhausen, G. (2010). Implicit self-stigma in people with mental illness. *Journal of Nervous and Mental Disease*, 198, 150–153.

Russell, E., Koren, G., Rieder, M., & Van Uum, S. (2011). Hair cortisol as a biological marker of chronic stress: Current status, future directions and unanswered questions. *Psychoneuroendocrinology*, 37, 589–601.

Sah, R., & Geracioti, T. D. (2013). Neuropeptide Y and posttraumatic stress disorder. *Molecular Psychiatry*, 18, 646–655.

Salovey, P., & Mayer, J. D. (1990). Emotional intelligence. *Imagination, Cognition, and Personality*, 9, 185–211.

Sanacora, G., Treccani, G., & Popoli, M. (2012) Towards a glutamate hypothesis of depression: An emerging frontier of neuropsychopharmacology for mood disorders. *Neuropharmacology*, 62, 63–77.

Sandman, C. A., Davis, E. P., Buss, C., & Glynn, L. M. (2011). Exposure to prenatal psychobiological stress exerts programming influences on the mother and her fetus. *Neuroendocrinology*, 95, 8–21.

SSapolsky, R. M., Romero, L. M., & Munck, A. U. (2000). How do glucocorticoids influence stress responses? Integrating permissive, suppressive, stimulatory, and preparative actions. *Endocrine Reviews*, 21, 55–89.

Sargin, D., Friedrichs, H., El-Kordi, A., & Ehrenreich, H. (2010). Erythropoietin as neuroprotective and neuroregenerative treatment strategy: Comprehensive overview of 12 years of preclinical and clinical research. *Best Practice & Research Clinical Anaesthesiology*, 24, 573–594.

Sassenberg, K. (2002). Common bond and common identity groups on the Internet: Attachment and normative behavior in on-topic and off-topic chats. *Group Dynamics*, 6, 27–37.

Scheier, M. F., & Carver, C. S. (1985). Optimism, coping, and health: Assessment and implications of generalized outcome expectancies. *Health Psychology*, 4, 219–247.

Schlotz, W., Hellhammer, J., Schulz, P., & Stone, A. A. (2004). Perceived work overload and chronic worrying predict weekend–weekday differences in the cortisol awakening response. *Psychosomatic Medicine, 66,* 207–214.

Schmid, D. A., Held, K., Ising, M., Uhr, M., Weikel, J. C., & Steiger, A. (2005). Ghrelin stimulates appetite, imagination of food, GH, ACTH, and cortisol, but does not affect leptin in normal controls. *Neuropsychopharmacology, 30,* 1187–1192.

Schmidt, N. B., & Keough, M. E. (2010). Treatment of panic. *Annual Review of Clinical Psychology,* 6, 241–256.

Schmidt-Reinwald, A., Pruessner, J. C., Hellhammer, D. H., Federenko, I., Rohleder, N., Schurmeyer, T. H., & Kirschbaum, C. (1999). The cortisol response to awakening in relation to different challenge tests and a 12-hour cortisol rhythm. *Life Sciences, 64,* 1653–1660.

Schueller, S. M., & Seligman, M. E. P. (2008). Optimism and pessimism. In K. S. Dobson and D. J. A. Dozois (eds), *Risk Factors in Depression* (pp. 171–194). San Diego, CA: Academic Press.

Schuler, L. A., & Auger, A. P. (2010). Psychosocially influenced cancer: Diverse early-life stress experiences and links to breast cancer. *Cancer Prevention Research, 3,* 1365–1370.

Schulkin, J. (2006). Angst and the amygdala. *Dialogues in Clinical Neuroscience, 8,* 407–416.

Schwarz-Bart, A. (1959). *The Last of the Just.* Woodstock & New York: Overlook.

Scott, D. J., Stohler, C. S., Egnatuk, C. M., Wang, H., Koeppe, R. A., & Zubieta, J. K. (2008). Placebo and nocebo effects are defined by opposite opioid and dopaminergic responses. *Archives of General Psychiatry, 65,* 220–231.

Seale, J. V., Wood, S. A., Atkinson, H. C., Lightman, S. L. & Harbuz, M. S. (2005.) Organizational role for testosterone and estrogen on adult hypothalamic-pituitary-adrenal axis activity in the male rat. *Endocrinology, 146,* 1973–1982.

Seery, M. D. (2011). Resilience: A silver lining to experiencing adverse life events? *Current Directions in Psychological Science, 20,* 390–394.

Segal, Z. V., Williams, J. M. G., & Teasdale, J. (2002). *Mindfulness-based Cognitive Therapy for Depression: A New Approach to Preventing Relapse.* New York: Guilford.

Segovia, G., del Arco, A., & Mora, F. (2009). Environmental enrichment, prefrontal cortex, stress, and aging of the brain. *Journal of Neural Transmission, 116,* 1007–1016.

Seidler, G. H., & Wagner, F. E. (2006). Comparing the efficacy of EMDR and trauma-focused cognitive-behavioral therapy in the treatment of PTSD: A meta-analytic study. *Psychological Medicine, 36,* 1515–1522.

Seligman, M. E., & Csikszentmihalyi, M. (2000). Positive psychology: An introduction. *American Psychologist, 55,* 5–14.

Seligman, M. E., & Maier, S. F. (1967) Failure to escape traumatic shock. *Journal of Experimental Psychology, 74* (1), 1–9.

Seng, J., Low, L., Sperlich, M., Ronis, D., & Liberzon, I. (2011). Post-traumatic stress disorder, child abuse history, birthweight and gestational age: A prospective cohort study. *BJOG: An International Journal of Obstetrics & Gynecology, 118,* 1329–1339.

Sequeira, A., et al. (2009). Global brain gene expression analysis links glutamatergic and GABAergic alterations to suicide and major depression. *PLoS One, 4,* e6585.

Serova, L. I., Tillinger, A., Alaluf, L. G., Laukova, M., Keegan, K., & Sabban, E. L. (2013). Single intranasal neuropeptide Y infusion attenuates development of PTSD-like symptoms to traumatic stress in rats. *Neuroscience*, *236*, 298–312.

Shad, M. U., Suris, A. M., & North, C. S. (2011). Novel combination strategy to optimize treatment for PTSD. *Human Psychopharmacology: Clinical and Experimental*, *26*, 4–11.

Shah, A. J., Veledar, E., Hong, Y., Bremner, J. D., & Vaccarino, V. (2011). Depression and history of attempted suicide as risk factors for heart disease mortality in young individuals. *Archives of General Psychiatry*, *68*, 1135–1142.

Shaham, Y., Shalev, U., Lu, L., De Wit, H., & Stewart, J. (2003). The reinstatement model of drug relapse: History, methodology and major findings. *Psychopharmacology*, *168*, 3–20.

Shalaby, A. M., & Kamal, S. M. (2012) Effect of rolipram, a phosphodiesterase enzyme type-4 inhibitor, on γ-amino butyric acid content of the frontal cortex in mice exposed to chronic mild stress. *Journal of Pharmacology and Pharmacotherpeutics*, *3*(2), 132–137. doi: 10.4103/0976-500X.95509.

Shanks, N., Windle, R. J., Perks, P. A., Harbuz, M. S., Jessop, D. S., Ingram, C. D., & Lightman, S. L. (2000). Early-life exposure to endotoxin alters hypothalamic-pituitary-adrenal function and predisposition to inflammation. *Proceedings of the National Academy of Sciences*, *97*, 5645–5650.

Shelton, R. C., & Miller, A. H. (2011) Inflammation in depression: Is adiposity a cause? *Dialogues in Clinical Neuroscience*, *13*, 41–53.

Sherman, A. C., Simonton, S., Latif, U., & Bracy, L. (2010). Effects of global-meaning and illness-specific meaning on health outcomes among breast cancer patients. *Journal of Behavioral Medicine*, *33*, 364–377.

Shimizu, N., Nakane, H., Hori, T., & Hayashi, Y. (1994). CRF receptor antagonist attenuates stress-induced noradrenaline release in the medial prefrontal cortex of rats. *Brain Research*, *654*, 145–148.

Shonkoff, J. P., Boyce, W. T., & McEwen, B. S. (2009). Neuroscience, molecular biology, and the childhood roots of health disparities: Building a new framework for health promotion and disease prevention. *Journal of the American Medical Association*, *301*, 2252–2259.

Shrestha, S., Hirvonen, J., Hines, C. S., Henter, I., Svenningsson, P., Pike. V. W., & Innis, R. B. (2012). Serotonin-1A receptors in major depression quantified using PET: Controversies, confounds, and recommendations. *NeuroImage*, *59*, 3243–3251.

Sibille, E., Pavlides, C., Benke, D., & Toth, M. (2000). Genetic inactivation of the Serotonin (1A) receptor in mice results in downregulation of major GABA (A) receptor alpha subunits, reduction of $GABA_A$ receptor binding, and benzodiazepine-resistant anxiety. *Journal of Neuroscience*, *20*, 2758–2765.

Siegel, S. (1999). Drug anticipation and drug addiction: The 1998 H. David Archibald Lecture. *Addiction*, *94*, 1113–1124.

Silvagni, A., Barros, V. G., Mura, C., Antonelli, M. C., & Carboni, E. (2008). Prenatal restraint stress differentially modifies basal and stimulated dopamine and noradrenaline release in the nucleus accumbens shell: An 'in vivo' microdialysis study in adolescent and young adult rats. *European Journal of Neuroscience*, *28*, 744–758.

Silver, R. C., Holman, E. A., McIntosh, D. N., Poulin, M., & Gil-Rivas, V. (2002). Nationwide longitudinal study of psychological responses to September 11. *Journal of the American Medical Association, 288*, 1235–1244.

Singhal, S., et al. (1999). Antitumor activity of thalidomide in refractory multiple myeloma. *New England Journal of Medicine, 341*, 1565–1571.

Sinha, R. (2008). Chronic stress, drug use, and vulnerability to addiction. *Annals of the New York Academy of Sciences, 1141*, 105–130.

Skilbeck, K. J., Johnston, G. A., & Hinton, T. (2010). Stress and GABA receptors. *Journal of Neurochemistry, 112*, 1115–1130.

Sklar, L. S., & Anisman, H. (1979). Stress and coping factors influence tumor growth. *Science, 205*, 513–515.

Skolnick, P., Popik, P., & Trullas, R. (2009). Glutamate-based antidepressants: 20 years on. *Trends in Pharmacological Sciences, 30*, 563–569.

Slavich, G. M., O'Donovan, A., Epel, E. S., & Kemeny, M. E. (2010). Black sheep get the blues: A psychobiological model of social rejection and depression. *Neuroscience & Biobehavioral Reviews, 35*, 39–45.

Slavich, G. M., Way, B. M., Eisenberger, N. I., & Taylor, S. E. (2010). Neural sensitivity to social rejection is associated with inflammatory responses to social stress. *Proceedings of the National Academy of Sciences, 107*, 14817–14822.

Smith, A. K., et al. (2011). Association of a polymorphism in the indoleamine- 2,3-dioxygenase gene and interferon-α-induced depression in patients with chronic hepatitis C. *Molecular Psychiatry, 17*, 781–789.

Smith, D. G., Davis, R. J., Gehlert, D. R., & Nomikos, G. G. (2006). Exposure to predator odor stress increases efflux of frontal cortex acetylcholine and monoamines in mice: Comparisons with immobilization stress and reversal by chlordiazepoxide. *Brain Research, 1114*, 24–30.

Smith, K. S., Virkud, A., Deisseroth, K., & Graybiel, A. M. (2012). Reversible online control of habitual behavior by optogenetic perturbation of medial prefrontal cortex. *Proceedings of the National Academy of Sciences, 109*, 18932–18937.

Smolderen, K. G., et al. (2009). The association of cognitive and somatic depressive symptoms with depression recognition and outcomes after myocardial infarction. *Circulation: Cardiovascular Quality and Outcomes, 2*, 328–337.

Smoller, J. W., Gardner-Schuster, E., & Covino, J. (2008). The genetic basis of panic and phobic anxiety disorders. *American Journal of Medical Genetics Part C: Seminars in Medical Genetics, 148C*, 118–126.

Song, Y. S., & Ingram, K. (2002). Unsupportive social interactions, availability of social support, and coping: Their relationship to mood disturbance among African Americans living with HIV. *Journal of Social and Personal Relationships, 19*, 67–85.

Sorrells, S. F., Caso, J. R., Munhoz, C. D., & Sapolsky, R. M. (2009). The stressed CNS: When glucocorticoids aggravate inflammation. *Neuron 64*, 33–39.

Sorrells, S. F., & Sapolsky, R. M. (2007). An inflammatory review of glucocorticoid actions in the CNS. *Brain, Behavior, and Immunity, 21*, 259–272.

Sotiropoulos, I., et al. (2011). Stress acts cumulatively to precipitate Alzheimer's disease-like tau pathology and cognitive deficits. *Journal of Neuroscience, 31*, 7840–7847.

Spalletta, G., Bossù, P., Ciaramella, A., Bria, P., Caltagirone, C., & Robinson, R. G. (2006). The etiology of poststroke depression: A review of the literature and a new hypothesis involving inflammatory cytokines. *Molecular Psychiatry*, *11*, 984–991.

Spear, L. P. (2009). Heightened stress responsivity and emotional reactivity during pubertal maturation: Implications for psychopathology. *Development and Psychopathology*, *21*, 87–97.

Stanton, A. L., Danoff-Burg, S., Cameron, C. L., & Ellis, A. P. (1994). Coping through emotional approach: Problems of conceptualization and confounding. *Journal of Personality and Social Psychology*, *66*, 350–362.

Stark, J. L., Avitsur, R., Padgett, D. A., Campbell, K. A., Beck, F. M., & Sheridan, J. F. (2001). Social stress induces glucocorticoid resistance in macrophages. *American Journal of Physiology – Regulatory, Integrative and Comparative Physiology*, *280*, R1799– R1805.

Steel, P. (2007). The nature of procrastination: A meta-analytic and theoretical review of quintessential self-regulatory failure. *Psychological Bulletin*, *131*, 65–94.

Steinman, R. M., & Cohn, Z. A. (1973). Identification of a novel cell type in peripheral lymphoid organs of mice. I. Morphology, quantitation, tissue distribution. *Journal of Experimental Medicine*, *137*, 1142–1162.

Steptoe, A., & Kivimäki, M. (2012). Stress and cardiovascular disease. *Nature Reviews Cardiology*, *9*, 360–370.

Steptoe, A., & Kivimäki, M. (2013). Stress and cardiovascular disease: An update on current knowledge. *Annual Review of Public Health*, *34*. (Epub ahead of print.)

Sterling, P., & Eyer, J. (1988). Allostasis: A new paradigm to explain arousal pathology. In S. Fisher, & J. Reason (eds), *Handbook of Life Stress, Cognition and Health* (pp. 629–649). Chichester: Wiley.

Sternberg, E. M. (2001). Neuroendocrine regulation of autoimmune/inflammatory disease. *Journal of Endocrinology*, *169*, 429–435.

Sternberg, E. M. (2006). Neural regulation of innate immunity: A coordinated nonspecific host response to pathogens. *Nature Reviews Immunology*, *6*, 318–328.

Stewart, J. (2000). Pathways to relapse: The neurobiology of drug- and stress-induced relapse to drug-taking. *Journal of Psychiatry and Neuroscience*, *25*, 125–136.

Stewart-Williams, S., & Podd, J. (2004). The placebo effect: Dissolving the expectancy versus conditioning debate. *Psychological Bulletin*, *130*, 324–240.

Stockmeier, C. A. (2003). Involvement of serotonin in depression: Evidence from postmortem and imaging studies of serotonin receptors and the serotonin transporter. *Journal of Psychiatric Research*, *37*, 357–373.

Straub, R. H., Dhabhar, F. S., Bijlsma, J. W., & Cutolo, M. (2005). How psychological stress via hormones and nerve fibers may exacerbate rheumatoid arthritis. *Arthritis & Rheumatism*, *52*, 16–26.

Sugama, S., & Conti, B. (2008). Interleukin-18 and stress. *Brain Research Reviews*, *58*, 85–95.

Sugiura, Y. (2004). Detached mindfulness and worry: A meta-cognitive analysis. *Personality and Individual Differences*, *37*, 169–179.

Suliman, S., Mkabile, S. G., Fincham, D. S., Ahmed, R., Stein, D. J., & Seedat, S. (2009). Cumulative effect of multiple trauma on symptoms of posttraumatic stress disorder, anxiety, and depression in adolescents. *Comprehensive Psychiatry*, *50*, 121–127.

Sullivan, R. M., & Gratton, A. (1998). Relationships between stress-induced increases in medial prefrontal cortical dopamine and plasma corticosterone levels in rats: Role of cerebral laterality. *Neuroscience, 83*, 81–91.

Sullivan, R. M., & Gratton, A. (2002). Prefrontal cortical regulation of hypothalamic-pituitary-adrenal function in the rat and implications for psychopathology: Side matters. *Psychoneuro-endocrinology, 27*, 99–114.

Suls, J., David, J. P., & Harvey, J. H. (1996). Personality and coping: Three generations of research. *Journal of Personality, 64*, 711–735.

Szyf, M. (2009). Epigenetics, DNA methylation, and chromatin modifying drugs. *Annual Review of Pharmacology and Toxicology, 49*, 243–263.

Szyf, M. (2011). The early life social environment and DNA methylation: DNA methylation mediating the long-term impact of social environments early in life. *Epigenetics, 6*, 971–978.

Taleb, N. N. (2007). *The Black Swan*. New York: Random House.

Talge, N. M., Neal, C., & Glover, V. (2007). Antenatal maternal stress and long-term effects on child neurodevelopment: How and why? *Journal of Child Psychology and Psychiatry, 48*, 245–261.

Tan, K. R., Rudolph, U., & Lüscher, C. (2011). Hooked on benzodiazepines: GABAAA receptor subtypes and addiction. *Trends in Neurosciences, 34*, 188–197.

Tangney, J. P. (1996). Conceptual and methodological issues in the assessment of shame and guilt. *Behaviour Research and Therapy, 34*, 741–754.

Tannenbaum, B., Tannenbaum, G. S., Sudom, K., & Anisman, H. (2002). Neurochemical and behavioral alterations elicited by a chronic intermittent stressor regimen: Implications for allostatic load. *Brain Research, 953*, 82–92.

Taubenfeld, S. M., Riceberg, J. S., New, A. S., & Alberini, C. M. (2009). Preclinical assessment for selectively disrupting a traumatic memory via postretrieval inhibition of glucocorticoid receptors. *Biological Psychiatry, 65*, 249–257.

Taylor, J., & John, C. H. (2004). Attentional and memory bias in persecutory delusions and depression. *Psychopathology, 37*, 233–241.

Taylor, S. E., Burklund, L. J., Eisenberger, N. I., Lehman, B. J., Hilmert, C. J., & Lieberman, M. D. (2008). Neural bases of moderation of cortisol stress responses by psychosocial resources. *Journal of Personality and Social Psychology, 95*, 197–211.

Taylor, V. A., et al. (2011). Impact of mindfulness on the neural responses to emotional pictures in experienced and beginner meditators. *NeuroImage, 57*, 1524–1533.

Teng, E. J., Bailey, S. D., Chaison, A. D., Petersen, N. J., Hamilton, J. D., & Dunn, N. J. (2008). Treating comorbid panic disorder in veterans with posttraumatic stress disorder. *Journal of Consulting and Clinical Psychology, 76*, 704–710.

Tennen, H., Affleck, G., Armeli, S., & Carney, M. A. (2000). A daily process approach to coping: Linking theory, research, and practice. *American Psychologist, 55*, 626–636.

Terrance, C., & Matheson, K. (2003). Undermining reasonableness: Expert testimony in a case involving a battered woman who kills. *Psychology of Women Quarterly, 27*, 37–45.

Thaker, P., et al. (2006). Chronic stress promotes tumor growth and angiogenesis in a mouse model of ovarian carcinoma. *Nature Medicine, 12*, 939–944.

Thoits, P. A. (2010). Stress and health: Major findings and policy implications. *Journal of Health and Social Behavior, 51*, S41–S53.

Thornton, L. M., Andersen, B. L., Crespin, T. R., & Carson, W. E. (2007). Individual trajectories in stress covary with immunity during recovery from cancer diagnosis and treatments. *Brain, Behavior, and Immunity, 21*, 185–194.

Tidwell, L. C., & Walther, J. B. (2002). Computer-mediated communication effects on disclosure, impressions, and interpersonal evaluations: Getting to know one another a bit at a time. *Human Communication Research, 28*, 317–348.

Tilders, F. J. H., & Schmidt, E. D. (1999). Cross-sensitization between immune and non-immune stressors: A role in the etiology of depression? *Advances in Experimental Medicine, 461*, 179–197.

Tromp D. P., et al. (2012). Reduced structural connectivity of a major frontolimbic pathway in generalized anxiety disorder. *Archives of General Psychiatry, 69*, 925–934.

Tsankova, N. M., Berton, O., Renthal, W., Kumar, A., Neve, R. L., & Nestler, E. J. (2006). Sustained hippocampal chromatin regulation in a mouse model of depression and antidepressant action. *Nature Neuroscience, 9*, 519–525.

Tseng, R. J., Padgett, D. A., Dhabhar, F. S., Engler, H., & Sheridan, J. F. (2005). Stress-induced modulation of NK activity during influenza viral infection: Role of glucocorticoids and opioids. *Brain, Behavior, and Immunity, 19*, 153–164.

Tsoory, M., Cohen, H., & Richter-Levin, G. (2007). Juvenile stress induces a predisposition to either anxiety or depressive-like symptoms following stress in adulthood. *European Neuropsychopharmacology, 17*, 245–256.

Tu, M. T., Lupien, S. J., & Walker, C. D. (2005). Measuring stress responses in postpartum mothers: Perspectives from studies in human and animal populations. *Stress, 8*, 19–34.

Turner, C. A., Akil, H., Watson, S. J., & Evans, S. J. (2006). The fibroblast growth factor system and mood disorders. *Biological Psychiatry, 59*, 1128–1135.

Tversky, A., & Kahneman, D. (1974). Judgment under uncertainty: Heuristics and biases. *Science, 185*, 1124–1131.

Tye, K. M., et al. (2013). Dopamine neurons modulate neural encoding and expression of depression-related behaviour. *Nature, 493*, 537–541.

Uchida, S., et al. (2011). Epigenetic status of Gdnf in the ventral striatum determines susceptibility and adaptation to daily stressful events. *Neuron, 69*, 359–372.

Ury, W. (1993). *Getting Past No.* New York: Bantam.

Uys, J. D., Muller, C. J., Marais, L., Harvey, B. H., Stein, D. J., & Daniels, W. M. (2006). Early life trauma decreases glucocorticoid receptors in rat dentate gyrus upon adult re-stress: Reversal by escitalopram. *Neuroscience, 137*, 619–625.

Vaiva, G., Ducrocq, F., Jezequel, K., Averland, B., Lestavel, P., Brunet, A., & Marmar, C. R. (2003). Immediate treatment with propranolol decreases posttraumatic stress disorder two months after trauma. *Biological Psychiatry, 54*, 947–949.

Van Ameringen, M., Mancini, C., Patterson, B., & Simpson, W. (2009). Pharmacotherapy for social anxiety disorder: An update. *Israel Journal of Psychiatry and Related Sciences, 46*, 53–61.

Van Boven, L., Loewenstein, G., Welch, E., & Dunning, D. (2012). The illusion of courage in self-predictions: Mispredicting one's own behavior in embarrassing situations. *Journal of Behavioral Decision Making, 25*, 1–12.

Van den Hove, D., et al. (2006). Prenatal stress and neonatal rat brain development. *Neuroscience, 137*, 145–155.

Van den Hove, D., et al. (2011). Differential effects of prenatal stress in 5-htt deficient mice: Towards molecular mechanisms of gene × environment interactions. *PLoS One, 6,* e22715.

Van Rossum, E. F., et al. (2006). Polymorphisms of the glucocorticoid receptor gene and major depression. *Biological Psychiatry, 59,* 681–688.

Varker, K. A., Terrell, C. E., Welt, M., Suleiman, S., Thornton, L., Andersen, B. L., & Carson, W. E., 3rd. (2007). Impaired natural killer cell lysis in breast cancer patients with high levels of psychological stress is associated with altered expression of killer immunoglobin-like receptors. *Journal of Surgical Research, 139,* 36–44.

Villa, P., et al. (2007). Reduced functional deficits, neuroinflammation, and secondary tissue damage after treatment of stroke by nonerythropoietic erythropoietin derivatives. *Journal of Cerebral Blood Flow & Metabolism, 27,* 552–563.

Virk, J., Li, J., Vestergaard, M., Obel, C., Lu, M., & Olsen, J. (2010). Early life disease programming during the preconception and prenatal period: Making the link between stressful life events and type-1 diabetes. *PLoS One, 5,* e11523.

Volkow, N. D., Wang, G. J., Fowler, J. S., Tomasi, D., Telang, F., & Baler, R. (2010). Addiction: Decreased reward sensitivity and increased expectation sensitivity conspire to overwhelm the brain's control circuit. *Bioessays, 32,* 748–755.

Volkow, N. D., Wang, G. J., Tomasi, D., & Baler, R. D. (2013). Unbalanced neuronal circuits in addiction. *Current Opinion in Neurobiology.* doi:pii: S0959-4388(13)00018-4.

Vollrath, M. (2001). Personality and stress. *Scandinavian Journal of Psychology, 42,* 335–347.

Wager, T. D., Scott, D. J., & Zubieta, J. K. (2007). Placebo effects on human mu opioid activity during pain. *Proceedings of the National Academy of Sciences, 104,* 11056–11061.

Walker, C. D. (2010). Maternal touch and feed as critical regulators of behavioral and stress responses in the offspring. *Developmental Psychobiology, 52,* 638–650.

Wang, J., Patten, S. B., Williams, J. V., Currie, S., Beck, C. A., Maxwell, C. J., & El-Guebaly, N. (2005). Help-seeking behaviours of individuals with mood disorders. *Canadian Journal of Psychiatry, 50,* 652–659.

Wang, R. P., et al. (2011). Toll-like receptor 4/nuclear factor-kappa B pathway is involved in myocardial injury in a rat chronic stress model. *Stress, 14,* 567–575.

Wankerl, M., Wüst, S., & Otte, C. (2010). Current developments and controversies: Does the serotonin transporter gene-linked polymorphic region (5-HTTLPR) modulate the association between stress and depression? *Current Opinion in Psychiatry, 23,* 582–587.

Wann, B. P., Audet, M. C., Gibb, J., & Anisman, H. (2010). Anhedonia and altered cardiac atrial natriuretic peptide following chronic stressor and endotoxin treatment in mice. *Psychoneuroendocrinology, 35,* 233–240.

Waselus, M., Valentino, R. J., & Van Bockstaele, E. J. (2005). Ultrastructural evidence for a role of gamma-aminobutyric acid in mediating the effects of corticotropin-releasing factor on the rat dorsal raphe serotonin system. *Journal of Comparative Neurology, 482,* 155–165.

Weaver, I. C., Champagne, F. A., Brown, S. E., Dymov, S., Sharma, S., Meaney, M. J., & Szyf, M. (2005). Reversal of maternal programming of stress responses in adult offspring through methyl supplementation: Altering epigenetic marking later in life. *Journal of Neuroscience, 25,* 11045–11054.

Webb, M., Burns, J., & Collin, P. (2008). Providing online support for young people with mental health difficulties: Challenges and opportunities explored. *Early Intervention in Psychiatry*, 2, 108–113.

Webster, J. I., Tonelli, L. H., Moayeri, M., Simons, S. S., Leppla, S. H., & Sternberg, E. M. (2003). Anthrax lethal factor represses glucocorticoid and progesterone receptor activity. *Proceedings of the National Academy of Sciences*, 100, 5706–5711.

Weinrib, A. Z., et al. (2010). Diurnal cortisol dysregulation, functional disability, and depression in women with ovarian cancer. *Cancer*, 116, 4410–4419.

Weinstock, M. (2007). Gender differences in the effects of prenatal stress on brain development and behaviour. *Neurochemical Research*, 32, 1730–1740.

Weiss, D. S. & Marmar, C. R. (1997). The Impact of Event Scale–Revised. In J. P. Wilson & T. M. Keane (eds), *Assessing Psychological Trauma and PTSD*. New York: Guilford, pp. 399–411.

Weiss, J. M., Glazer, H. I., Pohorecky, L. A., Brick, J., & Miller, N. E. (1975). Effects of chronic exposure to stressors on avoidance-escape behavior and on brain norepinephrine. *Psychosomatic Medicine*, 37, 522–534.

Welberg, L. A., Seckl, J. R., & Holmes, M. C. (2001). Prenatal glucocorticoid programming of brain corticosteroid receptors and corticotrophin-releasing hormone: Possible implications for behaviour. *Neuroscience*, 104, 71–79.

Wellman, P. J., Davis, K. W., & Nation, J. R. (2005). Augmentation of cocaine hyperactivity in rats by systemic ghrelin. *Regulatory Peptides*, 125, 151–154.

Whitbeck, L. B., Adams, G. W., Hoyt, D. R., & Chen, X. (2004). Conceptualizing and measuring historical trauma among American Indian people. *American Journal of Community Psychology*, 33, 199–130.

Wibral, M., Dohmen, T., Klingmüller, D., Weber, B., & Falk, A. (2012). Testosterone administration reduces lying in men. *PLoS One*, 7, e46774.

Williams, J. B., et al. (2009). A model of gene–environment interaction reveals altered mammary gland gene expression and increased tumor growth following social isolation. *Cancer Prevention Research*, 2, 850–861.

Williams, S., Sakic, B., & Hoffman, S. A. (2010). Circulating brain-reactive autoantibodies and behavioral deficits in the MRL model of CNS lupus. *Journal of Neuroimmunology*, 218, 73–82.

Willner, P., Muscat, R., & Papp, M. (1992). An animal model of anhedonia. *Clinical Neuropharmacology*, 15, 550A–551A.

Wills, T. A., & Shinar, O. (2000). Measuring perceived and received social support. In S. Cohen, L. G. Underwood, & B. H. Gottlieb (eds), *Social Support Measurement and Intervention* (pp. 86–135). New York: Oxford University Press.

Wilmink, F. W., Ormel, J., Giel, R., Krol, B., Lindeboom, E. G., van der Meer, K., & Soeteman, J. H. (1989). General practitioners' characteristics and the assessment of psychiatric illness. *Journal of Psychiatric Research*, 23, 135–149.

Wilson, C. J., & Deane, F. P. (2010). Help-negation and suicidal ideation: The role of depression, anxiety and hopelessness. *Journal of Youth and Adolescence*, 39, 291–305.

Wingfield, J. C., & Sapolsky, R. M. (2003). Reproduction and resistance to stress: When and how. *Journal of Neuroendocrinology*, 15, 711–724.

Winsky-Sommerer, R., Boutrel, B., & de Lecea, L. (2005). Stress and arousal: The corticotrophin-releasing factor/hypocretin circuitry. *Molecular Neurobiology*, 32, 285–294.

Wise, R. A. (2004). Dopamine, learning and motivation. *Nature Reviews Neuroscience*, 5, 483–494.

Wiseman, H., Barber, .P., Raz, A., Yam, I., Foltz, C., & Livne-Snir, S. (2002). Parental communication of Holocaust experiences and interpersonal patterns in offspring of Holocaust survivors. *International Journal of Behavioral Development*, 26, 371–381.

Witek-Janusek, L., Albuquerque, K., Chroniak, K. R., Chroniak, C., Durazo, R., & Matthews, H. L. (2008). Effect of mindfulness based stress reduction on immune function, quality of life and coping in women newly diagnosed with early stage breast cancer. *Brain, Behavior, and Immunity*, 22, 969–981.

Witt, S. H., et al. (2011). An interaction between a neuropeptide Y gene polymorphism and early adversity modulates endocrine stress responses. *Psychoneuroendocrinology*, 36, 1010–1020.

Wohl, M. J., Branscombe, N. R., & Reysen, S. (2010). Perceiving your group's future to be in jeopardy: Extinction threat induces collective angst and the desire to strengthen the ingroup. *Personality and Social Psychology Bulletin*, 36, 898–910.

Wohl, M. J. A., & Enzle, M. E. (2009). Illusion of control by proxy: Placing one's fate in the hands of another. *British Journal of Social Psychology*, 48, 183–200.

Wolak, J., Mitchell, K. J., & Finkelhor, D. (2003). Escaping or connecting? Characteristics of youth who form close online relationships. *Journal of Adolescence*, 26, 105–119.

Wolfe, N. (2011) *The Viral Storm: The Dawn of the New Pandemic Age*. California: Macmillan.

Wolkowitz, O. M., et al. (2011). Serum BDNF levels before treatment predict SSRI response in depression. *Progress in Neuropsychopharmacology and Biological Psychiatry*, 35, 1623–1630.

Woodward, S. H., Kaloupek, D. G., Streeter, C. C., Martinez, C., Schaer, M., & Eliez, S. (2006). Decreased anterior cingulate volume in combat-related PTSD. *Biological Psychiatry*, 59, 582–587.

Woody, E. Z., Szechtman, H. (2011). Adaptation to potential threat: The evolution, neurobiology, and psychopathology of the security motivation system. *Neuroscience & Biobehavioral Reviews*, 35, 1019–1033.

Wright, N. D., Bahrami, B., Johnson, E., Di Malta, G., Rees, G., Frith, C. D., & Dolan, R. J. (2012). Testosterone disrupts human collaboration by increasing egocentric choices. *Proceedings of the Royal Society B: Biological Sciences*, 279, 2275–2280.

Wrosch, C., Scheier, M. F., Carver, C. S., & Schulz, R. (2003). The importance of goal disengagement in adaptive self-regulation: When giving up is beneficial. *Self and Identity*, 2, 1–20.

Wyatt, S. B., Williams, D. R., Calvin, R., Henderson, F. C., Walker, E. R., & Winters, K. (2003). Racism and cardiovascular disease in African Americans. *American Journal of Medical Sciences*, 325, 315–331.

Xiao, W., et al. (2011). Inflammation and Host Response to Injury Large-Scale Collaborative Research Program: A genomic storm in critically injured humans. *Journal of Experimental Medicine*, 208, 2581–2590.

Xie, P., et al. (2009). Interactive effect of stressful life events and the serotonin transporter 5-HTTLPR genotype on posttraumatic stress disorder diagnosis in 2 independent populations. *Archives of General Psychiatry*, 66, 1201–1209.

Yamano, M., Ogura, H., Okuyama, S., & Ohki-Hamazaki, H. (2002). Modulation of 5-HT system in mice with a targeted disruption of neuromedin B receptor. *Journal of Neuroscience Research*, *68*, 59–64.

Yehuda, R. (2002). Current status of cortisol findings in post-traumatic stress disorder. *Psychiatric Clinics of North America*, *25*, 341–368.

Yehuda, R., & Bierer, L. M. (2009). The relevance of epigenetics to PTSD: Implications for the DSM-V. *Journal of Traumatic Stress*, *22*, 427–434.

Yoshimura, R., et al. (2011). The brain-derived neurotrophic factor (BDNF) polymorphism Val-66Met is associated with neither serum BDNF level nor response to selective serotonin reuptake inhibitors in depressed Japanese patients. *Progress in Neuropsychopharmacology and Biological Psychiatry*, *35*, 1022–1025.

Youngson, N. A., & Whitelaw, E. (2008). Transgenerational epigenetic effects. *Annual Review of Genomics and Human Genetics*, *9*, 233–257.

Youssef, F. F., et al. (2011). Stress alters personal moral decision making. *Psychoneuroendocrinology*, *37*, 491–498.

Ysseldyk, R., Matheson, K., & Anisman, H. (2010). Religiosity as identity: Toward an understanding of religion from a social identity perspective. *Personality and Social Psychology Review*, *14*, 60–71.

Zacharko, R. M., & Anisman, H. (1991). Stressor-induced anhedonia in the mesocorticolimbic system. *Neuroscience & Biobehavioral Reviews*, *15*, 391–405.

Zanardi, R., et al. (2001). Increased 5-hydroxytryptamine-2 receptor binding in the frontal cortex of depressed patients responding to paroxetine treatment: A positron emission tomography scan study. *Journal of Clinical Psychopharmacology*, *21*, 53–58.

Zarate, C. A., Jr, et al. (2006). A randomized trial of an N-methyl-D-aspartate antagonist in treatment-resistant major depression. *Archives of General Psychiatry*, *63*, 856–864.

Zhang, Y., Proenca, R., Maffei, M., Barone, M., Leopold, L., & Friedman, J. M. (1994). Positional cloning of the mouse obese gene and its human homologue. *Nature*, *372*, 425–432.

Zheng, J., Babygirija, R., Bülbül, M., Cerjak, D., Ludwig, K., & Takahashi, T. (2010). Hypothalamic oxytocin mediates adaptation mechanism against chronic stress in rats. *American Journal of Physiology – Gastrointestinal and Liver Physiology*, *299*, G946–G953.

Zilka, N., et al. (2012). Who fans the flames of Alzheimer's disease brains? Misfolded tau on the crossroad of neurodegenerative and inflammatory pathways. *Journal of Neuroinflammation*, *9*, 47.

Zohar, J., Juven-Wetzler, A., Sonnino, R., Cwikel-Hamzany, S., Balaban, E., & Cohen, H. (2011). New insights into secondary prevention in post-traumatic stress disorder. *Dialogues in Clinical Neuroscience*, *13*, 301–309.

Zohar, J., Yahalom, H., Kozlovsky, N., Cwikel-Hamzany, S., Matar, M. A., Kaplan, Z., Yehuda, R., & Cohen, H. (2011) High dose hydrocortisone immediately after trauma may alter the trajectory of PTSD: Interplay between clinical and animal studies. *European Neuropsychopharmacology*, *21*, 796–809.

INDEX